ULTIMATE VISUAL
HISTORY
OF THE WORLD

THE STORY OF HUMANKIND
FROM PREHISTORY TO MODERN TIMES

JEAN-PIERRE ISBOUTS

NATIONAL GEOGRAPHIC
WASHINGTON, D.C.

CONTENTS

THESE FIGURES, known as moai, were carved on Easter Island, eastern Polynesia, by the Rapa Nui people ca 1250–1500.

A YOUNG BUDDHIST monk opens the doors of Trongsa Dzong, ancestral home of Bhutan's monarchy.

THE STORY OF HUMANKIND

While the topic continues to be hotly debated, the general consensus in the scientific community is that humankind—in the sense of humans as cognitive beings—has been around for some 300,000 years. That is actually a very short period of time, given that the first living organisms—in the form of microbes—appeared on Earth some 3.7 billion years ago. The first animals began to emerge some 600 million years ago, followed by dinosaurs around 450 million years later.

Another way of imagining the story of our planet is to compress the whole 4.6 billion years of Earth history into 24 hours—a single day, starting from midnight. There are several ways to do that, but according to one scenario, the first multicell organisms appear shortly after 6 a.m. Then we have to wait a very long time, some 16 hours until 10 p.m. at night, for plants and animal life to emerge. At 10:45 p.m., the dinosaurs make their appearance, followed 45 minutes later by mammals. With just 20 minutes to go before the end of our Earth day, the dinosaurs are wiped out by a cataclysmic event (such as abrupt climate change as a result of an asteroid impact). It's only just before midnight, *at a minute to 12,* that *Homo sapiens* begins hunting and gathering.

Seen from this perspective, it is amazing to see what humans have accomplished in their short time on Earth. Starting from their humble beginnings, they learned how to cultivate their food, build their homes, organize their communities, and develop traditions of worship, and they discovered that they could trade the surplus of their agricultural yields, thus laying the foundation of international trade. In time, this growing prosperity freed certain individuals to focus on their creativity, such as producing tools, pottery, textiles, leather goods, sculpture, painting, monumental architecture, and, eventually, the art of writing.

Maya jade funerary mask

But after the Classical Age, it seemed as if humankind stalled. In some ways, the principles of life in Antiquity—when productivity was measured by what human hands could accomplish or the energy a horse could provide in a single day—remained valid until the mid-19th century. It was only with the Industrial Revolution that our lives became dependent on mechanization, just as our modern world is now increasingly dependent on automation.

The story of the amazing arc across these millennia is the subject of this book. It is a story told across the full canvas of human civilization, from Asia to Africa, from Europe to the Pacific, and from the Middle East—the birthplace of human civilization—to the Americas. It is an exciting story, filled with the rise and fall of dynasties and empires, the drama of wars and conflict, the stunning impact of new discoveries, the heroic deeds of men and women, and, above all, the power of ideas. Time and again, we will see that new ideas, whether in trade, economics, faith traditions, science, literature, or the arts, were the factors that helped human beings to advance, leapfrogging the boundaries of place and time into eras and territories unknown.

That is why today, in the third decade of the 21st century, an understanding of the forces that shaped our world is so important. No matter where we live on our planet, we are more interconnected than ever, not only through commerce and travel but also through the delicate strands of online communications that allow us to share ideas as never before.

This book is truly the story of our species—and how, against incredible odds, despite innumerable disasters and catastrophic conflicts, humans found a way to survive, and thrive. ■

– JEAN-PIERRE ISBOUTS,
Historian and author

CHAPTER 1

DAWN OF HUMANKIND

PREHISTORY—3000 B.C.E.

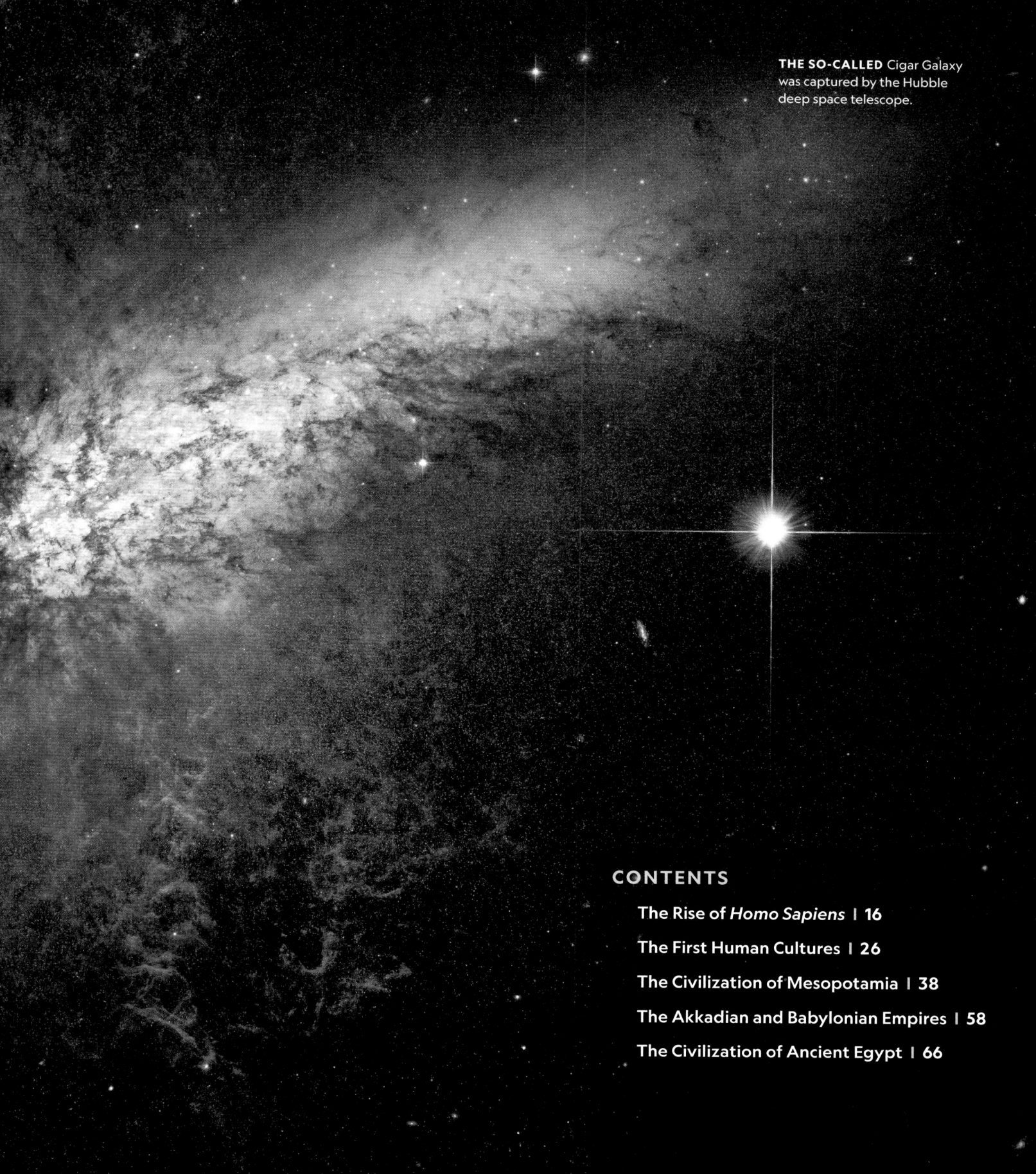

THE SO-CALLED Cigar Galaxy was captured by the Hubble deep space telescope.

CONTENTS

THE BEGINNING OF TIME

When did time begin? Astrophysicists would argue that moment came some 13.8 billion years ago, with the big bang that created the universe. From that time on, clouds of primordial elements, including subatomic particles, began to coalesce under gravitational force previously known as dark energy but more recently called the quintessence—literally, the quintessential element of life. This is what, in due course, produced the galaxies, stars, and planets that we see today. The interstellar drift produced by the big bang is continuing, so our universe is still expanding. Recently, the giant Hubble Space Telescope discovered something interesting: The rate of this expansion appears to be accelerating (known as the Hubble Constant). In 2016, Hubble also identified the farthest known galaxy in the universe: a constellation known by the prosaic name of GN-z11 in Ursa Major. The distance from Earth? An astonishing 32 billion light-years.

The Birth of Earth

Some nine billion years after the big bang, the planet we call Earth was still a giant molten rock. It was one of many objects, both large and small, that had come about by the collapse of a giant molecular cloud. Eventually that cloud coalesced into a sun, and thus the solar system was born. The detritus of this process—clumps of gas and dirt—eventually accreted into ever growing bodies of matter as they crashed into each other in their gravitational dance around the sun. That is when solar nebula started to work their magic. Combined with volcanic outgassing, these solar nebula produced the first hint of an atmosphere. At this stage, the solar system was still an unruly neighborhood of many careening shapes and objects, like billiard balls on a pool table. One of these balls was a planet-size body called Theia, which collided with the early Earth to ultimately form the moon. In 2019, scientists announced that moon rocks from the Fra Mauro highlands, collected by the crew of Apollo 14, contain minerals that could only have come from Earth or from an asteroid that collided with Earth.

After another billion years went by, the first signs of life began to stir on Earth. By then, the Earth had cooled, covering the inferno at its center with a hard crust that allowed liquid water (possibly introduced by meteorites) to flow. For example, scientists in Western Australia have discovered the fossilized remains of ancient microorganisms in sandstone strata that appear to be 3.48 billion years old. But the atmosphere still lacked oxygen, and without that, life could not begin. Fortunately, the Earth slowly cooled, allowing clouds to form, which in turn produced the rain that created the oceans. After another billion years, as the sun slowly grew in strength, the first algae and plants appeared with the ability to produce photosynthesis—the conversion of light energy into chemical properties, such as oxygen. But it still took another two billion years for complex, multicellular life to make its appearance. Around 541 million years ago, this culminated in the so-called Cambrian explosion, when an incredible variety of plant and animal life began to populate Earth. ■

AN ARTIST'S ILLUSTRATION of Earth's formation during the Hadean eon, 4.6 billion years ago

CAVE PAINTING of rhinoceroses from the Chauvet Cave in Vallon-Pont-d'Arc, France, ca 30,000 B.C.E.

A RECONSTRUCTION by John Gurche of *Homo habilis,* a Stone Age human species who lived 2.4 million to 1.4 million years ago

THE RISE OF
HOMO SAPIENS

In time, intelligent life made its appearance on Earth. This was the result of a long evolutionary process that began millions of years ago and produced several groups of ancestors known as hominids.

Hominids were primates with an average height of three or four feet. Their brains were only one-third the size of the modern human brain, which limited their cognitive ability. Nonetheless, they distinguished themselves by using primitive tools such as flints to hunt and gather their food. The earliest evidence—a group of fossilized animal bones bearing marks from stone tools—was found in 2010 in the Lower Awash Valley in Ethiopia and is now believed to be 3.4 million years old.

During the next phase, some of these hominids began to develop larger brains. This gave them the ability to communicate verbally with one another—for example, to coordinate an attack on prey or to form a community that would share the security and well-being of their offspring. One of the earliest groups of these humans, *Homo erectus* type, first appeared in Africa some 1.9 million years ago. This species enjoyed a particular advantage in that they could walk upright, leaving their hands free to wield tools and weapons and to gather foodstuffs. While the men were focused on

the hunt, the women became adept at scouring the fields for wild cereals and fruits, including almonds, acorns, and pistachios, sometimes covering large distances in order to find fresh sources of food. In the process, these early humans learned to develop more sophisticated tools, such as sharpened stones to dig out plants and roots and carve meat from animal carcasses. This greater access to higher nutrients, including proteins, may have accelerated brain development, which in turn allowed them to create better tools. Various skeletons have been found of prey such as deer, gazelles, and wild boar that appear to have been felled with bows and arrows or sharpened stone blades. Such tools also allowed these early humans to remove the hides of their prey to make clothing, which could be stitched together with wooden needles or spun flax.

Finally, between 300,000 and 200,000 B.C.E., the species *Homo sapiens* began to

THIS TWO-MILLION-YEAR-OLD hominid skull of *Australopithecus robustus* was found in Drimolen, South Africa.

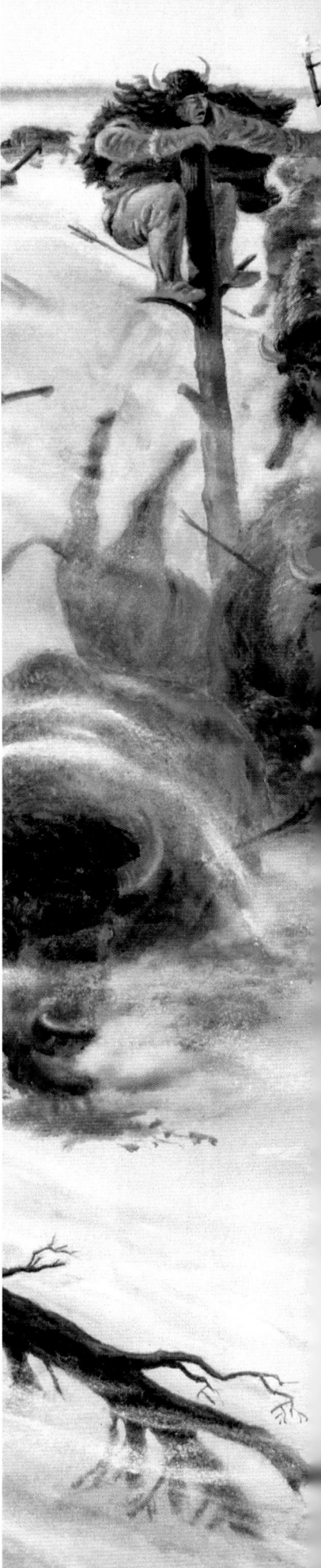

emerge almost simultaneously in Africa and Asia. These early humans had bigger brains than other humanoids, which gave them a critical edge with their rivals in the hunt for wild animals, the foraging of foods, and the preservation of fire. They also developed a more complex lifestyle, such as burying their dead according to set rituals; one typical example was found in the Wadi el-Mughara Caves on Mount Carmel, Israel.

Most important, the *Homo sapiens* species established the basic anatomy of human beings that has changed little between then and now, save perhaps for our average height.

The World After the Last Ice Age

Homo sapiens arrived just in time: The humanoids of planet Earth were about to be tested by an ice age that reached its most severe levels, the Glacial Maximum, some 22,000 years ago. These sharp climate changes tested the intellect of these early humans and challenged them to develop a number of survival strategies. For example, anthropologists believe that with the formation of ice and the drop of sea levels, so-called land bridges appeared between Europe, the Americas, and even parts of Asia and Australia that allowed large migrations. Many of these migrations were prompted by the search for new hunting areas as climate change also affected animal herds. For example, nomadic peoples are believed to have crossed from Siberia into the Americas some 14,000 years ago, in search of caribou, bison, and other animal herds. Some anthropologists believe that crossings to South America took place 12,000 to 15,000 years ago, and that a land bridge to Australia may have been used as much as 70,000 years ago. However, the prevailing opinion today is that early migration in Southeast Asia and the Pacific took place mostly by boat—in this case, bamboo rafts that allowed these early seafarers to move from island to island. Their nautical range increased as their flimsy vessels eventually gave way to sturdy, double-hulled outrigger canoes.

THE CHAUVET CAVE PAINTINGS reveal a great variety of animals, including reindeer, horses, bison, and aurochs, depicted in black charcoal and red paint made from the mineral hematite.

A MODERN ARTIST'S reconstruction of a group of hunters attacking bison at the close of the Ice Age, some 10,000 years ago.

NOTABLE DATES

ca 1,900,000 B.C.E.
Homo erectus appears in Africa

ca 300,000–200,000 B.C.E.
Homo sapiens emerges in Africa and Asia

ca 115,000 B.C.E.
Beginning of last ice age

ca 60,000 B.C.E.
Possible appearance of a land bridge to Australia

ca 40,000 B.C.E.
Homo sapiens emerges in Europe

ca 30,000 B.C.E.
Cave paintings in Chauvet Cave, France

ca 22,000 B.C.E.
Ice Age reaches its peak with greatest extent of ice coverage

ca 16,000 B.C.E.
Land bridge migration between Siberia and North America

ca 15,000 B.C.E.
Land bridge migration between Africa and South America

ca 12,000 B.C.E.
Last ice age ends

ca 11,500 B.C.E.
Clovis culture in the North American Southwest

ca 10,000 B.C.E.
Rising ocean waters separate Australia and New Guinea, Korea and Japan

ca 8000 B.C.E.
Indigenous people in Amazon basin domesticate cocoa and rubber trees

ca 8000 B.C.E.
Wheat and barley are cultivated in the Fertile Crescent

The cooler temperatures also forced these humans to husband fire as a source of warmth, and possibly as a means to cook their food, prompting major changes in their diet—which further encouraged their development as modern human beings. Their growing skills in the hunt for large animals may have contributed to the extinction of species such as the mammoth and the mastodon. The ferocity of this combat between man and beast is reflected in cave paintings from this era, such as the drawings of lions from the Chauvet Cave in southern France (ca 30,000 B.C.E.) or the colorful paintings of bison in the Altamira Cave in Cantabria, Spain—the oldest believed to be about 40,000 years old. Many similar cave paintings have been found in Mongolia, Indonesia, and India. These artists used a variety of pigmented materials, including blood, plant juices, egg whites, and charcoal.

When the last glacial age ended some 12,000 years ago, the climate began to warm, the ice receded, and the oceans stabilized, reaching their present form. Then humans were tested once more: The gradual warming of the Earth caused many animal species to become extinct, not only because of the hotter temperatures but also because of changes in vegetation and water sources and overhunting. These changes would have deprived many communities of their food supply were it not that the warmer climate also allowed entirely new edible crops and plants to prosper in the wild like never before.

The Rise of Domestication

The transition from the last ice age to the Neolithic or New Stone Age (ca 7000 to 2500 B.C.E.) witnessed what is perhaps the most critical transfor-

DEATH VALLEY

Another product from the early formation of Earth is Death Valley (at left), near the border of California and Nevada, today the hottest and driest place in the United States at 282 feet below sea level. During the Pleistocene epoch, this area of about 3,000 square miles was covered by water bodies that gradually evaporated, leaving deep salt deposits in their wake. The deposits include borax, a mineral widely used in detergents and cosmetics. The southern part of the valley has a number of towering rock formations, believed to be more than a billion years old. Researchers hypothesize that these formations were created by tectonic forces that mixed and compressed different layers of rock. This explains the striking contrast of colors and the reason that geologists refer to this area as the Amargosa Chaos, after the Amargosa River.

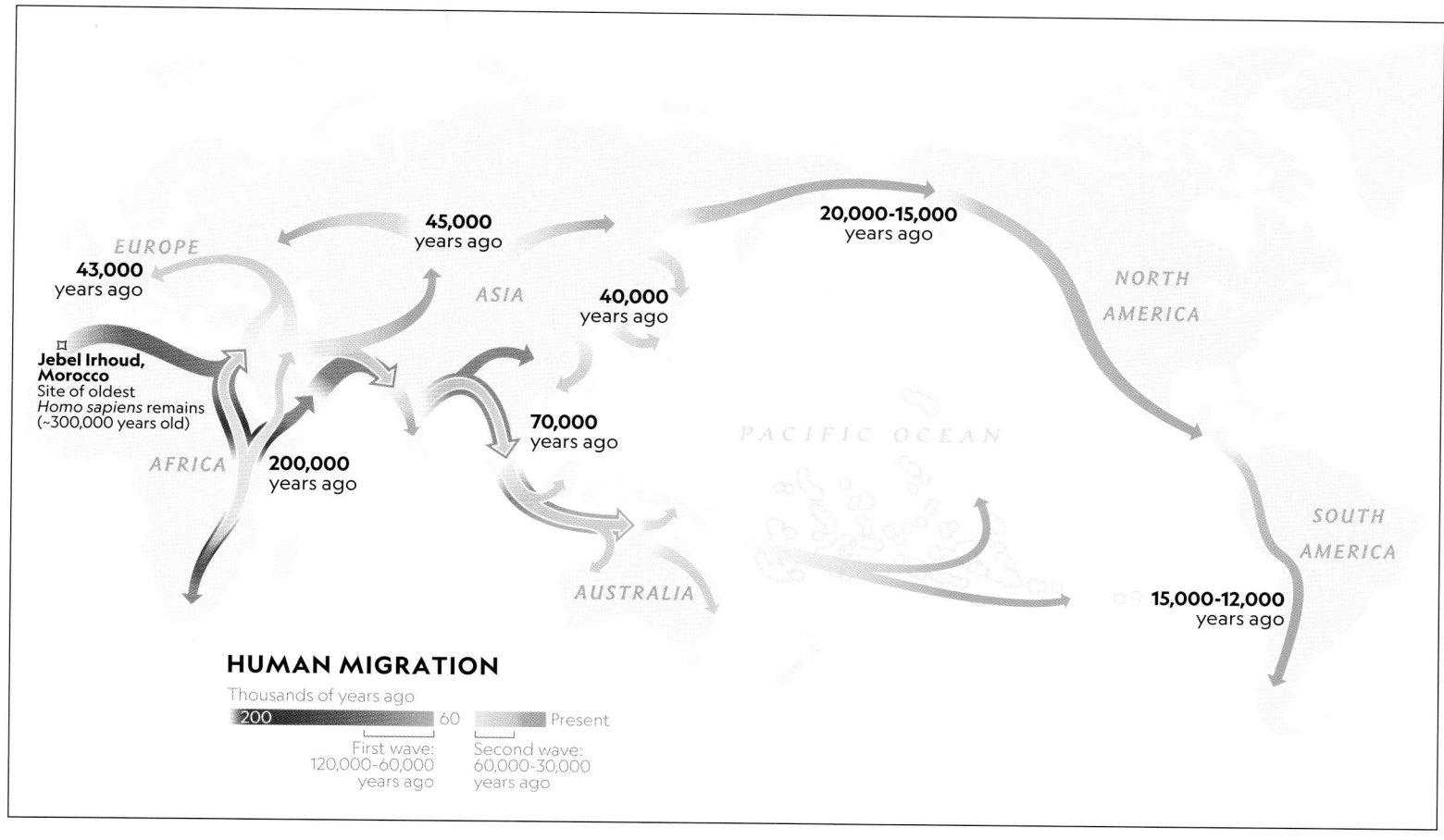

HUMAN MIGRATION

Thousands of years ago

200 ——— 60 ——— Present

First wave: 120,000–60,000 years ago

Second wave: 60,000–30,000 years ago

45,000 years ago

43,000 years ago

EUROPE

ASIA

40,000 years ago

20,000–15,000 years ago

NORTH AMERICA

Jebel Irhoud, Morocco
Site of oldest
Homo sapiens remains
(~300,000 years old)

200,000 years ago

AFRICA

70,000 years ago

PACIFIC OCEAN

SOUTH AMERICA

15,000–12,000 years ago

AUSTRALIA

mation in the human story. Slowly but surely, these early humans moved from a *destructive* to a *productive* lifestyle: from hunting and gathering to the domestication of animals and crops. In time, early farmers discovered that they could control the cycle of crop growth by careful tilling and seeding, creating domesticated varieties of cereals in the process. This included hulled wheat with strong spiked husks, like emmer and einkorn wheat, as well as barley. To cultivate crops marked a major psychological transformation for humans. No one could know if the planting of seeds would truly produce the cereals they needed to survive, which is why many early farmers continued to hunt to supplement their grown foods, especially during the winter.

Still, the benefits of farming over hunting were obvious. With a fairly predictable source of food, a man could settle his family in a hut and spare them the dangers and difficulties of long treks through unknown territory. As the surplus of

crops grew, humans could also feed and keep a number of animals, such as sheep, goats, and cattle. These domesticated animals not only served as a reliable source of milk, meat, wool, and hide but also could work as draft animals in the field. Thus, humans could take greater control of their destiny.

Still, choosing cultivation over the hunt was not as obvious as it may seem. Vegetation depends on rainfall, and rainfall is often uneven and unpredictable. In response, early settlements and villages would typically develop in close proximity to rivers or other natural sources of freshwater, such as springs. Springs are formed naturally by the downward pressure of layers of rock on groundwater, forcing it to the surface.

By 5000 B.C.E., agriculture was widespread throughout Africa, Asia,

A NEOLITHIC ICON of a boar was found in the archaeological site of Göbekli Tepe, Turkey.

THE TALL NEOLITHIC PILLARS at the temple of Göbekli Tepe, dated to the 10th millennium B.C.E., may be the world's oldest known monoliths.

and Europe. Barley and wheat remained the most popular crops, while sorghum was cultivated in Africa and rice and millet were grown in China and Southeast Asia. In the Americas, the cultivation of corn became a major source of food. North America experienced little domestication at this time, however, for the simple reason that its valleys were stocked with vast herds of bison, caribou, deer, and moose that had yet to experience the lethal threat posed by humans. For a long time, this provided the Native American tribes with a rich diet, though it also led to the slow decimation of animal herds. One by one, the wild horse, the mammoth, the giant bison, the mastodon, and even the camel became extinct on the American continent, only to survive and flourish in parts of Asia after their migration east across the few remaining land bridges. The horse, too, would not reappear in America until the arrival of the Spanish conquistadores in the 16th century.

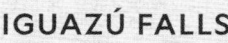

Elsewhere, notably in Africa, Asia, and Europe, agriculture encouraged the creation of permanent settlements. It allowed villagers to pool their resources, increasing harvest yields beyond subsistence levels. Such proto-villages also bestowed a sense of security, which enabled early farmers to share tools, seeds, and draft animals, while women found companionship and shared support in raising their offspring. As these villages prospered, eventually numbering some hundred people or more, tribal bonds began to develop.

What's more, the growing surplus of food allowed some members of the community to abandon farming and focus instead on crafts, for which there was a growing demand.

THESE MAMMOTH ivory figures from Malta, Siberia, are believed to date from the 21st to the 17th millennium B.C.E.

IGUAZÚ FALLS

One of the greatest world wonders is Iguazú Falls (at right), a vast complex of massive waterfalls fed by the Iguazú and Paraná Rivers on the border between Brazil and Argentina. Towering at a height of up to 269 feet, a large portion of the river plunges deep into in a U-shaped gorge known as the Devil's Throat. Geologists believe that these amazing falls were created some 100,000 years ago as a result of tectonic shifts, causing part of the Iguazú delta to drop, leaving a sharp crevice in place. Today, the water still cascades down at a rate of between 25,000 and 350,000 cubic feet per second. Regrettably, as a result of the construction of a dam in 1998 near Caxias, on the Brazilian side, the flow of water has been reduced, with potentially catastrophic consequences for the rich tropical plant life and wildlife.

MORE THAN 10,000
ARROWHEADS AND
SPEAR POINTS, KNOWN
AS CLOVIS POINTS,
HAVE BEEN FOUND IN
1,500 SITES ACROSS
NORTH AMERICA.

This is how a distinct class of craftsmen emerged, engaged in either the production of pottery, tools, farming implements, or textiles, or the brewing of beer. Others specialized in spinning sheep wool into textiles or weaving reeds into baskets. Such diversification naturally made communal life more complex. Before long, villagers understood that a central administrator was needed to set common values for barter and to rule over any disputes that might arise. A leader was chosen. As the village grew, the power and influence of this tribal chieftain increased as well. Thus, the foundation was laid for the emergence of city-states during the next millennium, led by a "king," who often served as chief priest of the city's patron god as well.

The development of settlements sowed the seeds for the rise of human civilization and the development of distinct cultures, such as the Clovis toolmaking culture in the North American Southwest (ca 11,500 B.C.E.); the Jomon culture of tools and potters in Japan (10,500 B.C.E.); and the Anatolian culture of 7250 B.C.E., which produced one of the first built cities at Catal Huyuk. ■

THE FUNCTION of this Neolithic life-size statue of a human being, found nine miles from Göbekli Tepe, Turkey, is still a mystery.

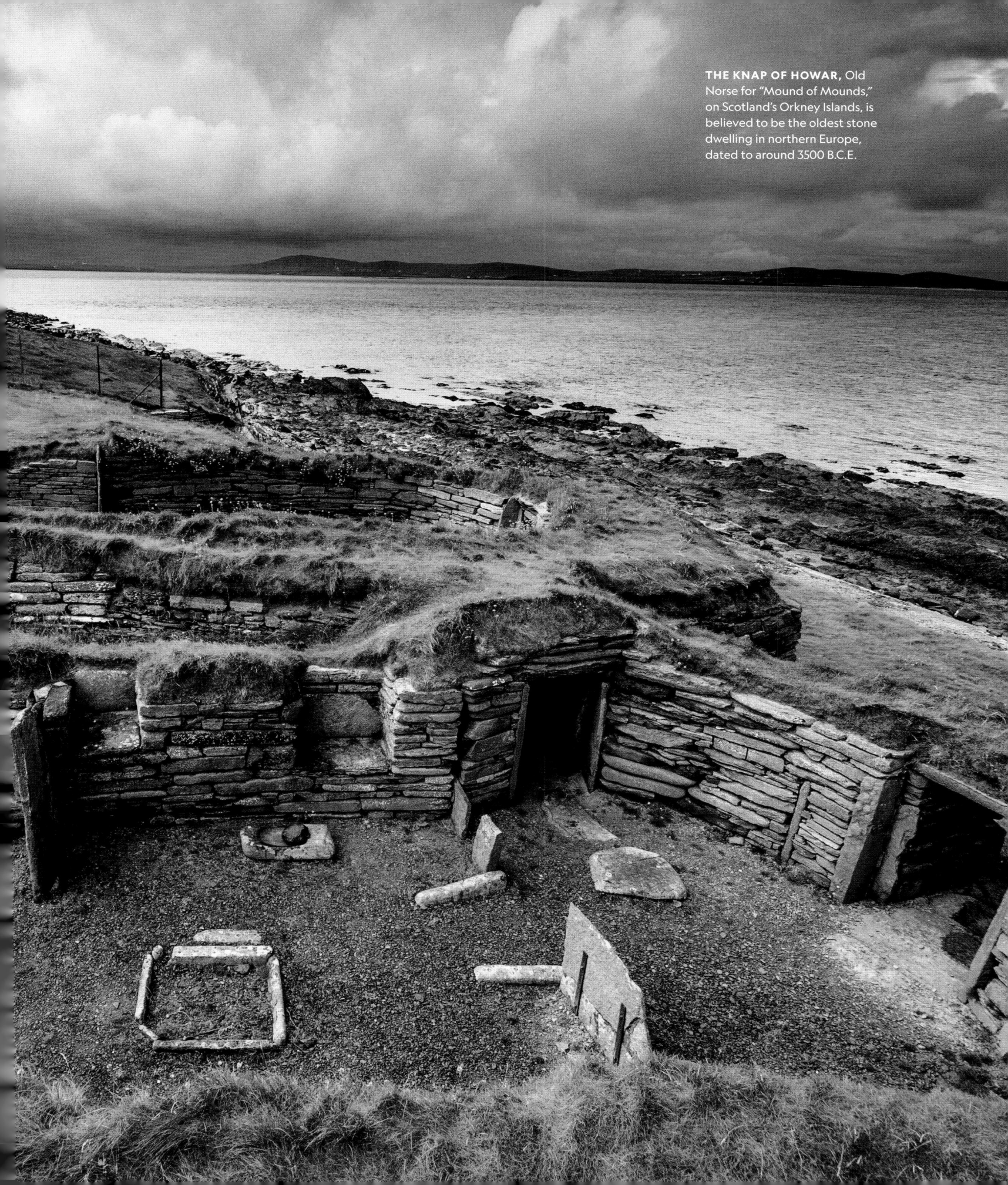

THE KNAP OF HOWAR, Old Norse for "Mound of Mounds," on Scotland's Orkney Islands, is believed to be the oldest stone dwelling in northern Europe, dated to around 3500 B.C.E.

A NEOLITHIC plastered skull from Ain Ghazal, ca 7200 B.C.E. Such heads were often buried beneath a dwelling, perhaps to ensure that the deceased's spirit would continue to guide the family.

THE FIRST HUMAN CULTURES

During the Neolithic or New Stone Age, the first human settlements arose in various parts of the Near East, Mesopotamia, and Asia, each of which would lay the foundation for early civilizations in the millennia to follow.

Ancient Jericho, located about 15 miles northeast of Jerusalem on a mound known as Tell es-Sultan, is perhaps the most impressive of these early settlements. Dating as far back as 8500 B.C.E., Jericho is often considered the oldest continuously inhabited city in the world. Sprawled across as many as 75 acres, Jericho soon had a population of some 2,000 people who lived in round huts, made not with reeds but with mud bricks—the earliest known use of mud baked in the sun. Even more remarkable is that this village was surrounded by a stone wall and a ditch, anchored by a mysterious tower. Thirty feet in diameter, the tower featured an internal staircase of stone steps that presumably led to its summit for observation, sacrifice, or some other type of religious rite.

Digging through the tell (a mound of successive layers of habitation) of Tell es-Sultan, archaeologists have identified no fewer than 21 successive settlements at Jericho. British archaeologist Kathleen Kenyon found massive, six-foot-thick walls, but these were demolished sometime before the sixth millennium B.C.E., most likely as a result of an earthquake. When the city was later rebuilt, it surrounded itself with a rampart of packed-mud walls—not much of a defense against a determined enemy. Nonetheless, the renown of its former walls may have inspired the story in the Bible whereby Joshua, the leader of the Israelites, was able to topple the walls with a mighty war cry, enhanced by priests blowing on rams' horns (Joshua 6:20). In and around Jericho, Kenyon discovered numerous fragments of sickle blades, which suggest that its inhabitants were farmers, cultivating such crops as barley, flax, einkorn, and emmer wheat. The discovery of arrowheads may indicate that these villagers were also engaged in the hunt to complement their diet.

Jericho was considered an exceptional settlement of the Neolithic Age, which spanned a time from ca 8500 to 4500 B.C.E., until the discovery of Ain Ghazal, near today's Amman in Jordan. The oldest excavated stratum at Ain Ghazal dates to about

AN EARLY PICTOGRAPHIC TABLET from Uruk, dated 3100–2900 B.C.E., deals with the administration of grain distribution.

7200 B.C.E., but this village was almost three times larger than Jericho. Its inhabitants raised a variety of crops and kept domesticated animals, including dogs, cattle, and pigs. The most astonishing feature of Ain Ghazal is its domestic structures. Unlike the mud-brick huts of Jericho, excavators found the remains of square houses made of stone, with each dwelling divided by walls to separate areas for various purposes. These walls were plastered to protect the family against moisture in winter and excessive heat in summer; in later centuries, the floors were plastered as well. This archetype of a farmer's home would remain common in the Near East for many thousands of years. Here too, skillful hands learned to spin sheep wool into textiles, weave reeds into baskets, and bake mud into bricks.

The 'Ubaid Culture

Some thousand miles to the east, in Mesopotamia, we see a similar development during the rise of the 'Ubaid culture (5200–3500 B.C.E.), named after the artifacts found at Tell al-'Ubaid in southern Mesopotamia. Among these are pottery samples that show a consistent and elegant geometric pattern applied with brown or black paint. Some of these vessels are equipped with handles and spouts. Originally pottery was produced by kneading clay so as to remove all pockets of air and rolling it into long strings or loops that could be coiled atop one another. In some cases, the clay was put on a flat, rotating platform, so that the potter could turn the clay and shape it equally on all sides. In the late third millennium B.C.E., Mesopotamian artisans

THE GARDEN OF EDEN

The Book of Genesis tells us that Adam and Eve dwelled in a beautiful Shangri-la, a garden called "Eden" (at left). Its meaning is uncertain, although a Babylonian cuneiform tablet uses *edinu* as a term for an "uncultivated plain." Some authors suggest that Eden may be linked to the Sumerian legend of a utopian land called Dilmun, sometimes identified with present-day Bahrain. Regardless of where this mythical land may have existed, the description in the Bible—as well as in the Quran, written many centuries later—leaves little doubt about the true significance of Eden: It was everything that the harsh Arabian desert was not. Many centuries later, when the Genesis tradition came under Persian influence during the Exile, the Garden of Eden acquired a new name: paradise, rooted in the Old Persian word *pardis*.

THE FORTIFICATIONS of Tell es-Sultan near Jericho date from the Middle Bronze Age IIA and IIB (1950–1550 B.C.E.).

NOTABLE DATES

ca 8500 B.C.E.
Earliest settlement of Jericho

ca 7200 B.C.E.
Foundation of Ain Ghazal, Jordan

ca 7000 B.C.E.
Neolithic or New Stone Age begins

ca 6500 B.C.E.
Legendary date of the founding of Ur

ca 6500 B.C.E.
Foundation of Catal Huyuk in Anatolia (Turkey)

ca 5500 B.C.E.
Communities in Near East learn to fire clay pottery

ca 5200 B.C.E.
Beginning of the 'Ubaid culture in Mesopotamia

ca 5000 B.C.E.
Legendary foundation of Eridu in Sumer

ca 5000 B.C.E.
Agriculture spreads in Africa, Asia, and Europe

ca 4500 B.C.E.
Communities with mud-brick dwellings become common

ca 4000 B.C.E.
Early farming settlements in Egypt

ca 4000 B.C.E.
People along the coast of Ghana, West Africa, develop pottery

ca 4000 B.C.E.
The woolly mammoth goes extinct in the Americas

A TERRA-COTTA FIGURE dating from 3500 B.C.E. was found at Tell al-'Ubaid near the ancient city of Ur in today's Iraq.

developed the fast-spinning potter's wheel, which allowed potters to use centrifugal energy to lift a clump of clay into a uniform shape, producing ever thinner walls in a great variety of shapes. Other potters would sometimes use a mold to create multiple versions of a particular design; terra-cotta olive lamps, for example, were often produced in quantity using a mold with a geometric or other nonfigurative motif.

Even more advanced is the layout of 'Ubaid villages. Until this time, settlements were a relatively haphazard affair. But 'Ubaid habitations show evidence of some form of planning. The houses, built of mud brick, are grouped around a shared courtyard and separated from other blocks by small alleyways. Strategically placed throughout the village are larger structures that may have provided storage for the villagers. In the center of the settlement is a mound, surmounted by what some scholars presume is a large shrine, dedicated to the patron god of the village. If this is true, it indicates the emergence of a faith system: the shared belief that human fate is controlled by otherworldly and vastly more powerful beings. Such sacred mounds in the heart of the settlement would become a common feature in communities throughout southern Mesopotamia.

The growth of settlements also fostered a sense of continuity with both the past and the future. This led to a funerary cult that recognized one's ancestors and the familial bonds of a clan. In some of these early cults, villagers initially buried the head of a deceased family member beneath the floor of their dwelling, perhaps to ensure that his spirit would continue to serve the family. After all tissue had decomposed, these ancestral heads were then covered with clay to restore their facial features. Near the end of the Stone Age, a new custom emerged: The entire body was interred until fully decomposed; then the bones were buried again in a ceramic box. This box, known as an ossuary, was often shaped in the form of a miniature house. The practice of secondary burial in stone ossuaries would continue well into Greco-Roman times.

Elsewhere, the deceased were carefully dressed, painted, and interred with their tools and jewelry, often with a stone slab marking the location of the grave. The bodies of the poor were usually interred in the soil, whereas the wealthy placed their dead in tombs.

THE SO-CALLED Royal Standard of Ur from around 2600 B.C.E., one of the most important artifacts from Sumer, depicts scenes of war and peace.

A COPPER ALLOY JAR with a spout is dated to the Late Uruk Period (3500–3100 B.C.E.).

> "LOOK AT IT STILL TODAY . . . THE OUTER WALL WHERE THE CORNICE RUNS, IT SHINES WITH THE BRILLIANCE OF COPPER; AND THE INNER WALL, IT HAS NO EQUAL."
>
> DESCRIPTION OF URUK IN THE *EPIC OF GILGAMESH*

The Rise of Cities

The advent of the Early Bronze Age around 3300 B.C.E. witnessed another set of important innovations. The development of the plow greatly increased agricultural yields. Copper ores were mined and alloyed with tin or other metals to produce bronze tools. By blending copper with tin, its melting point is reduced, thus making it easier to cast a particular shape. Bronze is also much harder than pure copper, which makes it an ideal metal for tools, arms, and armor. At the same time, trees were beginning to be planted in dedicated orchards for the production of a large surplus of olives and olive oil. To move these goods, the donkey emerged as the principal beast of burden.

Especially in dry climates, cultivation depends on a steady supply of water. This problem was tackled with the development of irrigation systems, which may rank as the greatest invention of the Early Bronze Age. The earliest canalization appears around 3000 B.C.E. in Mesopotamia, in the territory of Sumer (today's Iraq), where it was used to channel water from the Euphrates and Tigris Rivers to arable lands far inland. Such large-scale projects required planning, organization, and the cooperative use of capital and labor.

Not surprisingly, it is in Mesopotamia (literally "the land between the rivers") that we see the rise of the first major cities. One of the earliest and most powerful of these city-states was Uruk (the biblical Erech, and possibly the root of the word

CREATION EPICS OF MESOPOTAMIA

A narrative similar to Genesis can be found in the Babylonian creation epic, recorded on Akkadian tablets (at left) from the first millennium B.C.E., although their origins probably stretch back into the days of ancient Sumer. According to this epic, the Earth was formed by the god Marduk in six days after he vanquished the evil ocean goddess, Tiamat. Marduk first created the Earth and the firmament. Next, the epic tells us, "he constructed stations for the great gods, fixing their astral likeness as constellations." He then "caused the moon to shine" and appointed him "a creature of the night to signify the days." On the seventh day, Marduk created "a savage—'man' shall be his name. He shall be charged with the service of the gods."

IN MESOPOTAMIA, the Sumer culture reached its apogee in the city-state of Uruk, known as Erech in the Bible, nurtured by the waters of the Euphrates and the Tigris.

"Iraq"). Another was Eridu, which the Sumerian King List—a stone prism tentatively dated to 2100 B.C.E. documenting Sumer's rulers—identifies as the first city-state on Earth. The development of these early towns evolved over many centuries. Nevertheless, by the beginning of the fourth millennium B.C.E., a handful of prosperous communities had become so large and architecturally so sophisticated that they became true cities. They all boasted large agricultural markets where farmers could sell the region's surplus and where the worship of various regional deities slowly coalesced into a national cult. Inevitably this concentration of wealth also led to a growing bureaucracy to regulate and administer the expanding initiatives of public life. Thus, a hierarchical political system, a *res publica,* was born in which professional bureaucrats mediated between the populace and their supreme ruler.

From 3000 to about 2700 B.C.E, Uruk emerged as the dominant city-state of Sumeria. According to the Sumerian King List, Uruk was founded by a mythical ruler named Enmerkar, whose successor—the famous King Gilgamesh—was responsible for encircling the city with defensive walls. Uruk remained shrouded in legend until 1912, when a German team uncovered the remains of the city some 150 miles southeast of Baghdad, in Iraq. The excavations proved that the description

AFTER 3500 B.C.E., Sumerian merchants began to record their trade using a primitive pictographic script carved in soft clay, which eventually led to cuneiform writing.

A MAN in silhouette punts a shallow boat on the Euphrates River in Iraq.

A DIORITE HEAD found at Telloh, ancient Ngirsu, depicts Gudea, king of Lagash.

in the *Epic of Gilgamesh* was not poetic license. The walls of the ancient city ran for more than five miles in circumference. At its peak, Uruk covered an area of some 250 acres—by far the largest city-state in Sumer of this period.

The Growth of Trade

Many of these early cultures came about as a result of trade. Once early farming settlements began to produce an agricultural surplus, they looked for opportunities to trade that surplus for goods produced outside their community. In Mesopotamia, foodstuffs were exchanged for highly prized raw materials such as copper, seashells, and obsidian. Copper, discovered in Egyptian mines, was smelted and fabricated in numerous villages along the Nile. Obsidian, a natural glass found in volca-

nic areas in southeastern Turkey, was much prized throughout the Middle East for its use in blades and tools. In Mesopotamia, prosperity in trade produced a number of important city centers, such as Uruk, Lagash, Kish, Nippur, and Ur. By 2750 B.C.E., Ur's trade had made it the dominant city-state in all of southern Mesopotamia.

Meanwhile, in Egypt, Memphis (the capital of the Old Kingdom) traded its copper and turquoise for raw materials such as wood, gold, and the myriad chemicals needed in its mortuary temples, the center of Egypt's cult of the dead. Other major commodities were incense and ivory (Arabia and India), wine (Canaan and the Aegean), wood (Lebanon), cereals (Mesopotamia and Syria), and a red mineral known as carnelian (ancient Egypt and Greece).

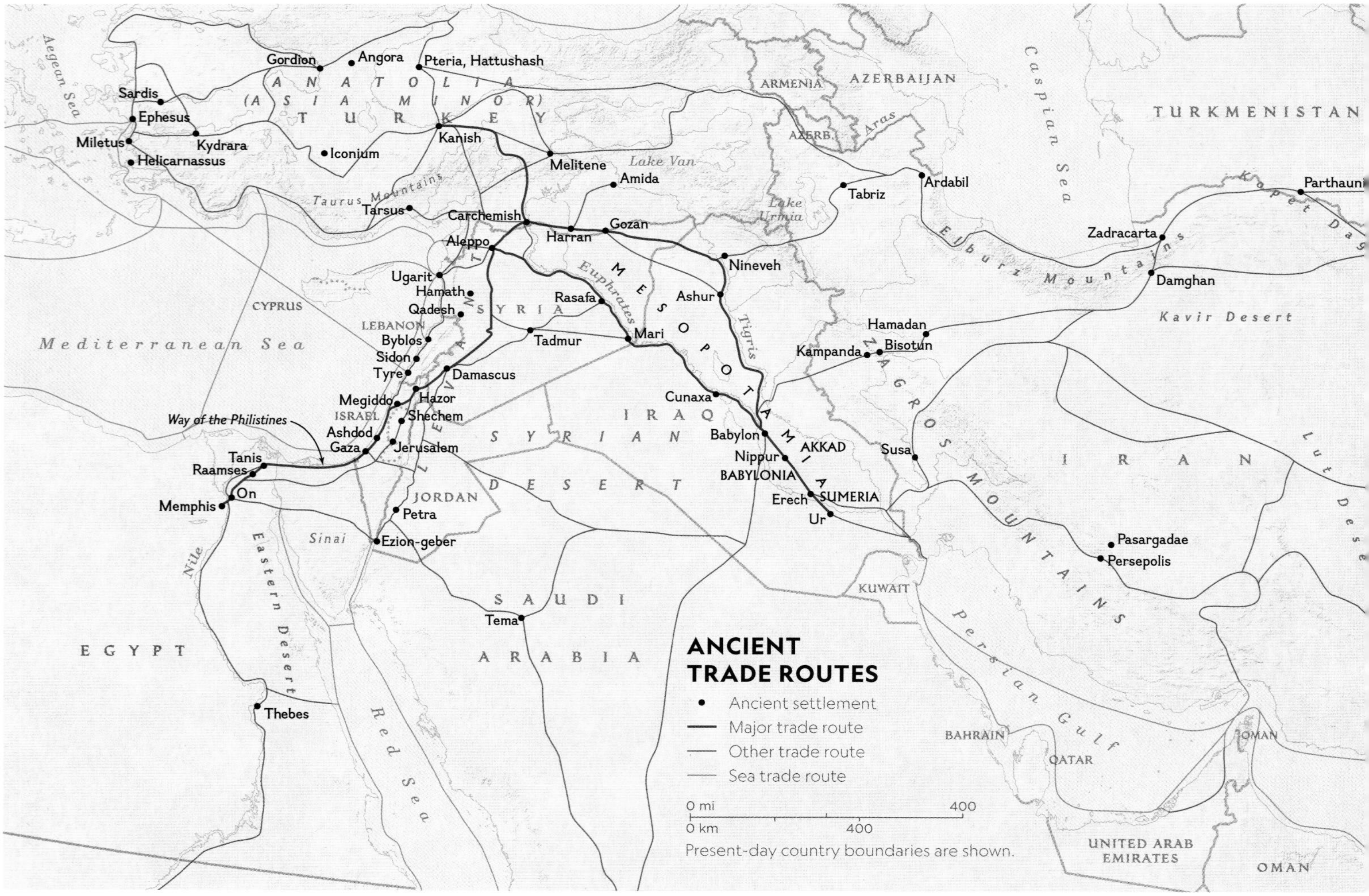

ANCIENT TRADE ROUTES

• Ancient settlement
━━ Major trade route
── Other trade route
── Sea trade route

0 mi 400
0 km 400
Present-day country boundaries are shown.

By the Middle Bronze Age, a number of trade "highways" were in use, each skirting the Arabian Desert. One was the Via Maris or Way of the Sea (*derekh ha-yam*) that ran from Egypt along the Mediterranean to the Jezreel Valley, the Transjordan, and onward to Syria, including the major trade centers of Aleppo, Harran, and Mari. From here, a southern route, running just below the Euphrates, brought goods to the Sumerian capital cities of Nippur, Uruk, and Ur. In the Book of Genesis, for example, Abraham used this route from Ur to Harran and from Harran down south to Canaan, the territory later known as Israel.

Meanwhile, Ur itself, which at the time was closer to the Persian Gulf, was the way station to trade with the nascent cultures of the Indus Valley. A northern route ran just north of the Tigris and

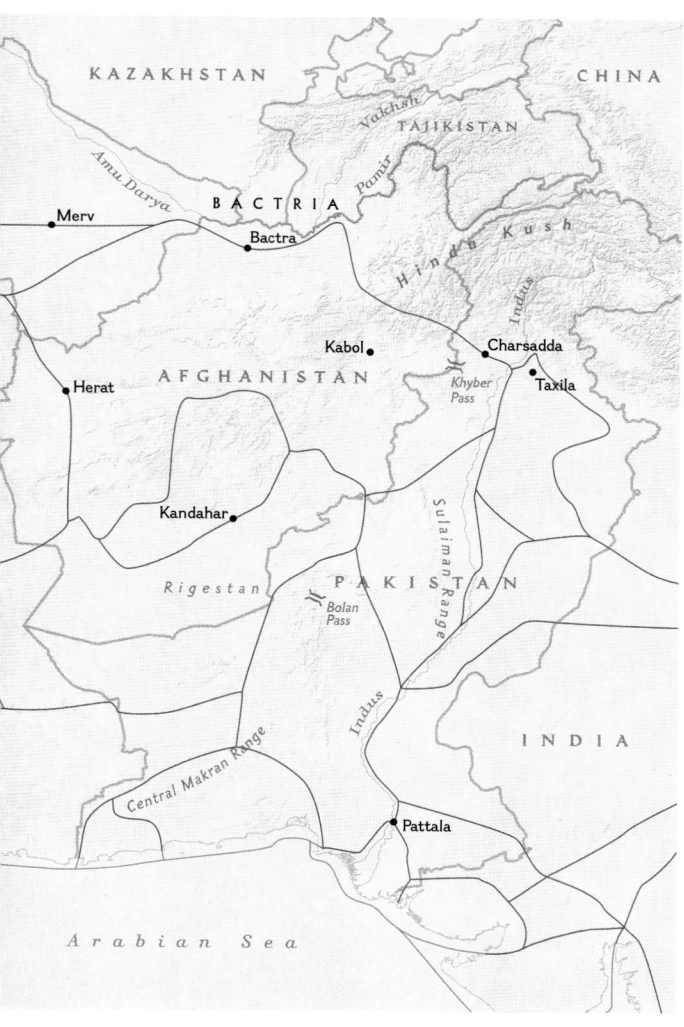

connected Harran with Ashur and Hamadan, where it branched off in the direction of Bactria and the markets of the East.

Another major road, the King's Highway (*derekh ha-melekh*) led from the Gulf of Eilat northward through the Negev and along the eastern bank of the Jordan to the city of Damascus, where it joined the Via Maris. Traders chose such well-traveled paths because they typically featured a number of watering holes, located strategically at a travel distance of no more than two days—the maximum time a rider on a donkey could travel without replenishing water bags.

Trade produced prosperity, which often aroused the envy of less fortunate towns and settlements. Cities began to compete with one another over such things as water rights, trade concessions, and fertile swaths of land. This spurred the development of another profession: the military. Affluent townships were able to throw up walls and other defensive works to protect themselves against marauders, which encouraged others in outlying areas to come and settle inside the relative safety of these fortifications. ∎

THE REMAINS of a ziggurat, built of sunbaked mud bricks, looms over the ancient site of Nippur in today's Iraq.

A MESOPOTAMIAN RELIEF from 2250–1900 B.C.E. depicts legendary King Gilgamesh of Uruk killing the Bull of Heaven.

THE CIVILIZATION OF
MESOPOTAMIA

Of all the early civilizations, the culture of Sumer in Mesopotamia (literally "the land between the rivers"), which was later continued in the Babylonian Empire, would have the greatest influence on the development of humankind.

Much of Sumer's activity was governed by its proximity to the Tigris and Euphrates Rivers. Unlike the Nile, however, the Euphrates and Tigris did not flood the countryside in predictable cycles. A field could bear fruit one year, only to be completely inundated during the next. It is therefore not surprising that there are countless references to a "great flood," often believed to have been orchestrated by divine power, in the literature of ancient Mesopotamia. The Sumerian King List is even organized in two separate periods: one before the Great Flood of 2900 B.C.E, and one after. Many of these flood stories have strong parallels with the story of Noah in the Book of Genesis.

In the *Atrahasis Epic,* for example, the gods decide to destroy humankind with an immense inundation. But the water god Enki takes pity on a man named Atrahasis and orders him to build a boat. This vessel, the god instructs him, should be filled with all of his possessions, including animals and birds.

The famous *Epic of Gilgamesh* offers an even closer parallel to the Noah story. In this account, Gilgamesh's ancestor Utnapishtim is told to build a large ship. "These are the measurements of the barque as you shall build her," the god Ea tells him. "Let her beam equal her length, let her deck be roofed like the vault that covers the abyss; then take up into the boat the seed of all living creatures." In Genesis, God tells Noah, "This is how you are to make it: the length of the ark three hundred cubits, its width fifty cubits, and its height thirty cubits. Make a roof for the ark, and finish it to a cubit above . . . And of every living thing, of all flesh, you shall bring two of every kind" (Genesis 6:14-19).

But did such a catastrophic flood actually take place? The Sumerian King List indicates that it must have happened before 2600 B.C.E. In 1922, while excavating the royal tombs of Ur near Tell al-Muqayyar in today's Iraq, British archaeologist Sir Leonard Woolley discovered a deep layer of "perfectly clean clay, uniform throughout, the texture of which showed that it had been laid there by

A MESOPOTAMIAN WEIGHT shows King Gilgamesh fighting two snakes.

"AFTER, FOR SEVEN DAYS [AND] SEVEN NIGHTS,
THE FLOOD HAD SWEPT OVER THE LAND . . .
ZIUSUDRA OPENED A WINDOW OF THE HUGE BOAT."

THE "GREAT FLOOD" IN THE ERIDU GENESIS TABLET

water." The layer was eight feet deep and then completely disappeared. His discovery prompted headlines around the world: Here, at last, was proof of the biblical Flood!

But in the years since, archaeologists have found evidence of many other greater and lesser floods in the area. It shows that the ancient "land between the rivers" was simply prone to frequent and sometimes catastrophic flooding. Modern research has found traces of an exceptionally large flood that must have occurred around 2900 B.C.E. Scientists base this theory on the radiocarbon dating of river sediments near Shuruppak (today's Tell Fara in Iraq). This vast deluge would undoubtedly have

Humbaba the giant

destroyed many of Sumer's incipient city-states and may have prompted a power shift from the city of Uruk to a fast-rising center on the Sumerian plain: the city of Ur, the putative birthplace of Abraham in Genesis. As documented by the Sumerian King List, "after Uruk was defeated, its kingship was carried off to Ur."

The City of Ur

Ur was an ancient city as old as Uruk, with settlements that dated back to the 'Ubaid period. Today, Ur lies 10 miles distant from the Euphrates, surrounded by bare desert, but in its heyday, the Euphrates flowed much closer, and Ur's surrounding fields were lush and fertile. By 2750 B.C.E., Ur had become the dominant city-state in all of southern Mesopotamia and the main center of its trade, including links with faraway territories like Egypt.

One reason for Ur's wealth was that its farmers began to develop a sophisticated system to better control the watering of the alluvial soil bordering the two great rivers. Naturally, such an ambitious and labor-intensive irrigation system required planning, equipment, and resources—in sum, it required organization. To accomplish this, the Sumerians formed a farmers' cooperative that after 3000 B.C.E. was in charge of a vast irrigation network across the Sumerian plains. So lush were Sumeria's vineyards and so fertile its groves that it was easy to imagine Sumer as the Garden of Eden on Earth.

THIS SEVENTH-CENTURY B.C.E. Assyrian tablet from Nineveh relates a part of the famous *Epic of Gilgamesh*, including the story of a great flood.

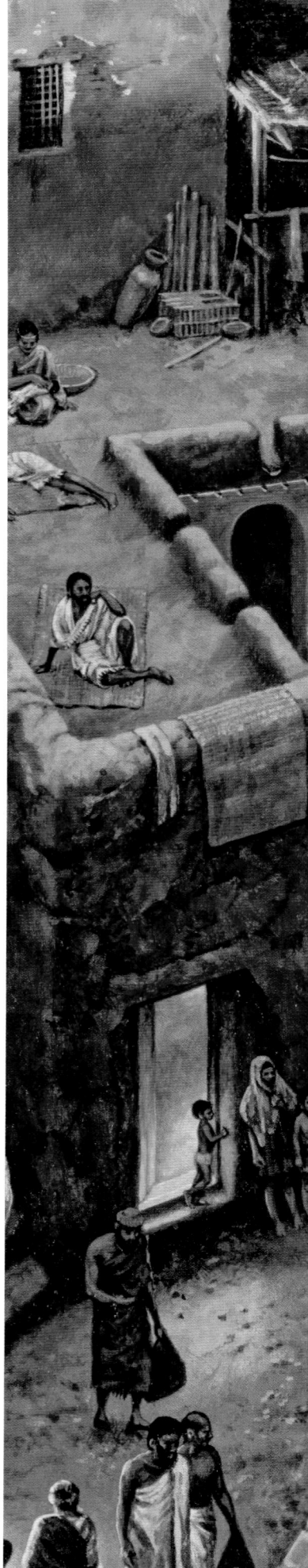

A MODERN ILLUSTRATION of the city of Ur at its peak during the Third Dynasty (ca 2113–2006 B.C.E.)

NOTABLE DATES

ca 3300 B.C.E.

Early Bronze Age begins

ca 3300 B.C.E.

First city-states emerge in Mesopotamia

ca 3200 B.C.E.

First examples of pictographic writing in Sumer

ca 3000 B.C.E.

Uruk becomes dominant city-state in Sumer

ca 2900 B.C.E.

Massive flood destroys most of the cities in Sumer

ca 2750 B.C.E.

Ur becomes the dominant city of southern Mesopotamia

ca 2560 B.C.E.

King Mesh-Ane-pada establishes the First Dynasty of Ur

ca 2350 B.C.E.

King of Lagash drafts the first code of law

ca 2100 B.C.E.

The Sumerian King List documents all kings of Sumer to date

ca 2000 B.C.E.

Epic of Gilgamesh is recorded

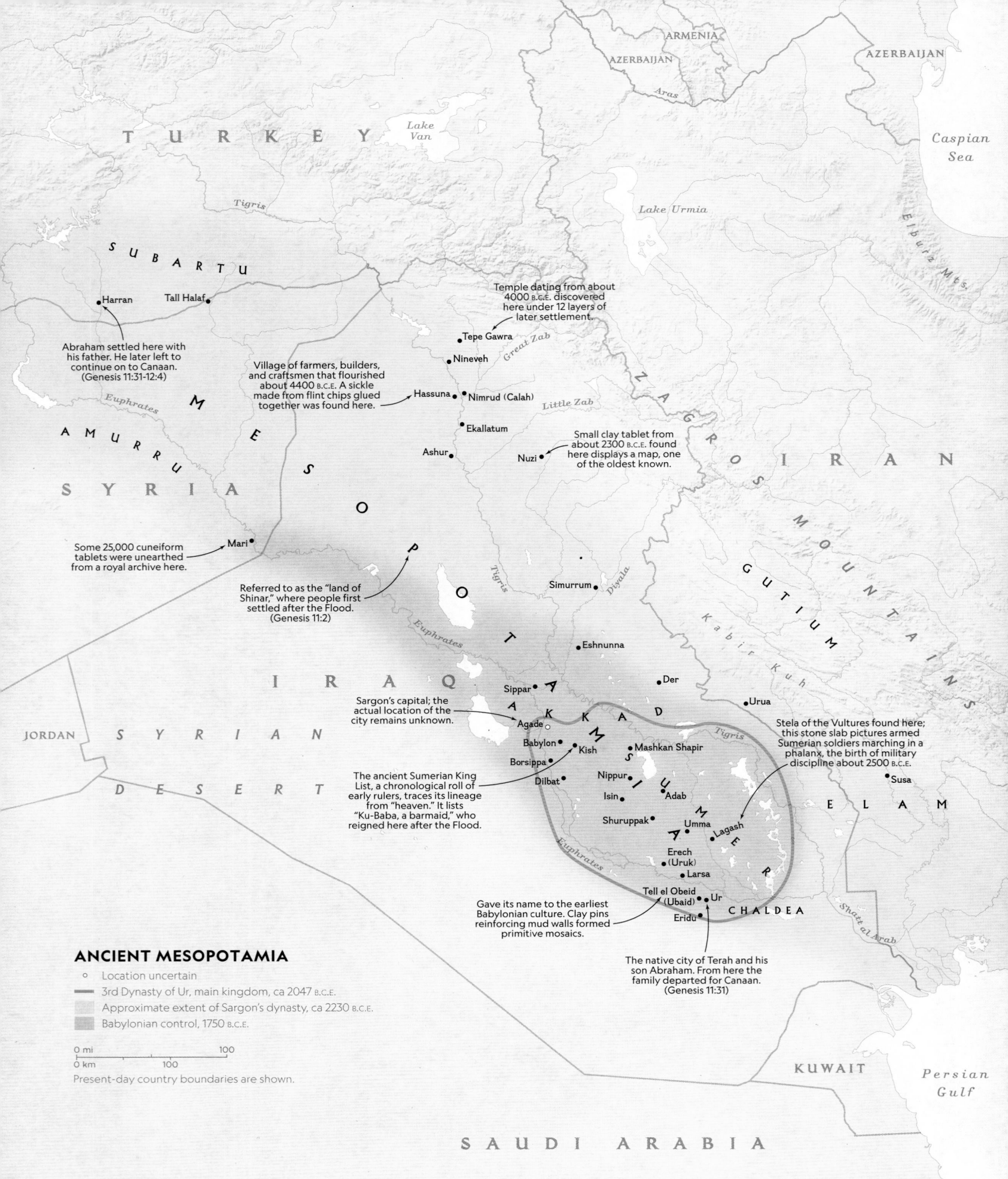

ARMENIA
AZERBAIJAN
AZERBAIJAN

Caspian Sea

TURKEY

Lake Van

Tigris

Aras

Lake Urmia

Elburz Mts.

SUBARTU

Harran •   Tall Halaf •

Abraham settled here with his father. He later left to continue on to Canaan. (Genesis 11:31–12:4)

M E S

Temple dating from about 4000 B.C.E. discovered here under 12 layers of later settlement.

• Tepe Gawra

Great Zab

• Nineveh

Village of farmers, builders, and craftsmen that flourished about 4400 B.C.E. A sickle made from flint chips glued together was found here.

Hassuna •   • Nimrud (Calah)

Little Zab

Euphrates

A M U R R U

• Ekallatum

S Y R I A

Ashur •

Small clay tablet from about 2300 B.C.E. found here displays a map, one of the oldest known.

Nuzi •

I R A N

Z A G R O S

O

Some 25,000 cuneiform tablets were unearthed from a royal archive here.

Mari •

Referred to as the "land of Shinar," where people first settled after the Flood. (Genesis 11:2)

P

Tigris

Simurrum •

Diyala

G U T I U M

M O U N T A I N S

Kabir Kuh

O

• Eshnunna

T

• Der

I R A Q

A

Sippar •

• Urua

Sargon's capital; the actual location of the city remains unknown.

Agade ○

M

Tigris

Stela of the Vultures found here; this stone slab pictures armed Sumerian soldiers marching in a phalanx, the birth of military discipline about 2500 B.C.E.

JORDAN

Babylon • • Kish

• Mashkan Shapir

A

K

K

A

D

• Susa

S Y R I A N

Borsippa •

Dilbat •

The ancient Sumerian King List, a chronological roll of early rulers, traces its lineage from "heaven." It lists "Ku-Baba, a barmaid," who reigned here after the Flood.

Nippur •

S

Isin •

• Adab

U

E L A M

D E S E R T

Shuruppak •

M

Umma •

A

• Lagash

Erech (Uruk) •

Euphrates

• Larsa

E

R

Shatt al Arab

Gave its name to the earliest Babylonian culture. Clay pins reinforcing mud walls formed primitive mosaics.

Tell el Obeid (Ubaid) •   • Ur

CHALDEA

Eridu •

The native city of Terah and his son Abraham. From here the family departed for Canaan. (Genesis 11:31)

ANCIENT MESOPOTAMIA

○   Location uncertain

———   3rd Dynasty of Ur, main kingdom, ca 2047 B.C.E.

Approximate extent of Sargon's dynasty, ca 2230 B.C.E.

Babylonian control, 1750 B.C.E.

0 mi   100
0 km   100

Present-day country boundaries are shown.

KUWAIT

Persian Gulf

S A U D I   A R A B I A

A similar development took place in another region blessed with a perpetual source of water: ancient Egypt. Here, only a modicum of irrigation was necessary, because each year, the Nile River rose like clockwork to deposit mineral-rich alluvial sediment over the adjoining fields. The result was a process of cultural growth very similar to what was happening in Mesopotamia, many hundreds of miles to the east. Thus, when the climate changed once more around 2500 B.C.E. and warmer temperatures robbed many regions in the Near East of their access to water, Egypt and Mesopotamia emerged as the two leading civilizations of the Early Bronze Age.

Similar changes in climate affected the area of Syria-Canaan, the principal territory of the stories in the Book of Genesis, which refers to famine no fewer than 24 times. As Egyptian records attest, this was not a rare occurrence and often led to social disorder, political instability, and wholesale migrations. The uncertainty of rainfall on which all agriculture depended was a principal factor, but other calamities—such as wind, mildew, disease, and insect pests—could also cause a harvest to fail. Since grain was the principal crop, a poor harvest had an immediate impact on a region's food supply. Archaeologists have found evidence of an extensive drought in the second millennium B.C.E that may be correlated to the story of Abraham's sojourn into Egypt. Some climatologists have linked this drought to persistent low flooding levels of the Nile during the Old Kingdom.

Early Religious Practices

Numerous clay figurines found in today's Iraq and Syria show that from the very beginning, the civilizations of ancient Mesopotamia were grounded in the collective worship of a pantheon of gods. Given that agriculture was the principal economic activity of ancient Sumer and the threat of flooding or drought was always present, it is not surprising that these earliest deities were closely

AN EXQUISITELY chiseled helmet made of hammered gold, found in the tomb of Meskalamdug in Ur

THE THRESHING FLOOR

In most agricultural communities of the Bronze Age, the threshing floor played a vital role in the village. It was usually composed of a bedrock surface in an elevated position, where the wind blew strongest. During harvesting, the sheaves were dropped on a pile; then the pile was passed over with a device known as a threshing board, a wooden slab studded with jagged stones or iron bits on the bottom. The repeated motion of the threshing board steadily removed the kernels of grain from the stalks, so that in due course, there remained a confused pile of grain, chaff (husks and stubble), and straw. As the afternoon breeze picked up, the farmer then threw the harvested wheat up in the air (at right), hoping for the wind to blow away the empty stalks and chaff from the heavier kernels. This motion was continued until all of the chaff had been dispersed, leaving only the pile of precious grain.

"ENDOWED WITH WISDOM BY ENKI AM I, THE MIGHTY KING OF NANNA AM I."

SUMERIAN HYMN OF PRAISE TO KING SHULGI, THIRD DYNASTY OF UR

intertwined with agricultural needs. Each god and goddess was believed to be responsible for a key element of crop growth—such as water (Enki), sun (Utu), earth (Ninhursag), air (Enlil), and fertility (Inanna). Many of these deities were revered as the patron god of a particular region. Enki, god of fresh water and wisdom, was worshipped as the patron god of the city of Eridu. In Uruk, the dominant gods were Inanna, the goddess of fertility, love, and war, and An, the god of heaven and ruler of the constellations.

In this early stage of human development, villages and their central shrines were relatively modest. An exception is the highly sophisticated central sanctuary found at the site of ancient Eridu, often considered the world's first major urban development. Located near Abu Shahrain in Iraq, some 12 miles southwest of Ur, Eridu was home to a large population of farmers and fisher-hunters, living in huts made of reeds or mud brick. At one end rose what is perhaps the first monumental structure in human history: a temple complex on a stepped terrace, accessible through stairways and dedicated to Enki. Inside, excavators found bone fragments of fish and other small creatures that may have been offerings to the deity. The Eridu shrine was destroyed and rebuilt at least 12 times over the centuries; archaeologist

A STATUETTE of the so-called Great Singer, from Tell Hariri in today's Syria, is dated to ca 2500 B.C.E.

EGYPTIAN CHILDREN ride a donkey near the great stepped pyramid of Djoser in Saqqara, designed by his court architect, Imhotep.

A MODERN
reconstruction of a
barque dedicated to
Enki, the Sumerian god
of water, magic, and
fertility and patron of
the city of Eridu

Fuad Safar, who began to excavate the site in 1946, estimated that the oldest sanctuary dates to before 5000 B.C.E.

Close to the sanctuary, Safar and his fellow archaeologist Seton Lloyd found a vast cemetery of individual mud-brick tombs, many well stocked with pottery, food, jewelry, and other artifacts. This necropolis may have been intended for the nobility of Eridu, who wished to be buried in the shadow of the city's great temple. Many of the tombs' 6,500-year-old bones were still in excellent condition. Men, women, and children had been carefully laid on their backs, accompanied by what appear to be personal items. In one instance, a small boy had been buried with his dog, a bone still in its jaws.

As Sumer's culture expanded, deities like Inanna, An, and Utu became recognized as gods throughout the Mesopotamian realm. When the region was conquered by Babylon many centuries later, its deities were absorbed and renamed—not unlike the way the Romans would adopt the gods of Greek mythology. Thus, Inanna became the Babylonian Ishtar, and Utu became Shamash. Ishtar was revered as the goddess of sexual love and is believed by some to be the patron goddess of prostitutes. In biblical times, Canaanite farmers would sometimes visit Ishtar shrines and mate with cult prostitutes to secure the harvest.

Early Sacrificial Cults

Sacrifice became an important part of these cults, as elsewhere in the ancient world. Animals— and possibly even humans—were sacrificed to the gods in order to secure the availability of water, earth, fertility, and other key elements of the harvest. By appeasing these deities with worship and sacrifice, it was believed, humans could assert some control over prevailing climate conditions so as to secure a good harvest.

THE COVER OF A COSMETIC BOX from Ugarit shows a fertility goddess, possibly Asherah, with rams, carved from elephantine ivory and dated ca 1200 B.C.E.

Eventually a form of national worship emerged, which inevitably fostered the emergence of a dedicated priesthood, whose task it was to develop and maintain an elaborate liturgy of cultic practice. This cadre grew into a powerful constituency; records from the Third Dynasty of Ur refer to a community of 62 priests, both male (*Ensi*) and female (*Nin*), whose rituals were accompanied by a dedicated choir and orchestra some 180 strong.

The earliest idols from Sumer are rather shapeless depictions of men and women with enlarged genitals, which suggests some form of fertility ritual. Over time, however, the Sumerian artists developed considerable artistry in shaping the images of their gods, as well as their earthly rulers. Archaeologists have discovered scores of figurines with outstretched or clasped hands, usually made of clay or gypsum, that appear to be worshippers (*orants*). Perhaps their primary function was to assure these gods that they were attended with around-the-clock worship. Excavations throughout Mesopotamia have yielded a veritable hoard of these votive statues. Most depict either a male or female worshiper dressed in fringed skirt or gown, hands tightly clasped in front of him or her, which may signify a Sumerian gesture of worship and piety.

Sumer's cult also extended into burial practices. The Royal Tombs, excavated by Leonard Woolley in 1922, contained the remains of 74 people, 68 of them women, whose bodies were arranged as if they were lined up in a funerary procession. This led Woolley to suggest a rather macabre scenario: On the death of the king, everyone in his entourage—wives, officials, and servants—was put to death as well so as to serve the deceased ruler in the afterlife. This royal retinue was equipped with every imaginable luxury. In one tomb, Woolley found a gold dagger, "its hilt of lapis lazuli decorated with gold studs"; in others, there were elaborate headdresses, a lovely harp trimmed in gold, board games, and cups and vessels of the finest materials. Woolley theorized that these tombs contained the bodies of King Abargi and Queen Puabi, together with their complete retinue.

Throughout Sumer, gods were worshipped in a dedicated structure known as a temple. In Uruk, for example, Inanna was venerated in the Pillar Temple at the heart of the city, while An, the god of heaven, was worshipped in a structure with multiple elevated levels known as the White Temple. Thus, the cult of these gods stimulated a new form of artistic endeavor: that of architecture.

Early Architecture

The concept of planned architecture originated at roughly the same time in both Mesopotamia and Egypt, but for different purposes. As we will see, in Saqqara, Egypt, Imhotep—the first named architect in history—designed a large complex of buildings as the principal mortuary precinct of his patron, King Djoser.

In Mesopotamia, the beginning of the third millennium B.C.E. also saw the rise of planned monumental architecture, but for a different reason: to honor the gods rather than deceased kings. Nor did the Sumerians as yet recognize the need for a professional architect, since most of the designing was left to skilled scribes. Nonetheless, monumental architecture was held in great esteem in the Sumerian city-states and considered one of the greatest gifts that the gods had bestowed on humankind.

Uruk is a key example. As evidenced by the *Epic of Gilgamesh,* it was one of the first planned cities

THIS GYPSUM FIGURE of a woman in prayer, known as an orant, dates from around 2400 B.C.E.

in human history with spacious streets, market squares, temples, and gardens, surrounded by a protective wall and linked to the nearby harbor via a canal. Zoned districts carefully distinguished between residential and commercial areas, civic centers, and religious precincts, all arranged with the temple at its core—not unlike the way medieval cities would slowly coalesce around their principal cathedral.

Through the late fourth and the early third millennium, these religious shrines grew from simple single-hall structures to sophisticated designs that, as in the case of ancient Egypt, aspired to the heavens. Their main purpose was to create a mediating space between the gods and people, between Earth and the firmament. Because the Earth's laws of gravity are universal, this naturally led to a pyramidal form, though the Mesopotamian solution differed from the design of Egyptian pyramids. In the Egyptian Old King-

dom, architects sought to create a perfect pyramidal shape with smooth triangular shapes on all four sides, rising from a square base to a single point on top. In Mesopotamia, by contrast, pyramids were shaped as a series of receding platforms with tapered walls, rising from a square, oval, or rectangular mound of rammed earth. And unlike the Egyptian pyramids, the summit was shaped as a flat platform, accessible through a series of external ramps and stairways.

Archaeologists have uncovered the remains of 32 of these ziggurats, including very large specimens near Baghada and Nasiriyah in Iraq and Khuzestan Province in Iran. The ziggurat's exposed facades were usually covered with glazed or colored brick that either extolled the deity to whom

THE RECONSTRUCTED
mud-brick staircase of the
ziggurat of Ur, Mesopotamia,
rebuilt by King Ur-Nammu
during the Third Dynasty of Ur
(ca 2113–2006 B.C.E.)

the ziggurat was dedicated or the king responsible for its construction. Some have astrological references, which suggests that ziggurats were also used for celestial observation. One of the most impressive examples is Ur's 80-foot-high ziggurat, dedicated to the moon god, Nanna. This ziggurat, partly restored, can still be admired near the excavations of Tell al-Muqayyar near Baghdad, though it suffered from bombing during the 2003 Iraq War. It is possible that the Mesopotamian ziggurat is the inspiration, if not the setting, for the story of the Tower of Babel. But Sumer's building prowess was not limited to the construction of temples alone. The Royal Tombs, excavated by Leonard Woolley in 1922, feature fully developed arches some 3,000 years before their reappearance in Roman architecture.

The Development of Writing

Perhaps the greatest contribution of Sumerian civilization was its development around 3200 B.C.E. of an early form of pictographic writing. The impetus was trade: Merchants needed some way to document who owed what to whom, and for how much. At first, traders carved small symbols in soft clay representing the type and quantities of goods they traded, such as sheaves of wheat and barrels of beer. These symbols eventually evolved into a primitive script of pictures, or pictograms, that are essentially abbreviated icons for a particular product, number, or value. In time, people began to understand that when these pictograms are placed together, they could become a sentence: an abstraction of a complete and logical thought. As a result, these pictographic sets became sufficiently familiar to a large group of people that they became standardized in what today we would call an alphabet. As their use grew, pictograms became abbreviated and stylized, so that by the third millennium, there were about 600 symbols, known as cuneiform script, that literate people could read and write. The term "cuneiform" refers to the wedge-like shape, made by a pen or stylus, with which the stylized symbols were impressed into soft clay. So successful was

the revolution of cuneiform script that unlike the far more difficult hieroglyphics of Egypt, it was adopted by virtually all other developing language groups in greater Mesopotamia—Akkadian, Hittite, Elamite, and other tongues.

The importance of this development can hardly be overstated. Unlike parchment or paper, clay tablets are durable and often survive fire. That is why entire libraries of ancient cuneiform tablets have survived to this day, while thousands of parchment scrolls of much later eras have been lost to fire, destruction, or simple decay.

As local and international trade grew, a system other than bartering was needed to put a value on a particular transaction. Until the Persian period in the sixth century B.C.E., most commercial transactions involved the exchange of

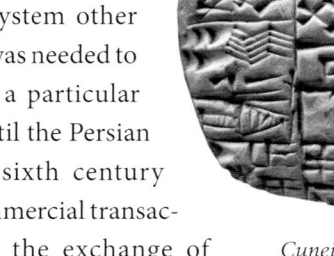

Cuneiform script tablet

chunks of precious metal. According to Bronze Age Egyptian inscriptions (as well as the Laws of Hammurabi), the going rate for a mature male slave was 20 "silver pieces," roughly the equivalent of two years of paid labor, which is reflected in the story of Joseph in Genesis. Most of the currency at the time was silver mined in Egypt, though not yet in the form of actual coins. Merchants would simply take various pieces of silver (and other precious metals) such as ingots, rings, or jewelry, and weigh them on a scale, using ceramic weights. Some of the oldest scales found in the Near East date back to 3000 B.C.E. For example, the Assyrian daric was a large weight, sometimes cast in the form of a lion, which weighed 2 pounds, 4 ounces, and equal to the value of a mina, which was the equivalent of 60 shekels. The words

THE BABYLONIAN Code of Hammurabi, one of the oldest written legal codes, was recorded on numerous stelae around 1754 B.C.E.

"mene," "tekel," and "parsin," which in the biblical story of Daniel appeared on the wall of Belshazzar's banqueting chamber, are actually units of measure equivalent to the mina, shekel, and half mina.

Law and Science

Another important development that emerged from Mesopotamia was the development of common code of rules to govern the behavior of a community and ensure the uniform application of justice. Around 2350 B.C.E., the ruler of the city-state of Lagash was the first to draft a legal code of conduct, which in turn inspired the Code of Ur-Nammu (21st century B.C.E.), the Code of Lipit-Ishtar (ca 1860 B.C.E.), and the famous Code of Hammurabi (ca 1754 B.C.E.). The Laws of Eshnunna, written around 2000 B.C.E., attempt to establish equitable prices and penalties for transactions, including marriage.

Another area where Mesopotamia made a major contribution in the third millennium B.C.E. was the concept of theoretical and practical science. Sumerian scientists developed the first calculator, the abacus, to help compute complex calculations in the exchange of trade. They also developed the first mathematical tables using a sexagesimal system, based on the value of 60. This system survives to this day in our division of one hour into 60 minutes, one minute into 60 seconds, and a circle into 360 degrees.

The so-called Standard of Ur, a block of wood decorated on both sides, shows another Sumerian invention: wheeled transportation. Though the chariot pictured on this artifact was still rolling on solid wooden wheels (the spoked wheel did not appear until 1800 B.C.E.), Sumer had thus created a seminal form of transport for thousands of years to come.

Another subject of scientific endeavor was astronomy. Excavators have found tablets that appear to record observations of the planet Venus and the constellations of various stars using circular planispheres or star charts. These tablets clearly show that at this point, astronomical observations were still pure science. Astrology—the divining of future events on Earth based on the relative movements and positions of celestial objects—did not become a major preoccupation until after 1000 B.C.E. In the heyday of Babylonian civilization, its astronomers could accurately predict the position of the sun, the moon, the planets, and various

> "IF [A HUSBAND] MADE [HIS WIFE] BEAR CHILDREN AND TAKES ANOTHER WIFE, HE SHALL BE DRIVEN FROM HIS HOUSE AND FROM WHATEVER HE OWNS."

THE LAWS OF ESHNUNNA

prominent stars. They also developed a planetary model that could accurately predict solar eclipses and created a lunar calendar that most cultures in the Near East adopted. A thousand years later, Babylonian records of comets, eclipses, and other celestial observations were still studied by Greek and Roman scholars and by scientists until well into the Middle Ages. Similarly, Sumer's myths, poems, and epics of gods were updated and copied during the subsequent Akkadian period.

Babylonian scholars were also the first to develop the principle of the time-mile, a measure of both distance and the time needed to cover it, which is still used in modern astronomy today in the form of the light-year. Units of measurement, however, were different from the ones we use today. Many Near Eastern cultures used the cubit, which equals approximately 18 inches. According to the first Book of Kings, for example, the Temple built by Solomon was 60 cubits long, 20 cubits wide, and 30 cubits high (1 Kings 6:2). This translates into a building with a length of 90 feet, a width of 30 feet, and a height of 45 feet. Other ancient measures include a finger (0.73 inches), a hand-breadth (3 inches), and a span (9 inches). ■

A BABYLONIAN PLANISPHERE, inscribed with cuneiform text, shows a schematic representation of star constellations in eight separate segments.

STARS ILLUMINATE the sky over Mount Taftan, an active stratovolcano in the Sistan and Baluchestan Province of Iran.

A BRONZE HEAD of an Akkadian ruler from 2250–2200 B.C.E. is believed by some to depict King Sargon the Great, first ruler of the Akkadian Empire.

THE AKKADIAN AND BABYLONIAN
EMPIRES

The exceptional wealth and culture of Sumer was bound to invite envy, rivalry, and conquest. Thus, around 2300 B.C.E., Mesopotamia was invaded by a group of people from the north known as the Akkadians.

A prolonged drought had led to excessive evaporation in Mesopotamia's irrigation networks, causing increased saline levels and a dramatic drop in crop yields. But the greatest disruptive force was the invasion by a warlike people known as the Akkadians, led by a king whose fame would later achieve mythical proportions: Sargon of Akkad. Sumer's city-states were no match for Sargon's battle-hardened Akkadian veterans. Having already vanquished the kingdom of Mari, Sargon turned on Uruk, Lagash, Eridu, and Ur, defeating them in short order. Sargon then joined these city-states into one political unit, the first unified body politic the region had ever known. By 2280 B.C.E., this Akkadian Empire stretched from the Taurus Mountains in today's southern Turkey to Lebanon in the west and the Persian Gulf in the east. The Akkadians are the first population group to be known as Semites, since their language would form the basis for the development of Hebrew, Aramaic, Assyrian, and Syriac.

Sargon's grandson Naram-Sin fought hard to keep intact the empire that had been bequeathed to him. Some of the restless city-states had risen in open rebellion upon the death of Sargon, and foreign tribes were pressing at the borders. In the ancient Near East, a "tribe" (such as the Elamites and Gutians) constituted a group of people with a shared ancestry, culture, and language but often with fluid political or geographic affiliations. Initially, Naram-Sin's campaigns against the Gutians were successful. This is attested by a magnificent limestone slab, or stela, now a prized possession of the Louvre in Paris. It shows the triumphant king at the top of a mountain summit under the protection of two astral deities, reveling in his victory over the Lullubi (a group of people who lived at the border between today's Iraq and Iran).

The stela marks only one of Naram-Sin's victories. By 2218 B.C.E., at the end of his reign, the Akkadian Empire still controlled all of Assyria, Syria, and major parts of today's Turkey. The orientation of these conquests was

A STONE PLAQUE from around 2450 B.C.E. depicts Enannatum I, Ensi or "king" of Lagash.

"I TOOK THE STELA OF NARAM-SIN AND CARRIED IT OFF, BRINGING IT TO THE LAND OF ELAM."

INSCRIPTION ON THE VICTORY STELA OF NARAM-SIN

KING NARAM-SIN of Akkad, wearing a horned tiara, towers over his vanquished enemies in this pink sandstone stela of around 2250 B.C.E.

no accident, for it followed the direction of the main international caravan routes.

The Rise of Hammurabi

Around 2150 B.C.E., the Akkadian period came to an end when Naram-Sin's son, Shar-kali-sharri, was no longer able to resist the Gutians, who succeeded in capturing major parts of southern Mesopotamia. The central government system established by Sargon dissolved. Instead, the Gutians delegated regional authority to native governors, provided their tribute was paid on time. As it happened, the city of Lagash was governed by an ambitious viceroy named Gudea, who ordered his sculpted likeness to be placed in strategic locations throughout Lagash-controlled territory. Statues of the governor, made of a black granite-like stone called diorite, can today be found in museums from London to New York.

Head of Hammurabi

The powers of these governors steadily grew, and by the beginning of the 21st century B.C.E., much of Sumer's ancient territory was once again in native hands. King Ur-Nammu of Ur presided over a brief but glorious restoration known as the Third Dynasty of Ur (ca 2113–2006 B.C.E.). A vast new public works program was begun, including a large-scale reconstruction of the city's irrigation networks, as well as the construction of the ziggurat dedicated to Nanna. King Ur-Nammu also developed one of the first legal codes in history, which would greatly influence the Code of Hammurabi some 300 years later.

But this revival was short-lived. During the reign of King Ibbi-Sin, who ascended the throne in 1963 B.C.E., Mesopotamia was visited by a new wave of invasions, this time by Elamites who hailed from what today is the Iranian plateau. This

A MODERN ARTIST'S impression of the Great Harbor in the City of Ur as it may have appeared around 2000 B.C.E.

A MODERN RECONSTRUCTION of Babylon shows the temple complex with the tower of the god Marduk at its center.

> "THOU, MARDUK, ART THE MOST HONORED OF THE GREAT GODS. THY DECREE IS UNRIVALED, THY WORD IS ANU."
>
> **AKKADIAN CREATION EPIC**

conflict led to a profound destabilization of the region, when much of the population was forced to flee. It is possible that the Elamite invasion forms the historical context for the Genesis story of Abraham's father, Terah, who fled Ur for the city of Harran in today's southern Turkey. Harran (*harranu* in Akkadian, which means "crossroads") was one of the farthest outposts of the Sumerian trade network.

Next, Mesopotamia experienced a measure of stability under the rule of a king named Hammurabi, who built a small city called Babylon into the capital of a major empire. Located astride the Euphrates, the city

Foundation peg with lion

was divided along its left and right banks, with steep embankments to contain the river's seasonal floods. Estimates suggest that by 1770 B.C.E., Babylon was the largest city in the world, with a population exceeding 200,000. Remnants from this fabulous city have been excavated in Hillah, Iraq, about 53 miles south of present-day Baghdad.

King Hammurabi is best known for codifying the legacy of many centuries of Sumerian and Akkadian legislation into a law known as the Code of Hammurabi (ca 1754 B.C.E.). Scholars now believe that King Hammurabi's chief contribution was to document laws that had already been in place for centuries. Among Ham-

THE QUEEN OF THE NIGHT

Sumer's sculptors became quite skilled in fashioning the human body in clay or gypsum. The British Museum owns an intriguing plaque of baked clay, known as the "Queen of the Night" (at right), which may represent Ishtar or her sister and rival, Ereshkigal, queen of the underworld. Made in the first half of the 18th century B.C.E. during the reign of King Hammurabi, the goddess wears a horned cap, symbol of divinity, while clutching the rod and ring of justice in her hands. The association with the night was probably suggested by the presence of an owl on either side of her, combined with the dark-painted background. Her full nudity makes the identification of Ishtar likely. Ishtar, known as Inanna in Sumer, was revered as the goddess of sexual love. In a curious coincidence, she may have been associated with the planet Venus, named after the Roman goddess of love.

"THE FIRST DUTY OF
GOVERNMENT IS TO
PROTECT THE POWERLESS
FROM THE POWERFUL."

HAMMURABI, SIXTH KING
OF THE FIRST DYNASTY OF BABYLON

murabi's 282 laws was a provision that "if a female slave has claimed equality with her mistress because she bore children, her mistress may not sell her" (Hammurabi, §146). This is reflected in the story of Sarah and the slave-girl Hagar, who, after she bore Abraham's son, began to look on her mistress with contempt. Because Israelite law dictated that Sarah couldn't dismiss Hagar outright now that she had born a son by Abraham, Sarah made her life so miserable that she ran away to the desert (Genesis 16:4-7).

In many ways, the Torah or Law that—according to the Bible—was revealed to Moses on Mount Sinai is a continuation of the Babylonian or Egyptian laws of the time, but with one important distinction: It recognizes God, rather than the ruling king, as the ultimate arbiter of human behavior.

Hammurabi continued to expand his reach until Babylon controlled much of southern Mesopotamia, ousting the hated Elamites in the process. This is the time historians refer to as the First Babylonian Dynasty, or Old Babylonia. But the empire began to disintegrate after Hammurabi's death, and eventually it fell victim to another rising power: that of Assyria. ∎

A BABYLONIAN RELIEF of a woman with her baby is dated to the 18th century B.C.E.

A MODERN IMPRESSION of the palace courtyard in Mari, a major city in northern Mesopotamia, shows a woman feeding birds.

THE GOLD THRONE of Tutankhamun (r. 1335–1325 B.C.E.) shows the king with his wife, Ankhsenamun.

THE CIVILIZATION OF ANCIENT
EGYPT

While Mesopotamia was in its ascendancy, Egypt was rising as another leading civilization of the Bronze Age, based on a process of growth similar to what was happening to the east. Egypt's civilization, too, first stirred along the banks of a great river: the Nile.

Unlike the Euphrates and the Tigris, the Nile rose dependably each year to deposit mineral-rich alluvial sediment across the fields bordering the river, which the Egyptians referred to as *kemet,* or "black land." In Egypt, therefore, there was no need for a complex irrigation system like the one developed by the Sumerians; the river provided all the irrigation the soil required, except for small canals to carry the water into the adjoining fields.

Climatologists suggest that before the Neolithic Age, Egypt was far greener than it is today. Archaeologists have discovered rock drawings that indicate the presence of nomadic shepherds in the Sahara as early as the ninth millennium B.C.E., when the world was just recovering from the last ice age. When the ice retreated, the seas rose, as did the temperatures—some believe by as much as 15°F. Consequently, the desert—which the Egyptians called *deshret,* or "red land"—began to encroach on the moist swamps and steppes of northern Egypt. Were it not for the great Nile River, all of Egypt may have been reduced to sand dunes, absorbed in one unbroken desert across

northern Africa and into the Arabian Peninsula. Fortunately, in the words of the Greek historian Herodotus, Egypt was given "the gift of the Nile," fed by spring rains in the African highlands. Without that river, Egyptian civilization may never have emerged.

By the fifth millennium B.C.E., when human settlements sprang up along the Euphrates River in Mesopotamia, a comparable evolution took place in the Nile Valley. Much of the local population consisted of nomadic herders, moving their sheep and goats from one pasture to the next. Excavations in the marshy Faiyum area west of the Nile and north of present-day Cairo have uncovered fragments of spears that suggest a significant local involvement with hunting and fishing. Elsewhere, the remnants of emmer wheat and barley indicate the development of farming communities, possibly using crop seeds imported from Mesopotamia.

During the later Neolithic period, there is

A DELICATELY CRAFTED amulet with the *wedjat,* the Eye of Horus, was found in the tomb of King Tutankhamun.

> "FOR ANY WHO SEES EGYPT . . . MUST RECOGNIZE, IF ONLY WITH COMMON POWERS OF OBSERVATION, THAT THE EGYPT TO WHICH THE GREEKS GO IN THEIR SHIPS IS AN ACQUIRED COUNTRY, THE GIFT OF THE NILE."
>
> HERODOTUS, *THE HISTORIES*

increasing evidence of trade with both Mesopotamia and the Aegean. Copper, discovered in Egyptian mines, became a sought-after commodity that was smelted and fabricated in numerous villages along the Nile. These prehistoric villages consisted of homes and workshops built with mud brick, often grouped around a central shrine, as in Eridu. In time, the communities began to coalesce into regions, or nomes, each run by a tribal chieftain. By 3300 B.C.E., these nomes had allied themselves into two distinct separate kingdoms.

Tutankhamun's golden sandals

The Unified Kingdom

The first kingdom, known as Lower Egypt, encompassed a territory, bisected by the Nile, from the Mediterranean to an area roughly near today's Cairo. This was the region of the Nile Delta, permeated with tributaries of the Nile that over the centuries had deposited layers of rich alluvial sediment. It was a fertile land filled with green pastures and shaded by date palms that would attract nomadic tribes from as far as Canaan and Syria, including the Israelites, in times of drought.

The other kingdom is referred to as Upper Egypt. It ran along the narrow ribbon of fertile land bordering the Nile, past its cataracts into Nubia to a line just north of present-day Khartoum. In this far more forbidding landscape, sustained by the life-giving artery of the river, the pharaohs built some of their greatest monuments, including Abydos, Thebes, and Abu Simbel.

Third-century B.C.E. Egyptian historian Manetho tells us that around 3100 B.C.E.—just as Uruk gained ascendancy in the delicate framework of city-states of Sumer—a mythical king named Menes (who may have been King Narmer) gathered sufficient strength to unify the two lands of Upper and Lower Egypt. This is borne out by a ceremonial plaque, known as the Narmer Palette, discovered near the ancient city of Kom el-Ahmar. On one side, King Narmer wears the white miter, or *hedjet,* of Upper Egypt; on the other, the red crown, or *deshret,* of Lower Egypt. Later, the

A VIEW of the tranquil waters of the Nile River near Luxor, Egypt, source of the ancient kingdom's fertility and prosperity

THIS COLONNADE is part of the temple of Abydos, built by King Seti I (r. 1290–1279 B.C.E.).

NOTABLE DATES

ca 4000 B.C.E.

Early farming settlements in Egypt

ca 3300 B.C.E.

Nomes of Egypt are organized in two separate kingdoms

ca 3100 B.C.E.

Egyptians develop mummification to preserve the dead

ca 3100 B.C.E.

Hieroglyphic writing emerges in Egypt

ca 3000 B.C.E.

Egyptians build ships using mortise and tenon joints

ca 2920 B.C.E.

Narmer unifies Egypt into one kingdom; First Dynasty begins

ca 2650 B.C.E.

King Djoser of the Third Dynasty assumes throne in Egypt

ca 2650 B.C.E.

Imhotep builds the mortuary complex of Djoser in Saqqara

ca 2575 B.C.E.

Old Kingdom Period of Egypt begins

ca 2550 B.C.E.

King Khufu (Cheops) builds Great Pyramid in Gizah

ca 2125 B.C.E.

Political upheaval marks Egypt's First Intermediate Period

THE GREAT complex of Ramses II was relocated to Abu Simbel in 1968 during the construction of the Aswan High Dam.

"[KING MENES] LED
THE ARMY ACROSS
THE FRONTIER AND
WON GREAT GLORY."

EGYPTIAN HISTORIAN MANETHO

pharaohs would combine both crowns into one headdress, known as the *pschent*.

Narmer founded the First Dynasty of Egypt (2920–2770 B.C.E.), the beginning of 31 dynasties over a span of 3,000 years. Each king or pharaoh was revered as a god, the living descendant of the sun god Re on Earth.

Narmer's son Aha solidified the unified kingdom by building a capital city at Memphis, not far from modern Cairo. According to Herodotus, Narmer himself had marked the spot by constructing a dam in the Nile, thus enabling his son to build on the reclaimed land. Under the leadership of Memphis, Egypt's cultural development soon began to rival the great cities of Sumer in architecture, literature, sculpture, and science. Memphis traded its copper and turquoise, mined in the Sinai, for raw materials such as wood, gold, and the myriad chemicals needed in its mortuary temples, the center of Egypt's cult of the dead.

Egypt's Religious Cults

If there is one thing that the ancient Babylonian and Egyptian civilizations had in common, it was a recognition of the need for a national system of worship. In both cultures, a wide variety of local beliefs and practices were eventually amalgamated into a common foundational myth. These myths saw the world ruled by a community of gods and goddesses,

TWO GILDED wood figurines from the tomb of King Tutankhamun

A GOLD PENDANT set with semiprecious stones and colored glass depicts Horus, the falcon god.

each with their own peculiar interests and passions that often mimicked the desires of the mortals down below. The need for such a national cult went well beyond the human yearning for spirituality. Kings were quick to recognize that national worship could unify the peoples under their sway but also authenticate themselves as divinely appointed rulers. In both Mesopotamia and Egypt, the king became the principal intermediary between the gods and humans. Two millennia later, imperial Rome would go even further and anoint each emperor a god upon his death.

The king, and his retinue of noblemen and high officials, formed an elite that in many ways paralleled the pantheon of Egyptian gods. Only they enjoyed the privilege of elaborate funeral practices, which they believed secured their memory and shepherded them to their rightful place in the afterlife. Indeed, the mortuary cult of Egypt's royal dynasties and aristocracy became the central

focus of its civilization. Egyptians believed that embalming and preserving the mortal remains of the deceased could preserve the integrity of a person's soul and body, his or her *ka* and *ba*. Sensational discoveries in the Valley of the Kings at Luxor, such as the tomb of Tutankhamun in 1922, have revealed that Egyptian burial customs for the elite included not only embalmment but also the interment of luxury goods and provisions for the afterlife. All this was governed by an elaborate set of rituals and magic spells, described in the Egyptian *Book of the Dead*.

Ordinary Egyptians did not have access to this mortuary cult. Unlike in ancient Greece and Rome, most Egyptian temples were not open to the public beyond the open forecourt. Therefore, we actually know very little about the worship of average Egyptians. But one glimpse can be found in the mysteries of the Osiris cult, which was concentrated in Abydos, located in Upper Egypt. Osiris was the god of death and resurrection, just

EGYPT'S MORTUARY CULT

The secret of Egypt's embalming procedure was to remove all moisture from the body, thus eliminating the principal agent of decay. Scholars believe that Egyptians may have arrived at this solution by observing the natural desiccation of corpses after burial in Egypt's dry desert sands. To imitate this process, Egyptian embalmers created a compound called natron, including sodium carbonate, bicarbonate, sodium chloride, and sulfa. Internal organs, always the first to decay, were removed and stored in so-called canopic jars (at right), the lids of which were often shaped in the forms of the divinity to whom protection of the organs was consigned. The entire embalmment process usually took 70 days.

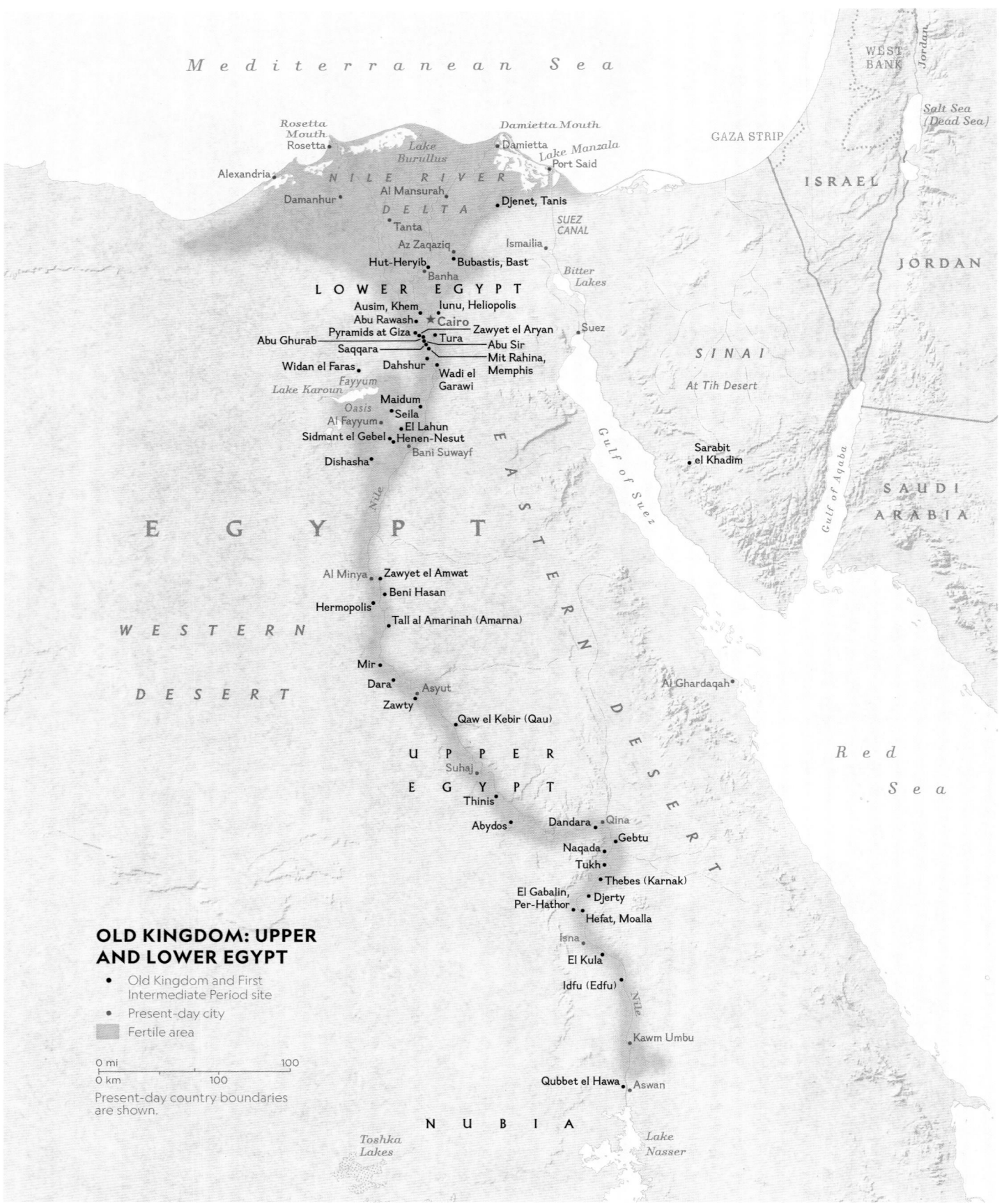

Mediterranean Sea

WEST
BANK
Jordan

Salt Sea
(Dead Sea)

GAZA STRIP

ISRAEL

JORDAN

Rosetta
Mouth
Rosetta

Lake
Burullus

Damietta Mouth
Damietta
Port Said
Lake Manzala

NILE RIVER

Alexandria

Damanhur

Al Mansurah

Djenet, Tanis

DELTA

SUEZ
CANAL

Tanta

Ismailia

Az Zaqaziq

Bitter
Lakes

Hut-Heryib
Bubastis, Bast

Banha

LOWER EGYPT

Ausim, Khem
Iunu, Heliopolis

Abu Rawash
★ Cairo

Pyramids at Giza
Zawyet el Aryan

Abu Ghurab
Tura

Saqqara
Abu Sir

Widan el Faras
Dahshur
Mit Rahina,
Memphis

Wadi el
Garawi

Suez

SINAI

At Tih Desert

Lake Karoun
Fayyum

Maidum

Oasis
Seila

Al Fayyum
El Lahun

Sidmant el Gebel
Henen-Nesut

Dishasha
Bani Suwayf

Sarabit
el Khadim

EGYPT

Nile

Gulf of Suez

Gulf of Aqaba

SAUDI
ARABIA

WESTERN

Al Minya
Zawyet el Amwat

Beni Hasan

Hermopolis
Tall al Amarinah (Amarna)

DESERT

EASTERN

Red

Mir

Al Ghardaqah

Dara

Asyut

Sea

Zawty

Qaw el Kebir (Qau)

DESERT

UPPER

Suhaj

EGYPT

Thinis

Dandara
Qina

Abydos
Gebtu

Naqada

Tukh

Thebes (Karnak)

El Gabalin,
Per-Hathor
Djerty

Hefat, Moalla

Isna

El Kula

Idfu (Edfu)

Nile

**OLD KINGDOM: UPPER
AND LOWER EGYPT**

● Old Kingdom and First
Intermediate Period site

● Present-day city

Fertile area

Kawm Umbu

Qubbet el Hawa
Aswan

0 mi   100
0 km   100

Present-day country boundaries
are shown.

Toshka
Lakes

NUBIA

Lake
Nasser

AN INLAID PECTORAL, or chest ornament, from the New Kingdom Period includes the name of King Tutankhamun.

as Horus was the god-king of Egypt, ruler of the sky. Pharaoh's reign unfolded between these two poles. While alive, he was the personification of Horus; in death, he became Osiris.

The cult center of Abydos tried to allow common men and women to experience a measure of the official cult. Each year, a great procession took place that carried a statue of Osiris from his temple to his tomb, in view of all those who had come to witness it. This was followed by elaborate mysteries and rituals at night; all those who had made the long journey to the shrine were invited to attend. For this reason, many Egyptians yearned to make a pilgrimage to Abydos at least once in their lifetime as a way to secure their own passage to the underworld upon their death.

The Pyramids

One of the earliest mortuary shrines of Egypt's Old Kingdom (2575–2134 B.C.E.) can still be seen in Saqqara, which served Memphis as the necropolis for its noblemen. Here, King Djoser of the Third Dynasty (2650–2575 B.C.E.) began what is possibly the oldest example of a planned architectural complex still extant today. Its purpose was to create a mortuary facility where the pharaoh, after

his death, would continue to be worshiped in a series of religious festivals. The city, like its king, would have to withstand the test of time and therefore would have to be immortal, so it was built of stone, rather than mud brick.

The tour de force of this design, created by Djoser's architect Imhotep, is a massive, stepped pyramid that in its heyday rose to 180 feet. Imhotep achieved this stupendous height by stacking a series of limestone blocks of diminishing size. Deep inside this massive structure was the burial chamber for the pharaoh, hacked out of sheer bedrock. To adorn this vast complex, Imhotep created certain architectural features that would remain valid in Egyptian and European architecture for the next 5,000 years: fluted pilasters and columns, capitals adorned with lotus or papyrus leaves, and ornamental friezes decorated with reliefs. Many of these buildings were built in limestone rather than baked brick and remain in astonishingly good condition to this day.

Why Djoser chose a pyramid to mark his tomb continues to be a subject of scholarly debate. One prevailing theory is that the shape naturally emerged from the use of a mastaba, or "stepped mound," to mark the grave of a nobleman. These mounds may have symbolized the primeval mound from which the Earth was originally created and to which the deceased were destined to return. Others have argued that Imhotep's pyramidal shape represented the hierarchical arrangement of a unified Egyptian society under the benevolent rule of King Djoser. Still others have put forth the theory that pyramids were used for astronomical observations or for manipulation of the projection of sunlight, given that Ra, the ancient sun god, was a leading deity in the Egyptian pantheon.

The Saqqara stepped pyramid set the trend for pharaohs to come; some 135 pyramids have been identified in Egypt. Eventually the stepped design was clad with a veneer of limestone so as to create a smooth surface. A small interior access way, designed with several false turns to confuse tomb robbers, led to the chamber in which the pharaoh's sarcophagus was placed. Smaller pyramids and tombs were built nearby to house the royal family and the pharaoh's closest advisers. The greatest examples of these Egyptian pyramids are still standing in Giza, near Cairo, including the pyramids of Khufu (or Cheops) and Khafre (or Chephren). In addition, ancient Egyptians were masters in carving rare stones such as porphyry, an extremely hard and durable igneous rock. Another expensive variant was alabaster, a soft-banded mineral made of calcite, often used as canopic jars (urns to hold the entrails from an embalmed body). Alabaster was also used to carve delicate, almost translucent flasks to hold precious fluids such as perfumes and fine oils. ■

DROUGHT AND FAMINE

One consequence of cultivation was that communities without access to irrigation canals or water wells became entirely dependent on rainfall. The uncertainty of precipitation, as well as factors such as wind, hail, mildew, disease, and insect pests, could cause a harvest to fail. In addition, farmers often had to cultivate on rocky terrain or loose topsoil that was vulnerable to the elements. Since wheat and barley were the principal crops in most Bronze Age civilizations, a poor harvest had an immediate impact on the region's food supply, often causing famine. As Egyptian records (at left) attest, this was by no means a rare occurrence, often leading to social disorder and wholesale migrations. Archaeologists have found evidence of an extensive drought during the Old Kingdom that some climatologists have linked to persistent low flooding levels of the Nile.

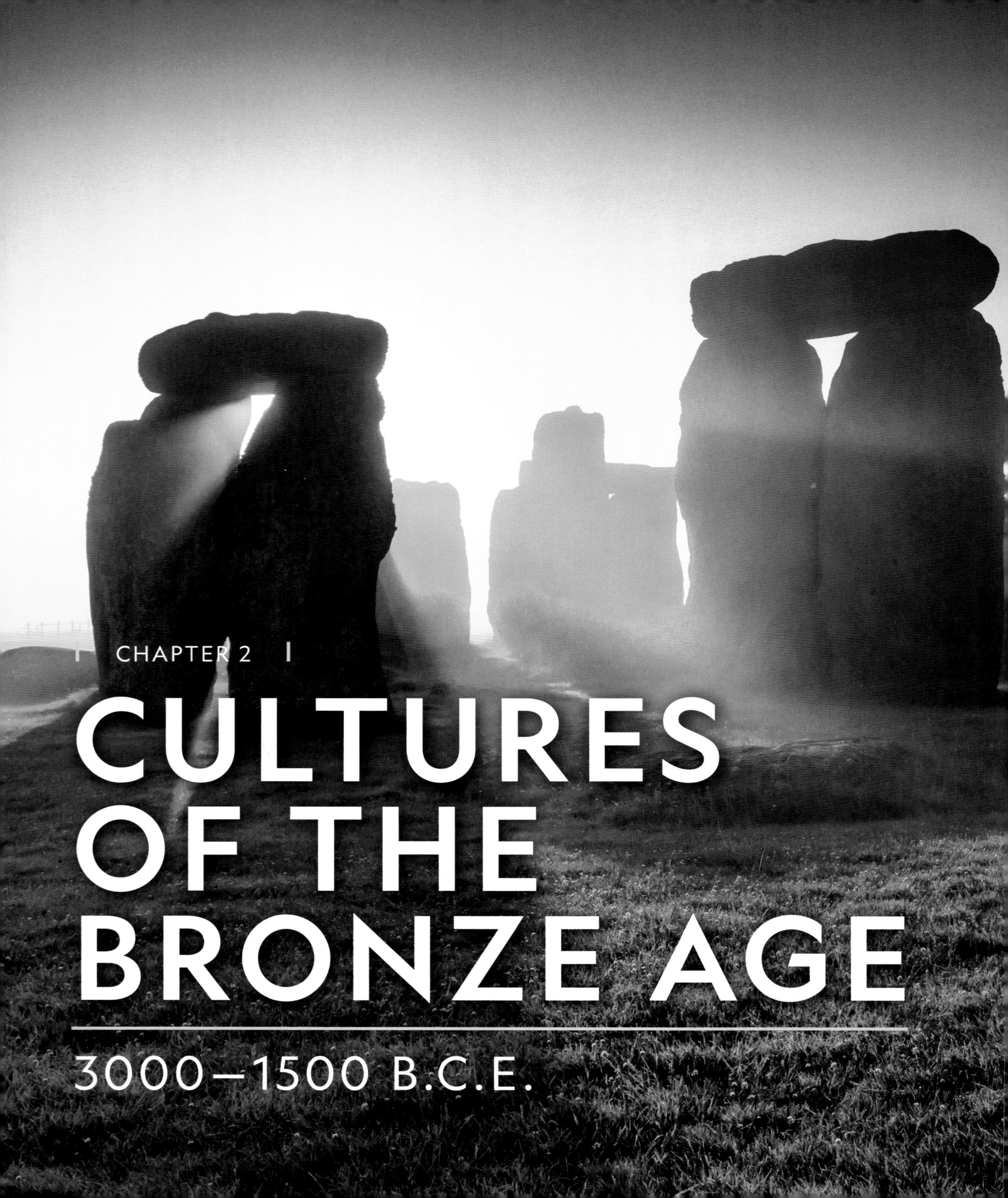

CHAPTER 2

CULTURES OF THE BRONZE AGE

3000–1500 B.C.E.

A VIEW of the stone circle of Stonehenge in Wiltshire, Great Britain, at sunrise

CONTENTS

THE RISE OF CIVILIZATION

Around the time of the first Mesopotamian settlements, several early cultures also sprang up in China. The Yellow River (or Huang) civilization is often cited as one of China's earliest cultures, though recent discoveries have shown that similar developments took place elsewhere, notably in the Yangtze River basin and along the Liao River. The name "Yellow River" refers to the fact that the land along its banks is often covered by a yellow dust called loess, deposited by winds and floods. This dust fertilizes the land with many rich minerals, thus creating a fecund soil for cultivation, particularly the growth of millet grain.

One of the oldest sites of the Yellow River culture is the village of Yangshao, discovered in 1921. From there, the culture soon spread into today's provinces of Shaanxi, Shanxi, and Henan. Historians believe that this is evidence of migration. The people did not build permanent settlements but moved on to new lands once the soil was exhausted. Indeed, the Yangshao people do not appear to have kept large domesticated herds save for pigs and dogs, but they probably augmented their diet with hunting and fishing.

The Yellow River Civilization

The Yellow River culture produced some exquisite pottery in deep red or black tones, often adorned with animal motifs, as well as markings that some believe may have been the first attempt at developing a script. They also developed the Chinese tradition of carving beautiful objects in jade and mastered the casting of vessels in bronze, using alloys of copper and tin.

Another unique feature was the early production of silk and hemp for use as garments and perhaps decoration. Silk was spun from the secretions of caterpillar that feed on mulberry bushes. These secretions produce a thread that skilled hands turned into shimmering textures, making silk one of China's most famous assets. The civilization experienced its greatest flowering from 5000 until 3000 B.C.E., when it was overtaken by the Majiayao culture to the west.

During the Middle Bronze Age, international trade grew steadily throughout Southeast Asia and the Middle East, but the stability of this nexus was disrupted by a number of mass migrations, often involving invasions by warring tribes. The Egyptian Empire, whose sphere of influence extended to Nubia in Africa and Syria-Canaan in the Near East, suffered incursions by the Hittites and the Sea Peoples. A similar disruption took place during the Warring States period in China, under the Zhou Dynasty, and in the Mediterranean Basin.

In India, this new era led to the Vedic period, which would produce some of the greatest scripture of Asia, based on ancient Harappan and Aryan traditions. These so-called Vedas would become the foundational text of Hinduism. In the Levant, ancient Judaism, born in the highlands of Syria-Canaan, would eventually produce Hebrew Scripture, including the Torah; the Jewish Law (also know as the Pentateuch); and the Books of the Prophets, which describe the history of the kingdoms of Israel. ∎

THE YA FU square lei wine vessel with flanges is a masterpiece from the late Shang Dynasty, 13th to 11th century B.C.E.

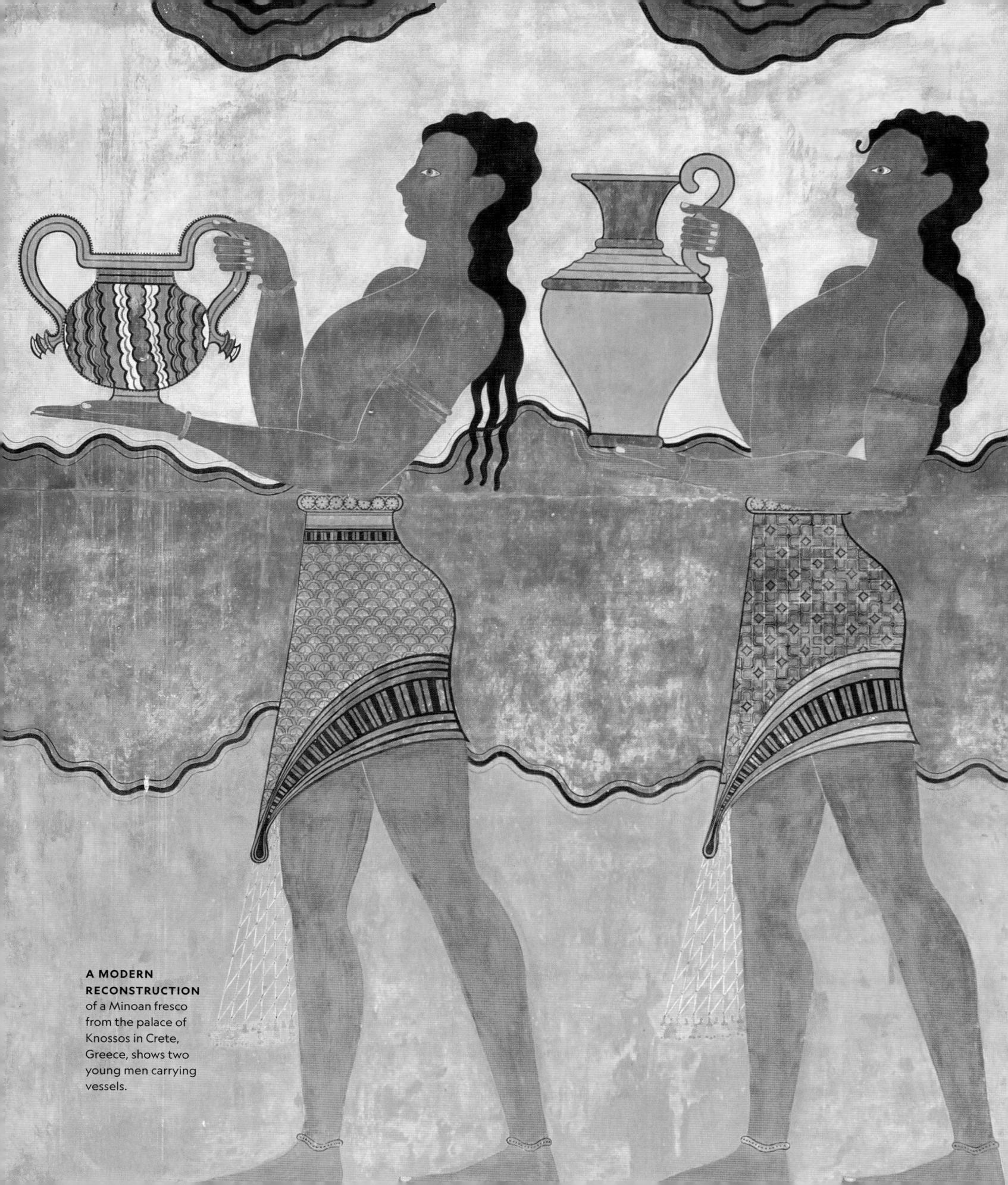

A MODERN RECONSTRUCTION of a Minoan fresco from the palace of Knossos in Crete, Greece, shows two young men carrying vessels.

A BUST from Mohenjo Daro in today's Pakistan shows a priest king wearing a cloak decorated with trefoil.

EARLY CULTURES IN
ASIA

From the middle of the third millennium B.C.E., early agricultural civilizations emerged in China and the Indus Valley that in some ways bore a remarkable similarity to the cultural origins of Mesopotamia and Egypt.

Just as Egypt's civilization is rooted in the legend of King Menes, or Narmer, so too does China trace the birth of its civilization to the mythical dynasty of Xia (ca 2070–1600 B.C.E.) in the Yellow River basin. In a striking parallel to the rise of Sumer, the unification of the tribes living along the Yellow River was prompted by a great flood, or perhaps a series of floods. According to Chinese myth, this was a time when the region was ruled by demigods known as the Three Sovereigns. Some texts also refer to the so-called Five Emperors, who each bestowed gifts on the land, such as fire, farming, architecture, medicine, and the invention of silk culture. When excessive flooding threatened the agriculture of the Yellow River, including the cultivation of rice, one of these rulers, Emperor Yao, is said to have ordered a man called Gun, a member of the Xia clan, to protect the land from any future floods. Gun then began the construction of large dikes to help channel the Yellow River, a project that took many years and was eventually continued by Gun's son Yu (known in Chinese texts as Yu the Great). When these dikes failed to stem the flooding, Yu came up with another idea: build a network of irrigation canals that not only carried the water farther inland but also gave the river (and its tributaries) an exit to the sea. After 13 years, Yu succeeded in stopping the floods, which boosted the agricultural output and the prosperity of the region.

Yu's position was further strengthened when he led his tribal militia against the Miao tribe, which had repeatedly invaded and harassed the Xia. For this and other achievements, Emperor Shun (who had succeeded Yao) appointed Yu as his heir. Thus, China's First Dynasty, the Xia, was born.

What these texts show is that the founding legends of both Mesopotamia and China are bound up in stories of agriculture, the threat of floods, and the invention of irrigation. But in other many respects, the prehistory of China is very different from that of Mesopotamia or Egypt. Bordered by desert and mountain ranges to the north and

A BRONZE SCULPTURE of a woman riding two Brahman bulls from Harappan is dated to 2000–1750 B.C.E.

> ## "IN THE NEXT TEN DAYS, THERE WILL BE NO MISFORTUNE. THERE WILL BE NO HARM; THERE WILL PERHAPS BE THE COMING OF ALARMING NEWS."
>
> **INSCRIPTION ON A SHANG DYNASTY ORACLE BONE**

west and by the Pacific Ocean in the east, China's civilization would rise in isolation, largely untouched by events in other parts of the world. Indeed, archaeologists have failed to uncover any incontrovertible evidence of the Xia Dynasty, which is why most Western historians believe that the story of the Xia forms part of China's founding myth. Indeed, modern archaeologists caution that prior to 1300 B.C.E., there are very few remains that could reliably attest to the existence of a ruling dynasty.

The Xia Dynasty was reportedly overthrown by King Tang, the first ruler of the Shang Dynasty. The Shang era witnessed urban development along the principal rivers as well as the rise of an elaborate funerary cult, as in Egypt. Shang kings were buried in great splendor, with precious robes

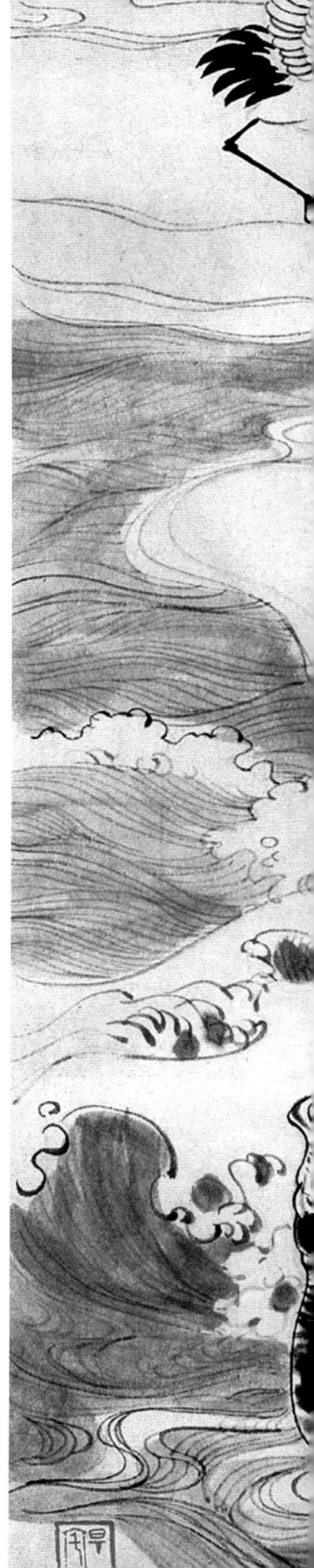

Presumed Xia Dynasty bronze coin

and jewelry, and accompanied by prisoners and slaves who were presumably sacrificed during the funeral ceremony. The growing luxury at the court prompted the need for a rise in taxes, which placed a heavy burden on the population. This explains why, when invaders from the west toppled the last Shang king, Di Xin in 1046 B.C.E., they were received as liberators by the population (or so their texts claim). Thus, the Zhou Dynasty was born.

Early Chinese Writing

Many question marks remain about the prehistory of ancient China. For example, historians don't agree when China's unique character-based alphabet was first developed. As in Sumer, the first attempts at writing involved the use of pictorial symbols, which may have begun as early as the Shang Dynasty, or even many centuries earlier. For example, Shang kings appeared to have used scribes or priests to make notations on animal bones. According to a prevailing theory, these notes involved questions that the king wished to submit to the gods. After the question was written, the bone was heated until it broke apart, thus allowing augurs to divine the response from the structure of the cracks—hence, the term "oracle bone." Many such bones, as well as bronze vessels inscribed with early characters, have been uncovered from this era. This emerging Chinese alphabet used neither standard pictures nor characters, but iconic representations called glyphs that may have one or several attributes,

BRONZE AGE DYNASTIES OF CHINA

- Xia Dynasty, ca 2000 B.C.E.
- Shang Dynasty, ca 1600 B.C.E.
- Zhou Dynasty, ca 1045 B.C.E.

GOBI DESERT

Yellow

Korea

Bo Hai

Yellow Sea

Yangtze

East China Sea

0 mi 400
0 km 400

Each dynasty is shown at its maximum extent.

A DEPICTION of Da Yu, or Yu the Great, legendary founder of the Xia Dynasty

THIS 348-FOOT MONUMENT in Zhengzhou, China, is dedicated to two of the earliest Chinese emperors, Yan Di and Huang Di.

depending on their meaning. Much about these glyphs remains unclear, however, because Chinese writing would not be standardized until the reign of the Qin Dynasty (221–206 B.C.E.).

Similarly, our knowledge of Chinese culture under the Shang and Zhou Dynasties is limited. Based on excavations to date, archaeologists have suggested that these societies were heavily stratified, with an upper layer of a wealthy elite lording over the vast masses of peasants, laborers, and slaves. These kings treated their subject peoples as mere serfs and exploited them ruthlessly for their crops and taxes. Indeed, much of the urban development was reserved for the wealthy, whereas most peasants lived in mud huts, huddled together in small villages.

The Shang, however, were noted for their interest in astronomy. In Anyang, in today's Henan Province, excavators found oracle bones dated to the Middle Shang Dynasty (1339–1281 B.C.E.) that appear to refer to stars and stellar constellations. Some texts refer to the sighting of a comet around 2296 B.C.E. It is possible that the Chinese lunar calendar was the result of these ancient astronomical observations.

A TORTOISE ORACLE SHELL from the Shang Dynasty is inscribed with Chinese characters suggesting a divination ritual.

The Indus Valley Civilization

As in the case of Sumer, Egypt, and China, the first civilization on the Indian subcontinent emerged along the fertile soil of a major river: the Indus. Originating in the Tibetan Plateau, the Indus River runs through northwest India and much of Pakistan to merge with the Arabian Sea, with an annual flow that is twice that of the Nile and three times that of the Tigris and Euphrates. When we include the tributaries of the Ghaggar-Hakra River, the Indus

THE TOMBS OF YINXU

The spectacular discovery in 1976 of Tomb 5 at Yinxu (at right), which unlike other tombs of this era had not been disturbed by grave robbers, revealed the wealth of the Shang Dynasty as no other excavation has ever done. Inside, excavators found more than 200 bronze ritual vessels, pottery, jade figures, and hair combs and pins, as well as a large cache of bronze weapons. Numerous inscriptions referring to a Lady Fu Hao suggest that the tomb belonged to the consort of King Wu Ding (r. 1250–1192 B.C.E.), who apparently was renowned for her martial skills as military commander. This, some believe, would explain the presence of so many weapons.

> "TRUTH CANNOT BE SUPPRESSED AND ALWAYS IS THE ULTIMATE VICTOR."
>
> **THE *YAJUR VEDA*, ANCIENT VEDIC TEXT**

Valley civilization (ca 3300–1900 B.C.E.) unfolded over a much larger territory than the other Bronze Age civilizations. Fed by seasonal monsoons, these rivers encouraged widespread farming and the growth of a considerable agricultural surplus. Date palms are believed to have been the first tree crops, followed by the cultivation of cereals. The abundance of monsoons, however, also discouraged the development of irrigation networks of the type then used in Sumer, which often led to extensive flooding. Some historians believe that this may have been the incentive for the development of walled cities. Some of the leading cities of the time include Harappa and Mohenjo Daro in today's Pakistan and Ropar, Kalibangan, and Dholavira in modern India.

Archaeologists first came into contact with the Indus Valley culture in the 1920s after the discovery of Harappa during the period of the British Raj. They were struck by the similarities between Sumer (which was also being excavated by British archaeologists at this time) and the Indus Valley civilization, which subsequently was called the Harappan civilization. For example, the population of the Indus Valley also mastered the art of crafting tools in bronze by blending copper and tin, and carved sculptures and seals using carnelian, a semiprecious gemstone. Elegant pottery, evidently produced on a

A MOTHER GODDESS STATUE was produced by the Indus Valley civilization in Mohenjo Daro in today's Pakistan.

THE BRONZE AGE
Harappa archaeological site in today's Punjab, Pakistan, was a center of the Indus Valley civilization.

MOHENJO DARO
in the province of Sindh, Pakistan, was once one of the largest settlements of the Indus Valley civilization, built around 2500 B.C.E.

RIGHT: This figure of a young dancer from Mohenjo Daro is one of the most famous artifacts from the Indus Valley civilization.

potter's wheel and adorned with geometric motifs, was found as well. In Mohenjo Daro in the south and Harappa in the north, excavators even discovered complete towns with homes and other structures built of baked brick, connected to running water and drainage systems. Many homes had private bathrooms, fed by wells with drainage pipes leading to sewers.

However, in a striking departure from Egyptian and Mesopotamian models, the Indus Valley civilization does not seem to have produced any monumental architecture, such as palaces or temples. This was not for lack of technology, because the Indus culture did produce large granaries, dockyards, and walls, built with dried brick. Given

that many of the homes in these cities were relatively equal in size, some scholars have posited that the Indus culture was remarkably egalitarian, without a hierarchical system supporting a royal elite or a caste of priests, as in the case of Sumer and Egypt. The cities appear to have been laid out on a grid pattern, which suggests the presence of some form of central planning that governed daily life in Harappan society.

Another unique aspect of the Indus culture was its concern for the use of standard weights and measures, no doubt necessitated by the extensive trade in the region. Their measurement system appears to have been decimal in nature, while weights were organized around a unit of 28 grams. Excavators have also found many jewelry items, including bangles and necklaces made of shell, agate, and ceramics. Local artisans excelled in crafting beautiful figurines in gold, stone, bronze, and clay, including the famous "Dancing Girl," dated between 2500 and 1900 B.C.E. Other figurines depict animals that may—or may not—have any religious significance. In 2006, archaeologists announced evidence of Harappan dentistry, based on the discovery of 11 drilled molar crowns in the skulls of nine adults.

Some scholars estimate that at its peak, during the so-called Mature Harappan Period (ca 2600–1900 B.C.E.), this civilization may have had a population of five million. At one point, Mohenjo Daro may have had a population of as many as 40,000 inhabitants before it was ravaged by floods; archaeological strata show that the town was rebuilt at least nine times. Soon after, however, the valley went into gradual decline when it experienced a steep drop in rainfall and salinization, similar to the climate change experienced in the

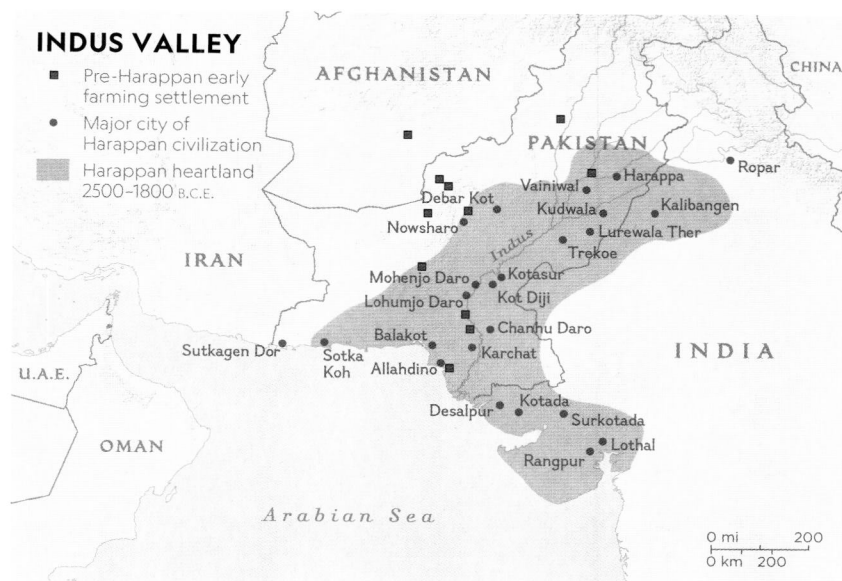

Middle East at this time. In the middle of the third millennium B.C.E., for example, a period of extended drought so ravaged the region's fields that it prompted the abandonment of many Early Bronze Age cities and forced much of the population back into a nomadic lifestyle. ■

WEAPONS OF WAR

The principal weapon for hunting and war during the Bronze Age was archery, one of the oldest and most reliable arms. First developed after the last ice age, the bow was a simple device that allowed archers to build up tension by pulling the bowstring, thus creating the energy needed to propel the arrow toward its target. To ensure that the arrow ran straight and true, arrows were often equipped with fletching at the end of the shaft, and its killing power was augmented with a bone or bronze arrowhead (at right) made of bone or bronze. By the end of the ninth century B.C.E., the composite bow became widespread in Asia and the Middle East. This weapon used laminated layers of wood to create a bow of tremendous propellant strength that could outrange traditional bows by far. Even as other arms were developed, the bow and arrow continued to be favored for the hunt many centuries later.

A MARBLE HEAD from Amorgos, Greece, is typical of the mysterious sculpture crafted by the Cycladic civilization of the third millennium B.C.E.

EARLY CULTURES IN
EUROPE

The four great civilizations of the Bronze Age—those of Egypt, Mesopotamia, China, and India—were by no means the only regions where early cultures emerged. In Europe too, domestication and cultivation led to the formation of village settlements.

Around 11,500 B.C.E., the Clovis culture, prominent in the Great Plains, spread across North America, while other early cultures followed in the Great Lakes region and in today's Louisiana around 3000 B.C.E. This is also when agricultural villages appeared in Central America and the Amazon region, around the lakes of southern France and Slovenia, and along the Danube in central Europe. Austronesians from Taiwan are believed to have settled in the Philippines at this time, while the Hittites established their first communities in Anatolia (today's Turkey) and the Phoenicians settled along the coast of modern Syria.

During this period, Europe saw the emergence of a mysterious phenomenon: the placement of large megaliths, or giant stones, according to a particular pattern. Among others, these configurations have been found on Malta, in France's Brittany region, and throughout Britain. The most famous of these concentrations is the monument of Stonehenge located in the county of Wiltshire, some eight miles north of Salisbury. Derived from the Old English words *stanhen gist,*

meaning "hanging stones," Stonehenge began around 3100 B.C.E. as a circular ditch, and between 2500 and 2000 B.C.E. grew into the concentric circles we see today. While at first the markers were built of timber, around 2600 B.C.E. the builders began to replace the wooden pillars with tall stones, made of dolerite. Each stone was originally taller than six feet in height and weighed about four tons. Later, 30 new stones were brought in, and these are the ones we see today. These sarsen stones are about 13 feet high and configured in several arrangements: the outer circle is a row of megaliths connected by lintels, and the inner circle is a group of five huge stone arches arranged in the form of a horseshoe. The lintel stones were fastened with joints, rather unusual for this period. Quite possibly the stones were quarried at the Preseli Hills in Wales.

The meaning of Stonehenge and similar configurations is not clear. While some megaliths in Britain have been associated with burial sites,

A LATE MINOAN vessel of the 16th century B.C.E. reveals the popularity of nautical motifs, including octopuses and dolphins, on the pottery of the period.

> ## "THOSE HUGE RUDE MASSES OF STONE, SET ON END, AND PILED EACH ON OTHER, TURN THE MIND ON THE IMMENSE FORCE NECESSARY FOR SUCH A WORK."
>
> **IRISH STATESMAN EDMUND BURKE ON STONEHENGE**

many appear to have a close identification with celestial observation, including an alignment with the winter and summer solstices. In one burial chamber in Newgrange, Ireland, for example, the rays of the sun reach the far wall at the end of the tomb only during the winter solstice. At Stonehenge, the summer solstice marks the moment when the sun rises directly over a 16-foot-tall stone at the end of the entrance gate. Some scholars suggest that the monuments were created by Druids as giant solar clocks to mark the beginning of the seasons for the benefit of farmers in the region. Druids were priests who exerted considerable religious and power in ancient Celtic cultures. Others reject this theory, since Celtic culture emerged only after the 12th century B.C.E., when Stonehenge had already stood for a millennium or more. There is no question, however, that Stonehenge and other megalith monuments would play a major role in Celtic culture.

The Menhirs of Carnac

Another mysterious grouping of Neolithic stones can be found in Carnac on the southern coast of Brittany, in France. More than 3,000 prehistoric megaliths or "menhirs" have been found here, often arranged in perfectly straight lines, hewn from local rock. The stones are arranged in three main groups of alignment, the meaning of which is not clear. According to a local myth, the megaliths were once the soldiers of a Roman legion who were turned to stone by Merlin, King Arthur's court magician. A similar legend suggests they were pagan soldiers who were stopped in their tracks by Pope Cornelius. But archaeologists believe that the stones are much older, going back as early as 4000 B.C.E., when Brittany was populated by pre-Celtic tribes. In addition to the stones, there are also a number of dolmens, tomb-like structures composed of giant stones. This clearly underscores the funerary character of the Carnac site; indeed, some historians believe that the stones were erected to mark the ancestors of leading families.

Today, most scholars agree that Carnac was an

THE AMESBURY ARCHER skeleton was found near Stonehenge and is tentatively dated to 2400 B.C.E.

STONEHENGE, begun around 3100 B.C.E. as a circular ditch on the Salisbury Plain, is one of Europe's most famous megalith monuments.

NOTABLE DATES

ca 3200 B.C.E.

Cycladic culture emerges in the central islands of the Aegean

ca 3100 B.C.E.

Construction of Stonehenge in Wiltshire, England, begins

ca 3000 B.C.E.

Rise of the Minoan civilization on Crete

ca 3000 B.C.E.

Agricultural villages appear in France, Slovenia, and Danube Valley

ca 2500 B.C.E.

Overland trade routes develop between Balkans and Spain

ca 2000 B.C.E.

Aryan-speaking Indo-Europeans spread in Balkans, Greece, and Italy

ca 1850 B.C.E.

Minoans develop an alphabetic script known today as Linear A

ca 1800 B.C.E.

Bronze casting spreads in British Isles and Scandinavia

ca 1700 B.C.E.

Aryan-speaking people move from Turkey and Ukraine to Scandinavia

ca 1613 B.C.E.

Massive volcanic eruption on Thera destroys Minoan civilization

ca 1600 B.C.E.

Mycenaean culture becomes dominant power in the Aegean

THE STONE ROWS of Ménec in Carnac, France, are believed to have served as a spiritual center.

important spiritual center of some sort. Some have identified it as gathering place of Druids, perhaps in connection with some form of celestial observation. Others have linked the stones to fertility rites, similar to Neolithic practices that archaeologists have discovered in ancient Mesopotamia. Another theory, more outlandish, suggests that the stones were established to protect the land against invaders, like a Neolithic equivalent of the "Dragon's Teeth" built by German forces along the Atlantic coast during World War II. Exactly how these monoliths would have deterred an army of Stone Age infantry is not clear, however.

The Cycladic Civilization

Another equally mysterious culture of this time appeared on the Cyclades islands, located in the Greek Aegean Sea. Here, villagers also cultivated emmer wheat and barley, possibly influenced by agricultural developments in

Egypt, as well as olives and grapes, while keeping herds of sheep, goats, and pigs. They also had an active fishing fleet that operated with slender boats propelled by oars or sails. Indeed, sailing boats appear on Egyptian frescoes and reliefs as early as 3200 B.C.E., followed shortly thereafter by the use of square-rigged sailing boats in Sumer.

Perhaps the most distinctive feature of the Cycladic civilization is its sculpture. Archaeologists have found scores of marble figurines with arms folded and blank, unadorned faces, save for a sharply carved nose. While some scholars have tried to identify these figures as idols related to some religious practice, the majority opinion among archaeologists today is that their purpose was funerary, given that they were almost always found in graves of both men and women. This may also explain why many

A DELICATE CYCLADIC figurine of a woman from ca 2500 B.C.E. was found in Amorgos, Greece.

THE MYSTERY OF ATLANTIS

Few places have weaved a spell as mysterious as the island of Atlantis, reportedly once home to a powerful, technologically advanced nation until its sudden destruction. Atlantis, said fourth-century Greek philosopher Plato, was a strong naval power that conquered most of the known world in both Europe and Northern Africa. Plato claimed his description was based on papyrus records in Egypt. But the true purpose of his Atlantis story is to juxtapose the city of Athens, a paragon of democracy and peaceful stability, with its very opposite, a city-state ruled by a despotic, warlike tyrant. In recent years, some authors have sought to associate Atlantis with the Greek volcanic island of Thera, also known as Santorini (at right). Thera was destroyed ca 1613 B.C.E. as a result of a massive eruption of its volcano. Remnants of ash and pumice have been found as far as Egypt.

THE WRITING SYSTEM OF THE MINOAN CIVILIZATION, KNOWN AS LINEAR A, IS A MYSTERY AND YET TO BE DECIPHERED.

figurines are shown with folded arms. Another favorite motif of these sculptors was the depiction of musicians, with the figure playing a harp. Their highly stylized appearance is often strikingly similar to 20th-century modernist sculpture.

The Cycladic artist also produced tools, weapons, and ornaments in bronze, evidence of an active international trade, given that Greece lacks any copper or tin ores. A Late Bronze Age ship discovered in 1982 at Uluburun, on the southern Turkish coast, contained copper and tin ingots, as well as blackwood from Africa. The ship also carried Canaanite jars filled with olives and glass ingots of cobalt blue turquoise—the earliest glass ingots discovered thus far.

The Minoan Civilization

Over time, the nexus of trade activity in the Aegean shifted south, to the island of Crete. Its importance was no doubt due to its geographic location, perched at the nexus of trade between Anatolia, the Cyclades, and Egypt. In addition, Crete was blessed with many natural harbors and fertile regions where farmers grew figs, olives, barley, wheat, and chickpeas, while raising pigs, goats, sheep, and cattle. The Cretans also mastered the process of fermenting wine from grapes and began the tradition of pressing oil from olives to be used in a range

THIS FAMOUS CYCLADIC marble statue is known as the Harpist or Lyre Player.

A VIEW of the Cyclades, a Greek island group in the Aegean Sea and center of Greece's earliest civilization

of domestic applications. Fruit grew in abundance, including apples, pears, and grapes. Date palms may have been native or imported from Egypt, while pomegranates were transplanted from the Near East.

By the late third millennium B.C.E., Crete had become a thriving culture of traders, farmers, and artisans who eventually produced a monarchy of sorts. These Cretan kings used the wealth of the island to construct a string of elaborate palaces in places like Malia, Phaistos, Zakros, and Knossos, which rank as the first examples of monumental architecture in Europe. As in ancient Egypt, these massive construction projects created a new social layer composed of builders, woodworkers, stone-masons, metalworkers, and artists.

We do not know the name of this civilization or that of its royal dynasty, so when British archae-ologist Arthur Evans started to excavate its remains at the beginning of the 20th century, he decided to name it himself. The labyrinth-like layout of the palace of Knossos reminded him of the mytholog-ical story of King Minos, who is described in the histories of Herodotus as the founder of a "sea empire." Evans therefore coined the phrase "Minoan civilization," which historians have used ever since, even though there is no evidence that Minos was a historical figure who lived on the island. Today, the Minoan age is generally consid-ered the foundation for the flowering of Greek civilization and, consequently, European civiliza-tion as a whole.

Around 1700 B.C.E., Crete's prosperity came to an abrupt end when a violent earthquake destroyed the buildings on the island and lay waste to many of its fields. Fortunately, the continuing growth of regional trade allowed the Cretans to bounce back and begin what archaeologists refer to as the Sec-ond Palace period (1700–1450 B.C.E.).

Minoan Art and Architecture

During this period, the Minoan kings built palaces that were even more stupendous than previously built structures. The largest of these is the Palace of Minos at Knossos, spread over five acres with

multiple levels, each accessible through a monu-mental staircase. The roofs were generally flat, which is why reconstructions of this complex look surprisingly modern and somewhat reminiscent of the cantilevered style pioneered by Frank Lloyd Wright. The Knossos palace was built with unbaked brick and supported by wooden beams and pillars that anticipate the columns of Greek architecture, even though they tapered downward rather than upward. The royal chambers had a piped water supply, large terra-cotta bath, and

THE SO-CALLED AKROTIRI BOXER fresco discovered in 1967 appears to depict two young boys with boxing gloves, dated to around 1700 B.C.E.

even flushing toilets. Stores were kept in huge clay jars known as *pithoi*.

All of the rooms were airy, lit by light wells, and often decorated with bright frescoes that give us a glimpse of Minoan high society of the time. Women combed their hair in long, elaborate coiffures and wore colorful flounced dresses with tight-waisted, short-sleeve bodices that left much of their breasts exposed. Men were more modestly attired with a simple kilt cinched with a belt, though most wore leather boots to protect the feet against sharp rocks and undergrowth.

A frequent motif in these murals is the bull, which strengthened Evans's association of this culture with the story of the Minotaur, a mythical creature with the head of a bull and the body of a man.

Minoan alabaster jug

Some frescoes depict some form of bull sport whereby athletic young men and women compete in grasping the horns of a charging bull and then trying to jump over its back—not a sport for the timid. Other painted scenes show young athletic men engrossed in boxing and wrestling, wearing knuckle-wraps to protect their hands, or groups of people dancing to the sound of instruments, quite possibly bagpipes and sistrums, a handheld percussion instrument.

The quality of these frescoes is unprecedented in its vibrancy and detail, particularly in the depiction of people, animals, and nature. Also remarkable is their idyllic setting, and the fact that all pictures appear to show young or ageless adults, unlike the presence

EARLY WRITING

Ancient Egypt produced a system of hieroglyphics, while Mesopotamia developed the cuneiform script. None of these would ultimately survive. What did survive was a process of writing that began during the Minoan age. Though several early Minoan scripts have survived, a language known as Linear A began to emerge between 2500 and 1450 B.C.E. (top left). While this is still undeciphered today, we do know that in the centuries to come, Linear A would serve as the foundation of Linear B script, developed by the Mycenaean civilization (bottom left). This script, developed around 1500 B.C.E. as a system of 87 syllabic signs and more than 100 ideographic signs, would become the basis of written Greek and, hence, our modern alphabet.

THE THRONE ROOM of the Minoan palace of Knossos was restored by British archaeologist Arthur Evans.

of the very young and the very old in Egyptian paintings. The virtuosity of these artists is matched by Minoan cups, fashioned of gold, which show the capture of bulls for use in the bullring. These cups were found in Sparta, on mainland Greece, which testifies to the reach of the Minoan civilization.

Indeed, as its influence expanded, the Minoan elite began to colonize the region. Among others, they may have been the ones who built the town of Akrotiri on the volcanic island of Thera (also known as Santorini), first excavated in 1967. The style of Akrotiri's homes and pottery, and the presence of paved streets and drainage systems, all point to a Minoan origin.

Around 1613 B.C.E. Thera's volcano erupted, casting a large cloud of ash as far as Egypt and Greenland. Even crops in China were affected. The town of Akrotiri was buried under layers of pumice, preserving many of its structures similar to the way the ash and lava from Vesuvius covered the Roman cities of Pompeii and Herculaneum. Soon after, the Minoan civilization went into decline. This allowed a new culture to flourish, that of Mycenae on the Greek mainland, which would soon expand its influence to trading partners throughout the

THE MINOAN "BULL-LEAPING" FRESCO from the palace of Knossos on Crete, now restored, is dated to ca 1450 B.C.E. **LEFT:** The "Snake Goddess," ca 1600 B.C.E., is one of several figurines found in Crete that may have been used for worship at home.

A VIEW of ancient Mycenae on the Peloponnese in Greece, center of the Mycenaean civilization

eastern Mediterranean. The fate of Thera has inspired some to connect it to the mythical land of Atlantis.

The Mycenaean Civilization

Mycenae is located on a landmass called the Peloponnese, a large peninsula attached to the mainland of Greece. By 1600 B.C.E., the city had become the dominant power in Greece. Even today, after excavations conducted in 1876 by Heinrich Schliemann, the site of ancient Mycenae is impressive to behold. Its capital enclave was surrounded by a wall of huge stones in the center of which stood the Lion Gate. This massive portal, covered by a 12-ton lintel, was topped by sculptures of twin lions guarding a Minoan-style column, symbol of the sacred earth of Greece. One of Mycenae's rulers was the legendary King Agamemnon of Homer's poem *The Iliad*.

Two centuries later, Mycenaean earthenware pottery could be found throughout

Mycenaean gold goblet

Egypt and Mesopotamia. This is the time when the slender, double-handled clay amphora makes its appearance as a container for precious substances. These vessels probably contained commodities from the prosperous international trade of the time—tin (necessary for the amalgamation of copper into bronze), olive oil, or wine.

Most of these goods entered the Fertile Crescent through the port of Tell el-Ajjul, which has been identified with the biblical city of Sharuhen, while Hazor was a main conduit for trade with Syria, Anatolia, and even Mesopotamia. The trade activity also spurred a new form of simplified writing. Largely under the influence of Mycenae, the first syllabic signs of the Linear B alphabet, the first attested form of written Greek, began to emerge. The importance of Mycenae was due in no small measure to the tension between Egypt and the Hittite Empire, which the Greek city was able to exploit as a "neutral party." ■

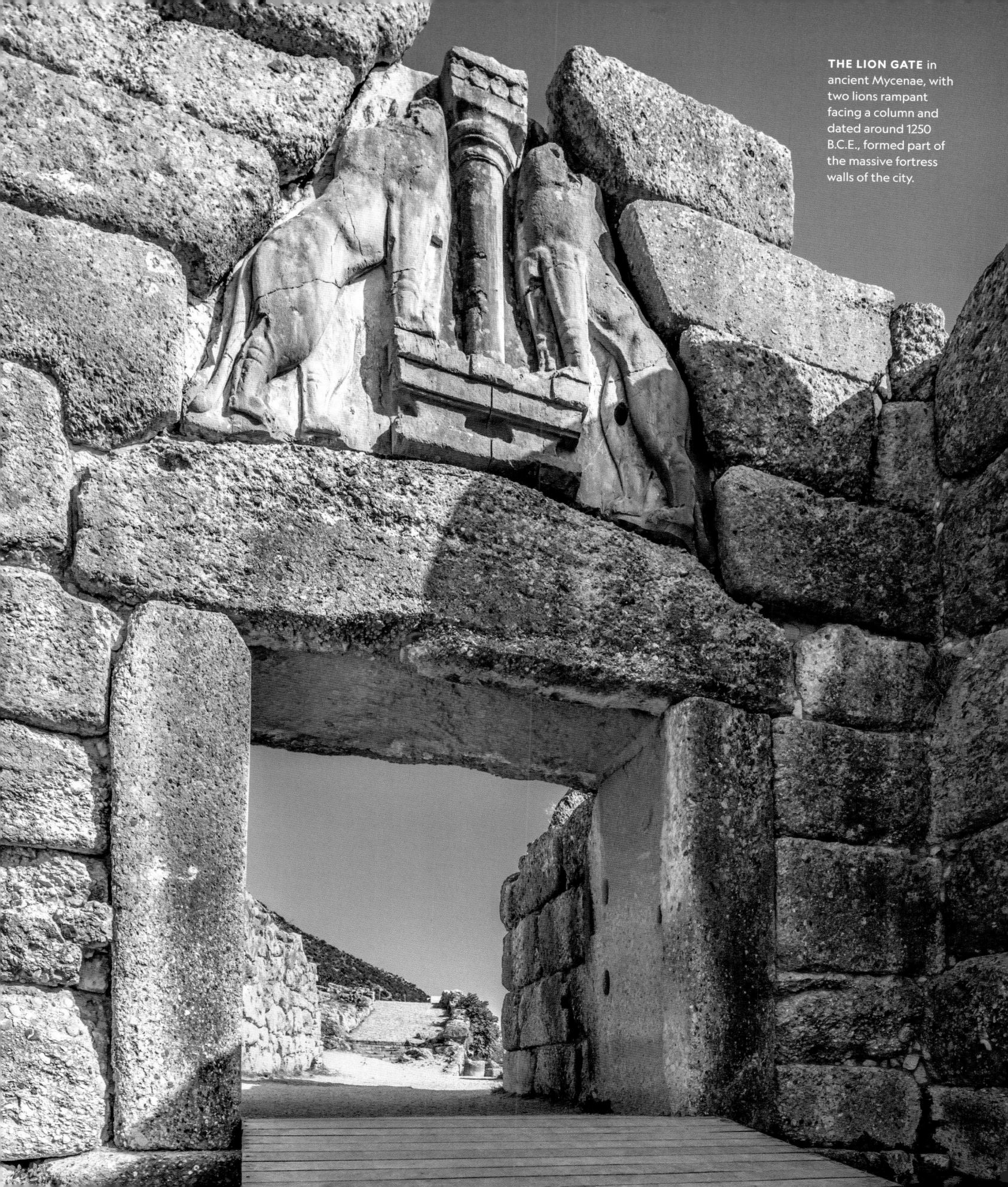

THE LION GATE in ancient Mycenae, with two lions rampant facing a column and dated around 1250 B.C.E., formed part of the massive fortress walls of the city.

CHENG TANG (r. 1675–1646 B.C.E.) was the first king of the Shang Dynasty (ca 1600–1046 B.C.E.).

ASIA
IN THE LATE BRONZE AGE

During the Late Bronze Age, the Shang Dynasty in China and the Vedic era in India produced major developments in trade, ceramics, writing, and religious ideas that would lay the foundation for the flowering of Asian civilization.

I n China, the Shang Dynasty (ca 1600–1046 B.C.E.) was reaching its zenith. It had made great strides in the casting of bronze for a variety of tools and artifacts, including large vessels and weapons, and had begun the development of an early writing system. That is one reason that the Shang (also known as Yin) is the first dynasty in Chinese history to be attested by some tokens of archaeological evidence. For example, at Anyang, the last Shang capital, archaeologists have uncovered the remains of several palaces, as well as 11 royal tombs, in addition to scores of artifacts made of jade, stone, bronze, and ceramics. And yet our knowledge of this dynasty is limited, because much information is derived from ancient texts such as the *Book of Documents,* the *Zuo zhuan,* and the *Bamboo Annals,* which often do not distinguish between legend and historical fact.

Nor was the Shang Dynasty the only prominent civilization in China at the time. Chinese and Western excavators have discovered the remains of other cultures, such as the Erlitou culture of Yanshi (ca 2100-1800 B.C.E), located south of the Yellow River. At its peak, around 1600 B.C.E.,

Yanshi was a walled city sprawled across nearly 500 acres that remained dormant until its discovery in 1957. Another important civilization was the Erligang culture of Zhengzhou, traces of which have been found across China in the form of pottery, bronze, and jewelry. A key center of Erligang culture was Panlongcheng in the Yangtze Valley. What these discoveries suggest is that at this time in history, Chinese history did not evolve in a linear sequence of dynasties but as a confluence of several contemporary cultures, each contributing to the genesis of an authentic Chinese civilization.

One of the most hotly debated topics in Chinese prehistory today is the origin of Chinese writing. As we saw, the emerging Chinese alphabet used iconic representations called glyphs, of which the oldest extant samples have been found in Anyang and are dated to around 1200 B.C.E. These are mostly inscriptions on bronze vessels, on stones or horns, or on oracle bones. While some scholars interpret these

A SACRIFICIAL BOWL in the shape of a bronze elephant from the Shang Dynasty is dated to the 12th century B.C.E.

symbols as evidence of a fully developed system of writing, others believe that a true Chinese alphabet was still in its infancy.

The principles of Chinese architecture, notably its post-and-beam-system, were already in place, as revealed by the excavations of the royal palace of Yinxu. This system refers to the practice of creating a building with large, load-bearing wooden beams, fitted and joined using large wooden pegs. At Yinxu, excavators found as many as 53 pavilions supported by thick wooden posts placed on large stone bases, built on rammed earth. Servants' quarters and storage space were provided by nearby rooms carved in underground pits.

Shang jade dragon

The Shang Military

Indeed, one of the distinguishing features of the Shang Dynasty was its military prowess. A great variety of arms have been excavated, including dagger-axes, spears, composite bows, and helmets made of bronze or leather. The Shang even deployed the chariot around the same time that this horse-drawn war vehicle appeared in the Near East, particularly the Hittite Empire of Anatolia, which some historians believe may suggest some form of contact between China and the Middle East. Other historians contest that claim, pointing to the relative isolation of the Shang Dynasty and its limited trade with outside territories. There is also evidence that the use of chariots was limited to commanders and the royal entourage, quite in contrast to the subsequent Zhou Dynasty, which deployed chariots on a large scale.

Another reason for the abundance of Shang weaponry was the dynasty's fondness for elaborate sacrificial ceremonies, in which both humans and animals were put to death. There is evidence, for example, that upon the death of a prominent member of the royal family, hundreds of slaves and servants were killed to serve the deceased—not unlike the human remains found by Woolley at the Royal Tombs of Ur. Large numbers of horses were interred as well. All this suggests that belief in the afterlife was strong in the Shang civilization and that the social divisions of life on Earth were thought to be continued in the hereafter.

HORSES AND CHARIOTS from the Shang Dynasty were discovered in a burial pit at Guangxi Zhuangzu, China.

CHINESE ARCHAEOLOGISTS
at work excavating an ancient
Shang graveyard in Anyang,
Henan Province, China

NOTABLE DATES

ca 1600 B.C.E.

The Erlitou culture rises in
Henan and Shanxi, China

ca 1500 B.C.E.

Shang Dynasty reaches its
apogee at Zhengzhou,
Henan Province

ca 1500 B.C.E.

Jomon culture in Japan
produces human figurines
in clay

ca 1500 B.C.E.

Aryan-speaking Indo-
Europeans migrate from Asia
to India on horseback

ca 1500 B.C.E.

Hindu sages develop the
Vedas, the earliest sacred
Hindu writings

ca 1500 B.C.E.

The Hindu caste system
emerges in India

ca 1500 B.C.E.

Early Chinese alphabet uses
iconic representations called
glyphs

ca 1400 B.C.E.

Shang Dynasty develops a
calendar with a 365¼-day
year in 12 months

ca 1300 B.C.E.

The royal palace of Yinxu is
the oldest example of
Chinese architecture

ca 1200 B.C.E.

Shang military introduces
chariots with spoked wheels

ca 1046 B.C.E.

Zhou Dynasty replaces the
Shang Dynasty in China

THESE FIVE HEADS reveal the artistry of the Shang Dynasty in fashioning a wide variety of artifacts in bronze as well as in gold, jade, and clay.

Shang religion revolved around animism and ancestral worship. While the Chinese acknowledged the presence of a "High God," they also attributed important powers to the sun and prominent geographical features, such as mountains and rivers. But the most important influence on a person's life was exerted by one's ancestors, as well as the ancestry of the prevailing dynasty. In response, the Shang developed a range of divination rituals, such as the heating and cracking of oracle bones to determine the will of ancestors before embarking on any projects or initiatives.

Over the centuries, the Shang were able to extend their sphere of influence westward, so that by the 12th century, they also controlled the Wei River Valley, populated by a people known as the Zhou. Though the Zhou tribal leader, King Wen, became a Shang vassal, he was assuaged with lofty titles such as "Count of the West," in the hope that this would solidify his fealty to the ruling dynasty. Those hopes were misplaced. When Wen's influence increased throughout the realm, the Shang King Di Xin threw him in prison, which only inflamed tensions among the Zhou. Di Xin realized his mistake and ordered Wen's release, but the damage was done. Wen began to build up his forces,

A SHANG DYNASTY bronze wine vessel from the 12th century B.C.E., probably cast from ceramic molds, is remarkable for its intricate surface decoration.

securing the support of surrounding tribes in this enterprise. Wen died before his army could rise in revolt, but his son, King Wu, continued the arms buildup until he had amassed an army of about 50,000. When most of the Shang army was moved east to deal with threats in that area, Wu saw his chance. In 1046 B.C.E., he led his army to the Shang capital city of Yin. In desperation, King Di Xin conscripted some 170,000 slaves in the defense of the city, but as soon as the Zhou forces appeared on the horizon, many of these defected to Wu's side or refused to fight altogether.

Jade figure, 1200 B.C.E.

The resulting clash, an event known as the Battle of Muye, was one of the bloodiest engagements in Chinese history. Though Di Xin still commanded a superiority in men and weaponry, Wu's highly motivated troops were able to defeat him. The Shang king retreated to the Deer Terrace Pavilion of his palace, covered himself with jewelry, and immolated himself with fire.

Thus ended the Shang Dynasty, giving way to the next Chinese dynasty, that of Zhou (1046–256 B.C.E.). Though its power would wane after 771 B.C.E. in the western part of its realm, this dynasty continued to rule in the eastern part—known as Eastern Zhou—until the Classical era, making it the longest-ruling dynasty in Chinese history.

India During the Vedic Era

From the second millennium B.C.E. onward, a prolonged drought spread through South Asia, eradicating much of the prosperity of the Indus Valley civilization, as well as settlements in today's Afghanistan and Iran. Part of this aridification was climate change and the absence of rainfall, whereas the decline of Indian monsoons prompted part of the Ghaggar-Hakra River system to dry up. Harvests failed at a growing rate, and by 1500 B.C.E., most agricultural cities of the Indus civilization had been abandoned.

EARLY POTTERY

The development of clay pottery was vitally important for cooking, as well as the storage of precious foodstuffs such as grains, figs, dates, salted fish, and oil, allowing a family to feed itself during the long periods between harvests. These early pots (at right) were fired in an oven known as a kiln, which drained the clay of any remaining moisture and allowsed it to harden. When kiln technology became more widespread, villages and townships learned to fire their own pottery from clay. In the process, they developed their own patterns of production and decoration that distinguished one region from another. The repertoire grew from storage jars, mixing vessels, and cooking pots to more sophisticated designs such as wine warmers or sieve jugs, with a strainer built in the vessel's spout to restrain the sediment. Clay vessels broke easily, but these potsherds found a new purpose as tools to scoop water, eat a stew, or dig the soil.

THESE HUMAN SKULLS were discovered in a pit during the excavation of a Shang city near Zhengzhou, Henan Province, China.

A MODERN PHOTOGRAPH
shows a Dalit, or Untouchable, woman from India with a veil covering her face.

At some time thereafter, a growing number of Indo-Aryan tribes moved into the Indian subcontinent. Some scholars believe that these people originated from steppes along the Black Sea in what today is Ukraine and slowly spread through Europe and part of Asia. They argue that even though these tribes were genetically diverse, they shared a unique culture and language referred to as *aryā*, or "noble." In time, these Indo-Aryans blended with local cultures to plant the seeds of most languages in Europe, Iran, and India. Other historians dispute this theory and claim that the Indo-Aryan culture was a continuation of the Indus Valley civilization and therefore an uninterrupted development of an indigenous Indian movement.

Whatever the case may be, there is little question that the Aryan tribes introduced a social class system known as castes, which by and large

AN INDUS VALLEY SEAL from the 26th century B.C.E. shows a horned animal.

continues to this day. Perhaps these castes came about because of the racial differences between the light-skinned Aryans and the native Indians, who were darker. Aryans identified themselves by two classes, the Brahmans (priests) and Kshatriyas (warriors). They lived largely separate from the indigenous people known as *dasas*, or "dark ones," who were organized in two groups: a mercantile class called Vaishyas, and the majority of peasants and laborers called Shudras. Many centuries later, these were followed by another group called the Untouchables, who were literally outcasts and charged with the most menial tasks imaginable. In an effort to combat the Indian caste system, Gandhi made a point of staying with the Untouchables of Delhi whenever he ventured into the city. ∎

EXCAVATING SETTLEMENTS

After a Bronze Age settlement was destroyed or abandoned—as a result of earthquake, drought, or act of war—it was often rebuilt by successive generations. These new arrivals typically built their mud-brick or stone structures on top of the ruins of the preceding epoch. Across the centuries, a city could thus rise to form a veritable mound (at right). Digging through such a tell, archaeologists in many cases have been able to identify successive periods of habitation as individual strata, or layers of debris, almost like layers in a cake. The role of pottery in stratigraphy is crucial for modern archaeologists, since after 6000 B.C.E., the craft of making stylistically consistent pottery became the domain of trained artisans. The classification of these styles—using the distinguishing features of color, material, and decoration and the shapes of the rim, handle, and sometimes spout—allows excavators to identify a given stratum in terms of date and culture.

AN 18TH-DYNASTY wall painting from the Tomb of Unsu in Thebes shows farmers at work sowing and harvesting.

EGYPT
IN THE LATE BRONZE AGE

For more than a thousand years, Egypt had ruled as the dominant power of the Near East, with its trade and cultural influences stretching as far as Mesopotamia, Greece, Nubia, and beyond. But during the Middle Kingdom, Egypt entered a period of steady decline.

What sustained Egypt's remarkable civilization across these vast spans of time? The answer is its exceptional role as the largest grain-producing region in the Near East. Egypt's two main cereal crops were emmer (or spelt) wheat, used for baking bread, and barley. Bread was the most important ingredient of a person's diet in ancient times (and in many regions of the world even today). While barley was grown primarily for beer or animal fodder, poor families often had to make do with barley as a wheat substitute. Barley was also fermented to brew beer, which explains why bread and beer were the two staples of the Egyptian worker's diet. This was complemented with lentils, beans, cabbage, and occasionally fish. Sheep, goats, and fattened calves were preferred sources of meat, though only wealthy families were able to eat meat on a regular basis.

The Nile River also enabled rapid transportation across the spine of Lower and Upper Egypt. The sensational discovery of a group of boats in Abydos in 2000 suggests that, as early as 3000 B.C.E., the ancient Egyptians had mastered the art of assembling a wooden hull using curved wooden planks, joined together with mortise and tenon joints and sealed with reeds. These ships were essentially river barges, though some scholars claim that they could have sailed along the Mediterranean coast as far as Syria and the gateway to northern Mesopotamia.

Mass Migration

Egypt's wealth served as a powerful magnet for immigrants, particularly in lands that were often scourged by drought and famine. Egypt's Middle Kingdom (ca 2040–1630 B.C.E.) witnessed numerous mass migrations from throughout the known world. Among others, the biblical story of Jacob's tribe in Egypt may have been inspired by several immigration waves from Syro-Canaan to Egypt, as documented by Egyptian records of the era. For example, an 18th-century B.C.E. roster of an upper-class household in Thebes lists 80 servants, including weavers

A PECTORAL, or chest ornament, with falcons and a scarab includes the name of King Senwosret II of the 12th Dynasty, Middle Kingdom.

"HAIL TO THEE, O NILE! YOU CREATE THE GRAIN, YOU BRING FORTH THE BARLEY, ASSURING PERPETUITY TO THE TEMPLES. IF YOU CEASE YOUR TOIL AND YOUR WORK, THEN ALL THAT EXISTS IS IN ANGUISH."

HYMN TO THE NILE, LATE SECOND MILLENNIUM B.C.E.

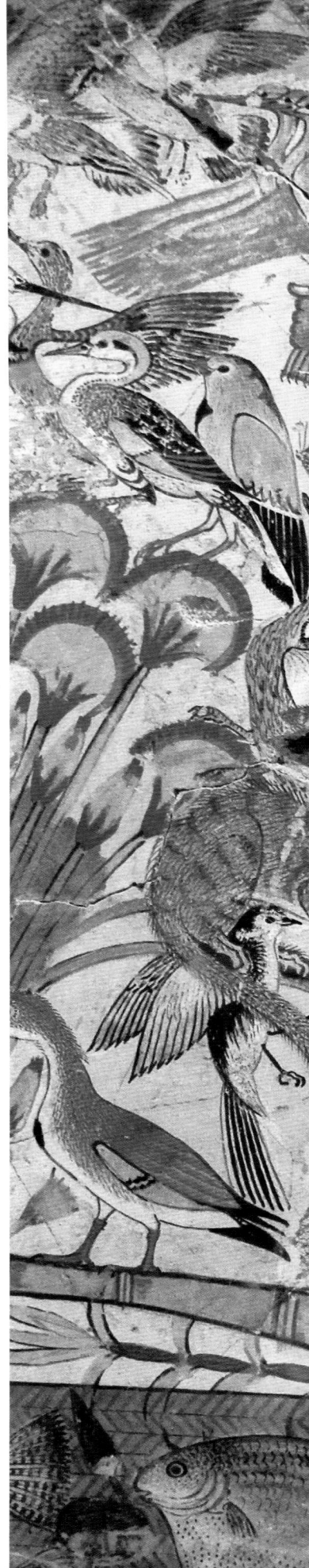

and spinners, of whom no fewer than 40 names are of Semitic origin, such as "Aqaba" and "Menahem." Because Egyptians had trouble pronouncing these foreign names, "guest workers" from abroad were immediately given Egyptian names. We see this in the story of Joseph, who was renamed Zaphenath-paneah (Genesis 41:45).

A vivid impression of foreign immigrants was discovered in a tomb found near the hamlet of Beni-Hasan, some 200 miles south of Cairo, apparently belonging to a local governor named Khnumhotep II, who lived during the reign of King Amenemhet II. The tomb was decorated with brightly colored scenes typical of an Egyptian nobleman's life—hunting in the marshes, overseeing the harvest, or heading out for a night of celebration.

One of the tomb's wall paintings depicts a long train of people, surrounded by their livestock, who are strikingly different from the lithe and elegantly dressed Egyptian figures. Accompanying hieroglyphs note that these are the Abiru, which literally means "sand dwellers" and should probably be translated as "migrants." Most Egyptians believed that servants from the East were inferior and often treated them with contempt. "Their tongues

AN ANCIENT EGYPTIAN
figure showing a woman filtering barley to make beer is dated to the Old Kingdom, Fifth Dynasty, ca 2400 B.C.E.

are separate in speech, and their natures as well," reads a 14th-century B.C.E. Egyptian document.

Even as Egypt's economic and political power during the Middle Kingdom entered a period of steady decline, its civilization still dazzled the world. The quality of Egypt's art remained unchallenged, exemplified by a magnificent black granite statue of Pharaoh Sesostris (or Senwosret) III of the 12th Dynasty, completed around 1850 B.C.E. The heavy eyelids, the somber expression, and the firm mouth of the king suggest a weariness with power that stands in stark contrast to the formalized portraits of the Old Kingdom. Another exquisite work from this period is the statue of the official Ankhrekhu. Though the features are realistic, the hair, hands, and vestments are stylized in an almost modern manner.

Senwosret III exemplifies the 12th-Dynasty kings who, of necessity, turned away from grandiose funerary monuments to concentrate on Egypt's economy and infrastructure. Senwosret himself pushed through a number of agricultural initiatives, including the digging of the Bahr Yusuf canal in the Faiyum and the broadening of a bypass canal at the first cataract of the Nile. He also expanded Egypt's territory southward, at the expense of Nubia and conducted a punitive campaign against Syria. But the pyramids built by the rulers of the next dynasty, the 13th (ca 1755–1630 B.C.E.), are small, pitiful affairs built of mud brick, with only a thin

THIS VIVID WALL PAINTING of a man hunting in the fields was found in the tomb of Nebanum in western Thebes, dated around 1356 B.C.E. (New Kingdom, 18th Dynasty).

BLACKENED LIDS
highlight this pharaoh's striking eyes in a wooden sculpture from the 13th Dynasty.

veneer of limestone. For example, the pyramid of Khendjer (or Userkare, ca 1740–1747 B.C.E.) is but a shadow of the grand pyramids of Khufu and Khafre in Giza, which by this time were more than 800 years old.

The Disintegration of Egypt

The gradual disintegration of Egypt's central authority led to the Second Intermediate Period (ca 1630–1520 B.C.E.), when the wave of poor immigrants pressing at Egypt's borders became overwhelming. This was partly due to the poor governance by the kings of the 13th Dynasty, who lacked the energy and initiative of previous kings. Another factor was a prolonged period of drought that also plagued South Asia, which led to insufficient flooding of the Nile River and further destabilization of the kingdom's economy. Pharaoh's authority to rule over his people depended on his stewardship of the annual flooding of the Nile. If the inundation was too deep, seeds could not germinate; if it was too shallow, there was not enough silt to support a full harvest. Each year,

therefore, kings and commoners alike prayed fervently for a perfect Nile flooding, even using "Nilometers" to measure the level of the river.

The resulting collapse of Egypt's central authority provoked a wave of immigration from the east, including a large number of tribes from Canaan, Syria, and Anatolia. Egypt's initial response was to deter these immigrants by building a string of forts along the eastern delta. But eventually Egypt's kings changed their mind and welcomed these immigrants, possibly because of a growing labor shortage. As early as the 12th Dynasty (ca 1991–1793 B.C.E.), the pharaohs had expanded their operations at gold mines in the eastern desert as well as the turquoise mines of southern Sinai in an attempt to enlarge their depleted coffers.

But during the 13th Dynasty, the number of refugees flooding Egypt's borders dissolved all sense of central authority. Indeed, since Egypt's kings were essentially powerless to stop them,

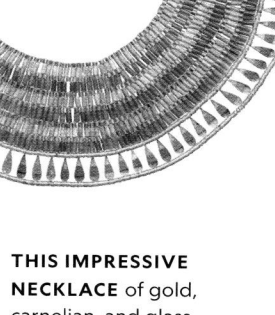

THIS IMPRESSIVE NECKLACE of gold, carnelian, and glass paste once belonged to Princess Neferuptah of the 12th Dynasty (ca 1991–1793 B.C.E.).

BRONZE AGE TRADE

The principal commodities of trade in the Bronze Age were copper and turquoise (Egypt), incense and ivory (Arabia and India), wine (Canaan and the Aegean), wood (Lebanon), cereals (Mesopotamia and Syria), and carnelian and obsidian (central Turkey). Egypt in particular required imports of a range of raw materials not available in Egypt: timber, marble, and countless precious metals and gems (at right). In addition, the mummification process used various exotic chemicals and spices, including the "gum, balm and myrrh" that the Ishmaelites carried to Egypt in the story of Joseph in Genesis. Balm was the gum of the balsam tree (*Commiphora opobalsamum*) that grew in southern Arabia and was mostly used for its medicinal qualities. Myrrh is the resin of a bush of thorns (*Commpihora myrrha*) that grew along the Arabian and African coasts on the Red Sea. It was used as a perfume agent in oils and as incense in the temple.

> "THE LAND [IS] BEING CAST AWAY . . . [BY] ASIATICS WHO PERVADE THE LAND . . . [THEY] HAVE COME DOWN INTO EGYPT, FOR A FORTRESS LACKS ANOTHER BESIDE IT, AND NO GUARD WILL HEAR."

THE PROPHESIES OF NEFERTI

these immigrants from Syria and Canaan were free to settle in the Nile Delta as they liked. In time, their Semitic chieftains began to dominate the trade and agriculture of this region, gradually displacing Egyptian control of the area. The third-century B.C.E. Egyptian historian Manetho refers to these Semitic tribes as Hikau-khoswet (Hyksos in Greek), which means "desert princes." Manetho also claims that these foreign tribes took control of Egypt's Lower Kingdom as the result of a military invasion, but modern research has shown that their domination of the region was a gradual process that took nearly a century.

The Hyksos in Ancient Egypt

By 1630 B.C.E., the Hyksos had effectively replaced the old Egyptian monarchy in the north with their own dynasty: the 15th Dynasty (1630–1520 B.C.E.). The first king was Sheshi, who established the dynasty. In response, Egyptian nobility was forced to abandon the Middle Kingdom capital of el-Lisht and move south to Thebes, former capital of the 11th Dynasty, to establish the 17th Dynasty.

A MIDDLE KINGDOM statuette of a hippopotamus is dated to the reign of King Senwosret II of the 12th Dynasty, Middle Kingdom.

18th Dynasty (ca 1539–1292 B.C.E.) depicts women pressing flowers to make perfume.

EGYPTIAN BOYS wade through a pool filled with the ruins of Memphis, capital of Egypt's Old Kingdom.

Here, they would set up a court in exile and plot their eventual restoration.

The Hyksos kings did not hesitate to arrogate the title of pharaoh for themselves. Having sacked the ancient royal capital of Memphis, they decided to build a capital city of their own, known as Avaris. Excavations by archaeologist Manfred Bietak have conclusively established that Avaris was located at Tell el-Dab'a in the eastern Nile Delta. Little remains, however, since most Hyksos palaces were built in mud brick and washed away by flooding over subsequent centuries. Nonetheless, Bietak's team was able to excavate the foundations of a 200-foot mud-brick palace, arguably the largest Hyksos structure ever found in the delta, probably built during the reign of King Khayan ca 1600 B.C.E.

Craving the legitimacy of the ancient monarchy they had ousted,

A scarab of King Sheshi

the Hyksos kings worked hard to imitate them. In the few portraits and statuettes that have survived, they have the same traditional attributes as the pharaohs of old. The Hyksos Dynasty lasted only a single century, spanning the reign of six kings. We know their foreign-sounding names from the so-called Turin King List papyrus, probably composed during the reign of Ramses II. Among them is a king called Y'qb-Hr (or Yaqub-Her), a name that bears an obvious resemblance to the Semitic name of Jacob from Genesis.

It is plausible to imagine that the story of Joseph in Genesis is set in the Lower Egypt kingdom of the Hyksos pharaohs rather than any other place and time in Egypt's history. The idea that an immigrant from Canaan could rise to the post of grand vizier of Egypt, which some scholars have dismissed as preposterous, is less astonishing when we consider that most other officials at

THE INVENTION OF THE CHARIOT

The horse-drawn chariot was possibly developed by the Hittites in their home territory of Anatolia (modern Turkey) and subsequently introduced in the Near East. The first reference to a chariot in ancient sources appears in an 18th-century Hittite text, where a chariot is drawn by as many as 40 teams of horses. The Hittites' enemy, the Egyptians, took heed and began to build chariots of their own that they ultimately used to stem the Hittite invasions (at right). These Egyptian-built chariots would figure prominently in the story of the Exodus, as well as in the climactic Battle of Qadesh, where Ramses II deployed thousands of his chariots against an equal number in the Hittite army. The battle ended in a draw, upon which Ramses and Hittite King Hattusilis III entered into a nonaggression pact, the first in recorded history.

"WE HAVE FINISHED LETTING THE BEDOUIN TRIBES OF EDOM PASS THE FORTRESS OF MER-NE-PTAH HOTEP-HIR-MAAT, SO AS TO KEEP THEM ALIVE, AND TO KEEP THEIR HERDS ALIVE."

REPORT FROM INENA, EGYPTIAN BORDER OFFICIAL, 13TH CENTURY B.C.E.

the court of Avaris would have hailed from Syria-Canaan as well.

Meanwhile, in the southern capital of Thebes, the disenfranchised 17th Dynasty of Egypt continued to plan the reconquest of Lower Egypt. Sometime around 1570 B.C.E., Pharaoh Seqenenre

THE DYNASTIES OF ANCIENT EGYPT
(B.C.E., OR BEFORE THE COMMON ERA)

Early Dynastic Period
2920–2575

Old Kingdom
2575–2134

First Intermediate Period
2134–2040

Middle Kingdom
2040–1640

Second Intermediate Period
1640–1550

New Kingdom
1550–1070

Third Intermediate Period
1070–712

Late Period
712–332

Greek Period
332–30

Roman Period
30 B.C.E.–395 C.E.

cast off his battle fleet and floated toward the Nile Delta to invade the north. Years of hard fighting followed, led on the Theban side by Seqenenre's successor, Kamose, and the first king of the new 18th Dynasty, Ahmose I. The conflict became the Sixty Years' War—a war of attrition that caused untold havoc upon the placid fields of the Nile. But in time, Pharaoh Ahmose I was able to capture the Hyksos capital of Avaris.

Ahmose gave leave to his troops to rape and pillage to their heart's content. "I carried off one man and three women from there," a captain named Ahmose wrote home; "His Majesty gave them to me as slaves." In 1999, Manfred Bietak uncovered a complex of buildings near Tell el-Dab'a, presumed site of Avaris, that revealed a thin layer of burned earth—testimony to the fury of King Ahmose's wrath. But Pharaoh didn't stop there. Knowing that he had the Hyksos on the run, Ahmose ordered a pursuit to erase the foreign threat from Egypt's borders. Once in Canaan, the retreating Hyksos made a last desperate stand at Sharuhen, which may be modern Tell el-Far'ah in the southern Negev. The Egyptian king easily destroyed and sacked the city. ∎

THIS FIGURE of a man named Djehutera dates to the Second Intermediate Period, when Lower Egypt was controlled by Hyksos kings.

MEMBERS OF a Semitic tribe, dressed in colorful striped garments, ask permission to enter Egypt in a mural from the tomb of Khnumhotep in Beni-Hasan, who served Pharaoh Amenemhet II (1876-1842 B.C.E.).

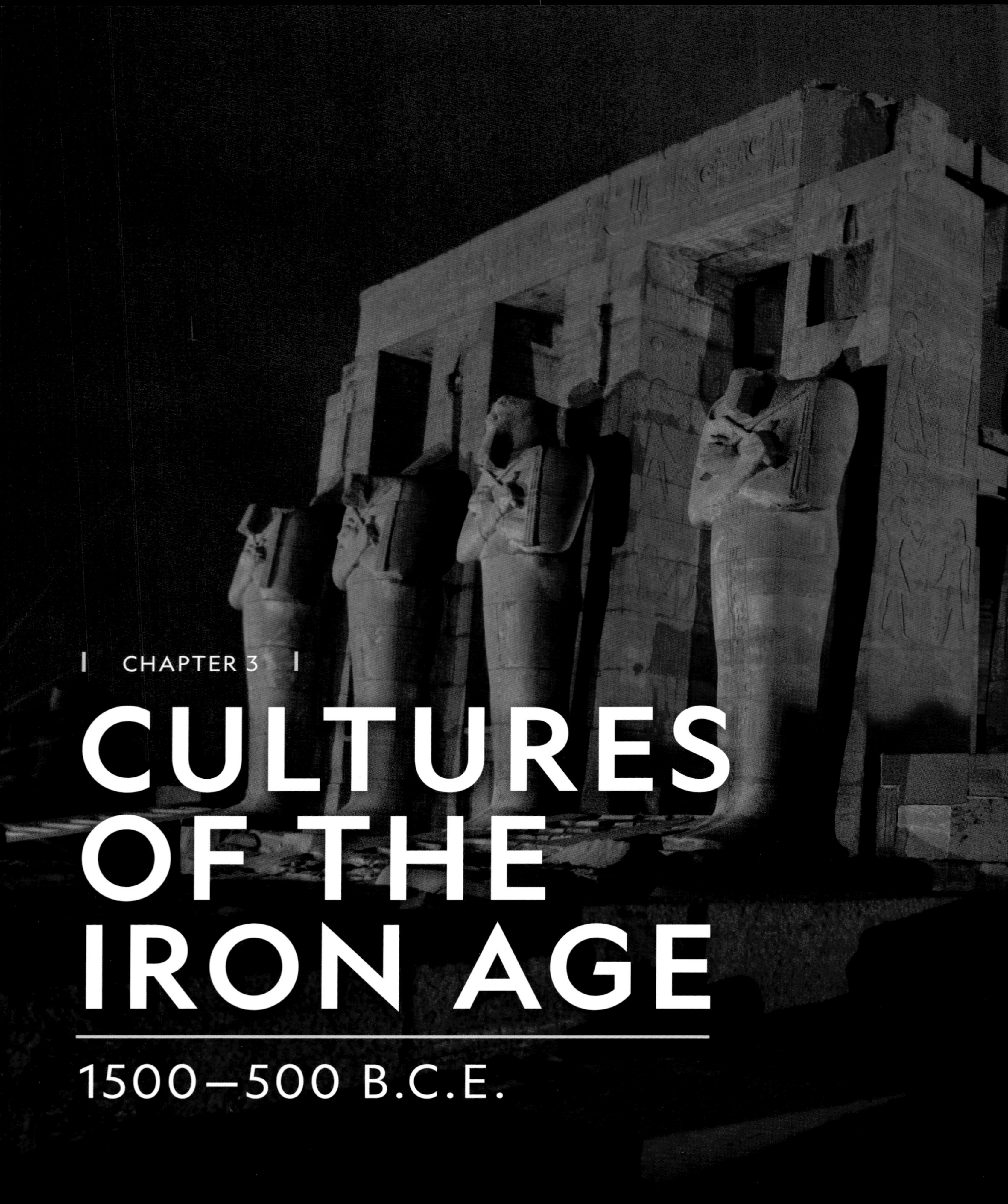

CULTURES OF THE IRON AGE

1500–500 B.C.E.

COLOSSAL STATUES guard the pylons of the Ramesseum, the mortuary temple of Ramses II in the necropolis of Thebes.

CONTENTS

THE IRON REVOLUTION

The transition to the second half of the second millennium B.C.E. coincided with major changes in the technology of the period, prompted by the gradual replacement of copper and bronze, the dominant metals for tools and arms, with items made of iron. Previously, iron had been available only in small quantities and accessible only to major powers such as Egypt. The idea that it was the Hittites who perfected ironwork in Anatolia before introducing it throughout the Near East has now been abandoned by most archaeologists, particularly since similar developments took place elsewhere in the world. The adoption of iron tools in Europe, for example, was almost simultaneous with the introduction in the Near East. In China, by contrast, the Iron Age did not begin until after the 10th century B.C.E., although in India, iron metallurgy was practiced as early as the 16th century B.C.E., as evidenced by objects from Hyderabad and Lahuradewa. In Africa, where bronze was hardly ever used (with the exception of the Egyptian colony of Nubia, today's Sudan), the introduction of iron came only around 550 B.C.E. after a long period in which stone remained the primary material for tools.

Regardless, the introduction of iron led to a rapid development in smelting and blacksmithing techniques, which produced a wide variety of iron objects for cooking, leisure, farming, and war. For example, farmers began to use a curved, hardwood plow fitted with an iron plowshare, which greatly facilitated the preparation of topsoil, particularly in regions of dry farming, for it broke the earth more deeply prior to seeding. Scholars therefore describe the period between 1200 and 1000 B.C.E. as the first Iron Age (Iron Age I), following the Bronze Age.

The Development of Alphabets

Another, and perhaps even more important, innovation of this era was the emergence of linear alphabets—in contrast to the pictographic and cuneiform writing of the Bronze Age—that produced three distinct variations: (1) the Phoenician alphabet, which took form in the 11th century B.C.E.; (2) the Hebrew alphabet, which emerged in the 10th century B.C.E.; and (3) distinct Aramaic alphabets that would become widespread after the sixth century B.C.E. under the influence of both the Phoenician and Hebrew models. Because of Phoenicia's extensive trade contacts with the Mediterranean world, the Phoenician alphabet would strongly influence the emergence of the Greek alphabet, the basis for our modern Latin-based style of writing.

Politically, the beginning of the Iron Age was also a time of great instability and turmoil, caused by the wholesale movement of peoples throughout the world—including, conceivably, Hebrew refugees from Egypt. An inscription in the Great Temple of Karnak from 1200 B.C.E. is one of the first to alert the nation to this development, citing the influx of five distinct groups of migrants. For more than a thousand years, Egypt had ruled as the dominant power of the Near East. But near the end of the Middle Kingdom (ca 1975–1640 B.C.E.), the unity of the realm began to crumble. ∎

THIS SCULPTURE of a Seated Buddha was created in Gandhara between the first and third centuries C.E.

A COLORED MURAL from the tomb of Nefertari depicts Osiris, the Egyptian god of cultivation and the afterlife, wearing the *atef,* his feathered white crown.

A POLYCHROME SCULPTURE from near Leh, India, depicts Maitreya, the Buddha who, according to Buddhist tradition, will appear in the future to succeed the present Gautama Buddha.

INDIA
THE CRADLE OF HINDUISM AND BUDDHISM

During this period, the Indian subcontinent became the birthplace of several traditions that would produce four of the world's major religions, including Hinduism and Buddhism, as well as related movements such as Jainism and Sikhism. These religions would soon radiate throughout Southeast Asia.

Perhaps the most important development in the religious sphere during this period originated in India. From about 1500 B.C.E. onward, the mostly pastoral communities in northwestern India produced a series of texts known as the Vedas. These Vedic texts are a collection of hymns, prayers, and rituals combining ancient Harappan and Aryan beliefs that were first organized in a canon during the rise of the Janapadas or Indian kingdoms, beginning with the kingdom of Kuru. The Vedic period, which lasted to 500 B.C.E., is a watershed moment in the history of India, for its culture would lay the basis of Hinduism at about the same time that ancient Judaism was stirring in Canaan. Today, Hinduism is the world's third largest religion, with more than a billion adherents.

Hinduism is a polytheistic religion with many greater and lesser divinities. The principal gods are the Trimurti or Hindu triad of Brahma, Vishnu, and Shiva. Brahma is the creator of the world; Vishnu is revered as the god of love, a hero of the downtrodden, and a savior of humankind; and Shiva is a somewhat ruthless deity who governs birth and death. The role of these gods, as articu-lated by the great 19th-century Hindu sage Swami Vivekananda, is to illustrate that the divine exists in all beings and that sharing the essence of this innate divinity will foster love and social harmony among all people. Unlike other religions, Hindu-ism does not recognize any central authority. Instead, it is manifested in many different tra-ditions, often blended with local currents of Taoism, Buddhism, Jainism, or even ancient animism, as in Bali.

Hindu deities are either masculine (*Deva*) or feminine (*Devi*). In Hindu art they are often shown with multiple ana-tomical attributes to symbolize their supernatural knowledge or with multiple arms to express excep-tional powers. For example, a god or goddess can be depicted with multiple faces to signify extraor-dinary powers. Some gods are also shown with animal attri-butes, such as Shiva's son Gane-sha, who has the head of an elephant, or the god Hanuman, who is shown as half monkey,

A SCULPTURE from Kashmir dated to the seventh century C.E. shows Brahma, the Hindu god of creation, and the Four Vedas.

> "DO NOT BE LED BY OTHERS, AWAKEN YOUR OWN MIND, AMASS YOUR OWN EXPERIENCE, AND DECIDE FOR YOURSELF YOUR OWN PATH."
>
> THE ATHARVA VEDA

half human. This conveys the idea that in the Hindu pantheon, there are no true boundaries between humans and animals; both have souls that can pass back and forth between the species.

Much of the Vedic texts is concerned with what happens to the soul after death. Scholars believe that in the beginning, these Vedic sages used a variety of hallucinogens to induce altered states of consciousness so as to unlock their inner spirit. Eventually they developed other techniques to explore their inner consciousness, including the technique we now know as yoga.

Hindu god Ganesha

This is why ancient India probably became the first culture to formulate the idea that human consciousness may be transcendental, and potentially immortal. As a result, Indian sages concluded that our consciousness can reach total happiness only if every form of material craving is utterly quenched or snuffed out, like the flame of a candle. This is captured in the word "nirvana," which literally means "quenching." It has served ever since as the ultimate goal of Hinduism, as well as Buddhism, Jainism, and Sikhism. For these traditions, nirvana is a state of a profound spiritual peace, quiet, and freedom from want. How followers can attain this nirvana is a point of contention between these traditions.

The Lord Buddha

Around 460 B.C.E., a philosopher and teacher known as Siddhārtha Gautama developed a philosophy that sought to navigate a middle way between excessive asceticism and physical indulgence. While the historical facts about his life are uncertain, most scholars agree that Gautama, later known as Buddha ("Enlightened One"), probably lived during the era of the Mahajanapada, a cluster of 16 kingdoms in northern India between the sixth and fourth centuries B.C.E. This was a fertile period of many rival *śramaṇa* movements, of "seekers of a higher purpose," and indeed Buddhist texts often show Buddha in debates with adherents of other philosophies. Some scholars have argued that since this period coincides with

A MODERN PHOTOGRAPH of a Hindu holy man teaching in the Amer Fort near Jaipur, India

THE HINDU GOD SHIVA killing Andhakasura for trying to abduct his consort, Parvati, is the subject of this carving from the Hoysaleswara Temple in India.

NOTABLE DATES

ca 1500 B.C.E.
Aryan-speaking Indo-Europeans migrate into India

ca 1500 B.C.E.
Hindu sages create Vedic texts, including hymns, prayers, and liturgy

ca 1400 B.C.E.
People in northern India begin working in iron

ca 1400 B.C.E.
India's Aryans establish the foundation of Hinduism

ca 800–500 B.C.E.
Scattered clans merge into larger states along the Ganges River

ca 800 B.C.E..
Indian teachers compile the Upanishads, sacred Hindu texts

ca 700 B.C.E.
Indian Sushruta performs surgery on cataracts and noses

ca 600 B.C.E.
Several kingdoms in India battle for power

ca 543 B.C.E.
Rise of the Magadha Kingdom of northeastern India

ca 520 B.C.E.
Parts of northwestern India are conquered by Persia

ca 500 B.C.E.
Mahavira (or Vardhamana) develops principles of Jainism

ca 460 B.C.E.
Siddhārtha Gautama (the Buddha) teaches compassion and wisdom

A MONK PRAYS at Bodh Gaya in the Mahabodhi temple complex in Bihar state, India.

the Persian conquest of the Indus Valley, the Buddha's ideas may have been partly a reaction to Achaemenid culture.

Although Buddhist foundational texts ascribe many miracles and supernatural events to Buddha's life, what is generally accepted is that Gautama was deeply affected by the suffering he witnessed among the people, and withdrew into a monastic lifestyle of yoga and meditation. This experience led to his awakening to full enlightenment at age 35 while seated under the so-called Bodhi tree in Bodh Gaya, India.

According to Buddhism, nirvana is the culmination of a long cycle of birth, death, and rebirth known as Saṃsāra (Sanskrit for "wandering"). In this view, humans are condemned to experience an endless cycle of reincarnation, with the

Standing Buddha from the first or second century C.E.

soul aimlessly "wandering" through the universe until, through progressive enlightenment, it finds ultimate release, known as moksha. Buddhism therefore sees the cycle of life through the prism of inevitable human suffering and nirvana as an ultimate resolution of that process. The Buddhist believer achieves that state by reaching ever greater stages of enlightenment, ultimately leading to complete self-denial.

Hinduism, by contrast, sees this process differently. For Hindus, Saṃsāra is above all the journey of the soul, known as atman, sustained by the creative force, known as Brahman. Although the body changes as it moves through various reincarnations, the soul always remains pure, provided it allows itself to be guided by Hindu gods who help humans to gain self-perfection. It is this state of knowing

THE RAMAYANA AND MAHABHARATA

The Vedic period in India (ca 1000–500 B.C.E.) produced the principal foundational texts of Hinduism—not only the Vedic texts but also the *Ramayana* and *Mahabharata*, Hindu epics written in Sanskrit. As in the case of many biblical texts, these multilayered poems went through many centuries of transmission and enrichment until they reached their current form between 400 B.C.E. and 400 C.E. The *Mahabharata* describes the conflict between two families of cousins, the Kauravas and the Pandavas, during a conflict known as the Kurukshetra War. With more than 200,000 individual verses, it is the longest known epic poem in history. A subset of the *Mahabharata*, the Bhagavad Gita, is considered by many an epic in its own right and was often quoted by Gandhi. The *Ramayana* (at right) tells the story of a legendary prince, Rama, who was exiled from the Kosala Kingdom by his father, King Dasharatha, and after many adventures is able to return to Kosala to be crowned king. Both epics convey the moral teachings of Hindu sages that exerted a strong influence on Hinduism and other Asian religions.

"DO NOT DWELL IN THE PAST, DO NOT DREAM OF THE FUTURE, CONCENTRATE THE MIND ON THE PRESENT MOMENT."

THE GAUTAMA BUDDHA

one's soul, and having achieved perfect harmony with that soul, that constitutes moksha—a place "where there is no old age nor death, no pain nor disease." As part of that journey, Hindus seek solace in the guidance of priests as well as a variety of ceremonial rituals that are mostly absent in Buddhism. That is why Hinduism is a religion in the traditional sense of the word, whereas Buddhism could be described as a more philosophical movement.

Both Buddhism and Hinduism operate with a foundational belief in reincarnation. The Bhagavad

Shakyamuni Buddha meditating

Gita explains that the soul will discard the old body and take on a new one, just as a person may discard old clothes for new garments. While the body is purely a vehicle to dispose of, the soul itself is indestructible and goes through many different lives in a cycle of birth and death. The quality of the next life, however, is determined by the sum of a person's deeds (or karma) in a previous life. A righteous person may look forward to a new life full of happiness, whereas those who behaved badly may return as a lower creature, such as an animal. ∎

THE CHAKRA SYSTEM

Some 2,000 years ago, Indian gurus identified a continuous flow of energy in the body that they called *prana*, or "life force." According to some chakra (Sanskrit for "wheel") systems, there are specific energy centers throughout the human body, running along the spinal cord from the base to the head (at left). They are believed to form the bridge between two dimensions of our being: the physical body (*sthula sarira*), made of matter, and the "subtle body" (*suksma sarira*), which consists of our consciousness. The Chinese concept of Qigong is similar, except that Chinese theory believes these life energies or meridians can (literally) be pinpointed and activated using acupuncture. Traditional chakra theories, by contrast, posit that as centers of energy, chakras do not have a definitive node and must therefore be managed in different ways, such as yoga.

MONKS PASS a sculpture of the Reclining Buddha in Buddha Park, also known as Xieng Khuan, near Vientiane in Laos.

THE GREAT CHINESE PHILOSOPHER Confucius (ca 551–479 B.C.E.) taught during the Spring and Autumn period of the late Eastern Zhou Dynasty.

CHINA
IN THE IRON AGE

A key period in Chinese history, the Zhou Dynasty witnessed the rise of important developments in the arts, philosophy, and science, including the foundation of Taoism by Lao-Tzu and the teachings of Confucius. Confucianism would become the foundation of Chinese learning and political theory.

In many respects, the Zhou Dynasty continued the cultural legacy of the dynasty it had replaced, perhaps in an effort to bolster its legitimacy. The Shang arts, language, and religious ceremonies were maintained in much the same vein as they had under the previous regime. Politically, however, the Zhou kings experienced much instability from both forces within and threats without. When Emperor Wu's premature death put an inexperienced heir on the throne, several princes in the eastern provinces rose in rebellion. This revolt was quelled, but the unrest set a pattern, and in the coming years, subject provinces would increasingly gain authority at the expense of the central state. This process was accelerated when the Zhou regime adopted a fengjian policy of devolving much of its power to the rulers of the four main provinces, who essentially governed as feudal potentates. Under their rule, agricultural estates were tended by peasants who received only part of the harvest, with the remainder confiscated by the local government.

At the same time, the Zhou kings developed a doctrine that became known as the Mandate of Heaven—the idea that the emperor was a divinely ordained son of the heavenly powers and answerable only to the gods. There was, of course, a flip side to that premise: As a man endowed with divine powers, the emperor was responsible for the proper cycle of seasons and the success of the harvest. As in the case of the pharaohs in Egypt, that meant that he would also be blamed if floods or drought brought widespread famine and misery. Whenever these occurred, it was widely believed that the emperor had failed in his responsibility of vouchsafing the nation's prosperity or that he had incurred the enmity of the heavens. This would inevitably result in popular unrest and revolt, as Chinese history would show.

Indeed, over time, the power of the local governors became so great that they were virtually on a par with the emperor, leading to an inevitable power struggle. When this rivalry broke into open warfare, King You made the fateful decision to exile his spouse, Queen Jiang, in favor of his

AN ANIMAL MASK is dated to the Western Zhou Period of China (1046–771 B.C.E.).

> "THE PEOPLE SUFFER FROM FAMINE BECAUSE OF THE MULTITUDE OF TAXES CONSUMED BY THEIR SUPERIORS. IT IS THROUGH THIS THAT THEY SUFFER FAMINE."
>
> **LAO-TZU,** *TAO TE CHING (THE BOOK OF THE WAY AND VIRTUE)*

beautiful mistress, Bao Si. Enraged, the queen's father, the Marquis of Shen, led an attack on the Zhou royal palace at Haojing, sacking the place and killing You. A group of nobles then declared the marquis's grandson, Ping, the king of a new, independent realm. This marked the end of the Western Zhou period, forcing the old regime to move east to continue its rule as the Eastern Zhou Dynasty. But this territory also fell prey to internal rivalries, leading to bloody partitions in what would later be called the Spring

Zhou Dynasty nephrite

and Autumn period. The last Zhou king, Nan, was killed when the Qin tribe invaded his capital, Wangcheng, in ca 256 B.C.E. The turmoil continued until some 35 years later, when the king of Qin, Ying Zheng, combined the various tribes and kingdoms into a single state, thus becoming the first emperor of a unified China.

In sum, the role of the Zhou Dynasty in Chinese history is less important in a political than in a cultural sense. The Zhou emperors continued to support the evolution of an authentic Chinese culture in art, architecture, engineering, and writing, transmitting many traditions from previous periods to subsequent generations and eventually China's Classical era. For example, a chancellor of Wei named Sunshu Ao invented a vast catchment reservoir in today's Anhui Province to preserve rainfall and protect the land against periods of drought. Later, this was expanded into an extensive system of irrigation canals that successfully diverted the flow of the Zhang River.

THESE ZHOU PERIOD figures are some of the earliest known Chinese depictions of human beings.

Chinese Philosophy

The most significant contribution of the Zhou Dynasty to Chinese civilization, however, was its cultivation of an indigenous Chinese philosophy. With his book *Tao Te Ching,* the author and philosopher Lao-Tzu founded a school of thought called Taoism. Taoism strives to achieve complete harmony with the spontaneous forces of the universe, known as *dao,* or "the Way." To do so, Taoist followers pursue three virtues: compassion, frugality, and humility.

Historians do not agree when Lao-Tzu is

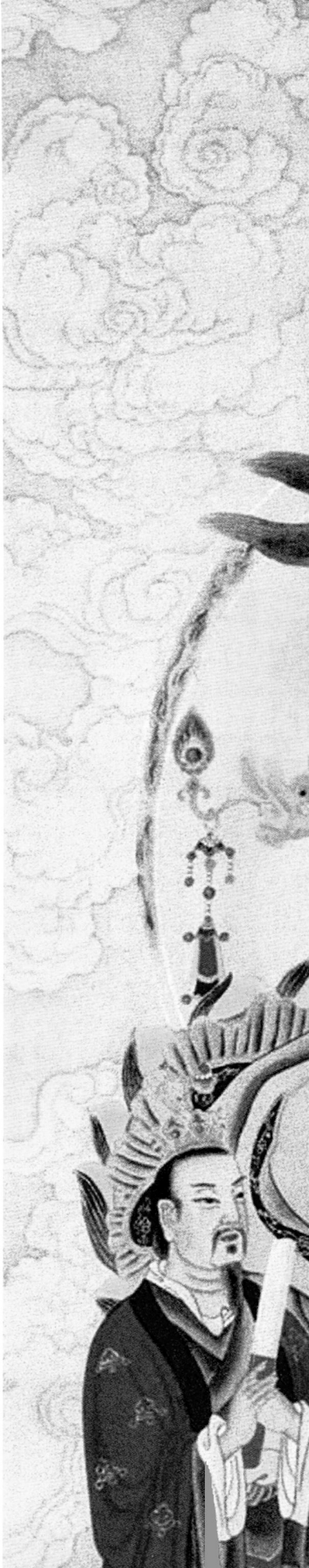

LAO-TZU, another great philosopher from the Zhou period, was the founder of Taoism.

NOTABLE DATES

ca 1046 B.C.E.
Shang Dynasty is toppled by the Zhou Dynasty

ca 1000 B.C.E.
Iron metallurgy spreads in China, producing better tools

ca 771 B.C.E.
China is divided in Eastern and Western Zhou kingdoms

ca 770–476 B.C.E.
States struggle for domination in Spring and Autumn period

ca 600–200s B.C.E.
Chinese texts are written with brush and ink on silk, wood, and jade

ca 551 B.C.E.
Kong Fuzi, or Confucius, is born in Qufu, modern-day Shandong

ca 500 B.C.E.
Construction of the Qi Wall, a 370-mile rammed earth barrier, begins

ca 453 B.C.E.
Beginning of the Warring States period

ca 400s B.C.E.
Farmers develop large-scale irrigation systems

ca 390 B.C.E.
Shang Yang centralizes the Qin government

ca 365 B.C.E.
Chinese astronomer Xi Zezong discovers Jupiter's moons

ca 221 B.C.E.
King of Qin, Ying Zheng is first emperor of a unified China

THE *ANALECTS* is an ancient Chinese book with sayings attributed to Confucius, completed in the third century C.E., that would serve as the foundational text of Confucianism. **BELOW:** A bronze plaque with animal heads was produced during the Western Zhou period in China.

believed to have written his works; traditionally he is dated to the last phase of the Zhou Dynasty, while some scholars associate him with the Tang Dynasty in the fourth century. But his philosophy would exert a powerful influence on other movements, including Confucianism and Buddhism, and gained a broad religious following during the subsequent Han Dynasty.

An even more influential philosopher was the teacher, author, and philosopher Confucius (Kǒng Fūzǐ in Mandarin), who is believed to have lived during the Spring and Autumn period of the late Eastern Zhou Dynasty. Confucius's ideas are less a religious or philosophical doctrine than a social and moral compact for Chinese society. His teachings stress the importance of self-study and education, social justice, loyalty to family, and a deep respect for ancestors and the elderly, organized in a hierarchical system of Chinese society. Children should revere their parents, the wife should defer to her husband, and the peasantry should obey those who are placed above them, including noblemen and mandarins. In a political sense, Confucius endorsed the traditional view of the Mandate of Heaven, buttressing the authority of imperial power at the expense of local barons and dukes. Having witnessed the brutality of internecine wars during the Zhou period, he believed that only a strong central government could prevent the chaos and violence of decades past. But to see Confucianism in strictly political terms would be a mistake. Above all, Confucius emphasized the importance for the individual to cultivate righteousness through learning and self-study and to strive for moral rectitude and compassion toward others. "Respect yourself, and

"FIX YOUR MIND ON TRUTH, HOLD FIRM TO VIRTUE, RELY ON LOVING KINDNESS, AND FIND YOUR RECREATION IN THE ARTS."

CHINESE PHILOSOPHER CONFUCIUS

others will respect you," he wrote. Similarly, he urged those in government to use justice and compassion and to place the good of the people above all else. Much of his thought can be captured in his famous adage, "Do not do unto others what you do not want done to yourself," which eventually became known as the Golden Rule.

The influence of Confucianism on the subsequent development of Chinese society can scarcely be overstated. Scholars tend to distinguish this following in two main currents: the ethical strand, which imbued Chinese society with a moral canon stressing the innate goodness of human beings, and a political or legal strand, which supported the idea of centralizing the state around a strong ruler, framed by a set of laws. In the 16th century, Jesuit missionaries translated some of the Confucian texts and brought them to Europe, where they were avidly studied during the Enlightenment.

Although Confucian philosophy was essentially secular in nature, this did not prevent the spread of so-called Confucian temples, which served more as centers of academic learning than places of worship. These temples were often used as sites where candidates for service in the imperial administration took their exams. Over time, some of these temples became amalgamated with other strands of Chinese thought and religions, including Taoism and Buddhism. ∎

A RICHLY DECORATED covered jar was produced during the Warring States period of the Eastern Zhou Dynasty, 453–221 B.C.E.

CHINESE ARCHITECTURE

Unlike Western architecture, Chinese builders almost never used vaulting to cover large spaces, opting instead for traditional beam-and-post timber-frame structures (at right). Whereas Western architecture emphasizes height and depth, Chinese architecture stresses the axial symmetry of horizontal lines, both individually and in relationship to other buildings in the complex. And while in the Western tradition the principal elevation is the most important feature, Chinese architecture uses curtain walls or door panels to enclose a building, deemphasizing the importance of load-bearing walls in favor of the roofline, which often feature dramatically curving eaves. Color is also a paramount feature of Chinese architecture, particularly in the later imperial periods when deep reds are for the building elevation, and the glazed tiles covering the roof are colored imperial yellow. The horizontal emphasis of the building is accentuated by curving eaves at its principal corners, often adorned with ceramic figurines.

AN UNFINISHED BUST
represents Nefertiti, the
beautiful royal consort
of King Akhenaten
(1353–1336 B.C.E.).

THE NEW KINGDOM OF
EGYPT

During the New Kingdom, Egypt's kings embarked on an aggressive program of territorial expansion, creating buffer states to protect the country from foreign invasions and bolster Egypt's role in international trade. Some believe that the Exodus took place in this period.

I n Egypt, meanwhile, the Hyksos episode continued to haunt the kings of the 18th Dynasty (ca 1539–1292 B.C.E.). These warrior kings, forged by battle, vowed never again to suffer the humiliation of foreign occupation. They raised new, professional armies and built strongholds along the eastern border, the Upper Nile, and the frontiers with Nubia. Egypt's security was further bolstered by the creation of a buffer zone of vassal states, including Canaan, Edom, Moab, and Syria, to be ruled by proxy through local governors. The era of a new Egypt, the Imperial Egypt of the New Kingdom, had begun.

During the reign of King Thutmose III, several tribal kingdoms, notably the Mitanni and the Hittites (located in today's Turkey and Syria), began to challenge Egypt's sphere of control. In response, the king gathered his armies and around 1468 B.C.E. met the rebellious Hittites near the Canaanite battleground of Megiddo in the Jezreel Valley. Riding "in a chariot of fine gold, adorned with his accoutrements of combat," the Pharaoh and his troops executed a pincer movement around the ancient Megiddo fortress that confused and ultimately routed the enemy. "Thou hast

smitten the Sand-dwellers as living captives!" exult the king's inscriptions in Karnak, carved around 1460 B.C.E. "Thou has made captive the heads of the Asiatics of [Canaan]."

All this wealth and glory nearly came to naught when Amenhotep IV assumed power in 1353 B.C.E. Shocking the nation, Amenhotep turned his back on the traditional Egyptian deities and ordered his people to venerate one god: the sun god, Aten. After changing his name to Akhenaten, the pharaoh even moved his court from Thebes to a brand-new capital city in central Egypt named Akhetaten ("the Horizon of Aten"), now identified with el-Amarna. There he ruled with his wife, Nefertiti. Artwork from this era shows the king and his family in a strange new style that emphasizes a pear-shaped body, protruding stomach, heavy eyelids, and elongated skull. The exception is the

A FUNERARY STELA depicts the officer Meri-Amun-Nacht paying tribute to King Ramses II (ca 1279–1213 B.C.E.).

"PLEASE, MY KING, SEND ARCHERS AGAINST THE
MEN WHO ARE COMMITTING THESE CRIMES . . .
THE HABIRU ARE TAKING THE CITIES OF THE KING!"

ABDIHEBA, EGYPTIAN GOVERNOR OF JERUSALEM, TO PHARAOH AKHENATEN

breathtaking polychrome bust of Nefertiti that today is the pride of Berlin.

The king's complete devotion to religious affairs threatened Egypt's control of the vassal states of the east. Once again, Hittite forces began to probe into Egyptian-held territory. The small Egyptian garrisons stationed in Canaan and Syria were powerless to resist them. When Akhenaten died around 1336 B.C.E., he was little mourned, and the court promptly abandoned el-Amarna and returned to Memphis. There, Akhenaten's ultimate successor, the boy king Tutankhaten, was crowned pharaoh. He soon changed his name to the now famous Tutankhamun ("the Living Image of Amun"), and the old priesthood and worship of Amun was reinstated.

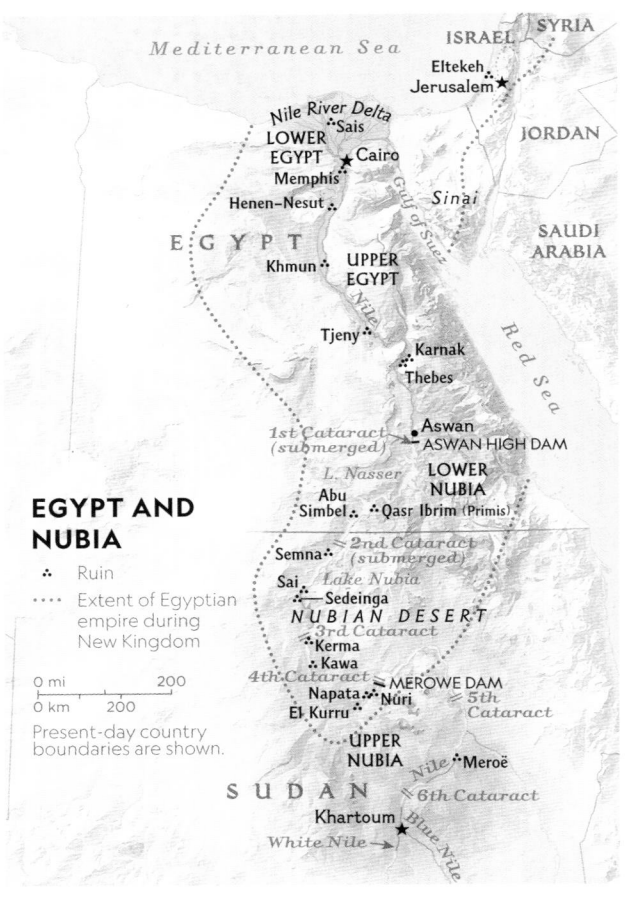
Ramses II

The Warrior Kings

The military-minded 19th Dynasty (1292–1190 B.C.E.) realized that only a massive new military effort could fully restore Egypt's power in the East. King Seti I saw the need for new military garrisons close to the vulnerable eastern border. The ideal place, as the Hyksos kings had discovered centuries earlier, was the eastern Nile Delta. One of these was a city later known as Pi-Ramesses or Per-Ramesses-Aa-nakhtu ("the house of Ramesses, great in victory"), which the Book of Exodus refers to as "Rameses." It was probably built on the remains of an old royal summer palace near one of the Pelusiac branches of the Nile.

Pi-Ramesses has been identified today as the large field bordered by palm trees near the village of Qantir, just north of the provincial capital of Faqus, some 70 miles north of Cairo. Since much of the land here is privately owned by local farmers, archaeologists are required to fill in their excavations with earth once their work is done and return the land to the farmers for cultivation. Therefore, all that is visible is a mound, not far from the place where Manfred Bietak discovered the remains of the Hyksos-era city of Avaris. Perhaps this close proximity enabled Seti's builders to reuse the spolia of the Hyksos capital—

EGYPT AND NUBIA

A RELIEF depicts King Akhenaten during worship of the god Aten, shown as a sun disk bathing the king with its rays.

NOTABLE DATES

ca 1550 B.C.E.

Pharaoh Ahmose steadily ousts the Hyksos from Egypt

ca 1473 B.C.E.

Hatshepsut, Thutmose's wife, becomes pharaoh

ca 1455 B.C.E.

Thutmose III leads the first of 16 campaigns into Syro-Canaan

ca 1400 B.C.E.

Egyptians develop water clocks, later known as clepsydras

ca 1345 B.C.E.

The Amarna Letters, a group of cuneiform tablets, are written

ca 1325 B.C.E.

King Tutankhamun dies; his tomb is discovered intact in 1922

ca 1279 B.C.E.

Reign of Ramses II (1279–1213 B.C.E.) begins

ca 1274 B.C.E.

Ramses II battles Hittites to a draw at Battle of Qadesh

ca 1250 B.C.E.

Swarms of locusts destroy crops in the Nile Valley

ca 1224 B.C.E.

Ramses' son Merneptah ascends the throne in Egypt

ca 1200 B.C.E.

First use of flax to make linen in Egypt

ca 1180 B.C.E.

Invasion of Egypt by the Sea Peoples is repulsed

A BAS-RELIEF from the temple of King Seti I depicts the king with Hathor, the mother goddess of ancient Egypt's pharaohs.

> ## "NOW A NEW KING AROSE OVER EGYPT . . . HE SAID TO HIS PEOPLE, 'LOOK, THE ISRAELITE PEOPLE ARE MORE NUMEROUS AND MORE POWERFUL THAN WE.'"
>
> **EXODUS 1:8-9**

masonry, columns, and decorative remains—to expedite the construction of the new one.

King Seti I died around 1279 B.C.E. and was succeeded by his son Ramses II, still in his teens. Blessed with a long reign—as long as 66 years by some estimates—Ramses II would become the most powerful king of the 19th Dynasty. Not only did he continue to build the supply city begun by his father—now modestly named after himself, as Pi-Ramesses—but he started the construction of a second city in the eastern delta. Dedicated to the patron god of his family and dynasty, it was called Per Atum, "house of Atum," or "Pithom" as the Bible calls it. Ramses' close association with his towering figure no doubt enhanced his own personality cult, as witnessed by scores of statues that have been recovered from this period.

According to the Book of Exodus, Israelite slaves were conscripted to work on the construction of Pi-Ramesses and Per Atum under ever more oppressive conditions. "The Egyptians became ruthless in imposing tasks on the Israelites," according to Exodus (1:13), "and made their lives bitter with hard service in mortar and brick and in every kind of field labor." This sets the stage for the greatest saga in the story of ancient Israel: the release from Egypt and the subsequent settlement in Canaan, the land of milk and honey. No record of the Exodus in Egyptian tablets has been found, but that is not unusual; the new dynasty did not make a habit of recording its defeats. There are, however, ample records of Semitic immigrant workers in Egypt, who may have drifted back to Syria-Canaan in the 13th century B.C.E. for a

AN EARLY SUEZ CANAL

A first Suez passage may have originated during the reign of Pharaoh Senwosret III of the 12th Dynasty, when an irrigation canal, built around 1850 B.C.E., produced a navigable link during the flood season. During the Late Period, Pharaoh Necho II of the 26th Dynasty then decided to build a proper canal in earnest. This navigable link between the Mediterranean and the Red Sea was accomplished by digging a canal from the Pelusiac branch of the Nile through Wadi Tumilat (near the frontier city of Pelusium) to the Bitter Lake (at right) and from there to the Red Sea. A city named Per-Temu-Tjeku was built to guard the waterway and serve as a storage facility. Despite his great achievements, we have only one sculpture of Necho in the round, a bronze statuette that shows the king kneeling in prayer or during a sacrifice.

variety of reasons—including, perhaps, Ramses' harsh policies of conscripting labor.

The Invasion of the Sea Peoples

By the 12th century B.C.E., the proud walls of Mycenae lay in ruins. The maritime trade that propelled the Greek city-states to prosperity was all but gone. A shadow of death was stealing across the Mediterranean basin, destroying everything in its path. Eventually this wave reached Anatolia, obliterating the Hittite Empire (which not even Ramses II had been able to bring to heel) before turning its sights on Syria, Canaan, and Egypt. One of the Ugaritic tablets records a frantic plea from Ammurapi, the king of Ugarit, to the king of Cyprus. "Enemy boats have arrived," the king exclaims, "the enemy has set fire to the cities and wrought havoc."

The principal agents of this upheaval were groups of marauding tribes that scholars group together under the name Sea Peoples. Ugaritic texts refer to them as the Shiqalaya, "they who live on boats." Assyrian records describe them as Ahhlamu, or "Wanderers." All these appellations suggest that the Sea Peoples were not an organized army but a motley band of predatory raiders whose origins have never been firmly ascertained. For example, contemporary records speak of tribes such as the Teresh or Tyrsenoi, who may have originated in Anatolia; the Sherden, sometimes identified with Sardinia; and the Shekelesh, who may have been of Sicilian origin. The group also included a tribe called the Peleset, more commonly known as the Philistines, possibly with roots in Crete.

The motive for their destructive swath across the ancient Near East is

A FOUNDATION STONE from ca 1275 B.C.E. documents the victory of King Adad-Nirari I of Assyria over the Mitanni.

AN AERIAL VIEW of Luxor at sunrise reveals the sprawling complex of the temple of Karnak.

A HALLWAY of the mortuary temple of Ramses III (ca 1187–1156 B.C.E.) at Medinet Habu reveals a profusion of Egyptian hieroglyphics.

"AS FOR THOSE WHO REACHED MY FRONTIER, THEIR SEED IS NOT, THEIR HEART AND THEIR SOUL ARE FINISHED FOREVER AND EVER."

RAMSES III ON THE SEA PEOPLES

not clear. There are indications, however, that the vast famine that swept through South Asia also affected the northern part of Asia Minor in the 13th century B.C.E. Harvests failed, and trade across the Aegean Sea was disrupted. Perhaps this famine jolted the great mass of poor and marginalized folk into a desperate search for food that, once bolstered by success, soon degenerated into a naked quest for loot and plunder. What is clear, however, is that the vast migration of Sea Peoples and other migrant communities caused a major realignment of the Near East. In the words of Hittitologist Gary Beckman, "No land could stand before their arms." The great city of Ugarit was utterly destroyed.

By 1175 B.C.E., the Sea Peoples had conquered most of the coastal regions of modern Syria and Lebanon. They next turned their attention to the last great power in the region: the land of Egypt, with its countless temples and treasures. As it happened, Egypt at the time was ruled by Ramses III, an able king and highly accomplished military commander. A series of reliefs on Ramses' funerary temple in Medinet Habu, west of Thebes, gives a detailed account of what happened next. "They came with fire prepared before them, forward to Egypt," the hieroglyphics reveal. Ramses III, however, was ready: "The chiefs, the captains of infantry, the nobles, I caused to equip the harbor-mouths, like a strong wall, with warships, galleys, and barges." As soon as the Sea Peoples appeared on the horizon, they divided their forces into a classic

THE SEARCH FOR KING TUT

After the excavations of the late 1800s, many archaeologists thought that the Valley of the Kings in Egypt had yielded all its secrets. However, British archaeologist Howard Carter (at right) was eager to find the tomb of an obscure king from the 18th Dynasty who was born in 1344 B.C.E. as the son of Pharaoh Akhenaten and died in ca 1325 B.C.E. Having cleared debris from a rubble-filled stairway in the valley, Carter discovered the top of a doorway, sealed with plaster. On it were the undisturbed seals of the royal necropolis, a sight that made Carter's heart race with excitement. As his team cleared the stairway, the entire door was exposed, and the seals of Tutankhamun were revealed. Carter's hunch was right: He had found the tomb of the unfortunate boy king.

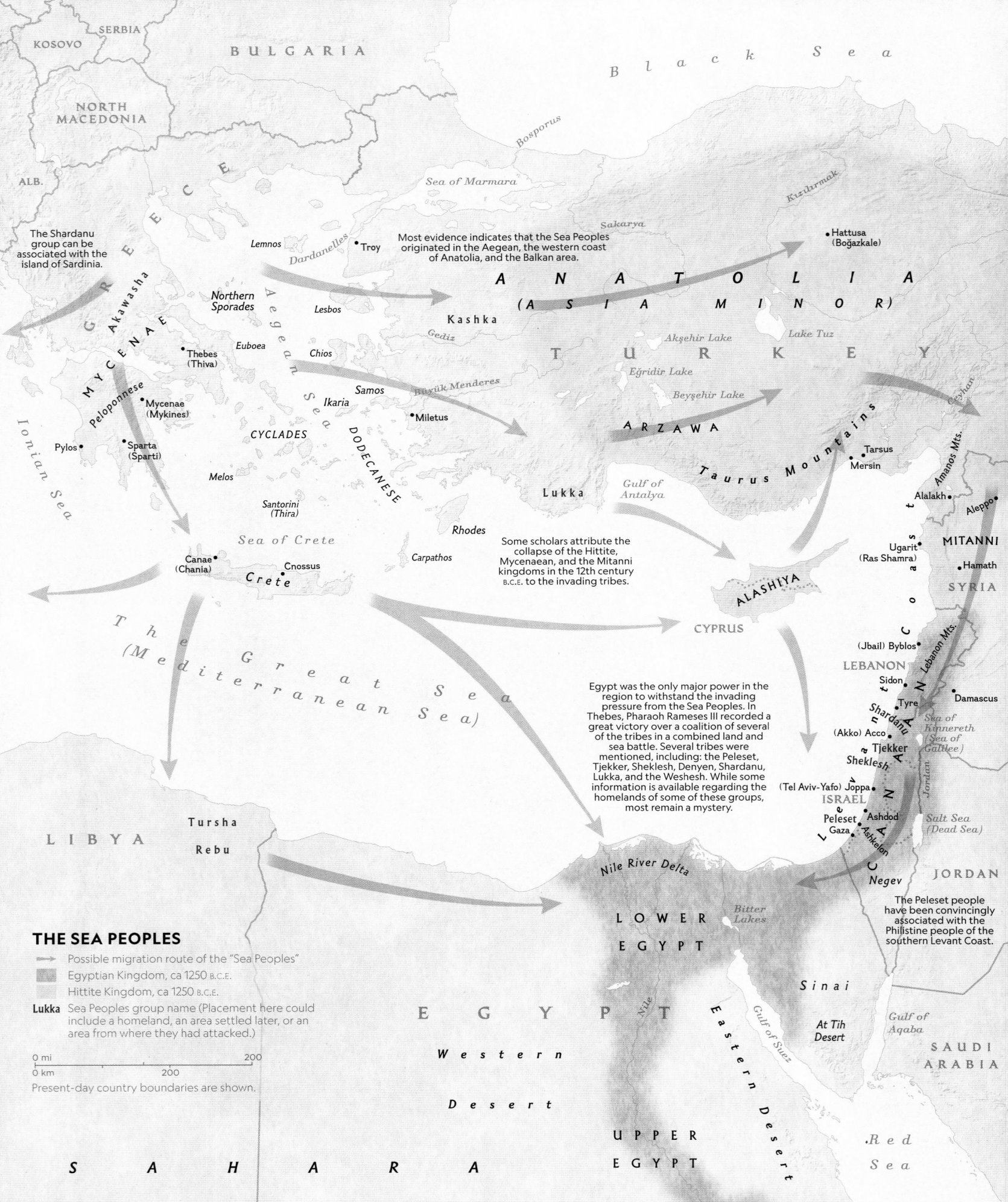

SERBIA

KOSOVO

BULGARIA

Black Sea

NORTH
MACEDONIA

Sea of Marmara

Bosporus

Kızılırmak

ALB.

Sakarya

The Shardanu
group can be
associated with the
island of Sardinia.

Most evidence indicates that the Sea Peoples
originated in the Aegean, the western coast
of Anatolia, and the Balkan area.

• Hattusa
(Boğazkale)

Lemnos

Dardanelles
• Troy

A N A T O L I A
(A S I A   M I N O R)

G
R
E
E
C
E

Akawasha

Northern
Sporades

Lesbos

Kashka

Akşehir Lake

Lake Tuz

T U R K E Y

MYCENAE

Chios

Euboea
• Thebes
(Thiva)

Eğridir Lake

Gediz

A
e
g
e
a
n
S
e
a

Beyşehir Lake

Samos

ARZAWA

Amanos Mts.

Peloponnese

• Mycenae
(Mykines)

Ikaria

• Miletus

CYCLADES

D
O
D
E
C
A
N
E
S
E

Büyük Menderes

Lukka

*Gulf of
Antalya*

Tarsus •

T
a
u
r
u
s

M
o
u
n
t
a
i
n
s

• Mersin

Ceyhan

Alalakh •

• Aleppo

MITANNI

Pylos •

• Sparta
(Sparti)

Melos

Santorini
(Thira)

Rhodes

Some scholars attribute the
collapse of the Hittite,
Mycenaean, and the Mitanni
kingdoms in the 12th century
B.C.E. to the invading tribes.

• Ugarit
(Ras Shamra)

• Hamath

SYRIA

*Ionian
Sea*

Canae
(Chania) •

Cnossus
•

Sea of Crete

Carpathos

ALASHIYA

*C
o
a
s
t*

Crete

CYPRUS

(Jbail) Byblos •

*L
e
b
a
n
o
n
M
t
s
.*

T
h
e

G
r
e
a
t

S
e
a

LEBANON

Sidon •

• Damascus

(
M
e
d
i
t
e
r
r
a
n
e
a
n

S
e
a
)

Egypt was the only major power in the
region to withstand the invading
pressure from the Sea Peoples. In
Thebes, Pharaoh Rameses III recorded a
great victory over a coalition of several
of the tribes in a combined land and
sea battle. Several tribes were
mentioned, including: the Peleset,
Tjekker, Sheklesh, Denyen, Shardanu,
Lukka, and the Weshesh. While some
information is available regarding the
homelands of some of these groups,
most remain a mystery.

P
H
O
E
N
I
C
I
A

Shardanu

• Tyre

*Sea of
Kinnereth
(Sea of
Galilee)*

(Akko) Acco •

Tjekker

Sheklesh

Jordan

LIBYA

Tursha

Rebu

(Tel Aviv-Yafo) Joppa •

ISRAEL

C
A
N
A
A
N

Peleset
Gaza •

• Ashdod
Ashkelon •

*Salt Sea
(Dead Sea)*

Negev

JORDAN

Nile River Delta

The Peleset people
have been convincingly
associated with the
Philistine people of the
southern Levant Coast.

L O W E R

E G Y P T

*Bitter
Lakes*

Sinai

THE SEA PEOPLES

→ Possible migration route of the "Sea Peoples"

Egyptian Kingdom, ca 1250 B.C.E.

Hittite Kingdom, ca 1250 B.C.E.

Lukka Sea Peoples group name (Placement here could
include a homeland, an area settled later, or an
area from where they had attacked.)

0 mi   200

0 km   200

Present-day country boundaries are shown.

E G Y P T

W e s t e r n

Nile

*At Tih
Desert*

*Gulf of
Aqaba*

Gulf of Suez

*E
a
s
t
e
r
n

D
e
s
e
r
t*

SAUDI
ARABIA

D e s e r t

U P P E R

E G Y P T

*Red
Sea*

S A H A R A

pincer movement: the infantry attacked on land, while the naval force staged an amphibious assault along the coast. The strategy had confounded cities all along the coasts of Turkey, Syria, and Canaan, but the invaders would face a far more capable opponent in Ramses.

As the vivid illustrations at Medinet Habu testify, Ramses rallied his troops to meet the Peleset infantry on Egypt's eastern border. The Philistine land army was defeated, whereupon the battle shifted to the Nile Delta. This was a problem, for Egypt had never fought a naval battle in home waters. The Egyptians were land warriors, not a seafaring people. Ramses, however, had manned his river galleys "from bow to stern with valiant warriors bearing their arms." As soon as the Philistine ships came within range, clouds of Egyptian arrows rained down on them, and the Philistines withdrew.

Repulsed from Egyptian shores, the Philistines pointed their ships back east, probing for a safe place to land. They chose the southern coast of Canaan. Here were cities such as Ashkelon, Ekron, Ashdod, Gath, and Gaza, which were all conquered by force. For example, the excavations at Tel Miqne, site of ancient Ekron, showed that after its founding in the Early Bronze Age, the town was destroyed during the Sea Peoples' invasions of the late 13th century B.C.E.

By 1150 B.C.E., all of these coastal cities were organized in a Philistine confederacy known as Philistia. One stela by eighth-century B.C.E. Assyrian king Adad-nirari reads: "I ordered the numerous army of Assyria to march against Palestine [Pa-la-áš-tu]," which shows that by that time, the term "Philistia" was already being mutated to "Palestine."

Modern excavations have shown that these early Philistine settlements shared a strong cultural tradition with Cyprus and Aegean regions under influence from Mycenae, as witnessed by the red and black geometric style of their pottery (known as Mycenaean IIIC). But the Philistines also introduced innovations of their own, such as the use of unperforated loom weights in their

looms; a fondness for the Greek custom of mixing water with wine; the worship of a number of foreign female deities; and a diet heavily dependent on pork, supplied by large herds of swine.

And so, by the middle of the 12th century B.C.E., a major group of people began to compete for the scarce water and land resources of Canaan. It was only a matter of time before these headstrong people would come into conflict with the equally determined Israelite settlers, and it is this conflict that absorbs the biblical narrative until the advent of the Israelite monarchy. ■

THIS VIEW of the interior courtyard of the mortuary temple of Ramses III at Medinet Habu shows the polychrome ornamentation of Egyptian temples.

A 13TH-CENTURY ISRAELITE MASK was discovered in the complex of Tel Hazor in northern Galilee.

THE BIRTH OF ANCIENT
ISRAEL

During the Iron Age of the Near East, groups of Israelites settled in the highlands of Canaan and eventually took control of the country, establishing a monarchical tradition in the north and the south. The Hebrew Bible refers to this period as the "kingdoms of Israel."

The epic saga of Israel's monarchy, from the entry into the Promised Land to the capture of Jerusalem by neo-Babylonian King Nebuchadnezzar in 586 B.C.E., is the subject of the collection in Hebrew Scripture known as the Nevi'im, or "Books of the Prophets." The first two books, known as Joshua and Judges, tell the story of the Israelite conquest and settlement in Canaan. Modern research has revealed that the Israelite "invasion" was probably less violent and abrupt than the Book of Joshua suggests. Though there are clear signs of military conquest during the early Iron Age in places such as Hazor, elsewhere archaeologists have failed to identify evidence of the type of destruction described in Joshua. Indeed, much of the debris found at large settlements can be dated to a later phase, when Canaan was invaded by the Philistines. As a result, most scholars accept that the "conquest" of Canaan may have been a process of gradual settlement over many generations.

According to the Bible, the Israelites entered Canaan and defeated most of the forces arrayed against them, taking the townships of Azekah, Makkedah, Libnah, Lachish, Eglon, Hebron, Debir, and even Hazor—capital of King Jabin. Next, Joshua devoted himself to dividing the newly conquered lands among the 12 tribes, including "the hill country and all the Negeb . . . as far as Baal-gad in the valley of Lebanon below Mount Hermon" (Joshua 11:16-17). The division was made by drawing lots.

Though inevitably this is the subject of debate, a majority of scholars agree that the highlands of Canaan show a substantial population increase in Iron Age I, between 1200 and 1000 B.C.E.—the time span of the Book of Judges. According to archaeologist Lawrence Stager, modern excavations have identified a population increase from 27 to 211 sites, an almost eightfold increase. What's more, many of these settlements were only 2 acres in size, compared with the 12-acre spread of older, established Canaanite communities. All this points to

THIS IVORY PLAQUE in the Phoenician style, depicting a cherub with wings, was found in the royal enclave of Samaria and is dated to the reign of King Ahab in the ninth century B.C.E.

"SO JOSHUA DEFEATED THE WHOLE LAND,
THE HILL COUNTRY AND THE NEGEB AND THE
LOWLAND AND THE SLOPES, AND ALL THEIR KINGS;
HE LEFT NO ONE REMAINING, BUT UTTERLY DESTROYED
ALL THAT BREATHED."

JOSHUA 10:40

the growth of new settlers with a primary focus on farming rather than the steady expansion of existing communities. This would corroborate the biblical account of tribes such as Ephraim and Manasseh, who bitterly complained of their being restricted to the highlands (with its poor terra rossa topsoil), while the better armed Canaanites controlled the far more fertile lowland valleys (Joshua 17:16).

In response, the highland tribes turned to terracing—the artificial creation of flat, arable plots on the hillside, supported by retaining walls of boulders and dry-laid stones. Terraced soil was not suitable for cereals like wheat, but perfectly fine for the production of olive oil and grapes.

These terraces may be the *meromei sadeh,* the "heights of the field" of the Naphtali extolled in the "Song of Deborah" (Judges 5:18); similar terracing can still be seen today in parts of the West Bank. At the same time, the diversity of animal bones found at these sites indicates that the new settlements also raised sheep, goats, and cattle.

What we may deduce from these discoveries is that a new and distinct culture was emerging in the highlands during Iron Age I. The sense of stability proved illusory, however. Soon, another threat appeared on the horizon, this time as a result of invasions from the east.

The Kingdoms of David and Solomon

What made the Philistines so successful in battle was their military discipline and unified command structure. Israel's forces, by contrast, were a quarrelsome lot in which each tribe prized its independence. In due course, the tribes realized that in order to defeat the Philistines, they had to act in unison. They chose Saul from the tribe of Benjamin to be their king and supreme commander. Saul was initially successful in driving the Philistines from the highlands. But despite Hebrew triumphs at the Battle of Bozez and Michmash, the conflict evolved into a protracted war of attrition. The tribes began looking for a new leader who could lead them to victory. They found him in a shepherd blessed with musical skills named David, who often entertained Saul with his singing and harp playing.

"DEBORAH PRAISES JAEL" is an engraving by French 19th-century artist Gustave Doré.

THE PALACE COMPLEX of Hazor, in northern Galilee, is believed to have been destroyed in the 13th century B.C.E. at the time of the Israelite settlement in Canaan.

NOTABLE DATES

ca 1214 B.C.E.
Victory slab of Merneptah is the first monument to refer to "Israel"

ca 1150 B.C.E.
Philistines consolidate their territory in Canaan

ca 1000 B.C.E.
Hebrew alphabet emerges

ca 1000 B.C.E.
Putative date of the unified kingdom of Israel

ca 931 B.C.E.
Putative date of Solomon's kingdom splitting into two: Israel and Judah

ca 880 B.C.E.
King Omri of Israel builds the new capital of Samaria

ca 853 B.C.E.
Assyrian King Shalmaneser III invades Israel

ca 743 B.C.E.
Ministry of the prophets Amos and Hosea begins

ca 721 B.C.E.
Rump state of Samaria falls to King Sargon II

ca 640 B.C.E.
King Josiah's reign leads to renaissance of Judah

ca 622 B.C.E.
High priest Hilkiah discovers Book of the Law

ca 586 B.C.E.
Neo-Babylonian King Nebuchadnezzar destroys Jerusalem

THE 590-YARD TUNNEL of Hezekiah ran from the Gihon Spring to the Pool of Siloam, thus providing Jerusalem with access to water in times of siege.

One day, the Philistines fielded a fearsome new weapon: a giant named Goliath, carrying a huge bronze spear. The Israelites were frozen in fear—except young David. Armed with only a sling, he picked a stone from a riverbed and slung it at Goliath's head. David's aim was true: The stone struck the giant and killed him, prompting the Philistines to flee. Saul was compelled to place young David at the head of his army but soon began to fear him as a rival. The king even began to plot to kill him, leaving David with little choice but to flee. But after Saul and his sons were killed at Mount Gilboa, David was proclaimed the new king of the Israelite tribes.

Thus began the Davidic era, which in the centuries to come would gain mythic proportions and serve as a beacon of messianic hope in troubled times. Before confronting the Philistines, David first wanted to create a capital as the center of a unified kingdom of Israel. His choice fell on the Jebusite city of Jerusalem. It was located on the boundary between the southern and northern tribes and was easily defended because it sat on a hill surrounded by valleys. What's more, it enjoyed its own source of freshwater, the spring of Gihon. Alarmed, the Philistines marched on Jerusalem to crush the new king before he became too powerful. But David was able to defeat the Philistines, not once but twice, pushing them back to their original homesteads along the coast. Eventually, all of the regions in Canaan, including the Jezreel Valley, the Shephelah, and the Galilee, came under David's control.

A TEL DAN INSCRIPTION, discovered in 1993 and dated around 850 B.C.E., includes the phrase *bytdwd*, which many scholars believe refers to the "House of David."

According to the Books of Samuel and the Books of Kings, David then expanded his territory until Israel became the dominant state in the Levant, absorbing the nations of Ammon, Moab, and Edom that had vexed the Israelites in years past. Modern research has questioned this claim. Some scholars believe that legends were woven around David to exalt him as an ideal king, as successful in peace as in war. In their view, David's

JERUSALEM

The name Jerusalem first appears in Egyptian records of the second millennium B.C.E., as well as in the 14th-century Amarna Letters, where the city is referred to as "Uru-Salim" ("foundation of Salim" or "Shalem," a figure who is sometimes identified as a Canaanite god of twilight). The Hebrew name, Yerushalayim ("Jerusalem"), has been alternatively translated as "Heritage of Salem" (*yerusha shalom*) or "Abode of Peace" (*shalom* instead of *shalem*). Excavations suggest that the area south of Temple Mount (Golden Gate, at right) was inhabited as early as the third millennium B.C.E., possibly by Canaanites of unknown origin. Egyptian records show that in the Late Bronze Age, Jerusalem's rulers paid tribute to the Egyptian crown.

> ## "SO ALL THE ELDERS OF ISRAEL CAME TO THE KING AT HEBRON . . . AND THEY ANOINTED DAVID KING OVER ISRAEL."
>
> 2 SAMUEL 5:3

greatest achievement is not the extent of his putative realm but the fusion of the quarrelsome tribes into one nation.

That unification process was continued by his son and heir, King Solomon, who created a modern administrative apparatus, dividing his realm into 12 districts that deliberately cut across tribal boundaries so as to further centralize power in Jerusalem. To pacify tribal sensibilities, Solomon continued his father's policy of marrying wives from many tribes, as well as from those nations with whom he struck an alliance. One of these foreign wives was an Egyptian princess, daughter of Pharaoh (1 Kings 11:1), who was probably Siamun of the 21st

Astarte amulet

Dynasty (ca 978–960 B.C.E.). In centuries past, it was Pharaoh who married daughters from foreign potentates. The fact that the situation was now reversed vividly illustrates the decline of Egyptian power during this time.

The Northern Kingdom

Solomon is also credited with the design of the First Temple in Jerusalem. At the time, it was probably the most impressive structure ever built in Canaan. Measuring some 120 feet in length and 55 feet in width, its exterior was adorned with "carved engravings of cherubim, palm trees, and open flowers" (1 Kings 6:29). The temple was fronted by a spacious courtyard that contained a

WORLD TRADE IN THE MIDDLE BRONZE AGE

Tablets from Sumer (at left) and Old Babylon depict a flourishing trade throughout the known world. Egypt traded with the Levant, the eastern part of the Mediterranean, via a route later known as the Way of the Philistines. The road hugged the Mediterranean Sea all the way to Byblos and Ugarit, where it turned inland toward either Aleppo and Harran, or Mari. From here, a southern route, running just below the Euphrates, brought goods to the Sumerian capital cities of Nippur, Uruk, and Ur. Ur itself, which at the time was closer to the Persian Gulf, was the way station to trade with the nascent cultures of the Indus Valley. The northern route ran north of the Tigris and connected Harran with Ashur and Hamadan, where it branched off in the direction of Bactria and other markets.

THIS LAVISH ILLUSTRATION of "The Visit of the Queen of Sheba to King Solomon" was painted by British artist Sir Edward John Poynter in the early 1900s.

A MODERN ILLUSTRATION shows the First Temple in Jerusalem with the altar for priestly sacrifice at right.

sacrificial altar and a bronze vessel, known as the Sea of Bronze. This vessel rested on 12 bronze oxen, each group of three facing the four points of the compass.

Solomon's unified kingdom did not last. According to biblical texts, after his death, his successor, a weak man named Rehoboam, summoned all the tribal leaders to Shechem to renew the treaty of unification. When the elders insisted on a reduction in taxes and forced labor, Rehoboam refused, and the tribes broke away with the cry, "To your tents, O Israel!" (1 Kings 12:14-16). They decided to form their own kingdom, the Northern Kingdom, which they defiantly called Israel so as to rob the south of its legitimacy. Solomon's former minister for forced labor, Jeroboam, was crowned king of this new nation. As a result, King Rehoboam now saw his kingdom reduced to the small footprint of Judah and Benjamin, which henceforth would be known as "the kingdom of Judah."

Some historians have questioned the biblical claim that Judah came about as a result of a split in the Unified Monarchy after the death of King Solomon. That doesn't rule out the sequence of events as the Bible depicts them. What it does say is that from a strictly historical perspective, Judah's statehood may have emerged more slowly, becoming a true independent polity only by the late ninth century B.C.E.

What is generally accepted is that Pharaoh Shoshenq, founder of the 22nd Dynasty (945–715 B.C.E.) used the political instability of this time to invade Judah and threaten to take Jerusalem. Deprived of any meaningful force to combat Pharaoh's

THE NINTH-CENTURY B.C.E. Moabite Stela, discovered in Dhiban, Jordan, in 1868, is one of the first historical attestations of Israel's kings.

KING JEHU OF ISRAEL prostrates before King Shalmaneser III of Assyria in a detail from the Black Obelisk of Shalmaneser III.

"twelve hundred chariots and sixty thousand cavalry," Rehoboam sued for terms, which allowed Shoshenq to make off with "the treasures of the house of the Lord" (2 Chronicles 12:3; 1 Kings 14:25). For Rehoboam, there was only one small comfort: Not content with raiding Jerusalem, Shoshenq continued north and invaded the kingdom of his erstwhile guest Jeroboam, plundering all the way to the North's mightiest fortress, that of Ma-ke-thu, or Megiddo.

Despite this upheaval, the Northern Kingdom would enjoy a period of great cultural and economic growth that culminated in the reign of King Omri. Aware of the ever present threat on his borders, Omri ended the long-simmering tensions with Judah and concluded a peace treaty with King Ittobaal of Phoenicia. This deal was sealed by marrying Omri's son Ahab to the Phoenician princess Jezebel. Omri then defeated his hostile neighbor to the east, Aram-Damascus, bringing peace to his kingdom. His military prowess is acknowledged by the famous Moabite Stela, which admitted that "Omri

Gilded bronze bull

humbled Moab for many years." So prominent was Omri's reign that even after the king's death, Assyrian texts referred to Israel as *bit humri,* "the house of Omri."

Omri also made his mark by building a new palace complex in Samaria to rival the Davidic palace in Jerusalem. This new acropolis rose on a summit in the hills of Ephraim, close to Shechem, known as Samaria. During excavations by Harvard's Clarence Fisher in the early 20th century, excavators uncovered a monumental palace that was much enlarged in later years. Amid the ruins, fragments of the original ivory ornamentation, crafted by Phoenician artisans, were found in situ. In a 2007 article, archaeologist Norma Franklin theorized that caverns underneath this structure may have been the tombs of Omri and his descendants, but others have challenged this idea.

In religious matters, however, the Northern Kingdom faced a problem: It was cut off from the Temple in Jerusalem, the acknowledged center of ancient Judaism, and the locus of its sacrificial cult. The first Book of Kings relates how worship of the Jewish God

"JEZEBEL AND AHAB
Met by Elijah" is an 1863
canvas by British painter
Sir Frederic Leighton.

THE REMAINS of the palace of King Omri at the acropolis of ancient Samaria, capital of the Northern Kingdom

"SO [JEROBOAM] TOOK COUNSEL, AND MADE
TWO CALVES OF GOLD. HE SAID TO THE PEOPLE,
'YOU HAVE GONE UP TO JERUSALEM LONG ENOUGH.
HERE ARE YOUR GODS, O ISRAEL.'"

1 KINGS 12:28

was increasingly challenged by Syro-Phoenician practices, including the worship of Baal Melkart and Asherah (or Astarte), and historians agree that this is probably what happened. Jeroboam reactivated the ancient shrines of Dan and Bethel for Yahweh worship and even developed religious festivals to compete with the ones in

*Phoenician ivory
of a woman*

Jerusalem. But the king also installed gold calves, the traditional idol of the Canaanite god El. When the Dan sanctuary was discovered in 1992, archaeologists found a stone platform that may be the *bamah,* or "high place," where the gold calf could have been placed.

The Southern Kingdom

Though much smaller than the Northern Kingdom and bereft of the ample resources of Israel's valleys, the Southern Kingdom of Judah was nevertheless able to survive. One reason may be that Judah's kings were more deft in international diplomacy during a time of growing conflict among foreign states, particularly Assyria. Another factor could be that Judah was simply too small and insignificant to play a major role in international affairs. And while Judah's agricultural economy was far more modest than that of the North and largely limited to the Shephelah Valley, it did find a way to exploit a native form of dry farming on the southern highlands, using iron tools to optimize the plowing and planting of topsoil. Part of this strategy involved the careful husbandry of rainfall. The Book of Chronicles, a parallel history to the Books of Kings, claims that in the eighth

century, King Uzzia "hewed out many cisterns . . . both in the Shephelah and in the plain, and he had farmers and vine-dressers in the hills and in the fertile lands, for he loved the soil" (2 Chronicles 26:10).

The eighth and seventh centuries also saw the rise of many prominent prophets in Judah, including Amos, Micah, and Jeremiah, but remarkably, their ministry was not primarily targeted against any pagan idolatry. By contrast, these prophets directed their scorn on the growing gap between rich and poor. Amos, a shepherd from Tekoa near Bethlehem, was alarmed by the wealthy landowners' land speculation at the expense of small subsistence farmers. "Because you trample on the poor and take from them levies of grain," the prophet inveighed, "you have built houses of hewn stone, but you shall not live in them"—a prophesy that may have inspired Jesus' parable about the rich man storing up his grain in barns (Amos 5:11; Luke 12:18-20).

The first mention of the name Judah outside the Bible appears on the Nimrud Tablet, discovered by British excavator George Smith during the excavations of Nimrud in 1873. Written around 733 B.C.E. during the reign of the great Assyrian warlord Tiglath-Pileser III, it describes the foreign tribute flowing into the imperial coffers as a result of the king's conquests. One of these vassal kings is "Jehoahaz of the land Judah (Yaudaya)," also known (without the theophoric Jeho or Yahweh) as King Ahaz. The tablet reveals that a new threat had appeared on the horizon: the military might of the Assyrian Empire. ■

THIS PORTRAIT from the sixth century B.C.E. depicts King Nebuchadnezzar II of Assyria, who was responsible for the destruction of the First Temple in Jerusalem.

THE RISE OF THE ASSYRIAN
EMPIRE

From the ninth through the sixth centuries, the military might of the Assyrian Empire disrupted the power balance of the Middle East, conquering, colonizing, and even depopulating large swaths of Aram-Damascus (Syria), Phrygia, Phoenicia, Israel, and ultimately Judah.

Around 1285 B.C.E., a new kingdom, called Assyria, had begun to coalesce around the city of Ashur, located on the Tigris River in Upper Mesopotamia. During the Middle Assyrian period (1365–1056 B.C.E.), the Assyrian kings exploited the waning of Egyptian and Hittite influence by steadily expanding their territory at the expense of the Old Babylonian Empire. First, they conquered the Elamites and pushed into today's Arabia before turning toward the nexus of international trade, the coastal cities on the Mediterranean, including Tyre, Sidon, Berytus (today's Beirut), and Arvad. King Ashur-bel-kala then launched a daring invasion of Babylonia proper and succeeded in capturing the ancient city of Babylon.

This was the situation when, as we saw, a wave of mass migrations swept over the Middle East, which did not fail to affect the Assyrian Empire. After Ashur-bel-kala's death, the realm went into decline and was only narrowly able to keep control of the vital trade routes along the Tigris River. What saved the Assyrian nation, however, was its tremendous military discipline and advanced

technology. This allowed King Adad-nirari II to launch a vast effort to reconquer the lands lost during the previous century. The king retook the Hittite and Hurrian homelands and went on to reconquer much of Babylonia. With Assyrian control thus restored, one more tantalizing opportunity beckoned: the strategic trade highways running south to Syria, Israel, and Egypt. It was left to King Ashurnasirpal II to exploit this opportunity. Finding little opposition for his massive forces, the king plowed through Aram-Damascus, Phrygia, Phoenicia, and the Northern Kingdom of Israel, levying a heavy tribute on his conquered vassals. As a result, vast wealth poured into the Assyrian coffers. Ashurnasirpal put it to good use by restoring ancient Babylonian temples and ziggurats and building a vast new palace complex in the city of Kalhu or Nimrud (known as Calah in the Bible), which he made his capital. In 1845, British explorer Austen Henry Layard uncovered Ashurnasirpal's palace. When the sand and dirt had been cleared away, Layard was stunned to see vast interior walls covered from top to bottom with

A DELICATE polychrome glazed jar from the eighth century B.C.E. was excavated in Ashur in northern Iraq.

"AS FOR OMRI, KING OF ISRAEL,
HE HUMBLED MOAB MANY [YEARS],
FOR CHEMOSH WAS ANGRY AT HIS LAND."

THE MOABITE STELA

reliefs and paintings depicting the king's victories. This form of decoration set a trend that subsequent Assyrian kings would emulate. Soon Nimrud became the nucleus of an Assyrian culture that was renowned for science, architecture, and the arts. In 1223 B.C.E., for example, Assyrian astronomers were the first to record a solar eclipse.

The death of the king around 858 B.C.E. and the succession by Shalmaneser III led to a dozen revolts among Assyria's restless subjects. Among the rebels was King Ahab of the Northern Kingdom of Israel, who had allied the kingdom with Syria and Egypt in a desperate attempt to shake off the Assyrian yoke. These coalition forces met Shalmaneser's army in the Battle of Qarqar around 853 B.C.E. According to Shalmaneser's impressive stela, discovered in 1861 and now in the British Museum, the coalition fielded more than 4,000 chariots, half of them supplied by Ahabbu or Ahab. Obviously the figures are exaggerated, but there is little doubt that the battle was one of the largest armored clashes to date. Nor was the outcome ever in any doubt. Shalmaneser's Black Obelisk, excavated in 1846, shows Ahab's successor, King Jehu, kneeling before the Assyrian king and his patron, the winged god Ashur. The inscription reads "tribute of Jehu son of Omri" (*ia-ú-a mar hu-um-ri-i*). Elsewhere, Assyrian records refer to the Northern Kingdom as *bit humri*—the "house" or "dominion" of Omri.

The Assyrian Deportations

In the eighth century B.C.E., Assyria's policy toward its subject peoples changed. Whereas before, the kings had been satisfied with collecting tribute from vassal states, the rapid population growth in the Assyrian plateau demanded an outright colonization of its outlaying empire. This task fell on King Tiglath-Pileser III, who ascended the throne in 745 B.C.E. and promptly mobilized his troops. It is this threat that had compelled King Pekah of Israel to ally himself with Aram-Damascus in an anti-Assyrian coalition, which in turn led King Ahaz of Judah to choose the side of Assyria instead. But Tiglath-Pileser rapidly conquered the Northern Kingdom, and this time he engaged in the wholesale deportation of the native population so as to make room for Assyrian settlers. "King Tiglath-Pileser of Assyria came," says the second Book of Kings, "and he carried the people captive to Assyria" (2 Kings 15:29). A vivid image of these deportations was captured on a stone relief from Nimrud that shows the king in his chariot, calmly observing his soldiers as they force-march their captives to an uncertain fate in Assyria.

Only the rump state of Samaria remained of what was once the proud kingdom of Israel. This region too would fall victim to deportation after King Sargon II captured the Samarian citadel in the final decade of the

A FREESTANDING STATUE of King Ashurnasirpal II was found in the palace of Nimrud, which became the king's capital.

ASHUR, located on the Tigris River in Upper Mesopotamia, was the first capital of the Assyrian Empire.

NOTABLE DATES

ca 911 B.C.E.

King Adad-nirari II of Assyria initiates conquest

ca 883 B.C.E.

Reign of King Ashurnasirpal II begins in Assyria

ca 870 B.C.E.

King Ashurnasirpal II invades Syria and Israel

ca 853 B.C.E.

Battle of Qarqar pits Assyria against Egypt, Syria, and Israel

ca 850 B.C.E.

King Shalmaneser III invades the Northern Kingdom of Israel

ca 745 B.C.E

King Tiglath-Pileser III colonizes the Northern Kingdom

ca 721 B.C.E.

Rump state of Samaria falls to King Sargon II

ca 612 B.C.E.

Medes and Babylonians sack Nineveh

ca 612 B.C.E.

Neo-Babylonian Dynasty takes over the Assyrian Empire

ca 605 B.C.E.

Neo-Babylonians defeat Egyptians and Assyrians at Carchemish

ca 575 B.C.E.

Ishtar Gate of Babylon is built

ca 586 B.C.E.

Neo-Babylonian King Nebuchadnezzar destroys Jerusalem

"I CARRIED OFF [TO] ASSYRIA THE LAND OF BÉ̞T-HÅUMRIA (THE 'HOUSE OF ISRAEL'), ITS AUXILIARY [ARMY], [AND] ALL OF ITS PEOPLE."

STELA OF TIGLATH-PILESER III

eighth century. According to the Bible, the prisoners were settled "in Halah, on Habor, by the river of Gozan," today identified with the Khabur River, one of the largest tributaries of the Euphrates in Syria (2 Kings 17:6). Sargon's annals claim that some 27,000 Israelites were thus uprooted. In their stead, Samaria was settled with colonists from places like Cuthah (possibly Tell Ibrahim, northeast of Babylon). This is one reason that the Jews of the New Testament held the Samaritans, or Cuthaeans, in such contempt, for although these foreign farmers had assimilated with the remaining Samarian population and eventually adopted Jewish practices, they possessed a Babylonian bloodline.

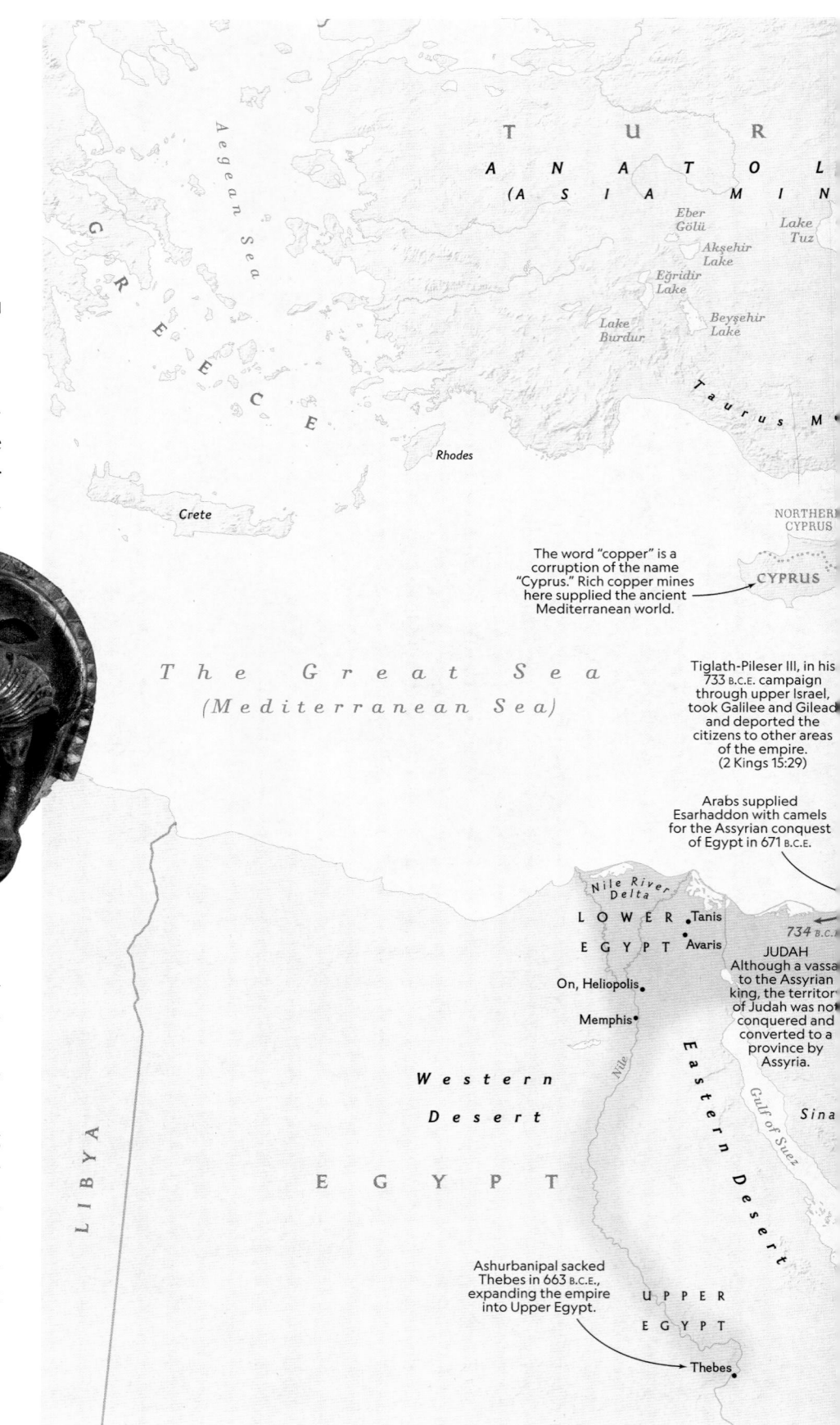

Assyrian lion

The kingdom of Judah would fall victim to the invaders as well, but not before the nation experienced a brief renaissance during the reign of King Josiah. Josiah rose to the throne after the 55-year reign of King Manasseh. As archaeologists Israel Finkelstein and Neil Asher Silberman have shown, Manasseh oversaw a strong recovery of Judah's agricultural economy, particularly in the export of olive oil to Assyria. The growing prosperity also allowed Manasseh to reinforce the kingdom's outlying fortresses facing Egypt, particularly in Arad, as evidenced by excavations there.

The word "copper" is a corruption of the name "Cyprus." Rich copper mines here supplied the ancient Mediterranean world.

Tiglath-Pileser III, in his 733 B.C.E. campaign through upper Israel, took Galilee and Gilead and deported the citizens to other areas of the empire. (2 Kings 15:29)

Arabs supplied Esarhaddon with camels for the Assyrian conquest of Egypt in 671 B.C.E.

JUDAH
Although a vassal to the Assyrian king, the territory of Judah was not conquered and converted to a province by Assyria.

Ashurbanipal sacked Thebes in 663 B.C.E., expanding the empire into Upper Egypt.

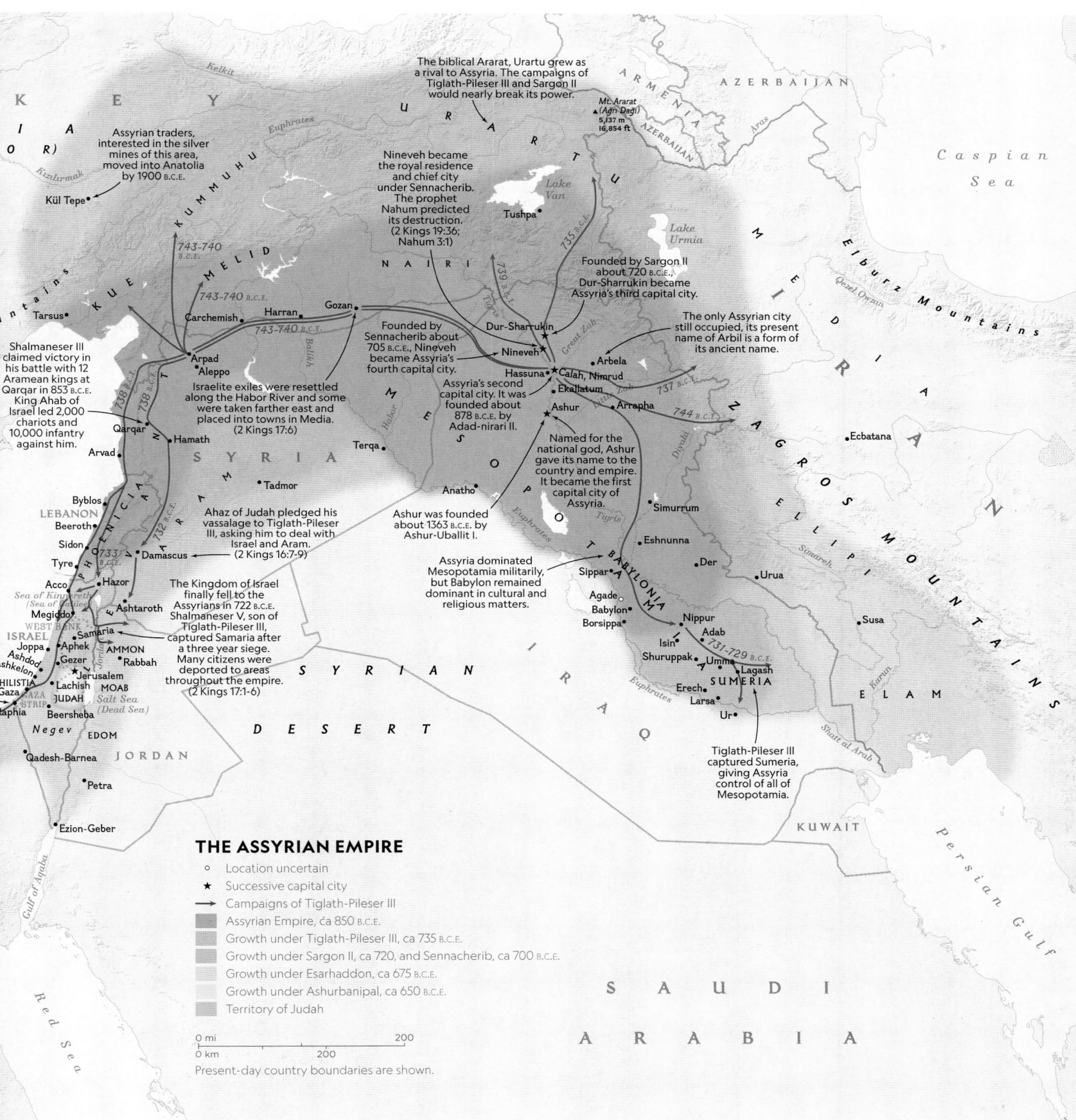

THE ASSYRIAN EMPIRE

The biblical Ararat, Urartu grew as a rival to Assyria. The campaigns of Tiglath-Pileser III and Sargon II would nearly break its power.

Assyrian traders, interested in the silver mines of this area, moved into Anatolia by 1900 B.C.E.

Nineveh became the royal residence and chief city under Sennacherib. The prophet Nahum predicted its destruction. (2 Kings 19:36; Nahum 3:1)

Founded by Sargon II about 720 B.C.E., Dur-Sharrukin became Assyria's third capital city.

The only Assyrian city still occupied, its present name of Arbil is a form of its ancient name.

Shalmaneser III claimed victory in his battle with 12 Aramean kings at Qarqar in 853 B.C.E. King Ahab of Israel led 2,000 chariots and 10,000 infantry against him.

Founded by Sennacherib about 705 B.C.E., Nineveh became Assyria's fourth capital city.

Israelite exiles were resettled along the Habor River and some were taken farther east and placed into towns in Media. (2 Kings 17:6)

Assyria's second capital city. It was founded about 878 B.C.E. by Adad-nirari II.

Named for the national god, Ashur gave its name to the country and empire. It became the first capital city of Assyria.

Ahaz of Judah pledged his vassalage to Tiglath-Pileser III, asking him to deal with Israel and Aram. (2 Kings 16:7-9)

Ashur was founded about 1363 B.C.E. by Ashur-Uballit I.

Assyria dominated Mesopotamia militarily, but Babylon remained dominant in cultural and religious matters.

The Kingdom of Israel finally fell to the Assyrians in 722 B.C.E. Shalmaneser V, son of Tiglath-Pileser III, captured Samaria after a three year siege. Many citizens were deported to areas throughout the empire. (2 Kings 17:1-6)

Tiglath-Pileser III captured Sumeria, giving Assyria control of all of Mesopotamia.

Legend

- ○ Location uncertain
- ★ Successive capital city
- → Campaigns of Tiglath-Pileser III
- Assyrian Empire, ća 850 B.C.E.
- Growth under Tiglath-Pileser III, ca 735 B.C.E.
- Growth under Sargon II, ca 720, and Sennacherib, ca 700 B.C.E.
- Growth under Esarhaddon, ca 675 B.C.E.
- Growth under Ashurbanipal, ca 650 B.C.E.
- Territory of Judah

0 mi ——— 200
0 km ——— 200

Present-day country boundaries are shown.

A LION LEAPS at the chariot of King Ashurnasirpal II in this ninth-century B.C.E. relief from Nimrud.

Thus, when his grandson Josiah (or Yoshiyyáhu, "healed by Yah") succeeded him around 640 B.C.E., the new king found a replenished treasury and a well-functioning economy. This allowed him to focus on two areas: religious reform and territorial expansion. During the renovation of the temple, the Bible tells us, the high priest Hilkiah discovered an ancient scroll that contained "the book of the law"—quite possibly an early version of what would become the Book of Deuteronomy (2 Kings 22:8). The discovery of the scroll spurred an attempt to create a canon of the full Torah, the Five Books of Moses—a process that would not be completed until after the Babylonian Exile.

Assyrian ivory of a woman

The Fall of Assyria

Meanwhile, the political situation was changing. The old Assyrian Empire was steadily crumbling, and Egypt was still recovering from Assyrian occupation. Josiah seized the ensuing power vacuum by invading the Assyrian provinces in the north, thus combining Judah and Israel into a united monarchy. This conquest, as some scholars have argued, was extolled by Josiah's panegyrists as a "restoration" of the legendary Davidic Kingdom, an idea that was subsequently woven into the fabric of Deuteronomist history by Josiah's scribes.

But the king overreached. When in 612 B.C.E. the Medes and Babylonians rose in rebellion and sacked Assyria's capital of Nineveh, the Egyptian pharaoh (either Psammetichus I or Necho I) came to the aid of the hard-pressed Assyrian forces to secure Egypt's trade routes at all costs. Surprisingly, Josiah decided to back the side of the rebels. In an ill-considered move, the king attacked the supply lines of the Egyptian army near the fortress

THE ASSYRIAN MILITARY MACHINE

Though at its core the Assyrian army continued to rely on infantry and archers, Ashurnasirpal II was arguably the first to use cavalry units to spearhead and screen the movement of infantry and its chariot forces. He is also credited with the development of the armored battering ram (at right). This large wooden framework placed on wheels was equipped with a heavy metal-clad ram suspended from chains, which a platoon of soldiers could cause to swing against the walls or gates of an enemy city. If the target city was built on an elevation, slaves would be deployed to build a large earthen ramp that would bring the siege machine close to the city walls. The Romans adopted the Assyrian siege tower but updated it with new technology, including the provision of various types of catapults and heavy crossbows. The earthen ramp built by the Romans to drive the siege towers of the 10th Legion to the walls surrounding Herod's fortress of Masada, on the Dead Sea, is still visible today.

"FALLEN,
NO MORE TO RISE,
IS MAIDEN ISRAEL;
FORSAKEN ON HER LAND,
WITH NO ONE TO
RAISE HER UP."

AMOS 5:2

of Megiddo. Judah's forces were defeated, the king was fatally wounded, and the kingdom of Judah became, once more, a vassal state of Egypt, like the Canaan of old. All of Josiah's grand ambitions had come to naught.

Seven years later, however, a new coalition of Medean and Babylonian forces defeated the Assyrians at the famous Battle of Carchemish. Unfortunately, the new Babylonian king, Nebuchadnezzar II, was every bit as rapacious as his Assyrian predecessors had been. He too was determined to restore the Assyrian Empire under the rule of Babylon. All of the former vassal states, including Judah, were summoned to pledge their fealty to Babylon or accept the consequences.

When King Josiah's successor, King Jehoaikim, began to plot a rebellion, Nebuchadnezzar's wrath was kindled. A clay tablet from the palace of Babylon states that "in the seventh year, in the month of Kislimu [the winter of 598 B.C.E.], the king of Akkad [Nebuchadnezzar] mustered his troops, marched to the Hatti-Land [Syria-Canaan] and encamped against the city of Judah [Jerusalem]." Jerusalem enjoyed a brief respite while the Babylonian king rushed his troops southward to defeat a rebellion by Egyptian King Apries, but in 586 B.C.E., Nebuchadnezzar returned and captured the city after a bitter struggle. The Jerusalem Temple was destroyed, and almost all inhabitants were killed or marched into captivity. The Israelite kingdoms were no more, and the great Babylonian exile had begun. Some three decades later, the Babylonian Empire fell to the king of Persia. ■

ANCIENT CULTURES OF THE
AMERICAS

Around 1500 B.C.E., agricultural cultures began to rise along the rivers of Central America. The most prominent of these Mesoamerican cultures was the Olmec civilization along the Gulf of Mexico, which developed a flourishing trade, the first written language in this hemisphere, and even pyramids.

What was happening in the rest of the world while all these great movements were taking place in Asia and the Middle East? As we saw, some 20,000 years ago, large groups of nomadic tribes are believed to have crossed a land bridge from northern Asia into North America in their hunt for game. Most of these peoples remained hunters and gatherers for millennia to come, in part because of the vastness of the continent and the instability of the climate after the last ice age. During the so-called Paleo-Indian period, a great number of tribes hunted species that are now extinct, such as the mastodon and the ancient bison. In time, however, these tribal groups embraced domestication and began to cultivate plants and cereals, particularly in more temperate climates. In the process, they developed distinct cultural and linguistic traditions.

Around 1200 B.C.E., at the same time of the beginning of great migrations in the Near East, major agricultural cultures began to form along the rivers of Central America. The most prominent of these so-called Mesoamerican cultures

was the Olmec civilization, which emerged along the Gulf of Mexico. The term "Olmec" is derived from the Nahuatl word Ōlmēcatl, which means "rubber people," presumably in reference to the many rubber trees in this region.

Like many similar agricultural communities in Asia and the Near East, the Olmecs developed prosperous communities by exploiting the rich alluvial soil of the Coatzacoalcos River basin. This river system provided both ample sources of water and a transportation network for trade in produce, jade, obsidian, and magnetite, a magnetic mineral. Over time, the Olmecs began to develop monumental urban centers grouped around pyramids. One of the largest of these is the Great Pyramid of La Venta, Tabasco, which today is still 100 feet high. Inside, excavators found pottery, figurines, mosaics, and polished serpentine blocks. There are also records written in glyphs that are still to be deciphered.

The question of Olmec writing eluded historians until 2006, when archaeologists published the discovery of the oldest known writing sample in the Western Hemisphere: the Cascajal Block, believed

AN INUIT CARVING in whalebone of a reindeer was found in Kinngait (formerly Cape Dorset) on Baffin Island, Canada.

THE OLMEC ARE BELIEVED TO HAVE DEVELOPED THE PANTHEON OF GODS THAT LATER WOULD BE ADOPTED IN VARIOUS FORMS BY THE MAYA AND THE AZTEC.

to be written with pictograms from the Olmec civilization. Found in Veracruz, Mexico, and dated to the first millennium B.C.E., the block has several linear rows of characters that may denote certain animals, pottery, tools, and food—particularly corn. Archaeologists speculate that the Olmec religion had great respect for animals, including serpents and jaguars, which may have been revered as deities or as the ancestors of human beings.

The most famous feature of the Olmec civilization, however, is it fondness for giant stone heads that may represent either kings or prominent deities. Since many appear to be wearing helmets, some historians claimed that the heads represented famous ballplayers, but this theory has now been largely abandoned. Nonetheless, some dozen rubber balls have been found at an archaeological site six miles east of the Olmec center of San Lorenzo Tenochtitlan, which suggests that the Olmecs were indeed avid ball-playing fans.

Equally impressive are Olmec masks, usually carved in jade, that betray an astonishing command of human physiognomy. Art historians consider these and other Olmec artifacts the first authentic art style of the Americas, not only because of their striking realism but also because of their virtuosity in different materials, including clay, basalt, bone, and jade. The Olmecs are also credited with the development of the corn-based tortilla, a mainstay of Central American cuisine today.

Anthropomorphic plaque, possibly by Olmec artisans

The Olmec civilization flourished from 1200 to 400 B.C.E., at which point it quite suddenly went into decline. What prompted this process has never been fully revealed, but most historians attribute the sudden drop in population to climate change, a series of earthquakes, or the silting up of the river system due to excessive farming. Others believe that volcanic eruptions may be the reason that the Olmec settlements were eventually abandoned.

Ancient Cultures in North America

Though none achieved the same level of sophistication of the Olmec civilization, by 1000 B.C.E. a number of other early cultures were emerging throughout the Americas. One of the most prominent was the Chavín culture in the Andes mountains, which excelled in finely woven textiles and artifacts of gold, silver, and copper. Other cultures include the Adena people in the Ohio River Valley and the Cochise culture of today's New Mexico and Arizona. In the Arctic, the Inuits and Aleuts founded a number of settlements, and in California, Pinto Indians developed triangular points for their spears to hunt game.

One of the leading cultures of this period is the one that arose in the Lower Mississippi Valley from around 1100 B.C.E. Modern excavations suggest that this culture was spread over a 100-mile area across the Mississippi Delta and the Gulf Coast and centered in a prehistoric site referred to as Poverty Point by archaeologists.

THIS CARVED MONUMENT was found in the Olmec archaeological site of La Venta in today's Mexican state of Tabasco.

NOTABLE DATES

ca 1500 B.C.E.

Agricultural cultures form along the rivers of Central America

ca 1500 B.C.E.

Metalworking begins in Peru

ca 1500 B.C.E.

People in today's western Mexico bury their dead in shaft tombs

ca 1400 B.C.E.

First development of a ball game by people of Chiapas, Mexico

ca 1400 B.C.E.

Olmec influence expands from the Gulf of Mexico to the Pacific

ca 1300 B.C.E.

The site known as Poverty Point is built in today's Louisiana

ca 1300–600 B.C.E.

Multiple eruptions from Los Humeros volcano in eastern Mexico

ca 1250 B.C.E.

Cahokia (near today's St. Louis) is the largest city in North America

ca 1000 B.C.E.

The Mississippian culture develops large earthen mounds

ca 900 B.C.E.

Olmec Cascajal Block is oldest form of writing in Western Hemisphere

ca 900 B.C.E.

Chavín culture rises in Chavín de Huántar, high in the Andes

CHAVÍN DE HUÁNTAR is a major archaeological site in Peru with ruins from the Chavín culture, which emerged around 900 B.C.E.

Today recognized as one of only 24 UNESCO World Heritage sites in the United States, Poverty Point consists of a remarkable group of earthen ridges and mounds across 402 acres, grouped in six concentric, C-shaped arrangements. The diameter of these ridges was quite large, measuring up to three-quarters of a mile. This explains why local archaeologists became aware of these ancient structures only when they were revealed in aerial photographs. The innermost concentric ridge embraces a large plaza, which was once marked with wood posts.

The sheer vastness of this monument suggests that it emerged over time, between 1600 and 1300 B.C.E. Its purpose, however, continues to be debated. Were these vast ridges used for cultivation so as to protect crops from inundation during flooding, or were they the foundations of settlements, raised high above the ground so as to protect them from invaders? The presence of holes along with what appear to be earth ovens would suggest that the monument definitely contained residences, but whether these were permanent is difficult to ascertain. That is why, as in the case of Stonehenge, some historians believe that the site was a shrine of some sort that invited tribal assemblies at particular points in the year. The concentric ridges could have been built to ward off evil spirits. Others suggest that the place had an astronomical purpose.

Over the subsequent centuries, during the so-called Woodland period of pre-Columbian cultures in North America, the continent witnessed the rise of a great number of sites that straddled both hunter-gatherer and cultivation activity. This period is distinguished by the development of pottery in a great variety of forms and using a number of different forms of manufacturing. These tribes also developed tools of bone and stone and became adept at leather crafts, as well as the weaving of indigenous textiles. Their primary weapons used in the hunt

Chavín-style pin ornament

CROP YIELDS IN EARLY CULTURES

The typical landholdings of a peasant family probably ranged around four acres. A farmer (at right) in Antiquity likely realized a return of 1:5, that is, five times the original seed planted. Scholars have calculated that the annual yield of a single acre was 1,320 pounds (600 kg). Allowing for crop rotation, this means that the average farmer would have needed at least .625 acre per person in his household. Some historians believe it took 11 bushels of wheat to feed an adult in a year. That means families of four or five needed at least 5.5 to 6.5 acres of land to feed their families, and this was *before* taxes. Recent UN estimates have reached the same conclusion.

THE FAR-FLUNG MISSISSIPPIAN TRADE NETWORK EXTENDED NORTH TO THE GREAT LAKES, WEST TO THE ROCKY MOUNTAINS, AND SOUTH TO THE GULF OF MEXICO.

were spears, until the bow and arrow became the weapon of choice.

The Woodland period was followed from ca 700 by the Mississippian culture, which emerged in the river valley south of today's St. Louis and throughout the Southeast. Its most prevalent cultural trait was the design of large earthen mounds in the form of pyramids or flattened platforms. One of the largest of these is in Cahokia, located near today's East St. Louis in Illinois. Built from around 1000 C.E. onward, the large mounds in this area are recognized today as a UNESCO World Heritage site. Forensic evidence suggests that the local settlers cultivated maize and traded the surplus with surrounding regions across a large trading network. At its peak, around 1200 C.E., Cahokia may have been the largest urban concentration in North America, with a population of 20,000. More than three hundred years later, after the arrival of Europeans, the Mississippian cultures had all but vanished. Only the Natchez people still retained some practices until the 18th century. ■

A CROSS-SHAPED ornament from Chavín de Huántar is tentatively dated to around 500–200 B.C.E.

A MODERN ARTIST'S IMPRESSION of the Native American Cahokia site near St. Louis, Missouri, reveals a sprawling complex with multiple mounds.

THE ISHTAR GATE with its glazed figures of bulls once towered over the Processional Way of Babylon, leading to the sixth-century B.C.E. temple of Marduk.

EUROPE
DURING THE IRON AGE

After the growth of early cultures during the Bronze Age, the Iron Age witnessed the arrival of several highly influential movements in both northern and southern Europe that would lay the foundation for the great civilizations of Antiquity.

As in other regions, mass migrations would also shape the principal demographic makeup of continental Europe. The most important of these were the Indo-European movements from the area of the Black Sea and the Balkan Peninsula into east and southeast Europe from about 4000 B.C.E. onward. This migration provided the primary impetus for the development of the various Indo-European languages in the millennia to come. Several proto-cultures flourished during this time, including the community in today's Bulgaria that was responsible for producing the Varna Necropolis treasure of ca 4500 B.C.E., one of the oldest gold treasures ever found. Discovered in 1972, the Varna site has so far yielded 294 graves filled with pottery, flint and obsidian plates, beads, and gold and copper artifacts.

By 2000 B.C.E., there were several Bronze Age cultures in today's Germany, Denmark, Sweden, Norway, and Britain, many of them developed by migrants from other regions. For example, modern isotope tests of the tooth enamel of a skeleton recovered at Stonehenge suggest that some of these people originated in the Alpine region of today's Switzerland.

As elsewhere in the world, trade served as an important catalyst. This included the exchange of amber, recovered from the Baltic Sea, as well as tin from Cornwall and copper from the Great Orme mine in north Wales. In time, this exchange led to the rise of the so-called Atlantic Bronze Age, a term that denotes the steady growth of trade and cultural links among regions of southwestern Europe. Coastal communities in France, Britain, Portugal, and Andalusia built cliff castles and round houses with strikingly similar characteristics. Italy saw the development of the Nuragic civilization on Sardinia and Corsica, distinguished by the use of dolmens and menhirs to construct Nuragic towers, as well as the Canegrate culture in today's Po Valley. During the Iron Age, the Villanovan culture

AN ANTHROPOMORPHIC figure was excavated in the Varna Necropolis in Bulgaria, one of the oldest archaeological sites in eastern Europe.

"SING TO ME, MUSE, AND TELL THE STORY OF . . .
THE WANDERER, BLOWN OFF COURSE TIME AND AGAIN,
AFTER HE PLUNDERED THE PROUD HEIGHTS OF TROY."

HOMER, *THE ODYSSEY*

emerged in Etruria (today's Tuscany, Latium, and Umbria). By the eighth century B.C.E., this would produce the Etruscan civilization, the most important cultural development on the peninsula before the rise of Rome.

By contrast, the decline of Mycenae and the collapse of its Bronze Age trade had plunged Greece into its Dark Ages. Many of Mycenae's magnificent palaces and cities were abandoned or destroyed. The cause of this collapse has mystified generations of historians. Today, some believe the Sea Peoples may have been responsible, but this theory is contested by the fact that other regions of Greece, such as Attica and the Ionian islands, continued to prosper.

Golden mask of Agamemnon

Other scholars have argued that a series of earthquakes were at fault. Whatever the case may be, both Mycenae and one of its main competitors, the city of Troy in the northwestern part of today's Turkey, were left in ruins. Ancient Greek historians believed that this was the result of a Trojan War between the two rivals, which according to Herodotus took place in 1250 B.C.E. The legend of this war inspired Homer's famous epic poems, *The Iliad* and *The Odyssey,* composed between ca 900 and 750 B.C.E.

The Celtic Civilization

In central Europe, the most important development at the dawn of the Iron Age was the arrival of the Celts (or *Keltoi* in Greek), who settled around 800 B.C.E. near Hallstatt in Gmunden, today's Upper Austria. Located in an idyllic setting between the Hallstätter See and the soaring slopes of the Dachstein massif, the Hallstatt culture developed a flourishing business in trading salt, a locally mined mineral that was much in demand for the preservation of meat. This brought the Celts in contact with many regions as far as the Mediterranean, which broadened their territorial reach and allowed them to develop growing townships such as the Heuneburg settlement in southern Germany. Discovered in 1846, the Celtic necropolis of Hallstatt has yielded more than 1,000 graves that are remarkable for their similarity in terms of their wealth and grave attributes. It seems that at this stage, the Celtic community was

CELTIC STANDING STONES are found throughout Ireland, Scotland, and parts of England, often with inscriptions in Celtic or Latin.

AN EVENING VIEW of Hallstatt on the Hallstätter See, where the Celts first settled around 800 B.C.E.

NOTABLE DATES

ca 1400 B.C.E.
Stonehenge in Britain assumes the form it has today

ca 1320 B.C.E.
Ship sinks off coast of Uluburun, Turkey's oldest known shipwreck

ca 1300 B.C.E.
Mycenae is the dominant power in the Aegean

ca 1290 B.C.E.
City of Troy is destroyed by Mycenaeans

ca 1285 B.C.E.
Oral traditions of the Trojan War begin to circulate

ca 1200 B.C.E.
First signs of raiders, the Sea Peoples, in the eastern Mediterranean

ca 1200 B.C.E.
Proto-Celtic tribes settle in eastern Europe

ca 1150 B.C.E.
Mycenae's power is challenged by invading Dorian Greeks

ca 1150 B.C.E.
Dark Age of Greece begins

ca 1100 B.C.E.
First evidence of the Phoenician alphabet

ca 1000 B.C.E.
Rise of the Villanova culture in Italy, precursors of the Etruscans

ca 800 B.C.E.
Use of iron to make arms spreads through Europe

A CIRCULAR CELTIC TOWER is surrounded by the pastoral landscape of Scotland.

> "THE WHOLE [CELTIC] RACE . . . IS MADLY FOND OF WAR, HIGH-SPIRITED, QUICK TO BATTLE . . . EVEN IF THEY HAVE NOTHING ON THEIR SIDE BUT THEIR OWN STRENGTH AND COURAGE."

STRABO, GREEK GEOGRAPHER

mostly egalitarian, without the cult of a princely elite, as in other parts of the world at that time.

These excavations show that the Celts were highly skilled in the forging of bronze weapons and tools, and they used four-wheeled wooden wagons for transportation. When iron became available in large quantities, the Celts quickly became expert metalsmiths, producing household tools and agricultural blades, swords, and lances of iron. This gave them a strong military superiority which they used to spread across Europe, moving into Germany, France, and Scandinavia. By 400 B.C.E., Celtic tribes had penetrated as far

Celtic torque with bull heads

as France and the Low Countries, and by 500 B.C.E. into the Iberian Peninsula, and even the British Isles, where they would have a decisive influence on the development of an English culture before the arrival of the Romans.

The Birth of the Modern Alphabet

Egyptians developed hieroglyphic or hieratic (cursive) systems for writing, while the Mesopotamian culture had perfected the cuneiform script originally developed by Sumer. But the Mediterranean world chose neither. Instead, it adopted the first instance of a truly alphabetic script, known

WHO WERE THE SEA PEOPLES?

The first mention of large groups of invading migrants in Egypt, known as Peleset (*P-r-s-t* in Egyptian hieroglyphics), which would play such a disruptive role in Canaan and early Israel, can be found at the mortuary Temple of Ramses III at Medinet Habu. These inscriptions inspired 19th-century Egyptologist Emmanuel de Rougé to coin the phrase *les peuples de la mer*. Their rise is also attested by contemporary Assyrian records, which refer to the Sea Peoples (at right) as *Ahhlamu*, or "Wanderers." Their wholesale migration may have been caused by the decline of the Mycenaean civilization, the collapse of the Hittite Empire, or the great eruption of the volcano at Thera. According to the Bible, the Philistines came from Caphtor (either Crete or Cyprus), which may not be far from the truth (Amos 9:7, Jeremiah 47:4).

A PHOENICIAN SHIP, similar to the type introduced during Iron Age II.
BELOW: The Gezer Calendar, discovered at Tell el-Jazari, is one of the oldest examples of Hebrew writing, dated to the 10th century B.C.E.

as the Phoenician alphabet, first documented around 1050 B.C.E. The Phoenician dialect owed much to the same northwestern "Indo-Semitic" that formed the basis of Hebrew and Aramaic and was, by varying degrees, also spoken in Phoenician, Moabite, and Edomite dialects. This alphabet spread rapidly through Phoenician trade routes in the Mediterranean basin, including Greece. The oldest example of written Hebrew is a small tablet from Gezer, dated around 925 B.C.E., describing a calendar of agricultural seasons. The key challenge of any form of writing is to accurately grasp the phonemes ("significant sounds") by which spoken language communicates its meaning. Semitic scripts such as Old Hebrew and Phoenician emphasized the different pronunciation of consonants rather than vowels. For example, an inscription on a bronze arrowhead from the 11th century states that the weapon belongs to "d" (meaning

"Ada"), who was the son of "b'l" (meaning "Bala"). Greece had experimented with its own written language, known as Linear B, but around 800 B.C.E., the Greeks adopted the Phoenician alphabet as well. Classical Greek, however, places a greater emphasis on vowels. In response, the Greeks adopted separate symbols for A, E, I, O, and U that, by and large, we continue to use in our modern alphabets today.

The Fall of Babylon

While Greece was slumbering in its Dark Ages, Nebuchadnezzar's dream of recreating Babylonia's storied past in a vast neo-Babylonian realm turned out to be doomed to failure. Perhaps the king had a premonition about its short time span, because back at home in Babylon, he launched into a frenzied program to rebuild the city in a fashion that would put the Assyrian capitals of Nineveh and Ashur to shame. One of the king's most impressive monuments, the Ishtar Gate, is still visible today

A GILDED STATUE is believed to be a votive figure dedicated to a Phoenician deity.

A MODERN ILLUSTRATION
of the Processional Street of
Babylon shows the Ishtar Gate as it
would have appeared in the sixth
century B.C.E.

in the Pergamon Museum in Berlin after extensive restoration. The huge gateway was one of eight gates that led to the city's inner precinct. Begun in 575 B.C.E., the gate was covered with glazed color tiles that depicted dragons and a type of oxen known as aurochs, symbols of the Babylonian gods Marduk and Adad. Excavated by German archaeologist Robert Koldewey, the current restoration contains many of the original bricks.

Shortly after the Ishtar Gate was completed, however, the neo-Babylonian Empire began to crumble. The trouble began in the kingdom of Anshan, today's Iran, which had been ruled by a dynasty that traced its origins to a legendary figure named Achaemenes (the later Persian dynasty would become known as the Achaemenids). In 553 B.C.E., Anshan's vassal king decided to rise up against his overlord, the king of the Medes, and in short order he proceeded to conquer all of the Median Empire. The king's name was Cyrus II. Thus began an era that in the span of a mere four centuries would see the rise of three vast empires: those of Persia, Greece, and Rome. ■

THIS CELTIC SCULPTURE features two stylized faces.

AN ARCHER, possibly a member of the Persian Guard, marches on a wall of molded enameled brick from Darius's palace at Susa, dated around 510 B.C.E.

THE PERSIAN
EMPIRE

For more than two centuries, the Achaemenid Dynasty would rule the largest empire in history, fostering an unprecedented level of peaceful coexistence and commercial activity. The Persians built a central road network and postal system and had a high degree of religious tolerance.

I n 540 B.C.E., Cyrus turned his armies against the neo-Babylonian realm, now ruled by King Nabonidus. A man who preferred to dwell in his library rather than in the barracks, Nabonidus had placed his son Bel-shar-usur at the head of his army. (Bel-shar-usur may have inspired the character of Belshazzar in the Book of Daniel.) But when the Persian troops led by Cyrus massed on the border, Nabonidus rushed back to reassert his authority once more, even going so far as to cancel the annual Babylonian New Year's Feast, for which he incurred the wrath of the Babylonian priesthood.

By October 539 B.C.E., Cyrus had reached the city of Babylon itself. According to the Verse Account of Nabonidus, a Babylonian tablet recovered in 1924, the citizens of Babylon simply opened the gates to let the Persian conquerors march in. Cyrus's own chronicle, a clay cylinder in the Babylonian tradition, credits Marduk, the Babylonian supreme god, with his stupendous victory. This betrayed his shrewd use of claiming divine patronage to legitimize his conquests, a practice that is also reflected in the biblical account. According to Second Isaiah, the Hebrew

exiles anointed him as the "servant of YHWH" (Isaiah 44:21), just as Cyrus would be honored as the "chosen one" of Marduk in Babylon, and his grandson Darius would soon be welcomed as the new "son of Ra" in Egypt.

For more than two centuries, the Persian or Achaemenid Empire was ruled from its capital in Pasargadae as the largest empire in history. If projected on a modern map, the empire would have encompassed today's Turkey, Syria, Iraq, Iran, Israel, Jordan, and Lebanon, as well as Russia, Armenia, Afghanistan, and much of Central Asia, including northern India. By some estimates, this commonwealth embraced some 50 million people.

In this great realm, a culture clash seemed inevitable. Under King Astyages, Media had become a center of a new and fervent monotheism, Zoroastrianism, whereas the court of King Croesus of Lydia was known for its Hellenistic tendencies, even offering sanctuary to Greek exiles. Yet Cyrus was not like other

A SIGLOS depicting King Darius I (r. 521–486 B.C.E.) is one of the earliest forms of struck coinage.

> ## "I RETURNED TO THE SACRED CITIES ON THE OTHER SIDE OF THE TIGRIS, THE SANCTUARIES WHICH HAVE BEEN RUINS FOR A LONG TIME . . . AND ESTABLISHED FOR THEM PERMANENT SANCTUARIES."
>
> **KING CYRUS, CYRUS CYLINDER**

Mesopotamian leaders. He understood that an occupied people, bereft of their political identity, would instinctively transfer their collective aspirations to a national cult if allowed to do so. In order for these cults to flourish and remain a stabilizing force, they required religious leadership and a central place of worship. Therefore, Cyrus gave strict instructions to allow each occupied people to worship freely, correctly believing that religious observance can be a powerful stabilizing force regardless of political circumstance.

The Cyrus cylinder

Religious Tolerance in the Persian Empire

In the case of Jewish worship in Judah, however, there was a problem. The religious elite of Israel no longer lived in Jerusalem but as refugees along the banks of the rivers of Babylon; here were the scribes, the priests, and the scholars, busy finishing the Deuteronomistic history of Israel and the final composition of the Pentateuch. Even worse, the principal sanctuary of Judaism, the Temple in Jerusalem, was a heap of ruins. Cyrus's decision to release the exiles in Babylon and sanction a reconstruction of the temple (Ezra 1:2) was therefore very much the product of an uncanny political mind. In fact, according to the text of the Cyrus Cylinder, the Persian king also undertook religious restorations in other places, including the return of the "gods of Sumer and Akkad," and willingly paid for the "repair of their dwelling places."

The exiles from Judah and the Northern Kingdom were now free—free to pack up their families and belongings and return to their homelands. The first caravans duly set out, although many Jews chose to remain in Babylon. According to Josephus, the first century C.E. Jewish historian, many Jewish expatriates were "unwilling to leave their possessions." These communities in exile, however, remained faithful to the Covenant Law and the worship of Yahweh and in the centuries to come would serve as important centers for the study of Jewish Law.

Those who did decide to return now found themselves in the sub-province of

DUTCH BAROQUE ARTIST Rembrandt van Rijn created the dramatic oil painting "Belshazzar's Feast" in 1635.

THE CITY OF PERSEPOLIS in today's Iran was chosen by Cyrus the Great as the capital of the new Achaemenid Empire, but it was Darius I who built much of its palace complex.

NOTABLE DATES

ca 560 B.C.E.

King Croesus of Lydia mints first gold and silver coins

ca 550 B.C.E.

King Cyrus II of Anshan conquers the kingdom of Media

ca 539 B.C.E.

Babylon surrenders to King Cyrus II

ca 525 B.C.E.

King Cambyses, son of Cyrus, conquers Egypt

ca 522 B.C.E.

Darius I usurps throne in Persia, making the Zoroastrianism state religion

ca 515 B.C.E.

People of Yehud (Judah) complete Second Temple with Persian funds

ca 500 B.C.E.

Royal Persian road stretches 1,600 miles from Sardis to Susa

ca 490 B.C.E.

Carthage founds colonies on Atlantic coast of Africa

ca 480 B.C.E.

King Xerxes I wins Battle of Thermopylae and sacks Athens

ca 466 B.C.E.

Athenian-led Delian League liberates its Ionian colonies from Persian rule

ca 459 B.C.E.

Hall of a Hundred Pillars in Persian city of Persepolis

ca 366 B.C.E.

Egypt revolts against Persian rule

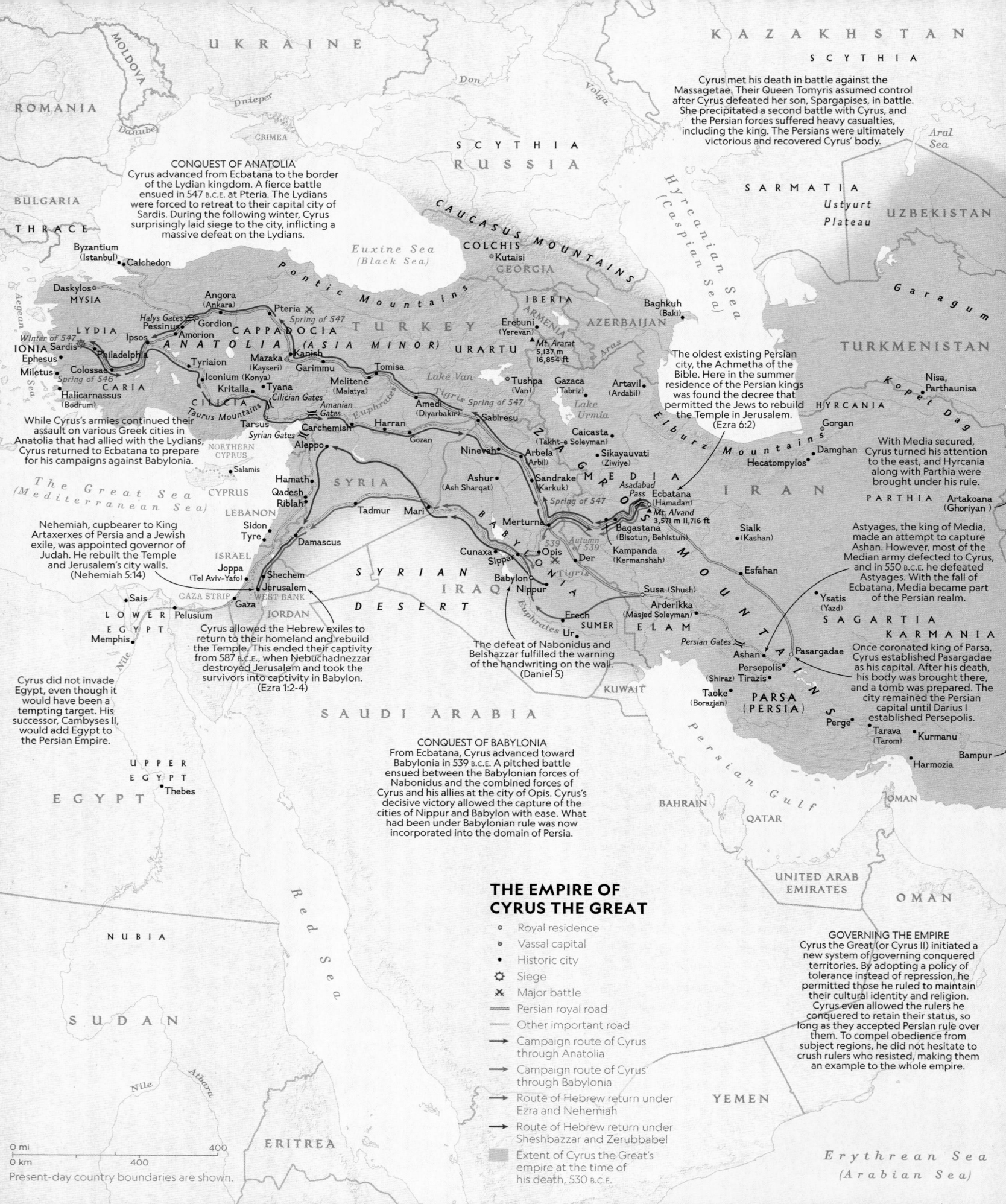

KAZAKHSTAN

UKRAINE

MOLDOVA

ROMANIA

BULGARIA

THRACE

SCYTHIA

RUSSIA

SCYTHIA

Cyrus met his death in battle against the Massagetae. Their Queen Tomyris assumed control after Cyrus defeated her son, Spargapises, in battle. She precipitated a second battle with Cyrus, and the Persian forces suffered heavy casualties, including the king. The Persians were ultimately victorious and recovered Cyrus' body.

Don

Dnieper

Danube

CRIMEA

Volga

Aral Sea

SARMATIA

Ustyurt Plateau

UZBEKISTAN

CAUCASUS MOUNTAINS

COLCHIS

Kutaisi

GEORGIA

IBERIA

ARMENIA

AZERBAIJAN

Hyrcanian Sea (Caspian Sea)

Garagum

CONQUEST OF ANATOLIA
Cyrus advanced from Ecbatana to the border of the Lydian kingdom. A fierce battle ensued in 547 B.C.E. at Pteria. The Lydians were forced to retreat to their capital city of Sardis. During the following winter, Cyrus surprisingly laid siege to the city, inflicting a massive defeat on the Lydians.

Euxine Sea (Black Sea)

TURKMENISTAN

Byzantium (Istanbul)   Calchedon

Daskylos   MYSIA

Pontic Mountains

Angora (Ankara)

Pteria ✕ *Spring of 547*

TURKEY

Baghkuh (Baki)

Nisa, Parthaunisa

Kopet Dag

Pessinus   Amorion

Ipsos   Gordion

Halys Gates

Winter of 547

IONIA   Sardis
LYDIA

CAPPADOCIA

ANATOLIA (ASIA MINOR)

Erebuni (Yerevan)

URARTU

▲ Mt. Ararat 5,137 m 16,854 ft

Artavil (Ardabil)

HYRCANIA

Gorgan

The oldest existing Persian city, the Achmetha of the Bible. Here in the summer residence of the Persian kings was found the decree that permitted the Jews to rebuild the Temple in Jerusalem. (Ezra 6:2)

Damghan

Ephesus   Philadelphia
Colossae
Miletus

Mazaka (Kayseri)   Kanish

Tyriaion

Garimmu

Tushpa (Van)

Lake Van

Gazaca (Tabriz)

Lake Urmia

Elburz Mountains

Hecatompylos

IRAN

Iconium (Konya)

Melitene (Malatya)

Tomisa

Spring of 547

Caicasta (Takht-e Soleyman)

PARTHIA

Artakoana (Ghoriyan)

CARIA

Kritalla   Tyana

CILICIA

Amedi (Diyarbakir)

Sabiresu

Halicarnassus (Bodrum)

Cilician Gates

Taurus Mountains

Amanian Gates

Harran

Gozan

Nineveh

Arbela (Arbil)

Sikayauvati (Ziwiye)

Sandrake
Karkuk

With Media secured, Cyrus turned his attention to the east, and Hyrcania along with Parthia were brought under his rule.

Tarsus   Syrian Gates

NORTHERN CYPRUS

Salamis

Aleppo

Carchemish

Ashur (Ash Sharqat)

ZAGROS   MEDIA

Asadabad Pass

Ecbatana (Hamadan)

Damghan

Sialk (Kashan)

Esfahan

While Cyrus's armies continued their assault on various Greek cities in Anatolia that had allied with the Lydians, Cyrus returned to Ecbatana to prepare for his campaigns against Babylonia.

Aegean Sea

The Great Sea (Mediterranean Sea)

CYPRUS

Hamath

SYRIA

Qadesh
Riblah

LEBANON

Tadmur   Mari

Merturna

Spring of 547

▲ Mt. Alvand 3,571 m 11,716 ft

Bagastana (Bisotun, Behistun)

Kampanda (Kermanshah)

Astyages, the king of Media, made an attempt to capture Ashan. However, most of the Median army defected to Cyrus, and in 550 B.C.E. he defeated Astyages. With the fall of Ecbatana, Media became part of the Persian realm.

Nehemiah, cupbearer to King Artaxerxes of Persia and a Jewish exile, was appointed governor of Judah. He rebuilt the Temple and Jerusalem's city walls. (Nehemiah 5:14)

Sidon
Tyre

Damascus

ISRAEL

Joppa (Tel Aviv-Yafo)

Shechem

Jerusalem

SYRIAN DESERT

Cunaxa

Babylon

Opis

Sippar

Nippur

Autumn of 539

BABYLONIA

Tigris

Susa (Shush)

Der

Arderikka (Masjed Soleyman)

Ysatis (Yazd)

SAGARTIA

KARMANIA

Once coronated king of Parsa, Cyrus established Pasargadae as his capital. After his death, his body was brought there, and a tomb was prepared. The city remained the Persian capital until Darius I established Persepolis.

Sais

GAZA STRIP   WEST BANK

Gaza

JORDAN

Cyrus allowed the Hebrew exiles to return to their homeland and rebuild the Temple. This ended their captivity from 587 B.C.E., when Nebuchadnezzar destroyed Jerusalem and took the survivors into captivity in Babylon. (Ezra 1:2-4)

LOWER EGYPT   Pelusium

Memphis

IRAQ

Erech

Ur

SUMER

Euphrates

ELAM

Persian Gates

Ashan

Persepolis   Tirazis

(Shiraz)

Pasargadae

Taoke (Borazjan)

PARSA (PERSIA)

Perge

Tarava (Tarom)

Kurmanu

Bampur

Cyrus did not invade Egypt, even though it would have been a tempting target. His successor, Cambyses II, would add Egypt to the Persian Empire.

The defeat of Nabonidus and Belshazzar fulfilled the warning of the handwriting on the wall. (Daniel 5)

KUWAIT

SAUDI ARABIA

Harmozia

UPPER EGYPT

Thebes

EGYPT

CONQUEST OF BABYLONIA
From Ecbatana, Cyrus advanced toward Babylonia in 539 B.C.E. A pitched battle ensued between the Babylonian forces of Nabonidus and the combined forces of Cyrus and his allies at the city of Opis. Cyrus's decisive victory allowed the capture of the cities of Nippur and Babylon with ease. What had been under Babylonian rule was now incorporated into the domain of Persia.

BAHRAIN

QATAR

Persian Gulf

UNITED ARAB EMIRATES

OMAN

Red Sea

NUBIA

THE EMPIRE OF CYRUS THE GREAT

∘ Royal residence
⊙ Vassal capital
• Historic city
⚙ Siege
✕ Major battle
═ Persian royal road
┄ Other important road
→ Campaign route of Cyrus through Anatolia
→ Campaign route of Cyrus through Babylonia
→ Route of Hebrew return under Ezra and Nehemiah
→ Route of Hebrew return under Sheshbazzar and Zerubbabel
▨ Extent of Cyrus the Great's empire at the time of his death, 530 B.C.E.

GOVERNING THE EMPIRE
Cyrus the Great (or Cyrus II) initiated a new system of governing conquered territories. By adopting a policy of tolerance instead of repression, he permitted those he ruled to maintain their cultural identity and religion. Cyrus even allowed the rulers he conquered to retain their status, so long as they accepted Persian rule over them. To compel obedience from subject regions, he did not hesitate to crush rulers who resisted, making them an example to the whole empire.

YEMEN

SUDAN

0 mi ___ 400
0 km ___ 400

Present-day country boundaries are shown.

ERITREA

Nile

Athbara

OMAN

Erythrean Sea (Arabian Sea)

Yehud, part of the fifth Persian satrapy known as 'Abar nahara ("Beyond the [Euphrates] River") and ruled by a governor called Sheshbazzar. Quite possibly, this new viceroy was a descendant of King Jehoiachin and therefore a member of the house of David. Sheshbazzar's actual domain, however, was much smaller than the former kingdom of Judah. Yehud was now bordered to the north by the tribal boundary just north of Bethel, to the east by the Jordan River (including Jericho), and to the south by a frontier that ran well short of Hebron, depriving the sub-province of Israel's ancient patriarchal city. It was also a very poor province, which explains why the new Temple had barely risen above its foundations some 20 years after the first return of exiles.

This provoked the ire of the Prophet Haggai, whose book probably originated during the early years of the reign of the new Persian king, Darius I. Pointing to poor harvests and drought as signs of the Lord's wrath, the prophet asked, "Is it a time for you yourselves to live in your paneled houses, while this house lies in ruins?" (Haggai 1:4). Under the pressure of these admonitions, the Temple was

completed at last. In 515 or 516 B.C.E., the people of Yehud were able to dedicate the new Temple in Jerusalem. What's more, under the leadership of Ezra and Nehemiah, Yehud was now, for all practical purposes, governed by the religious elite of a priesthood. The ancient ideal of a Davidic monarchy, ruled by a messiah, had been replaced by that of a Jewish theocracy whose authority was

A MODERN IMPRESSION of the palace of Susa, built by the Achaemenid Dynasty of Persia to demonstrate its might

THE GOLD OF THE ACHAEMENIDS

To demonstrate its might, the Achaemenid Dynasty of Persia built palaces at Pasargadae, Persepolis, and Susa. Each of these sites has yielded archaeological remains in abundance, including life-size bas-relief sculptures that deliberately aimed to surpass their Assyrian predecessors. But their signature art was undoubtedly their virtuosity with precious metals, particularly the manufacture of beautifully detailed gold and silver vessels. A favorite motif was a drinking cup fashioned in the shape of an animal—such as the mythological winged lion, the symbol of Achaemenid rule (at right). The famous Oxus treasure is a collection of 170 objects from the fifth and fourth centuries B.C.E.

> ## "WHAT A MAN DOES OR PERFORMS, ACCORDING TO HIS ABILITY, BY THAT I BECOME SATISFIED WITH HIM."
>
> **KING DARIUS I OF PERSIA**

rooted in the sacrificial system of the newly restored Temple. This idea—that the cult system organized around the Temple had absorbed and replaced the need for a Jewish political identity—would become the dominant theme of the Second Temple period (515 B.C.E.–70 C.E.).

The Achaemenid Period

The Persian or Achaemenid period introduced a number of innovations, including a network of royal roads, a central postal system, a national army (equipped with portable pontoon bridges), and a new degree of religious tolerance and diversity. The new empire reached its peak under King Darius I, who built a new capital in Persepolis (today's Farz Province of Iran), as well as a stupendous new palace in Susa (the biblical Sushan),

where the stories of Daniel and Esther are set.

Still, Darius faced a number of revolts in virtually every corner of his empire. Worse, the growing tensions between Persia and Greece over the Persian occupation of the northern Aegean led to an all-out war, which ended in a Persian defeat at the famous Battle of Marathon in 490 B.C.E. This did not settle the argument, however. The clash between the two leading civilizations of their time continued until 466 B.C.E., when the Athenian-led Delian League liberated its Ionian colonies (on today's Turkish coast) from Persian rule. After that, hostilities petered out as the Greek city-states and Persia, exhausted by their military adventures, settled into an uneasy coexistence. Fortunately, this did not prevent an active cultural and commercial exchange, as we will see shortly.

POTTERY OF THE IRON AGE

Stylistically, pottery production in the Fertile Crescent was long influenced by the superb kilns of Egypt. Particularly during the New Kingdom, Egyptian craftsmen produced beautifully styled ceramic vessels (at left), painted in elaborate polychrome patterns, which military governors brought with them as they took up their posts in towns throughout the Egyptian Empire. As Egypt's economic and political influence declined, the culture of Mycenae, located on the mainland of Greece, became more prominent. This is when the slender, double-handled clay amphora made its appearance as a container for precious substances, such as olive oil and wine, during long seaborne voyages. The prominent role of Mycenae in this Mediterranean commerce is attested by numerous pottery samples found in Canaan, easily identifiable by their red and black geometric style.

THE STAIRS OF THE TRIPYLON, or Triple Gate, in the palace of Persepolis, led to the Council Hall.

THE APADANA is a large hypostyle hall of open verandas at the palace of Persepolis, which may have served as King Darius's audience chamber.

Among others, this era would see one of the most important inventions of the ancient world: the struck coin. Exactly who first developed the idea of minted currency is a matter of debate, though most historians agree it occurred first in Lydia (today's northwestern Turkey) during the sixth century B.C.E., possibly during the reign of King Alyattes. The first coins were struck using electrum (an alloy of silver, gold, and copper) with little more than a symbol, such as an animal, as ornamentation. From there the practice moved to the Persian interior, where it produced the gold daric and the subsequent adoption of coins throughout the empire. Originally called the Babylonian shekel, the daric was a gold coin of 8.4 grams. It replaced actual weights, such as the mina weighing two pounds, four ounces, which had previously served as currency. The

Persian cup with winged lions

words "mene," "tekel," and "parsin," which Daniel deciphered on the wall of Belshazzar's banqueting hall, are units of measure equivalent to the mina, shekel, and half-mina (Daniel 5:25).

In the fifth century, the Athenian drachma became the coin of choice throughout the Mediterranean world, usually bearing the image of an owl, symbol of the city's patron, Athena. Many cities followed suit by issuing the silver tetradrachm (four drachmas) coin or the even larger decadrachm (10 drachmas). From the third century onward, in the wake of Alexander's conquest, coins were struck with the likeness of the local ruler, which has been a boon for archaeologists in trying to date a particular layer in excavations. This custom would become the norm during the 400-year history of the Roman Empire, and a practice that continues into modern times. ∎

THUS SPAKE ZARATHUSTRA

When Cyrus the Great conquered the kingdom of the Medes, he encountered temples (at right) dedicated to a legendary priest named Zarathustra (Zoroaster). Like Moses before him, Zarathustra preached that there was but one God—a Lord of Heaven and Light named Ahura Mazda, or "Wise Lord"—and that life on Earth is essentially a struggle between good and evil. To please the Wise Lord, Zoroaster said, one must be honest, ethical, and compassionate; to defy such virtues is to cater to the Devil (Ahriman). Zoroaster also preached that a new savior named Saoshyans would come to raise the dead, preside over a Last Judgment, and herald eternal life. Zarathustra's teachings were compiled in a collection of sayings known as the Avesta, but only one book, known as Vendidad, has survived. Zoroastrianism exerted considerable influence on the new Persian Empire, including Jewish scholars in Babylon and Judea.

CHAPTER 4

THE CLASSICAL AGE

500 B.C.E.–300 C.E.

THE ACROPOLIS with the fifth-century B.C.E. Parthenon, dedicated to Pallas Athena, looms over modern Athens by night.

CONTENTS

BIRTH OF THE CLASSICAL ERA

From the sixth century onward, human civilization reached a new level of sophistication in a variety of fields that improved the quality of life for peoples throughout the world. Amazingly, this process took place not only in Europe but also in China, Africa, and the Middle East. In response, many historians refer to the period between 500 B.C.E. and 500 C.E. as the Classical Age. Within that thousand-year time span, humankind made great strides not only in art, architecture, and science but also in philosophy and political ideas. Even as the power of these nations waned, their cultural influence remained strong. For example, the culture of Greece—known as Hellenism—was perpetuated by the Romans in their ever growing empire across Europe and the Near East. And in China, the Qin Dynasty marked the zenith of the great cultural developments that had preceded it, particularly in Chinese literature, philosophy, the arts, and architecture. During this millennium, much of the world shared a common heritage of language, trade practices, and even a common currency, which would produce the foundation for the civilization of the High Middle Ages in Europe.

Exactly what prompted the rise of the Classical Age, notably in Greece, has been endlessly debated. Some historians point to the precedent of the Cycladic, Minoan, and Mycenaean civilizations in the region. But many of the fruits from these cultures were disrupted by the Greek Dark Ages between 1100 and 800 B.C.E., beginning with the fall of the Mycenaean civilization. During this period, international trade collapsed, monumental building ceased, towns were abandoned, and writing in Linear B all but disappeared. Only by the eighth century was Greek civilization ready to emerge once more, as shown in its foundational epics, Homer's *Iliad* and *Odyssey*.

The Recovery of Ancient Greece

The first signs of economic recovery were signaled by the growing adoption of iron smelting, developed in the Levant and introduced to Greece by traders from Cyprus. Archaeological excavations show that after 900 B.C.E., weapons were increasingly made of iron rather than bronze. By the beginning of the eighth century, grave items interred in cemeteries in Athens, Lefkandi, and Olympia reveal a variety of goods, including quality pottery produced with improved glazing techniques. The presence of luxury goods made of ivory, amber, and gold in these graves clearly shows that international trade was growing once more. Indeed, it was the resumption of trade that prompted the need for a more efficient system of writing so that merchants could document the terms and quantity of goods being exchanged. Much of the trade in the Mediterranean at the time was controlled by Phoenicians, who had developed a unique cargo ship for this purpose. Propelled by either rowers or large sails, the Phoenician galley was a fast ship with a slender hull of one or two levels and a low draft, perfectly suited for either coastal or river traffic. Homer's epic, *The Iliad,* specifically refers to oarsmen-propelled galleys that brought the Greek warriors to the coastline of Troy. It was therefore not surprising that the Greeks adopted the Phoenician alphabet for their writing, as it allowed for the use of vowels in addition to consonants. ■

A TERRA-COTTA WARRIOR from the tomb complex of Emperor Qin Shi Huang of China. This warrior was one of an army of terra-cotta figures found buried in the tomb.

A GREEK RED-FIGURED LEKYTHOS from ca 460 B.C.E. depicts Theseus and Ariadne being woken up by Athena.

THE CLASSICAL AGE OF
GREECE

From the sixth century onward, a new civilization emerged in ancient Greece that would have a strong influence on the rest of the world, not only in Europe and the Near East but also in India and other regions in East Asia.

Before the great flowering of ancient Greece could come about, the Greek city-states still had many political obstacles to overcome. The continuing tension between the traditional aristocracy and the growth of an educated urban class led in 561 B.C.E. to a coup by populist leader Peisistratos and his sons, who established an autocratic regime in Athens. Though ruling as a tyrant, Peisistratos was careful to abide by the laws, and in the words of Greek historian Herodotus, he "administered the State under the established constitution, governing both fairly and well." As a champion of the lower classes, the Hyperakrioi, Peisistratos did everything in his power to curtail the influence of the nobility, restricting their privileges while distributing many of their lands to the poor. The aristocracy, including the nobleman Cleisthenes, responded by appealing to the king of Sparta, Athens's leading rival, for help. The king, Cleomenes I, was happy to oblige; already, his policy had brought most of the Peloponnese into the Spartan sphere of influence. The invitation to intervene in Athens therefore held the tantalizing prospect of bringing all of Greece under Sparta's sway.

True enough, the coup to topple Peisistratos's son Hippias succeeded, but now Athens found itself in danger of becoming one of Sparta's puppet states. In response, Cleisthenes offered his fellow Athenians a radical proposition: abjure any form of single-man rule and instead adopt a form of government where all citizens shared in power. This novel type of self-rule was coined "democracy," based on the Greek words *dêmos* (people) and *krátos* (power)—"people power," in short. Thus, by 508 B.C.E., Athens had become one of the world's first functioning democratic states. Several attempts by Sparta to nip this rebellion in the bud and subjugate Athens to Spartan control failed, opening the way for Athens to experience its Golden Age.

Indeed, in the span of only half a century, Athenians would revolutionize the fields of art, architecture, science, and philosophy and lay a lasting foundation for Western civilization. Much of this development was led by Athenian statesman Pericles, a member of the same Alcmaeonid family that had produced Cleisthenes.

THIS FOURTH-CENTURY B.C.E. bust is believed to represent Greek philosopher Plato.

> "IT WAS THE ATHENIANS . . . WHO, HAVING CHOSEN THAT GREECE SHOULD LIVE AND PRESERVE HER FREEDOM, ROUSED TO BATTLE THE OTHER GREEK STATES."

GREEK HISTORIAN HERODOTUS

But Athens's position was still precarious, given that it faced threats on two fronts: Sparta and the Peloponnese, on the one hand, and the Persian Empire, on the other. During the preceding century, Persia's King Cyrus had conquered most of the Greek cities on Asia Minor, in particular Ionia, thus bringing Persian might to the doorstep of Athens. By the beginning of the fifth century, the deep resentment of the Ionian Greeks against their Persian overlords erupted in a revolt, with active support from Athens. Though this rebellion was suppressed, it had caused great damage to Persian prestige and its continuing political and economic control.

The Greco-Persian Wars

In response, Cyrus's successors decided to launch several punitive campaigns against Greece in an attempt to bring it to heel. The first invasion, instigated in 492 B.C.E. by King Darius I, initially met with spectacular success: The Aegean islands as well as much of Macedon and Thrace were brought under Persian control. But when in 490 B.C.E. the Persian infantry landed in Attica near the town of Marathon, some 26 miles northeast of Athens, the Athenians dealt the superior Persian forces a stunning defeat. As legend has it, a Greek herald named Pheidippides ran straight from Marathon to Athens to bring the happy news to its anxious citizens, which in modern times would inspire the marathon race.

Vowing revenge, Darius's son Xerxes led an even larger invasion force 10 years later. Two major battles, on land at Thermopylae and at sea near Artemisium, ended in a defeat for Athens and its allies of the Delian League. Fortunately, Xerxes failed in his effort to also destroy the allied fleet at the Battle of Salamis, and now the battle lines were drawn: the awesome power of the Persian Empire versus the fractious and brittle alliance of Greek city-states. Recognizing the mortal danger, all of Greece—including Sparta, Athens, Corinth, and Macedon—banded together to defeat the Persian foe. The result was a cataclysmic battle fought near the city of Plataea in Boeotia in 479 B.C.E. After several days of hard fighting, the Greeks defeated a portion of the Persian infantry and then descended on the Persian camp to engage in wholesale slaughter. Capitalizing on their military momentum, the Greek allies destroyed the Persian fleet at Mycale and evicted the

A GREEK SIXTH-CENTURY B.C.E. BAS-RELIEF from Sparta shows figures from Greek mythology.

THE SACRED ISLAND OF DELOS, revered as the birthplace of Apollo, was a major pilgrimage destination well into the second century C.E.

NOTABLE DATES

ca 561 B.C.E.

Peisistratos establishes autocratic regime in Athens

ca 508 B.C.E.

Athens creates a democratic constitution

ca 492 B.C.E.

Persian King Darius I conquers Aegean islands, Macedon, and Thrace

ca 490 B.C.E.

The Greeks defeat the invading Persian army at Marathon

ca 480 B.C.E.

Persian King Xerxes I sacks Athens but is defeated by Greek fleet near Salamis

ca 478 B.C.E.

Athens forms the Delian League as the leading power of Greece

ca 460 B.C.E.

Pericles rules as leader of Athens until 429 B.C.E.

ca 438 B.C.E.

The Parthenon is completed in Athens

ca 428 B.C.E.

Greek philosopher Plato is born

ca 406 B.C.E.

Deaths of Euripides and Sophocles end great era of Greek drama

ca 399 B.C.E.

Socrates dies by drinking hemlock

"THE BATTLE of Thermopylae in 480 B.C.," painted by American artist Stanley Meltzoff in 1963

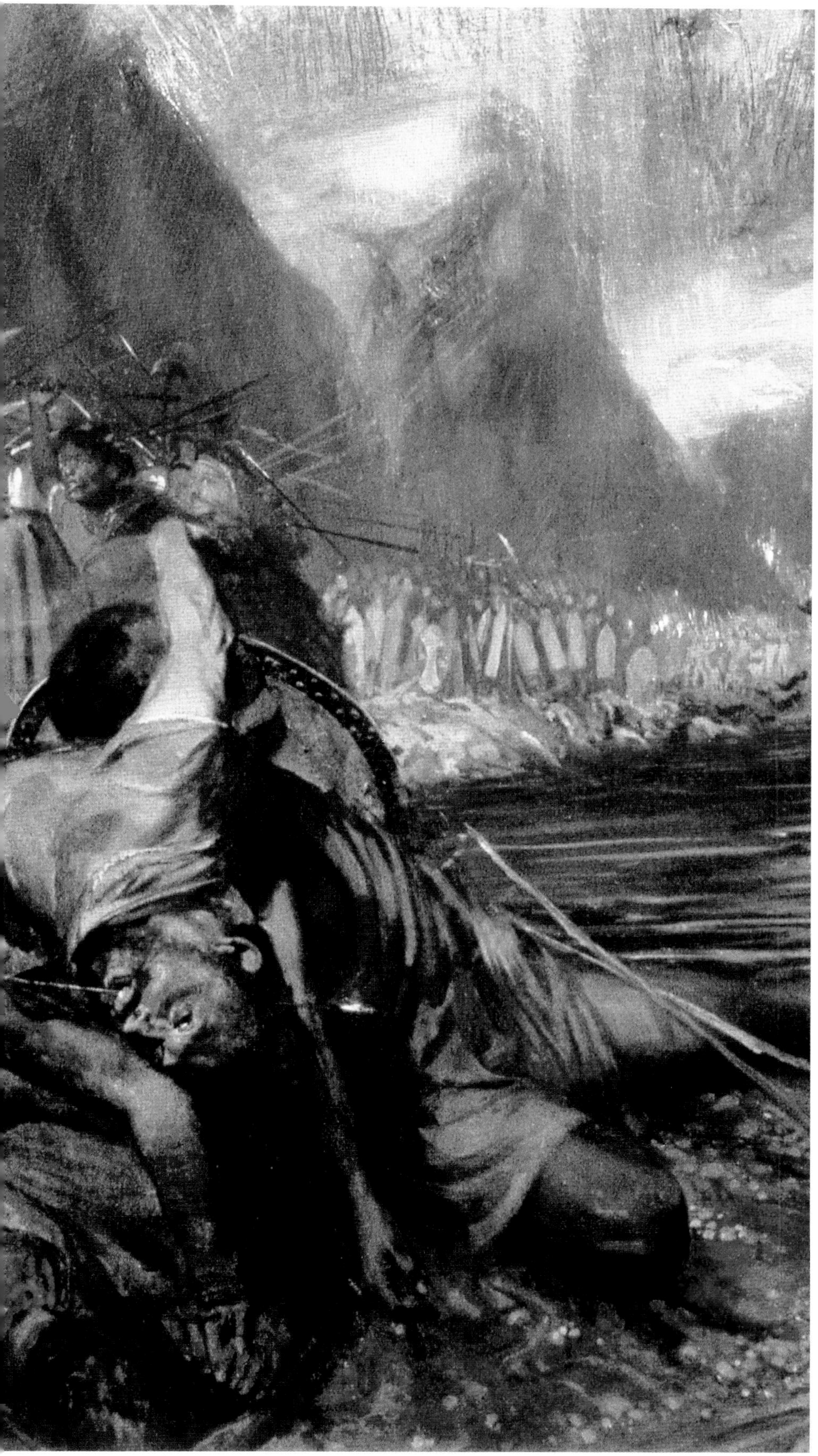

"WE HAVE FORCED EVERY SEA AND LAND TO BE THE HIGHWAY OF OUR DARING, AND EVERYWHERE, WHETHER FOR EVIL OR FOR GOOD, HAVE LEFT IMPERISHABLE MONUMENTS BEHIND US."

PERICLES' FUNERAL ORATION, CA 429 B.C.E.

Persians from Byzantium. Athens now reigned supreme in the region and exploited the moment to form the Delian League—an alliance of all the coastal regions around the Aegean Sea, unified in their opposition against the Persians. Over the next three decades, this league succeeded in driving the Persians from the coastal regions of Asia Minor and Europe altogether.

Originally, the Delian League was based on the sacred island of Delos, where the alliance was established and all members remitted their dues. But in 454 B.C.E. Pericles decided to move the league treasury to Athens, thus establishing the city as the undisputed center of the Greek sphere of influence. Although this inflamed the tensions between Athens and Sparta, the vast tribute now flowing into the city's coffers would help build the greatest monument of Antiquity and the centerpiece of the Golden Age: the Acropolis.

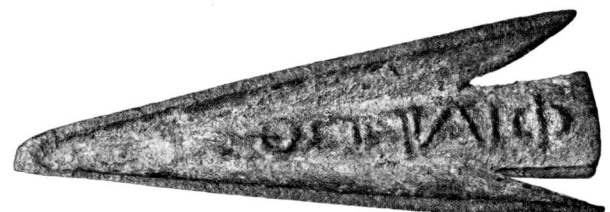

A GREEK BRONZE ARROWHEAD, inscribed with "Philippo," a name possibly related to King Philip II of Macedon, is dated to the first half of the fourth century B.C.E.

THE THOLOS, a lovely circular temple in the sanctuary of Delphi, Greece, was dedicated to Athena, the goddess of wisdom and war.

BELOW: The "Aphrodite of Cnidus" is one of several variations on a sculpture by Greek sculptor Praxiteles from the fourth century B.C.E.

The Golden Age of Athens

Greek life unfolded against the backdrop of a highly developed mythology of many gods and goddesses, though scholars do not agree to what extent this polytheism exerted a direct influence on daily life. Certainly the heroic stories of these immortals and their heroes formed the foundation for Greek identity and were passed from generation to generation, just as these sagas served as an inexhaustible supply of motifs for potters, painters, and sculptors alike. At the head of the Greek pantheon stood Zeus, the supreme god who, though married to Hera, was legendary for his pursuit of young mortal women. Poseidon was the god of the seas and earthquakes, while Helios controlled the sun and Apollo served as the god of music, poetry, and oracles. The lovely Aphrodite governed matters of the heart, while Hades ruled the underworld, a domain known as Hades.

Certain cities and trades adopted gods as their patrons. Thus, Apollo was worshiped at the sanctuary of Delphi, which contained the most famous oracle in Antiquity. Here, petitioners from all over the known world came to pose their questions. These were answered by a medium, a woman sorceress named the Pythia, after she entered into a trance to hear the god's whispers in her heart. Poseidon was the patron of sailors and seafarers, who would make sacrifices in his honor to secure a safe journey. Dionysus was the god of wine, fertility, and theater and the focus of the so-called Dionysian Mysteries, where women could flaunt convention and surrender themselves to religious ecstasy and sensuous pleasure. Since the earliest Dionysian ceremonies took place in a theater, led by a chorus, they would ultimately produce staged drama—and the birth of modern theater.

MONUMENTAL DOORWAYS
attest to the former splendor of
the Tachara Palace of Persepolis,
built by King Darius I of Persia.

THE FIFTH-CENTURY B.C.E. PARTHENON, a temple dedicated to Pallas Athena, is the most outstanding example of the Greek Doric style of architecture.

An equally prominent deity was Pallas Athena, who naturally served as the patron goddess of Athens. Her area of responsibility in the Greek pantheon was wisdom and warfare—an odd combination, perhaps, but one that made perfect sense to Athenians. As in cities elsewhere, Athena had traditionally been venerated in a temple, which in pre-Archaic times had been constructed of wood or mud brick. Such a temple usually consisted of a single-chamber megaron, accessible through a simple vestibule. From the eighth century B.C.E. onward, as the prosperity of the city-states grew, these simple structures gained a more monumental character. Key elements, such as the columns and supporting walls, were now built in stone rather than wood, even though they still bore the shape of their wooden precedent; the hollow grooves on the columns, for example (known as fluting), were still reminiscent of the bark of trees from which the wooden columns had originally been carved.

By the sixth century, the Greek temple was reaching its classic form. It now consisted of a central nave, the naos, which contained the cult statue of the god to which the temple was dedicated. This nave was preceded by a vestibule, the pronaos, screened by an elaborate porch. This facade typically supported a triangular gable facing the pitched roof, the pediment, where sculpture groups illustrated key scenes from mythology. In addition, the columns supporting the entablature were now extended to create a continuous colonnade around the structure, known as the peristyle. Most important, architects searched for the perfect ratio of proportions between length and elevation, as well as individual elements such as base, column, capital, frieze, and pediment. This, some scholars believe, let them to the so-called golden rule in architecture, also known as the rule of Phi: a proportion of 1:1.618.

The most perfect expression of this carefully modulated system is the Parthenon temple on the central mound of Athens known as the Acropolis. Pericles initiated construction of this massive yet elegant temple in 447 B.C.E. when Athens was at the apex of its wealth and power, replacing an

THE BIRTH OF MODERN THEATER

In ancient Greece, Dionysus was the god of wine and fertility, but Dionysian performances also produced our modern theater. Originally, Greek religious plays were performed in open-air theaters (at right) by a chorus of some 50 actors, singing verses in unison. Around 530 B.C.E., an actor named Thespis decided to expand the chorus with himself performing in the role of the principal character. The playwright Aeschylus added a second character, and Sophocles added a third character. As a result, the chorus was moved to the background, and the idea of a plot or "tragedy" emerged, performed on stage by different protagonists.

"WEALTH STAYS WITH US A LITTLE MOMENT,
IF AT ALL; ONLY OUR CHARACTERS ARE STEADFAST,
NOT OUR GOLD."

GREEK TRAGEDIAN EURIPIDES

older temple that had been destroyed during the previous Persian invasion. The name "Parthenon" refers to the presence of living quarters within the temple for young, unmarried women (*parthénes*) who served the goddess.

The temple was designed in the so-called Doric order, with plain round capitals and fluted columns without a base. The columns did not taper to the top in a straight line but instead revealed a slight swelling in the center, known as entasis, to suggest the heavy weight they were supporting. These and other refinements have prompted some art historians to refer to the Parthenon as a monumental sculpture rather than a building. Though a large statue of Pallas Athena was installed in the inner sanctum, modern research has revealed that the temple served as the central treasury of the Delian League rather than as a place of worship.

The Parthenon has served ever since as the seminal work of Doric architecture, but in subsequent decades, the Greek temple paradigm was enhanced with a number of refinements. In response to the robust, masculine Doric order native to western Greece, the east—notably the Ionic coast of Asia Minor—produced a more feminine order, known as Ionic. The columns became more refined, carved with slender fluting, and with a capital adorned with scrolls or volutes. At the

A GREEK *KOUROS,* or youth, in the Archaic style shows how quickly Greek artists mastered the art of realism between the sixth and fifth centuries B.C.E., as evidenced by the caryatid maidens at right.

same time, the columns were placed on a rounded base, with two convex moldings. A third and even more ornate architectural style, known as the Corinthian order, originated in the fourth century, whereby the capital was raised and decorated with two rows of acanthus leaves, culminating in four scrolls. All three orders—Doric, Ionic, and Corinthian—were adopted by Roman architects in later centuries.

Greek Sculpture and Pottery

At the same time that Greek architects were defining the principles of classical architecture, Greek sculptors were revolutionizing the way that the human form could be shaped in marble. Early Greek sculptures from the Archaic period were cast in the same stiff, formulaic poses that characterized Egyptian sculpture. Indeed, the stylized representation of young men, known as *kouroi*, betrays the influence of Egyptian statues. But as the fifth century progressed, Greek sculptors such as Phidias, Praxiteles, and Lysippos embarked on an unprecedented effort to articulate the human form—including such details as muscle, sinews, and bone—in marble. The culmination of this effort is the group of sculptures that once adorned the east pediment of the Parthenon. These groups represent various deities as they witness the birth of Athena from the head of Zeus. In these figures, all sense of rigidity has disappeared; for the first time, the human body is reproduced with startling realism, down to the detail of the linen chiton, the clingy garment that the

THE PORCH of the Erechtheion temple in Athens contains the famous columns in the shape of robed maidens, known as caryatids, which would be replicated for many centuries to come.

A COLOSSAL HEAD OF ZEUS marks the funerary complex or Hierothesion of King Antiochus I at the sanctuary of Nemrut Dagi in southeastern Turkey.

goddesses wore. Long credited to the sculptor Phidias, these exceptional works of art were taken from the Parthenon in the early 19th century on orders of Thomas Bruce, the Earl of Elgin. Known since as the Elgin Marbles, the group is exhibited in the British Museum in London, though the Greek government continues to strenuously petition various world bodies for their return. The sheer realism and plasticity of Greek sculpture would not be matched until the Italian High Renaissance and the art of Michelangelo Buonarroti.

The same Greek focus on beauty and grace would also produce the loveliest forms of pottery in human history. From the eighth century onward, both Athens and Corinth began to dominate the international market for ornamental pottery with a broad repertoire of forms, including the amphora and pithos, used as storage vessels; the krater for mixing water and wine; the kylix and kantharos used as drinking cups; and the slender lekythos and alabastron, designed to store delicate perfumes and ointments. Vessels were also produced as grave markers and to receive funerary offerings, and other beautifully painted vases served as trophies at sport competitions, a custom that continues to this day.

What made Greek pottery so exceptional was not only the artistry of the form but also the decoration. During the Archaic period, vases were painted in black paint on the ochre-colored background typical of fired clay. Artists eventually realized that it is difficult to realistically depict human figures that way because black does not allow for more than mere silhouettes. The solution, which originated in the late sixth century, was to do the reverse: paint the background black and draw the figures in delicate outlines against the ochre base. This technique, known as the red-figured style (compared to the earlier black-figured style), set the trend of ancient pottery for centuries to come. By the fourth century, Greek red-figured vases and drinking cups had become the fashion on affluent

tables throughout the Mediterranean, including the Near East and Persia.

Greek Philosophy and Science

The stabilization of Greek society during the Golden Age, in both an economic and political sense, also gave a new impetus to scholarship, particularly in the fields of philosophy, mathematics, geometry, medicine, ethics, and rhetoric. Scholars have often debated what prompted this explosion of intellectual activity across so many disciplines in so short a time frame. Some believe that these sages must have been in contact with the scientific traditions of the Near East, particularly in geometry, astronomy, and physics. Others argue that the Greeks deserve the full credit for developing this next level of human reason. Physics, for example, was the focus of the School of Miletus, founded by Thales of Miletus, whom Aristotle once called the "first philosopher." According to ancient reports, Thales could predict a solar eclipse and even taught the Egyptians how to measure the height of their pyramids. Pythagoras developed Greek cosmology and posited the idea that everything in nature was governed by certain mathematical principles so as to achieve universal harmony. By contrast, Heraclitus argued that nature functions through the unity of opposites in both a physical and moral sense.

"THE DEATH OF SOCRATES" was painted by French artist Jacques-Louis David in 1787.

ITALIAN RENAISSANCE artist Raphael placed Aristotle (modeled after Leonardo da Vinci) and Plato in the center of his 1511 fresco "The School of Athens" in the Vatican in Rome.

Hippocrates founded a school of medicine and sought to discover the source of many illnesses, which in Antiquity were often considered the result of either sinful living or evil spirits. The Hippocratic Oath, which originated between the fifth and third centuries B.C.E., is still taken by physicians today as a pledge to practice at the highest possible ethical standard.

Perhaps the most prominent philosopher was Socrates, who laid the foundation for Western ethics, including ideas about how society should function and citizens should behave toward one another. But his stinging critique of the Athenian government made him, in the words of his pupil Plato, a "gadfly" of the state. As a result, Socrates was forced to either repudiate his teachings or drink poison hemlock; he chose the latter. Typically, his last words were to remind his friend Crito to settle a debt (a rooster) to his friend Asclepius.

For modern scholars, the challenge of understanding Socratic ideas is that none of his writings have survived; all that we know about him is derived from secondary sources, including Plato's *Apology.* That may also explain why Plato would become the most influential Greek philosopher for many centuries to come. Among others, he founded the Academy, the first institution of higher learning in the Western world, grounded in his faith in human reason to overcome all challenges. At the same time, Plato advocated the idea that all human beings carry within themselves a spark of the divine, which would inspire philosophers and theologians from Porphyry to St. Augustine, and produce the Neoplatonic school during the Renaissance. So profound was the impact of Greece's imagination that the works of its artists, architects, philosophers, and mathematicians continued to reverberate throughout the ancient world for centuries. ∎

THE ORACLE OF DELPHI

The Oracle of Delphi was one of Antiquity's oldest oracles. According to a Greek myth, it was founded by Apollo after he slew the snake Python, guardian of the goddess Gaia. From the eighth century B.C.E. onward, the site began to function as an oracle, allowing privileged pilgrims to solicit the god's wisdom on a variety of matters. The heart of the Delphi sanctuary was a massive temple dedicated to Apollo, towering high over many lovely treasuries that the Greek city-states had built here in honor of the god. On special days in the year, the temple became an oracle when a special medium (at right), called the Pythia, received a select group of visitors with her attendant priests. Under influence from mysterious fumes, the Pythia's body would begin to writhe and convulse while she uttered strange sounds and cries. It was therefore left up to the priests to interpret these utterances and produce a response, which gave them tremendous power—particularly if the question pertained to important political matters.

A GILDED BRONZE STATUE, now in the National Museum in Khartoum, Sudan, is believed to represent an unidentified king of Kush.

THE CLASSICAL AGE OF
AFRICA

Until now, most of the leading civilizations had unfolded in Europe and the Near East. But from the eighth century B.C.E. onward, Africa began to play a greater role as well, particularly with the emerging power of the kingdoms of Nubia and Carthage.

Of all the emerging kingdoms in Africa, the Kushite kingdom of Nubia began to challenge the hegemony of Egypt and eventually overtake it. As we saw, Nubia (originally known as Medjay in ancient Egyptian hieroglyphics) had long been dominated by ancient Egypt in terms of its culture, language, and even the practice of building pyramids as funerary monuments. There was extensive trade between the two realms, and many Egyptians and Nubians intermarried. Some historians believe that several pharaohs of the 12th Dynasty were of Nubian origin. But Egypt had inexorably entered a period of decline; during the 21st Dynasty, it was Pharaoh, in this case King Siamun, who married his daughter to King Solomon by way of securing a treaty, rather than the other way around. Egypt experienced one last gasp at glory under King Shoshenq I of the 22nd Dynasty, who, according to the Bible, deployed "twelve hundred chariots and sixty thousand cavalry" to invade both Judah and Israel around 925 B.C.E. But many of the monuments that Shoshenq built to document his reign remained unfinished, which suggests that the king must have died shortly after this invasion. At that time, the 22nd Dynasty was based in the city of Tanis, in the northeastern Nile Delta, using "spolia"—sculptures as well as masonry—taken from Pi-Ramesses, the city begun by the 19th Dynasty under Ramses II. But after the death of the last king of the 22nd Dynasty, Osorkon V, the unified kingdom started to disintegrate. Trade had suffered as a result of the collapse of Mycenaean and Assyrian power, and various factions began to vie for the throne. The result was civil war. During the 23rd Dynasty (ca 830–715 B.C.E.), various "kings" established themselves at the head of city-states in Tanis, Leontopolis, Thebes, and Hermopolis.

The Kushite Kingdom

The Nubians, who had long chafed under their role as Egypt's vassal, saw their opportunity and seized it with both hands. During the eighth century B.C.E., they established the independent kingdom of Kush with a capital in the city of Napata (near today's Karima, Sudan). Fifty years later, the Kushites attacked their erstwhile overlord and penetrated deep into Egypt,

A NUBIAN FIGURE made of clay was probably used as an object of fertility worship.

> "EGYPTIANS DO EVERYTHING IN WAYS THAT ARE OPPOSITE TO OTHERS . . . AMONG THEM THE WOMEN FREQUENT THE MARKET AND CARRY ON TRADE, WHILE THE MEN REMAIN AT HOME AND WEAVE."
>
> **GREEK HISTORIAN HERODOTUS**

going as far as Thebes. Here they remained for 20 years while King Piye gathered his forces and moved northward, defeating the remaining Egyptian rulers in Sais, Leontopolis, and Tanis. Egypt, for all intents and purposes, had now become a Nubian kingdom, with Piye establishing the 25th Dynasty. Ironically, this conquest restored Egypt as a unified nation, with the same territorial reach it had once enjoyed under the aggressive kings of the New Kingdom—albeit under Nubian rule. Just like the Hyksos kings of the Second Intermediate

Gold bracelet from Shoshenq II

Period, the Nubian kings quickly adopted the lifestyle and glamour of the Egyptian court, building temples and palaces along the Nile in ancient places such as Memphis, Kawa, and Karnak. They also developed their own script, Meroitic, inspired by Egyptian hieroglyphics, and even revived the lost art of building pyramids.

But when the Nubian pharaohs tried to extend their power into the Near East, they quickly ran afoul of the Assyrian colossus, which then straddled the Levant from Judah to the Persian Gulf. After Nubian king Shabaka fomented a rebellion against Assyria in the Israelite city of Ashdod, King Sargon II struck back and defeated the Nubian forces. King Taharqa tried again to stem the Assyrian tide, even aiding King Hezekiah of Judah during Sennacherib's siege of Jerusalem, but the Assyrian might was too strong and the Nubians were pushed back to Egypt.

Sennacherib's successor, King Esarhaddon, decided it was time to eliminate Egypt as a rival once and for all. In 671 B.C.E., he invaded Egypt with a large force. Taharqa and his court had little choice but to flee southeast to their Nubian homeland, some 300 miles away. There they built a new capital, Meroë, on the eastern banks of the Nile, close to today's Shendi in Sudan.

Astonishingly, this defeat turned out to be a blessing: It allowed the Nubians to create a kingdom that no longer needed to imitate Egyptian culture but could develop an indigenous

A GNOME-LIKE STATUE depicts the Egyptian god Bes, the protector of mothers and households.

THIS IS ONE of roughly 100 pyramids of the necropolis of Meroë, capital of the Kingdom of Kush, built from the third century B.C.E. onward.

NOTABLE DATES

A GUARDIAN illuminates one of the many hieroglyphics on a wall from the tomb of a Nubian king.

"GOD HAS GIVEN TO MAN
NO SHARPER SPUR
TO VICTORY THAN
CONTEMPT OF DEATH."

ROMAN HISTORIAN LIVY,
WRITING ABOUT HANNIBAL

civilization on its own terms. Blessed by the nearby presence of gold, iron, and copper mines, the new Kushite Kingdom quickly became a central nexus of trade throughout the region, thus establishing one of the first important kingdoms of Central Africa. Egyptian gods were discarded in favor of native Nubian deities, and an indigenous architectural style emerged, particularly in the royal cemetery of Meroë. Here, archaeologists have discovered the remains of no fewer than 200 pyramids. Meroë, said fifth-century Greek historian Herodotus, was "a great city" and "the mother city of all other Ethiopians." And so it would remain until Meroë's clash with Roman forces under Augustus, which remarkably ended in a peace treaty of 22 B.C.E.

Carthage in North Africa

Meanwhile, another city was making its influence felt: Carthage, located near today's Tunis on the coast of North Africa, which was founded as a colony of Phoenician traders in 814 B.C.E. In 750 B.C.E. the city had severed its ties with the Phoenician homeland and quickly established itself as a growing power in the Mediterranean. Later legends, repeated in Rome's foundational epic of the *Aeneid* by the poet Virgil, claimed that the city was founded by a beautiful queen named Dido, who fell in love with the *Aeneid*'s hero, Aeneas.

A SCULPTURE of a recumbent lion clutching a head reveals the quality of Nubian art.

"I HAVE COME NOT TO MAKE WAR ON THE ITALIANS,
BUT TO AID THE ITALIANS AGAINST ROME."

CARTHAGINIAN GENERAL HANNIBAL

Released of its colonial bonds, Carthage soon became the most strategic trading port between the Mediterranean and the African interior. Buoyed by its wealth, it gradually extended its territorial reach until it became the center of a Punic empire (based on the Latin word *Punici,* or "Phoenicians"), stretching across North Africa to Sicily and even Spain. As the city of Carthage grew, its port was extended to two large, ultramodern harbors, protected by massive walls running 23 miles in length. The harbor became the base for the largest navy of its time, a fleet of 220 warships, which soon dominated much of the seaborne traffic in the Mediterranean. This was bound to bring Carthage

Phoenician head, second century B.C.E.

into conflict with Greece and later with an upstart republic called Rome. For many years, the stoic Roman orator Cato the Elder was heard to mutter in the Roman Senate, *Carthago delenda est,* "Carthage must be destroyed."

This was easier said than done. During much of the third century B.C.E., Rome and Carthage had been locked into three devastating Punic Wars. During the second conflict, between 218 and 210 B.C.E., Carthage's commander, Hannibal, had launched his famous invasion of Rome with an army that could field no fewer than 37 elephants. The Roman forces suffered a devastating defeat at Cannae, but Hannibal never succeeded in capturing the city of Rome itself. Finally,

THE INTRODUCTION OF CAMELS

The thriving markets of Africa and the Near East forged paths to lands beyond, including the Chinese Empire. The Spice Route through Persia, for example, carried Chinese bolts of silk and finished silk garments, as well as elephant tusks, amber, pearls, and spices from India, but most of these goods were carried on donkeys. Archaeological evidence has shown that camels did not become widespread until the late eighth and early seventh centuries B.C.E. The introduction of camels was a major innovation, because their splayed hooves enabled them to trod over sand, including the African Sahara, and their humps could store up to 25 gallons of water, good for two to three weeks of travel. A typical caravan of the Roman Imperial period would be composed of some 100 camels, each laden with about 500 pounds of cargo and capable of traveling 20 to 30 miles a day (at right).

THE REMAINS OF CARTHAGE
near today's Tunis, once the most
powerful city in North Africa
before its fall to Rome

WHEN EXCAVATORS opened these ancient Phoenician jars, they found the remains of human sacrifices.

in 146 B.C.E. Cato got his wish: Carthage was destroyed in a huge massacre that reportedly claimed the lives of 200,000 inhabitants.

Surprisingly, the city bounced back under Roman rule and rapidly became a leading center of trade once more. Some historians believe that Carthage was the largest city in the preindustrial era, with a population of half a million inhabitants or more. A series of books written by the Punic General Mago around 300 B.C.E. describes Carthage's agricultural bounty, with acres of orchards that yielded olives, pomegranates, figs, dates, and almonds, in addition to grapes that were fermented into a form of sherry. Amphorae with Punic markings containing olive oil or wine have been found all over the Mediterranean. Later, Carthage would become an important center of early Christianity as well. The city was the birthplace of church fathers such as Tertullian and Lactantius, as well as the residence of theologian Augustine of Hippo. From 251 C.E. onward, the city would host a number of important church synods, or councils, that, among matters, confirmed the biblical canon for the Latin Church. ∎

AN ARTIST'S IMPRESSION of the port of Carthage around the third century B.C.E., when it ranked as the leading trading hub in the Mediterranean

SOME OF the original pigments are still visible on this terra-cotta statue from the tomb of Emperor Qin Shi Huang of China.

THE CLASSICAL AGE OF
CHINA

In the third century B.C.E., the Qin Dynasty was able to once more unify the disparate states of China by establishing a strong centralized government. This would form the basis for China's first Golden Age under the Han Dynasty, which would rule for more than 400 years.

Could it be an accident that China entered its Classical Age at around the same time that Greek culture dominated the West? The putative links between China and Europe during the late Zhou and Qin Dynasties have been endlessly debated, perhaps because some modern historians are charmed by the idea that the world of Confucius could somehow be in contact with the world of Socrates. But most scholars—including Chinese historians—believe that China in this period continued to live in splendid isolation until the Silk Road of the second century C.E. enabled the first caravans to traverse the 5,000-mile distance.

After the split of the Zhou kingdom in 453 B.C.E., China was ruled by several different states during what is known as Zhànguó Shídài, the Warring States period (ca 453–221 B.C.E.). In the final phase of this era, Ying Zheng, head of the Qin kingdom, launched a series of campaigns to expand its territory to the east. In short order, the states of Han, Zhao, Yan, Wei, and Chu succumbed to Qin might, until the last power, the kingdom of Qi on the Yellow Sea, was conquered in 221 B.C.E. As a result, China was once more unified, though this time as a functioning political entity, a true empire. Cognizant of that historic fact, Zheng declared himself Qin Shi Huang, "First Emperor of Qin." Some historians believe that *Qin* may in fact be the root of the Western name of China, transmitted via Indo-Aryan as *Sina* and subsequently as *Thinai* in Greek.

Though the Qin Dynasty ruled for only 15 years, making it the shortest major dynasty in Chinese history, its impact was profound. Its first challenge was to severely curtail the power of the feudal aristocracy and centralize administrative control in its capital of Xianyang. To do so, it launched a number of ambitious public works projects that employed thousands of peasants—not unlike the way modern China has moved from Third World to First World status by virtue of lavish urban and infrastructure projects. One of these Qin initiatives was a plan to create an interlocking system of defensive walls along its northern border, which eventually produced the Great Wall of China. Work was also begun on a national road network and an extension of existing canals.

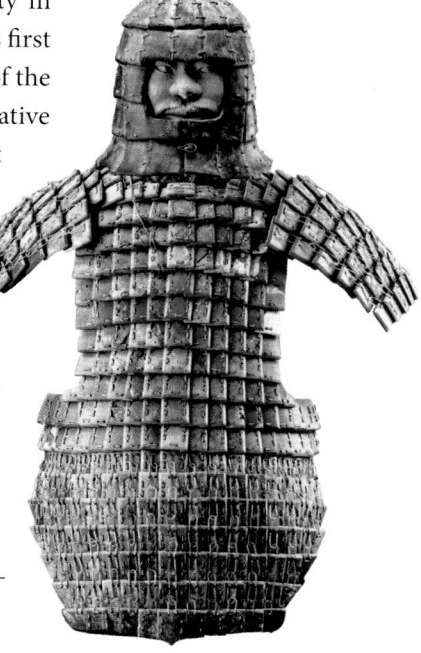

THIS MODEL OF A SOLDIER wearing an armor of stone, woven with copper wire, was found near the tomb of Qin Shi Huang's terracotta army.

> "NOW THAT MY MIGHT RULES ALL WITHIN THE SEAS . . .
> WHERE WILL I FIND BRAVE MEN TO GUARD THE
> FOUR CORNERS OF MY LAND?"
>
> **EMPEROR GAOZU, HAN DYNASTY**

The Qin administration may have taken its cue from the Persian Empire by introducing many innovations to streamline its economy, such as a standard system of currency, weights, and measures—including such details as the standard length of chariot axles. It also moved to standardize the characters of the Chinese alphabet, adopting a more stylized "lesser-seal" calligraphy that would remain largely intact as bold-form writing until modern times. At the same time, the military in the former states was raised to Qin standards, notably in the use of cavalry, the short sword, and the crossbow. Virtually all of these initiatives would be adopted and retained by subsequent dynasties, so the influence of the Qin era is far greater than its short life span would suggest. In particular, the central administrative system of the Qin Dynasty would remain in operation for many centuries, not unlike the way that the imperial state forged by Augustus would rule Europe for hundreds of years.

One would think that the revolutionary changes brought by Qin Shi Huang would have made him a revered figure, but the opposite is true. Folk songs from this period suggest considerable public resentment against the totalitarian nature of the new government, including its decision to shut down schools of philosophy and the wholesale burning of books except for those that supported government policy. Many workers complained about the horrific conditions under which they toiled on the Great Wall and other construction projects. At least three attempts were made to assassinate the emperor, which explains why he became increasingly obsessed with death and the afterlife—even ordering the creation of a terracotta army of about 8,000 warriors and cavalry to guard his future tomb.

In 210 B.C.E., word reached Qin Shi Huang that a secret elixir had been developed by Taoist sages that could confer the immortality that he so desperately sought. Unfortunately, the precious liquid was kept in a secure place on a remote island in the east and guarded by a fearsome sea monster. Undeterred, the emperor set out to find the secret potion, but died along the way. The news was kept secret until Prime Minister Li Si could safeguard the accession of one of the emperor's weaker sons, Huhai, whom he thought he could control. Instead, Huhai—now ruling under the name Qin Er Shi or "Second Generation of the Qin"—embarked on a

A MODERN CHINESE BRONZE STATUE depicts Qin Shi Huang, who in 221 B.C.E. unified the Chinese Empire.

THE INFLUENCE of philosopher and statesman Confucius would stretch across the two millennia of Chinese history and endures even today.

NOTABLE DATES

ca 500 B.C.E.

Legendary foundation of Japanese Yamato monarchy

ca 475 B.C.E.

Zhou kingdom splits during Warring States period

ca 221 B.C.E.

Ying Zheng, king of Qin, unifies China as an empire

ca 218 B.C.E.

Qin Shi Huang begins Great Wall of China

ca 210 B.C.E.

Qin Shi Huang dies while in search of elixir of youth

ca 206 B.C.E.

Liu Bang (Gaozu) establishes Han Dynasty in China

ca 150 B.C.E.

Development of junk ships enables Chinese exploration by sea

ca 119 B.C.E.

Han Dynasty adopts standard wuzhu coin

ca 82 B.C.E.

Chinese *Book of Han* identifies Japan as realm of 100 kingdoms

ca 65 C.E.

Buddhism begins to penetrate China from India

110 C.E.

Oldest known use of paper for writing in China

132 C.E.

Chinese astronomer Zhang Heng develops planetarium

A SYSTEM OF DEFENSIVE WALLS that ultimately produced the Great Wall of China was consolidated in 220 B.C.E. by Emperor Qin Shi Huang.

wildly extravagant scheme of public works, including the insane order to have the city walls covered with lacquer. This soon required a major increase in taxes, which prompted the old feudal lords to revolt. Desperate to maintain their control of the empire, Qin mandarins ordered Li Si's execution while forcing the emperor to commit suicide and then foisted his nephew on the throne. It was to no avail, for revolts now roiled the nation. In 206 B.C.E. the Qin capital of Xianyang was destroyed by Xiang Yu, a peasant leader, and a second rebel leader, Liu Bang, was installed as emperor. He adopted the imperial name of Gaozu or Kao-tsu, meaning "the High Ancestor of Han." Thus began the Han Dynasty, that would rule China for the next 426 years.

The Han Dynasty

The four centuries of Han rule are commonly regarded as the first Golden

A bronze Hu wine vessel

Age of China's Antiquity. Many innovations from the Qin rulers were stabilized and vested as an integral part of Chinese identity. The Han culture persists to this day; many Chinese identify as Han Chinese, and characters in the Chinese alphabet are known as Han characters. At the same time, the Han period firmly established the position of emperor at the pinnacle of the nation's administration, assisted by educated ministers and mandarins in the capital and landed aristocracy across the far-flung districts of the land. In a nod to the nobility, which was still smarting from the oppressive nature of the Qin regime, some of these districts—known as *jún*—were allowed to retain the status of semi-autonomous provinces until, in due course, the local lords were brought to heel.

To finance the new empire and its central court, the economy was reorganized and nationalized on an

THE TERRA-COTTA ARMY OF QIN SHI HUANG

After Emperor Qin Shi Huang unexpectedly died in 210 B.C.E., he was buried in a tomb together with an army of terra-cotta soldiers, horses, and chariots, distributed over three separate burial pits (at right). Given the vast scope of this enterprise, scholars believe that work on this mausoleum began soon after Emperor Qin ascended the throne. Some estimate that it would have taken some 700,000 workers to build the complex, which also included terra-cotta figures of court officials and servants. The terra-cotta army was discovered in 1974 by farmers digging a water well near Mount Li in Xi'an, Lishan Province.

unprecedented scale, including the manufacture of silk, iron, liquor, and salt, as well as new Chinese inventions such as paper. The laws were altered to allow all sons of a landowner to share in the inheritance, which provided for a more equitable form of land distribution and contributed greatly to social stability. With the shift to the standard wuzhu coin in 119 B.C.E., China also moved to a fully monetary economy, with poll and property taxes paid in coin rather than in kind. To sustain this currency flow, the official mint produced as many as 220 million coins a year. Like the Roman denarius, the Chinese wuzhu would remain the currency of choice in Asia for many centuries until the advent of the Tang Dynasty in 618 C.E. Han rulers also gradually extended their sphere of influence over Korea and part of Vietnam, while the development of a trade route later known as the Silk Road greatly facilitated commerce with the West. Long before this route was built, however, Chinese merchants had already been in contact with Persia and Rome to the west, as well as with the island group of Japan to the east.

Buoyed by this affluence, Chinese science and technology prospered as never before. Blast furnaces and forges poured forth wrought iron, cast iron, and steel, which in turn produced farm implements such as iron plowshares and seed drills that greatly increased harvest yields. The invention of chain pumps enabled the development of irrigation systems that could bring water to fields in higher elevations. In the second century C.E., Chinese engineers also designed the junk ship, using sails that were reinforced with horizontal rods or battens and steered by a stern-mounted rudder. These sturdy vessels allowed Chinese traders to venture out of the rivers and coastal areas into the open sea. The junk would remain a

Woman with a mirror from the Han Dynasty (ca 206 B.C.E.– 220 C.E.)

fixture of the Chinese maritime tradition and is still used today, though mostly as pleasure yachts for tourists.

Most important, however, the Han emperors abrogated the Qin suppression of Confucian scholarship. They reopened schools of philosophy, realizing that these academies would produce the skilled administrators the empire needed to sustain its economic and political growth. Gaozu went out of his way to invite men of letters to the capital of Chang'an (today's Xi'an), followed by the founding of the first Imperial University in 124 B.C.E. Individual schools were established, each focused on a particular discipline in traditional Chinese literature, such as the *Book of Spring* and *Autumn Annals* or the *Book of Ceremonies.* The Han Dynasty even cultivated the Chinese equivalent of historian Herodotus in Sima Qian (ca 145–90 B.C.E.), who sought to document China's 2,000-year history in his *Records of the Grand Historian.* But when Sima defended a military officer whose troops had suffered a defeat against the Hsiung Nu, a tribal group in the eastern Eurasian Steppe, Emperor Wu was deeply displeased. The hapless historian was tried and duly castrated.

Arts and Religion of the Han Period

The Han Dynasty proved fertile ground for religion as well. An elaborate liturgy emerged, based on the worship of key deities (such as the so-called Five Powers); of the rule of spirits (*shen*) living in mountains, rivers, and trees; and of one's ancestors as part of China's long tradition of ancestor worship. Many Han shrines and temples arose to accommodate the worshippers. Beliefs centered around the idea that each person has two souls: a body-soul, or *po,* that went to the grave with the deceased, and the spirit-soul, or *hun,* that would live on in the afterlife.

At the pinnacle of this religion

A CLASSIC JUNK BOAT, propelled by sails reinforced with horizontal rods, or battens, plies the waters of Hong Kong harbor.

惠承 三

A GROUP OF SHEPHERDS with their flock travel across the ancient Silk Road near Tashkurgan, close to the borders of Tajikistan, Afghanistan, and Pakistan.

晋皇甫謐

A MODERN PORTRAIT depicts Huangfu Mi, also known as Shi'an, a renowned scholar and physician during the Late Han Dynasty and successive periods.

stood the emperor as both high priest and the intermediary between heaven and earth. Only in 57 C.E. did Buddhism begin to penetrate China from India, with the first Buddhist temple built outside the capital of Luoyang during the reign of Emperor Mingdi. The first Buddhist tracts were translated into Chinese, including the *Shurangama Sutra* and the *Perfection of Wisdom*.

Of all the Han arts, none was as beloved as poetry, especially a form of rhymed verse known as *fu* ("rhapsody"). The fu format enabled the poet to explore a subject, such as love, in great depth and from a variety of angles, using both verse and prose. It became a favored form of discourse at court, particularly if it took the form of a tribute to the glory and wisdom of the emperor. After the Chinese revolution in the 20th century, fu poetry was harshly suppressed as a bourgeois form of art and only recently has been rehabilitated as a prominent form of Chinese literature.

The equivalent of fu poetry in the visual arts was a new interest in expressing themes from everyday life rather than the formulaic motifs of ceremony and mythology from previous dynasties. Han artists excelled

A GOOSE-SHAPED POT with polychrome decoration is dated to the period of the Han Dynasty.

THE "FLYING HORSE OF GANSU," dated to the second century C.E., was discovered in 1969 near the city of Wuwei, Gansu Province.

in the ancient art of jade carving, pottery, lacquer-ware, and terra-cotta sculpture and delighted in the depiction of genre scenes, such as hunting or fishing or even landscapes. Many earthenware figures of everyday women and men, not unlike the Greek Tanagra terra-cotta figurines of the late fourth century B.C.E., have survived from this era.

The Chinese invention of paper led to an explosion of calligraphy in ink and brush. It also replaced silk as a new and much cheaper support for painting. Serendipitously, these innovations coincided with a growing demand for paintings. The prosperity and social stability of the Han era had created a new layer of patrons who were eager to flaunt their newfound wealth through the acquisition of works of art.

The Birth of the Japanese Monarchy

Like China, Japan spent the years of its prehistory in relative isolation. During the early Jōmon period, so called because of the "cord-marked" nature of its pottery, hunter-gatherers used land bridges between Asia and the Japanese archipelago to settle on the four main islands of Honshu, Hokkaido, Kyushu, and Shikoku. Around 800 B.C.E., these people began to cultivate rice. This shift from hunting-gathering to agriculture was completed in the Yayoi period (300 B.C.E.–250 C.E.). At this time, iron weapons and tools from China were introduced to the Japanese homelands, as well as new technologies such as glass-making and silk production.

Some modern scholars believe that these changes were accompanied by a mass immigration from the Asian continent, especially from Korea, since modern Japanese are more genetically similar to the Yayoi than the Jōmon people (who continue to live in Japan as a minority, known as the Ainu). Indeed, the Yayoi period would see a virtual explosion in Japan's population, rising from two to four million people. Exactly how the archipelago was ruled during

A 17TH-CENTURY CHINESE PAINTING on silk depicts Emperor Wudi leaving his palace.

THE KUMANO NACHI TAISHA in the Kii Mountains of Japan is a major Shinto shrine that combines Buddhist and Shinto influences.

> "THEN GOING TOWARD THE SOUTH, ONE ARRIVES AT THE COUNTRY OF YAMADAI, WHERE A QUEEN HOLDS HER COURT."
>
> CHEN SHOU,
> *RECORDS OF THE THREE KINGDOMS*

these centuries is not clear. A Chinese history book from around 82 C.E., known as the *Book of Han,* describes Wa or Japan at this time as a patchwork of more than a hundred kingdoms, but this number could have a purely symbolic significance. Archaeologists have discovered numerous fortified villages, which suggests that this was a period of conflict between warring regions. A later Chinese history, the *Wei Zhi,* or *Records of the Three Kingdoms,* dated to the third century C.E., claims that Japan was ruled by a legendary priestess-queen called Himiko, who established a kingdom known as Yamatai-koku. One account reports that the queen, who never married, lived in a castle attended by 1,000 women—rather exceptional by the patriarchal standards of ancient Asia.

Around this time, the first Chinese traders and envoys decided to reconnoiter this strange Japanese archipelago. One official described how after "going south by water for twenty days" he arrived at an island called Toma, where "there were about fifty thousand households." From there, the envoy traveled south, "ten days by water and one month by land," until he

THIS BRONZE BELL is an important artifact from the Yayoi period (300 B.C.E.–300 C.E.), when Chinese metallurgy was introduced to Japan.

A STONE BUDDHA from the Northern Zhou period attests to the enduring influence of Buddhism during the classical period.

reached Yamatai, a magnificent capital city ruled by Queen Himiko and her elaborate court. Modern scholars have cast doubt on this legendary kingdom, and efforts to identify it by archaeological means have not yet produced results. Instead, excavations suggest that ca 400s C.E., a tribal region known as the Yamato, based in the region of modern-day Kyoto, gradually took control of much of the country. This Yamato period, which lasted until about 700 C.E., was attended by new waves of immigrants from the Korean peninsula. Some historians have posited the theory that the Korean immigration amounted to a military takeover of the Japanese archipelago, led by cavalry, but this theory is now largely discounted.

This era is also notable for the rise of numerous *kofun*, or large mounds, in which leading noblemen were entombed upon their death. The idea of burying the ruling elite in mounds originated in both China and Korea but found its most widespread expression in Japan, with major mounds built near Kyoto, Osaka, and Nara. Some of these mounds, such as the burial ground of Emperor Nintoku, are as much as 90 feet high and 1,200 feet long. Archaeologists have identified close to 20,000 such mounds of variable height and size, which is why many historians refer to the Yamato era as the Kofun period.

Japanese history, however, sees its origins very differently. It argues that the first Japanese "emperor"—a title obviously influenced by Chinese precedent— ascended the Chrysanthemum throne on February 11, 660 B.C.E., a date still celebrated as Japan's National Foundation Day. As a result, the Imperial House of Japan, also known as the Yamato Dynasty, claims to be the oldest continuous hereditary monarchy in the world. Most modern historians respectfully dispute this chronology and believe that the Japanese monarchy emerged during the late Kofun period, with Emperor Kinmei as the first historically attested ruler. Ancient records suggest that this unification process evolved over time as more local chieftains pledged their loyalty to the Yamato regime. As this early kingdom grew, it assiduously sought recognition

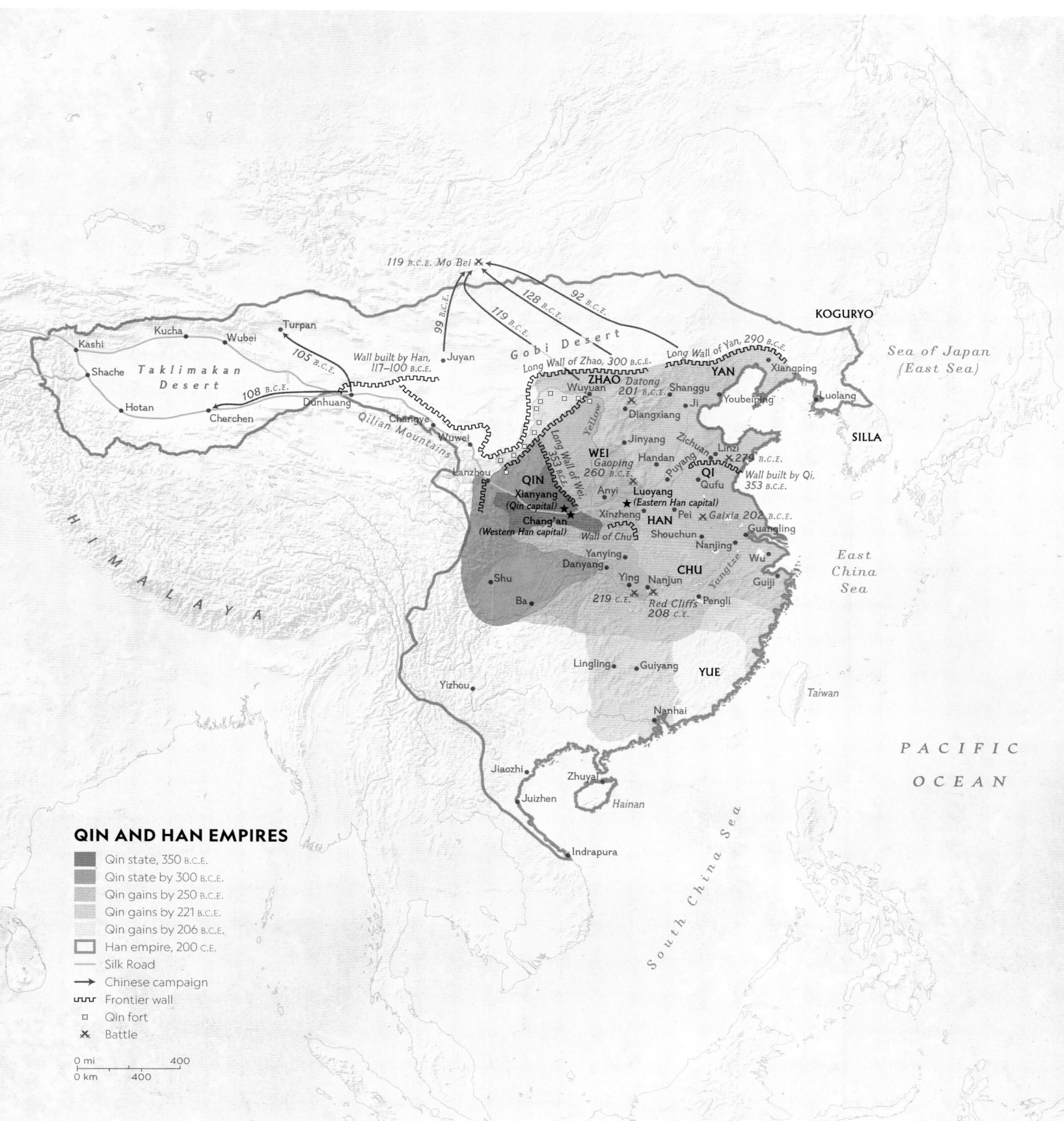

119 B.C.E. *Mo Bei* ✖

KOGURYO

Sea of Japan (East Sea)

99 B.C.E.   119 B.C.E.   128 B.C.E.   92 B.C.E.

Gobi Desert

Long Wall of Yan, 290 B.C.E.

Turpan

Kashi   Kucha   Wubei

Shache

Taklimakan Desert

105 B.C.E.   Wall built by Han, 117–100 B.C.E.   Juyan

Hotan

108 B.C.E.   Cherchen   Dunhuang

Xiangping

SILLA

Luolang

Long Wall of Zhao, 300 B.C.E.

ZHAO *Datong*   **YAN**

Wuyuan   *201 B.C.E.*   Shanggu

Diangxiang   Ji   Youbeiping

Qilian Mountains

Changye   *Yellow*

Wuwei

Jinyang   Zichuan   Linzi ✖ *279 B.C.E.*

Lanzhou

WEI   Handan   Puyang   **QI**

Gaoping   Anyi   Wall built by Qi, 353 B.C.E.

260 B.C.E.   Qufu

QIN

Xianyang ★   Luoyang ★ *(Eastern Han capital)*

(Qin capital)

Chang'an   Xinzheng   **HAN**   Pei ✖ *Gaixia 202 B.C.E.*

(Western Han capital)   Wall of Chu   Shouchun   Guangling

Long Wall of Wei, 353 B.C.E.

Yanying   Nanjing   Wu

Danyang   *East China Sea*

Shu   Ying   Nanjun   Guiji

Ba   *219 C.E.* ✖ ✖   Pengli

Red Cliffs 208 C.E.   *Yangtze*

CHU

HIMALAYA

Lingling   Guiyang   **YUE**

Yizhou

Nanhai   *Taiwan*

PACIFIC OCEAN

Jiaozhi

Zhuyai   *Hainan*

Juizhen

Indrapura   *South China Sea*

QIN AND HAN EMPIRES

- ▮ Qin state, 350 B.C.E.
- ▮ Qin state by 300 B.C.E.
- ▮ Qin gains by 250 B.C.E.
- ▮ Qin gains by 221 B.C.E.
- ▮ Qin gains by 206 B.C.E.
- ▢ Han empire, 200 C.E.
- —— Silk Road
- → Chinese campaign
- ⌐┐ Frontier wall
- ▫ Qin fort
- ✖ Battle

0 mi   400
0 km   400

ROWS OF torii gates, known as Senborn Torii, lead to the sacred precinct of the Fushimi Inari-taisha shrine at the base of Inari Mountain in Kyoto, Japan.

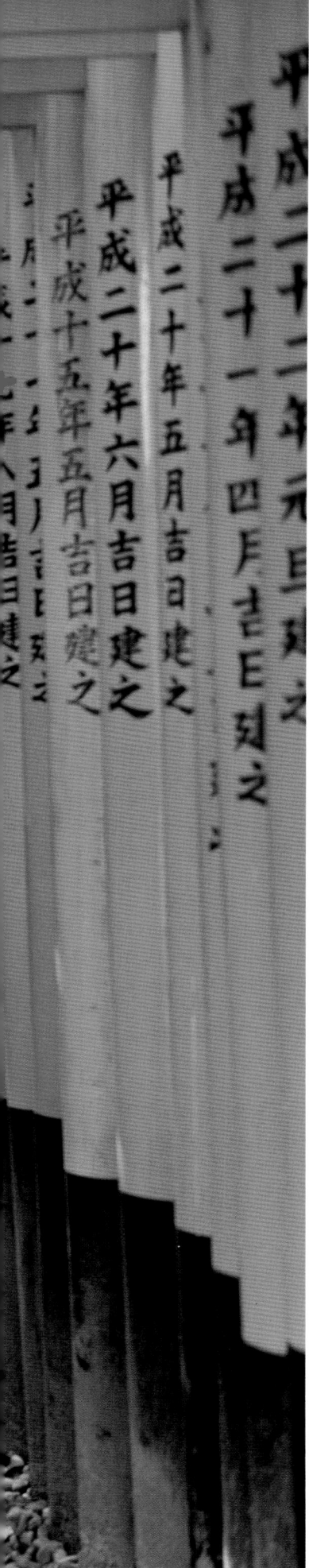

> "WHEN WISE MEN ARE ENTRUSTED WITH OFFICE, THE SOUND OF PRAISE ARISES. IF CORRUPT MEN HOLD OFFICE, DISASTERS AND TUMULT MULTIPLY."

PRINCE SHŌTOKU OF JAPAN, ASUKA PERIOD

as a sovereign power from imperial China, which was eventually granted. Among others, this included a letter from Prince Shōtoku of Japan, son of Emperor Yōmei, to Emperor Yang of Sui, China, which opens: "From the sovereign of the land of the rising sun to the land of the setting sun," the first known reference to Japan as the "land of the rising sun." These contacts also prompted a steady stream of Chinese scholars, craftsmen, architects, and engineers, who left a deep Chinese imprint on Japanese art, architecture, and literature.

The Yamato cult was closely intertwined with a native religious tradition known as Shinto ("Way of the Gods"),

Dogu figurine, Jomon Period

which, like Chinese religious ideas of the time, revolved around the worship of gods (*kami*), spirits (*shin*), nature, and ancestors. According to Shinto cosmology, the Japanese island group was created by two gods, a male (Iazanagi) and female (Izanami), who were charged by the other gods to produce a wondrous land. They thrust their spear into the ocean, and the droplets that fell from it created the Japanese archipelago. Only in the sixth century C.E., after Chinese monks brought the teachings of Buddha to Japan, was Buddhism adopted as the official religion of the nation, though Shinto religion continued to prosper, particularly among the common people. ■

PERFUMES FROM THE EAST

Among the luxuries imported from the East were balm and myrrh, used as aroma agents in temples as well as in affluent homes (at right). Balm was the gum of the balsam tree (*Commiphora opobalsamum*) that grew in southern Arabia and was mostly used for its medicinal qualities. Myrrh is the resin of a bush of thorns (*Commpihora myrrha*) that grew along the Arabian and African coasts on the Red Sea. It was used as a perfume agent in oils and as incense in temples. In Roman Palestine, myrrh (mixed with oil) was used for purification of the deceased prior to burial (as in the case of Jesus). It was also an adhesive and therefore used as the last and final step of burial preparation before the body was wrapped in linen.

THIS PORTRAIT of Alexander the Great forms part of the Alexander Mosaic in the House of the Faun in Pompeii, inspired by a painting by Philoxeilos of Entrea.

THE EMPIRE OF
ALEXANDER
THE GREAT

In the West, long-simmering tensions between Greece and Persia erupted once more when in 334 B.C.E. young Alexander, son of King Philip II of Macedon, invaded Persia with a force of more than 40,000 soldiers and changed the face of the world forever.

With the help of his flying cavalry, as well as stout phalanxes of Macedonian hoplites (heavy infantry), Alexander dealt a crushing defeat to the army of Persian King Darius III at the Battle of Issus in 333 B.C.E. Alexander proceeded to advance deep into the Persian realm. One by one, Syria, Phoenicia, Judah, and Egypt were added to the territory of the young Macedonian warrior, with only Tyre, Gaza, and Samaria offering meaningful resistance. Then his army turned east, capturing the great Mesopotamian cities of Babylon, Susa, and Persepolis before reaching the Upper Indus River Valley. The result was an empire even greater than its Persian precedent, covering some two million square miles.

As vast as Alexander's empire was, it would not outlive its founder. Just 11 years after the Battle of Issus, as Alexander was busy plotting a new campaign on the Arabian peninsula, he contracted a mysterious disease that has never been accurately diagnosed. After 14 agonizing days, he died in Darius's palace in Babylon.

His death was so sudden that no one had prepared for an orderly succession. Alexander's son by his Bactrian wife, Roxanne, was not born until two months after his death. This led to a power struggle between Alexander's leading generals, known as the Diadochi, or "successors." A protracted civil war ensued, which by 305 B.C.E. had produced four distinct realms: Anatolia (today's Turkey), headed by the Attalid Dynasty of General Lysimachus; the home territories of Greece and Macedon, ruled by the heirs of General Antigonus; the empire of Mesopotamia, led by the heirs of General Seleucus; and Egypt, ruled by General Ptolemy. Few of these generals were content with their allotments, however, and war erupted again. Between 315 and 312, Antigonus and Seleucus I, who had temporarily aligned himself with Ptolemy, came to blows. In

A FIFTH-CENTURY terracotta relief from Tarantino, Italy, depicts the torso of a young man.

"IF IT WERE NOT MY PURPOSE . . . TO TRAVERSE AND CIVILIZE EVERY CONTINENT, TO SEARCH OUT THE UTTERMOST PARTS OF LAND AND SEA, TO PUSH THE BOUNDS OF MACEDONIA TO THE FARTHEST OCEAN . . . I SHOULD NOT BE CONTENT TO SIT QUIETLY."

ATTRIBUTED TO ALEXANDER THE GREAT BY ROMAN HISTORIAN PLUTARCH

301 B.C.E., Antigonus was vanquished at the Battle of Ipsus, and Ptolemy established the Ptolemaic Dynasty. His kingdom now ranged from Egypt to Phoenicia and Syria, including Judah, which served as a buffer against any future encroachment by his rivals.

The Spread of Hellenism

Politically, Alexander's empire had fallen apart, but as a cultural entity, it remained intact. Although local languages continued to be spoken, Greek (in a patois known as *koiné*) became the dominant language of international trade, politics, and the arts. In addition, Alexander had founded new cities, or *poleis,* throughout his realm, from which Hellenistic culture would radiate into the surrounding region. These cities were usually planned on the grid pattern developed by Hippodamus of Miletus. They featured such quintessential Greek institutions as a theater; a market, or agora; temples dedicated to Zeus, Apollo, or other Greek gods; and a gymnasium where young men were educated and trained in sports. Sometimes existing cities were entirely rebuilt in the Greek fashion, such as Akko (renamed Ptolemais) and the Ammonite capital of Rabbath-Ammon (today's Amman in Jordan), which was reestablished as Philadelphia.

In Egypt, Alexander founded a city on the Mediterranean coast near the village of Rhakotis that would bear his name: Alexandria. Designed

Alexander the Great

by his architect Dinocrates, it was designated by Ptolemy I as the new capital of Ptolemaic Egypt. It then became the principal center of Ptolemy's attempt to fuse both the Egyptian and Greek culture into a new syncretic civilization. Laid out in the usual grid pattern, Alexandria boasted a man-made causeway to the island of Pharos, which held the tallest lighthouse of the ancient world. It soon became the principal port in this part of the Mediterranean—assisted by the fact that its primary competitor, Tyre, had been thoroughly destroyed. Not surprisingly, this is also where Alexander's body was eventually put to rest, in a gold sarcophagus filled with honey.

By the mid-third century, Alexandria had truly become the Athens of the Middle East. Here were a university, an astronomical observatory, a zoo, a botanical garden, and, above all, a magnificent library of more than 400,000 volumes— possibly the greatest concentration of learning in Antiquity. Its population, too, became increasingly diverse as its prosperity attracted tradesmen, bankers, scholars, and literati from throughout the former Alexandria Empire.

Throughout much of the known world, Hellenism now ruled supreme. Greek literature, theater, and philosophy were studied in academic centers, while Greek art had a profound influence on artists from Egypt to India. Literacy rates rose, particularly in coastal areas, as did standards of

THE DORIC TEMPLE of Concordia in Agrigento, Sicily, exemplifies the archetype of a Greek sanctuary that would be replicated throughout the Mediterranean world.

THE RECENTLY EXCAVATED Roman amphitheater in Alexandria, Egypt, was rebuilt in the second century C.E. by Hadrian, the Roman emperor.

"THREE CLASSES INHABITED THE CITY:
FIRST THE NATIVE EGYPTIANS;
SECONDLY, THE MERCENARY CLASS;
AND THIRD, THE TRIBE OF THE ALEXANDRIANS,
WHO . . . ARE STILL GREEKS BY ORIGIN AND MINDFUL
OF THE CUSTOMS COMMON TO THE GREEKS."

ROMAN GEOGRAPHER STRABO ON ALEXANDRIA

living. A currency system was introduced, using coins bearing the Attic owl, which greatly facilitated international trade. This booming trade in turn necessitated an expansion of sea routes. New roads were laid as well, and existing ones were restored and expanded.

But near the end of the third century, international tensions threatened to disrupt the peace once more. The newly crowned Seleucid king, Antiochus III, decided to recover the lost lands. In a series of military campaigns that lasted

Silver drachma with the owl, symbol of Athena

nearly two decades, the king reconquered much of Asia Minor before pushing east, eventually leading his armies as far as Kabul in today's Afghanistan. According to Greek historian Polybius, he then crossed the mountains of Hindu Kush and entered India, where he forced the Indian king, Subhashsena, to terms.

Having thus recovered most of the original Alexandrian empire in the east, Antiochus believed himself to be invincible, if not a reincarnation of the

THE SYNAGOGUE

As the Jewish Diaspora—the dispersal of Jews throughout the Alexandrian Empire—spread, the need rose for local community halls where Jewish expatriates could observe the Sabbath, celebrate Jewish festivals, and host other community functions. The result was the synagogue, from the Greek *synagogē*, or "house of assembly"—*beit knesset* in Hebrew. These early synagogues usually consisted of a rectangular hall with benches on either side (at right). The end wall facing Jerusalem contained a niche known as the Ark, where the scrolls of the Torah were kept. One of the oldest such synagogues has been found in Egypt, dating to the third century B.C.E.

> "WHATEVER POSSESSION WE GAIN BY OUR SWORD CANNOT BE SURE OR LASTING, BUT THE LOVE GAINED BY KINDNESS AND MODERATION IS CERTAIN AND DURABLE."

ALEXANDER THE GREAT

great Alexander himself. From this point on, his coins proclaim him as Antiochos Megas, "Antiochus the Great." Drunk with victory, he next turned his forces against the former Alexandrian possessions in the south: Ptolemaic Syria. At first he was repulsed, but in 198 B.C.E. the king succeeded in defeating Ptolemy V Epiphanes at the Battle of Paneion, close to the source of the Jordan. Syria, including Galilee and Judea, was now forcefully brought into the Seleucid Empire.

But then Antiochus III overreached: He plotted an ill-fated attack on Greece, which at that time happened to be a province of an emerging new power called Rome. Antiochus was beaten and forced to remit crippling reparation payments to Rome. By the time his son Seleucus IV acceded to the throne, the Seleucid Empire was on the verge of bankruptcy.

The Mauryan Empire of India

After the Vedic period, India had witnessed a renewed period of urbanization when new towns sprang up along the Ganges River, particularly in the Central Ganges plain. Trade contacts were reestablished, which boosted the growth of the population and the rise of large, heavily fortified

THE EMPIRE OF ALEXANDER THE GREAT

city-states. As in the case of China, this was accompanied by an effort to standardize weights, measures, and currency in the form of punch-marked coins. Writing too became more widespread using both Brahmi and Kharosthi alphabets. Among the various kingdoms of the time, the Nanda Kingdom soon rose to become the dominant power in the north, stretching from Bengal in the west to the Vindhya Range in the south and the Punjab in the west. Greek historian Plutarch claims that at one point, the Nanda army numbered 200,000 infantry, 80,000 cavalry, and 6,000 war elephants.

This is the moment when the forces of Alexander the Great steadily moved eastward into the plains of Punjab, and a great clash between the East and West seemed inevitable. But then Alexander's army threatened mutiny while camped at Hyphasis (today's Beas River), perhaps because the soldiers knew that the Nanda forces were five times larger than their own. As a result, this is as far as Alexander ever got. He accepted the demands of his soldiers and led his army southward, along the lower Indus River, before finally turning west and on the road back to Babylon. That is where, three years later, he lay on his deathbed.

Less than a year would pass before an orphan from rural Patna (today's Bihar) named Chandragupta Maurya would seize the opportunity left unfulfilled by the young Greek prince. Knowing that much of the north was still mobilized to deter any new probes by the Greeks, Chandragupta forged alliances with local rulers. Having amassed a formidable army of his own, he launched a campaign to evict the Nanda Dynasty. In 305 B.C.E. he

RIDERS MOUNTED ON ELEPHANTS cross the Ganges River near Sonpur in the Indian state of Bihar at dawn. **BELOW:** A Mauryan-Sunga coin is dated to the second century B.C.E.

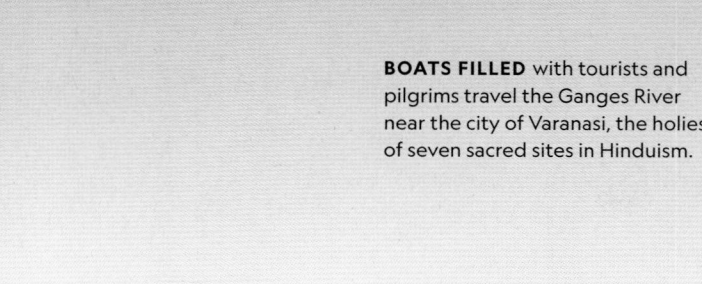

BOATS FILLED with tourists and pilgrims travel the Ganges River near the city of Varanasi, the holiest of seven sacred sites in Hinduism.

"ONCE ONE HAS MADE A DECISION, ONE SHOULD NOT TURN BACK AND REVISIT IT. THOSE THAT KEEP TURNING TO LOOK BACK AT THEIR DECISIONS DO NOT MAKE HISTORY."

CHANDRAGUPTA MAURYA, FOUNDER OF THE MAURYA EMPIRE

conquered the Nanda possessions in today's Afghanistan and Pakistan after defeating the forces of Seleucus, the Greek general who had taken control of the eastern part of Alexander's empire. It was left to his son and grandson to complete the conquest of southern India, so that for a brief moment, the Indian subcontinent was unified.

Even as his realm was expanding, Chandragupta focused on developing his nation by using many of the scientific and engineering ideas that the Greeks had introduced. He organized the development of large irrigation networks to expand India's agricultural base and thus produce sufficient food for the vast number of peoples now under his control. He also set about to create land routes to transport the surplus for trade, spurning the water routes that had traditionally served as India's principal infrastructure. According to a Greek ambassador at his court, this project included the construction of a thousand-mile highway between the Maurya capital of Pataliputra in Bihar

THE FOURTH-CENTURY B.C.E. MAURYAN HEAD of a bodhisattva (a person dedicated to the path of Buddha) betrays a strong influence of Greek models.

"SANDROCOTTUS, HAVING THUS ACQUIRED A THRONE, WAS IN POSSESSION OF INDIA."

MARCUS JUNIANUS JUSTINUS, *PHILIPPIC HISTORY*

to the city of Taxila in the northwest. Other roads reached out to Nepal, Sasaram, and Karnataka.

Archaeological discoveries from this era are scarce, but what has been found testifies to the exceptional skill of Mauryan artists, who often used Greek sculpture and painting as their model. A key example is the life-size rendering of a female deity, known as the Didarganj Yakshi, dated between the third century B.C.E. and second century C.E.

Unfortunately, the Maurya Empire did not last. Chandragupta's grandson Ashoka was compelled to wage a bloody war against the state of Kalinga, in which an estimated 100,000 soldiers perished. Ashoka was so repelled by the bloodshed that he converted to the peaceful tenets of Buddhism. He also gave up hunting, outlawed animal sacrifice, and restricted himself to a vegetarian diet. For the remainder of his reign, the king focused on building monuments to the Buddha, including a series of columns throughout his kingdoms that became known as Ashoka's pillars. He also sent Buddhist missionaries to Sri Lanka, from where the movement spread rapidly throughout Central Asia. But after his death in 232 B.C.E., the empire split up into separate kingdoms once more. It would not be reunited until the rise of the Gupta Empire some 500 years later. ∎

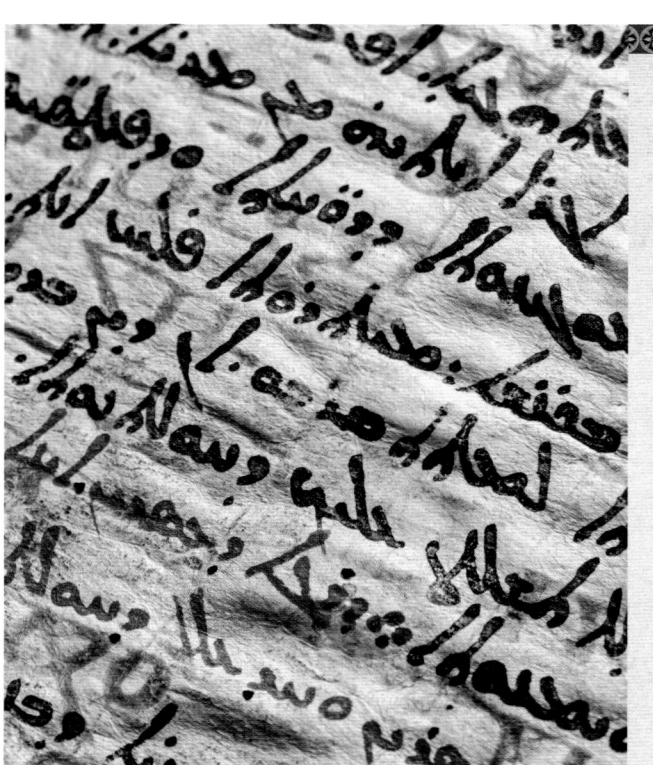

Depiction of an Indian demi-goddess

ARAMAIC

Modern research has shown that Aramaic (at left), the language of the Aramaeans that originated in Mesopotamia, shares deep roots with Semitic languages such as Hebrew and Phoenician. Scholars believe that Aramaic was already in use in the Assyrian Empire in the eighth century B.C.E., gradually replacing the ancient Akkadian language. In the sixth century, the Achaemenid conquerors of Babylonia deliberately chose Aramaic as the new lingua franca of their realm. Aramaic became the dominant language of the Near East, including Judea. The later books in the Hebrew Scriptures, such as the Book of Daniel, are written in Aramaic, while the Gospels include no fewer than 26 words in Aramaic spoken by Jesus.

THE GREAT STUPA of the Ashoka Temple in Sanchi, Madhya Pradesh, is one of the oldest stone structures in India, first built in the third century B.C.E.

THE FIRST CENTURY C.E. COLOSSEUM, one of Rome's most famous landmarks, is officially known as the Flavian Amphitheater but was soon associated with a colossal statue of the Emperor Nero that once stood nearby.

THE ROMAN
EMPIRE

At its height, the Roman Empire was one of the most powerful empires in the world and its city the largest urban area in history. With its military, its engineering, its currency, and its imperial bureaucracy, Rome would rule Europe and the Near East for nearly 500 years.

ronically, as late as the fourth century B.C.E., few people had heard of Rome. Its capital city was little more than a group of settlements scattered across seven hills rising along the Tiber River. According to Rome's founding myth, the city was originally established by two brothers, Romulus and Remus, who were raised by a she-wolf, though archaeologists believe that Rome's beginnings are more prosaic, with origins going back to the 10th century B.C.E. Nevertheless, we have no reason to doubt the claim of Roman historians such as Livy that around 509 B.C.E. the citizens of Rome were fed up with their kings and decided to establish a republic.

This republic, like its precedent in Athens, was unquestionably more inclusive than the monarchies of its time, but it was hardly a democracy in the modern sense of the word. Most of Rome's political power remained in the hands of a landed aristocracy that controlled the Senate, which soon became the principal executive and legislative body. During the next five centuries, which historians call Rome's Republican period, the city slowly but steadily expanded its commercial and territorial influence, aided by the fact that in the

East, Greece and Persia were too busy fighting each other to take any notice. As we saw, this prolonged clash between the Greek and Persian superpowers culminated in the final battle between Alexander the Great and King Darius III of Persia, which ended in the latter's defeat in 333 B.C.E.

As a new world order emerged in the East, no one paid much attention to the Roman Republic or the fact that it steadily took control of the Italian peninsula after the defeat of its last main enemy, the Samnites of southern Italy, in 290 B.C.E. On Rome went, pushing from the southern tip of Italy to Sicily, which brought it into conflict with Carthage during the Punic Wars. By the beginning of the second century, Rome emerged triumphant and found that much of the East lay ready for conquest as well.

The Growth of the Roman Empire

The reason was the growing hostility between the Ptolemaic and Seleucid Empires, each ruled by successors of Alexander the Great, which reached a flash point in 200 B.C.E. when Seleucid King Antiochus III decided

A BUST from 130 C.E. shows Roman emperor Hadrian in the idealized neo-Hellenistic style favored during his reign.

"I CAME, I SAW, I CONQUERED."

JULIUS CAESAR,
BY ROMAN HISTORIAN PLUTARCH

to invade Ptolemaic Palestine. Egyptian King Ptolemy V was defeated, after which Galilee and Judah were absorbed in the Syrian eparchy, or prefecture, of Samaria. When Antiochus III embarked on his ill-fated invasion of Greece, Rome was ready: It intervened and imposed such crippling war indemnities on Antiochus that his successor, Antiochus IV, was forced to start looting temples throughout his realm, including the Temple in Jerusalem, in order to come up with the payments. In response, the Jews, under the leadership of the Maccabees and the *Hasidim* (the pious ones), rose in revolt. The success of this Maccabean Revolt would lead to nearly a century of Jewish independence.

Coin with Caesar

The outcome of these years of turmoil was that Rome gradually became the dominant power in the Mediterranean Basin. Rome's aristocracy, which had traditionally drawn its riches from extensive landholdings, now became fabulously wealthy. Senators eagerly sought appointments to the provinces overseas, where they could make a fortune from the sale of local trade monopolies, kickbacks, and other lucrative concessions. This further widened the gap between Rome's ruling elites and Italy's vast majority of peasants, most of whom tilled the land as little more than serfs. Worse, as Rome's expansion required the levy of more and more legions, landowners were forced to import slaves by the thousands to work as field hands. This further distanced the nobility from the people, or plebs, and lay the foundation for large-scale unemployment in the years to come. In response, the people clamored for the redistribution of public lands, but no real action was taken until the rise of a man named Julius Caesar.

The Rise of Caesar

Though a nobleman who traced his lineage to the goddess Venus, Caesar had early on aligned himself with the populist cause. In 59 B.C.E., following a period of great political upheaval, Caesar had deftly created a triumvirate, or "reign of three men." This included the famous general Pompeius Magnus, or Pompey the Great. When Pompey's legions intervened in the Third Mithridatic War, the Roman general found himself tantalizingly close to Syria, still ruled by the Seleucid Dynasty, and Palestine, now an independent Jewish kingdom ruled by the Hasmonean House. Pompey decided to invade Syria, march on its capital of Antioch, and depose the ruling king, Antiochus XIII. The purpose of this strategy was to create a buffer state between Rome's principal source of grain, Egypt, and the empire of the Parthians, heirs to the ancient Persian Empire.

As it happened, civil war had broken out in the Hasmonean Kingdom of Judea after the death of Queen Salome Alexandra in 67 B.C.E. Her two

A PENSIVE first-century C.E. portrait of a woman with a stylus and wax tablet from Pompeii has sometimes been identified as the Greek lyric poet Sappho.

THE THEATER COMPLEX at Lepcis Magna near today's Khoms, Libya, is one of the best preserved Roman theaters in the world.

NOTABLE DATES

ca 280 B.C.E.
New Roman Republic controls the Italian Peninsula

ca 189 B.C.E.
Rome defeats Antiochus III, taking Roman rule into Asia Minor

ca 63 B.C.E.
Roman general Pompey conquers Judea

ca 44 B.C.E.
Julius Caesar is assassinated on the Senate floor

ca 42 B.C.E.
Caesar's assassins, Brutus and Cassius, are defeated at Battle of Philippi

ca 30 B.C.E.
Egypt is annexed as a Roman province, ending its 3,000-year history

ca 27 B.C.E.
Octavian, now named Augustus, is ruler of the Roman Empire

ca 14 C.E.
Augustus dies and is succeeded by Tiberius

ca 41 C.E.
Emperor Caligula is assassinated and succeeded by Claudius

68 C.E.
Emperor Nero commits suicide and is succeeded by Galba

79 C.E.
Pompeii and Herculaneum destroyed by eruption of Mount Vesuvius

116 C.E.
Trajan extends Roman Empire into Parthia

122 C.E.
Hadrian's Wall built in Britain

THE ROMAN EMPIRE

North Sea

Caledonia
Hibernia

Hadrian's Wall

Eburacum
Deva
Lindum
Viroconium
BRITANNIA
Glevum
Isca Silurum
Verulamium
Londinium
Camulodunum
Dubrae
Isca Dumnoniorum
Noviomagus
Portus Itius
Gesoriacum
Bagacum

Germania

Vistula

MAGNA GERMANIA
12 B.C.E.–9 C.E.
Noviomagus
Vetera
Colonia Agrippinensis
Bonna
GERMANIA INFERIOR
Augusta Treverorum
Mogontiacum

Rhine R.
Elbe

Juliobona
Rotomagus
Augustodurum
Noviodunum
Lutetia
LUGDUNENSIS
Cenabum
Durocortorum
BELGICA
GERMANIA SUPERIOR
Argentorate
Vindobona
Castra Regina
Carnuntum
Aquincum
Brigetto

Darioritum
Juliomagus
Portus Namnetum
Caesarodunum
Augustodunum
Limonum
Loire
Seine
Vesontio
Aventicum
RAETIA
Curia
Cambodunum
NORICUM
Teurnia
Iuvavum
Savaria
Virunum
PANNONIA SUPERIOR
PANNONIA INFERIOR
Mursa
Viminacium
Siscia
Sirmium
Singidunum

Danube
ATLANTIC OCEAN

Mediolanum
AQUITANIA
Gallia
Lugdunum (Lyon)
Vienna
Lake Geneva
ALPES GRAIAE ET POENINAE
Octodurum
Axima
Segusio
ALPES COTTIAE
Rhône
A L P S
Lake Como
Aquileia
DALMATIA
MOESIA SUPERIOR
Illyricum

Burdigala
Mediolanum
Cremona
Placentia
Genoa
Bononia
Ravenna
Ariminum
Florentia
Pisae
Ancona
Arretium
Perusia
Castrum Novum
Po
Salonae
Adriatic Sea

Brigantium
Lucus Augusti
Asturica
Bracara Augusta
Portus Cale
Salamantica
LUSITANIA
Legio VII Gemina
Pompaelo
Clunia
Numantia
Caesaraugusta
Ebro
Dertosa
Tarraco
NARBONENSIS
Nemausus
Tolosa
Narbo
Arausio
Arelate
Massilia
Forum Julii
Cemenelum
ALPES MARITIMAE
Saturnia
Cosa
Veii
Rome
Ostia
Capua
Puteoli
Misenum
Neapolis
ITALIA
Corfinium
Beneventum
Pompeii
Paestum
Dyrrhachium
Apollonia
Brundisium
Taranto
Thurii

Hispania
Tagus
Emporiae
Rhodae
Barcino
Scallabis
Emerita Augusta
Olisipo
Toletum
TARRACONENSIS
Saguntum
Valentia
Palma
Balearic Islands
CORSICA
Aleria
Olbia
SARDINIA
Carales
Tyrrhenian Sea
Croton
Messana
Rhegium
Catana
Syracuse
SICILIA
Ionian Sea

Pax Julia
Italica
Corduba
Hispalis
BAETICA
Malaca
Gades
Carteia
Tingis
Carthago Nova
Panormus
Lilybaeum
Agrigentum

Rusaddir
Cartennae
Caesarea
Sitifis
Portus Magnus
Utica
Carthage
MAURETANIA CAESARIENSIS
Lambaesis
Thamugadi
Theveste
Thugga
Hippo Regius
Hadrumetum
Thapsus
Mediterranea

MAURETANIA TINGITANA
Sala
Volubilis

Oea
Leptis Magna
Sabratha
AFRICA
Charax

THE ROMAN EMPIRE

Roman territory, 201 B.C.E.

Gains by 100 B.C.E.

Area ruled by the time of Julius Caesar's death, 44 B.C.E.

Area ruled by the time of Caesar Augustus' death, 14 C.E.

Gains by Emperor Trajan, 117 C.E.

Region temporarily held by Rome, with dates

Vassal of Rome

ᴨᴨᴨ Fortified frontier

—— Roman road

★ Empire/kingdom capital

⊙ Provincial capital

◡ Legion headquarters

⚓ Major naval base

Sarmatia

Scythia

Caspian Sea

Dnieper

Don

Volga

Dniester

Caucasus Mountains

Olbia

★ Panticapaeum

BOSPORAN
KINGDOM

Chersonesus

Pityus

Lake
Sevan

ARMENIA
114–117 C.E.

Parthia

Black Sea

Trapezus ⚓

Apulum

Troesmis ⚓

Sarmizegetusa
Regia

Tomis

Sinope

Satala

Lake
Van

Lake
Urmia

DACIA

Durostorum

Tropaeum
Traiani

Amisus

Pompeiopolis

Amastris

Megalopolis

Tigranocerta

Amida

Oescus

Novae

MOESIA
INFERIOR

Heraclea
Pontica

Zela

ASSYRIA
116–117 C.E.

Danube

Serdica

Hadrianopolis
(Edirne,
Adrianople)

BYTHINIA ET
PONTUS

Gangra

CAPPADOCIA

Melitene

Tigris

Philippopolis

THRACIA

Byzantium
(Istanbul, Constantinople)

Ancyra

Caesarea

Edessa

MESOPOTAMIA
115–117 C.E.

Nicopolis

Perinthus

Nicomedia

Nicaea

Dorylaeum

Samosata

Ctesiphon

Stobi

Cyzicus

Prusa

Anatolia
(Asia Minor)

Cyrrhus

Heraclea

Thessalonica

ASIA

GALATIA

Euphrates

MACEDONIA

Pergamum

Antiochia

Iconium

Tarsus

Antiochia

Dura Europos

EPIRUS

Smyrna

Aphrodisias

LYCIA

CILICIA

Seleucia

SYRIA

Palmyra

Ambracia

Ephesus

Miletus

Laodicea ⚓

Raphaneae

Nicopolis

Delphi

Athens

Attalia

Emesa

Corinth

ACHAEA

Cnidus

Rhodus

Myra

Salamis

Tripolis

Heliopolis

Persian
Gulf

Sparta

Aegean Sea

CYPRUS

Damascus

Paphos

Tyrus

CRETA

Gortyn

Caparcotna

Caesarea

Bostra

mean Sea

Jerusalem

JUDEA

Dead Sea

Gaza

Pelusium

ARABIA

Petra

Nicopolis

Ptolemais

Cyrene

Alexandria

Memphis

CYRENE

Oxyrhynchus

Hermopolis

Nile

AEGYPTUS

Ptolemais

Coptus

Thebae

Red Sea

0 mi   400

0 km   400

Modern names appear in parentheses.

sons, Hyrcanus II and Aristobulus II, both vied for the throne. In response, Pompey decided to conquer the kingdom for Rome and install Hyrcanus as a vassal prince. Thus, Jewish independence came to an end and would not be reinstated—save for brief periods of rebellion—until the 20th century.

The triumvirate of Caesar, Crassus, and Pompey lasted six years but ended in civil war once more. After Pompey broke their alliance and accused Caesar of usurping his authority, Caesar and his 13th Legion crossed the Rubicon River into Rome's home territory. Pompey fled to Greece, where he hoped to raise new armies, but Caesar gave chase and defeated him at the Battle of Pharsalus in 48 B.C.E.

A grateful Senate voted to give Caesar the title of dictator—a magistrate with extraordinary powers. Caesar accepted and promptly set sail for Egypt, where Pompey had reportedly fled in

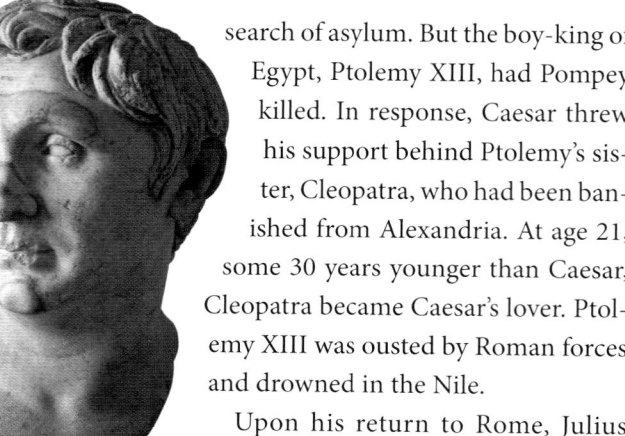

Pompey the Great

search of asylum. But the boy-king of Egypt, Ptolemy XIII, had Pompey killed. In response, Caesar threw his support behind Ptolemy's sister, Cleopatra, who had been banished from Alexandria. At age 21, some 30 years younger than Caesar, Cleopatra became Caesar's lover. Ptolemy XIII was ousted by Roman forces and drowned in the Nile.

Upon his return to Rome, Julius Caesar was welcomed by ecstatic crowds. Seizing the moment, he forced a series of reforms through the Senate, including the redistribution of land to some 15,000 of his veterans. He also established a new calendar, the Julian calendar, which closely matches our modern one. The Senate responded by naming him *pater patriae*, Father of the Fatherland. The seventh month in the new calendar, called Quintilis, was renamed Julius, or "July," in his honor—a name that endures to this day.

The old aristocracy, however, was busy plotting

ROMAN ARCHITECTURE

Another way in which Augustus sought to fuse the empire into one nation was his attempt to impose a uniform aesthetic on all major urban centers using the Greek model of an ideal city, or *polis* (at left). The inspiration came from Alexander the Great, who founded countless poleis in the areas he conquered. Augustus revived this ideal, since much of Roman art and architecture was a re-creation of Classical Greece; to this the Romans applied their superior knowledge of construction technology. Whereas the Greeks primarily used the traditional post-and-beam structure to build their monuments, the Romans developed arches and vaults as the principal support system. They also added some quintessentially Roman buildings to the repertoire, such as public baths, a central forum, and sometimes even an aqueduct that could carry freshwater from faraway mountains to fountains in the city center.

"CAESAR GIVING CLEOPATRA the Throne of Egypt" was painted by Italian Baroque artist Pietro da Cortona in 1637.

FRENCH ARTIST Jean-Léon Gérôme painted "The Death of Caesar" in 1867, showing the conspirators in a jubilant mood after Caesar's assassination.

> "WHO WOULD NOT WANT TO LEARN HOW, AND UNDER WHAT FORM OF GOVERNMENT, ALMOST ALL OF THE INHABITED WORLD WAS CONQUERED AND BECAME SUBJECT TO THE RULE OF ROME?"
>
> **GREEK HISTORIAN POLYBIUS,** *THE HISTORIES*

its revenge. On March 15, 44 B.C.E, the Ides of March, the conspirators struck just as Caesar entered the Senate. The dictator was reportedly stabbed more than 20 times and died on the marble pavement.

Julius Caesar's assassination sent shock waves through the empire and precipitated the Second Roman Civil War, which lasted more than a decade. In the end, Caesar's 18-year-old grand-nephew, Gaius Octavian, emerged as the victor.

The Pax Romana

During the next four decades, a long reign by any measure, Octavian succeeded in establishing the Roman Empire as a thoroughly integrated body politic led by a single individual, ruling as emperor. At the same time, he established the Julio-Claudian family as a dynasty that was to rule for much of the first century. Ironically, by killing Julius Caesar, the aristocrats had precipitated the very thing they had hoped to avoid: the end of the Roman Republic. But the concentration of power into a monarchical system had practical benefits. The Roman Empire had become too vast to be managed by the quarrelsome and ever-shifting factions of the Roman Senate. The new empire needed a strong hand.

Octavian, on whom the Senate bestowed the reverential title Augustus, or "August One," in 27 B.C.E., could wield that strong hand. He stabilized the Senate and other

Caesar's grand-nephew Octavian

government institutions, brought an end to the tensions between the plebs and the aristocracy, and established a system of international administration that would function largely unchanged for the next 300 years. At the same time, Augustus extended Rome's territorial gains until, in Lionel Casson's words, a person could travel "from the burning sun of Mesopotamia to the mists of Scotland" without ever crossing a national frontier. The result was a Pax Romana, a Roman Peace, whereby the subject peoples of this great new realm were finally free from the cycle of war.

Within this economic sphere, Greece was a leading exporter of white linen, olive oil, honey, and some of the best wine in the empire, as well as paintings and statuary. Syria was prized for popular snacks such as dates, figs, and sugared plums. Spain yielded silver, while the timber from Gaul (France) was considered second only to the cedar from Lebanon. Liquid commodities such as wine, olive oil, and *garum*—a fish sauce condiment that was as popular in ancient Rome as ketchup is today—were transported throughout the empire in amphorae, many of which have been found almost intact from shipwrecks off the coast of Asia Minor—today's Turkey. Egypt was the linchpin of this great global economy as the empire's principal breadbasket, with grain ships leaving for Rome almost daily. The country was also famous for its glass, jewelry, alabaster, porphyry, and granite, as well as the fine quality of its papyrus. Other regions in the Near East provided products such as almonds, walnuts, coconuts, apricots, and peaches.

Most of these commodities poured into Rome as in-kind tribute. It has been estimated that at its peak in the second century C.E., Roman treasury receipts from overseas tribute totaled 1.5 billion sesterces, roughly the equivalent of $6 billion today. This did not include import duties, which were levied whenever a shipment crossed from one Roman province into another. Much of this wealth was used for imports from outside the empire because the Romans had by this time developed a keen appetite for luxury goods from the East. As in the European Union today, this economic activity was sustained by a common currency: the denarius, a coin that figures prominently in the Gospels (for example, Matthew 20:2).

By the second century C.E., most people in the empire could not imagine living in a world other than the Roman commonwealth, accustomed as they were to the stability and economic benefits of a single market, a single currency, and a single security system stretching from the Atlantic coast to the Arabian Gulf. ∎

ROMAN HIGHWAYS

In order to enable his legions to move across the empire at speed, Augustus initiated a vast effort to build a comprehensive road network. Traditionally, roads were the responsibility of cities and townships that relied on them—including villages that needed a road to the nearest town to bring their produce to market. Main roads, to the extent that these existed, were limited to the principal caravan routes; these often dated back hundreds of years, such as the Way of the Philistines along the Mediterranean coast and the King's Highway from Damascus to the Egyptian border. The Romans were the first to conceive of a systematic road network that would link all principal cities within the empire. At its peak, this road system covered some 250,000 miles, of which some 50,000 miles were paved (at left), an astonishing achievement by the standards of Antiquity. Under Trajan, no fewer than 29 major highways connected the city of Rome in all directions of the compass.

THE SECOND-CENTURY C.E. ARCH of Septimius Severus looms over the Roman Forum with the temple of Saturn in the background.

A MOCHE FRIEZE appears to depict a divine being with the severed head of a prisoner.

THE CLASSICAL AGE IN
THE AMERICAS

The era of great classical cultures was not limited to Asia, Africa, or Europe. In Central and South America too, new civilizations rose that produced some of the most impressive and most enigmatic monuments of this period.

Perhaps the most famous of these cultures was the Nasca civilization that produced the so-called Nazca Lines: huge figures of animals as well as geometric forms carved in the soil. Known as geoglyphs, some of these shapes measure as much as half a mile across. Among them are the outlines of monkeys, dogs, lizards, hummingbirds, and spiders, while other shapes seem to suggest mysterious spirals, trapezoids, and rectangles. What is so remarkable about these drawings is not only their astonishing size, but also that they seem to be made up of a single continuous line.

In fact, the only way to truly appreciate these giant shapes is to see them from the air. This has prompted some to suggest that the Nazca Lines are the work of aliens from other planets or the work of human hands guided by some alien intelligence. Modern scholars dismiss this notion, of course, but it is true that no one has yet figured out what the purpose of these drawings might be. Equally puzzling is the fact that these giant forms—believed to have been made between 200 B.C.E. and 600 C.E.—have been preserved to a remarkable degree across the intervening 1,500 years. The reason, experts speculate, is the extreme

dryness of the land itself: Located in southern Peru, the lines are carved on a plateau that is mostly devoid of precipitation.

This extreme aridity may be the reason these figures were drawn in the first place. Some historians speculate that the Nazca Lines started as the beginning of a system of reservoirs and irrigation canals, tapping into the groundwater from subterranean aquifers and the Río Grande de Nasca drainage system. In time, this involved the construction of an elaborate system of subterranean aqueducts, known as *puquios*. As the years passed, these canals may have acquired a religious significance, perhaps because—as in ancient Mesopotamia—they were dedicated to gods that were intimately associated with the primary conditions of cultivation.

We do know that the Nasca culture was a highly sophisticated civilization that produced exquisite cotton textiles and various shapes of richly decorated pottery. What's more, the Nasca diet was extraordinarily varied; archaeologists have found the remains of

THESE GOLD FIGURES illustrate the virtuosity of the Moche artisans.

"BECAUSE OF CLIMATE CHANGE, THE NAZCA LINES,
WHICH ARE ONLY 10 TO 30 CM DEEP,
ARE IN DANGER OF BEING WASHED AWAY."

VIKTORIA NIKITZKI, MARIA REICHE CENTRE

sweet potato, fish, squash, beans, manioc, and the most important staple in the diet, corn. This was complemented with meat from llamas (used as pack animals) as well as guinea pigs, as evidenced by numerous sacrifices found at the ancient Nasca site of Cahuachi, near the coast of the central Andes. Here, Italian and American archaeologists have discovered an elaborate acropolis of 40 mounds that contained large adobe structures. The excavators identified the site as a sacred destination for pilgrimage. They base this theory on the presence of only a few permanent housing structures and the fact that most food was apparently brought in and consumed on site. There is even some evidence of

Moche ornament from Sipan

hallucinogenic beverages, extracted from the San Pedro cactus, which may have been imbibed as part of religious ceremonies. Some historians believe that the Cahuachi shrine was devoted to the ritual worship of fertility and water so as to secure a successful harvest.

Another curious aspect of Nasca religion is the use of a skull as a funerary marker. Some believe these skulls are trophy heads of enemies killed in battle—a motif that also appears on Nasca pottery. Others believe that these are simply objects of funerary rituals, similar to the use of plastered skulls in the Late Stone Age in the Near East.

The Moche Culture of Peru

The Moche culture was a civilization that flourished in the valleys and coastline of northern Peru at this time. Like the Nasca, Moche society was based primarily on cultivation, sustained by a network of irrigation canals fed by local rivers. The Moche people were also impressive builders who erected an adobe pyramid on the Rio Moche, which would rank as the largest pre-Columbian structure in Peru until the advent of Spanish explorers. Here, archaeologists found many beautiful frescoes, though much of the site was destroyed by Spanish conquistadores and presumably robbed of any burial implements, particularly those made of silver and gold. Moche ceramics, too, were of a very high quality. Its potters used molds to produce a number of complex shapes, usually decorated with scenes from warfare, irrigation, textile making, or couples making love.

It was not until 1987 that excavators succeeded in uncovering an intact Moche burial site. This tomb, excavated near Sipán, contained the remains

AN ANCIENT GEOGLYPH of a spider is a typical example of the mysterious Nazca Lines that originated between 200 and 600 C.E.

288 THE CLASSICAL AGE

THE ANCIENT MAYA
stepped pyramid known as
El Castillo at Chichén Itzá,
in today's Mexican state of
Yucatán, was dedicated to
the serpent deity Kukulkan.

NOTABLE DATES

ca 600 B.C.E.

Rise of the Maya civilization

ca 250 B.C.E.

Maya alphabet numbers
500 glyphs

ca 200 B.C.E..

First appearance of Nazca
Lines

ca 100 B.C.E.

Beginning of the Moche
culture in Peru

ca 100 C.E.

Construction begins on the
Maya Pyramid of the Sun
in Teotihuacan

ca 250 C.E.

The Maya develop city-states
buoyed by trade

ca 300 C.E.

Lord of Sipán of Moche
Kingdom is buried near Sipán

ca 400 C.E.

Moche Kingdom covers 400
miles of Peru's coastal region

ca 500 C.E.

The Hopewell culture fades
in the Ohio Valley

ca 500 C.E.

Teotihuacan, Mexico, is the
largest city in the Americas

ca 500 C.E.

Maya civilization flourishes on
the Yucatán Peninsula

ca 700 C.E.

Pyramid of the Magician is
built in Uxmal (Mexico)

MULTIPLE MOCHE INDIAN MUMMIES were discovered at the stepped pyramids of the El Brujo archaeological site, located north of today's Trujillo, Peru.

"THERE WAS NEITHER MAN, NOR ANIMAL, BIRDS, FISHES, CRABS, TREES, STONES, CAVES, RAVINES, GRASSES, NOR FORESTS; THERE WAS ONLY THE SKY."

CREATION NARRATIVE FROM THE MAYA *POPUL VUH*

of a king, carbon-dated to 300 C.E., who is tentatively identified as the "Lord of Sipán." It also held the remains of several other people (presumably servants) and was richly adorned with objects made of gold and silver. Another tomb, discovered in 2005 at the El Brujo archaeological site near Trujillo, contained the remains of a prominent woman. Her grave was also decorated with numerous artifacts and included the skeleton of a teenage girl who bore signs of death by a garrote, suggesting that she was a servant girl put to death in order to serve her mistress in the afterlife.

The Moche culture flourished from about 100 to 700 C.E., reaching its apex around 400 C.E. when its kingdom commanded nearly 400 miles of coastal territory. Some 900 years later, the Inca culture of Peru would still use roads carved by Moche engineers nearly a millennium earlier.

The Maya Civilization

The most impressive culture in the Americas of this period was undoubtedly the Maya civilization. From about 700 B.C.E., the Maya developed a society whose accomplishments matched those of Greece and Persia in writing, science, mathematics, art, and architecture,

A MOCHE STAR-SHAPED ORNAMENT is believed to be part of a calendar

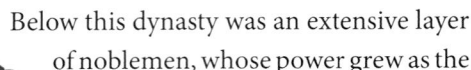

including the construction of the most impressive pyramids in Latin America. At its zenith, the Maya controlled a territory equal to Guatemala, Belize, southeastern Mexico, and the western parts of El Salvador and Honduras. This region was anchored by a number of city-states, including Teotihuacan in the Valley of Mexico, Tikal in today's Guatemala, Copán in western Honduras, and Calakmul on the Yucatán Peninsula. Some historians have compared this political structure to that of prehistoric Mesopotamia or that of preclassical Greece, where city-states maintained a delicate balance of power using a variety of alliances.

Maya dignitary from Campeche

While much of the Maya civilization remains shrouded in legend, historians generally believe that at its peak, the realm was governed by various hereditary "divine kings" who mediated between the gods and the mortals on Earth, similar to the role that Chinese emperors played in this period.

Below this dynasty was an extensive layer of noblemen, whose power grew as the centuries progressed. They drew their wealth and power from their landholdings, where peasants worked to cultivate a great variety of crops, using canals and terraced hillsides to draw sufficient water. This was a particular challenge in the north, which suffered from very low levels of precipitation, compared to the south where plentiful rain produced dense rainforests.

In between ranged a series of volcanic highlands that not only boasted highly fertile topsoil but also produced a hard volcanic glass known as obsidian, much prized for the tips of arrows and spears. Obsidian soon became an eagerly sought material in the intercity trade. As in the case of the Nasca and Moche, the principal Maya staple was corn, which they crossbred with wild grain to increase the size of the ears.

The Maya civilization introduced many other

MAYA MEDICINE

Anticipating Indian chakra techniques, the Maya practiced holistic healing methods that emphasized the balance between body and spirit. Their focus was on sustaining the uninterrupted flow of *ch'ulel,* or "life force," similar to the Indian idea of prana and the Chinese concept of qi. As Maya scholar Bonnie Bley wrote, "This life force was everywhere. It permeated from mountains, rivers, houses, plants, to people, and was said to come from a spiritual divine authority." As a result, much of Maya medical practices revolved around the innovative use of herbs and plant extracts, as in the case of Chinese medicine. Special healers (at right), known as *h'men,* were trained in the use of these herbs and tried to restore the balance of mind and body in those who were ill. Today, physicians increasingly recognize that a person's emotional and spiritual health can have a major impact on his or her physical condition.

THIS MAYA MURAL is one of several impressive ones in the Templo de las Pinturas (Temple of the Paintings) from the acropolis of Bonampak in today's Mexico, dated to ca 790 C.E.

A MASK from 672 C.E. made of malachite, a green mineral, is believed to depict a female ruler, Lady Tz'akbu Ajaw, also known as the Red Queen.

inventions to the Americas, including the most sophisticated writing system on the continent to date. Though the Maya script is often called hieroglyphic because of its iconograph resemblance to Egyptian writing, the comparison is misleading. As a system of logosyllabic signs—in which each symbol represents a complete word rather than a phonetic element of that word—it is perhaps more akin to the writing that was being canonized in China at this time. By about 250 C.E., the Maya alphabet consisted of about 600 glyphs that remained in use until the arrival of the Spanish conquistadores. Texts were written on ceramics, stone markers called stelae, and a form of paper made from tree bark, known as *amatl*. Unfortunately, after the arrival of the Spanish conquerors, Catholic prelates ordered many of the Maya texts destroyed as tokens of a pagan culture. Thousands of Maya codices are believed to have been lost in this manner, with the exception of three books, now held in museums in Madrid, Dresden, and Paris. As one prominent Maya historian, Michael Coe, has written, imagine if "all that posterity knew of ourselves were to be based upon some prayer books and 'Pilgrim's Progress.' " This also explains why the remaining Maya texts were not fully deciphered until the end of the 20th century.

The Maya Pyramids

The most impressive product of the Maya civilizations was its penchant for building pyramids. Their principal purpose, scholars believe, was to provide monumental tombs for Maya royalty or to provide ceremonial shrines for the worship of a particular god. As in ancient Egypt, the practice of building these large structures may have emanated from the tradition of creating burial mounds. Unlike Egyptian pyramids, however, the Maya pyramids were topped by the flat platform for either worship or astronomical observation, similar to the ziggurats of Mesopotamia. In Teotihuacan, for example, the Pyramid of the Sun (a name later coined by the Aztecs) was built beginning in 100 C.E. along the so-called Avenue of the Dead. Originally rising to a height of 216 feet and finished with lime plaster, it is the third largest pyramid in the world. Many

A RECTANGULAR sculpted stone block known as Altar Q depicts the 16 Maya rulers of Copán, located in present-day Honduras.

THE POLYCHROME clay bowl with the head of a jaguar from ca 250–600 C.E. was found in Tikal in present-day Guatemala.

A MAYA ASTRONOMICAL TEXT DESCRIBING THE MOVEMENT OF VENUS, DATED BETWEEN 1021 AND 1154 C.E., IS BELIEVED TO BE THE OLDEST PRE-HISPANIC DOCUMENT OF THE AMERICAS.

of its sides were decorated with colorful murals, which have worn off over time. The exact purpose of this pyramid, or the identity of the deity to which it may have been dedicated, has not yet been established. At its peak, Teotihuacan was one of the largest cities in the Americas, with a population of more than 125,000 people.

Another famous Maya pyramid is the structure in Uxmal, today located some 40 miles south of Mérida in the state of Yucatán, Mexico. Built in the late classical age from around 500 C.E., the so-called Pirámide del Adivino (Pyramid of the Magician) forms part of an elaborate acropolis, surrounded by buildings with smooth ashlar walls and ornate friezes in the local Puuc style.

Maya chocolate-making pot

What makes this pyramid so unusual is the oval or elliptical shape of its walls, which were steadily expanded over the next 400 years. Though the original height of the pyramid is in dispute, most scholars accept that it once rose to at least 115 feet on a base of 225 by 160 feet, making it the most prominent Maya structure in Yucatán.

The Maya constellation of city-states lasted until around 850 C.E., when the civilization went into rapid decline for reasons that are not yet known. During the next decades, many of its magnificent buildings and pyramids were slowly reclaimed by tropical growth and rainforests, until they were rediscovered by explorers in the 19th century. ∎

A MAYA APOCALYPSE?

Among many of the Maya inventions was the development of an annual calendar of 365 days (detail at left), based on a careful observation of lunar and solar cycles as well as earlier Mesoamerican systems. This solar calendar was used in conjunction with another system known as the Tzolkin: a ceremonial year of just 260 days. Together, the two calendars were meshed to produce the so-called Calendar Round, which is still used in parts of Guatemala today. Maya astronomers also developed a longer vigesimal measure (based on a unit of 20), known as the Long Count, for documenting longer spans of time. For example, they determined that after the world was created in 3114 B.C.E., it entered a series of cycles, one of which was to end in 2012. This didn't mean that the world would end, but that a new cycle would begin.

A NIGHTTIME VIEW of Chichén Itzá in today's Mexico shows the head of the serpent deity Kukulkan, to which the pyramid was dedicated.

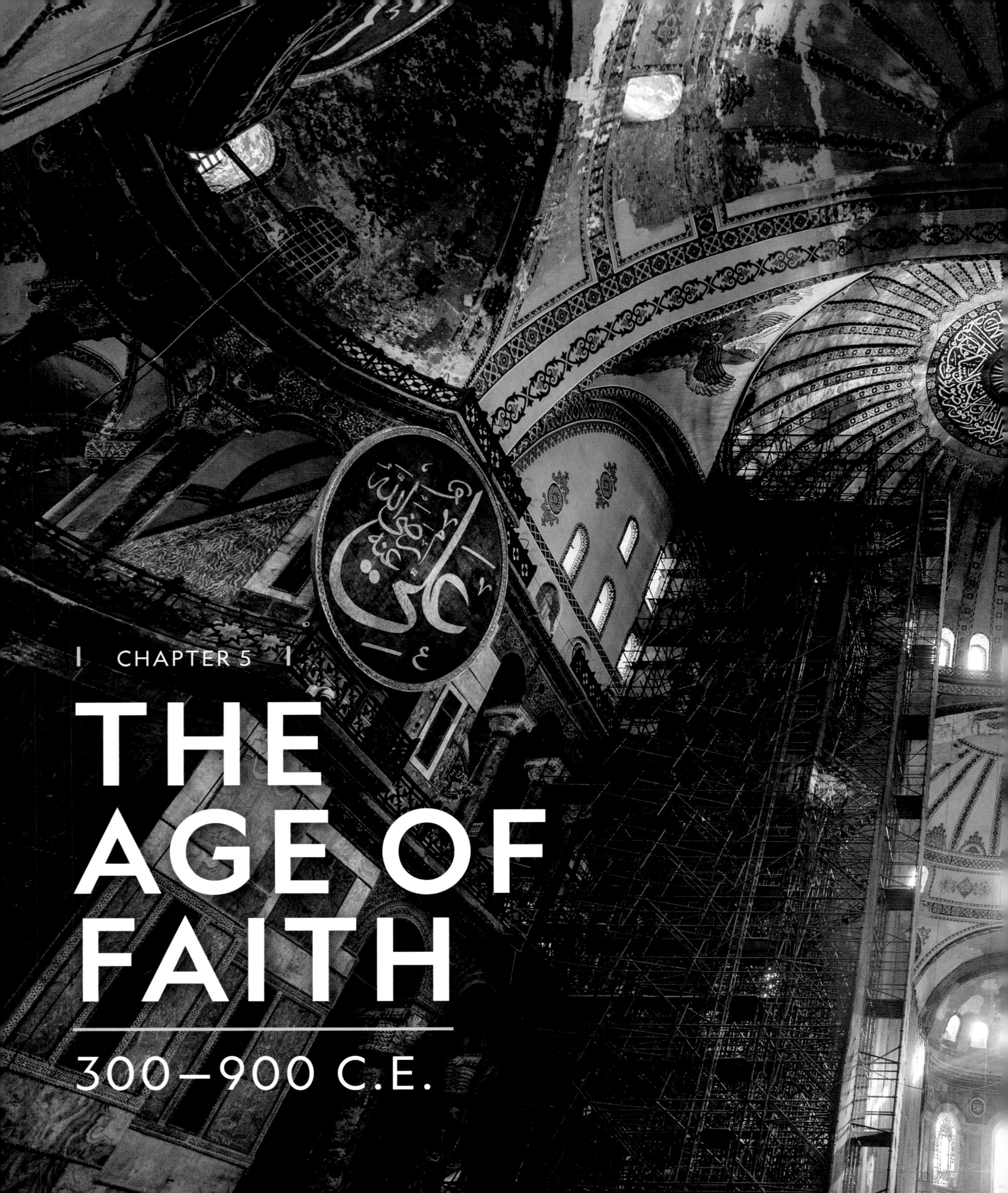

CHAPTER 5

THE AGE OF FAITH

300–900 C.E.

HAGIA SOPHIA in Istanbul, the last monumental masterpiece of Roman architecture, was built as a basilica by Emperor Justinian I between 532 and 537 C.E.

CONTENTS

THE RISE OF RELIGIONS

The period between 300 and 900 C.E. witnessed the astonishing spread of new religious ideas throughout the world. After Christianity took root in Europe, the Near East, and even parts of China, it was displaced by the rise of Islam in North Africa and the Sasanian Empire. Meanwhile, Buddhism grew rapidly throughout India, China, and Southeast Asia. This process coincided with the collapse of ancient kingdoms and empires that saw their predominantly pagan imprint replaced with new faith traditions.

Nowhere was the transformative role of religious ideas more prevalent than in the Roman Empire—a vast realm that for centuries had served as the largest commonwealth ever known in history. Inevitably, this also led to the proliferation of different belief systems. Roman soldiers as well as sailors and merchants returned from their travels with new cult practices, including the worship of Isis, Cybele, and Mithras. The Mithraic Mysteries, a religion inspired by an Indo-Iranian angelic divinity known as Mithra or Mithras, were particularly popular in the Roman military. Its liturgy would typically unfold in a cave-like space known as a mithraeum. Here, up to 30 worshippers would sit and share a meal of bread and wine in front of an effigy of the god slaying a bull.

Judaism in the Diaspora

Another religion that had found adherents throughout the empire was Judaism. As part of the ongoing Diaspora, Jewish communities could be found in major cities of the empire, including in the city of Rome itself. Some of their synagogues were founded as early as the first century B.C.E., when Rome was still growing as an economic and political power in the Mediterranean. Scores of inscriptions found in local Jewish catacombs are in Greek rather than Latin. What's more, Jews enjoyed certain rights that were not available to other people in the empire—such as exemption from military service, rights of assembly, and the right to observe the Sabbath.

This tolerance for other faith traditions changed when the Roman Empire came under increasing pressure from barbarian tribes. In the third century C.E, the growing peril of invasions became so dire that a complete overhaul of the imperial system that Augustus created was needed. Instead of one ruler, four rulers—two emperors and two vice emperors, or caesars—were appointed to lead Roman forces at critical fronts throughout the realm. Each emperor established a forward headquarters near sensitive frontiers; one of these was just a few miles distant from a city called Byzantium—the future Constantinople. When in 305 C.E. Emperor Diocletian decided to abdicate, a 20-year civil war erupted among various pretenders to the throne. In 312, the two remaining imperial claimants, Constantine and Maxentius, met for a decisive clash at a crossing over the Tiber River, known as the Milvian Bridge. This battle would have far-reaching consequences for the spread of a new religion called Christianity. ■

A SCULPTURE OF THE SEATED BUDDHA is dated to the fifth-century C.E. Gupta period in India.

A BRONZE PANEL from around 200 C.E. shows the Indo-Iranian angelic divinity Mithras slaying a bull.

A 12TH-CENTURY BYZANTINE MOSAIC of Jesus was created for Hagia Sophia in Constantinople, today's Istanbul.

THE BIRTH OF
CHRISTIANITY

Though suppressed in its native Judea, the teachings of a Jewish rabbi named Jesus of Nazareth inspired a movement called Christianity that spread rapidly throughout the Roman Empire. In the fourth century, it would become the sole religion of the Roman realm.

According to the Nativity narratives in the Gospels of Matthew and Luke, Jesus was born to a maid named Mary (or Miriam in Aramaic), who lived in the village of Nazareth in Galilee. She was betrothed to a man named Joseph (or Josef). Joseph is traditionally described as a carpenter, but it is more likely that he was a farmer who supplemented his income with woodworking jobs. While growing up, Jesus must have observed his father as he toiled on his land—sowing seeds, pruning the orchard, and reaping the harvest—which explains why so many of these themes would return in Jesus' parables during his ministry. Recent research suggests that because of his woodworking skills, Joseph and his son Jesus may have been involved in the construction of Sepphoris, the new capital built by Herod Antipas (Herod the Great's son) just six miles north of their hamlet of Nazareth. At the time of King Herod's death in 4 B.C.E., his kingdom was divided among his sons (and one sister) into four separate territories. While Judea was to be ruled by his son Archelaus, Galilee and Perea (the Transjordan) was given to Antipas.

When Jesus was about 32 or 33 years old, he decided to join the movement of John the Baptist, a dissident preacher who lived on the other side of the River Jordan in the region of Perea, also ruled by Herod Antipas. The Gospel of Luke dates John's ministry to the "fifteenth year of the reign of Emperor Tiberius, when Pontius Pilate was governor of Judea, and Herod was ruler of Galilee" (Luke 3:1). The most plausible date is therefore the year 28 C.E.

Like many other religious movements at the time—such as those of the Zealots and the Essenes—John the Baptist rejected the sacrificial cult at the Jerusalem Temple and the corruption of the Temple priesthood and clamored for a return to a society wholly ruled by the precepts of the Torah, the Jewish Law. John injected urgency into his campaign by warning that the nation's lawlessness—primarily its neglect of the Jewish Law—was bound to invite the wrath of the Lord, who would send a fearsome, divinely appointed commander—the Messiah—to eject the foreign occupiers and install a true reign of God. Shocked by his words, many listeners agreed to repent and accept John's ritual of

A SIXTH-CENTURY SILVER CHALICE with Coptic text was produced for a Christian community in Egypt.

"THE SPIRIT OF THE LORD IS UPON ME, BECAUSE HE HAS ANOINTED ME TO BRING GOOD NEWS TO THE POOR."

GOSPEL OF LUKE 4:18

purification: immersion and baptism in the water of the River Jordan. Jesus, too, agreed to be baptized.

At some time thereafter, Jesus decided to develop his own ministry in his native Galilee. Initially, those in his following were some of the Baptist's disciples who gravitated to Jesus and referred to him as "Rabbi" and "Messiah" (John 1:38-41). In Galilee, he recruited additional disciples from among the local fishermen. In the initial phase, Jesus focused much of his activity on the area confined by Bethsaida, Chorazin, and Capernaum, all within a day's walking distance. He taught a new compact for the social and spiritual renewal of Jewish society, known as the Kingdom of God. In this, he was perhaps inspired by prophets like Amos, Micah, and Hosea, who also urged their followers to focus not on the sacrificial cult

Tyrian half-shekel

but on the core pillars of the Torah: compassion, social responsibility, and faith in God. His preaching drew large crowds, not least because Jesus sometimes engaged in miraculous feats, such as exorcisms.

But after several months—the chronology is not clear—Jesus realized that little had changed in his native Galilee in response to his sermons and miracles. "Woe to you!" he cries in the Gospels of Luke and Matthew, denouncing the very cities—such as Capernaum and Chorazin—on which he had focused his ministry (Matthew 11:21; Luke 10:13). In response, he decided to go to Jerusalem as the Passover festival was nigh. Like the prophet Jeremiah, he would appeal to his fellow Jews in Judaism's most sacred sanctuary, the Temple. But when Jesus reached the sanctuary, he was shocked to find that the massive forecourt was filled with moneychangers doing brisk business converting Roman currency into Temple shekels. He began to drive them out, and it is likely that this violent demonstration prompted the warrant for his arrest. Later that night, he was apprehended by Temple guards on the Mount of Olives and brought to the house of the high priest Caiaphas for an indictment. For reasons that are still debated, Caiaphas decided to refer the case to the Romans, with the charge that Jesus had claimed to be the King of the Jews. This was a grave political offense that was bound to invoke retribution by the Roman authorities. And so it came to pass: Jesus was interrogated by the Roman prefect, Pontius Pilate, and condemned to die on the cross. According to Church tradition, he was crucified on the last day of Passover, a Friday, and hastily buried before sundown and the beginning of the Sabbath.

Soon after, however, reports began to circulate

THIS CANVAS of "St. Joseph, the Carpenter" was painted by French Baroque artist Georges de la Tour in 1642.

THE SYNAGOGUE of ancient Capernaum, built of blocks of white limestone, has been dated to the late third century C.E.

NOTABLE DATES

37 B.C.E.
Reign of King Herod the Great (37–4 B.C.E.) begins

4 B.C.E.
Putative date of birth of Jesus

6 C.E.
Augustus annexes Judea as a Roman province

26 C.E.
Pontius Pilate appointed procurator of Judea

ca 28 C.E.
Jesus joins movement of John the Baptist in the Jordan

30–33 C.E.
Jesus is tried and crucified on orders of Pilate

ca 50 C.E.
Paul begins journeys through the Eastern Roman Empire

64 C.E.
Nero blames Christians for Great Fire of Rome

185 C.E.
Bishop Irenaeus proposes Gospel canon of Matthew, Mark, Luke, and John

249 C.E.
Emperor Decius persecutes all who refuse to worship Roman gods

261 C.E.
Emperor Gallienus ends persecution of Christians

313 C.E.
Constantine issues Edict of Milan, tolerating all religions

476 C.E.
Fall of Western Roman Empire

THESE CAVERNS are believed to have formed part of the lower level of the Antonia Fortress, even though they were later incorporated in a Roman city gate built in the second century C.E.

that Jesus had risen from the dead and had appeared to his disciples in different locations (Mark 16:6, John 20:26-27). The news of Jesus' resurrection galvanized the Apostles. They came out of their places of hiding and returned to Jerusalem. There, they resolved to continue Jesus' work and propagate the good news of the Kingdom in Judea and beyond.

The Early Apostolic Movement

Until this moment, Christianity had spread throughout the Mediterranean basin haphazardly and in the face of occasional suppression by local and state authorities. As early as the first century, the Sadducee priesthood in Jerusalem had noted with alarm that the "Jesus following" led by the Apostles was still alive. They had believed that by crucifying Jesus, his Messianic movement had been suppressed. The idea that Jesus had been resurrected from the dead

Emperor Augustus

was a further provocation, because the Sadducees (unlike the Pharisees) firmly rejected the immortality of the soul, let alone the possibility of physical resurrection.

In every respect, Jesus' followers continued to live as Jews by observing the Sabbath, praying at the Temple, and preparing and eating kosher foods. But as the Sadducee persecution intensified after the murder of a disciple called Stephen, many followers fled from Jerusalem to find sanctuary elsewhere, in places like Cyprus, Phoenicia, Damascus, and Antioch. While the deacon Philip moved to Samaria, Jesus' main disciple, Peter, left for Lydda and Joppa. Only a core group remained in Jerusalem, soon to be led by a man named James, Jesus' brother.

Not satisfied with this dispersal, the high priest Caiaphas ordered the disciples arrested wherever they could be found. One zealous young man named

THE "HERESY" OF ARIANISM

Relieved from the scourge of Roman persecutions, the nascent Church was next tormented by internal disputes over the divine nature of Christ (at right). What did it mean that Christ was both human and divine?

A prominent presbyter from Alexandria named Arius sought to resolve the matter by claiming that since Christ was "begotten by the Father," he could therefore not be of the same divine substance as the Father. In other words, Father and Son could not be consubstantial. The simple logic of this solution appealed to many believers. Arius's ideas became a major Arianist movement that prompted a synod in Nicaea, in today's Turkey. A majority of bishops voted for the "consubstantiality clause," which today is still recited in the Nicene Creed. But Arianism continued to spread, particularly among the converted barbarian tribes of Europe.

"THUS THE PIOUS EMPEROR, GLORIFYING IN
THE CONFESSION OF THE VICTORIOUS CROSS,
PROCLAIMED THE SON OF GOD TO THE ROMANS."

EUSEBIUS, *THE LIFE OF CONSTANTINE*

Saul offered to go to Damascus, where a large group of apostolic disciples had reportedly found refuge. Caiaphas authorized this mission (even though it fell outside his jurisdiction), but on the way to Damascus, Saul had a change of heart. He heard a voice saying, "Saul, why do you persecute me?" (Acts 9:4). This was the turning point: From this time forward, Saul—later called Paul—devoted himself wholeheartedly to advancing the apostolic mission. He undertook three major journeys to Asia Minor and Greece, where he (as well as other early proselytizers) established communities of followers of Jesus, who were soon called Christians (*Christianos* in Greek).

Along the way, Paul made an astounding discovery: While many Jewish communities rebuffed his message of Christ as the Messiah, many Gentiles were quite receptive. This was not without precedent. Though most Apostles—like other observant Jews—refrained from contact with Gentiles because they did not honor the Jewish purity laws, Peter had received a vision in Joppa that suggested that the prohibition against the conversion of Gentiles was lifted. But there was a crucial difference: Peter and other Apostles welcomed Gentiles as converts provided they also agreed to become practicing Jews. Paul, however, found that while many Gentiles were attracted to Christian spirituality, they weren't interested in adopting Jewish customs as well (such as the need to be circumcised and eat only kosher foods). In response, Paul decided that Gentiles who wanted to be "baptized" as followers of Christ need *not* adopt Judaism as well. "Real circumcision is a matter of the heart," he wrote in his letter to the Romans; "it is spiritual, not literal" (Romans 2:29). As a result, Paul consciously released the early Christian movement from its Jewish roots, thus laying the foundation for a new and separate religion: Christianity.

The Growth of Christianity

Although Rome refused to recognize Christianity as an officially tolerated faith, the movement continued to grow. Rather than meeting in public, followers gathered in each other's homes to talk about Jesus' teachings and share in table fellowship. This idea of private assembly is the root meaning of the Greek word *ekklesia,* or "gathering," which later would be translated as "church." By the end of the first century, there were as many as 300,000 Christians in Asia Minor alone.

But modern research has shown that there were actually multiple Christian movements circulating in the third and fourth centuries. Some of these did not agree with Paul's interpretation that Jesus' quintessential purpose was to redeem humankind by virtue of his death and resurrection. Many of these were Jewish Christians. The Christian community in Rome, for example, existed well before Paul's arrival on the scene. Some of these movements blended Platonic ideas with Christology in the belief that deep meditation and immersion in the divine would ultimately lead to a secret knowledge (*gnosis* in Greek) of God. This idea was popular, for it agreed with the premise in Greek philosophy that each human being carried a spark of the divine inside. For these so-called Gnostic Christians, this also explained the reason that Jesus often spoke in parables. Other Christians, such as the Docetists, believed

THIS OSSUARY, a box for the second burial of skeletal remains after the body has decomposed, is believed to have contained the bones of the high priest Caiaphas.

THE SPREAD OF CHRISTIANITY, 600-1200

- Roman Catholic area of influence ca 1054
- Eastern Orthodox area of influence ca 1054
- Area of shared influence
- ✝ Roman patriarchate (Pope)
- ✝ Orthodox patriarchate
- ✝ Nestorian patriarchate
- — Silk Road
- — Other route
- ⤳ Nestorian influence
- COPTIC CHURCH Monophysite church

0 mi ————— 400
0 km ————— 400
Present-day country boundaries are shown.

Map labels:

Ireland — IRELAND (ÉIRE), Waterford
U.K., York, Chester
BRITISH ISLES, Great Britain
Celtic Sea, Bristol Channel, The Wash
Land's End, London, Dartmouth
Channel Islands, Boulogne
English Channel, Strait of Dover
ATLANTIC OCEAN, Point St.-Mathieu
Bayeux, Rouen, Rennes, Paris, Reims, Verdun, Orléans, Tours, Vézelay
Bay of Biscay
Bordeaux, Clermont, Lyon
León, Pamplona, Toulouse, Narbonne, Albi, Nîmes, Marseille
Pyrenees, ANDORRA
Zaragoza, Barcelona
Duero, Ebro, Tagus, Toledo
SPAIN, The Reconquista returned the prevalance of Christianity 1050-1250.
Valencia, Granada, Cartagena
Alboran Sea
Balearic Sea, Balearic Is.
Corsica, Sardinia, Cagliari
FRANCE, Loire, Garonne, Rhône, Seine, Rhine

North Sea
DENMARK, JUTLAND, Roskilde, Lund, Bornholm
SWEDEN
Baltic Sea, Rügen
Frisian Islands, FRISIANS, NETHERLANDS
Hamburg, Lübeck, Danzig (Gdańsk), POMERANIA
Bremen, Brunswick (Braunschweig)
WENDS
Bruges, Lille, Cambrai, Liège, BELGIUM, Cologne, LUX., Trier, Mainz
Converted to Christianity ca 900-1100
Converted to Christianity ca 800
SAXONS
GERMANY
ALLAMANNI, Nuremburg, Ratisbon (Regensburg), Prague
Converted to Christianity ca 880-1039
CZECHS, CZECHIA (CZECH REP.)
Metz, Strasbourg, Basel
SWITZERLAND, ALPS
Converted to Christianity ca 600
Danube, Main
Milan, Turin, Venice, Genoa, Po
Ligurian Sea, Pisa, Livorno, Florence, Ravenna
Converted to Christianity ca 1125
Neman, PRUSSIA
Converted to Christianity ca 1230-1280
BELARUS
Posen (Poznań), POLAND, POLES, Lublin, Kraków
Oder, Vistula, Bug
Converted to Christianity ca 966-1034
Converted to Christianity ca 988-1015
Kyiv
UKR
EUROPE
SLOVAKIA, Vienna, Pressburg (Bratislava), AUSTRIA
Buda and Pest (Budapest), HUNGARY, MAGYARS
CARPATHIAN MOUNTAINS
Dniester, Southern Bug
Converted to Christianity circa 950-1050
MOLDOVA, Prut, Mureș, Tisza
SLOVENIA, CROATIA, Drava, Sava, Danube
ROMANIA
BOSNIA AND HERZEGOVINA, Zara (Zadar), Belgrade
SERBIA, Spalato (Split), Ragusa (Dubrovnik)
Converted to Christianity ca 863-900
Converted to Christianity ca 900
MONTENEGRO, SERBIA, Niš
BULGARIA
Contention between Rome and Constantinople came to climax in 1054. Papal legate Cardinal Humbert delivered a Bull of Excommunication, effectively dividing the church between East and West.
KOS., Sofia, BULG.
NORTH MACEDONIA
ITALY, Adriatic Sea, Rome ✝, Naples, Bari, Brindisi, Dyrrhachium (Durrës)
ALBANIA
Thessalonica (Thessaloniki)
Constantinople (Istanbul) ✝ (Kocaeli), Nicomedia
Gallipoli, Cyzicus, Nicaea (Iznik)
GREECE, Athens, Peloponnese
Aegean Sea
Pergamum (Bergama), Sardis, Smyrna (Izmir), Miletus, Laodicea (Denizli)
Tyrrhenian Sea
Palermo, Messina, Sicily, Syracuse (Siracusa)
Ionian Sea
Tunis, ALGERIA, TUNISIA
Gulf of Hamamet, MALTA
Mediterranean Sea
Gulf of Gabes
Gulf of Sidra
AFRICA, LIBYA, SAHARA, EGYPT
Candia (Irakleio), Crete, Rhodes
Alexandria ✝, COPTIC
Bosporus
LIVONIA

that Jesus' physical presence had been an illusion and that he had always been a divine being. By contrast, the Ebionites—a group that may have originated in the Jerusalem community—held true to their Jewish roots and believed that Jesus had always been a mere mortal.

On top of that, Christianity had to cope with Roman intolerance and occasional persecution. After the Great Fire of Rome in 64 C.E., when rumors circulated that Emperor Nero had deliberately set the fire in order to build a new planned city, Nero passed the blame on to Rome's Christian communities. Scores of Christians were arrested and executed.

Scholars do not agree, however, to what the extent the Roman prohibition of Christianity was enforced in the second and third centuries. There were doubtless episodes of violent conflict, often instigated by local communities that harbored suspicions about Christian worship and its practice of eating "Christ's body" and drinking "Christ's blood." What's more, the Christian emphasis on love (*agapè* in Greek, meaning charitable love), regardless of class boundaries, was often ridiculed

The Antioch Chalice

in a society where classes were rigorously separated and love in a religious context was often associated with Dionysian rites.

The most damning aspect of Christianity in the eyes of many Romans, however, was Christians' refusal to offer sacrifices to the Roman gods, and particularly the reigning emperor. This reinforced the impression of Christianity as a foreign cult profoundly at odds with Roman interests. Little wonder, then, that Roman historian Tacitus referred to Christianity as a "deadly superstition," and Pliny the Younger called it "a superstition taken to extravagant lengths." In 250, Emperor Decius went so far as to order that all citizens obtain a *libellus,* certified proof of faithful sacrifice to Roman gods, on pain of death. Scores of Christians submitted. Those who refused to comply, including Pope Fabian, the 20th pope since Peter, were promptly executed.

The Byzantine Empire

And yet Christianity continued to expand. As archaeological excavations have shown, Christian chapels sprang up in unexpected corners of the

SECRET SYMBOLS OF CHRISTIANITY

In response to Roman persecution, Christians developed secret emblems and symbols to identify them as a member of the flock. One such emblem was the *ichthys* symbol—the Greek word for fish—rendered as a word or in the stylized form of a fish (at left). The fish signified the apostolic task of serving as "fishermen of men," and the word "ICHTHYS" served as a Greek acronym of the phrase *Iēsous* (Jesus), *Christos* (Christ), *Theou* (God), *'Yios* (Son), *Sotēr* (Savior). Another seemingly innocent logo was the twin Greek characters A (alpha) and Ω (omega), based on the statement, "I am Alpha and Omega" (Revelation 22:13). The cross as the universal sign of Christianity was a later development.

AN EARLY SIXTH-CENTURY marble head depicts Ariadne, Byzantine empress and consort of Emperor Zeno.

MANY OF ISTANBUL'S MOSQUES built after the fall of Constantinople to Sultan Mehmed II in 1453 are modeled after the Hagia Sophia basilica, as in the case of the Sultan Ahmed Mosque, completed in 1616.

"THE PEOPLES WHO FALL UNDER THE SWAY OF OUR IMPERIAL CLEMENCY SHOULD PROFESS THE FAITH . . . COMMUNICATED BY THE APOSTLE PETER."

THEODOSIUS I'S EDICT OF 380, MAKING CHRISTIANITY ROME'S OFFICIAL RELIGION

empire, founded by unknown missionaries well beyond the orbit of the original Apostles. For example, Christianity was introduced into Egypt via Alexandria, which had a large Jewish community, and from there it spread rapidly among both Greek and Coptic-speaking communities. The faith also spread northward, using the ancient trade routes of Mesopotamia along the Tigris and Euphrates Rivers. By the middle of the second century, Edessa had become an important center of Christian activity. Church tradition claims that the Apostle Thomas carried the Gospel to India, although scholars believe that it was actually the work of Syriac missionaries who revered Thomas as their patron saint. By the time church theologian Pantaenus of Alexandria traveled to India around 180 C.E., he found many flourishing Christian communities.

Constantine's Edict of Milan of 313 C.E. removed all limits on religious expression in the Roman Empire, but this religious tolerance toward other faiths was short-lived. Less than 90 years later, Emperor Theodosius II outlawed all pagan cults, including the Roman state religion. In all, it had taken 350 years for the ideas of a Galilean rabbi to conquer the world and become the sole religion of the Roman Empire.

In the meantime, the Roman Empire itself had undergone a transformation. Constantine recognized that the future of the empire lay in the East rather than the West. While much of Gaul and Spain was under pressure from barbarian hordes, the population centers of Asia Minor were enjoying robust growth. As a result, Constantine decided to build a new Roman capital, Roma Nova, near the town of Byzantium, originally founded by Greek settlers in 657 B.C.E. The new capital—eventually renamed Constantinopolis, or

"city of Constantine" in Greek—rose in less than 20 years, a stupendous achievement. Less than a century later, Constantinople would become a Christian city, endowed with churches and chapels rather than pagan temples.

Under Emperor Theodosius II, the tables were now turned as Rome's ancient cult become outlawed and Christianity was proclaimed the sole religion of the empire. Christian clergy throughout the realm needed no further prompting. They began to ransack pagan temples, destroying thousands of statues of Roman deities while making off with a vast haul of silver, gold, and other treasure. In Alexandria, Bishop Theophilus personally supervised the wholesale destruction of a cultural complex known as the Mouseion, including the still functioning Alexandrian Library. The culture of Roman Antiquity had effectively come to an end.

And so had the breadth of its territory. When the Roman Empire stood at its zenith, a citizen could travel from the moors of Britain to the deserts of Mesopotamia without ever crossing a border. By the fifth century, the western part of the realm had shrunk to a shadow of its former self. In 405, a mass migration of Germanic tribes, possibly fleeing from Huns invading from farther east, plunged into Gaul, causing havoc on a vast scale. In 410, Roman control of Britain evaporated. That same year, Rome was sacked by the Visigoths, followed by Vandals in 455. Spain was carved up between Vandals and other tribes. The last Roman co-ruler in the west, Romulus Augustulus, was deposed in 476. Only the empire in the east anchored on Constantinople, now known as the Byzantine Empire, would last for another thousand years. ■

THE SIXTH-CENTURY RELIQUARY CROSS of Justin II, also known as the Crux Vaticana, is believed to be the oldest reliquary claiming to contain a fragment of the True Cross.

A HEIAN PERIOD sculpture in lacquered and gilded wood of the Buddha Amitabha, or "celestial Buddha," was created by a Japanese artist in the 11th or 12th century.

THE RELIGIONS OF
THE EAST

India's Gupta Dynasty practiced religious tolerance, as did the Tang Dynasty of China, where Buddhism continued to coexist with Confucianism. By the ninth century, the Church of the East had become the largest Christian territory of its time.

While the Roman Empire went into decline, India attained new heights with its own Classical Age. After many centuries in which the Indian subcontinent was ruled by separate kingdoms, the region came together once more under the so-called Gupta Dynasty. Its founder is usually identified as Shri-Gupta from Uttar Pradesh, even though we have few contemporary documents or archaeological evidence that can attest to his rule. Scholars therefore do not agree on the precise dates of his reign, but most accept that it must have occurred at some point in the middle or end of the third century C.E. His successors, including Chandragupta I and his son Samudragupta, continued to conquer other Indian kingdoms, relying on new military innovations such as the use of mounted archers and elephant-borne heavy cavalry. Several gold coins from this era depict Gupta kings on horseback, wielding a bow and arrow, thus emphasizing the critical role of this weapon in their conquests. Some historians believe that the Gupta fascination with military strategy even led to the development of chess (*caturanga*).

A stela known as the Allahabad Pillar notes that scores of border kingdoms were compelled to pledge obedience to Samudragupta and duly pay tribute. In addition, it notes that many of these vassal kings offered their daughters in marriage, not unlike King Solomon's practice of marrying the daughters of subject kings so as to cement their loyalty. The pillar also describes the king's great interest in the arts, including music and poetry, and refers to him as the "king of poets."

Subsequent kings, including Chandragupta II, further expanded Gupta territory until it ranged from the Ganges to the Indus River, including today's northern Pakistan. Chandragupta also made an effort to restore indigenous Indian rituals and a sense of Indian identity to stem the growing Greco-Roman influence percolating into the subcontinent. Deeply beholden to the well-being of his people, he established hospitals and houses for the

A NINTH-CENTURY CLAY SCULPTURE depicts the dual-form Hindu god Harihara, in which the right half represents the god Shiva (Hara) and the left the god Vishnu (Hari).

"ALL THE PEOPLE WITHIN THE FOUR SEAS MAY,
WITHOUT EXCEPTION, DEVELOP ENLIGHTENMENT
AND TOGETHER CULTIVATE FORTUNATE KARMA."

EMPEROR WEN OF SUI DYNASTY

poor and increased Gupta patronage of the arts, in particular sacred art.

Another remarkable aspect of the Gupta Empire is its religious tolerance, even though the House of Gupta itself was devoutly orthodox Hindu. The Gupta style of art and sculpture, deeply influenced by Greco-Roman models, found expression not only in Hindu themes but also in Buddhist and Jain motifs. For example, Chinese scholar Fa-hien (or Faxian), who traveled through India and Central Asia between 402 and 414 C.E., was amazed by the quality of Buddhist sculptures by Gupta artists,

Head of a Buddha

even though Hinduism remained the principal religion of the land. In addition, Chandragupta II's court was known for its patronage of illustrious literati, including Sanskrit poet and playwright Kālidāsa, who were known as the *Navaratna,* or "Nine Jewels." Significantly, it was during this period that the epic stories of the Ramayana and the Mahabharata reached their final form. Science enjoyed royal patronage as well. A Gupta scholar, the astronomer Aryabhata, was one of the first to postulate that the Earth moves around the sun and that the moon is lit by reflected sunlight. Indian mathematicians are also credited with developing the decimal system, beginning with zero.

Much of the prosperity of the Gupta Dynasty was due to the continuing trade contacts with the Eastern Roman Empire and its insatiable appetite for luxury products from the East. Thus, Gupta traders not only carried silk, ivory, and pearls westward but also fine objects of gold, precious furs, and sought-after spices such as pepper, from trading centers such as Benares, Paithan, and Pataliputra.

By the middle of the fifth century C.E., the empire began to suffer increasing incursions from neighboring tribal entities, including the Kidarites from Bactria (modern Afghanistan and northern Pakistan). Some scholars have compared the Kidarites to the Huns, who invaded the Roman realm around the same time and contributed to the fall of the Western Roman Empire. Although the Gupta King Skandagupta was able to defeat the Kidarite forces around 455 and eventually push them back across the border, the effort to repel these and other invasions drained the

EMPEROR WEN OF SUI, from the "Thirteen Emperors Scroll," was painted by Tang Dynasty court artist Yan Liben.

THIS GUPTA MONUMENT with figures of Buddha as well as bodhisattvas was designed under the influence of Greco-Roman architecture.

NOTABLE DATES

ca 220 C.E.
End of the Han Dynasty in China

ca 300 C.E.
Chandragupta I expands control over most of India

ca 320 C.E.
Chinese develop the stirrup for greater control on horseback

ca 400 C.E.
Yamato culture spreads across the Japanese archipelago

ca 400 C.E.
The Hindu epic *Bhagavad Gita* assumes its final form

ca 400 C.E.
Hinduism gradually replaces Buddhism as dominant religion in India

ca 450 C.E.
Huns invade the Gupta Empire of India

ca 538 C.E.
Missionaries carry Buddhism to Japan

ca 581 C.E.
Sui Dynasty achieves a reunification of China

ca 618 C.E.
Tang Dynasty initiates one of China's most important epochs

ca 710 C.E.
Beginning of the Nara period in Japan

ca 840 C.E.
Emperor Wuzong bans all religions other than Taoism in China

treasury and sent the empire into its inevitable decline. Around 500, a new invasion, this time led by the Huns, led to a protracted war of attrition that prompted the breakup of the Gupta Empire.

In the seventh century, a new kingdom under King Harsha emerged in the north. Unlike the Gupta kings, Harsha was a devoted Buddhist, but he did not impose his religious beliefs on his people. In sharp contrast to the rulers of the Byzantine and Chinese Empires, Harsha followed the precedent of the Gupta Dynasty and allowed the people to pursue the faith of their choice. But after Harsha's death, the kingdom crumbled once more, leaving India unprepared for the Muslim armies that descended from the north. In 712, the Islamic forces were able to penetrate as far as the Indus River Valley.

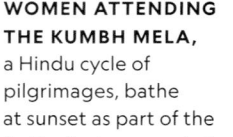

Gold Gupta coin

But India was very far from the capitals of the Islamic Empire, so that for several centuries, the traditional religious diversity of India remained undisturbed. This tolerance was prompted in no small degree by the fact that trade was largely in the hands of Hindu merchants, particularly in the south. But all that would change when Muslim Turks invaded India around 1000.

Buddhism Spreads Through China

In China, meanwhile, Buddhism continued to grow under the reign of the Tang Dynasty. As we saw, Buddhism first reached China from India during the Han Dynasty from about 57 C.E. onward, and the key Buddhist tracts would not be translated into Chinese until the second century. Soon after, nomads invaded China's borders and

WOMEN ATTENDING THE KUMBH MELA, a Hindu cycle of pilgrimages, bathe at sunset as part of the festival's atonement ritual.

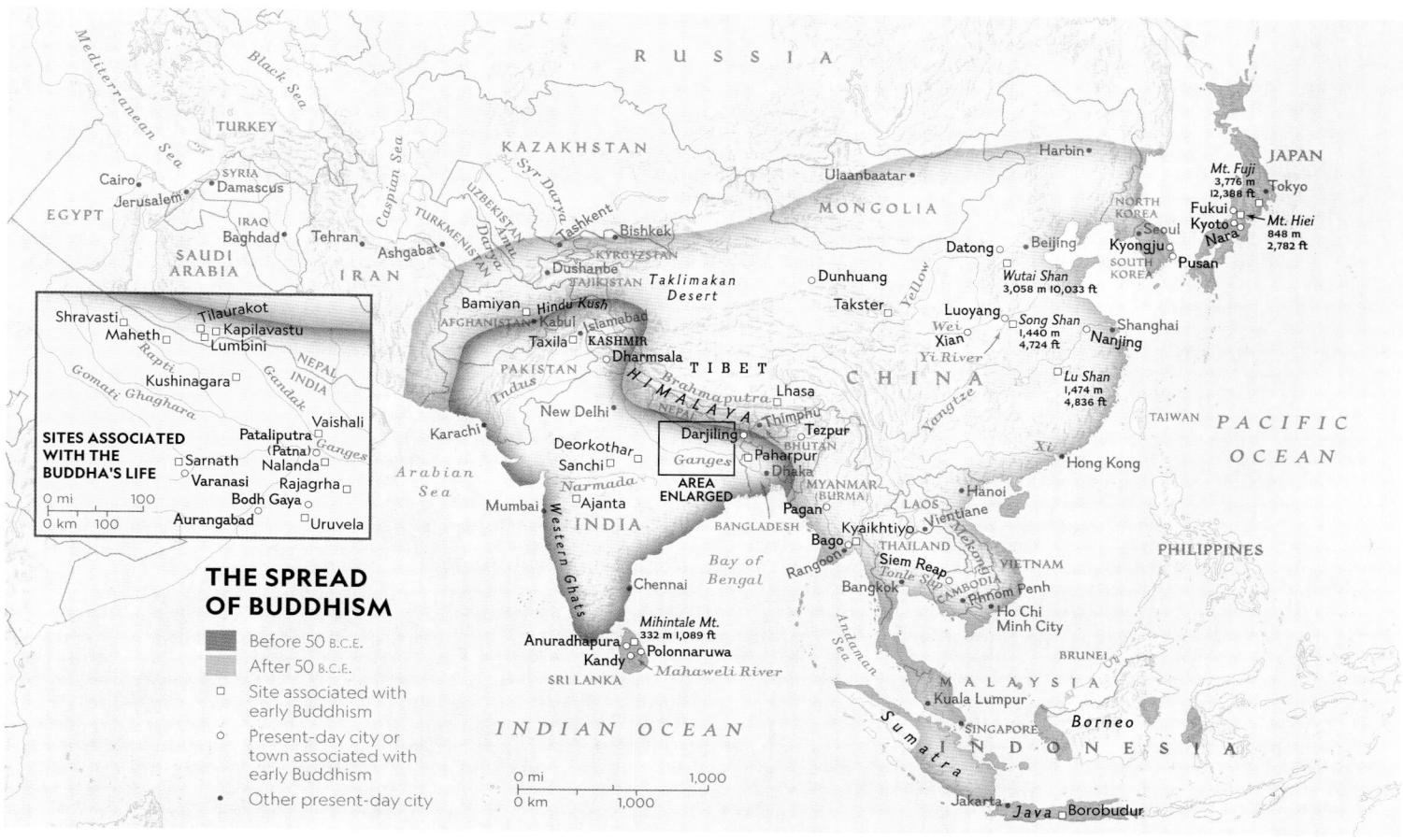

THE SPREAD OF BUDDHISM

Before 50 B.C.E.

After 50 B.C.E.

▫ Site associated with early Buddhism

○ Present-day city or town associated with early Buddhism

• Other present-day city

SITES ASSOCIATED WITH THE BUDDHA'S LIFE

in 220 C.E. brought about the collapse of the Han Dynasty. For the next three centuries, China was plunged in a dark period of great political and civil tensions. The nation disintegrated into rival kingdoms, each vying for expansion at the expense of others. It is sometimes argued that this extended period of social unrest produced a strong need for a deeper and more meaningful spiritual movement than the mostly intellectual Confucianist tradition. Buddhism met that need, which may explain its rapid spread during this time, even though Buddhism continued to coexist with indigenous Chinese religions such as Taoism.

Only in 581 C.E. was Yang Jian (who ruled under the regnal name of Emperor Wen of Sui) able to drive out foreign invaders and unify China once more. His Sui Dynasty then set about to thoroughly modernize the nation by improving China's land and water routes, which had crumbled from neglect during the preceding ages. Among others, Yangdi, the second Sui emperor,

oversaw the construction of the Jing-Hang Grand Canal, which eventually would run from Beijing to Hangzhou. This waterway, the oldest and longest canal in the world, greatly facilitated the transport of precious grain from the Yangtze Valley to the Sui cities in the north. The canal also facilitated the rapid spread of ideas, including Buddhism. Wen himself was a practicing Buddhist who believed that this faith tradition could act as a powerful unification force for his far-flung nation, just as Christianity and Islam had unified the lands under Byzantine and Caliphate rule. This is when one of the most important texts of Chinese Buddhist teachings, the *Móhē zhǐguān,* or *Great Treatise on Concentration and Insight,* by Chinese Buddhist sage Zhiyi was composed. In

A TANG DYNASTY MIRROR of bronze and silver is decorated with lotus flower motifs and mythical animals.

> ## "WITH HISTORY AS A MIRROR, ONE CAN UNDERSTAND THE RISE AND FALL OF A NATION."
>
> **EMPEROR TAIZONG, TANG DYNASTY**

601 C.E., Emperor Wen even secured important relics of the Buddha, which he donated to Buddhist temples throughout China.

The Golden Era of the Tang Dynasty

The Sui Dynasty lasted for only 37 years, but Buddhism continued to flourish under the subsequent Tang Dynasty as the dominant ideology, albeit in a thoroughly Sinicized fashion. A growing network of Buddhist monasteries offered educational opportunities to children of the poor and the wealthy alike, while providing lodging for travelers and offering work for tenant farmers on their lands. Buddhist monasteries thus fulfilled much of the same social and economic functions that

Benedictine monasteries would serve in Europe during the Middle Ages.

Many Chinese today revere the Tang Dynasty as a Golden Age of Chinese history, and they have a point. For a nation that had suffered from unrest and civil war for many centuries, the Tang Dynasty offered a period of stability that allowed its population to grow, its trade to prosper, and its arts to reach unprecedented heights of skill and beauty. Part of this political stability was perhaps due to the decision of Tang rulers to delegate administrative power to skilled mandarins and officials rather than to the traditional landed gentry. Some estimates suggest that the population of the Tang capital of Chang'an (today's Xi'an) grew to more

THE INVENTION OF GUNPOWDER

Chinese chemists (at left) were busy developing various elixirs that were hoped to confer immortality—or at least an extension of the human life span—when by chance they stumbled on a different commodity altogether. A key ingredient of their chemical experiments was saltpeter (or potassium nitrate), which one alchemist decided to blend with charcoal and sulfur. The resulting concoction, when brought in contact with an open flame, exploded in a spectacular flash—so much so that the alchemist's hands and face were burned and the house in which he and his assistant were working burned to the ground. This is believed to have happened in the 900s, though it took decades before the Chinese recognized its military potential. When some 50 years later, the Mongols invaded, they were met with "flying fire," the 10th-century equivalent of rocket-propelled missiles. But it would take at least another century before the Chinese developed the cannon, which reached Europe in the 15th century.

> "I ENVY YOU, WHO FAR FROM STRIFE AND TALK ARE HIGH-PROPPED ON A PILLOW OF BLUE CLOUD."
>
> **LI BAI, NOTED TANG DYNASTY POET**

than one million, which would have made it the largest city in the world of its time.

At the same time, the Tang emperors embarked on the greatest territorial conquest since China's initial unification. In less than half a century, its armies conquered parts of India, northern Korea, parts of Afghanistan and Persia, and the territory of modern Vietnam. The result was a new Chinese empire that controlled more than 80 million people and proudly radiated its political and cultural power through Asia and beyond. The reconstruction of the Silk Road through the strategic Gilgit Valley in Tibet restored trade links to Persia and the Islamic and Byzantine Empires, which abetted a rising demand among Chinese urban elites for luxury products from the West. Thousands of foreign merchants were allowed to settle in Chinese cities and set up their business. In 748 C.E., a Buddhist monk named Jian Zhen wrote a breathless report of the frenzied commerce of the port of Guangzhou, marveling at "big ships" that arrived from Borneo, today's Indonesia, and Persia, loaded with "spices, pearls and jade piled as high as a mountain."

Chinese literature and especially poetry flourished once more. By one count, the Tang Dynasty produced nearly 50,000

AN INTRICATELY ENGRAVED gilt silver flask is testimony to the skill of Tang Dynasty artisans.

THE GIANT WILD GOOSE
Pagoda in southern Xi'an, Shaanxi, China, is a Tang Dynasty structure originally designed in 652 and rebuilt in later periods.

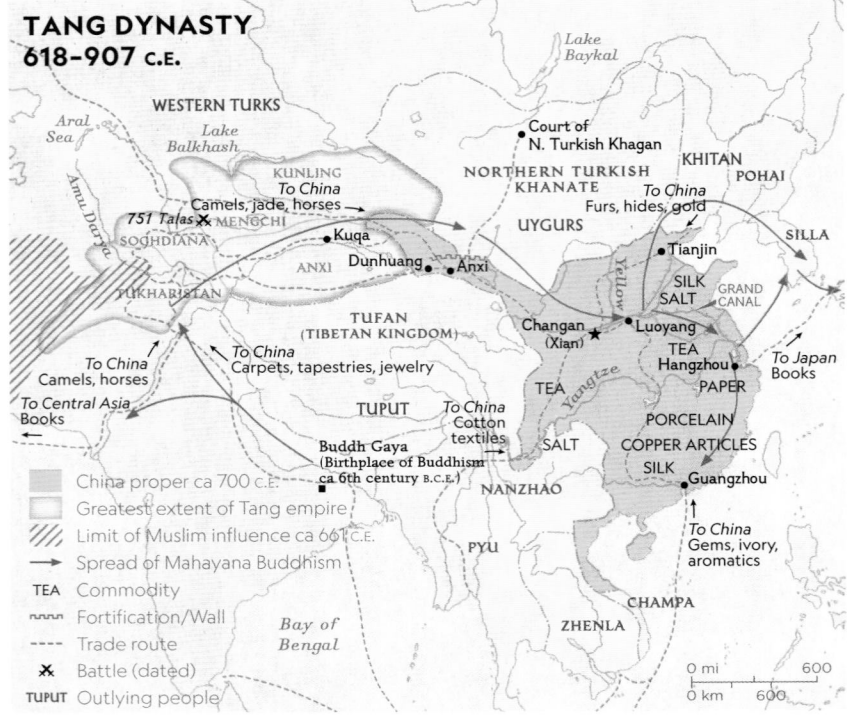

TANG DYNASTY
618–907 C.E.

Camels, jade, horses — To China
751 Talas ✕ MENOCHI
SOGHDIANA
Kuqa
Dunhuang • Anxi
To China — Furs, hides, gold
UYGURS
Tianjin
SILK
SALT
GRAND CANAL
SILLA

TUKHARISTAN
ANXI
To China
Camels, horses
To Central Asia
Books
TUFAN
(TIBETAN KINGDOM)
To China
Carpets, tapestries, jewelry
Changan (Xian) ★
Luoyang
TEA
Hangzhou
PAPER
To Japan
Books

TUPUT
To China
Cotton textiles
TEA
Yangtze
PORCELAIN
COPPER ARTICLES
SILK

Buddh Gaya
(Birthplace of Buddhism
ca 6th century B.C.E.)
SALT
NANZHAO
Guangzhou

WESTERN TURKS
KUNLING
To China
NORTHERN TURKISH KHANATE
KHITAN
POHAI
Court of
N. Turkish Khagan

Aral Sea
Lake Balkhash
Amu Darya
Lake Baykal

PYU
To China
Gems, ivory, aromatics
CHAMPA
ZHENLA
Bay of Bengal

China proper ca 700 C.E.
Greatest extent of Tang empire
Limit of Muslim influence ca 661 C.E.
Spread of Mahayana Buddhism
TEA Commodity
Fortification/Wall
Trade route
✕ Battle (dated)
TUPUT Outlying people

0 mi   600
0 km   600

THE HORSE, here executed in porcelain and colored glazes, was one of the most popular motifs in Tang art, reflecting the Tang Dynasty's military conquests as well as its prosperous trade links.

poems in either the *Jinti shi* style of seven-character lines or the more traditional *Guti shi* style used in classic Confucian poetry. In fact, poetry was deemed such an integral element of Tang culture that it was featured on civil service entrance exams for students aspiring to a role in the Tang administration.

Chinese scientists and engineers excelled as well. Tang chemists were encouraged to develop a range of new materials, including fireproof cement for glass and porcelain, as well as a waterproof cream to protect underwater divers. Bamboo pipes were used to carry natural gas from deep wells into the homes of the elite. In 747 C.E., Emperor Xuanzong commissioned the construction of an "air-conditioned" hall in his palace, using a combination of fountains and fans powered by water.

Other emperors focused on fostering the growth of another major Chinese science, holistic medicine. Emperor Gaozong is credited with funding the development of a major encyclopedia of Chinese pharmacy going back some 3,000 years. Completed in 657 C.E., the work cataloged 833 different herbs, minerals, and extracts for such diseases as diabetes and ulcers. Two years later, a Chinese dentist named Su Gong first published the use of tin and silver amalgams to fill dental cavities. Similar experiments by Chinese alchemists led to the invention of gunpowder.

Tang medical expertise, unprecedented for its time, was disseminated through a network of imperial medical schools where aspiring physicians had to pass a state exam in order to be licensed. In sports, the Tang period shone as well. Chinese noblemen readily embraced polo, an equestrian team sport developed by Iranian nomads that became highly popular among the Parthian aristocracy. Known as *chovgan* (the name still used in Iran today), the game was probably introduced by Persian merchants via the Silk Road. At the peak of its popularity in the Tang period, Chinese noblemen competed in acquiring the best-trained Persian horses.

Tang Art

At the same time, Tang artists excelled in a great variety of forms, including painting, calligraphy, and the use of a new material called porcelain. Much of this endeavor was actively supported by the state through the foundation of art schools, including the establishment of the eighth-century Hanlin Academy in Chang'an. In 847 C.E., historian Zhāng Yànyuǎn compiled China's first official history of art, *Lidai Minghua Ji,* or *Famous Paintings of Successive Dynasties.* While Zhāng extolled the creativity and invention of Chinese artists, he also stressed that painters did not work in a vacuum and had to abide by ethical and political norms. Indeed, many Tang artists (both painters and calligraphers) were also Confucian scholars or poets. An artist's work, it was believed, should express not only creative skills but also the quality of his or her character.

One particularly popular motif of the Tang period was the landscape, painted as a mural or on silk. Two styles emerged: the ink-and-wash

A 16TH-CENTURY REPRODUCTION captures the beauty of an original landscape by Tang artist Li Zhaodao.

IN THIS TIMELESS IMAGE, a long caravan of traders makes its way across the Taklamakan Desert, near Dunhuang, China.

"DRIFTING, DRIFTING, WHAT AM I MORE THAN
A SINGLE GULL BETWEEN SKY AND EARTH?"

DU FU, NOTED TANG DYNASTY POET

style popularized by the painter Wang Wei, and the blue-and-green landscape style developed by, among others, the artist Li Zhaodao. Li is believed to be the artist who painted the best-known work from this period, "The Emperor Ming Huang's Journey to Shu," dated between 720 and 740 C.E., and today known only through copies. In art of this style, human figures play a secondary role; the main emphasis is on the majesty on the land-scape, in this case the soaring cliffs of the Sichuan Mountains. Other works from this period depict Bud-dhist themes, many of which were lost during the great Buddhist sup-pression by Emperor Wuzong.

One of the most important cycles of

Tang Dynasty covered jar

Buddhist painting was discovered in the Cave Temples of Dunhuang, also known as the Mogao ("peerless") caves in northwestern China. Exca-vated out of cliffs close to the Silk Road, these caves were originally created and decorated by Buddhist monks and followers in order to obtain karmic merit. The nearly 500 caves still contain more than a thousand depictions of the Buddha in various poses. A number of texts in Sanskrit, Tibetan, and even Hebrew suggest that these caves were not solely used for Buddhist vener-ation, but also allowed Taoist, Con-fucian, and Christian travelers on the Silk Road to pause for worship. Indeed, with the exception of Emperor Wuzong, the Tang Dynasty

THE DEVELOPMENT OF CHINESE PORCELAIN

Tang porcelain (at right) was the product of a long process of experimentation over many centuries. During the Tang era, por-celain (or "high-fired ware" as the Chinese called it) obtained its unique glazing and translucency by firing kilns to as high as 2,200°F. Because of the difficulty of this process and the delicate, shell-like texture of the material, it soon became the most sought-after form of pottery in affluent homes, replacing standard low-fired earthen-ware. A popular motif in this time was the porce-lain horse, a reflection of the importance that the Silk Route played in sustaining the empire's wealth. Today, Tang horses made of porcelain or another Chinese material, jade, are among the most sought-after objects by Chinese and West-ern collectors.

was remarkable for its religious tolerance, in contrast to what was happening in other parts of the world. While Confucianism remained the official ideology of the state, Tang emperors and the aristocracy actively sponsored the development of Buddhist monasteries, temples, and schools, as had been the case during the preceding Sui Dynasty. Similarly, these elites tolerated a growing Christian presence, with Chinese missionaries fanning out to Korea, Japan, and other nations in the East. This is why by the ninth century, the Church of the East (or the East Syriac Church, as it is sometimes called) had become the largest Christian movement of its time in geographical terms, stretching from Mesopotamia and Persia to India and China.

The Tang Dynasty is also credited with developing the world's first movable print technology in the form of block prints. Scholars generally agree that the world's oldest printed book is the *Diamond Sūtra,* a Chinese translation of a Mahayana Buddhist sutra in Sanskrit. It was produced in 868 C.E. by printing carved wooden blocks on strips of paper, which were then collated in a scroll. The book dwells on a number of Buddhist themes, such as the emptiness of phenomena in human life, and exerted an immense influence on Chinese thought. Among others, it prompted numerous other translations, as well as 800 commentaries by noted Chinese Buddhist sages such as Xie Lingyun, Zhiyi, and Sengzhao. The book was discovered in 1900 in the so-called Library Cave of the Dunhuang cave complex, among nearly

THIS EARTHENWARE TOMB GUARDIAN from the Tang Dynasty, executed with a three-color glaze, was meant to ward off grave robbers and safely transport the deceased to the afterlife.

A COPY OF "THE EMPEROR MING HUANG'S JOURNEY to Shu," originally dated between 720 and 740 C.E. and attributed to renowned Tang artist Li Zhadao

青綠開山迥
迴岐道路長
水人多結案行
子自開禪綠
迴名和利那
好芳與忙年
小失姓民北宗
丘未唐
甲午新秋
尚題

THE SHITENNŌ-JI TEMPLE in Osaka, Japan, was founded in 593 and is considered the first Buddhist temple in Japan, though it has been rebuilt many times.

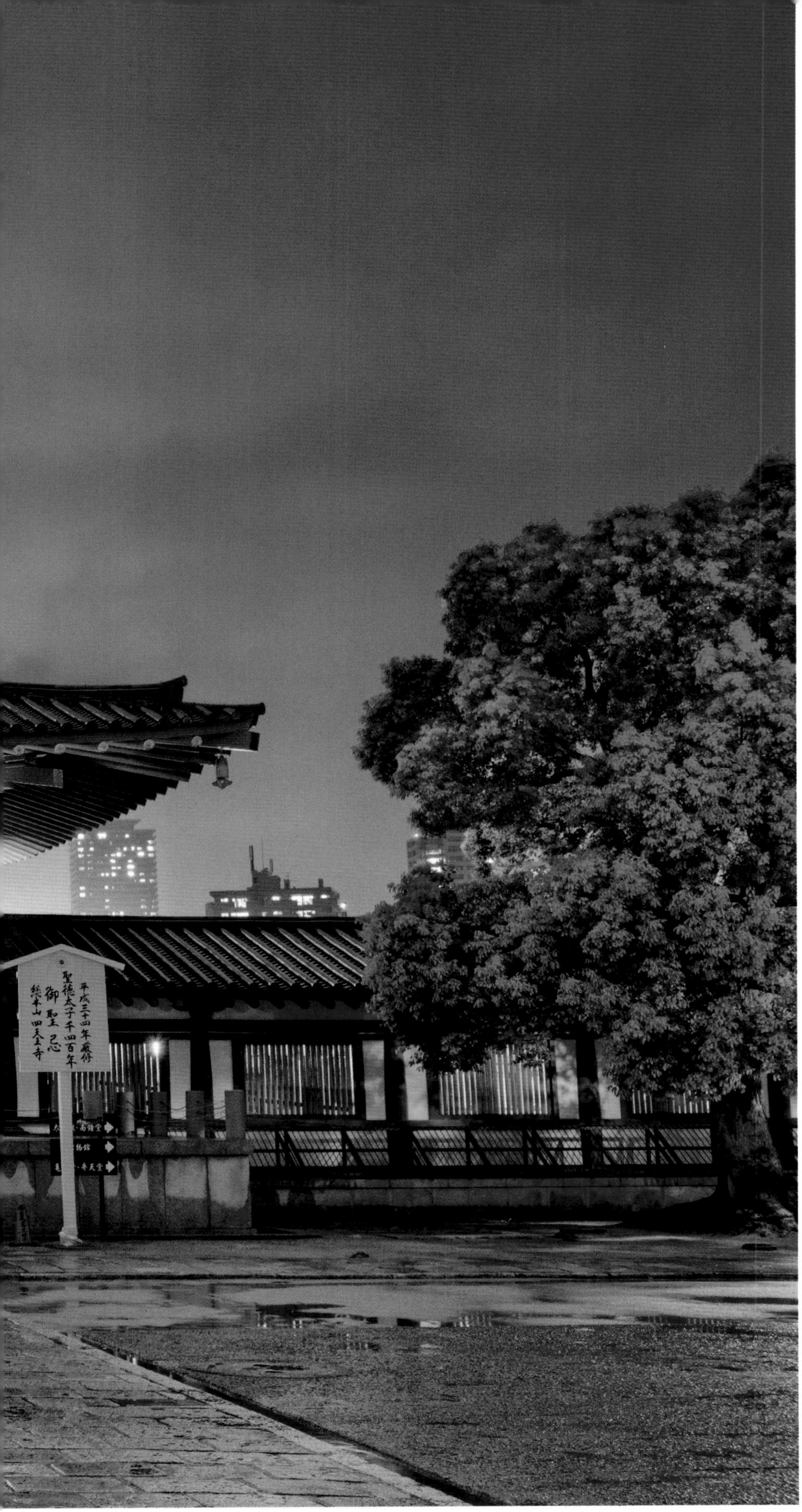

"RESEMBLANCE REPRODUCES THE FORMAL ASPECT OF OBJECTS, BUT NEGLECTS THEIR SPIRIT; TRUTH SHOWS THE SPIRIT AND SUBSTANCE LIKE PERFECTION."

JING HAO, RENOWNED CHINESE LANDSCAPE ARTIST

50,000 ancient manuscripts, paintings, and other objects.

In the 840s, the growing interest in Buddhism prompted a reaction under the reign of Emperor Wuzong. A committed Taoist, Wuzong banned all other forms of worship. Surprisingly, this suppression was prompted not only by religious concerns but also by urgent financial motives. Under the Tang emperors, monasteries had enjoyed tax-exempt status, which Wuzong believed deprived the state of badly needed tax receipts. Spurred by one of his advisers, the Taoist monk Zhao Guizhen, Wuzong ruthlessly persecuted Buddhist monks and nuns who refused to release the wealth of their order and return to life as laypersons. Wuzong defended his policy as a pious return to the authentic Chinese traditions of Confucianism and Taoism. By 845, most of the roughly 4,000 Buddhist temples in China had been destroyed, and many thousands of shrines lay in ruins.

Not content with this "cleansing" of Chinese soil, Wuzong also turned his ire against other "foreign" influences, including Nestorian Christianity,

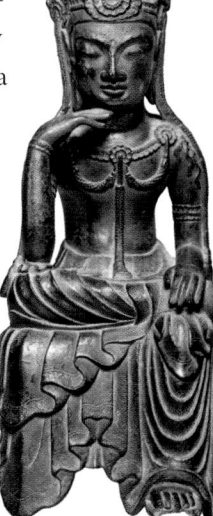

A MAITREYA SCULPTURE, depicting the Buddha of the Future, was cast in Japan during the late Asuka or early Nara period (600–710).

EMPEROR SHŌMU ruled Japan as its 45th emperor from ca 724 to 749, according to the traditional chronology of Japan's monarchy.

extent it was different from the preceding Kofun era, there is no question that the Asuka period (a term not coined until 1900) saw the growing power of the emperor based in Yamato Province. A convenient starting date for this period is 538, when Buddhism was introduced to Japan by missionaries from China and Korea. From this point on, Buddhist ideology increasingly began to contest the indigenous Shinto religion, greatly abetted by the ruling Japanese elites. Fifty years later, this process culminated in the takeover of the central government by the Buddhist Soga clan. They elevated a Yamato prince, Shōtoku Taishi, to the status of regent, though nominally still serving under Empress Suiko.

Shōtoku and his successors set about to thoroughly transform Japan using Confucian and Buddhist models from China. Among others, the prince established the Confucian Twelve Level Cap and Rank System to distinguish separate classes of Japanese officialdom, so named after the silk caps worn by prominent officials. Below these elites lived the vast mass of Japanese peasant farmers, artisans, fishers, potters, and weavers. In 604, the prince also developed the so-called Seventeen-Article Constitution. Although it was more of a Buddhist and Confucian moral code than an actual legal codex, it is probably one of the first constitutions adopted by a state in history.

In all other areas, Chinese influence on Japan continued unabated. The Asuka rulers adopted the Chinese writing system, its calendar, its irrigation technology, and even its weaving methods. Similarly, the principles of Chinese beam-and-post architecture were adopted. One example is the impressive Shitennō-ji temple in today's Osaka, considered one of the oldest Buddhist temples in Japan, even though its pavilions have been rebuilt several times. The complex includes a beautiful five-story pagoda (a tower used to store relics or sacred writings), as well as the Golden Pavilion that houses an image of the Bodhisattva Guanyin, the goddess of mercy.

Despite this pervasive Chinese influence, however, the Asuka rulers refused to accept the

Manichaeism, and Zoroastrianism. These religions never recovered from this wholesale destruction. Nestorian Christianity went in a deep decline, while Buddhist influences steadily waned. Some 60 years later, the Tang Dynasty itself came to an end.

The Late Classical Age in Japan

In Japan, the Kofun period was followed by a phase in which the nation was increasingly ruled by the Yamato clan, whose militias had expanded their control over the Japanese archipelago in the preceding centuries. Though scholars differ about the specific dates of this period or indeed to what

THIS MURAL from the seventh-century Takamatsuzuka Tomb in Asuka, Japan, depicts the "Beautiful Women of the Asuka Period."

THE BYŌDŌ-IN, a Buddhist temple just outside Kyoto built during the Heian period, is surrounded by a lovely *Jōdo-shiki* (Buddhist style) garden and pond.

"HARMONY IS TO BE VALUED, AND THE AVOIDANCE
OF WANTON OPPOSITION TO BE HONORED."

PRINCE SHŌTOKU, "THE SEVENTEEN-ARTICLE CONSTITUTION"

subordinate role that Japan had always played in relation to its great neighbor China. Shōtoku even claimed equality with the Chinese emperor, which his Chinese counterpoint of course rejected out of hand. From that moment, the political relationship between Japan and Chinese began to deteriorate, even though on a cultural and economic level the exchange of products and ideas continued as before.

The strong control of the Soga clan inevitably led to a reaction, which arrived in 645 in the form of a palace coup. The result was a period of great change, known as the Taika Reform in Japan, during which Emperor Tenji sought to wrest control from the powerful landowning clans. This led to a series of punishing taxes on produce as well as silk, cotton, and other products, which served to erode the wealth of the landed gentry. To seal the imperial control over the country, Japan was now divided into provinces to be ruled by government-appointed officials rather than by hereditary noblemen. Formerly known as Wa, Japan was now called Nihon, or Nippon, the name it still has today.

The Nara Period of Japan

During the subsequent Nara period (710–794), the Japanese imperial seat was moved to Heijō-kyō, the modern city of Nara. In its layout and architectural style, the new capital closely followed the model of Chang'an, the Chinese capital of the Tang Dynasty. Heijō-kyō eventually grew to a population of 200,000 people, making it the first major urban center in Japanese history. Near the end of the eighth century, the capital moved once more, this time to Heian-kyō, the "Capital of Peace" in modern Kyoto, where it would remain for the next 1,000 years.

Thanks to the adoption of Chinese characters during the Asuka period, Japanese culture now experienced a great flowering of poetry, or *waka*. The oldest and most famous of these poems is the *Man'yōshū,* the "Collection of Ten Thousand Leaves," possibly compiled around 759 by the statesman and poet Ōtomo no Yakamochi. The work is universally recognized as a unique blend of Confucian, Taoist, and Buddhist themes that are beautifully harmonized with indigenous Japanese motifs, taken from Shinto sacred literature. At the same time, the poem provided the impetus for the development of an authentic Japanese writing system by simplifying and stylizing Chinese characters to Japanese syllables.

Japanese art and architecture did not reach their apogee until the subsequent Heian period (794–1185), often known as the Golden Age of Japan's classical era. The court, in modern-day Kyoto, was now dominated by the Fujiwara clan, which became the nation's leading art patrons. Japanese artists and designers were encouraged to strive for indigenous themes and art forms inspired by Japanese rather than Chinese ideas and traditions. One example is the fondness for so-called *yamato-e* genre scenes, inspired by rural motifs. Other forms of inspiration were found in Japanese history, such as the cataclysmic Sea Battle of Dan-no-ura of 1185, when the ruling Taira clan was defeated by the ships of the Minamoto clan.

Meanwhile, sculptors continued to create images of Buddhist deities, but in wood rather than bronze. Fashion underwent changes too: Women of the ruling elites applied white rice powder to their faces, blackened their teeth, and wore an elaborate kimono dress known as *jūni-hitoe.*

In sum, by the ninth century, Japan was emerging from under the shadow of its former Chinese overlord as a proud and sovereign nation. ∎

FEMALE DEITIES play an important role in the Japanese Shinto religion, as shown by this simple but affectionate 12th-century figure in polychrome wood.

EUROPE
IN THE DARK AGES

After the fall of the Roman Empire in the West, Europe disintegrated into a number of fiefdoms led by the Visigoths, Ostrogoths, and other tribes. Many of these had already converted to Christianity and were thus instrumental in introducing the faith to Europe.

As the Roman Empire continued to disintegrate in the West, various tribes moved in to fill the vacuum. One of these was a group of Gothic tribes, living in what today is modern Germany, who by the third century were occupying large tracts of Europe north of the Danube. From here, they steadily staged a number of violent incursions into southern Europe, pushing through the Balkans to plunder their way to Athens and moving as far as Cyprus. A century later, after the Goths had split into the Thervingi and the Greuthungi, separated by the Dniester River in today's Romania, they in turn were routed by invaders. These were the Huns, a warlike people from east of the Volga River in Russia, who pushed the Goths farther into former Roman territory.

This is when a missionary named Ulfilas began his evangelizing efforts among the Gothic tribes. He soon realized he needed a Bible in the Gothic language if his efforts were to bear fruit. During the next several years, Ulfilas painstakingly translated the Bible from Greek into Gothic script, using many characters that he himself devised. This rare translation, which would serve as a foundation of Gothic script, was partially preserved in a rare sixth-century document known as the Codex Argenteus. On the strength of this Gothic Bible, Ulfilas was able to make large-scale conversions among the Gothic tribes.

Eventually, the Goths split into Visigoths, nominal allies of Rome, and the fearsome Ostrogoths, who considered Rome their sworn enemy. Both, however, were Christians, largely as a result of Ulfilas's efforts. The Visigoths would settle farther southwest, along the Loire River and in Aquitaine, from where they made their way to Spain. For the next three centuries, Spain would be ruled as a Visigoth kingdom, though often beset by dynastic strife as various factions fought for control of the throne.

Another missionary named Patrick carried the Christian gospel to Ireland, a territory that had never been conquered by the Romans and was therefore untouched by either Roman polytheism or Byzantine Christianity. Patrick and his followers were harassed and repeatedly imprisoned by the lords of local clans, while suffering fierce opposition from the local druids and magicians. Struggling

A SIXTH-CENTURY BROOCH of an eagle was crafted by an Ostrogoth artist.

"ALL THOSE WHO DO NOT APPEAR AT THE RIVER TOMORROW FOR BAPTISM WILL INCUR MY DEEPEST DISPLEASURE."

CLOVIS I, THE FIRST KING OF A UNIFIED FRANCE

against great odds, Patrick nevertheless succeeded in converting many thousands of men and women, among not only the peasantry but also the local nobility. Another legendary figure named Brigit is credited with founding the first monastery in Ireland near Kildare, welcoming both men and women.

The Hun Invasions

In Roman Gaul, meanwhile, several monks including Martin of Tours and a cleric named Cassian began to establish monasteries in Ligugé, Marmoutier, and Marseilles, thus laying the foundation for the monastic orders and abbeys that would sustain Europe during the Dark Ages.

Nonetheless, large areas of fifth-century Europe still remained untouched by Christianity. As the

"ST. MARTIN Cutting a Piece of His Cloak" is a painting by an unknown artist in the Cathedral of Tours, France.

Visigoth gold coin

vestiges of Roman law and order slowly dissipated, so did the social fabric of society—a process that was accelerated by the great popular upheavals of barbarian peoples throughout this period. Ironically, many of these barbarian tribes had already converted to Christianity and were thus instrumental in planting the faith in the areas they conquered. Visigoth King Alaric, for example, besieged and sacked Rome in 410, but made sure that churches were not harmed. In 428, the Vandals, likewise Arian Christians, invaded northern Africa and swept away Roman control of the Mediterranean. As they battled to invest the city of Hippo in 430, the theologian Augustine, a fervent advocate of Catholic doctrine and author of several highly influential works, lay dying. According to tradition, the Vandals burned the city but left Augustine's church and library untouched.

Then Attila the Hun (r. 434–453) swept into western Europe, and his followers had no such compunction about Christianity. Pushing pagan and Christian tribes alike into Gaul and beyond, they crossed the Alps and threatened the Italian peninsula itself. An unusual alliance of Visigoths and Germanic Alemanni, a ferocious tribe renowned for their military prowess, joined with Roman forces to try to stop the Huns, but to no avail. In 452, Attila was approaching Rome when the reigning pope, Leo I, rode on horseback to meet him. What transpired next is uncertain, but Attila was persuaded to turn back—his wagon trains already loaded with booty from northern Italy. For this, Pope Leo is often called "Leo the Great," though he himself adopted the title used previously by the chief priest of Rome's pagan cult: Pontifex Maximus. This title is still used by popes to this day.

A 12TH-CENTURY COPPER AND ENAMEL PLAQUE depicts Byzantine commander Heraclius defeating King Khosrow II of Persia.

NOTABLE DATES

313 C.E.

Ulfilas, missionary to the Gothic tribes, is born

406 C.E.

Germanic tribes cross the Rhine

410 C.E.

Visigoth King Alaric sacks Rome

415 C.E.

Cassian founds the Abbey of St. Victoire in Marseille, France

430s C.E.

Patrick is appointed bishop of Ireland

451 C.E.

Brigit, founder of the first monastery in Ireland, is born

452 C.E.

Pope Leo I persuades Attila the Hun not to sack Rome

486 C.E.

King Clovis I of the Franks begins unification of France

523 C.E.

King Yusuf As'ar Yath'ar of Yemen converts to Judaism

614 C.E.

Persian general Shahrbaraz invades Byzantine Palestine

627 C.E.

Byzantine commander Heraclius defeats Persian King Khosrow II

654 C.E.

Visigothic Law Code serves as basis for medieval Spanish law

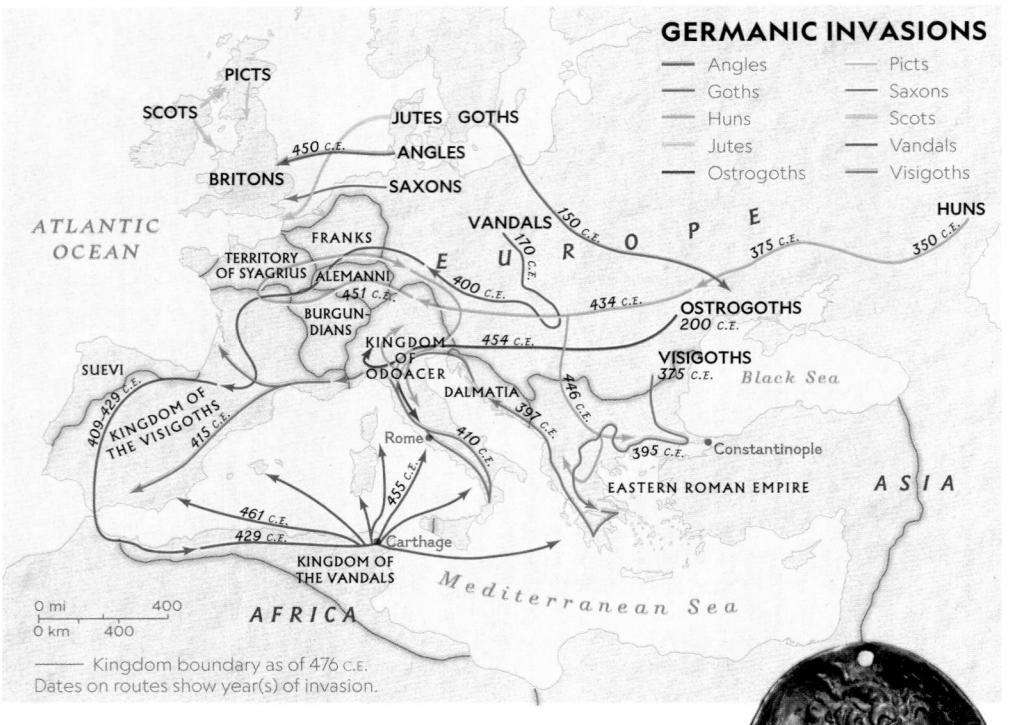

GERMANIC INVASIONS

Legend:
- Angles
- Goths
- Huns
- Jutes
- Ostrogoths
- Picts
- Saxons
- Scots
- Vandals
- Visigoths

PICTS
SCOTS
JUTES GOTHS
ANGLES
BRITONS
SAXONS
ATLANTIC OCEAN
FRANKS
TERRITORY OF SYAGRIUS
ALEMANNI
BURGUNDIANS
VANDALS
150 C.E.
170 C.E.
400 C.E.
451 C.E.
E U R O P E
HUNS
350 C.E.
375 C.E.
434 C.E.
OSTROGOTHS 200 C.E.
KINGDOM OF ODOACER
454 C.E.
VISIGOTHS 375 C.E.
Black Sea
SUEVI
409-429 C.E.
KINGDOM OF THE VISIGOTHS
415 C.E.
DALMATIA
446 C.E.
397 C.E.
410 C.E.
Rome
395 C.E.
Constantinople
EASTERN ROMAN EMPIRE
A S I A
455 C.E.
461 C.E.
429 C.E.
Carthage
KINGDOM OF THE VANDALS
Mediterranean Sea
AFRICA

0 mi 400
0 km 400

— Kingdom boundary as of 476 C.E.
Dates on routes show year(s) of invasion.

AN ILLUSTRATION
from the *Breviary of Alaric,*
a book of Roman law
compiled by the Visigoth
king Alaric II in 506

Leo's dramatic intervention also boosted the prestige of the Roman papacy, which since the reign of Theodosius had been in danger of being overshadowed by imperial authority. During the Council of Chalcedon, the Catholic bishops solemnly agreed that the Apostolic See of Rome should be considered supreme, followed by the authority of Constantinople in second place.

Another prominent tribe were the Franks. The meaning of the word "Frank" is uncertain, though eventually all of France (or Frankreich in German, literally "Frankish realm") would be named after them. Evicted from their native territory in the Rhineland by the Hun invasions, they originally settled in southern Gaul. Here, they assimilated with the local culture and ultimately produced linguistic adaptations of Latin that would evolve into the Romance languages of today. As more and more Frankish fiefdoms were settled near such Roman centers as Tournai, Camb-

Attila, king of the Huns

rai, and Le Mans, it was left to a strong leader to forcefully combine these into a sole Frankish kingdom. That man was Clovis I, a son of the Merovingian King Childeric I. Trained as a commander in Rome's legions, Clovis turned against Syagrius, the Roman prefect in charge of Gaul, and defeated him at the Battle of Soissons. Beginning with the Battle of Soissons in 486, Clovis steadily brought virtually all of Roman Gaul under his sway, which is why French historians consider him the first true king of a united France. The name Clovis would eventually become "Louis" in French and be proudly adopted by 18 French kings.

A committed pagan, he refused to be baptized, although his consort, Princess Clotilde of Burgundy, was a Catholic. Clotilde gave birth to two sons and had each baptized in secret, but the first son died, and the second very nearly perished from an illness. This only hardened Clovis's opposition to Christianity. But eventually he realized that the world had changed, with France surrounded by Christian kingdoms. He may also have seen an opportunity to unify the people of France under a Catholic banner. On Christmas 496, he was baptized near Reims. Almost all of France's subsequent kings were anointed in Reims Cathedral.

Thus, France became a Catholic country.

The Persian-Byzantine Wars in the East

At this point, the East was gripped by a series of cataclysmic wars that would ultimately forge a path for a new faith, known as Islam. The root cause of these tensions was not only a contest over control of Mediterranean trade, but also the growing intolerance of Byzantine emperors, now ruling the former Roman Empire in the East,

AN AERIAL VIEW shows the Old Town of Sanaa, capital of today's Yemen, with its main gate, known as Bāb al-Yaman (Gate of Yemen).

> ### "THEY SHOT FROM THEIR BALLISTAS WITH SUCH VIOLENCE THAT ON THE TWENTY-FIRST DAY THEY BROKE DOWN THE CITY WALL."
>
> ANTIOCHUS STRATEGOS,
> *THE PERSIAN CONQUEST OF JERUSALEM*

against other faiths. For example, Egypt had always harbored large Jewish communities, even though Byzantine Egypt was by now largely Christian, in a tradition known as Coptic Christianity (the word "Copt" is rooted in the Greek word for Egypt, *Aigyptos*). But as Byzantine hostility towards its Jewish population grew, many Jews decided to leave and settle along the Red Sea, moving as far as Yemen. In 523, the King of the Himyarites in Yemen, Yusuf As'ar Yath'ar (r. 517–525) took the extraordinary step of converting to Judaism, thus creating the first sovereign Jewish state since the fall of the Hasmoneans in Judea.

Sassanid horse head in gilded silver

Unfortunately, Yath'ar (also known as Dhu Nuwas) now proceeded to oppress the Christians in his kingdom. This set the stage for increasing hostility between Yemen and a Byzantine proxy in the area, Ethiopia. These tensions were exacerbated by the fact that Ethiopia was also Yemen's principal rival in the Red Sea trade.

In 523, Yath'ar destruction of several Christian communities in Zafar and Najran sparked an all-out war between Yemen and Ethiopia. The Ethiopian general Abreha crossed the Red Sea, invaded southern Arabia, and proclaimed himself King. In response, local Arabian chieftains asked for help

THE VIKINGS

Just as the various English fiefdoms began to coalesce into a single kingdom, the British Isles were targeted by seaborne Scandinavian warriors known as the Vikings .These Norse seafarers were motivated to leave their homesteads in Denmark, Norway, and Sweden by the growing population in Scandinavia and the lack of good farmland to sustain them. Using their shallow-draft Viking ships (at right) to great effect, they sailed not only to England but also to today's Germany, Russia, and even Constantinople in an ever escalating bid for loot. Some historians believe that the Vikings used their navigational skills to explore Iceland, Greenland, and even North America. By the 10th century, however, most Vikings had assimilated into the population they had conquered.

from the other superpower in the region, the Sassanian Empire of Persia. The Persian troops easily vanquished the Ethiopian forces and occupied Yemen in the process, thus expanding Persia's sphere of influence at the expense of the Byzantine Empire. It was here, in the southern Arabian region of the Hijaz, that history's next chapter would be written.

Heraclius, seventh-century Byzantine

Over the ensuing decades, centuries-old tension between the Byzantine and Persian powers continued to escalate. War broke out once more when the Byzantine Emperor Tiberius II attacked the Persian-occupied lands bordering the former Byzantine territory of Armenia. This was an attempt to restore Byzantium's wealth and prestige, but instead it led to a prolonged period of warfare between the two powers until a new Persian king, Khosrow II, faced a rebellion within his own realm. Uncertain of the quality and loyalty of his troops, Khosrow, in an unexpected move, turned to Byzantium, his former enemy, for help. Emperor Maurice sent troops to support the king, and received Persia's agreement to cede Armenia to Constantinople. This peace did not last long, however. In 602, Maurice was overthrown by a commander named Phocas, which prompted the Persian king to launch a "war of revenge" against the Byzantine usurper.

This time, the Persian troops gave no quarter. the Persian armies marched into Asia Minor. Antioch was invested in 611, followed by much of Armenia, Syria, and the Caucasus kingdom of Lazica. In 614, the Persian general Shahrbaraz entered Palestine, looting and burning his way toward Jerusalem. At that time, the Christian transformation of the holy city was in full swing, with a majestic Church of the Holy Sepulchre

THE CAROLINGIAN RENAISSANCE

The most powerful figure in early medieval Europe is unquestionably Charles the Great, or Charlemagne, who succeeded his father, Pepin the Short, as king of France. Charles gradually expanded his territory until he became de facto ruler of much of western Europe. Charles was crowned by Pope Leo III (at left) with the title of Holy Roman Emperor in an attempt to revive the splendor of the Western Roman Empire, albeit in a Christian mold. Architects harked back to Roman models, such as the Palatine Chapel in Aachen, inspired by the Basilica of San Vitale in Ravenna. Carolingian scholars freely copied texts by Roman and Greek authors, and artists developed a manuscript illumination inspired by classical sculpture, including the famous Aachen Gospels (820).

THE ARCH OF CTESIPHON, known as Taq-I Kisra or Arch of Khosrow, is the only remaining monument from the great capital city of the Persian Sassanid Empire.

rising on Golgotha. Streets that had once been filled with Jewish worshippers during holy festivals were now crammed with monks, prelates, and pilgrims from all parts of the Byzantine Empire.

The patriarch of Jerusalem, Zacharias, was wholly unprepared for the Persian invasion. The city's stout walls were breached by the Persian catapults in less than three weeks. More than 65,000 Christians were killed in the massacre that followed. Those who survived were rounded up and, in a replay of the Babylonian captivity, dispatched into exile. Most churches were burned to the ground, including the Church of the Holy Sepulchre. The True Cross, believed to have been used in Jesus' crucifixion, was carried back to Persia as ordinary loot.

In a calculated move, General Shahrbaraz handed control of Jerusalem back to the Jewish patriarchate. However, in 616 the Persians reneged on their promise of Jewish autonomy, and Palestine was incorporated into the local Persian satrapy.

Persia's rule was short-lived, however. Another Byzantine commander, Heraclius, overthrew the usurper Phocas and seized power as the new emperor, vowing to reclaim Christian territories. In 622, Heraclius and his forces plowed through Asia Minor to restore it to Byzantine sovereignty. They then moved into Mesopotamia and dealt Khosrow II a stinging defeat at the Battle of Nineveh in 627. The triumph was complete when in 630 Heraclius solemnly returned the True Cross to Jerusalem. For a moment, it appeared as if Heraclius had restored the vast reach of the Roman Empire. But appearances were deceiving, for soon another and far more powerful army would appear on the borders of the Byzantine Holy Land, led by caliph 'Umar ibn al-Khattab. ∎

THE SULTAN AHMED MOSQUE, or Blue Mosque, as seen from the Hagia Sophia in Istanbul

THE RISE OF
ISLAM

A merchant named Muhammad receives divine revelations calling him to propagate a faith of total surrender to a single God that will unify all of Arabia. His successors carry the banner of Islam into bordering territories, eventually conquering much of the Byzantine and Persian Empires.

Annexed by Rome in the second century C.E., the province of Arabia Petraea originally stretched from Damascus to Sinai in the south and to the mountain chain of Harrat al Uwairidh in the east, a territory roughly equivalent to today's Sinai, Jordan, and the northernmost corner of Saudi Arabia, including a slice of Syria and Lebanon. Governed from Petra and later Bostra, Arabia was at the edge of civilization as the Romans knew it; beyond this frontier, the Arabian Peninsula fell away to the southern desert, controlled by a number of smaller fiefdoms and tribes.

Ethnically, the Arabian tribes descended from two legendary ancestors, 'Adnan in the north and Qahtan in the south. Though the descendants of Qahtan considered themselves the purer strain (also known as *al-'Arab al-'Aribah,* or "the true Arabs"), both the 'Adnan and Qahtan traced their lineage back to Ishmael, son of Abraham. Many of these tribes were either settlers (*al-hadar*) around oases or caravan posts or Bedouin nomads (*al-badiyah*) wedded to a nomadic lifestyle focused on the herding of sheep, camels, and goats. These

Bedouin were known to terrorize the settled tribes with sudden raids. Animosity between these settlers and nomads ran deep, borne by a history of violent strife that would continue well into the Islamic era.

Throughout this checkerboard of interlocking tribal fiefdoms ran the principal caravan routes. Here, for example, was the Hijaz, a region of small cities such as Medina (then called Yathrib) and Mecca (or Makkah), home of the cubelike structure called the Kaaba, where several pagan deities were venerated. Despite being hemmed in by three monotheistic faiths—Judaism, Christianity, and Persian Zoroastrianism—the Arab tribes still clung to their ancient pagan beliefs. Their deities featured a supreme god named Allah (derived from *al-ilah,* "the god") who was, like Zeus or Jupiter, the father of the gods, the ruler of the heavens.

In 570, a young woman from Mecca named Amina gave birth to a baby boy and named him Muhammad. Tragically, her husband, Abdullah, a member of the Hashemite clan, had died a few months earlier while visiting

A LUSTERWARE VASE with ornamental relief and metallic highlights illustrates the virtuosity of Islamic artists around the 12th century.

> "RECITE IN THE NAME OF YOUR LORD WHO CREATED.
> HE CREATED MAN FROM A (BLOOD) CLOT.
> RECITE, FOR YOUR LORD IS MOST BOUNTIFUL."

**MUHAMMAD'S FIRST REVELATION
AS DESCRIBED IN THE QURAN (96:2-5)**

Yathrib. When Amina herself died soon after, the orphan boy was raised by a succession of Hashemite relatives and eventually became a trader like many others in Mecca. Thus, he traveled widely along the principal trade routes to Petra, Bostra, and other caravan markets.

Along the way, he must have come into contact with Jewish communities, which were heavily involved in the regional trade. Here too were dissident Christian monasteries of Monophysite, Arian, and Nestorite Christians who had settled in Arabia, beyond the reach of Byzantine orthodoxy, to cater to the needs of passing travelers. We may therefore presume that Muhammad became familiar with both the Jewish and Christian faiths, and possibly their Scriptures as well.

The Birth of Islam

Muhammad married a wealthy widow named Khadija and soon enjoyed a life of affluence. But as tradition tells us, he became uncomfortable with the primitive idolatry and pagan rituals of his Arab tribe. He remembered that his grandfather had often retreated to a lonely cave in the hills of Jebel-an-Nur to meditate, and he began to do the same. In 610, shortly before the Persian conquest of the Holy Land, this is where, according to Islam, Muhammad began to receive divine revelations,

THE DOME OF THE ROCK

Legend tells us when Caliph 'Umar conquered Jerusalem after a seven-month siege, he was asked to spare the people in the city. Remarkably, he agreed. He asked to be taken to Temple Mount, site of the former Jewish Temple and the reputed location of Muhammad's ascension into heaven, which had been turned into a garbage dump. According to a Muslim historian, 'Umar unfurled his cloak, filled it with debris, and began to clear the site. Temple Mount then became the Muslim al-Haram al-Sharif, the Noble Sanctuary of Muhammad's heavenly visit, as well as the traditional location of Abraham's sacrifice. Here, the Umayyad caliph Abd el-Malik built the iconic Dome of the Rock (at left). Its design combines circular and octagonal motifs to symbolize the transition from the Earth to the divine. Below the dome is a cave, the Well of Souls, where Muslims believe the souls of the dead will gather in anticipation of the Last Judgment.

A NIGHTTIME IMAGE captures the circumambulation of pilgrims around the Kaaba in Mecca, an ancient shrine revered as the holiest place in Islam.

NOTABLE DATES

570 C.E.
Prophet Muhammad is born in Mecca

610 C.E.
Muhammad begins to receive divine revelations

622 C.E.
Muhammad and his followers move to Yathrib during the Hijrah

630 C.E.
All of Arabia is unified under the banner of Islam

631 C.E.
Muhammad establishes the pilgrimage (hajj) to Mecca

632 C.E.
Muhammad's death prompts power struggle between Medina and Mecca factions

636 C.E.
Muslim Caliph 'Umar defeats Byzantine forces at Battle of Yarmuk

637 C.E.
Persian capital of Ctesiphon falls to Muslim invaders

650s C.E.
The first canon of the Quran is compiled

661 C.E.
Rise of the Umayyad Dynasty

732 C.E.
Charles Martel stops the Muslim armies at Poitiers

800 C.E.
Charlemagne is crowned Holy Roman Emperor by Pope Leo III

MUSLIM WOMEN pray on the eve of the first day of Ramadan, a month of prayer, togetherness, and fasting (or *sawm*), which is one of the Five Pillars of Islam.

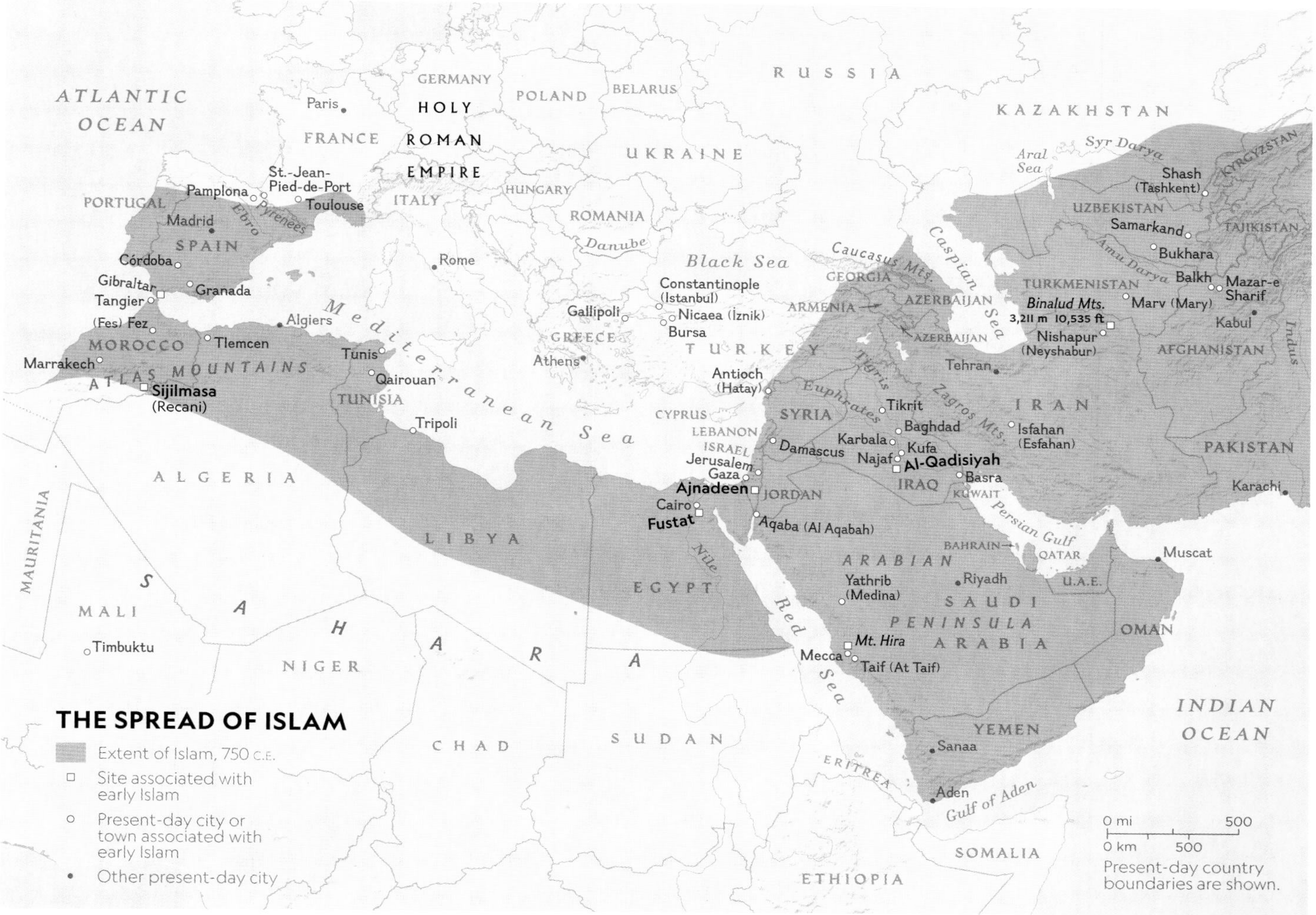

THE SPREAD OF ISLAM

- Extent of Islam, 750 C.E.
- □ Site associated with early Islam
- ○ Present-day city or town associated with early Islam
- • Other present-day city

Present-day country boundaries are shown.

urging him to propagate a faith in one God. As one of Muhammad's biographers describes it, the Word of God came to him in dreams through the angel Gabriel. Muhammad would continue to experience these revelations for the next 25 years, first in Mecca and later in Medina. In the process, he began to understand that these revelations were the makings of a book of holy scripture that would become the Quran (or Koran). Muhammad told others of his visions, reciting them as they had been told to him. The root of the word "Quran" is the Arab verb *qara'a*: "to recite." Soon a community of believers began to grow up around his teachings, and Muhammad recognized that this could produce a new religion: one that could unify the fragmented Arab world.

Muhammad's teachings, however, were not embraced by most citizens of Mecca. The city itself was already a pilgrimage destination; in its center stood the Kaaba, which was dedicated not only to the worship of Allah but other local gods as well. As the threat against Muhammad and his followers grew, they decided to leave Mecca and settle in Yathrib. The date of this journey, the Hijrah, in 622 is reckoned as Year 1 A.H. (or *Anno Hegirae*) in the Muslim calendar.

Muhammad's sojourn in this city, soon renamed Madinah-tun-Nabi (the City of the Prophet, or Medina), made him a statesman of considerable renown. Using Medina as his base, Muhammad gradually expanded his reach, often following pitched battles.

As the Muslim faith grew and attracted large numbers of converts, it took on a more distinctly Arab

A SILVER BOX
containing texts from the Quran, the holy scripture of Islam

A PAGE WITH A *SURAH*
(chapter) from the Quran
with prayer beads to
assist in *tasbih*,
meditative prayer

armies reached the city. Afterward, the cross—or, rather, pieces of it—entered the realm of legend, with many churches in the East and West claiming to possess fragments.

Muslim forces took over Jerusalem in 638. But unlike in earlier sieges, the city's residents, including Christian and Jewish citizens, were not persecuted. 'Umar's Pact of Guarantee granted Christians "safety for their persons, their goods, churches, crosses—be they in good or bad condition—and their worship in general." The Jews were accorded religious freedom as well. It soon became Islamic policy throughout the empire to treat the "People of the Book" with a circumspection befitting their status as co-believers in God's revelation, even though their beliefs differed from Islamic interpretation. Scholars believe that this policy of tolerance was as much a matter of politics as religion. Military success had the effect of overwhelming the Arab armies. Stretched all over the Middle East, 'Umar and his successors had no

character. During daily prayer, Muslims had once faced Jerusalem; now the faithful turned in the direction of Mecca, home to the Kaabah, the historical shrine of Allah, which had been revealed to Muhammad as having been built by Abraham and Ishmael. When the Prophet finally succeeded in conquering Mecca in 630, he rededicated the Kaaba to the worship of Allah as the one and only God.

The Muslim Conquest

After Muhammad's death in 632, Islam's influence continued to expand. His successor, the caliph Abu Bakr, chosen in 632, suppressed tribal revolts throughout the Hejaz and southern Arabia and pushed eastward to unify all of the Arabian Peninsula under the banner of Islam. The next caliph, 'Umar ibn al-Khattab, who succeeded in 634, went beyond the borders and brought the Islamic conquest into the Byzantine and Persian realms. Long years of conflict had exhausted these two superpowers. Khosrow II had died in 628, succeeded by a string of weak and inept rulers, and Byzantium's financial and military resources were strained, leaving Palestine and Syria vulnerable to attack. 'Umar's forces first plunged into these territories in 634. When the Byzantine and Muslim armies clashed at last in the Battle of Yarmuk in 636, Muslim forces emerged victorious. Reportedly, Emperor Heraclius was able to rush to Jerusalem and retrieve the True Cross before the Muslim

PRINCIPAL CALIPHATES OF THE ISLAMIC EMPIRE

Rashidun Caliphate
632–661

Umayyad Caliphate
661–750

Abbasid Caliphate
750–1258

Fatimid Caliphate
(909–1171)

Almohad Caliphate
(1121–1269)

Mamluk Sultanate
(1261–1517)

Ottoman Caliphate
(1517–1924)

Please note: Caliphates are not always contiguous because of rival or overlapping dynasties.

"AT THE ENTRANCE to the Temple Mount of Jerusalem" is an 1886 painting by German artist Gustav Bauernfeind.

THIS 1808 ILLUSTRATION from a book by 19th-century Indian author Mirza Muhammad Rafi' Bazil depicts the death of Abu Bakr, Muhammad's successor and the first of the *Rashidun*, or "rightly guided" caliphs.

choice but to govern by proxy, relying on local systems of government already in place.

'Umar himself was killed in 644 by a Persian slave. Six prominent leaders in Mecca then selected a new ruler, 'Uthman ibn Affan. Unlike Abu Bakr and 'Umar, who like Muhammad were members of Mecca's Hashemite middle class, 'Uthman was a nobleman from the Umayyad clan. His selection infuriated the faction from Medina, who remained steadfast in their support of Muhammad's young cousin (and son-in-law) 'Ali.

Eighth-century bird, Umayyad caliphate

'Uthman's rule is distinguished by his decision to create the official canon of the Quran as an authoritative collection of all revelations received by Muhammad. He also expanded the Islamic Empire by completing the conquest of the former empire of Persia and pushing the Arab armies into Libya. But on his death in 656, a majority in Mecca clamored for a return of a caliph drawn from the middle class, like Abu Bakr and 'Umar, rather than the ranks of nobility. Later, they would become known as *al-sunnah wa-l-jamaa*, followers of the traditions (*sunnah*) of the Prophet. Arrayed against them was the continuing faction in Medina who were supporters of 'Ali, or *shi'at 'Ali*. Here lay the seeds of the first great schism in Islam—that between Sunnis and Shiites. Years of civil strife followed, until the Umayyad Dynasty seized power and ended the tradition of electing a caliph by majority vote. To solidify their rule, the Umayyads moved the capital of the Islamic empire from Mecca to the city of Damascus, where their power was unchallenged.

Islamic Art and Science

The Umayyad Dynasty introduced a great flowering of Arab culture throughout the Islamic empire. Muhammad had always maintained that the religion of Islam was a worldly religion. To pursue science and investigate the mysteries of the natural

LA CONVIVENCIA IN SPAIN

The three Abrahamic faiths—Judaism, Christianity, and Islam—enjoyed a rare period of peaceful coexistence in the Islamic-ruled region of Al-Andalus (today's Andalusia) in southern Spain. During the struggle between the Umayyads and the Abbasids for control of the Islamic Empire, Umayyad nobleman Abd-al-Rahman III fled to Al-Andalus and took control of the region. The city of Córdoba became an unprecedented center of learning with the establishment of the University of Córdoba by Rahman's son, al-Hakam II. One of his ministers was a Jewish physician named Hasdai ibn Shaprut, who brought numerous Jewish scholars to Moorish Spain. The Library of Córdoba grew to 400,000 books, including Greek works that otherwise would have been lost to civilization. The prayer hall of the Great Mosque of Córdoba (at right) has 856 columns. In the 16th century, a Renaissance nave was built in its center.

world was to admire the magnificent creation of God himself. This was the main impetus for what some scholars have called the "second Islamic conquest," namely, the acquisition and preservation of countless works from Antiquity that otherwise would have been lost to the world. Islamic scholars now pursued every field of science, from medicine to astronomy, from agriculture to algebra. Among others, Islamic astronomers refined an instrument known as the astrolabe, which enabled the user to fix the position of the time as well as the position of the sun and stars. The astrolabe was of use not only to mariners but also to devout Muslims, who wished to identify the direction of Mecca for their prayers.

At the same time, Islam developed an artistic style that abided by the Muslim prohibition on the depiction of living creatures but was no less imaginary in its creativity. They derived inspiration from the calligraphy of the Quran, combined with nonfigurative geometric patterns known as arabesques—the intricate interlacing of floral motifs, including foliage and fruits—which also served to perpetuate Arabic as the lingua franca of the Islamic Empire. With their beguiling curvilinear patterns, arabesques were eminently suited for the decoration of curved objects such as vessels,

ASTROLABES, including this Persian device, were used for maritime navigation and to determine the direction of Mecca for prayers.

A WOMAN AND HER CHILD enter the lavishly decorated tomb of 18th-century Sufi poet Sachal Sarmast near Khairpur, Sindh Province, Pakistan.

FRENCH ARTIST Charles Auguste Steuben painted "The Battle of Poitiers of October 732, Won by Charles Martel" in 1837.

> ## "DO NOT QUARREL, AND DO NOT CREATE DIFFERENCES AMONG YOURSELVES. HOLD FAST TO THE ROPE OF GOD."

'UTHMAN IBN AFFAN, THIRD CALIPH

plates, and lamps. Elsewhere, Islamic artisans adopted the Persian technique of color glazing to develop lusterware, pottery covered by a metallic, iridescent veneer with lustrous rainbow-colored effects. Persia itself, meanwhile, became known for delicately knotted carpets, a tradition that endures to this day. Textiles, copper, and precious metals also proved to be a popular medium for Muslim artists.

Dinar from Umayyad caliphate

But the greatest achievement of early Islamic art was the building that still stands in the center of Temple Mount in Jerusalem: the shrine referred to as the Dome of the Rock (known as Qubbet es-Sakhra to Muslims). Marking the rocky outcropping that Muslims identified as the place of Abraham's near-sacrifice of his son, the monument's large dome is embraced by an ambulatory in the form of an octagon. Sixteenth-century ruler Suleyman the Magnificent then covered the exterior with majolica tiles. In 1958, the dome was covered with gilded aluminum plates—a project that was completed only in 1964, three years before the Six Day War in which Israeli forces took control of East Jerusalem.

As the Dome of the Rock rose on the platform where the Jewish Second Temple had once stood, the Islamic armies continued their relentless advance under the command of Umayyad caliphs. After meeting fierce resistance from the Berbers of North Africa, these tribes were persuaded to convert to Islam. The former Roman capital of Córdoba was taken in 711, followed by Toledo. The Muslim viceroy of North Africa, Musa ibn Nusayr, then made plans to carry the Islamic banner through Spain and France and into the heartland of Europe.

The Islamic Invasion of Europe

Terrified by the seemingly unstoppable Muslim steamroller, communities throughout northern Spain and France coalesced around their Christian centers, whether village church or monastery. Suddenly Christianity not only represented faith and charity but also security—thus restoring a sense of regional identity where, in the aftermath of the Western Roman Empire's fall, there was none. As a result, the Islamic conquest had the unintended effect of shaping Christian centers with an indigenous, truly "European" character.

The king of the Franks, Charles Martel, decided to draw a line in the sand over which the Muslims would not pass. Indeed, the Islamic armies were checked at the Battle of Poitiers. But it was left up to the greatest ruler of this era, King Charles the Great (or Charlemagne), to finally drive the Muslims back into southern Spain. There, the Umayyad caliphs initiated a period of great cultural prosperity and interfaith collaboration known as the Convivencia.

Charlemagne, meanwhile, extended his reach across all of France and parts of Germany. In 800, he was crowned Holy Roman Emperor by Pope Leo III—a hereditary title much coveted by Europe's kings. Charlemagne used his authority to harmonize Latin liturgy across most of western Europe and to foster a new flowering of the arts, known as the Carolingian Renaissance.

Unfortunately, Europe's growing prosperity came at a cost, for it soon invited a new wave of invaders—the Vikings from the north, the Slavs from the east, and the Saracens from the south—all intent on destroying Europe's fragile new identity on the cusp of the continent's rebirth. ∎

A FUNERARY PORTRAIT from Faiyum, Egypt, depicts a bearded man from the third century C.E.

AFRICA

IN THE AGE OF FAITH

Africa experienced a major revival in the kingdom of Aksum, heir to the Nubian kingdom of Kush, located in today's Eritrea and northern Ethiopia. Meanwhile, the kingdom of Ghana in West Africa, known as Wagadou, became an important nexus for trade with the Muslim Empire.

After the fall of the Nubian kingdom of Kush in the third century, another polity rose in its stead: the kingdom of Aksum. Located between the Nile and the Red Sea, Aksum deftly exploited its proximity to the main maritime trade routes to establish a number of trading cities. This prompted an age of great prosperity, proudly identified by 126 obelisks—some as high as 110 feet—which its proud kings established all over their realm. Having converted to Christianity in the fourth century, Aksum remained Christian territory until the Muslim conquest of Egypt in 641, which isolated Aksum from other Christian domains on the Mediterranean. In 651, Arabs used their new bases in Egypt to invade Aksum, but they were defeated by massed ranks of Nubian archers. The outcome of this clash was the Treaty of Baqt, a remarkable document that recognized Aksum as a Christian domain even as the surrounding territory slowly succumbed to Islam. This Nubian territory would remain Christian until the 13th century.

Over the preceding centuries, prosperous towns had also sprung up elsewhere—particularly along the Senegal and Niger Rivers. Here was the city of Jenne-Jeno or "Ancient Djenné," located in today's Mali, which at its peak numbered a population of 10,000. This was the realm of the kingdom of Ghana, or Wagadou, whose merchants traded with their Muslim clients in luxury items such as ivory, salt, and even gold, which was mined farther south. This trans-Saharan trade boosted the wealth of Ghana's kings, who used their prosperity to embark on a policy of territorial expansion. By the eighth century, Ghana ruled a veritable empire in West Africa, including both today's Mali and Mauritania. Although these rulers eventually converted to Islam, they retained many of the local practices, including the veneration of idols so despised by Arab Muslims.

Archaeological evidence of the Ghana Empire had been scant until French archaeologists began excavations in modern Mauritania in the 1950s and 1960s. Their discoveries suggest that the empire's capital was based in Koumbi Saleh, close to the Sahara. According to inscriptions, the city was as much as six miles wide and included 12 mosques.

A PERFUME BOTTLE
from Meroë, capital of the Nubian Kingdom of Kush

> ## "[THE KINGDOM OF GHANA] COULD PUT 200,000 MEN INTO THE FIELD, MORE THAN 40,000 OF THEM ARCHERS."
>
> **AL-BAKRI, A MUSLIM HISTORIAN**

Trade also brought prosperity to East Africa, where cities such as Mombasa and Mogadishu had long served as key ports for traders from the Arabian Peninsula and the East. From here, Muslim traders sailed to Quilon in southern India and as far as Canton, China. They returned laden with silk, paper, tea, and porcelain. Some scholars believe that attempts to reproduce Chinese porcelain—a hopeless effort, since kaolin clay was not available outside China—then led Muslim artisans to develop lusterware, which had a similar delicate sheen. The lusterware process soon spread from the east of

Meroitic vase from al-Kadada, Sudan

Africa into Spain, Syria, and Italy, where it was known as majolica.

Coptic and Muslim Egypt

East Africans embraced Islam with equal vigor, so that the skyline of its cities soon featured scores of mosques and minarets. Here, the locals spoke Bantu languages, but Arab traders referred to them as Swahili ("coastal people" in Arabic), and the name stuck. By the ninth century, Swahili had become an integral part of the Islamic world, filled with glittering cities that stood in sharp contrast to the crumbling towns of Europe.

Meanwhile, dissident churches continued to

ISLAMIC NONFIGURATIVE ART

Under Muslim rule, Africa and the Near East experienced a cultural flowering inspired by Greek, Roman, and Christian models. Islam was, at the time, a worldly religion that encouraged the pursuit of science as the study of God's magnificent creation. But Islam did not permit the representation of living creatures in art or sculpture. In the Hadith, the "Sayings of the Prophet (Muhammad)," Allah is quoted as saying, "And who is more unjust than those who try to create the likeness of My creation?" Islamic scholars interpreted this to mean that any human attempt to imitate God's creation was weak and meaningless. Consequently, Islamic artists in Africa and elsewhere were forbidden to paint living beings and concentrated on abstract forms of expression (at left), although in regions of the empire, notably Persia, this proscription was ignored.

A YOUNG WOMAN
from the island of Lamu,
on the northern coast of
Kenya, proudly wears
her niqab, or Islamic veil.

NOTABLE DATES

429 C.E.

Vandals settle in North Africa

451 C.E.

Coptic Church splits from the
Eastern Orthodox Church

500 C.E.

Kingdom of Aksum controls
much of North Africa

543 C.E.

First Christian mission
established in Nubia

641 C.E.

Muslim conquest of Egypt

650 C.E.

Kingdom of Ghana rules
much of West Africa

661 C.E.

Muhammad's fourth
successor, 'Ali, is assassinated

707 C.E.

The Faras Cathedral in Nubia
is rebuilt

786 C.E.

Shiite Muslims flee to the
Maghreb, Morocco

800 C.E.

City of Jenne-Jeno in Niger
Delta has 10,000 inhabitants

801 C.E.

Berbers establish a separate
state in North Africa

971 C.E.

Al-Azhar University is
founded in Cairo

PIGEONS FLOCK to the courtyard of the 10th-century Mosque of al-Hakim in Cairo, Egypt, named after the sixth Fatimid caliph, Al-Hakim bi-Amr Allah.

"IF GOD AND CHRIST
WERE EQUAL
THEN CHRIST SHOULD BE
CALLED GOD'S BROTHER,
NOT GOD'S SON."

ARIUS, PRIEST AND FOUNDER OF ARIANISM

prosper both within and outside the borders of the Byzantine Empire. The Coptic Church, which had split from the Eastern Orthodox Church after the Council of Chalcedon of 451, became the dominant Christian movement in Egypt. When the Christian kingdom of Armenia was overrun by Persia and Byzantium refused to come to its aid, Armenian bishops abandoned the Chalcedon principles and opted for Monophysitism. Monophysists were also particularly strong in Syria.

The ongoing controversy about the dual nature of Christ entered a new phase when the patriarch of Constantinople, Nestorius, proposed that Jesus was a mortal man until he was touched by the logos and became divine. Nestorius thus found himself opposed by both the Byzantine Nicene orthodoxy, which claimed that God and Jesus were of the same substance, and by the still powerful Monophysite movement, which argued that Jesus had been a divine being from the beginning. Nestorius vigorously objected to the Byzantine practice of referring to the Virgin Mary as Theotokos (God-bearer). Mary, Nestorius argued, should be exalted as the mother of Jesus, as Christotokos (Christ-bearer).

Fiercely opposed by Nestorius's opposite number in Alexandria, Bishop Cyril, the Nestorian theology was condemned by the Council of Ephesus in 431, and Nestorius was removed from his see. That did not stop his theological vision from catching on like wildfire. Nestorianism grew by leaps and bounds throughout the Byzantine Empire. When the movement was condemned as heresy by the Council of Chalcedon in 451, its adherents fled to Sassanid Persia, eventually forming what became known as the Church of the East. The Persian city of Nisibis became its intellectual center, attracting many scholars from the school of Edessa, one of the earliest centers of Christian exegesis in the East.

11th-century Abbasid-Fatimid bangle

In Egypt, however, the Islamic conquest precipitated a long decline, which was halted only after the Shia Fatimids took over the Islamic Empire in the 10th century. The Fatimids concentrated their power in North Africa and in 969 moved their capital to the new city of al-Qāhira, modern Cairo. Suddenly, Egypt found itself once more at the nexus of a vast empire, this time an Islamic realm that stretched from the Red Sea to the Atlantic coast. This prompted a renaissance of Egyptian trade and manufacturing that had languished under Byzantine rule. Once again, Egypt's wheat and barley, as well as its fine cotton, linen, and flax, were in demand throughout the Islamic Empire. In addition, Egyptian craftsmen developed an exquisite form of glazed pottery in myriad forms.

The benchmark currency for much of this trade was the Fatimid dinar, a gold coin minted in Egypt. The Fatimids also revived Egyptian architecture by building two major projects in Cairo that remain to this day: the Al-Hakim Mosque, completed in 1010, and the Al-Azhar University, one of the world's oldest surviving academic institutions, founded in 971.

Originally Fatimid rule was tolerant of other faiths, and many Jewish and Christian officials were welcomed in the Fatimid administration. Such tolerance also allowed the caliphs to use Jewish bankers to bankroll their armies, including the recruitment of large numbers of Mamluks. But the virulent suppression of non-Muslim faiths, including Judaism and Christianity, by the Fatimid caliph Al-Hakim, also known as "the Mad Caliph," was bound to elicit a reaction. This came in the form of a papal decree by Pope Urbanus II. ∎

THE ANCIENT MOSQUE OF DJENNÉ

Although archaeological remains from the great cultures of sub-Saharan Africa are scant, the city of Jenne-Jeno ("Ancient Djenné") in today's Mali is one of the best-known archaeological sites of the region. Settled as early as 250 B.C.E., it became renowned for its production of terra-cotta figures, including archers, mounted riders, and young women in a variety of forms. Its greatest monument is a mosque built of sun-dried mud bricks (at left), decorated with a unique pattern of bundled palm sticks that protrude from the wall surface. These serve as scaffolding for repairs, which are needed on a regular basis, given the fragility of the mud bricks. Indeed, the current version dates from 1907, though the mosque was originally built in the 13th century. When in 1996, *Vogue* magazine staged a photo shoot of scantily dressed women inside the mosque, the locals became outraged. The mosque has been off-limits to non-Muslims ever since.

AN AERIAL VIEW of Cairo at sunset shows the Coptic quarter with several Christian churches and monasteries.

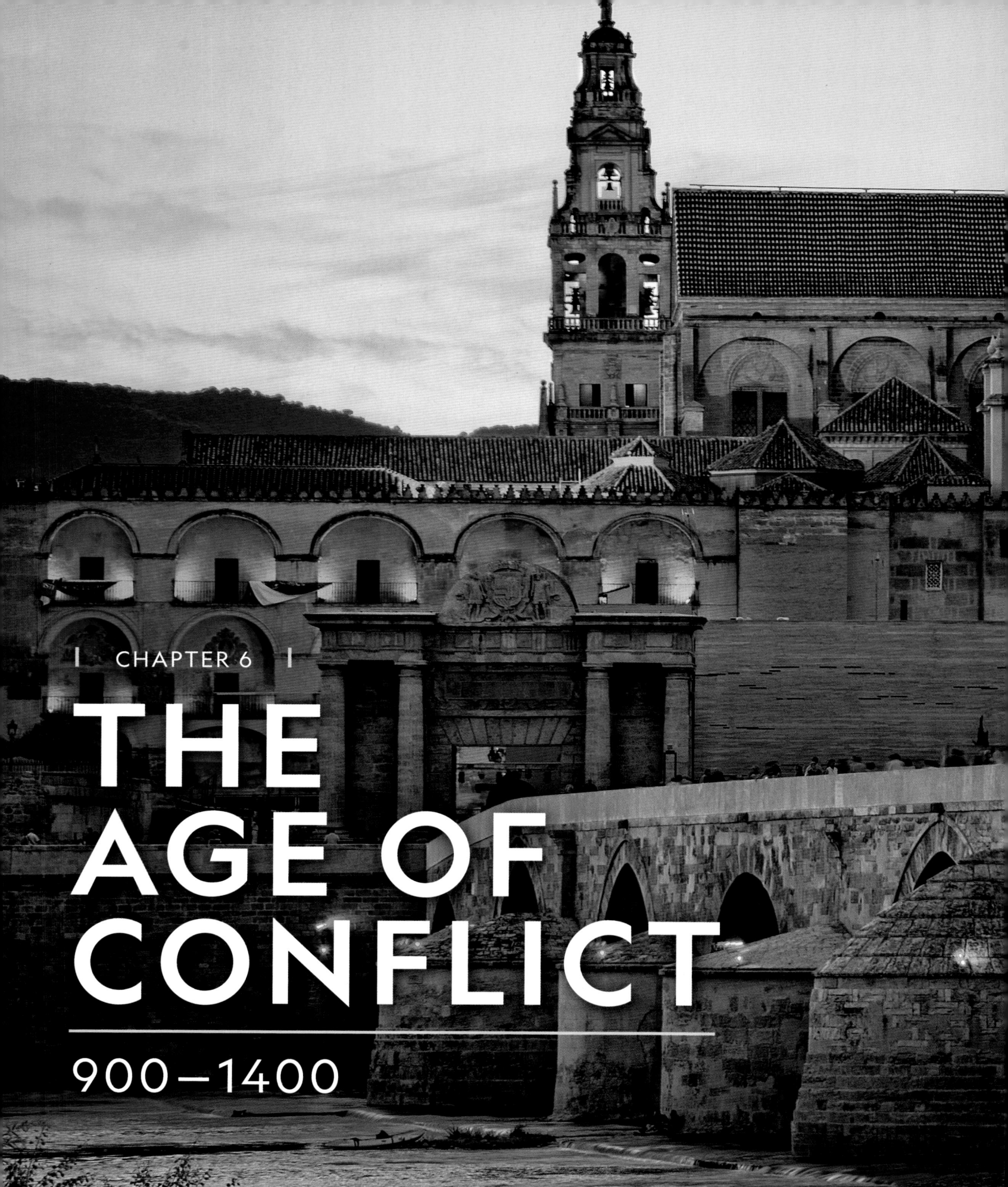

CHAPTER 6

THE AGE OF CONFLICT

900–1400

AN EVENING VIEW shows the Roman bridge over the Guadalquivir River and the Mosque-Cathedral of the city of Córdoba, symbol of the period of the Convivencia in Moorish Spain.

CONTENTS

THE ORIGINS OF CONFLICT

Between the 11th and 13th centuries, the world was convulsed by conflicts that radically reshaped the alignment of nations. Escalating tensions between Christian pilgrims and their Muslim hosts in the Holy Land prompted a series of clashes that would launch the Crusades and ultimately bring the Ottoman Empire to the doorstep of Vienna. This laid the foundation for the nation-states of Europe and fostered an economic recovery after the long period of decline during the European Dark Ages (500–1000).

In Southeast Asia, a powerful empire arose in the region of Funan, located in the southern part of the Mekong Delta. This was the Khmer Empire, whose rulers would conquer a territory akin to modern-day Cambodia, Myanmar, Vietnam, and the Yunnan Province of China. Its most prominent leader, Jaya-varman II, also founded a city known as Yashodharapura, where Khmer architects under King Suryayarman II would build one of the most famous Asian monuments: Angkor Wat.

The Mongol Invasions

Perhaps the biggest and most disruptive series of conquests were the Mongol invasions that terrified much of Southwest Asia, the Near East, and even Europe. In 1206, its principal warlord, Genghis Khan, united all of the quarrelsome tribes of Mongolia before conquering the Xia and Jin territories of China. From there, Mongol armies plunged into Tibet, Korea, and much of modern China, and many years later reached as far as modern-day Russia, Poland, and Bulgaria.

In the Americas, a similar process took place as a Nahua tribe identified as the "Mexica" broke out of the central Valley of Mexico and conquered much of their neighboring lands, establishing what today we call the Aztec Empire. Farther to the south, a Peruvian group living in the Cusco Valley of the Andes Mountains also used its military and economic superiority to establish themselves as the dominant power of the western regions of South America. They produced perhaps the most significant civilization in the Americas after the Maya, the Inca civilization, which among others built the stunning citadel of Machu Picchu.

In the 13th century, another civilization reached its zenith: the Christian Church in Europe. Never before did the Church hold such sway over almost every aspect of life, both sacred and secular. The power of Rome radiated from every monastery, church, and cathedral into medieval society, affecting every individual. This era of the Church triumphant produced the first great architectural tradition since Roman times: the Gothic cathedral.

In the Islamic Empire, meanwhile, the rule of Muhammad's immediate Arab successors—the so-called Four Rightly Guided Caliphs—had been replaced with a dynasty of Umayyad aristocrats. These Umayyads moved the capital of the new empire from Mecca to the city of Damascus, where their power was unchallenged. The Umayyads then introduced a great flowering of Muslim culture. Muhammad had always maintained that the religion of Islam was a worldly one. Therefore, to pursue science or to investigate the beauty of the natural world was to admire and appreciate the magnificent creation of God himself. ■

A KNIGHT'S CROSS was struck to commemorate the First Crusade (1096–1099).

A FRAGMENT of the sculptural detail from Borobudur on Java, Indonesia, reveals the richness of this great Buddhist monument.

SALA DIN VS

A PORTRAIT of Muslim commander Salah-ad-Din ("Saladin" in Western parlance) was painted by Italian artist Cristofano dell'Altissimo in 1568.

A WORLD
AT WAR

European Christendom launched a series of military expeditions against Muslim control of Palestine. Meanwhile, the Khmer Empire spread over much of Southeast Asia, and the Mongol warrior Genghis Khan launched a series of conquests that ultimately produced the largest empire in human history.

The Crusades were a unique series of European military expeditions to recover the Holy Land, which encompassed today's Egypt, Israel, and Jordan, from Muslim rule. Even though in the end, Crusader control of these lands was elusive, the Crusades are important for two reasons. First, these expeditions found broad and enthusiastic support among kings, nobility, and the people, thus galvanizing Europe and allowing it to break out of its isolation during the Dark Ages. Second, the organization of these massive international campaigns provided a new impetus to European trade relations while laying the foundation for the emerging nation-states of France and Britain in the future.

A principal motive for organizing these expeditions was the fact that Muslim rulers became more hostile toward Christians in their territories, particularly Western pilgrims to the Holy Land—which encompassed today's Egypt, Israel, and Jordan. As we saw, until the Islamic conquest, these lands formed part of the Byzantine Empire and had long welcomed large numbers of Christian pilgrims from throughout western Europe as well as Byzantine lands. The early Muslim dynasties, including the Umayyads, continued to respect these Christian pilgrims because Islam too recognized the importance of pilgrimage as exemplified in the hajj to Mecca, one of the Five Pillars of Islam. For example, when a French prelate named Arculf arrived in Egypt in 679 during Umayyad rule, he was able to roam freely, visiting several Coptic monasteries in Egypt before continuing to Bethlehem and Jerusalem. Along the way, he recorded his impressions in a notebook known as *Historia Ecclesiae*. Published after his return, the book became a sensation and prompted a new wave of pilgrims eager to visit the Holy Land.

The growing tension between the Byzantine and Islamic realms did not deter these pious travelers, though many were forced to travel by sea via Alexandria rather than use the overland route through Asia Minor and Syria. Conditions for pilgrims improved further during the caliphate of Harun al

A 13TH-CENTURY gilded bronze statuette depicts a mounted knight in armor, ready for battle.

"WE HAVE MINGLED BLOOD WITH FLOWING TEARS,
AND THERE IS NO ROOM LEFT IN US FOR PITY."

IBN AL-ATHIR ON THE FALL OF JERUSALEM

Rashid, who corresponded regularly with his counterpart in Europe, Charlemagne. Prodded by the French king, Rashid even agreed to build a number of pilgrim hospices in Jerusalem and ensure that Christian pilgrims were given full access to holy sites.

The Path to War

This benevolent attitude changed after the enlightened Muslim caliph died at the beginning of the ninth century. Stories of pilgrims being abused soon spread through Europe, including the horrific experience of a nobleman named Frotmond who was so savagely robbed and beaten that he was left for dead on the road. Matters went from bad to worse in the wake of the Fatimid conquest of the Islamic Empire by

13th-century sword

Gawhar al-Siqilli in 969. His Shia rule, bent on enforcing Islamic orthodoxy, showed little tolerance toward Christians, particularly Christians from Islam's sworn enemy, Byzantium. In response, the Byzantine emperor John I Tzimiskes launched an invasion to free the Holy Land from Muslim rule and briefly took Nazareth and Caesarea before he was repulsed.

Perhaps in retaliation, the sixth Fatimid caliph, Al-Hakim, launched a persecution campaign from 996 onward, targeting both Christian churches and Jewish synagogues.

The Church of the Holy Sepulchre, painstakingly rebuilt after the Persian sack of 614, was once again torn down in 1008. The demolition was so thorough that even the foundations were destroyed, down to the bedrock. Other churches in

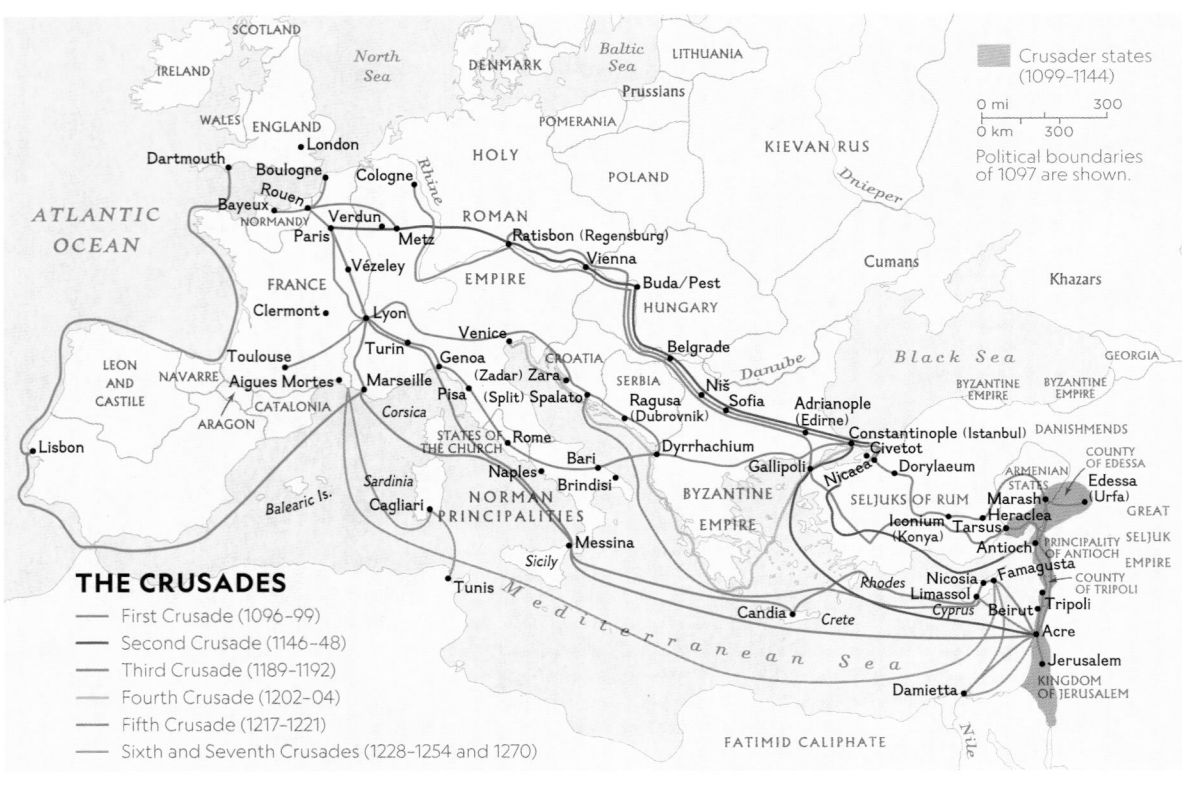

THE CRUSADES

— First Crusade (1096–99)
— Second Crusade (1146–48)
— Third Crusade (1189–1192)
— Fourth Crusade (1202–04)
— Fifth Crusade (1217–1221)
— Sixth and Seventh Crusades (1228–1254 and 1270)

Crusader states (1099–1144)

Political boundaries of 1097 are shown.

A 19TH-CENTURY ILLUSTRATION depicts the 1098 Battle of Antioch between the Crusader forces of Bohemond of Taranto and the army of the Muslim commander Kerbogha of Mosul during the First Crusade.

NOTABLE DATES

1095

During Council of Clermont, Pope Urban II formally calls for a Crusade

1099

Frankish Crusaders capture Jerusalem, the start of 88-year Crusader rule

1150

King Suryavarman II completes Angkor Wat

1162

Temüjin, the future Genghis Khan, is born in Delüün Boldog, Mongolia

1177

Angkor Wat is changed from a Hindu to a Buddhist temple complex

1187

Salah-ad-Din besieges Jerusalem and captures the city

1191

During Third Crusade, Richard "The Lionheart" conquers Cyprus and Acre

1204

Fourth Crusader army diverts to Constantinople and sacks the city

1227

Mongol forces capture the western Xia region in China

1227

Genghis Khan dies, but his successors continue to expand the Mongol Empire

1258

The Mongols capture Baghdad and evict the caliphate

FRENCH 19TH-CENTURY ARTIST
François-Marius Granet painted this scene of Godfrey of Bouillon depositing the trophies of Askalon in the Church of the Holy Sepulchre.

Palestine were converted into mosques or changed into stables or depots. For this, Al-Hakim is sometimes referred to in Christian literature as "the Mad Caliph."

Christian pilgrims who still made it to the Holy Land against all odds came back with hair-raising stories of abuse, robbery, and beatings. One of these was a prelate named Gerbert, who in time would become Pope Sylvester II. Upon his return in 986, Gerbert issued an open letter calling on the Christian world to liberate the beleaguered Christian communities in Palestine. Thus, Europe slowly embarked on a path to war.

The First Crusade

When the Fatimid Dynasty was ousted by the even more violent Turkish Seljuqs, led by Malik Shah, the call for war rose all over Europe. In 1095, during the Council of Clermont, Pope Urban II formally called for a Crusade—which lit-

erally means "taking up the cross" in French—to deliver the Christians in the Holy Land from Muslim rule. The papal call succeeded beyond all expectations. Scores of knights and even greater numbers of foot soldiers rose to the occasion. Urban tried to excuse women, monks, and men of poor health from service, but to no avail. Their enthusiasm may have been motivated by the papal pledge of "plenary indulgence," which essentially allowed the Crusaders to plunder to their heart's content.

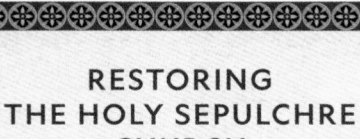

13th-century German helmet

In all, seven major Crusades and a number of lesser ones were launched between 1096 and 1291, mostly with limited success. Only the First Crusade, led by illustrious figures such as Duke Godfrey of Bouillon, King Philip I of France, and the brother of King William II of England, Robert Curthose, was able to make substantial gains against Muslim forces. In 1099, Jerusalem was taken

RESTORING THE HOLY SEPULCHRE CHURCH

After their conquest of Jerusalem, the first priority for the Crusaders was to rebuild the original Church of the Holy Sepulchre virtually from scratch. The new design restored the idea of combining two separate buildings—a basilica commemorating Golgotha with a rotunda surmounting Christ's tomb—into one structure, though two domes still mark these two functions from the outside. Furthermore, a bell tower was added. Allowing for various additions and restorations, this is the church (at right) that visitors to Jerusalem's Old City see today. While rebuilding the foundations, the architects discovered the remains of Hadrian's original temple dedicated to Venus. This was converted into a chapel dedicated to Empress Helena, Constantine's mother, while a separate crypt was hewn for the tombs of Crusader knights, including Godfrey.

> "I HAVE BECOME SO GREAT AS I AM BECAUSE I HAVE WON MEN'S HEARTS BY GENTLENESS AND KINDLINESS."
>
> SALADIN, COMMANDER OF MUSLIM FORCES

by Frankish Crusaders after both Jewish and Muslim inhabitants of the city united in a desperate defense of the city. Most of these defenders were massacred in the orgy of violence that followed.

Thus began a brief period of Christian rule, from 1099 to 1187, in the Holy Land, during which four separate Crusader states were established. One of these was the "kingdom" of Jerusalem, ruled by Godfrey of Bouillon. Godfrey refused to assume the title of king and was addressed instead as Advocatus Sancti Sepulchri, or Defender of the Holy Sepulchre, the location where Jesus was believed to have been crucified and risen from his tomb.

Saladin's Siege

The Muslim response was not long in coming. From 1100 onward, Crusader forces found themselves under increasing pressure from Seljuk Turkish armies. In 1144, Imad ad-Din Zengi, the governor of Mosul and Aleppo, invaded Edessa, defeating the first of the Crusader states. This news so alarmed the West that Pope Eugene III, joined by prominent clerics such as Bernard of Clairvaux, called for a Second Crusade. This campaign, led by King Louis VII of France and Bavarian monarch Conrad III, made it as far as Jerusalem but contributed little to the maintenance of Crusader power in the region other than prompting Muslims to declare a jihad against all Crusader states.

One of Zengi's lieutenants, Salah-ad-Din ("The Righteousness of the Faith," also known to the West as Saladin), took over the struggle with the greatest Muslim army yet assembled. He was outraged by continued attacks on unarmed Muslim

THE MOSQUE OF AL-HAKIM in Cairo, Egypt, was used by Muslim forces as a prison for captured Crusaders and later served as a stable for the horses of Saladin's cavalry.

"**RICHARD I** the Lionheart, King of England" was painted by 19th-century French artist Merry-Joseph Blondel in 1841.

pilgrimage and trading caravans, led by the militant Crusader knight Raynald of Châtillon. In 1187, he crushed the Crusader forces at the Battle of Hattin, leaving the knights with fewer than 15,000 men. Saladin then laid siege to Jerusalem with a force of nearly 80,000 Saracen warriors. The defenders had little choice but to capitulate, and on October 2, Saladin entered the city.

Copper dirham with image of Saladin

The fall of Jerusalem inevitably led to a call for a Third Crusade, this time led by Richard "The Lionheart" of England, but despite several attempts, Richard was unable to retake Jerusalem. Nevertheless, all was not lost. Given that both Richard and Saladin had a reputation for chivalry, an uneasy truce was declared that granted Christian pilgrims unimpeded access to holy sites in Jerusalem—the principal war aim of the Crusades to begin with.

From there on, the Crusader states were gradually rolled back until the knights clung only to their stronghold in Caesarea, near the place of Herod's great harbor. They were evicted at last by the Mamluk sultan Baibars in 1275. From that moment on, the Mamluks remained in control of the Holy Land until Jerusalem fell to another Islamic invader, the Ottoman Turks, in 1517. These Muslim rulers would remain in place for the next 400 years.

The Rise of the Khmer

During the heyday of the great classical empires, roughly from the first to the sixth centuries, the fertile region of the Mekong Delta was inhabited by a number of small states that had increasingly fallen under the spell of Indian culture. Indian caravans and traders brought not only textiles, silver, and gold but also new religious ideas such

THE CITADEL of Salah-ad-Din (or Saladin) near Al-Haffah in Syria formed part of the Crusader Kingdom of Antioch before it fell to Saladin's army in 1188 after a three-day siege.

as Hinduism and Buddhism, both of which found fertile soil along the Mekong River. Modern historians are not sure what these peoples called themselves, but Chinese cartographers referred to them as the Funan or Nokor Phnom, which means "Mountain Kingdom." The name was aptly chosen, since the Mekong Delta is bordered by the Dângrêk Mountains in the north and the southwestern valley runs into the Cardamom (or Krâvanh) and Elephant (or Dâmrei) Mountains. Here is the Phnom Aural, the highest peak of today's Cambodia, with an elevation of just under 6,000 feet.

Chinese records describe Funan as an agricultural region where people lived in stilt houses and cultivated rice, pearls, and spices. Apparently Funan also had a rich musical tradition. When in 263 C.E. Funanese musicians gave a performance for Emperor Jing of Eastern Wu, he was so impressed that he ordered the establishment of a conservatory of Funanese music near Nanking. Perhaps one reason for Funan's cultural prominence was that it had absorbed not only Indian but also Chinese and

A BRONZE FIGURE of a ruler or deity from Prakhon Chai in Buriram Province, Thailand

EVERY YEAR, Buddhist monks converge in Borobudur, Java, to pray at this Buddha shrine in Indonesia.

A DETAIL of one of the 504 Buddha statues that grace the ninth-century Buddhist monument of Borobudur, the world's largest Buddhist temple

Javanese influences. Indeed, many features of its later monuments would betray a strong influence of Javanese architecture, including the ninth-century Buddhist temple of Borobudur in central Java.

In the sixth century, things began to change. One of Funan's vassal entities, a loose confederation of city-states north and south of the Dângrêk Mountains that the Chinese called Chen-La, shook off Funan hegemony and began to grow as a major force in its own right. Historians believe that the largest ethnic tribe of Chen-La was a group of people who later would become known as the Khmer and who today account for about 97 percent of the population of Cambodia. But Chen-La was never a strong, unified polity in its own right, and for the next 200 years, several kings continued to compete for control of this highly fertile region with its lucrative trade links. It was only around 800 that a young prince named Jayavarman II launched an intense effort to unify Chen-La and steadily expanded his control of the greater Mekong Delta. By 802, his realm had become so large that he proclaimed himself *chakravartin* ("king of kings"), a divinely appointed ruler of what we now call the Khmer Empire.

The Development of Angkor Wat

In the years to come, Jayavarman II and his successors continued to expand the Khmer domains until at the peak of its power, the Khmer Empire controlled much of mainland Southeast Asia, including modern-day Cambodia, Myanmar, Vietnam, and the Yunnan province of China. As the empire grew, Jayavarman II also cast about for a proper capital and finally settled on the northern shore of the Great Lake, or

AN AERIAL VIEW of Borobudur, which guides pilgrims through passageways across nine platforms as a re-creation of the path to Nirvana. **BELOW:** Earthenware vessel with a trunk-shaped spout from the Funan-Chenla culture of the sixth to eighth centuries.

Tonle Sap. Known as Yashodharapura, the city steadily grew until it covered more than 400 square miles, almost 20 times the size of Manhattan and home to more than 750,000 people. Here, Khmer architects would build one of the world's most impressive monuments: Angkor Wat, Sanskrit for "Temple City."

At its center lies a massive temple complex, built by King Suryavarman II to honor the Hindu god Vishnu. Designed in the high classical style of Khmer architecture, it served as both the center of state religion as well as the seat of the royal administration. From here, the Khmers initiated the development of a highly sophisticated hydraulic network, fed by rainfall and reservoirs, that was used for transporting goods as well as the cultivation of rice. Khmer architects developed Angkor city based along an axial design, not unlike temple complexes in ancient Greece and Rome, that culminates in the main temple symbolizing Mount Meru, the home of the Hindu gods. Much of this architecture is built up of smooth, tight-fitting blocks, carved from standstone, without the use of mortar. Given this painstaking building method, it is quite astonishing that most of Angkor Wat was built over 30 to 40 years. Equally remarkable is the extensive decoration that runs along almost every surface of the complex, inspired by Hindu epics such as the Ramayana and the Mahabharata.

Unlike similar temples in Asia, Angkor Wat was never completely abandoned, in part because the extensive moats prevented the jungle from overwhelming the site. As a result, it was largely intact when the first European explorers arrived here, beginning with 16th-century Portuguese Antonio da Magdalena.

A SCULPTURE from the 12th-century Angkor Wat ("Temple City" in Sanskrit), capital of the Khmer Empire built by King Suryavarman II in today's Cambodia

MONKS VISIT the 13th-century Ta Prohm temple in Siem Reap, Cambodia, originally built as a Mahayana Buddhist monastery by Khmer King Jayavarman VII.

The Mongol Invasions

The most terrifying of all conquests in this period were undoubtedly the Mongol invasions of the 12th and 13th centuries. They were launched by a man who was born in 1162 in the mountains of Mongolia as the second son of a Kiyad chieftain. After his father was killed by Tatars when he was only nine years old, the boy—who was called Temüjin, or "man of iron"—grew into a gangly lad with dark, hollow eyes. Part of this was due to malnutrition. After his father's death, the tribe refused to accept either Temüjin or one of his brothers as new head of the clan, and so the family was exiled to the steppe. For the next few years, they subsisted on small game and edible legumes they found in the fields and forests of Mongolia, like the hunter-gatherers of old. At one point, Temüjin was even captured by one of the rival tribes and forced into slavery, though eventually he was able to escape with the aid of

Ghazan Khan gold coin

a guard who had taken pity on the boy.

As a result, young Temüjin was a close witness to the senseless violence and tribal warfare of Mongolia, where clans such as the Tatars, Merkits, Mongols, and Naimans competed bitterly for scarce resources. Perhaps the experience taught him the futility of internecine conflict and instilled in him a desire to unify the tribes of his country, not unlike the way Muhammad was inspired to unify the Arabian Peninsula by observing the relentless conflicts that scoured his native land.

Having married a young woman named Börte, Temüjin abandoned hopes of becoming head of his own clan and allied himself with a relative, Toghrul, the leader or Khan of the Keraites. It was a propitious move. When Börte was captured by a Merkit clan, Toghrul did not hesitate to give Temüjin a force of 20,000 warriors to reclaim her. Carefully plotting his strategy, Temüjin ambushed

RELIGIOUS TOLERANCE IN THE MONGOL EMPIRE

For the Mongols, religion was a personal affair that should not be subject to any political interference. The original Mongol tribes worshipped many deities, including the Mongol war god Begtse (at left). While some tribes were Buddhist, others adhered to Nestorian Christianity. According to one tradition, one of Genghis Khan's daughters-in-law, a Keriat princess named Sorkaktani-beki, was Christian. Her son, Prince Hulegu ("warrior" in Mongolian), believed that Christianity could play a strategic role in creating a buffer against the ever looming threat of Islamic Persia. Indeed, when Hulegu Khan invaded Persia in the mid-1250s, his army included scores of Christian soldiers and officers who hoped to restore Nestorian Christianity in the Persian Empire. Their hopes came to naught when the Mongol forces, led by a Christian general named Ked-Buka, were soundly defeated by vastly superior Islamic forces at the Battle of Ain Jalut in 1260, just a short distance from Jesus' hometown of Nazareth.

the Merkits and dealt them a stinging defeat, impressing everyone with his military acumen and calm leadership in battle.

Genghis Khan Launches the Conquest

This was the turning point. In 1186, Temüjin was chosen khan of the Mongol tribe and quickly rose to prominence by joining the Jin, rulers of northern China, in their war against the Tatars. The Tatar army was utterly destroyed. Temüjin then consolidated his power by leading successful attacks on the Naimans and the Uighurs, so that by 1206, Temüjin, now known as Genghis Khan or "Universal Ruler," had unified all of the warring tribes of Mongolia.

If he had halted his military campaigns at this point, Genghis Khan's name in history would have been secured. Instead, he marshaled his forces and in 1207 attacked the Chinese state that bordered Mongolia on the west, known as the Western Xia. The Xia were nominally allied with the Jin Dynasty, but Genghis Khan judged correctly that the Jin were too war-weary from their conflict with the Tatars to come to their aid. Despite a stout defense thrown up by the Xia forces, Genghis Khan captured their principal cities in 1211 and forced the Xia emperor to pledge fealty as a vassal. At that point it was obvious that the Jin Dynasty was going to be Genghis Khan's next target. Jin's emperor, Xuanzong, hastily mobilized his army along the Mongol border, but then the Jin commander, General Wanyan Jiujin, hesitated to invade. It was a mistake. Warned by a defector of the positions of Jiujin's forces, Genghis Khan crashed into the Jin army and killed vast numbers of enemy soldiers. He then moved on to the Jin capital of Zhongdu (today's Beijing), besieging the city in 1215 and forcing Xuanzong to flee.

Still, Genghis Khan refused to rest on his laurels. Although his Mongolian army was exhausted from years of relentless campaigning, the conqueror now set his sights on much of the remaining territories of Southwest Asia. Though he died in 1227, his successors continued his vision of a vast unified world by plunging into Tibet, Korea,

and much of modern China, turning them into vassal states.

The Mongols Invade Europe

Beyond these newly conquered lands lay the vast steppes of Russia, ruled from the capital in Kiev. In 987, its ruler, Vladimir I, had decided that the country should embrace Byzantine Christianity. Kiev, the heart of Russia, then entered a Golden Age as a leading center of Christian civilization in

A 13TH-CENTURY PORTRAIT of Genghis Khan ("Universal Ruler"), who unified the warring tribes of Mongolia and initiated a conquest that would extend through much of Southeast Asia and beyond

eastern Europe. Countless beautiful churches were built on the Byzantine model, topped by a series of domes painted in robin's-egg blue or covered with gold—the first tokens of monumental architecture ever built in the Ukraine, if not in Russia altogether. Kiev's prosperity also produced the Golden Gates of Kiev, built by Yaroslav the Wise in 1017.

To the Mongols, Kievan Rus' was an irresistible target. Starting in 1237, the Mongol general Subutai invaded the country and brushed aside the 80,000 Kievan troops who had been hastily assembled by King Mstislav III. Subutai then went on to destroy virtually all of the nation's major cities, sparing only Novgorod and Pskov.

Three Russian princes who had resisted the onslaught, including Mstislav III, were led underneath a wooden platform where Subutai and his generals were enjoying a hearty meal and crushed to death. "When we were journeying through that land we came across countless skulls and bones of dead men lying about on the ground," an eyewitness, the papal envoy Giovanni del Carpine, wrote in 1246: "Kiev had been a very large and thickly populated town, but now it has been reduced almost to nothing . . . the inhabitants are reduced to slavery."

Not surprisingly, news of the Mongol horrors soon spread through Europe, causing widespread panic. Much of the terror was inspired by the fact

EUROPEAN CAMPAIGN: Mongol raiding parties reach the outskirts of Vienna in December 1241. The death of Ogodei back in Mongolia saves Europe from further attack.

RUSSIANS Batu subdued Russia's feuding principalities by 1240. They remain vassals until Ivan III repels the Mongols in 1480.

Inspired by Persian astronomers, Kublai Khan commisioned an observatory to be built in Daidu. There the armillary sphere was used to measure angles between celestial objects. Under Kublai's 34-year rule, China makes many great strides in science.

Extent of Mongol Empire in 1294

JAPANESE CAMPAIGNS Two failed attempts, in 1274 and 1281, to invade Japan frustrate Kublai Khan's desire to expand his empire beyond the seacoast.

HORSES MEET ELEPHANTS Their horses shy in terror when mongols face a Burmese army mounted on 2,000 elephants.

MONGOLS IN JAVA Two years before his death, Kublai Khan sends a fleet of 1,000 ships against the island kingdom of Java. Facing intrigue and ambush, the Mongols once again return in defeat.

MONGOL CONQUESTS

✕ Major battle
→ Mongol military route
Present-day country boundaries are shown.

0 mi 400
0 km 400

that the Mongol armies appeared absolutely unstoppable. After Kievan Rus', today's Bulgaria and Hungary fell to the Asian invaders. Those who resisted these campaigns were put to death, sometimes in the most horrific fashion, such as being lowered into boiling vats.

Eventually the Mongol Empire became the largest realm at that time—larger even than the Persian or Roman Empires. Some kingdoms merely surrendered and were absorbed, such as the Buddhist Uighur Kingdom; others were conquered by the sword and suffered for it. At one point, after the defeat of Urgench, every Mongol soldier was charged with executing at least 24 people.

Nor did the Mongol army stop at the borders of Asia and Europe. In the 1250s, the Mongol hordes invaded today's territories of Iran, Iraq, and Syria, penetrating as far as Palestine. Baghdad, the nexus of the Islamic Empire, was taken in 1258 after a long and bloody siege. Two years later, however, the Mongol steamroller was finally checked when the Muslim Mamluks defeated the Mongols at the Battle of Ain Jalut, in the heart of Galilee. Nevertheless, the violent conquests continued elsewhere. Mongol armies raided Lithuania in 1277, followed by Poland in 1287, while on the other side of the globe, Mongols launched attacks against Myanmar and Java. In sum, modern historians calculate that the Mongol invasions led to the death of between 20 and 40 million people in all theaters of war.

The Mongol Legacy

Having reached its high mark, the Mongol Empire began to disintegrate. Nonetheless, Khan's successors continued to rule various lands for several centuries—similar, perhaps, to the way Alexander the Great's successors remained in power in many nations subdued during the Alexandrian conquest. In 1279, for example, Kublai Khan established the Yuan Dynasty of China, which also

BRITISH ILLUSTRATOR Cecil Langley Doughty created this modern impression of Mongol soldiers breaking through the Great Wall of China. **ABOVE:** This Mongol helmet was captured as a trophy by victorious Japanese forces during the Yuan invasion of 1274 or 1281, led by Kublai Khan.

A MODERN PHOTO depicts a Mongolian archer joining the Naadam Festival, which involves horse racing, archery, and Mongolian wrestling.

"[THE MONGOLS] ATTACKED RUS, WHERE THEY MADE GREAT HAVOC, DESTROYING CITIES AND FORTRESSES AND SLAUGHTERING MEN; AND THEY LAID SIEGE TO KIEV, THE CAPITAL OF RUS."

GIOVANNI DEL CARPINE, PAPAL ENVOY TO THE GREAT KHAN

controlled the region of Tibet as well as Korea. Persia would be ruled by another Mongol off-shoot, the Timurid Dynasty, into the 15th century. The longest-lasting Mongol territory, however, was the Mughal Dynasty, which continued to control much of India well into the 19th century.

Not all of the Mongol legacy was drenched in blood. Genghis Khan adopted the Uighur alphabet as the official written language of the Mongol Empire and restored the Silk Road as the key artery of trade between Europe and Asia. This has prompted some historians to coin this era, ironically, the Pax Mongolica ("Mongol Peace"). Furthermore, in most of his conquered lands, Genghis Khan established a meritocracy where local officials could rise in the Mongol administration regardless of class or rank, simply on the strength of their ability. As the Islamic conquerors had realized long before him, a vast empire could not be ruled by Mongols alone but depended on a cadre of indigenous, educated leaders. Women too were held in high esteem, and some were allowed to rise to positions of power and influence. In addition, the Khan recognized the importance of teachers, doctors, and priests to maintain the social harmony of the empire and exempted them from taxes. Indeed, once a region was conquered, the Mongols practiced broad religious tolerance, allowing everyone to worship as he or she saw fit. ∎

THIS FRESCO of
St. Thomas Aquinas was
painted by Italian artist
Fra Bartolomeo in the
early 16th century.

THE MEDIEVAL
WORLD

The High Middle Ages, the apogee of Catholic Christianity, witnessed a decisive power shift from the Greek Church in the East to the Latin Church of the West. For the next five centuries, Europe was the center of Christianity, convulsed by wars and the Black Death.

The 12th century marked the beginning of an economic revival throughout Europe, buoyed by the growth of international commerce. As the new nation-states of France and Britain came into their own, political stability encouraged trade contacts across the Continent, from the Italian states in the south (particularly Florence and Pisa) to the cities of the Hanseatic League in the north, including Bremen, Hamburg, and Lübeck. Then, in 1204, the sack of Constantinople by knights of the Fourth Crusade disrupted trade with the Islamic Ottoman Empire, which the mercantile cities of Venice and Genoa rushed to fill. By the early 14th century, Venice had all but replaced Constantinople as the principal European conduit to trade with the Ottoman Empire. The vast wealth that poured into the city lay the basis for the role Venice was destined to play in the Renaissance.

The rising prosperity also fueled a rapid growth of Europe's population, which had steadily declined after the fall of the Roman Empire. This population growth led to an urgent quest for more inhabitable space. Across Europe, large tracts of forests and marshlands were cleared and drained to make room for new settlements, which in time would emerge as cities in their own right. This was particularly true in Germanic-speaking lands, where the growing scarcity of arable land prompted many people to cross the River Elbe and settle east of the traditional Frankish boundaries. All of these developments produced a degree of economic activity that by some estimates would not be surpassed until the 19th century.

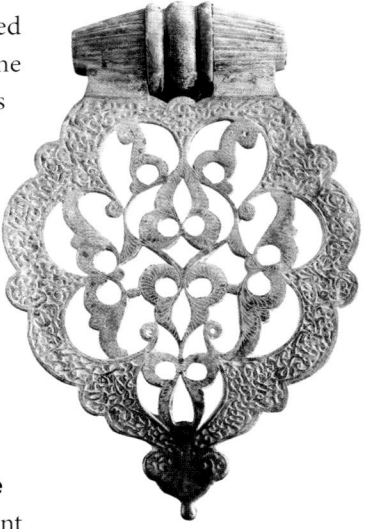

A 10TH-CENTURY DOOR KNOCKER from Seville in Al-Andalus, Moorish Spain, during the period of the Convivencia

The Changing Social and Political Landscape

Inevitably, these movements produced important social and political changes. For the first time since the fall of the Roman Empire, growth was stimulated by the mercantile cities rather than the Church or the temporal powers. It was a new middle class of merchants, craftsmen, artists, and other professionals who nurtured and sustained the European economy, and they demanded a voice in the way they were governed. Some cities such as Florence and Cologne shook off the rule by local princes or bishops and appointed city councils made up of the leading mercantile families.

> "WHEN I WAS IN SIN IT WAS BITTER TO LOOK ON LEPERS, BUT THE LORD BROUGHT ME AMONG THEM, AND I SHOWED MERCY TO THEM."

THE TESTAMENT OF FRANCIS OF ASSISI

In Germany, these became known as Imperial Free Cities, proud of the fact that they owed allegiance or tribute to no one save the emperor.

Following an ill-fated showdown with Pope Innocent III and the loss of Normandy after the Battle of Bouvines in 1214, King John of Britain was even compelled to sign the Magna Carta, which greatly curtailed the previously unchecked power of the English monarchy. Likewise, Emperor Frederick II of the Hohenstaufen Dynasty was forced to grant considerable autonomy to the various principalities under his sway.

Of course, the growing economy did not change the fact that illiterate peasants made up the vast majority of the European population, often living far from the social and spiritual safety net offered by cities and the Church. It was precisely to meet their needs that a new monastic movement was born. Unlike the monks of a previous era, these friars did not seek prayer and solitude behind monastery walls, but rather went out to engage with the ills and needs of the outside world. The first of these orders was founded in 1215 by Dominic Guzman, a Spanish priest and diplomat who had traveled extensively through Europe before settling in Toulouse. His order of the Dominicans would provide basic education to thousands of the poor and illiterate. By the same token, the Dominicans

FASHION IN THE MIDDLE AGES

Between 1200 and 1340, Europe experienced a great revival in trade, which led to the rise of distinct fashion trends, often set by the courts of France and England. Clothing became a barometer of wealth based on the particular colors and fabrics used. Crimson and purple, for example, were costly since these dyes had to be painstakingly extracted from beetles or sea snails. Ultramarine blue (at left), the most expensive color of all, was ground from crushed lapis lazuli and was adopted by the French court as its heraldic color. Fabrics too signaled the wealth of the wearer. Cotton was imported from India and therefore expensive. So was silk, a fabric developed in China, which was introduced to the Byzantine Empire in the sixth century and brought back to western Europe by the Crusaders. By contrast, garments of the most common folk were woven from flax or wool. Flax was a fiber from the flax plant and often home-spun into linen. Raw sheared wool from Scotland was shipped to the Low Countries and Italy, where it was washed, woven, and dyed into delicate fabrics.

"THE DELIVERANCE
of the Prisoners of
Carcassonne" was painted
by French artist Jean-Paul
Laurens in 1879.

NOTABLE DATES

1203
The University of Siena is founded

1204
Constantinople is sacked by militia of the Fourth Crusade

1213
The Council of St. Albans, precursor of the English Parliament, is founded

1220
Chartres Cathedral is completed

1225
The final version of the Magna Carta is issued

1230
Leprosy is introduced to Europe, possibly via Crusader ships

1231
The Inquisition is established in Lombardy

1252
Florence begins to mint its own currency, the gold florin

1266
Thomas Aquinas begins the *Summa Theologiae*

1300
Guillaume de Machaut, composer of the Ars Nova style, is born.

1309
The papal court moves to Avignon, where it will remain for more than 70 years

1337
Outbreak of the Hundred Years' War

THE DUOMO, or Cathedral, of Siena, Italy, is one of the most impressive monuments of 14th-century Romanesque architecture in Tuscany.

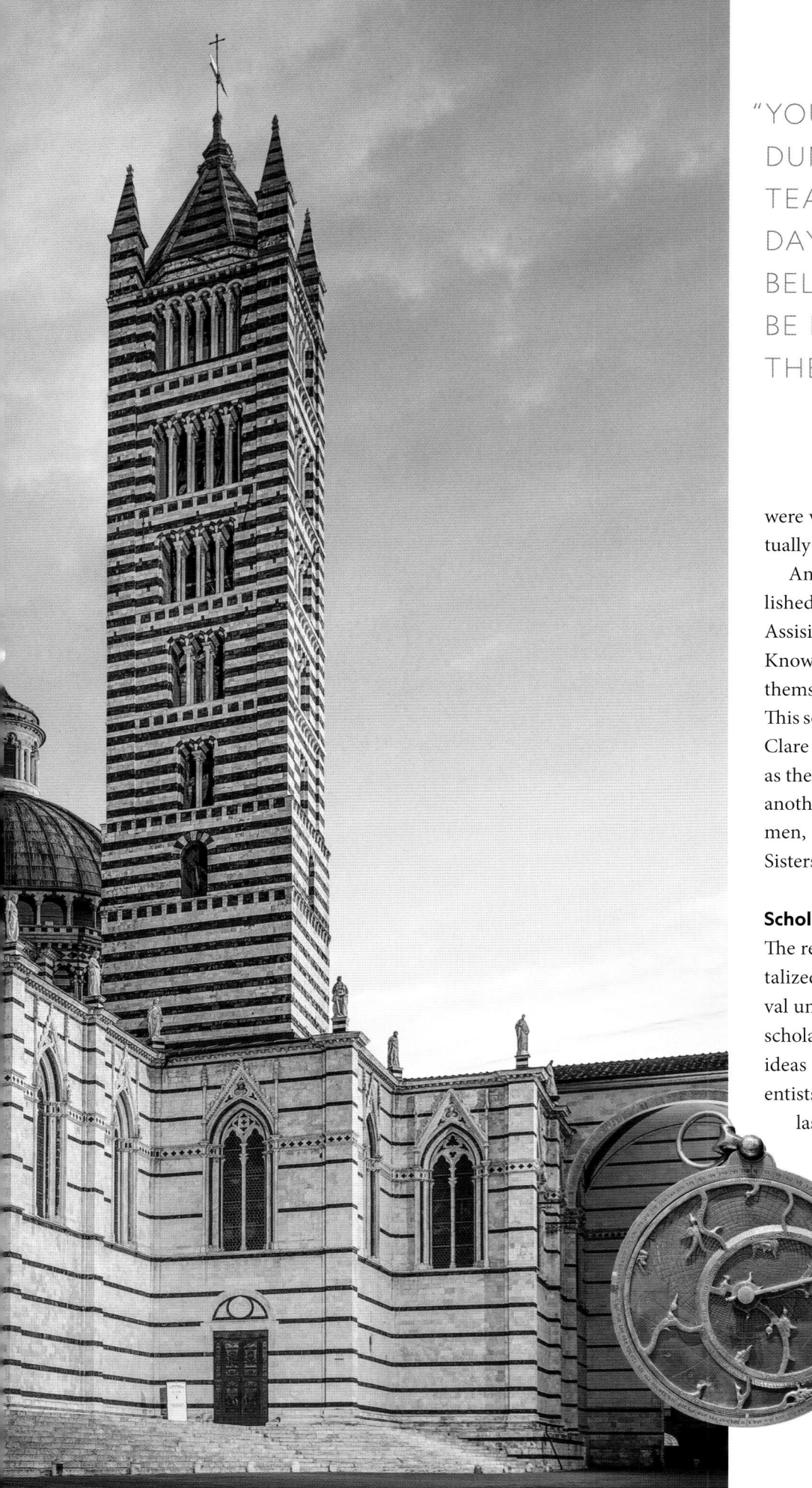

"YOU MAY CALL HIM A DUMB OX, BUT WITH HIS TEACHING HE WILL ONE DAY PRODUCE SUCH A BELLOWING THAT IT WILL BE HEARD THROUGHOUT THE WORLD."

**ALBERTUS MAGNUS
ON HIS STUDENT THOMAS AQUINAS**

were vigilant for any form of heresy, which eventually led to the formation of the Inquisition.

Another even more influential order was established by the son of a rich silk merchant from Assisi, Tuscany, named Francesco di Bernardone. Known as the Franciscans, these friars devoted themselves to ministering to the poor and the sick. This soon inspired a wealthy Assisi woman named Clare to create a similar order for women, known as the Poor Clares or Order of Poor Ladies. Later, another Franciscan order was established for laymen, known as the Third Order of Brothers and Sisters of Penance.

Scholastic Movement

The restoration of trade and prosperity also revitalized intellectual thought in Europe. As medieval universities grew, a new movement known as scholasticism emerged that sought to reconcile the ideas of Greek and Roman philosophers and scientists with the tenets of the Christian faith. Scholasticism was inspired in part by the rediscovery of the works of fourth-century B.C.E. philosopher Aristotle, which had been preserved in monasteries throughout Europe, as well as the great

THIS 14TH-CENTURY ASTROLABE
shows that the ancient instrument continued to be used in the Middle Ages in Europe and well into the age of global exploration.

"I HAVE NOW REIGNED ABOVE FIFTY YEARS IN VICTORY OR PEACE; BELOVED BY MY SUBJECTS, DREADED BY MY ENEMIES, AND RESPECTED BY MY ALLIES."

ABD-AL-RAHMAN III, REFLECTING ON HIS TOLERANT RULE IN AL-ANDALUS

Muslim libraries of Córdoba and Grenada. Aristotle, the tutor of Alexander the Great, appealed to the medieval European mind because of the practical and tangible quality of his writings. His oeuvre was the basis of almost every aspect of medieval intellectual endeavor, from ethics to physics, from music to poetry, and from political theory to rhetoric and logic.

The academic revival produced a new type of scholar: the intellectual cleric, steeped in Church doctrine as well as the classics, exemplified by 13th-century sages like Thomas Aquinas and 14th-century scholars such as William of Ockham, John Wycliffe, and Thomas à Kempis. Of all medieval scholars, Thomas Aquinas was perhaps the most influential. In 1245, he moved to Paris to continue his studies at the renowned University of Paris, which was rapidly becoming one of Europe's most influential centers of learning. In many of his subsequent writings, Aquinas argued that Aristotelian philosophy and Christian doctrine were essentially complementary rather than contradictory and that theology was a science, grounded in knowledge and observation like any other form of scientific endeavor. Many of these intellectuals were in close touch with one another, using Latin as their common language. Their scholarship would lay the foundation for the great humanists of the Renaissance, including Marsilio Ficino, Thomas More, and Erasmus.

The Islamic Convivencia in Moorish Spain

In the meantime, something extraordinary was happening in Al-Andalus (today's Andalusia) in Spain. Here, the Umayyad Dynasty initiated a period of considerable harmony among Muslims, Jews, and Christians, known as the Convivencia. Religious tolerance was a novelty for the Spaniards, who had known only the fanatical Arianist brand of Christianity espoused by the Visigoths. It did not come easily, for Spain was still tormented by different sects competing for power under Moorish rule, stoked by the rivalry of Toledo, Seville, and Córdoba. The 10th-century Umayyad caliph Abd-al-Rahman III put an end to the turmoil by suppressing the power of the feuding aristocrats. He then initiated a patronage of the arts that many successors to come would continue. A key example is a lovely ivory box, carved from a single elephant tusk and dated around 968, now in the collection of the Louvre in Paris. In the

AN ANONYMOUS 16th-century portrait depicts 14th-century scholastic theologian John Wycliffe, who completed a translation of the New Testament into English in 1382.

A DETAIL of a 13th-century Flemish tapestry shows a prelate reading a book in a pleasure garden filled with exotic flowers and animals.

THE COURT OF THE LIONS in the Alhambra complex in Granada is an exquisite example of delicate arabesques interwoven with the Moorish arcade.

SPANISH ARTIST
Dionís Baixeras i Verdaguer painted "Abd al-Rahman III Receiving the Ambassador at the Court of Cordoba" in 1885.

Judería, the Jewish quarter of Córdoba, Abd-al-Rahman employed Muslim artisans to build a synagogue for Córdoba's Jewish population.

At the same time, Córdoba became Europe's leading center of learning. Its library ultimately grew to 400,000 volumes, including works by Plato, Aristotle, Archimedes, and other Greek scholars who otherwise would have been lost to civilization. More than 5,000 calligraphists were employed in copying the works. Their efforts laid the foundation for the literary revival during the Renaissance.

The Convivencia was not without its challenges. Jews, Christians, and Muslims lived in separate quarters in Córdoba and elsewhere in Al-Andalus. There was little social contact outside the spheres of science,

11th-century ceramic ewer

government, and commerce. Taxes levied on Christians and Jews were higher than those Muslims were required to pay. Tempers rose when some Muslim imams ordered the bell towers of churches torn down—or at least cut in height—so that they would not rise higher than the minarets of the city's mosques. Christian theologian Eulogius wrote that devout Christians, including his own grandfather, would hold their hands over their ears whenever the cry of the muezzin rose over the city. But otherwise, the three faiths coexisted with a remarkable degree of tolerance.

This harmony came to an end in 1031 when a new wave of Berber armies entered Córdoba and the Abbasids began to assert their control over all of Islam. One Berber sect known as the Almoravids introduced a

> "IF THE EYE OF MAN . . . MARKS THE ABUNDANCE OF LIGHT FROM THE WINDOWS, IT ADMIRES THE INESTIMABLE BEAUTY OF THE GLASS AND THE VARIETY OF THE MOST COSTLY WORK."
>
> THEOPHILUS, *ON VARIOUS ARTS*

strict observance of the Quran, ending the worldly pursuits that had made Córdoba the center of human civilization. At the same time, the political unity of Al-Andalus disintegrated into separate fiefdoms, known as *taifas* (based on the Arab word *ta'ifah,* or faction). Public worship by Jews and Christians was curtailed; many families were forced to flee to Toledo and other more tolerant cities in the province or beyond.

Gothic Cathedrals

Undoubtedly, the medium in which the High Middle Ages found their greatest religious expression was the cathedral. Important changes in early 13th-century technology created a new idea of what sacred architecture should look like and what

purpose it was meant to fulfill. One important factor was the desire to open up the thick walls characteristic of Romanesque buildings to allow for the display of art in stained glass. In an age that prized preaching when the vast majority of the faithful were illiterate, these great sheets of light became the people's Bible—key moments from the Old and New Testament, illustrated in shimmering glass.

This innovation demanded a radically different approach to the mastery of load-bearing forces. The solution was to direct the weight of the vaulted roof into concentration points using diagonal ribs, which themselves were supported by massive compound piers running the full height of the church. These piers in turn transferred the

EARLY POLYPHONIC MUSIC

Gregorian chants originated as a fusion of Roman and Frankish song traditions, dating to the time of Charlemagne. Gregorian music is monophonic, which means that all voices in the choir sing in unison, in the same serene pitch and rhythm without any form of accompaniment. These liturgical songs were notated on often beautifully illuminated sheet music (at left), which uses simple rhythmic symbols to identify either a longa (long note) or a breve (short note). Some composers began to experiment with organum, an early polyphonic style whereby voices move in parallel motion, separated by perfect fourths, fifths, or octaves. Organum would lay the foundation for the Ars Antiqua, or early polyphony, which liberated composers to explore a variety of harmonic textures across variable rhythmic patterns. This produced the tradition of the motet, a sacred work meant to inspire piety and devotion.

THIS VIEW of 12th-century Notre Dame as seen from the south of the River Seine was taken before the fire that destroyed the central spire and much of the roof over the nave on April 15, 2019.

A VIEW OF A TYPICAL GOTHIC CHOIR shows how the weight of the roof is channeled via diagonal ribs into massive compound piers, which in turn are supported by exterior flying buttresses—thus opening up the wall for sheets of stained glass.

downward pressure of the vaults into exterior struts, known as flying buttresses, which became a dominant feature of Gothic cathedrals. Thus, whereas Romanesque builders had tried to contain the weight of the building within, the Gothic architects moved it outside. At the same time, the structural needs of this rib-and-pier system shaped the top of each window into a pointed arch, which soon became the most recognizable element of the Gothic style.

The invention of Gothic technology coincided with the rapid growth of urban wealth and the desire to express that wealth in magnificent monuments to God, often in competition with other cities. Thus, the period between 1190 and 1280, which historians refer to as High Gothic, saw an unprecedented outburst of building activity not only in France but also in Germany, England, Italy, and Spain. As cathedrals topped by soaring spires rose to become the dominant feature on every skyline, they proudly declared the shift from the monastery to the city as the dominant center of Christian activity.

The Hundred Years' War and the Great Plague

Europe's "long summer of the High Middle Ages," in the words of historian David Bentley Hart, came to an end in the mid-14th century when Europe was visited by the twin calamities of the Hundred Years' War and the Black Death. The Hundred Years' War was fought between England and France, between the Plantagenets and the House of Valois, for control of the French kingdom. The war was fought primarily on French soil, and countless French peasants suffered an unending scourge of pillage, destruction, and death. One of these peasant families lived in the village of Domrémy near the Meuse River, which served as the boundary between those who pledged their fealty to Burgundy (in alliance with the English invaders) and the so-called Armagnacs, people who remained loyal to the French Crown. As it happened, this family had a daughter named Jehanette, who in 1429 would gain fame as Jeanne

THE 15TH-CENTURY coat of arms of the Arc family during the Hundred Years' War

d'Arc, the young woman who led the French army on a series of stunning victories.

The Black Death originated in Mongolia and probably was carried by Mongol invaders and Genoese merchant ships from the Crimea to southern Italy and then rapidly spread throughout the Mediterranean. By 1351, the pandemic had penetrated deep into Europe, reaching eastern Europe and even Russia; only isolated areas in Poland and the Low Countries were spared. Medieval science was powerless to stop it. Some physicians believed the plague was carried by air from decaying corpses, aided by the humid conditions of summer; others believed that noxious fumes from sewers were at fault. Some civic authorities, such as the city of Pistoia, urged an evacuation of all healthy people from diseased neighborhoods. This sometimes worked, though not for reasons cited, for the plague was actually spread by black rats harboring infected fleas.

For most, this advice came too late. A society that had been so painstakingly built in the previous century was torn asunder as all social classes, from paupers to princes and bishops, were struck by the disease. As thousands died, the Christian order collapsed; thieves, rapists, and murderers roamed freely without any fear of retribution. Modern estimates vary wildly, but it is generally believed that some 25 to 30 percent of the European population was killed; worldwide, the population was reduced from some 450 million in the 13th century to around 375 million in the 14th century.

The long period of the plague produced a fatalistic mood among many Europeans. The 1353 collection of novellas *The Decameron* by Giovanni Boccaccio relates how seven young women and three young men entertain each other with tales of love and death while sheltering in a villa outside Florence, so as to escape the ravages of the Black Death. And yet, in the shadow of death that held Europe captive, the seeds of a great rebirth were about to be sown. ■

PLAGUE'S RELENTLESS ADVANCE

SECOND PANDEMIC

→ Plague route by sea

✱ European cities repeatedly hit by plague, 1347–1771; perhaps 50 million people died in all

LONDON
Plague was endemic in London beginning in 1348 and ending with the Great Plague of 1665 that claimed at least 68,000 lives.

MOSCOW
Brought by troops returning from a Russo-Turkish war in 1771, plague killed a reported 60,000 persons in Europe's last major epidemic.

CHINA
In the late 1320s a plague epidemic broke out in Central Asia and spread east to China. Records are vague but millions died by the century's end. Plague later spread west along caravan routes, reaching the Black Sea by 1347.

SICILY
Plague landed in western Europe at Messina, Sicily, in October 1347 when plague-ridden galleys arrived from Black Sea ports in the Crimea.

ISLAMIC WORLD
Starting with an epidemic in 1348, the population of the Muslim world suffered recurring plague outbreaks into the 19th century.

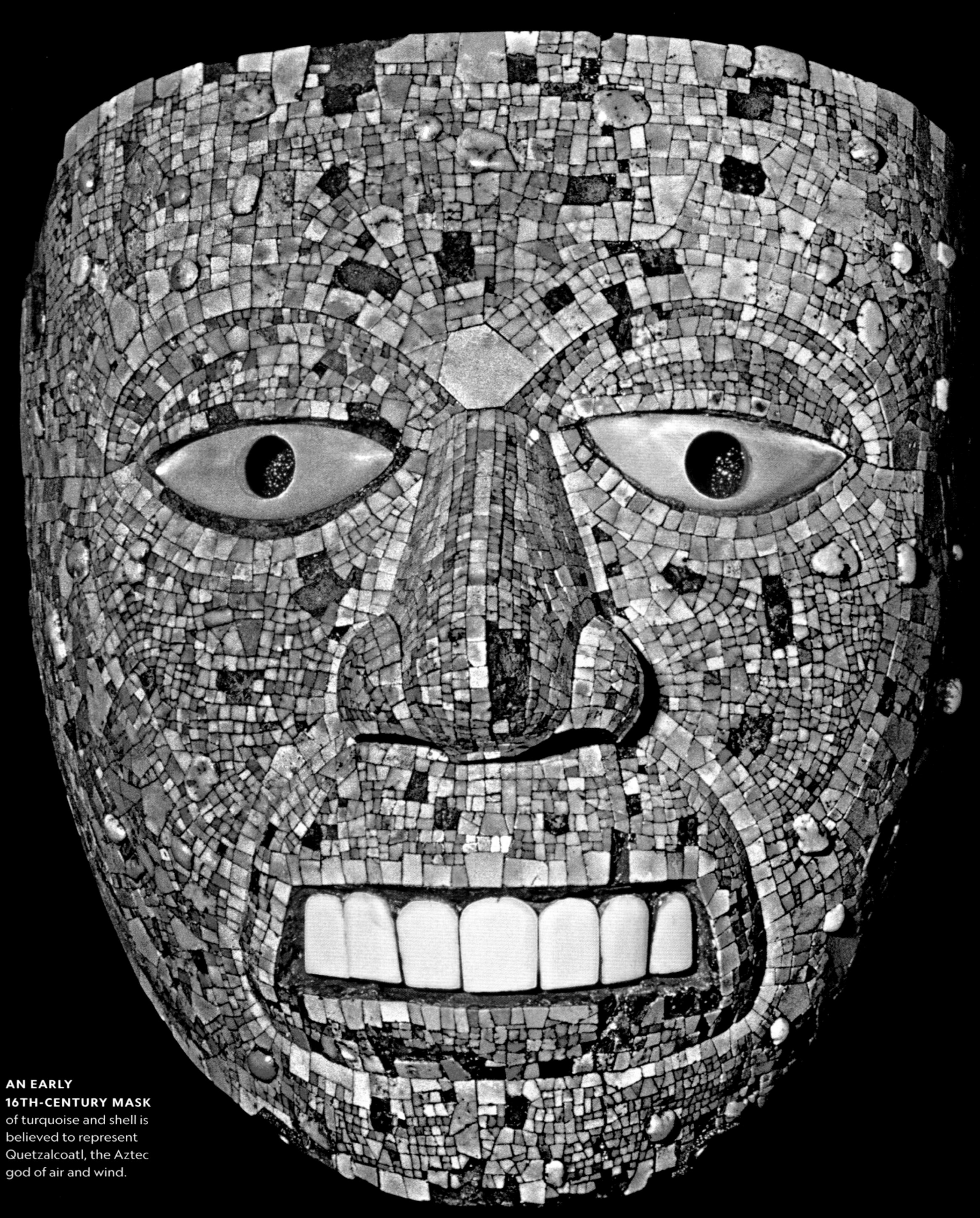

**AN EARLY
16TH-CENTURY MASK**
of turquoise and shell is
believed to represent
Quetzalcoatl, the Aztec
god of air and wind.

EMPIRES OF THE
AMERICAS

The era of great conquests in Asia and Europe found a parallel in the rise of major empires in the Americas, which produced considerable social upheaval as well as the birth of new cultural traditions. The most prominent of these were the Aztec and Inca civilizations.

The rapid decline of the Maya civilization after 900 C.E. left a power vacuum in Central America and led to a fragmentation of its empire into separate fiefdoms. One of these was the Toltec civilization, which rose in the 10th century around its capital city of Tula (or Tollan Xicocotitlan), located just north of modern-day Mexico City. It was laid out on a grid-like pattern that allocated separate zones for pyramids, temples, palaces, and residential areas. In time, the city became a magnet of trade for surrounding regions. As its population grew to 50,000, so did its diversity, absorbing many Mesoamerican cultural and linguistic traditions. According to one Toltec document, the city was ruled by a leader who combined the functions of high priest and king, known as Quetzalcoatl ("Feathered Serpent"). Religious traditions had always been important in this part of the world, and like the Maya, the Toltec practiced human sacrifice as a way to placate the gods. Large stone depictions have been found of Toltec officials killing their enemies as part of a sacrificial ritual. Human heads may also have been used as part of the Toltec fondness for ball playing;

one altar near a ball court was found to contain numerous human skulls.

Surprisingly, King Quetzalcoatl turned against such sacrifices, claiming that the bloodshed offended the gods rather than assuaging them. Many of his followers then ended the practice, while others—such as adherents of the cult of Tezcatlipoca—persisted with killing human beings as part of their worship. Nonetheless, Quetzalcoatl's supreme power was such that his death in the mid-950s—the records aren't clear—plunged the region into instability. The conflict between rival religious groups escalated, and many decided to leave Tula, prompting the Toltec civilization to go into a steady decline. This process was accelerated by the outbreak of a prolonged drought in the 11th century, which—as in other parts of the world—prompted large migrations of people in search of more fertile lands. For example, one group of Toltec "exiles" decided to settle in Cholula, the site of the largest Maya pyramid in the Americas.

THIS STATUE OF XIUHTECUHTLI, the Aztec god of fire, was found in the temple of Tenochtitlan, in the center of today's Mexico City.

"WE ARE OBLIGATED TO WORSHIP [OUR GODS]
AND MAKE SACRIFICES . . . FOR THEY GIVE US HEALTH
AND RAINS AND GOOD SEED TIMES AND SEASONS
AND AS MANY VICTORIES AS WE DESIRE."

KING MOCTEZUMA II, RULER OF THE AZTEC EMPIRE

The Aztec Empire

Another group on the move was a people that we today refer to as the Aztec. They wouldn't have used this term and most likely identified themselves as Nahua peoples, which today is still the largest indigenous group in Mexico and El Salvador. The Nahua spoke a language known as Nahuatl, the lingua franca of Mesoamerican trade, that probably originated in Aridoamerica, roughly the territory of northwestern Mexico. By 1325, the Nahua—more specifically, the Nahuatl-speaking group of the Mexica— had established themselves in the Valley of Mexico. Here, they built a new urban concentration on the shores of Lake Texcoco known as Tenochtitlan, which in time would become modern Mexico City.

This was a fertile region, and the Mexica soon developed a flourishing agriculture of a variety of crops, including corn, beans, and legumes. This was bound to invite envy from surrounding population groups still struggling from the aftereffects of the drought, and the Mexica found themselves defending their resources. This, some historians believe, is what sparked the Mexica (or Aztec) conquest: to secure the territories surrounding the city of Tenochtitlan through the development of buffer states. The Mexica then gradually expanded their influence through a combination of alliances and military conquest, so that by the early 15th century, the highland plateau of Central Mexico was dominated by the Mexica-led Triple Alliance of three major city-states: Tenochtitlan, Tlacopan,

LIFE IN THE AZTEC EMPIRE

To consolidate his conquest, the Aztec king Moctezuma I (at left, with captives) established an imperial administration as comprehensive as the Augustan imperial system. All taxes and tributes were collected by the central authority in Tenochtitlan, sidelining local aristocracies. Local rulers were allowed to stay in place provided they pledged total submission to the king; otherwise, they were replaced by governors appointed by the crown. Moctezuma also promulgated a set of laws to secure the social harmony of the lands under his control. Many offenses, such as adultery, warranted the death penalty. Schools were built everywhere to both indoctrinate the young and prepare them for military training. Religious observance was strictly enforced, including the sacrifice of human beings captured during Aztec wars of conquest.

A NIGHTTIME VIEW shows the five-tiered pyramid of Tula, the former capital of the Toltecs, topped by massive columns representing Toltec warriors

NOTABLE DATES

ca 1000

Toltec capital of Tula emerges as the leading power in central Mexico

ca 1000

Chimú state emerges in the Moche River Valley of Peru

ca 1175

After Tula is sacked, the Toltec Empire crumbles

ca 1200

Chimú rulers build an empire along the coast of Peru

1325

The Mexica establish Tenochtitlan, capital of the Aztec Empire

ca 1400

The Inca Empire expands from its center in the Cusco Valley

1428

King Itzcoatl's forces enlarge the Aztec Empire

1438

Inca ruler Pachacúti expands the Inca Empire through alliances and conquests

1450

Construction of the great Inca citadel of Machu Picchu begins

1487

King Ahuitzotl sacrifices 20,000 captives at the Great Pyramid of Tenochtitlan

ca 1500

The Inca Empire reaches the apex of its wealth and power

1519

Conquistador Cortés reaches Tenochtitlan

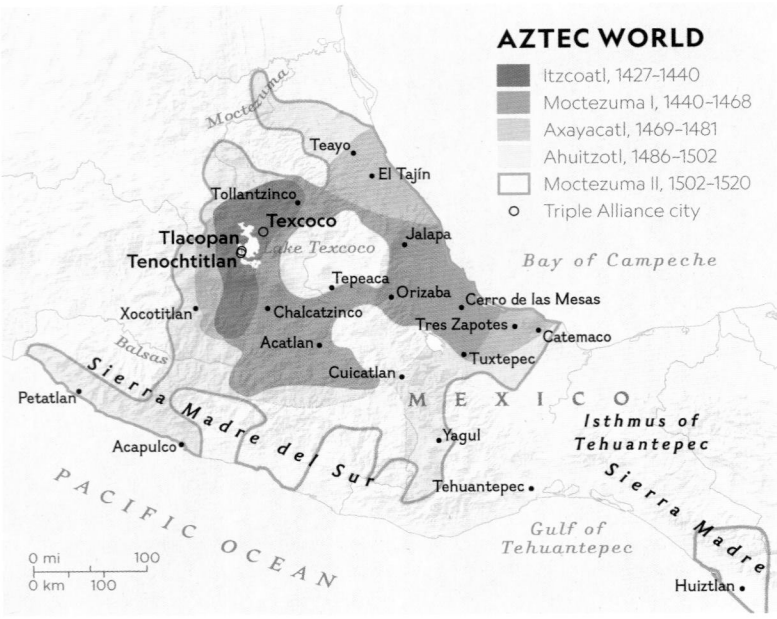

AZTEC WORLD

- Itzcoatl, 1427–1440
- Moctezuma I, 1440–1468
- Axayacatl, 1469–1481
- Ahuitzotl, 1486–1502
- Moctezuma II, 1502–1520
- ○ Triple Alliance city

and Texcoco. Each of the kings of these states were revered as the Huetlatoani, meaning "Great Leader" or "Emperor." But Tenochtitlan soon rose as the dominant power, and both Tlacopan and Texcoco were turned into vassal states.

The Mexica were renowned warriors who fell on their enemies with a fury that shocked much of the Mesoamerican world. This fostered their reputation as an irresistible force against which all resistance was futile. Indeed, Mexica soldiers were instilled with the belief that military conquest was a sacred duty demanded by the gods. The rate of these conquests accelerated under the Mexica king Itzcoatl in 1428, when Tenochtitlan's domain stretched from the Gulf of Mexico to the Pacific Ocean. It was the largest empire ever established in the Americas, covering 80,000 square miles and encompassing as many as six million people. The Aztec Empire remained in control of these lands until the arrival of the Spanish conquistadores in the 16th century.

Aztec gold pendant

The Inca Civilization

Just as the Aztec Empire had risen from the foundation of earlier civilizations, so too did the Inca Empire absorb an earlier culture, this one known as the Chimú civilization. The Chimú had emerged as the successors of the Moche Kingdom, located in modern-day Peru, which had ended around 700 C.E. Beginning from 1100, the Chimú tried to revive the economy in the region by excavating the dormant Moche irrigation systems, thus restoring the flow of water to the region's fields. One Chimú-built canal reportedly carried water over 50 miles to the city of Chan Chan, which at its peak in the 14th century sheltered about 35,000 people.

At around the same time, a pastoral tribe that spoke Quechua, a language of ethnic people in the Peruvian Andes, was living in the Cusco Valley in the Andes. According to one legend, Inca founder Manco Cápac wanted to find the center of the world—just as the god Zeus had done at Delphi in Greece. But whereas the Greek god had used two eagles from opposite ends of the Earth, Manco Cápac went around probing the ground with a gold staff. He traveled up and down the so-called Sacred Valley, banging away with his rod, until he came to Cusco. As soon as he set foot in this place, his staff miraculously disappeared into the soil. The king thereupon declared that he had found the navel of the world and ordered that capital of his kingdom be built on the spot.

Thus was born the civilization of the Inca. The name is derived from *inka,* the Quechua word for "king" or "ruler." Though it denotes the ruling class of these people, the Spanish conquerors used the term to identify all of the Inca territory as "Imperio inca," and the name stuck. The Incas became adept at cultivation.

A PAINTED BRAZIER depicts Chicomecóatl ("Seven Serpent"), the goddess of agriculture and maize, a mainstay of the Aztec diet.

A MODERN VIEW of the circular terraces of an Inca agricultural site at Moray in the Sacred Valley of Peru

In the Sacred Valley around Cusco, undulating emerald terraces cascaded off the rugged hills, fed by rivers that spring from surrounding gorges. Even today, this valley is one of the most fertile regions in Peru, where small villages blend with the hills as if they have always been part of nature. According to one theory, the Inca developed this valley in the shape of the Milky Way, which they believed was the most sacred phenomenon in nature.

Maize was their principal crop: a thick, juicy type of corn that was first domesticated in Mesoamerica some 10,000 years ago. But the Incas also cultivated peanuts, quinoa, chilies, tomatoes, squash, pumpkins, and, above all, potatoes. Botanists believe that the potato was first grown along Lake Titicaca some 6,000 years ago. The Incas raised this humble crop to a high art. At the peak of their empire, they grew more than one thousand varietals, each with its own name. Even today, Andean cuisine offers a wide variety of potatoes,

Aztec pectoral ornament with double serpents

from the *Milagro* to the *Luntus,* from the *Yana warmi* to the *Puku tarma.* The harvest was then distributed by pack animals using domesticated llamas and alpacas.

By 1400, the Inca population had outgrown the capacity of the terraced fields of the Sacred Valley, and the empire began to expand. Under the leadership of Pachacúti ("He Who Transforms the Earth"), who came to power in 1438, the Inca embarked on a series of conquests by conscripting all able-bodied men who were not needed for the harvest in the fields. While some territories were acquired by force, others voluntarily joined the Inca commonwealth because of its obvious economic and technological superiority. Over the next 100 years, the Inca Empire would eventually cover nearly a 3,000-mile swath of western South America, including large portions of modern-day Peru, Ecuador, Bolivia, Argentina, and Chile, making it the largest and most developed pre-Columbian civilization.

INCA TRADITIONS

According to Inca mythology, the gods were born at Lake Titicaca. Located at an altitude of 12,500 feet above sea level, it is the highest navigable lake in the world. Here, the sun god Inti (at right) was born on the Isla del Sol, and here too the sun gave birth to his son Manco Cápac, the first Inca ruler. Local guides still point to two large footprints that, they claim, were made when the sun god stepped on Earth to deliver Manco Cápac as well as his sister, Mama Ocllo, who also became his wife. Some of the Inca traditions are still adhered to by the Uros people, who live on tiny islands that are actually floating vessels of dried totora reeds. For example, their garments signal whether a man or woman is eligible. Young single girls wear brightly colored pompons, whereas married men wear bright red caps.

> "IN THE VARIETY OF ITS CHARMS AND THE POWER OF ITS SPELL, I KNOW OF NO PLACE IN THE WORLD WHICH CAN COMPARE WITH IT."
>
> HIRAM BINGHAM, FIRST TO STUDY MACHU PICCHU

Machu Picchu

Much of the Inca wealth was poured into building a magnificent citadel on an 8,000-foot ridge surrounded by soaring Andean peaks. Just as the sacred city of Delphi is embraced by the mountain of Parnassus, so too is Machu Picchu surrounded by the Urubamba and Vilcabamba ranges of the Andes. Though it was begun as an estate for Inca ruler Pachacúti, Machu Picchu rapidly gained importance as a major religious center. The Inca believed that the cosmos revolved around four principal elements: sun, wind, water, and stone. All four are represented on the citadel. Here, for example, was the Sun Temple, a large, perfectly circular building with two large windows that archaeologists coined the "solar observatory." One window was placed to face the sunrise during the December solstice, and the other catches the sunrise during the summer solstice in June. During these two days, which were probably holy days on the Inca calendar, the sunlight streamed directly into the temple. The temple also contains a sacred stone that resembles a sundial, which may have been used to calculate the days and seasons to guide the cultivation of the fields. Other structures include Pachacúti's palace and a large residential area to house the royal staff and their servants. Machu Picchu also had its own agricultural area, where farmers grew crops year-round, making the citadel virtually self-sufficient.

Bone shawl pin with birds

What is so remarkable about these Inca structures is that its builders used tight-fitting hewn stone, which relied on gravity rather than mortar for stability. Known as ashlar, this type of construction is time-consuming but very strong—a necessity given the frequency of earthquakes in this region. How the Inca stonemasons were able to create such tight-fitting walls, with each stone fitting into the next as in a three-dimensional puzzle, is one of the great mysteries of the Inca culture. Similarly, doors and windows are often trapezoidal, tilting inward as they rise for greater strength.

While today Machu Picchu can be reached by train, in Inca times it was accessible only through the so-called Inca Trail, which runs across two passes at an altitude of some 13,000 feet before moving through a cloud forest. Along the way was an Inca "resort" known as Wiñay Wayna ("forever young"), with mountain springs where travelers could refresh themselves.

Machu Picchu was first explored in 1911 by American explorer Hiram Bingham. His photos caused a sensation in the worldwide press. Since the Spanish conquerors never discovered the site, it is perhaps the best-preserved example of Inca civilization. ∎

AN EXAMPLE of the use of ashlar, tight-fitting hewn stones that rely on gravity rather than mortar for stability

A VIEW of the great 15th-century citadel of Machu Picchu, begun as a summer retreat for King Pachacúti before becoming a major Inca religious center

THE AGE OF DISCOVERY

1400–1700

CONTENTS

THE GREAT REVIVAL

Beginning in 1400, Europe experienced a revival of ancient Greek and Roman art, literature, and science in various fields of endeavor, ushering in the era of the Renaissance. In time, the Renaissance would lead to major new scientific discoveries as well as global exploration, while also sowing the seeds for the Reformation.

Nineteenth-century historians liked to depict the Renaissance as a miraculous explosion of creativity after centuries of medieval ignorance, but this is a simplification. In many ways, the 15th-century Renaissance was a continuation of the intellectual reawakening of the 13th century, following its temporary disruption by the social and political upheavals of the 14th century, including the plague. The humanists of the 15th century—writers such as Leonardo Bruni and Marsilio Ficino—would see themselves as the direct descendants of Dante, Petrarch, and Boccaccio, just as the first great Renaissance artist, Masaccio, drew his inspiration from 14th-century painter and architect Giotto di Bondone. In addition, the Florentine Renaissance was fostered to a considerable degree by a "brain drain" from Constantinople, capital of the Byzantine Empire, which in 1453 fell to the armies of Sultan Mehmed II. Scores of artists, scholars, and scientists fled the Islamic conquest to settle in Florence and other urban centers in Italy.

Reaction to the Established Order

The new focus on humanist inquiry also unleashed long-simmering resentment at a Church that had become self-absorbed and beset by corruption. With little interest in theological matters but deeply immersed in the power politics of the Italian peninsula, the Renaissance popes injected themselves into territorial disputes while trying to expand the geographic reach of the Papal States. The vast expenditures in the military and the arts required resources that the papacy did not have, dependent as it was on contributions from the faithful. In response, the popes turned to new financial instruments to fund their zest for aesthetic and military glory. Some of these instruments, such as the sale of indulgences, infuriated a priest and theologian at the University of Wittenberg. His name was Martin Luther, and his ire launched the Reformation.

Elsewhere in the world, new empires were on the rise. After 1354, a Turkish dynasty known as the Ottomans took control of the Islamic Empire and by the 16th century extended to much of the Mediterranean world, including North Africa, Persia, Anatolia, the Caucasus, the Balkans, and Greece. Reaching its heyday under the legendary reign of Suleyman the Magnificent, the Ottoman Empire then entered a slow decline but remained a potent force in the Middle East until the 20th century and its fall after World War I.

Similarly in China, the Mongol-led Yuan Dynasty was toppled in 1368 by the Ming Dynasty of Han Chinese, which remained in power well into the 17th century. In Russia, the Mongol and Tatar invasions had disrupted the power of Kievan Rus', but as the Mongolian tribes slowly assimilated with local communities, Moscow emerged as the new power center of the Russian heartland. ■

A BRASS ASTRONOMICAL SUNDIAL from the 16th century illustrates the growing interest in charting the celestial heavens.

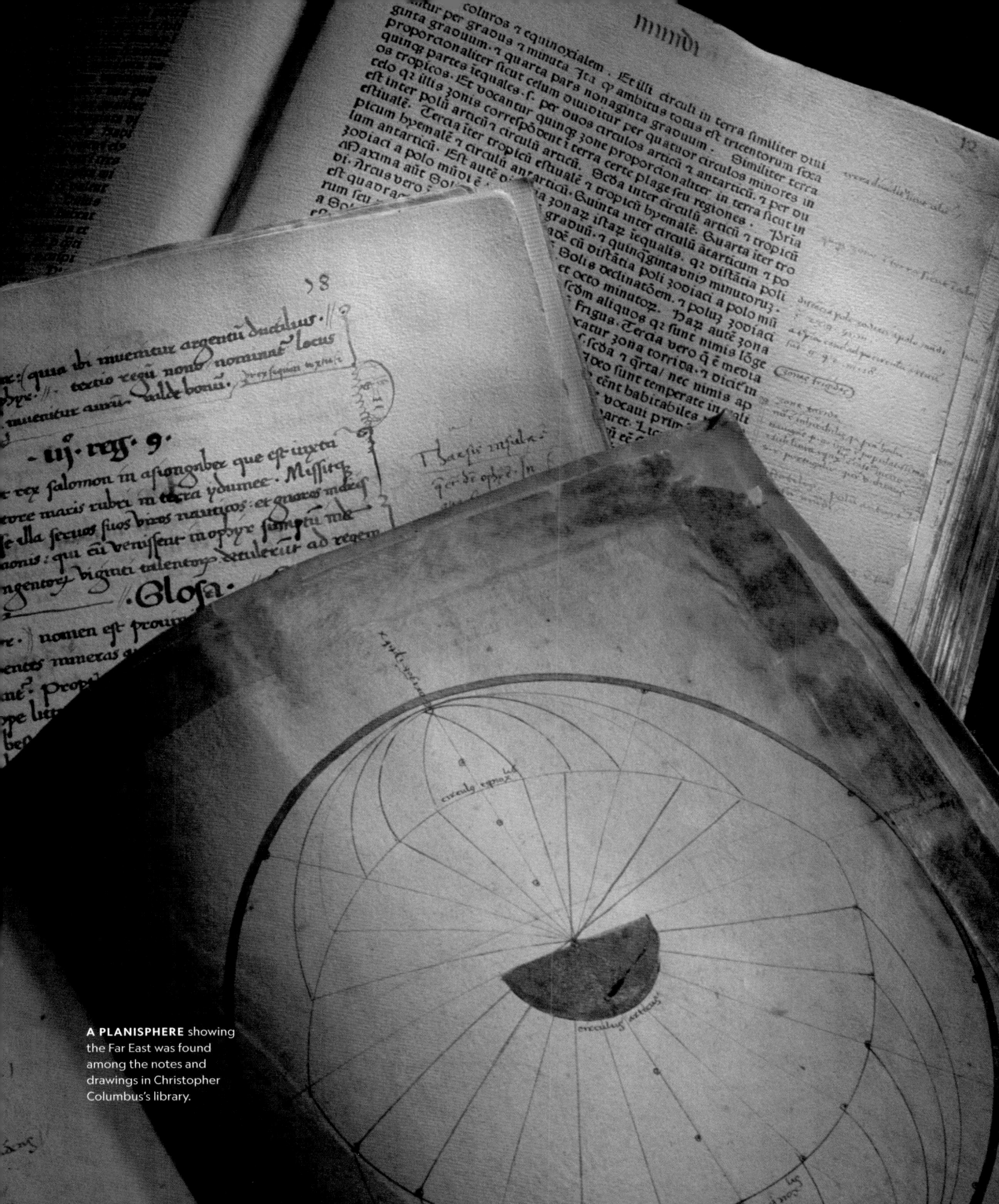

A PLANISPHERE showing the Far East was found among the notes and drawings in Christopher Columbus's library.

THE ERA OF THE
RENAISSANCE

From 1400 onward, beginning in Italy, western Europe was swept by a new passion for classical models that in the 19th century would come to be known as the Renaissance. In due course, this revolutionized all fields of human endeavor, including the visual arts, architecture, science, and literature.

n 1401, the Florentine Guild of Cloth Merchants, known as the Arte di Calimala, announced a competition to design a new set of bronze doors for the Baptistery of St. John, an 11th-century building opposite Florence Cathedral. All competitors were asked to submit a model for one of these panels, depicting Abraham's sacrifice of Isaac. The idea of creating such a competition was new, prompted by the fact that Florence had become a magnet for new generations of artists and sculptors. The guild wanted to exploit that plethora of talent and ensure that it got the best and the brightest for its work.

The response exceeded their expectations. No fewer than seven competitors submitted a design, but only the models of the winner and runner-up have survived. Both were young, aspiring goldsmiths: 24-year old Filippo Brunelleschi and 23-year-old Lorenzo Ghiberti. Both sculptors openly modeled their saintly figures on Roman art. In centuries past, the Church would have rejected such a brazen imitation of pagan models—certainly for a sacred subject. But remarkably, neither the Church authorities nor the wool guild objected. They rallied around the declared winner, Lorenzo Ghiberti, because his design was techno-

logically superior: The young artist was able to cast his model in one piece.

Most art historians mark the Baptistery Competition as the beginning of a movement that many centuries later would be known as the Renaissance. This is a French translation of a word coined by the 16th-century author Giorgio Vasari: *rinascità,* or "rebirth." As Vasari described it, it was a group of Florentine artists, scholars, and scientists who first broke with medieval ideas and doctrines that had restrained creative and intellectual endeavor. The result was a veritable rebirth of Western knowledge and learning, inspired by the great models of Antiquity.

Of course, Vasari's view was an exaggeration, but there is no question that the great humanists and artists of 15th-century Florence ushered in a new era of scientific discovery, artistic creativity, and geographical exploration. As Ghiberti set about to cast his great doors in bronze, Brunelleschi traveled to Rome to study Roman buildings. By carefully measuring extant monuments, he discovered the sophisticated system of proportions, known as the golden rule of 1:1.6, by which

A MEDAL of Byzantine Emperor John VIII Palaeologus was originally struck by Italian artist Pisanello around 1439.

the Romans were able to construct such monumental theaters, arenas, aqueducts, and basilicas all over Europe. That system had eluded the architects for more than a thousand years, including those who sought to build in a Roman-like manner and failed, thus producing the heavy, fortress-like style known as Romanesque. As Brunelleschi was sketching these Roman monuments on paper, he made another important discovery: the law of linear perspective, which would transform the search for realism in Renaissance art. For example, painter Masaccio and his collaborator Masolino revolutionized painting with their fresco cycle in the Brancacci Chapel in the Church of Santa Maria del Carmine in Florence, completed in 1427. For the first time, these artists used Brunelleschi's linear perspective to create a panorama of striking realism. In 1444, the great sculptor Donatello, a close friend of Brunelleschi, carved a free-standing statue of the biblical David that is commonly regarded as the first nude sculpture conceived in the round since Antiquity.

Donatello's "David"

Florentine artist Leonardo da Vinci then introduced the next phase, the High Renaissance, by largely abandoning geometric perspective in favor of a form of optical perspective that suggested space through the illusion of light, shadow, and atmospheric depth. This new form of realism, introduced in da Vinci's 1498 fresco of the Last Supper at the Santa Maria delle Grazie in Milan, made a huge impact on the artists of his time. Reproduced endlessly using the new technique of copper engraving, the work help accelerate the spread of Renaissance ideals all over Europe.

The Vatican did not try to suppress this new infatuation with pagan art and architecture. In fact, the opposite was true. Both Pope Julius II, an avid collector of Greek and Roman sculpture, and his successor, Leo X, turned Rome into the next great center of European art, based on the work of titans such as Raphael, Bramante, and Michelangelo Buonarroti. It was Bramante who first designed the outlines of a massive new basilica that would replace the Old St. Peter's church on Vatican hill, first built under Constantine the Great. Work on this monumental endeavor began during the papacy of Julius II in 1506 and was not completed until more than a century later, in 1626.

The Fall of Constantinople

For the last 500 years, ever since the Great Schism of 1054, the Church in Europe had been split between the Greek Byzantine Church, governed by the patriarch of Constantinople, and the Latin Church, governed by the pope in Rome. In time, these two denominations would become known as the Eastern Orthodox Church and the Roman Catholic Church, respectively—a situation that continues

THE MASSIVE DOME
over the central crossing of
the Florence Cathedral was
completed in 1446, based
on designs by Florentine
sculptor and architect
Filippo Brunelleschi.

NOTABLE DATES

1401
The competition for the
Florence Baptistery panel
doors is held

1424
Masaccio and Masolino begin
work on the Brancacci chapel
frescoes

1430
Thessalonica is conquered by
Ottoman forces

1444
Donatello completes the
bronze "David," first
freestanding nude since
Antiquity

1446
Brunelleschi's dome of the
Florence Cathedral is
completed

ca 1450
Johannes Gutenberg
develops the printing press

1453
Constantinople falls to the
forces of Sultan Mehmed II

1469
Piero de Medici is succeeded
by his son Lorenzo de Medici
"The Magnificent"

1506
Bramante begins work on the
new St. Peter's Basilica in Rome

1508
Michelangelo begins the
ceiling frescoes for the Sistine
Chapel

1517
Martin Luther publishes his 95
Theses on the castle church at
Wittenberg

to this day. But in the 15th century, Constantinople came under increasing threat from the Muslim Ottoman Empire to the south. Part of the reason was that the Byzantine Empire had never fully recovered from the sack of Constantinople by Crusaders in 1204. Its realm splintered into a number of Greek mini-states, including those of Nicaea and Epirus. The plague that devastated Europe also struck hard in Constantinople; by some estimates, more than half of the city's population died. Thus weakened, the empire was powerless to stem the encroachment of its enemies.

Despite a temporary thaw during the reign of Emperor Manuel II Palaiologos and Sultan Mehmed I, relations between the Byzantine and Ottoman domains rapidly deteriorated. In 1430, the Ottoman armies began their march on Byzantine territory in an effort to capture the Byzantine province of Attica, Greece. In response, the Byzantines rebuilt a huge wall, known as the Hexamilion, or Six-Mile Wall, along the Isthmus of Corinth to keep the Muslim armies at bay. However, Ottoman engineers had designed a huge mortar known as a bombard, which easily reduced the vast wall to rubble and led to the complete conquest of Greece by Muslim forces.

In 1451, new Muslim sultan Mehmed II ascended the throne at age 19 and almost immediately set his sights on the ultimate prize: the Byzantine capital of Constantinople. In preparation for the attack, he established a large garrison on the Bosporus, just a few miles north of Constantinople. Seeing this concentration of Muslim forces on their doorstep, the city was gripped by panic. The Byzantine army rapidly began to stockpile food and arms for the coming siege, while Emperor Constantine XI sent a mission to Rome in a desperate attempt to ask the pope to intervene.

THE ITALIAN RENAISSANCE

Pavia — Location of institution or birthplace of person of interest

Botticelli, 1445 — Person of interest and birth year

SISTINE CHAPEL, 1473 — Institution and founding year

0 mi ——— 100
0 km ——— 100
Boundaries as of 1454 are shown.

To sweeten the offer, the emperor pledged to implement a full reconciliation between the Greek and Latin Churches. But the pope, Nicholas V, no longer wielded the influence over Europe's kings that the papacy had enjoyed during the High Middle Ages. What's more, England, France, and Spain had exhausted themselves in the Hundred Years' War and felt little appetite to involve themselves in a conflict with the Islamic Empire. Thus, other than sending a few ships with supplies, the Western powers left the Byzantines to face the Muslim armies by themselves.

The Final Assault

To repulse the 80,000 troops that Mehmed II was about to hurl against the city, Emperor Constantine could muster only some 9,000 soldiers, 2,000 of whom were enlisted foreigners and mercenaries of dubious loyalty. What's more, the Muslim commanders also wielded 70 cannons and mortars—

including a monstrous bronze cannon cast by a renowned Hungarian founder called Orban—as well as a squadron of 1,500 Serbian cavalry. And to further deter anyone from coming to the emperor's rescue, Mehmed also deployed a fleet of some 126 galleys, boats, and transports to choke off the Golden Horn, the city's outlet to the sea. The Byzantines had erected a large chain across the bay, but the Ottomans built a huge road of wooden logs to transport the ships across Galata Hill, thus bypassing this barrier.

Still, the capture of Constantinople was not a forgone conclusion. The city was protected by stout walls, some dating back to Roman times. The Byzantines also had artillery; arguably, their cannons did not have the range of the Ottoman guns, but they did have the benefit of an elevated position from where they could direct plunging fire on the attacking Muslim forces. Indeed, when the assaults began, all were repulsed with heavy losses on the Ottoman side, which boosted the morale of the defenders. But the Turkish infantry was relentless. "They found the Turks coming right up under the walls and seeking battle," wrote an eyewitness, Venetian physician Nicolò Barbaro, "and when one or two of them were killed, at once more Turks came and took away the dead ones . . . without caring how near they came to the city walls." Next, Mehmed tried to dig tunnels underneath the walls, but the Byzantines found out about it and, with the help of an engineer, were able to dig mines in the opposite direction to thwart the Muslim soldiers.

On May 29, 1453, Mehmed launched an all-out offensive that breached the walls and pushed the defenders into the city. As the Ottomans closed in, Constantine XI threw off his imperial cloak and joined

A MODERN ILLUSTRATION shows how Ottoman workers built a huge road of wooden logs to transport their ships across Galata Hill, thus bypassing the chain across the bay of the Golden Horn.

DEFENDERS of Constantinople used terra-cotta hand grenades, known as Greek fire, in a desperate attempt to ward off Ottoman invaders.

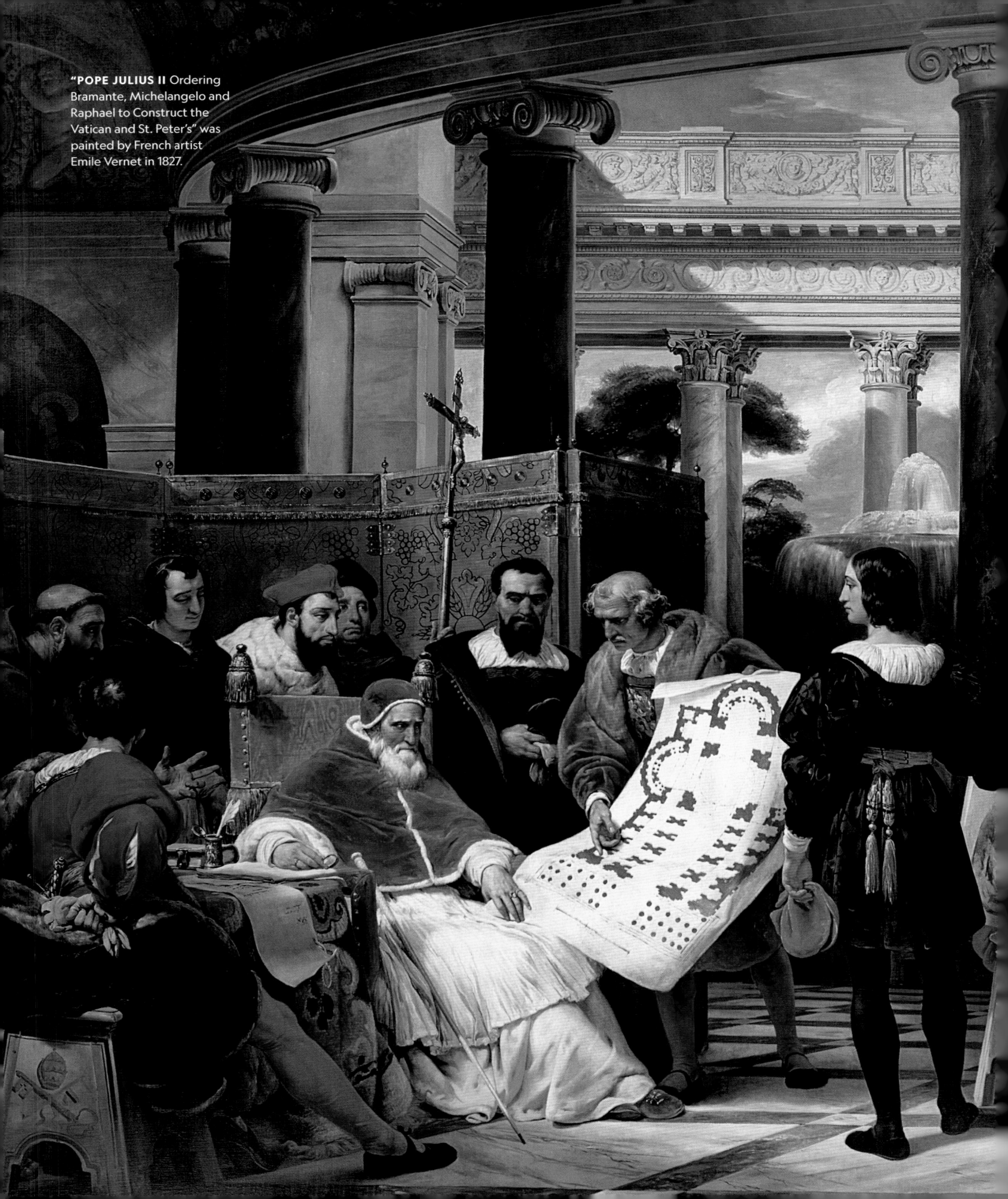

"POPE JULIUS II Ordering Bramante, Michelangelo and Raphael to Construct the Vatican and St. Peter's" was painted by French artist Emile Vernet in 1827.

"WHY DOES THE POPE, WHOSE WEALTH TODAY IS GREATER THAN THE WEALTH OF THE RICHEST CRASSUS, BUILD THE BASILICA OF SAINT PETER WITH THE MONEY OF POOR BELIEVERS?"

MARTIN LUTHER, NINETY-FIVE THESES

the defenders on the ramparts, where he died in battle. Thus, Constantinople fell and the Byzantine Empire ceased to exist. A three-day orgy of pillage, rape, and looting ensued. The sixth-century church of Hagia Sophia, built by Emperor Justinian, was converted into a mosque.

The Era of the Reformation

In the mid-15th century, a small group of powerful Roman families—principally the Rovere, the Borgia, and the Medici—gained control of the College of Cardinals through threats and bribery. This all but guaranteed that the popes of the Renaissance were men bent on enriching and empowering their families rather than on making urgent reforms in the governance of the Church. However, this also meant that the arts flourished under their patronage. By 1513, with Michelangelo, Raphael, and Leonardo da Vinci working at the Vatican, Rome had eclipsed Florence as the reigning center of European art, and it would retain this position well into the baroque era.

Unfortunately, these vast expenditures required resources that the papacy did not have, dependent as it was on contributions from the faithful. In response, the popes turned to new fundraising sources. One was the outright sale of ecclesiastical offices and the other, the purveying of so-called indulgences. An indulgence was a promissory note: Although it did not grant Christians forgiveness of their sins, it alleviated the penance that they would have to suffer in purgatory, the intermediate state between death and admission to heaven. Some clerical sources argued that a stay in purgatory could last several centuries, which widened the appeal of these indulgences.

By the early 16th century, the European-wide sale of indulgences reached a fever pitch as both Pope Julius II and Pope Leo X struggled to finance the construction of the St. Peter's Basilica, a monumental endeavor. One of these vendors was a Dominican friar named Johann Tetzel, who in 1516 began to offer indulgences for sale in Germany. This infuriated a theologian at the University of Wittenberg in Saxony, who utterly rejected the idea that wealthy individuals could "buy off" their repentance (or that of their relatives) in purgatory. His name was Martin Luther.

Born in 1483 in Eisleben, Saxony, Luther studied the medieval curriculum of rhetoric, grammar, and logic before entering an Augustinian monastery. But monastic life proved unsatisfying, and

GERMAN ARTIST Lucas Cranach the Elder painted this portrait of Martin Luther, titled "Luther as Professor," in 1529.

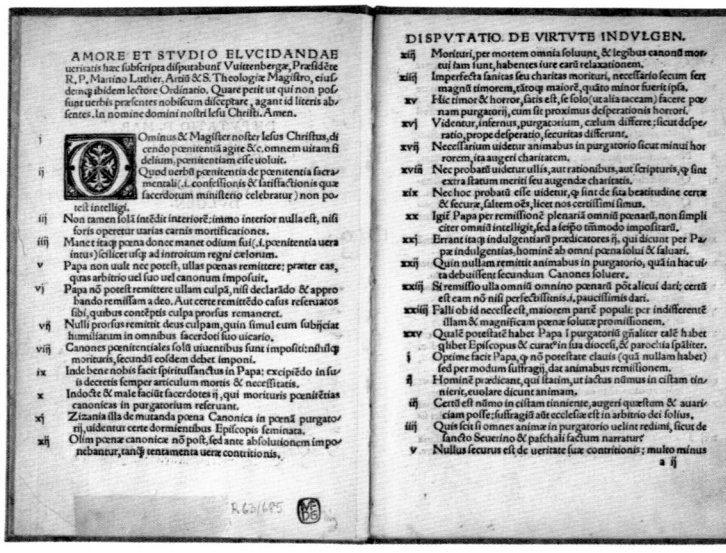

THE NINETY-FIVE THESES by Martin Luther were published in Basel in 1517 as a pamphlet in the original Latin and later translated in a book in German.

The Ninety-Five Theses

On October 31, 1517, Luther sent the Bishop of Mainz a copy of his Ninety-Five Theses, which attacked the sale of indulgences as theologically invalid. The whole point of confession and penance, Luther argued, was that Christians could contemplate the error of their sinful behavior. Furthermore, only God, not the pope, had the power to remit sins. Unfortunately, Bishop Albert of Mainz himself was deeply in debt and therefore dependent on the proceeds from Tetzel's fundraising. The bishop promptly ignored the letter, but the die was cast. Published in the form of pamphlets, Luther's Theses spread through Europe like wildfire, kindling a long-suppressed resentment against the willful abuses of the Catholic clergy and the papacy.

after he was ordained a priest, he was offered a position to teach theology in 1508 at the newly founded University of Wittenberg. It was here that he developed his doctrine of justification: that people can receive God's grace only through faith rather than through religious ritual or charitable works. This would become a key tenet of Lutheranism.

The situation escalated rapidly. In 1518, Luther was summoned to Rome to explain himself, but he refused to comply. The pope responded with a

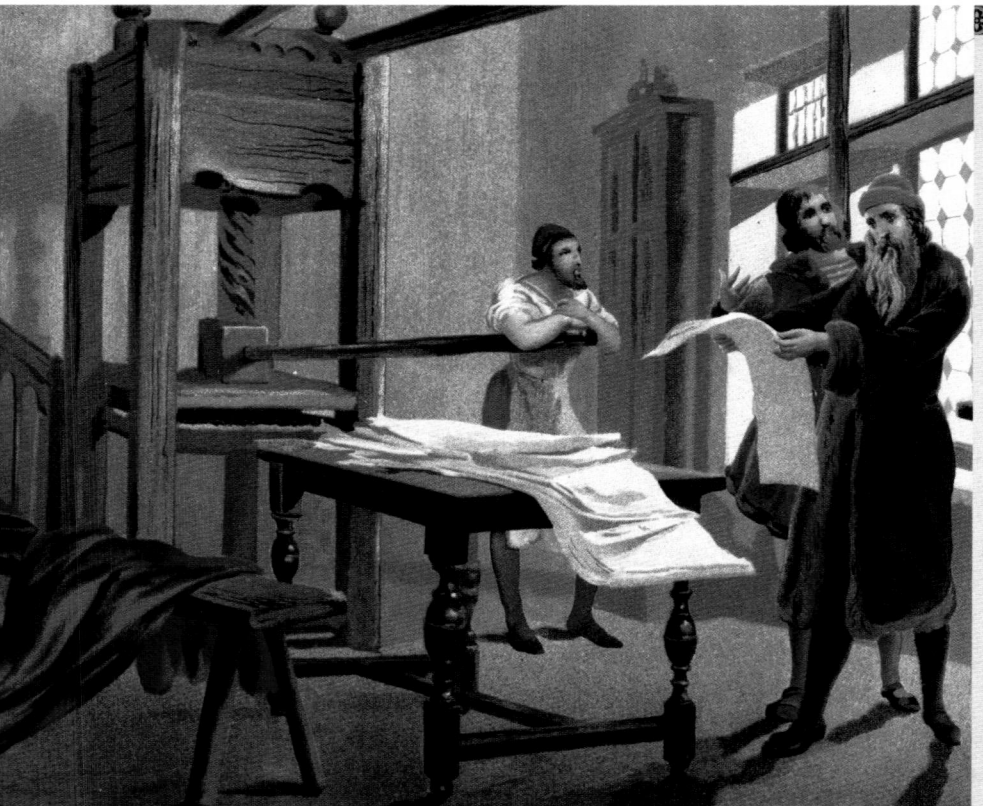

THE PRINTING PRESS

Until 1487, books were essentially bound, handwritten originals, copied laboriously from a source, as had been the case since before Antiquity. The first attempt to mechanize the book-copying process took place in China, where Bi Sheng experimented with various movable woodblock techniques during the Han Dynasty. In Europe, the invention of the printing press (at left) is usually attributed to Johannes Gutenberg around 1450. Gutenberg developed a mold to rapidly produce movable metal type in a uniform style—a typeface, in short. The Renaissance printing presses revolutionized the distribution of religious and political ideas and broke the monopoly on knowledge among the elites. One press could produce some 3,500 pages a day. Just 50 years after Gutenberg's invention, some 20 million printed books were already in circulation. The printing technology was a key factor in the rapid spread of the Reformation throughout Europe.

"**LUTHER NAILS** the 95 Theses to the Door of Wittenberg Cathedral, 31 October 1517" was painted by Belgian artist Ferdinand Pauwels in 1872.

THE COURT of the Holy Roman Emperor Charles V in Toledo, Spain, became a center of the initial Catholic resistance against the spread of the Reformation.

1520 encyclical that declared Luther's Ninety-Five Theses to be a work of heresy. Luther then cannily called upon German princes to stop paying ecclesiastic tribute to Rome—something they were only too eager to do—and to help create an indigenous German Church. The response was extraordinary. Many German kings and princes had long resented the dominant role of the Catholic Church in every aspect of life. When, in 1526, the rulers of the 300-odd German states were given the choice to opt for either Catholicism or Lutheranism, a majority chose to create an indigenous Lutheran Church. Thus, Germany was cleft by a division between a largely Protestant north and a predominantly Catholic south that to some extent remains to this day.

Gold coin with Ferdinand II and Isabella

The Reformation Spreads

From Germany, the reform movement spilled into the rest of Europe. Having fought an 80-year war to shake off Spanish rule, the Dutch Seven Provinces chose the Dutch Reformed Church as the official denomination of the new republic. Meanwhile, a theologian named Hans Tausen intro-

duced Luther's views to Denmark, and from there, Lutheranism spread to Sweden and Norway. As the Reformation grew, other movements sprang up, including one inspired by French theologian John Calvin, who fled to Switzerland to organize the movement known as Calvinism. Calvin broke with Luther over a number of issues, including the celebration of the Eucharist and the use of paintings and music in worship. Under his leadership, Geneva became the center of Calvinism. In France, too, the number of Calvinist adherents—known as Huguenots—grew rapidly. This sparked a bloody civil war in the second part of the 16th century during the rule of King Henry of Navarre and his consort, Marguerite de Valois.

Only Spain was able to resist the Reformation. In 1479, the dynastic marriage of King Ferdinand II of Castile and Queen Isabella of Aragon had unified the country under one crown. The royal couple was determined to transform the Iberian realm into a strong nation-state on the model of France and England, with Roman Catholicism as its unifying force. In 1492, they issued the Alhambra Decree, which forced non-Christians to either

MARTIN LUTHER'S HYMN

Martin Luther loved music, and he had little patience for those reformers who detested any form of art or music in liturgy. "My heart bubbles up and overflows when I hear music," he would say. In 1527, Saxony suffered from an outbreak of bubonic plague. In response, Luther composed a hymn (at right) inspired by Psalm 46, "Ein' feste Burg ist unser Gott" ("A mighty fortress is our God"). It was an instant hit that carried the Reformation into the farthest corners of Europe. Like many other composers, Johann Sebastian Bach transcribed it for his choral cantata BWV 80. In 1966, the hymn even appeared in the New St. Joseph Sunday Missal, a Catholic collection of church hymns. Today, "A Mighty Fortress" is an ecumenical song, sung by Christians of every confession.

THE PROTESTANT REFORMATION

Religions and Sects, 1560

- Anglican
- Calvinist
- Catholic
- Lutheran
- Eastern Orthodox
- Combination of Catholic, Lutheran, and Calvinist
- Islam
- ○ Large minority present

Counter-Reformation, 1648

- Area reclaimed by the Catholic Church
- Area lost to Protestant sects

0 mi ————————————— 200
0 km ————————————— 200

Boundaries circa 1560 are represented.

JOHN KNOX (CA 1514–1572)
The clergyman and activist was instrumental in steering Scotland toward Calvinism. He proclaimed the right to resist any Catholic ruler who acted to prevent Protestant worship.

JOHN WYCLIFFE (CA 1330–1384)
An Oxford professor, he argued that Scripture had superior authority to the pope. He also preached that the Bible should be available to common folk in their own language.

Charles V prosecuted a sporadic war with the Schmalkaldic League, a band of Protestant princes within the Empire. The Peace of Augsburg in 1555 allowed each prince to decide whether subjects would be Catholic or Lutheran.

The English Reformation came in two phases. Henry VIII (r. 1509–1547) threw off the authority of Rome without doctrinal changes. Puritan reformers later worked to make changes to the Anglican Church's theology.

ULRICH ZWINGLI (1484–1531)
His biblical sermons inspired Zürich into the Reformation.

JOHN CALVIN (1509–1564)
In authoring his *Institutes of the Christian Religion*, the scholar produced the best exposition of Protestant doctrine at the time.

The Anabaptist movement introduced the concept of the separation of church and state.

Philip II of Spain dedicated his reign to the reestablishment of the Catholic Christendom. To that end, he assembled a Grand Armada, 132 ships with 3,165 cannons, to attack Protestant England. Harassed by faster English ships, and decimated by powerful storms, only 67 galleons returned.

HUGUENOTS
French Calvinists were on the rise until the Catholic monarchy cracked down on them in 1572, massacring thousands.

PETER WALDO (CA 1140–1218)
A rich merchant, Waldo gave up his wealth to follow the apostolic model of poverty. Preaching the Gospel in French, his followers sought to purify the Church of worldly power, and focus on following Christ.

IGNATIUS OF LOYOLA (1491–1556)
Founder of the Jesuits, or Society of Jesus, the former soldier and nobleman dedicated his life to spiritual discipline in service to the pope.

SCOTLAND

North Sea

Lindesnes

Edinburgh • *Firth of Forth*

BRITISH ISLES

Ireland (England)

Newcastle •

Dublin •

Great

York •

Waterford •

Chester •

Britain

The Wash

St. Georges Channel

WALES ○

Bristol Channel

ENGLAND

London •

Land's End

Dartmouth •

English Channel

Channel Islands

Bruges •

HOLLAND

Amsterdam •

Bremen •

SPANISH NETHERLANDS ○

Boulogne •

Lille •

Ghent (Gent) •

Cologne •

Rhine

Cambrai •

Liège •

Bayeux •

Rouen •

Trier •

Mainz •

Point St.-Mathieu

Seine

Reims •

H R O E M

Rennes •

Paris •

Orléans •

Strasbourg •

Tours •

Basel •

Zürich •

FRANCE ○

SWISS CONFEDERATION

Geneva •

A L

ATLANTIC OCEAN

Lyon •

Milan •

Bay of Biscay

Bordeaux •

Turin •

Genoa •

Cape Finisterre

Garonne

Rhône

León •

Po

Oporto (Porto) •

Pamplona •

Toulouse •

Nîmes •

Valladolid •

Duero

Narbonne •

Pyrenees

Ligurian Sea

Pisa •

Salamanca •

Zaragoza •

Marseille •

Livorno •

PORTUGAL

Ebro

Manresa •

Lisbon •

Tagus

SPAIN

Barcelona •

Corsica (Genoa)

Toledo •

Guadiana

Balearic Sea

Valencia •

Balearic Is. (Spain)

Sardinia (Spain)

DENMARK AND NORWAY

Oslo
Drammen

SWEDEN

Uppsala

Skagerrak

Vänern

Vättern

Gotland

JUTLAND

Öland

Baltic Sea

Bornholm

Roskilde • • Lund
Copenhagen

In 1536, Denmark
officially adopted
Lutheranism as the state
religion. It was imposed
on Norway and Iceland,
both ruled from
Copenhagen.

Gulf of Finland

Tallinn

ESTONIA

Lake Piepus

Hiiumaa

Saaremaa

Gulf of Riga

Pskov

LIVONIA

Riga

Moscow

Moscow

COURLAND

Tula

Volga

Königsberg
(Kaliningrad)

PRUSSIA

Vilnius

LITHUANIA

RUSSIA

Neman

Rügen

Lübeck

Danzig
(Gdańsk)

POMERANIA

Grudziadz

Hamburg

MARTIN LUTHER (1483–1546)
On October 31, 1517, Luther nailed
his Ninety Five Theses questioning
Church dogma to the door of the
church. The former monk's belief
in salvation by faith in Christ alone
and the authority of scripture
ignited the Reformation.

Brunswick
Braunschweig

BRANDENBURG

Magdeburg

Posen
(Poznań)

Vistula

Warsaw

KINGDOM OF

POLAND AND

Pinsk

Prypyats'

Dnieper

Desna

Chernihiv

HOLY

Wittenberg

Elbe

SAXONY

Oder

SILESIA

POLAND

GRAND DUCHY

Kyiv

UKRAINE

Weser

MAN

Main

Nuremburg

JOHN HUSS (1369–1415)
An early Czech reformer,
he preached that Christ,
not the pope, is the head
of the Church. Emphasis
was placed on personal
faith and the authority of
the Gospels.

Prague

BOHEMIA

MORAVIA

Lublin

Kraków

OF LITHUANIA

GALICIA

Southern Bug

Dnieper

EMPIRE

Danube

Ratisbon
(Regensburg)

BAVARIA

Augsburg

PHILIPP MELANCHTHON
(1497–1560)
A teacher by trade, this
friend of Martin Luther
codified Protestant
thought. He authored the
Augsburg Confession.

AUSTRIA

Vienna

STYRIA

Pressburg
(Bratislava)

HUNGARY

CARPATHIAN MOUNTAINS

Dniester

BESSARABIA

MOLDAVIA

Prut

KHANATE OF CRIMEA

Karkinit Gulf

CRIMEA

TYROL

ALPS

CARINTHIA

CARNIOLA

Tisza

TRANSYLVANIA

Buda and Pest
(Budapest)

Mures

Olt

Balaklava

VENICE

Venice

Ravenna

CROATIA

Drava

Sava

Danube

WALACHIA

Black Sea

Florence

PAPAL STATES

Zara
(Zadar)

BOSNIA

Spalato
(Split)

SERBIA

Adriatic Sea

REP. OF
RAGUSA

Ragusa
(Dubrovnik)

Danube

BULGARIA

Rome

NAPLES
(Spain)

Bari

Dyrrhachium
(Durrës)

Thessalonica
(Thessaloniki)

OTTOMAN EMPIRE

Adrianople
(Edirne)

Bosporus

Tyrrhenian Sea

Naples

Constantinople
(Istanbul)

Gallipoli

Nicomedia (Kocaeli)

Nicaea (Iznik)

RENOWNED SPANISH ARTIST
Francisco Goya y Lucientes completed "The Court of the Inquisition" in 1819.

"THE KING'S MAJESTY JUSTLY AND RIGHTFULLY IS AND OUGHT TO BE SUPREME HEAD OF THE CHURCH OF ENGLAND."

HENRY VIII'S ACT OF SUPREMACY

accept baptism or leave the country. Thousands of Jews and Muslims who had lived in Spain for generations were forced to flee. To ensure that the conversos—Jews and Muslims who agreed to be converted—remained true to the Christian faith, the Spanish Crown activated the Inquisition. For the remainder of the 15th century, some 2,000 Spaniards were accused of heresy and burned at the stake.

In England, King Henry VIII had been faithful to Rome while married to Queen Catherine, the daughter of King Ferdinand and Queen Isabella of Spain. But when the queen proved unable to give him a male heir, King Henry planned to set her aside in favor of a woman at court named Anne Boleyn. Once it became clear that Pope Clement VII would not grant him an annulment, King Henry and his chancellor, Thomas Cromwell, pushed through the Act of Supremacy of 1534, which made the king the head of the newly formed Church of England, known as the Anglican Church. Thus empowered, Henry was able to marry Anne Boleyn, while Cromwell, a fervent reformer, pushed for the wholesale suppression of English abbeys and monasteries. Much of the centuries-old English monastic culture was destroyed, and scores of monks and nuns were forcefully evicted. In the coming decades, England would continue to oscillate between Reformist and Catholic sentiments, driven by Henry's whim. Over time, the Anglican Church would retain much of the original Catholic liturgy, albeit in a thoroughly English mold, as evidenced by the *Book of Common Prayer* of 1549. ∎

HÆC EST EFFIGIES LIGVRIS MIRANDA COLVMBI ANTIPODVM PRIMVS
RATE QVI PENETRAVIT IN · ORBEM ·

SEBASTIAN
VENETVS FA

ITALIAN RENAISSANCE
ARTIST Sebastiano del Piombo
painted this posthumous
portrait of Christopher
Columbus in 1519.

THE AGE OF EXPLORATION

From the early 16th century onward, European explorers pushed the boundaries of European commerce into the far corners of the world, discovering new lands in a way that would have a profound impact on the indigenous populations and ultimately the course of humankind.

Why did European explorers suddenly decide to push the boundaries of the continent into the far corners of the world? The reasons are manifold, but one key factor was the fall of the Byzantine Empire to the Ottoman Turks, which forced European merchants to identify new sea routes to the East that bypassed Muslim territory. That quest was necessitated by the rapid growth in the demand for spices from the "East Indies," as Asia was called. Spices had become increasingly important not only for medical, culinary, and cosmetic purposes, but also as a food preservative, given the rapid growth of the European population. By the 17th century, the search for stable sources of spices to vouchsafe food supplies had become such a priority that a fierce competition known as the Spice Race ensued among the European powers. The goal was to capture as many resource-rich territories in Southeast Asia as possible, as well as strategic victualing stations along the way. This development would eventually lead to the creation of large colonial empires in the 19th century.

Two other factors played a role. One was the avid search for gold and other precious metals to finance the growth of Europe's leading nation-states. It was the search for gold that had persuaded the Spanish Crown to finance Columbus's expedition to the Indies via a western, transatlantic route. That same quest would bring Spanish conquistadores to the shores of the Americas and lead Portuguese navigators to prowl the coasts of Africa.

Another key factor that is not always understood was the development of significant technological innovations rooted in the scientific curiosity of the Renaissance. For many centuries, European mariners had used the galley, a single-mast ship mostly suited for coastal traffic. But in 1450, the Portuguese developed the carrack, a galley built around a wooden frame (the caravel) and equipped with square-rigged sails on the foremast and lateen-rigged sails on the mizzenmast, which gave it the ability to tack fore and aft into the prevailing Atlantic winds. This made the vessel suitable for long-distance travel in blue waters. Little surprise, then, that at the close of the 15th century, Portugal was dominating the first phase of European

THIS 17TH-CENTURY GOLD BROOCH is one of several precious objects that were recovered from a sunken ship off the coast of Havana, Cuba.

> # "IN THIS ISLAND, THERE ARE MANY SPICES AND GREAT MINES OF GOLD AND OF OTHER METALS."
>
> CHRISTOPHER COLUMBUS AFTER HIS LANDING AT THE BAHAMAS

exploration, a position it would hold until well into the 16th century. It was a carrack, the *Santa María*, that carried Christopher Columbus to the Bahamas in 1492. For navigation, Columbus and later 16th-century explorers used a cross-staff, a device that measured the altitude of the sun and the stars, or an astrolabe, another device for calculating latitude at sea depending on the altitude of celestial bodies. Longitudes and latitudes were calculated with a quadrant and a plumb line, and a compass was used for dead reckoning.

The Discovery of the New World

Using their fleet of carracks, the Portuguese established themselves on the Atlantic islands of Madeira and the Azores and began to move steadily southward. Senegal, Cape Verde, and what is today Sierra Leone were taken in the next few decades, which established Portugal's reputation as the leading power in West Africa. In 1488, Bartolomeu Dias succeeded in reaching the southern tip of the African continent. He was followed by Vasco da Gama, who in 1498 rounded the cape and from there plotted a maritime course to India, stopping at ports in eastern Africa for provisioning. Goa, Malacca, and Hormuz all fell into Portuguese hands as key stations along the new sea route to the Indies.

Since Portugal had traveled east, Spain opted to go west, across the vast Atlantic Ocean, in

A MODERN ILLUSTRATION depicts Portuguese explorer Vasco da Gama handing the Samudra Sultan of Calicut (today's Kozhikode, India) a letter from the king of Portugal in 1498.

A LARGE assortment of spices are sold in open markets throughout Asia and the Middle East, as shown here in Nagpur, India.

NOTABLE DATES

1450
Portuguese invent the caravel and explore the western coast of Africa

1477
Ptolemy's *Geographica* is re-published in Rome

1488
Bartolomeu Dias succeeds in reaching the Cape of Good Hope

1492
Christopher Columbus lands in the Caribbean

1494
Treaty of Tordesillas divides New World in Portuguese and Spanish spheres

1499
Vasco da Gama rounds the Cape of Good Hope

1513
Juan Ponce de Léon discovers Florida

1519
Hernán Cortés reaches the Yucatán Peninsula in Mexico

1583
Jesuit Matteo Ricci reaches Beijing

1598
Dutch explorer Jan Huygen publishes an atlas of sea routes to the East Indies

1600
English traders form the East India Company

1620
An English colony is established in Plymouth, Massachusetts

"[THIS CITY] IS SO BEAUTIFUL AND HAS SUCH FINE BUILDINGS THAT IT WOULD BE REMARKABLE EVEN IN SPAIN."

SPANISH CONQUISTADOR FRANCISCO PIZARRO ON THE INCA CITY OF CUSCO

search of a new route to the East Indies. That was Columbus's primary mission. Five weeks after a victualing stop in the Canary Islands, he made landfall on the Bahamas, believing he had reached the East Indies. Instead, he had discovered the New World, which unleashed an intense competition between Spain and Portugal to explore and exploit the new territories. The Vatican now feared that these two major Catholic powers might find themselves in conflict. In response, Pope Alexander VI negotiated the Treaty of Tordesillas of 1494, by which the two explorer nations carved up the world between themselves. Portugal gained control over Africa, Asia, and the eastern part of South America (analogous to today's Brazil), while Spain received all lands to the west of that line—much of which was still to be explored.

Spain wasted no time in seizing the land apportioned to it. In 1513, Juan Ponce de Léon discovered a territory on the doorstep of North America's southernmost coast. Impressed by the profusion of exotic plants and flowers, he called it the "land of flowers," or *la Florida,* particularly because it was Easter season, known in Spanish as *Pascua Florida,* or "feast of flowers." Six years later, conquistador Hernán Cortés reached the Yucatán Peninsula and made contact with the Maya civilization. Soon after, rumors reached Spain that precious metals could be found aplenty among the Aztec and Maya civilizations. This spurred a new

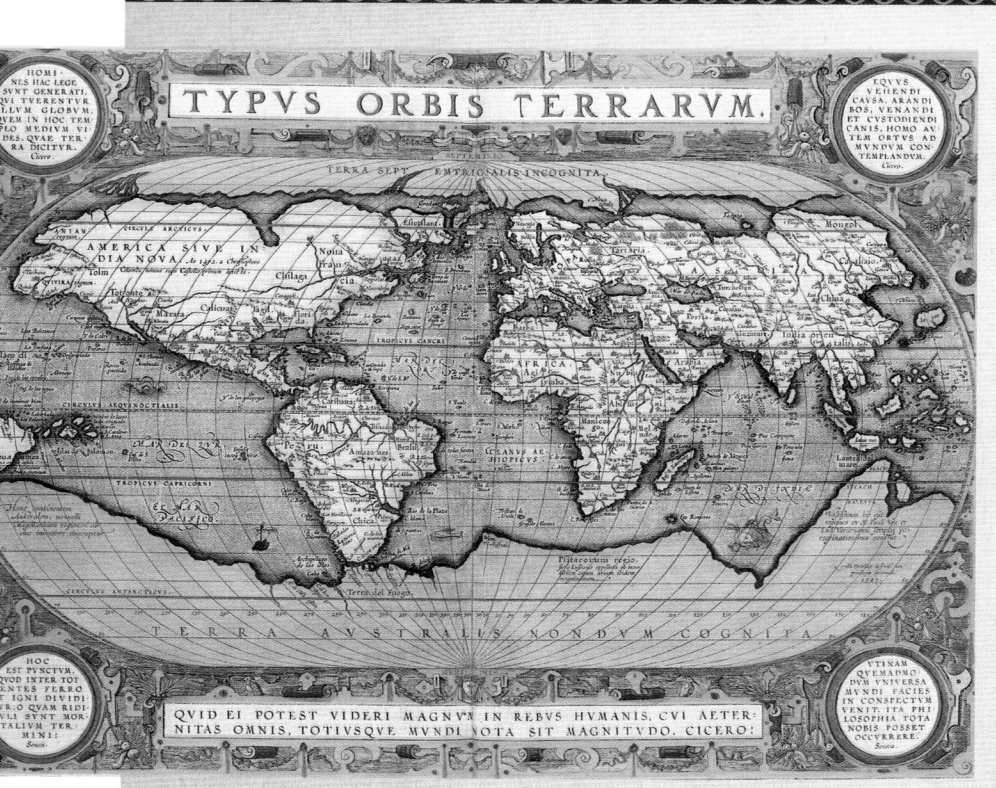

THE AGE OF CARTOGRAPHY

The rapid growth of European colonies in the New World prompted a high demand in Europe for ways to visualize these exotic new lands. In an age before photography and film, when the most important mass medium was the copper engraving, this need was satisfied by colored maps (at left). Maps, often adorned with small, scenic views around the borders, brought home the stunning differences among these infinite, untamed lands and the increasingly crowded conditions in Europe's urban areas. After cartographers such as the German Sebastian Münster and Flemish engraver Ortelius developed the first tentative maps of North and South America, often based on sketchy geographical data, maps became steadily more detailed and accurate as charting activity increased along both the Atlantic and Pacific coasts. Once these maps were engraved and printed on heavy paper, they were often hand-colored by artists so as to increase their commercial appeal and value.

A MODERN ILLUSTRATION depicts the crew of Columbus's ship *Santa María* unloading the vessel after it ran aground in today's St. Ann's Bay, Jamaica, in 1503.

ARCTIC OCEAN

ALASKA

GREENLAND

EUROPE

Gulf of Alaska

Hudson Bay

NORTH AMERICA

Island of Newfoundland

Québec *1608*

○ Port Royal *1605*

• Plymouth *1620*

Cádiz

Palos de la Frontera

In 1542, Portuguese explorer Juan Rodriguez Cabrillo charted the California coast, paving the way for the establishment of Spanish missions in "Alta California" in the 18th century.

Father Juan de Padilla, a Franciscan missionary, accompanied Coronado on his mission to the "Seven Cities."

Santa Fe *1608*

de Soto 1539-1543

○ St. Mary's City *1634*
○ Jamestown *1607*
○ Roanoke *1585*

From the early 17th century onward, various Protestant colonies were established in North America, including settlements by Puritans and Pilgrims in New England, Quakers in Pennsylvania, Huguenot Lutherans in New York, and Methodists in New Brunswick.

Canary Islands

Cabrillo 1542

Coronado 1540-42

Baja California

de Soto 1539-1543

De Soto brought priests with him on the first European expedition of inland North America.

Columbus 1492-93

Saltillo *1577*
Zacatecas *1548*
Tampico *1554*
Compostela *1542* Guadalajara
Navidad
Acapulco *1550*

MEXICO
Cortés 1519-1521
Veracruz *1519*
1521 Mexico City
Puebla *1531*

Gulf of Mexico

Florida
St. Augustine *1565*

1515 Havana

Cuba
Santiago de Cuba *1515*
La Isabela *1493*

Yucatán Peninsula

Jamaica

Hispanola
Santo Domingo *1496*

San Juan *1509*

Bahama Islands

ATLANTIC OCEAN

Lesser Antilles

Columbus 1493-96

Columbus brought Christian priests with him on his second voyage at the insistence of the pope, in order to colonize the New World with Catholic missions.

Caribbean Sea

Trujillo *1525*

VICEROYALTY OF NEW SPAIN

Spanish conquistador Hernán Cortés invaded Mexico in 1519, conquering the Inca Empire, and supported evangelizing efforts by Franciscan priest Gerónimo de Aguilar (assisted by La Malinche, a Mexican native).

1510 Nombre de Dios
1597 Portobelo
1519 Panama

Santa Marta *1525*
Maracaibo *1529*
Caracas *1567*
Cartagena *1533*
Cumaná *1522*

Cali *1536*
1537 Popayán
1534 Quito

Bogotá (Santa Fé de Bogotá) *1538*

Belalcázar 1533-39

Mouth of the Amazon

PACIFIC OCEAN

EQUATOR

From 1590-1661, the northeast coast of present-day Brazil was an area of conflict between the Portuguese, Dutch, and at times the French.

In 1615 the Portuguese take over the French town of São Luís do Maranhão.

1538 Guayaquil
1526 Tumbes
1532 Paita
1532 Piura
1532 Cajamarca
1534 Trujillo

Riobamba *1534*
Cuenca (Tomebamba) *1557*

Brieva and Toledo 1637-38

Belém (Feliz Lusitânia) *1616*
São Luís (São Luís do Maranhão) *1612*

Natal *1599*
Olinda *1535*
Recife *1537*

The evangelization of Peru began when missionaries arrived with Francisco Pizarro's military expedition.

PERU
Pizarro 1531-33

In the 17th century, Jesuits created mission towns or reducciones in Spanish Paraguay (including present-day Brazil and Argentina) as havens for natives desperate to escape slave hunters.

The first Jesuits in Spanish America arrive in Lima, 1568.

1537 Callao
1535 Lima
1572 Huancavelica

Cusco *1533*

SOUTH AMERICA

BRAZIL (TERRA DE SANTA CRUZ)

Salvador (São Salvador da Bahia de Todos os Santos) *1549*

VICEROYALTY OF PERU

1540 Arequipa
1541 Arica

La Paz *1548*
Sucre (La Plata, Chuquisaca) *1538*
Potosí *1545*

Lake Titicaca

Corumbá *1788*

Portugal's King John III gave the Jesuits permission to enter Brazil in 1549.

Almagro's 1535 expedition failed to establish Spanish control south of Cusco. Almagro's harsh treatment of native groups made it difficult for Valdivia to gain the trust of these peoples, five years later, as he established Spanish control in the south.

São Vicente *1532*

Rio de Janeiro *1565*

Asunción *1537*
Ciudad Real *1630*

In 1555, the French establish a colony in Guanabara Bay. In 1565 the Portuguese expel the French and establish Rio de Janeiro (São Sebastião do Rio de Janeiro).

Spanish conquistador Pedro de Valdivia invaded present-day Chile in 1541 and established various cities, including Santiago, under the banner of Catholicism. Present-day Argentina, first explored by Amerigo Vespucci in 1502, saw its first Catholic settlements in the 1570s around the Río de la Plata.

Valley of Copiapó
1550 Coquimbo
1544 Valparaíso
1541 Santiago
Concepción *1550*
1552 Valdivia

Córdoba *1573*
Mendoza *1561*

Buenos Aires *1536*

Río de la Plata

Initially, Brazil (originally named Ilha de Vera Cruz, and later renamed Terra de Santa Cruz) was established as 15 private captaincies. Two of the 15 prospered, while the other 13 captaincies failed. This led the king to make colonization a royal effort rather than a private one. Under the new organization Jesuits came to Brazil. They set up missions, saved natives from slavery, studied native languages, and converted many of them to Roman Catholicism.

Valdivia was captured and brutally killed, along with his priest, by the Mapuche in 1553 in modern-day Chile.

CONQUEST OF THE AMERICAS, 1492–1650

  Area under Spanish control in 1600
  Area under Portuguese control in 1600
→ Christopher Columbus 1492-93 (first voyage)
→ Christopher Columbus 1493-96 (second voyage)
→ Hernán Cortés 1519-1521
→ Francisco Pizarro 1531-33
····▶ Sebastián de Belalcázar 1533-39
·-·▶ Diego de Almagro 1535
··-·▶ Pedro de Valdivia 1540-1553
→ Hernando de Soto 1539-1543
→ Francisco Vásquez de Coronado 1540-42
→ Juan Rodríguez Cabrillo 1542
→ Domingo de Brieava and Andrés de Toledo 1637-38

• Settlement with year of founding; historical names in parentheses
○ Point of interest

0 mi ——————— 2,000
0 km ——————— 2,000

wave of explorations with the full support of King Charles V of Spain. In 1530, Francisco Pizarro landed in Peru with a force of 200 men and succeeded in defeating the far greater Inca forces. One by one, the indigenous civilizations of Central and South America were suppressed and replaced by colonial administrations. Many native tribes perished not by the sword but as a result of diseases introduced by Europeans. Smallpox is believed to be the cause of the death of half the population of Peru, which explains why Pizarro could defeat the Inca armies with a force of only 160 men.

Not wanting to be left behind, France decided to join the rush to the New World. In 1534, Jacques Cartier explored the Gulf of St. Lawrence and claimed much of this region for King François I,

thus establishing French Canada. In 1608, Samuel de Champlain founded a trading fort that would become Quebec City, the first permanent French settlement in North America.

The Settlement of the Americas

The principal driving force to colonize the New World was the quest for gold and any other precious metals. That quest was successful in some parts of South America. For example, vast deposits of pure silver were found and harvested from the mines of Potosí in the Andes, followed by mines in Zacatecas and Guanajuato in Mexico. This Spanish intake of gold and silver created an entirely new economy: a global economy based on hard currency such as the real, the crown, and the

A 1671 COLORED ENGRAVING shows the silver mines of Potosí (in today's Bolivia), which had become one of the largest and most affluent cities in Latin America, with a population of 200,000.

"PREPARE YOUR HEARTS AS A FORTRESS, FOR THERE WILL BE NO OTHER."

SPANISH CONQUISTADOR FRANCISCO PIZARRO

guilder, with a face value that matched their actual silver and gold content.

To their disappointment, however, the explorers of North America failed to find any such ores in their territory. They then struck about for goods that could justify the expense of maintaining early colonies and settled on fur. In Europe, and particularly in the colder climates of the North, fur from ermines, martens, mink, fox, and beavers was a precious commodity, usually reserved for the elite. It was the search for fur that led the French to establish settlements along the St. Lawrence River, where they could trade in pelts with local tribes such as the Montagnais and the Algonquin people.

Up to this point, England had not joined the race to the New World, for it lacked the resources or the political will to engage in costly expeditions. With the constant threat of a Spanish invasion, England had to husband its military and naval assets, and leave it up to swashbuckling privateers such as Sir Francis Drake to prey on Spanish ships laden with gold bullion. But after Drake succeeded in circumnavigating the globe, Queen Elizabeth recognized that England could not be left behind. In 1584, she granted Sir Walter Raleigh a royal patent to explore the east coast of North America. This territory was named Virginia, in honor of England's "Virgin Queen." Two early attempts to create a settlement on Roanoke Island, in today's North Carolina, failed because the land was

A CRUCIFIX made of black mineral may have belonged to a Catholic member of the Jamestown colony, founded in 1607.

A MODERN RECONSTRUCTION shows the interior of a Powhatan wigwam in the Indian Village near historic Jamestown.

poorly chosen, with little arable land in the vicinity. But in 1607, an English settlement on Chesapeake Bay named Jamestown (to honor the new English monarch, James I) proved to be more successful. King James also authorized a group of investors to form the Virginia Company, on the model of the English East India Company that was charged with importing spices from the East. Before long, Jamestown would begin to attract large numbers of men and women who wanted to escape England in the hope of a better life.

Coin struck in Jamestown

Other English settlements followed, including Popham (Maine, 1607), Bermuda (1609), Plymouth (1620), and various locations in Newfound-

ARTIST WILLIAM SEGAR, court painter of Queen Elizabeth I of England, painted this portrait of Sir Walter Raleigh in 1598.

land. Most of these were abandoned just a few years after their founding, but among those that endured were the colonies of Salem (1626) and Plymouth. These Puritan and Pilgrim communities were motivated not by the fur trade but by the need to escape religious persecution in England. Thus, the English foundation of New World settlements was not rooted in commercial interests but in a desire for unfettered political and religious freedom—an idea that would ultimately lead to the American Revolution.

The Exploration of Southeast Asia

As they fought their long war to throw off the Habsburg yoke of Spain's king, Philip II, the seven provinces of Holland decided to beat Spain at its own game by becoming a leading player in the Spice Race. They did so with a revolutionary design for a long-distance ship, known as the *fluyt,* first built by Dutch shipwrights in 1581. This was an agile, three-masted vessel in which most armament was thrown overboard so as to create a maximum amount of cargo space. Without rows and rows of cannons, these 80-foot ships became much easier to equip, maintain, and operate, and they cost about half as much as a Spanish galleon to build.

In 1596, a four-ship expedition led by Cornelis de Houtman explored the shores of Java, beginning a nearly four-century occupation of the island group known today as Indonesia. Five years later, Willem Janszoon discovered a large landmass that became known as Terra Australis Incognita ("Unknown Land in the South"), today known as Australia. In 1598, Dutch explorer Jan Huygen published a book detailing the principal sea routes to the East Indies, which eliminated Portugal's competitive edge and unleashed a European race to the East. To exploit their gains, Dutch traders formed the Vereenigde Oost-Indische Compagnie (VOC) in 1602, the first multinational corporation in history. For the next 200 years, the VOC would dominate European trade with Asia, dispatching 4,785 ships that carried 2.5 million tons of cargo,

virtually monopolizing the trade in spices. Not to be outdone, England focused on India, establishing a first foothold in 1608. By the end of the 17th century, England was in virtual control of the Indian subcontinent. A century later, James Cook exploited the fact that the Dutch had done little to capitalize on their discovery of the Australian continent and charted a course to Australia's west coast. He promptly named it "New South Wales." In 1788, a British convoy known as the First Fleet arrived with the first group of some 750 convicts (including 188 women), thus establishing Australia as a large-scale, open-air penal colony.

The Counter-Reformation

The flood of wealth from the New World galvanized a campaign in Spain and Italy that is often referred to as the Catholic Counter-Reformation, an effort to roll back the Protestant movement. For much of the early 16th century, many rulers and clerics still hoped that a permanent European split along the lines of faith could be averted. For more than a thousand years, Europe had been unified under the sign of the Latin cross; surely, such a remarkable solidarity should not be discarded lightly. Hope for reconciliation was further advanced by a perception in certain Catholic circles that the Lutherans and Calvinists were right on a number of issues. The papacy *had* become estranged from the urgent social and spiritual issues of the day. There was much corruption among the Catholic hierarchy, and many of the clergy had indeed strayed far from the precepts of the Gospels. Perhaps, then, the opposing parties could try to work out a compromise

Telescope that James Cook used on his Pacific voyages

TAOS PUEBLO, a settlement of Puebloan Native Americans in Taos, New Mexico, is considered one of the oldest continuously inhabited communities in the United States.

that would keep the Christian Church intact.

This is what happened in 1541 in the city of Ratisbon (today's Regensburg, Bavaria), where six theologians—three Catholics and three Protestants—sat down for a colloquy with the aim of forestalling a permanent split of the Church. To help matters along, Emperor Charles V of Spain was willing to accept two key Protestant demands: that clergy would be allowed to marry and that during the Eucharist, the cup of wine should be shared by the congregation, not just the officiating clergy. That Charles considered himself authorized to rule on such pivotal issues of Catholic doctrine underscores the tremendous influence that Spain—boosted by the fantastic wealth from its New World

Gold coin (ecu) of King Charles V

possessions—now wielded as the leading power of Europe. A tentative compromise was indeed reached among the six theologians, but the proposal was roundly rejected by both Martin Luther and the College of Cardinals. Its failure doomed the radical reform movement within Catholicism. If the Reformation could not be curbed by force of reason, it would be fought henceforth by the power of the sword.

This effort, known as the Counter-Reformation, unfolded on two levels. First, the Catholic Church launched an extensive effort to enhance the piety and devotion of its followers by developing a new generation of art and churches that used baroque illusionism to transport the faithful to heavenly ecstasy. This

"HERE I STAND. I CANNOT DO OTHERWISE. GOD HELP ME."

MARTIN LUTHER AT THE DIET OF WORMS

search for spiritual renewal was abetted by several new Catholic orders that emphasized the power of prayer and meditation while offering Catholic education of the young regardless of social status. Second, the Church actively encouraged the princes of Catholic nations to roll back the Reformation by military means. This produced the Thirty Years' War (1618–1648), one of the most destructive conflicts ever fought on European soil. In some states, the male population was reduced by half, not only by military action but also because of famine, disease, and malnutrition. After peace was finally concluded in 1648, many regions would take more than a century to recover.

Helmet of Charles V of Spain

The Counter-Reformation also gave a new impetus to the exploration and colonization of territories in the New World. When, upon his arrival in India in 1498, Portuguese explorer Vasco da Gama was queried about what he wanted there, his response was "Christians and spices." In the 16th century, that need to convert souls to Catholicism became urgent. New Spanish expeditions into the interior of North and South America were now invariably accompanied by monks and priests, including Jesuits, Dominicans, and Franciscans. When, in 1531, a Mexican peasant named Juan Diego claimed to have seen a vision of the Virgin Mary in Guadalupe, Mexicans converted by the thousands; by the late 1530s, there were eight million Christians in Mexico. ■

THE THIRTY YEARS' WAR

The Thirty Years' War (1618–1648) was one of the most destructive conflicts ever fought on European soil (at right). The immediate cause was the ongoing conflict between Protestant and Catholic states, after Calvinism continued its rapid growth in the north. Charles V, the Holy Roman Emperor, was desperate to preserve the loyalty of European principalities, while other European powers saw an opportunity to roll back the emperor's grip on Europe. Holland was in open rebellion against Spain. The Danish king, Christian IV, sided with Lower Saxony in an attack on imperial forces, soon joined by Swedish King Gustavus Adolphus. In 1635, Louis XIII of France launched an attack on Spanish troops in Germany and the Netherlands. The Portuguese exploited the moment to rise up against Spain as well. In the end, the Habsburg Empire was greatly diminished, splintered into more than 300 principalities.

A PORTRAIT of Suleyman the Magnificent, the 16th-century sultan of the Ottoman Empire, was painted by Italian artist Titian around 1530.

THE RISE OF NEW
EMPIRES

The era of the Renaissance was also witness to the rise of new empires in the Middle East, China, and Russia—each of which would exert a profound influence on developments around the globe, including growing tensions between East and West.

At the beginning of the 14th century, Osman I was the leader, or bey, of one of several Turkish principalities in what is today's northwest Turkey. He wasn't satisfied with his *beylik,* his domain, and decided to expand his territory at the expense of a string of Byzantine towns located along the Sakarya River. The Byzantine Empire was weak as a result of the 1204 sack of Constantinople and its subsequent loss of trade between East and West. Osman continued to roll up Byzantine lands until, at long last, forces led by the Byzantine general George Mouzalon tried to stop him. Osman's warriors dealt him a crushing defeat, and suddenly Osman had become a force to be reckoned with. Though he died in 1324, his successors continued his push into the weakly defended Byzantine lands, steadily creating a new realm that proudly bore the name of its founder: the Ottoman Empire, derived from "Uthman," the Arabic version of "Osman." Having captured the strategic Venetian port city of Thessaloniki, Ottoman forces turned north into Serbia and in 1389 destroyed the army of Prince Lazar Hrebeljanović of Serbia at the Battle of Kosovo.

At this point, the crowned heads of Europe became deeply alarmed. If the Turkish war machine was not checked, Ottomans could plow deep into Europe, just as the Mongol armies had threatened to do a century earlier. In response, these princes set aside their perennial rivalry and formed a coalition to stop the Muslim onslaught. They were encouraged to undertake this new "Crusade" by Pope Boniface IX in Rome, notwithstanding the fact that there was also a rival pope in Avignon who did everything in his power to undermine Rome's authority. Still, the Crusade was formed under the leadership of Sigismund, the prince elector of Brandenburg, using not only Balkan forces but also troops from Hungary, France, England, Burgundy, and the German states. Seldom has Europe been so unified as in these frightful days when Western civilization seemed to hang in the balance.

In 1396, the European army, about 15,000

AVALOKITEŚVARA, a bodhisattva who embodies the compassion of all Buddhas, is shown in this 10th-century gilded Chinese statue with a thousand arms and eyes.

> ## "WHAT MEN CALL SOVEREIGNTY IS A WORLDLY STRIFE AND CONSTANT WAR; WORSHIP OF GOD IS THE HIGHEST THRONE, THE HAPPIEST OF ALL ESTATES."
>
> **SULEYMAN THE MAGNIFICENT**

men strong, clashed with the 20,000 Ottoman troops during a prolonged siege of the fortress of Nicopolis in today's Bulgaria, close to the River Danube. Ottoman Sultan Bayezid I rushed reinforcements to the beleaguered stronghold, which routed the European alliance and sent its soldiers packing. Now, it seemed, all of Europe lay wide open to the Muslim conquest. And indeed, the Ottomans may very well have pushed on to Vienna were it not that in 1402 they were attacked by a rival Turkish force, the Timurid Kingdom, which succeeded in taking Sultan Bayezid prisoner. Europe—and the Byzantine Empire—was granted a reprieve while these two Turkish rivals sorted things out. By 1413, however, the Ottomans had emerged triumphant and their conquest began anew. Sultan Murad II, who had ascended the throne in 1421, defeated the last European Cru-

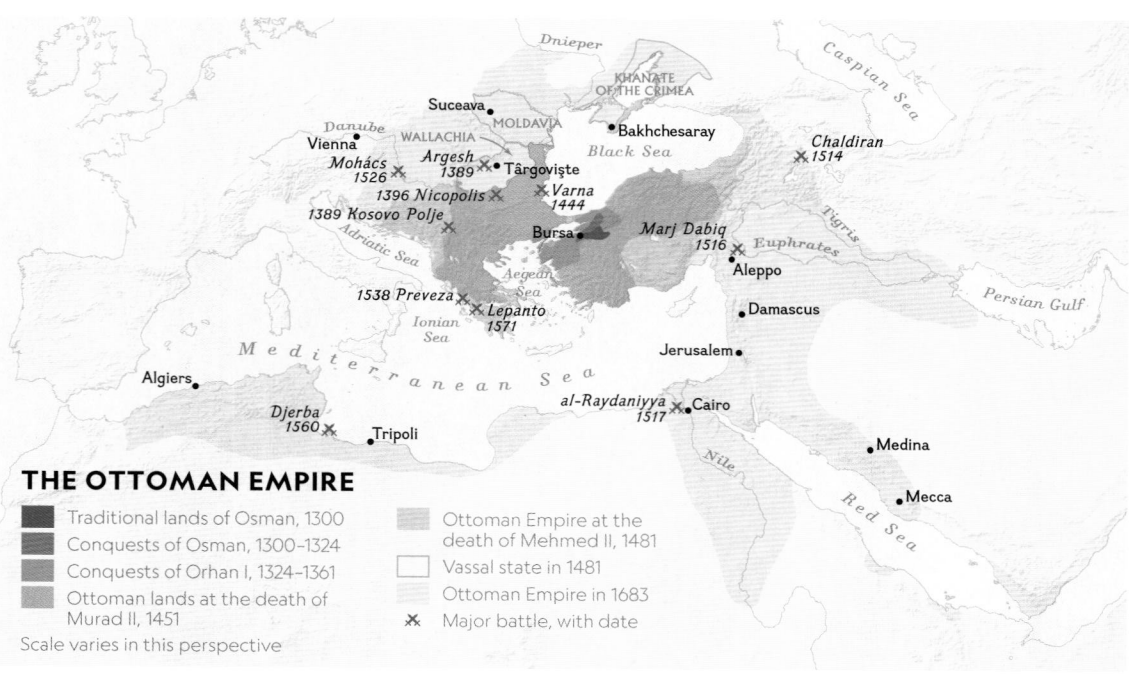

Turkish 15th-century helmet from Anatolia

sade at the Battle of Varna in 1444. Murad's son Mehmed II then decided to vanquish the Byzantine Empire once and for all, and he captured Constantinople in 1453.

In some ways, the Ottomans were more enlightened than their Arab or Syrian predecessors. Many high-ranking officials were freed slaves, while an elite corps of warriors known as Janissaries usually consisted of slaves or young Christian boys recruited for military service. Suleyman the Magnificent, who rose to power in 1520, pushed through many reforms in taxation, education, and criminal law, which is why he became known as "The Lawgiver" to his subjects. He also fell in love with a Christian woman named Hürrem Sultan (known as Roxelana in the West), who converted to Islam and became his spouse. An accomplished poet and artist himself, Suleyman also stimulated a revival

THE OTTOMAN EMPIRE

■ Traditional lands of Osman, 1300	▨ Ottoman Empire at the death of Mehmed II, 1481
■ Conquests of Osman, 1300–1324	□ Vassal state in 1481
■ Conquests of Orhan I, 1324–1361	▨ Ottoman Empire in 1683
■ Ottoman lands at the death of Murad II, 1451	✕ Major battle, with date

Scale varies in this perspective

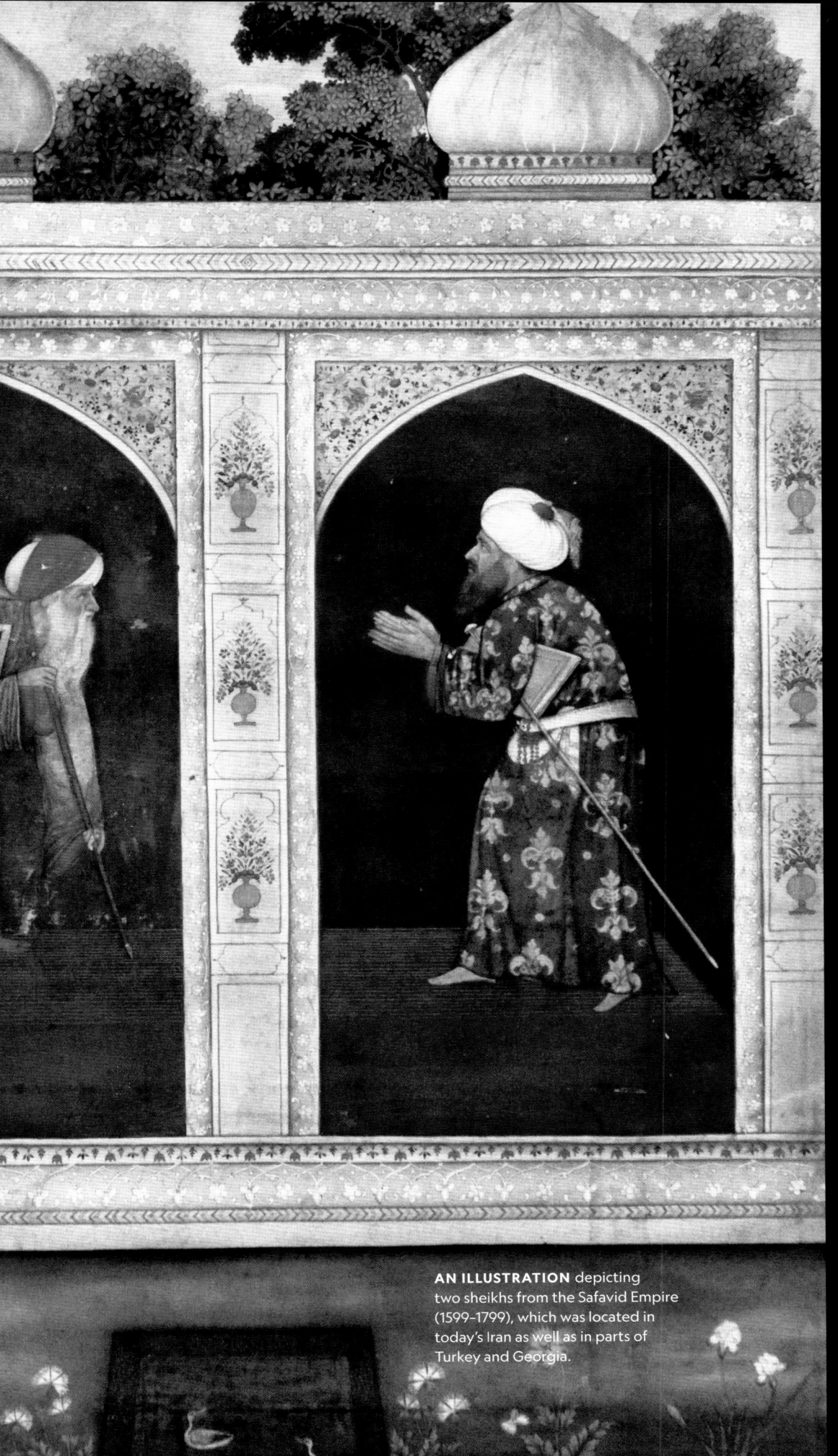

AN ILLUSTRATION depicting
two sheikhs from the Safavid Empire
(1599–1799), which was located in
today's Iran as well as in parts of
Turkey and Georgia.

NOTABLE DATES

1299
Osman I begins the Ottoman
Dynasty

1368
Zhu Yuanzhang topples Yuan
rule and begins Ming
Dynasty

1405
Chinese mariners travel
westward as far as Africa

1421
Emperor Yongle of China
formally establishes Beijing as
national capital

1444
Sultan Murad II defeats the
last European Crusade at
Battle of Varna

1453
Sultan Mehmed II takes the
Byzantine capital of
Constantinople

1520
Suleyman the Magnificent
begins 46-year rule of the
Ottoman Empire

1523
Mughal warlord Babur
invades India

1526
Ottoman forces defeat the
Hungarian army

1557
Portugal establishes a trading
base on Macao

1571
All-European navy defeats
the Ottoman Navy at the
Battle of Lepanto

A RARE CIRCULAR MAP with the Stephansdom (St. Stephen's Cathedral) in its center depicts the siege of Vienna by Turkish forces in 1530.

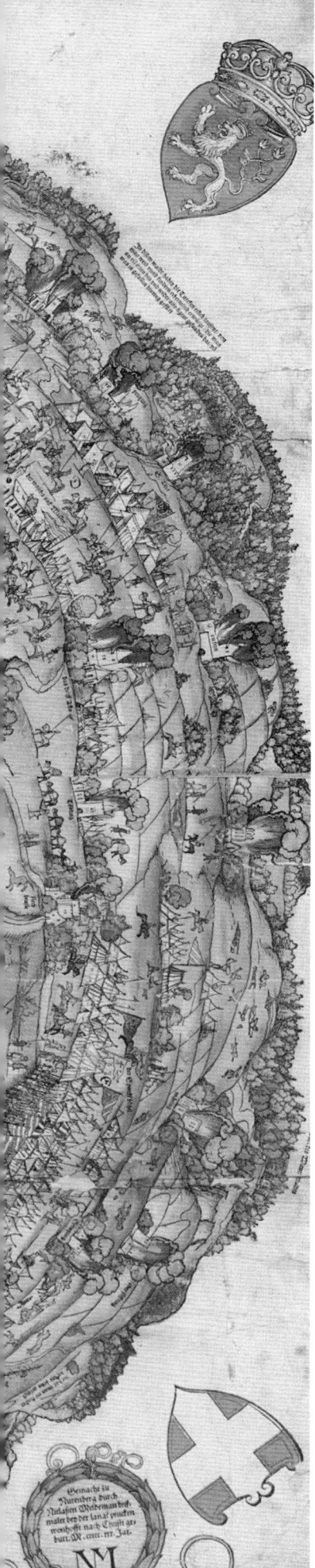

of Islamic arts through the empire and surrounded the Old City of Jerusalem with newly built walls that still stand today.

In the meantime, the Ottoman Empire continued to expand. Persia, Palestine, Egypt, and Hungary all fell to the Ottoman steamroller, and in 1529, Muslim forces led by Suleyman the Magnificent laid siege to Vienna, capital of the Habsburg Empire. But many Ottoman troops were worn down by the years of fighting and unaccustomed to the unusually heavy rains of early autumn. Much to Europe's relief, the Ottoman assault was repulsed, marking the farthest extent of the Ottoman penetration in Europe. Nonetheless, by this time, the Ottoman Empire reached from Algiers to Bahrain and from Yemen to Hungary, including large swaths of the Mediterranean Sea.

Ottoman expansion was decisively checked when a combined European flotilla defeated the Ottoman Navy at the Battle of Lepanto in 1571. In 1623,

Ottoman ewer, 18th century

Ottoman forces tried once more to take Vienna, but the Muslim army was repulsed and finally driven out of Europe save for Greece. The Ottomans would continue as one of the world's leading superpowers until the 19th century, when its territorial reach steadily began to crumble.

The Russian Empire

Another major power that rose in the aftermath of the Renaissance was Russia. As we saw, the polity known as Kievan Rus' had suffered greatly from the Mongol invasions. Some historians believe that nearly half of its population was killed. In the aftermath, the nation's cultural zenith shifted from Kiev to the Grand Principality of Moscow, which from 1283 onward was ruled by a Tatar puppet king named Daniel I. Nevertheless, the population remained faithful to their local culture and traditions and were finally able to shake off the Tatar yoke during the reign of Ivan III. Ivan

OTTOMAN JERUSALEM

After Palestine fell to Ottoman forces in 1517, the city of Jerusalem—which had been neglected under previous Muslim regimes—experienced a period of renewal during the reign of Suleyman the Magnificent. Ending the persecution of religious minorities, Suleyman ordered that Jews and Christians be allowed to worship as they saw fit. The Ottoman sultan also ordered the construction of Jerusalem's crenellated walls (at right), two and a half miles in length, on the remains of Herodian and Roman walls. The walls are equipped with seven gates that are still in use today. Encouraged by Ottoman tolerance, Jerusalem enjoyed a commercial and spiritual revival. A Jewish rabbi named Judah He-Hasid recruited Jewish Ashkenazi families throughout Poland, Germany, and Moravia (today's Czech Republic) and settled them in Jerusalem. His followers built the Hurva Synagogue, restored in 2010.

> ## "I HAVE CONQUERED OTHER NATIONS; YET I HAVE NOT BEEN ABLE TO CIVILIZE OR CONQUER MYSELF."
>
> **PETER THE GREAT, TSAR OF RUSSIA**

then embarked on several conquests that nearly tripled the size of his domain. In 1497, he proclaimed himself Ruler of All Rus. He solidified his throne by marrying the niece of the Byzantine emperor, thus positioning Moscow as the natural successor to Constantinople as capital of the Roman Empire and the Patriarchate of the Orthodox Church. To remind everyone of that fact, the Byzantine emblem of the double-headed eagle (known as the aquila, symbol of Roman military might) was adopted as the royal Russian coat of arms. In 1547, the new Grand Prince of Moscow, Ivan IV Vasilyevich (later known as Ivan the Terrible), even assumed the Byzantine title of Caesar or tsar, ruling from Moscow.

Well into the 17th century, Russia remained largely isolated from the great creative and scientific developments taking place in Europe, but that changed with the ascent in 1682 of Peter I. Known later as Peter the Great, Peter was determined to divorce Russia from its medieval past and turn it into a modern European nation. His famous "opening to the West" led to many important reforms in the fields of science, education, and the arts. The Russian alphabet was simplified, the Russian calendar was replaced with the Western Julian calendar, and state investment poured into Russian industries. Taking a cue from Louis XIV, Peter abandoned the system of local *uyezds,* or administrative subdivisions, and concentrated the government in a new capital, St. Petersburg, from where it oversaw eight newly created provinces. To curb the powerful influence of the Russian Orthodox Church, the tsar also forbade the construction of new monasteries and restricted the

AN AERIAL VIEW of St. Petersburg with the Church of the Savior on Spilled Blood shows the planned layout of the city, reportedly inspired by Tsar Peter the Great's visit to the canals of Amsterdam.

"TSAR IVAN IV THE TERRIBLE" was painted by Russian artist Viktor Mikhailovich Vasnetsov in 1897.

freedom of existing convents. Peter's successors continued this policy, so that by the end of the 18th century, some 560 out of 950 Russian monasteries had been closed.

Peter's Russia had by now grown to a huge nation that stretched from its borders with Poland to the Pacific Ocean. To reflect this fact, in 1721, Peter formally proclaimed the Russian Empire, confident in the belief that from this time forward, Russia would play a major role in European and global affairs. In this, as subsequent events would show, he was not wrong.

China After the Tang Period

For nearly three centuries, China enjoyed the peace and prosperity of the Tang Dynasty. Its population nearly tripled by 742, when a census recorded at least 50 million people. Chinese crafts flourished, not least because the Tang administration established numerous schools where children were trained to become skilled craftsmen, which in turn stimulated the economy and trade. But in 755, a revolt by a local governor, An Lushan, toppled the emperor and threw the nation in turmoil. Stability was eventually established, but the position of the emperor was weakened as more power flowed to the regional military governors. This inevitably made the empire vulnerable to foreign invasions, so that in the late Tang Period, numerous regions fell to neighboring states while its internal security was eroded by competing warlords.

After the Tang period came to an end in 907, China essentially broke up into multiple states during the so-called Five Dynasties and Ten Kingdoms Period, when the Han, Zhou, Jin, and Liang regimes competed for control of the strategic heartland of northern China. It was only in 960, with the rise of the Song Dynasty, that much of China was reunified once more, though a large

THE 10TH-CENTURY TOMB of Emperor Wang Jian of Shu is located in Chengdu, Sichuan Province, China.

Song Dynasty wine cup

part of its territory remained in control of the rival Liao Empire. But then a vassal Liao kingdom, that of Jin, rose up against its overlord, defeated the Liao, and next ousted the Song Dynasty, so by 1200, the Jin Dynasty had recovered most of the northern lands once ruled by the Tang Dynasty.

By the dawn of the 13th century, China was subject to the power play of three main constituencies: the Jin in the north, the Song in the south, and the Xia in the west. This was the situation when the Mongol conquest arose and rolled up each of these dynasties and produced a new dynasty, that of the Yuan, in their stead. China was now a single state once more, though its rulers were not native Chinese but Mongolian. Nonetheless, the Yuan emperors (who also had the largely honorary title of Great Khan of the Mongol Empire) worked to restore much of the trade that had sustained the great flowering of the Tang Period. Amazingly, the Silk Road now ran through a single polity, the Mongol Empire, in which roads and maritime connections were revived once more. It was during this time that a Venetian explorer, Marco Polo, visited China and recorded his impressions of the awesome splendor of the Chinese court.

There was, however, a flip side to the vastly improved connections throughout the empire. These ensured that the 14th-century plague, which some historians believe originated in Mongolia, was rapidly disseminated throughout the Mongol Empire and into Europe. According to some estimates, the Black Death killed some 35 million Chinese, or more than 30 percent of the population of China. Agriculture and most commerce collapsed. Thoroughly weakened, the Yuan Mongol regime fell prey to a growing number of peasant rebellions that culminated in the conquest of the Yuan capital of Khanbaliq—today known as Beijing—by rebel leader Zhu Yuanzhang in 1368. Yuanzhang then founded the Ming Dynasty, which would rule China until 1644.

The Ming Dynasty

The Ming emperors brought a desperately needed period of stability and restoration to China. Transport and irrigation canals, city walls, temples, and other monuments were carefully restored. Among others, this is the time when much of Beijing's fabled Forbidden City was built to house the imperial family as well as Ming administrators and staff. Fields in rebellious regions that had been destroyed by vengeful Yuan governors were slowly

PRINCIPAL DYNASTIES OF IMPERIAL CHINA

Xia Dynasty
ca 2070–ca 1600 B.C.E.

Shang Dynasty
ca 1600–ca 1046 B.C.E.

Zhou Dynasty
ca 1046–256 B.C.E.

Qin Dynasty
221–207 B.C.E.

Han Dynasty
202 B.C.E.–220 C.E.

Three Kingdoms Period
220–280 C.E.

Jin Dynasty
266–420

Sui Dynasty
581–618

Tang Dynasty
618–907

Five Dynasties Period
907–979

Song Dynasty
960–1279

Yuan (Mongol) Dynasty
1271–1368

Ming Dynasty
1368–1644

Qing Dynasty
163–1912

A GILT BRONZE SEAL with a Lion-Dog was crafted during the Song Dynasty in China.

nurtured to health. Peasants in these lands were given a three-year tax exemption to allow them to rebuild their farms. In particular, the Ming rulers sponsored the cultivation of tea, hemp, and cotton, which they considered vital ingredients for rebuilding the national economy. Unique Chinese craft industries such as the manufacture of porcelain and silk were once again actively patronized. The nation also became a formidable producer of iron, using native ore mines, with an annual estimated output of some 100,000 tons of iron. The Ming rulers also restored the

Ming Dynasty incense burner

examination system, the traditional venue for talented youngsters to be educated and trained for service in the imperial administration regardless of class or social status. The Ming academies would continue to function, with few changes, for the next 500 years.

Having suffered two centuries of Mongol rule, it is only natural that the Ming regime remained deeply suspicious of foreign contact, even as the age of European exploration brought ships from the West on China's doorstep. This explains why Ming emperors poured vast amounts of

A 10TH-CENTURY CHINESE PAINTING shows a caravan of Khitan people, a nomadic Mongolian tribe, at a rest stop.

A MONGOL ARCHER on horseback is the subject of this 16th-century Ming painting of ink and color on paper. The painting has numerous collecting seals, some of which appear to be forgeries so as to enhance the value of the work.

> "NATION SHATTERED, MOUNTAINS AND RIVERS STAY . . .
> LAMENTING THE TIMES, FLOWERS SHED TEARS."
>
> DU FU, TANG DYNASTY POET

treasure into expanding the Great Wall, adding some 5,500 miles of fortifications from the Jiayu Pass on the western frontier to the Shanhai Pass in the east, on the shores of the Yellow Sea. It also explains why they were hesitant to engage in trade with the West, even though the demand for Chinese silk and porcelain was growing rapidly. Only a few Western powers were eventually allowed to trade with Chinese merchants: the Portuguese via their settlement in Macao (1557) and the Dutch via Formosa (today's Taiwan). By contrast, the Ming rulers initiated many expeditions of their own, sending ships as far as Africa and the Persian Gulf; some records describe Chinese explorers visiting Mecca. One famous Chinese mariner, Zheng He, conducted several expeditions through-

out Southeast Asia, including a major embassy to India. As a result, the Ming regime would soon receive tribute not only from its traditional dependencies in Korea and Java but also from vassal kingdoms in Cambodia, Borneo, Sumatra, parts of India, and even Japan.

India during the Mughal Period

In 1483, a child named Babur was born in Andijan in the Fergana Valley, today located in Uzbekistan. His father was the ruler of Fergana Valley who traced his lineage across many generations to the great Genghis Khan himself. Thus, while Babur was of Mongol origin, he and his tribe were the product of the Turkic and Persian influences that circulated in the valley at the time. This is why he

MING PORCELAIN

As historian Bradley Smith once wrote, in 1433, China represented the height of human endeavor. Never before had a single nation with a population of 60 million achieved such cultural unity over so large an area. What's more, Ming China led the world in the manufacture of rice, silk, metals, coal, lacquerware, paper, and weapons, but its splendor was nowhere better expressed than in its porcelain (at right). The dynasty founded an imperial porcelain factory at Jingdezhen, which instantly became the center of Chinese ceramics production with its trademark glazed cobalt-blue wares. As technology improved, its decoration became more delicate, depicting birds, flowers, and other motifs inspired by Chinese landscape paintings. From the 1570s onward, Ming porcelain became the dynasty's most important export product and found ready buyers throughout the world. In Holland, the Ming blue-and-white ware even inspired the development of an indigenous style known as Delft Blauw.

> "O SOUL, THOU ART AT REST. RETURN TO THE LORD AT PEACE WITH HIM, AND HE AT PEACE WITH YOU."
>
> **INSCRIPTION AT THE ENTRANCE GATE OF THE TAJ MAHAL**

was known as a Mughal, a Persian corruption of the word "Mongol." This cultural mix would serve him well when he succeeded his father as ruler of Fergana in 1495 and promptly began to expand the borders of his realm. In 1523, he unleashed his mounted warriors on northern India, where they ran circles around the slow-moving Indian cavalry on elephants and eventually toppled the Turkish sultan ensconced in Delhi. Thus began the Mughal Dynasty of India, even though Babur himself continued his conquest eastward to Afghanistan, ultimately establishing his court in Kabul. Mughal control of India was then contested by the Afghan Dynasty of Sur between 1538 and 1555 until Babur's grandson Akbar returned with force and re-established the Mughal Dynasty in India for the next 300 years.

An able administrator, Akbar organized his vast territory in administrative districts in which Hindu officials found ready employment, even though the Mughals were Muslim. The tax for non-Muslims (including Hindus), known as the *jizya,* was sharply reduced, even abolished. Akbar even married an Indian princess named Mariam-al-Zamani, from the prestigious Rajput caste. To guide his administration, Akbar recruited talented men from a range of professionals to serve as his advisers, just as the Gupta kings had done before him. Serving as the emperor's *navaratnas,* or "nine jewels," this advisory council included a renowned musician named Tansen.

The Mughal Arts

The Mughal Dynasty presided over one of the most glamorous periods of India's history since the Gupta Empire, in which indigenous Indian styles

Hilt of a Mughal dagger with horse's head

blended harmoniously with Persian influences. The most famous architectural example is, of course, the magnificent Taj Mahal in Agra, on the south bank of the Yamnuna River. It was begun in 1632 by Mughal emperor Shah Jahan as a mausoleum for his second and most favored wife, Arjumand Bann Begum, whose regnal name as empress was Mumtaz Mahal. Mumtaz bore her husband no fewer than 14 children but died in childbirth after delivering her 14th child, Princess Gauhar Ara Begum, in 1631. Deeply distraught, Jahan ordered a building to be designed as a testament to his love for his wife. The result is a design that blends Persian motifs with indigenous Mughal styles, including the provision of four minarets to emphasize the strict spatial symmetry of the design. More than 20,000 workers were employed on the building, led by Jahan's court architect, Ustad Lahauri, but in the end it still took 22 years to build.

The Mughal Empire reached its zenith in the 17th century, when it ruled more than 100 million people on the Indian subcontinent. Shah Jahan also built a magnificent new capital in Delhi, including such marvels as the Red Fort with its undulating series of arches of red sandstone. But the Mughal period is particularly known for its exquisite painted miniatures, which were used as either book illustrations or stand-alone works of art. Influenced by the long tradition of Persian miniature painting, which ignored the Muslim prohibition on the depiction of human beings and other living things, Mughal artists were drawn to portraiture. Their beautiful renderings of kings and courtiers disporting themselves give us a privileged look of the splendor of the Mughal court. ∎

THE TAJ MAHAL in Agra, India, one of the most famous monuments in the world, was begun in 1632 by the Mughal emperor Shah Jahan as a mausoleum for his second and most favored wife, Arjumand Bann Begum.

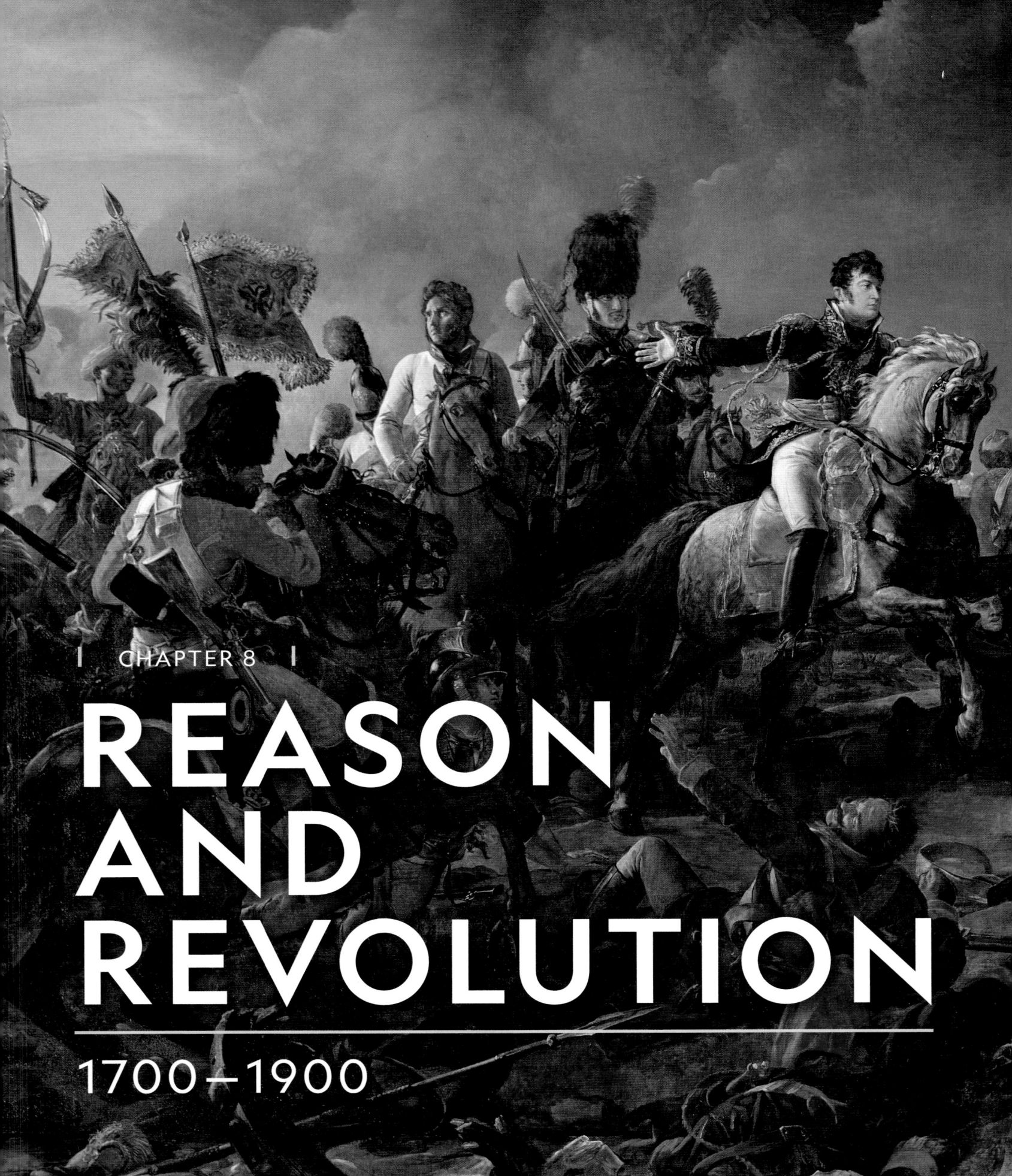

CHAPTER 8

REASON AND REVOLUTION

1700–1900

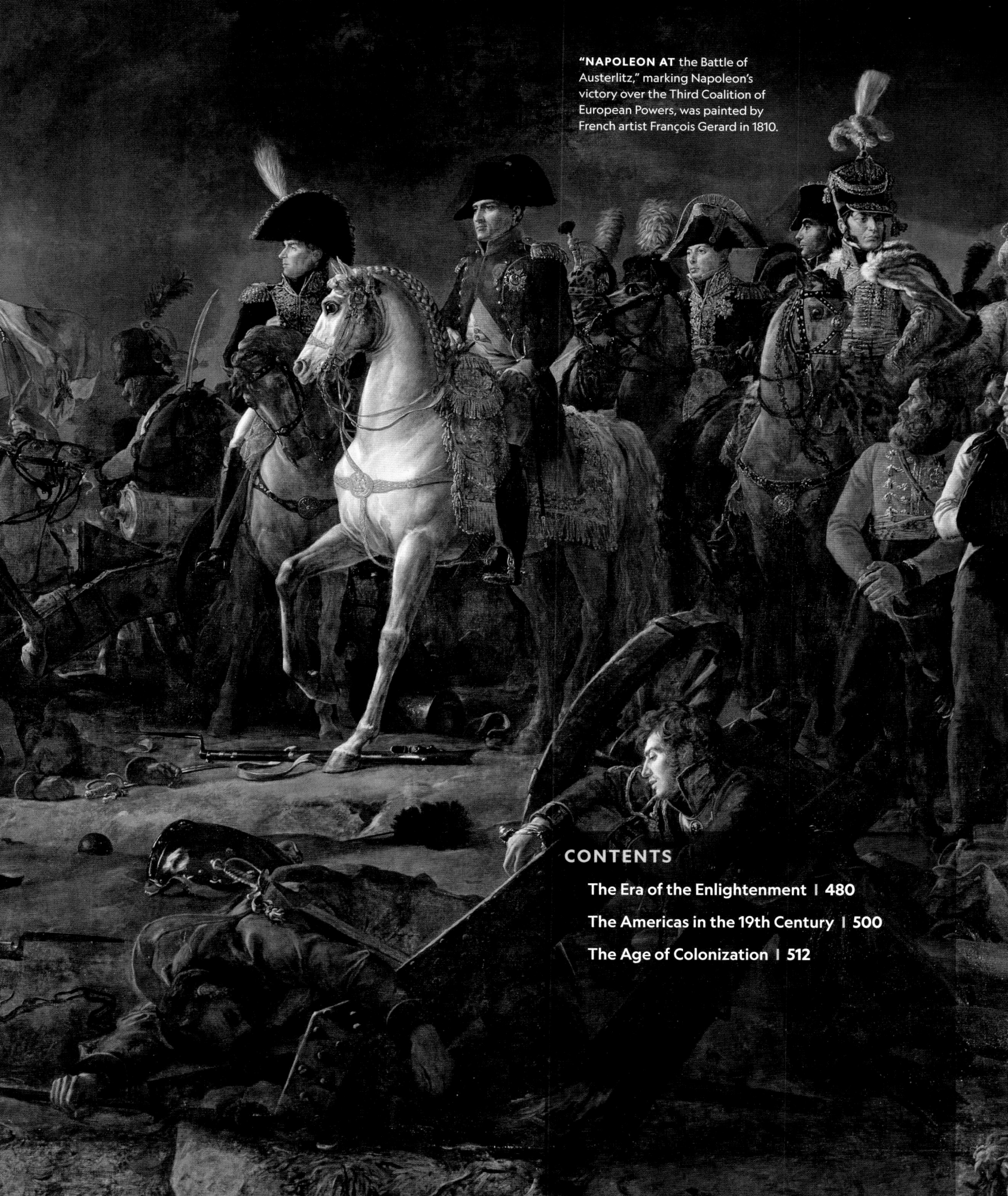

"NAPOLEON AT the Battle of Austerlitz," marking Napoleon's victory over the Third Coalition of European Powers, was painted by French artist François Gerard in 1810.

CONTENTS

THE AGE OF REASON

From the 17th century onward, the world was swept by new ideas about ethics, governance, and human rights that are collectively known as the Era of the Enlightenment. The Enlightenment was prompted in part by the chaos wrought by the Thirty Years' War. Many authors of the time asked a simple question: How could a faith rooted in Jesus' call for love produce such tremendous violence? Particularly among philosophers and scientists, the ravages of war prompted a deep skepticism about the lofty ideals of Christianity. As French 18th-century philosopher Voltaire wrote, "Of all religions, the Christian should inspire the most tolerance. And yet, until now, Christians have been the most intolerant of men." In response, these intellectuals set out to develop other ethical principles that could govern an ever more complex world.

The result of this quest was a movement that became known as the Enlightenment or, more appropriately, the Age of Reason. The term covers a number of disparate theories and ideas from the late 17th and 18th centuries. What these authors had in common was a search for a new moral and ethical foundation for humankind, using humanist principles first developed in the Renaissance.

The Rise of Science

The Enlightenment brought together thinkers from a range of disciplines. Some of its most influential writers were scientists like English physicist Isaac Newton; authors like French encyclopedist Denis Diderot or German writer Immanuel Kant; or pure thinkers such as Dutch philosopher Baruch Spinoza or English philosopher John Locke. But they shared a conviction that humankind had lost its moral compass and needed to find a new ideological framework to guide its ongoing advancement.

Many believed that such a foundation could only be found in human reason, devoid of any theological bias. Only reason, based on sound scientific methods and scholarly analysis, said French philosopher René Descartes, could guide humankind to discover universal truths and values. A mathematician by training, Descartes was convinced that the new emphasis on scientific knowledge would make all preceding ideologies redundant; only deductive logic should be the guiding beacon of human endeavor.

Most of these debates took place in literary salons or published pamphlets, far removed from daily life. But their influence on Europe's leaders and institutions was vast. Empress Maria Theresa of Austria, King Frederick II of Prussia, and Tsarina Catherine the Great of Russia were intrigued by these ideas and avidly engaged in correspondence with these philosophers. King Frederick the Great even employed Voltaire as an adviser. In the growing American colonies, the principles of Enlightenment would strongly resonate with leaders such as Benjamin Franklin and Thomas Jefferson and provide a major impetus for the American Revolution. In France, it would unleash forces that ultimately produced the French Revolution and the Napoleonic era. And in South America, it kindled a desire for independence from the Spanish and Portuguese Empires, resulting in a series of rebellions led by Simón Bolívar. The 19th century also saw the rise of the Industrial Revolution and the growth of European colonies. ■

THIS POWDER HORN from the American Revolution was engraved with the name of Thomas Kempton, a captain serving with the Massachusetts militia.

AMERICAN PAINTER Jean Leon Gerome Ferris, well known for his scenes from American history, was the artist of "Writing the Declaration of Independence in 1776," depicting Benjamin Franklin, John Adams, and Thomas Jefferson (standing).

THE ERA OF THE ENLIGHTENMENT

The idea of the Enlightenment as an opportunity to redefine the purpose of human existence animated many philosophers and scientists. Rationalism, deism, empiricism, and the encyclopédie movement all sought to find solutions for the great questions of their time.

Many modern historians believe that the ideas of the Enlightenment were essentially a reaction to the centuries-old influence of the Church. They cite the famous trial of Italian physicist and astronomer Galileo Galilei who, like Copernicus before him, had argued that it was the sun that stood at the center of our cosmos—not the Earth as taught by Christian doctrine. In 1613, he was forced by the Church to recant, even though scientifically he knew he was right. For many, this signaled that Christianity was an obstacle to science, too beholden to doctrine to tolerate independent research. What is often forgotten is that Galileo had relied heavily on observations by Jesuit astronomers. Moreover, many of Europe's brightest minds, the cream of the Enlightenment, had been educated in Jesuit institutions.

Other critics see the Enlightenment as a reaction to the devastation of the Thirty Years' War, the terror of the Inquisition, and the bloody suppression of Huguenots in France and Protestants elsewhere. They point to data showing that poverty, disease, and malnutrition in Europe were considerably worse in the 17th century than at any other time during the High Middle Ages and the Renaissance. It seemed, then, that humankind was moving backward rather than forward.

Most authors, however, interpret the Age of Reason as simply a logical extension of the European Renaissance, which unleashed human creativity and scientific pursuits unfettered by religious dogma. This did not mean, however, that the philosophers of the Enlightenment were agnostic or rejected the idea of God. Indeed, a movement called deism believed that rational thought could ultimately prove the existence of a divine being far better than divine revelation or the reading of Scripture. To make their point, English deists such as Lord Herbert of Cherbury and Matthew Tindal argued that while God created the universe, he also gave human beings the gift of reason and free will. As a result, they wrote, God chose not to intervene in human destiny but nevertheless expected men and women to live moral lives. This explained, in the deist view, why there was so much violence, tragedy, and evil in the world despite God's innate goodness—and why it was up to humankind, guided by rational

A LOUIS XIV marquetry clock of wood and brass appliqué in the style of André-Charles Boulle is dated to 1700.

> "REASON'S LAST STEP IS THE REALIZATION THAT
> THERE ARE AN INFINITE NUMBER OF THINGS
> THAT ARE BEYOND IT."
>
> BLAISE PASCAL, FRENCH PHYSICIST AND THEOLOGIAN

thought, to create order in the chaos. English philosopher John Locke, often recognized as the principal exponent of a movement called empiricism, added that since no single religion could ever claim to be absolutely perfect in its revelation, all nations should grant their citizens complete freedom in conscience, thought, and faith.

In France, the emphasis of the Enlightenment moved away from religion to the practical issues of the day, such as politics, relations among nations, and the pursuit of science. For example, Denis Diderot argued that if science should indeed serve as the basis of modern society, then an inventory of all knowledge should be made and published for the benefit of all the world. Thus was born an enterprise known as the *Encyclopédie* project, the first attempt since Pliny and Aristotle to create a categorical dictionary of human knowledge of the time. Coauthored with Jean le Rond d'Alembert, the *Encyclopédie* combined science, philosophy, and physics with entries on more mundane subjects, such as French trades and engineering devices.

Initially, aristocrats throughout Europe were smitten with these high-brow ideals and eagerly discussed them in salons, hoping that some of their intellectual élan would rub off. But French noblemen became increasingly alarmed by the *encyclopédistes'* call for equality, intellectual liberty, and anticlericalism, and with good reason. Many historians believe that Diderot's *Encyclopédie* planted the seeds for the French Revolution.

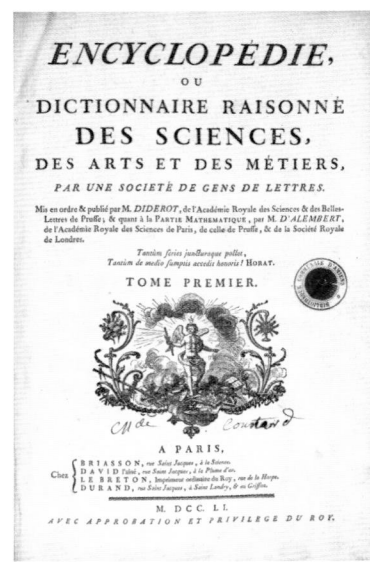

Title page of the Encyclopédie

The Roots of the American Rebellion

Since their foundation in the 17th century, England's colonies in North America had been allowed to manage their own affairs in what English politician Edmund Burke called a happy condition of "salutary neglect." Like a benign but mostly absent father, the British Crown allowed the settlers to manage things as they saw fit as long as the ships carrying sugar, tobacco, rice, and fur arrived in English ports on schedule. In response, the American colonists had built systems of governance and jurisdiction that paid lip-service to the crown but otherwise operated as largely autonomous states.

This changed with the accession in 1760 of George III, who was shocked to discover that England's treasury had been severely depleted by the Seven Years' War (1756–1763). A more stringent tax regimen was desperately needed to rectify this state of affairs, and in the king's view, the American colonists should pay their share. During the Seven Years' War, English soldiers and sailors had bled to keep these colonies safe from England's enemies, and now the colonists were expected to show their gratitude. Thus, from 1764 onward, George III's chancellor of the exchequer, George Grenville, initiated a series of acts with the goal of sharply increasing revenues from the overseas colonies. One of these acts invalidated the paper money printed by the local colonies on the grounds that all trade debts should be settled by "hard currency" such as the British pound. This

NOTABLE DATES

1648
The Treaty of Westphalia ends the Thirty Years' War

1651
Thomas Hobbes publishes his influential book *Leviathan*

1721
Johann Sebastian Bach writes the Brandenburg Concertos

1748
French philosopher Montesquieu writes *The Spirit of Laws*

1751
Denis Diderot and Jean le Rond d'Alembert publish first volume of *Encyclopédie*

1756
Outbreak of the Seven Years' War

1770
Outraged over increase in taxes, American colonists pelt British soldiers with rocks

1776
American Continental Congress declares independence from England

1781
Immanuel Kant writes *Critique of Pure Reason*

1789
The French Revolution begins

1793
Louis XVI and Marie-Antoinette are executed by guillotine

1799
Napoleon Bonaparte assumes power in France as First Consul

inevitably pushed many of the colonies to the point of bankruptcy.

In popular lore, it is the Boston Tea Party—when a group of rebels dumped some 45 tons of English tea in Boston Harbor—that marked the beginning of the American Revolution, but in fact it was Grenville's Acts that lit the fuse. This was followed by an even more controversial decree, the so-called Stamp Act of 1765, which levied taxes on anything that involved printed paper, including newspapers, pamphlets, wills, marriage licenses, and even playing cards. For many colonists, these "Intolerable Acts" left them no choice: Either they resisted, or they would be forced into penury.

The American Revolutionary War

King George and the British Parliament fatally misread the American colonists' motives and their plea to be treated as equals. Wiser counsel might have reminded them that the 13 Colonies now had a population of 2.5 million that was doubling every quarter-century and that soon America would be a political and economic power in its own right. Thus, when the colonies persisted in their protest, arguing that there could be no taxation without their representation as equals in British Parliament, the king ordered a military response.

Initial skirmishes around Boston led to an ignominious withdrawal of British forces. This was hailed as a great victory by the Continental Congress in Philadelphia, which now served as the de facto national assembly in control of the rebellion. Congress also voted to create a Continental Army by fusing many disparate colonial militias into a cohesive force, to be led by a Virginia officer

> # "OUR CRUEL AND UNRELENTING ENEMY LEAVES US ONLY THE CHOICE OF BRAVE RESISTANCE, OR THE MOST ABJECT SUBMISSION."
>
> **GEORGE WASHINGTON, AS COMMANDER-IN-CHIEF OF THE CONTINENTAL ARMY**

named George Washington. And on July 4, 1776, it took the extraordinary step of formally declaring independence from the British Crown.

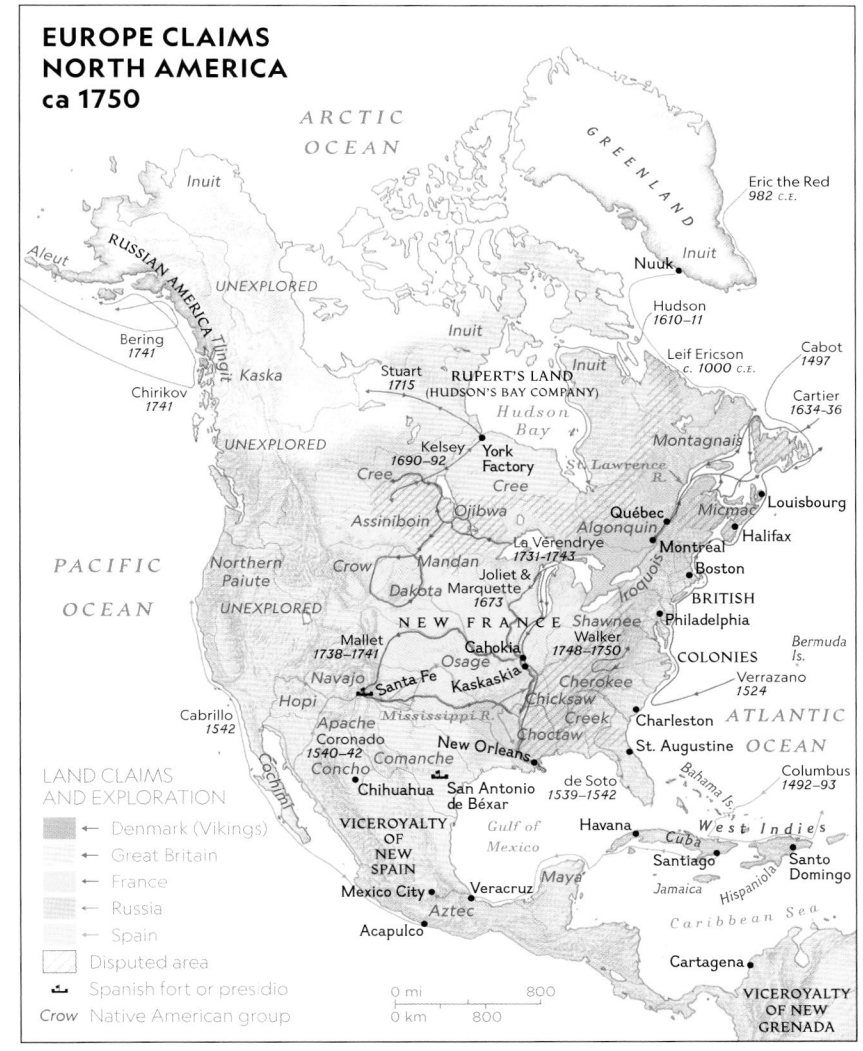

1763 cavalry pistol from the Revolutionary War

"By the God that made me, I will cease to exist before I yield to a connection on such terms as the British Parliament propose," Thomas Jefferson wrote, "and in this, I think, I speak the sentiments of America." Greatly influenced by Montesquieu's *De l'Esprit des Loix* (*The Spirit of Laws*), Jefferson took part in drafting the U.S. Constitution, which separated the government into legislative, judicial, and executive branches. Montesquieu's book also argued for an end to slavery, but it would take nearly another century before this aspect of Enlightenment theory would be written into American law as well.

But first, the American Revolution had to be won. Just two days before the declaration of independence, Britain had begun to disembark a vast invasion force on Long Island near Manhattan, under the command of Gen. William Howe. These redcoats—as the English infantry was called, given their red uniforms—soon brushed away the Continental defenders and quickly pushed into Manhattan, setting most of Washington's troops to flight. A war of attrition ensued, with Washington using guerrilla tactics to stage surprise attacks on the superior British troops while Howe steadily expanded his control over New York and New England. As winter fell, the Continental Army was reduced to 6,000 men, morale was low, and Congress was forced to evacuate Philadelphia. The outlook for American independence was bleak.

An extraordinary series of events—prompted by a combination of skill, courage, and pure luck— somehow saved the revolution. Up in Lake Cham-

plain near the Canadian border, with only a handful of brittle gunboats, the American general Benedict Arnold— later vilified for defecting to the British—was able to delay a vastly superior British fleet, thus defeating the Admiralty's much-vaunted Northern Strategy. On Christmas night, 1776, Washington crossed the Delaware River with a hardscrabble force of just 2,400 men in a surprise

---

EUROPE CLAIMS NORTH AMERICA ca 1750

LAND CLAIMS AND EXPLORATION

← Denmark (Vikings)
← Great Britain
← France
← Russia
← Spain
Disputed area
⚓ Spanish fort or presidio
Crow Native American group

0 mi   800
0 km   800

A COPY of Emanuel Leutze's famous 1851 painting "Washington Crossing the Delaware" by Eastman Johnson

"AGAINST SO POWERFUL
AN ATTACK, WE CANNOT
HOPE TO MAKE A VERY
LONG RESISTANCE."

BRITISH GENERAL CHARLES CORNWALLIS
AT YORKTOWN

attack on the British depot at Trenton, New Jersey. After more than an hour of sharp fighting, some 900 Hessian mercenaries, hired by the British Crown, were taken prisoner. The attack restored American morale, along with the confidence of Congress in its commander-in-chief.

Defeat at Yorktown

Enraged, General Howe ordered a highly experienced officer, General Cornwallis, to pursue the rebel forces and destroy them. Rather than occupying ground—which, with only some 35,000 troops, Howe could never hope to do—it was the destruction of Washington's army that now became the foremost British objective. This was articulated as the Southern Strategy, with the goal of bottling up Washington in Virginia where he could be attacked in a pincer movement by land and by sea. This strategy might have succeeded were it not for a surprising development: Benjamin Franklin, the American ambassador at the court of Versailles, was finally able to persuade King Louis XVI of France to come to the aid of the hard-pressed Continental forces. France had been itching for revenge after its humiliating defeat by British arms during the Seven Years' War. The king's foreign minister, Charles Gravier, Comte de Vergennes, was at last convinced that Washington stood an even chance of winning.

However, after scoring big victories in Charlestown and Richmond between 1780 and 1781, Cornwallis showed that the Southern Strategy was working; clearly, he had Washington on the run. Cornwallis then set out to fortify Yorktown, on Chesapeake Bay, as a base from which to supervise the final phase of the war. But unbeknown to him,

A PORTRAIT of Charles Cornwallis, British general during the American Revolutionary War, was painted by renowned English artist Thomas Gainsborough in 1783.

France had not only sent reinforcements of 5,500 troops but also ordered the French admiral de Grasse to throw a naval blockade around Yorktown. As Washington and Gen. Marie-Joseph du Motier of France, better known as the Marquis de Lafayette, led their combined armies to Yorktown, Cornwallis suddenly realized that the Americans had turned the tables on him: It was he, rather than Washington, who was now caught in a pincer movement.

On October 19, 1781, the British general surrendered his sword. Two years later, England, France, Spain, and America signed the Peace Treaty of Paris, establishing the United States as the first republic based on the Enlightenment ideals of freedom and democracy. American-born painter Benjamin West was commissioned to capture this momentous event in a painting.

Unfortunately, the British delegation refused to pose, and so this remarkable painting remained unfinished.

The Fall of the French Monarchy

By this time, France had replaced Spain as the dominant political power in Europe and Italy as the center of European culture. French, rather than Latin or Italian, was now the lingua franca of European science, diplomacy, music, literature, and art. But all the glitter of Louis XVI's court, including its new penchant for classicizing furniture and decoration known as Louis Seize, could not hide the fact that France was deep in debt. As in Great Britain, its opponent in the Seven Years' War, the cost of this global conflict had drained the French treasury, exacerbated by the monarchy's disastrous economic policies. The French Compagnie d'Occident (Company of the West), which was backed by the French Crown, is a telling example. Desperate to hold on to its possessions in North America, it had shipped 5,400 colonists to Louisiana. But many of these were conscripts,

THE DECEPTIVE ROLE OF MAPS

British officers had been trained with maps that showed Britain's geography in detail, at a scale that represented hundreds of square yards. Maps of North America showed territory that was measured in the thousands. For the 18th-century British officer, operating in unfamiliar territory using maps printed back in England, this difference was never made explicit. Therefore, the British—from the king on down to his ministers and generals—subconsciously transferred their sense of scale from their home maps to the maps of this new and unknown land where they were expected to fight. But North America was not a country; it was a continent, where the eastern seaboard (at left) alone stretched more than 1,500 miles. No British general ever grasped that simple fact, thus sustaining the illusion that such a vast territory could ever be subdued with only 35,000 men.

AN ANONYMOUS FRENCH ARTIST created this impression of "The Taking of the Bastille, 14 July 1789."

vagabonds, or criminals, since few French citizens looked forward to settling in the swampy fields and humid climate of the bayou. Inevitably, most of these settlers died of malaria or fled to the more temperate climate of Spanish Florida. In an effort to maintain the illusion of solvency, the company then issued paper currency in the form of promissory notes while spreading the (completely unfounded) rumor that gold had been found in the Mississippi Delta. In 1720, the bubble burst when the value of the notes was revealed to exceed the value of actual coinage in France's treasury. In 1731, the Compagnie d'Occident went bankrupt with a loss of more than 20 million livres. And yet this episode prompted Europe to begin using bank notes, of the type we use today, rather than the coins then in circulation.

In the 1780s, France's economic malaise was deepened by the expense of supporting the American Revolution and a string of bad harvests, which had a devastating impact on the French peasantry. Since France was an overwhelmingly agricultural nation, the deep recession plunged much of the population into despondency. It also fostered a

A COCKADE in the colors of the French Republic with the text *Égalité, Liberté* ("Equality, Freedom")

deep resentment against the French aristocracy, which continued its extravagant lifestyle as if nothing was amiss. Suddenly the ideals of Diderot's *Encyclopédie* didn't sound so far-fetched. "Freedom, brotherhood, equality or death" (*Liberté, fraternité, égalité ou la mort*) now became a spontaneous call for the people to rise and seize control of their government.

The French Revolution

When on July 11, 1789, King Louis XVI dismissed the liberal-minded finance minister, Jacques Necker, large-scale riots erupted in Paris that three days later led to the storming of the Bastille prison, the hated symbol of French absolutism. The protests soon spread to the countryside, where farmers and peasants turned against the feudal aristocracy, evicting them from their chateaux. On August 4, the newly formed parliament known as the Assemblée Nationale abolished the nobility's landownership altogether. While various parties jockeyed for control of this body, the king saw the writing on the wall. In June 1791, he attempted to flee with his highly unpopular queen, the Austrian

Marie-Antoinette. They got only as far as Varennes, 130 miles from Paris, where they were apprehended and brought back to Paris. One year later, the king was formally deposed, and on January 21, 1793, he was executed by guillotine on today's Place de la Concorde.

The irony is that Louis XVI was perhaps the most enlightened monarch of the Bourbon Dynasty. Despite fierce opposition from the French nobility, Louis had tried to abolish serfdom, lower the peasant tax, and adopt a greater tolerance toward Huguenot activity. In 1787, just two years before the Revolution, he had signed the Edict of Versailles, which granted Calvinists, Lutherans, and Jews full legal status and put an end to religious persecution in France. This was followed by a largely ceremonial Declaration of the Rights of Man and Citizen in 1789, which eliminated any form of persecution or discrimination on religious grounds within the French realm. Alas, it was all too little, too late.

The murder of these anointed royals sent shock waves through Europe. Almost overnight, the lofty ideals of the Enlightenment, admired by

VOLTAIRE'S WIT

The most influential French philosopher was François-Marie Arouet, better known as Voltaire (at left). Part of his appeal was that he expressed his ideas not only through philosophical tracts but also in novels, poems, and plays, which gained broad popularity throughout Europe. His smooth writing and sharp wit did not disguise his animus against the French First Estate, the Catholic Church, which he denounced as feudal, dogmatic, and intolerant of social change. As his fame spread, Voltaire corresponded with King Frederick the Great of Prussia, as well as the most powerful autocrat of all: Tsarina Catherine the Great of Russia. But the affection of these monarchs for Enlightenment ideals went only so far. While they liked to flirt with concepts such as equality and freedom, none dared to actually implement them as a matter of state policy.

Napoleon Bonaparte

The French Revolution was followed by a period of great turmoil known as the Reign of Terror. Hundreds of people, including noblemen and commoners suspected of "anti-revolutionary sympathies," were put to death, often based on spurious charges. Finally, in 1795, an executive council known as the Directoire ("Directorate") assumed the reins of the French government in an effort to restore political stability and rekindle the moribund French economy. Eager to reassert France on the European stage, it also got itself embroiled in military adventures that further eroded France's finances. The only significant outcome of these attempts to recapture *la gloire* was the rise of a war hero, a young artillery officer from Corsica. Hailing from minor Italian nobility known as the House of Bonaparte, Napoleon had adroitly used the chaos of the French Revolution to secure an appointment as general at the tender age of 24. He then led a stunningly successful campaign against Austria and the Italian city-states that greatly restored French national pride. Using his popularity as leverage, in 1799, Napoleon Bonaparte staged a daring coup that toppled the Directoire and got himself installed as First Consul of the French Republic. Worn out by the incessant political instability, the French people welcomed his autocratic regime with open arms.

Six years later, Napoleon went even further and crowned himself emperor of France during a carefully stage-managed ceremony in Notre Dame Cathedral, a scene that was later immortalized in a painting by Jacques-Louis David. But despite this sudden return to a hereditary monarchy, Napoleon always insisted that his regime remained true to the principles of the French Revolution, including the abolition of feudalism and the establishment of universal human rights. In fact, it was these lofty goals that motivated him to conquer much of western and central Europe.

Eyewitnesses of the time wrote that Napoleon did not strike a particularly impressive figure. Of middling height, just over five feet tall, he had

"THE EMPEROR NAPOLEON in His Study at the Tuileries" was completed by French artist Jacques-Louis David in 1812, showing the emperor in the uniform of a colonel of the Imperial Guard infantry.

so many in the upper classes, were exposed as the dangerous seeds of insurrection. Instead of fostering a new system of international security, as many had hoped, the Age of Reason had destroyed one of Europe's mightiest dynasties—and it wasn't done yet.

A 20-franc gold coin, 1803

LES INVALIDES in Paris, built by Louis XIV as a hospital and home for French veterans, contains the tomb of Napoleon Bonaparte.

a dark complexion that betrayed his Italian roots. As a man untroubled by social graces, invariably dressed in the drab uniform of a colonel in the Imperial Guard, he was—as even close friends admitted—often "ill-humored" and bored with idle conversation. But what never failed to mesmerize his audience were his eyes. In contrast to his swarthy features, they were blue-gray and radiated a fierce intellect and iron will. Few who met Napoleon came away without being impressed with the power of his personality.

As part of his strategy to restore French grandeur, Napoleon believed that France should get rid of any colonial possessions that didn't serve his political goals. Even though Nouvelle France, or New France, still occupied large territories in North America, from Canada to the Gulf of Mexico, in practice most of these were controlled by Native American tribes. Thus, in 1803, Napoleon negotiated the Louisiana Purchase with Thomas Jefferson, the third president of the United States. Despite its name, this sale didn't involve just Louisiana but much of Texas, Arkansas, Oklahoma, Missouri, Kansas, Colorado, Nebraska, Iowa, Wyoming, Montana, Minnesota, and the Dakotas—in all, some 828,000 square miles of North American territory. The purchase price was just $18 a square mile, or a total of $15 million. In one fell swoop, Jefferson was now much closer to realizing his vision of a United States from coast to coast.

The Napoleonic Wars

In Europe, many nations feared that a newly resurgent France would destabilize the continent and perhaps infect other nations with the seeds of revolution. In 1805, Imperial Russia, Britain, the Habsburg Empire, and others joined in a military alliance with the aim of containing Napoleon, who by then had swallowed modern-day Holland, Belgium, Luxembourg, and parts of Italy. But the coalition was no match for Napoleon's brilliant generalship. In 1805, the European allies were decisively beaten at the Battle of Austerlitz, even though the Russian and Austrian armies dwarfed the forces of Napoleon's Grande Armée. Vienna was invested, and all of Austria's lands in Bavaria and Italy were ceded to France.

The string of victories became a source of deep concern to Napoleon's erstwhile ally Prussia, and so in 1806, it was King Friedrich Wilhelm III of Prussia who forged a new coalition, this time including Russia, Saxony, Sweden, and Great Britain. In practice, however, it was the Prussian army that confronted Napoleon's forces, and they were ignominiously crushed by the French juggernaut at the Battle of Jena-Auerstedt of October 14, 1806. Napoleon quickly followed through by occupying Prussia all the way to the Russian border, where he defeated the forces of Tsar Alexander I on June 14, 1807. It seemed, then, that the Napoleonic steamroller was unstoppable. Europe's armies, which for centuries had trained to fight an opponent head-on, were ill equipped to counter Napoleon's uncanny talent for rapidly moving infantry and cavalry units across the battlefield, like pieces on a chessboard.

THIS UNIFORM was worn by Major Thomas Noel Harris at the Battle of Waterloo.

THE NAPOLEONIC CODE

Notwithstanding the violent upheaval of the Napoleonic Wars, the French emperor (at right) did implement a number of reforms in the countries under his sway, inspired by the principles of the French Revolution. A number of institutes of higher learning were created, thus restoring, to some degree, the proud tradition of European academia that had been eradicated by the suppression of Jesuit learning in 1767. In France and elsewhere, a uniform tax code was adopted that applied to everyone, including the nobility, the clergy, and other privileged classes. Another important contribution was the Napoleonic Code, which gave Europe its first uniform judicial grounding. Drafted by four leading legal experts in 1804, it replaced all existing feudal laws by establishing a common legal foundation inspired by the French Revolution's Declaration of the Rights of Man and of the Citizen, stating that all suspects shall be presumed innocent until proven guilty. It also granted freedom of worship to Huguenots, Jews, and other faith groups.

BRITISH ILLUSTRATOR William Holmes Sullivan created "The Battle of Waterloo, 18th June 1815" as a color lithograph in 1898.

> "THE BATTLEFIELD IS A SCENE OF CONSTANT CHAOS. THE WINNER WILL BE THE ONE WHO CONTROLS THAT CHAOS, WHETHER HIS OWN OR THAT OF HIS ENEMIES."
>
> **NAPOLEON BONAPARTE, EMPEROR OF FRANCE**

But then the French emperor over-reached. In November 1807, he invaded the Iberian Peninsula with the goal of cutting off Britain from its last remaining trade partners on the Atlantic, Portugal and Spain. But Napoleon's French soldiers were ill-equipped to fight in Spain's harsh climate and unfamiliar terrain. The conflict devolved into six years of attritional warfare, with Spanish and Portuguese forces actively supported by Great Britain. The Spanish population suffered unspeakable horrors, which inspired Francisco Goya's print series "Los Desastres de la Guerra" ("The Disasters of War") as well as his masterpiece, "The Third of May, 1808." Thus weakened, Napoleon made the fateful step of invading Russia in 1812 with an army of up to 685,000 French and auxiliary soldiers. It was perhaps the largest military force ever assembled in human history up to that point.

British shako worn during Battle of Waterloo

As expected, the French army made rapid progress through western Russia but was never able to defeat the Russian forces in a decisive battle. Using the same tactics that Soviet forces would employ in 1941 against the German Wehrmacht, the Russian army left a scorched earth in its wake to deny the invader the use of towns, wells, fields, and livestock. When in September, Napoleon finally reached Moscow, he found the city abandoned, with many of its buildings set on fire. As the fearful Russian winter set in, the French emperor led what remained of his army back to France, harassed by mounted Cossacks all the way. Nearly half a million French were either killed or captured, while Russian casualties amounted to 400,000—staggering numbers for the warfare of the time.

The disastrous Russian campaign was the turning point. Convinced that Napoleon was now fatally weakened, the European powers came together once more to defeat the emperor. At the 1813 Battle of Leipzig, their forces crushed Napoleon's army, which at this point was made up of barely trained young conscripts. France was invaded, and Napoleon was forced to abdicate. Surprisingly, the victors allowed Napoleon to be exiled to the island of Elba, off the coast of Tuscany, where he was installed as governor. This was a fateful mistake, for soon Napoleon was scheming to return to France and establish his empire once more. In February 1815, he did just that and quickly made his way to Paris to reassert his control of the French government. The grossly obese Louis XVIII, whom the European powers had foisted on the French throne in the hope of turning back the clock, fled in the nick of time. Thus began Napoleon's last 100 days, which ended when a vast army of British and Prussian forces, assisted by their allies, defeated the French army at the famous Battle of Waterloo on Sunday, June 18, 1815. This time, Napoleon was exiled to a remote island in the South Atlantic, known as St. Helena. Here, the French emperor died in 1821, at age 51, of stomach cancer. Since then, numerous conspiracy theories have argued that Napoleon was poisoned with arsenic, though recent studies question this idea. What is true is that his body was remarkably well preserved when it was moved back to Paris in 1840. Today, his remains rest in a magnificent tomb at Les Invalides, a former military hospital, in the center of Paris. ■

AN 1863 PHOTO depicts President Abraham Lincoln at the height of the American Civil War.

THE AMERICAS
IN THE 19TH CENTURY

The principles of the Enlightenment inspired not only the American and French Revolutions, but also a number of independence movements in Central and South America. Meanwhile, the newly formed republic of the United States was increasingly split on the issue of slavery.

Just as the European powers began to expand their colonial holdings in Africa and Asia, a series of revolutionary movements shook the Spanish and Portuguese colonies in Latin America. The spark that lit the fuse was Napoleon Bonaparte's 1808 invasion of Spain, which rippled across Spanish colonies in the New World. Napoleon's decision to put his brother Joseph on the throne of Spain severely eroded what legitimacy the Spanish Crown still exerted in its colonies. It didn't help that the territory of New Spain in the Americas was experiencing a severe economic downturn. Among others, in 1810, it emboldened a Jesuit-trained priest, Miguel Hidalgo y Costilla, to launch the Hidalgo Revolt, which gathered some 80,000 peasants into an ad hoc revolutionary army. This hardscrabble force was able to take a number of Mexican towns and villages but was thoroughly defeated on the doorstep of Mexico City. Hidalgo and a fellow revolutionary, José María Morelos, were captured and executed, but the seeds of revolt had been sown. After Napoleon's defeat, royalist elements in Mexico, fearing for their aristocratic privileges, formally declared their independence from Spain. Other revolutionary movements led to the foundation of today's Costa Rica, Honduras, Nicaragua, Guatemala, and El Salvador.

Simón Bolívar

In South America, the torch of freedom was lit by a Venezuelan nobleman, Simón Bolívar, who while studying in Europe had become deeply impressed by the ideas of the Enlightenment and the success of the French Revolution. Bolívar returned to Venezuela in 1807 and began plotting a coup, which in 1810 succeeded in deposing the Spanish colonial administration. The Spanish Royal Army soon mobilized, however, and pushed back against the revolutionary forces. In 1813, Bolívar was compelled to leave the country, but four years later, he returned with a much larger army to try to evict the Spanish colonial troops. Many years of battle still remained, but in 1819, Bolívar was declared president of a union of Venezuela, Colombia,

AN INFANTRY DRUM
used during the American Civil War

> "SLAVERY IS THE DAUGHTER OF DARKNESS;
> AN IGNORANT PEOPLE IS THE BLIND INSTRUMENT
> OF ITS OWN DESTRUCTION."
>
> **SIMÓN BOLÍVAR, VENEZUELAN REVOLUTIONARY LEADER**

Panama, and Ecuador, known as Gran Colombia. On June 29, 1821, a victorious Bolívar was finally able to enter Venezuela's capital of Caracas after defeating the Spanish forces at the Battle of Carabobo.

José María Morelos on a one-peso coin

Meanwhile, another revolutionary, Gen. José de San Martín of Argentina, was fighting to liberate the southwest of the continent. Having triumphed over Spanish forces in Chile, San Martín turned toward Peru. In 1821, he officially declared Peruvian independence, but staunch opposition compelled him to call for Bolívar's help. What transpired between the two men has never been ascertained, but in 1822, Martín left and Bolívar took over full responsibility for ousting the remaining Spanish troops.

The Colony of Brazil

Brazil continued to be ruled by a feudal aristocracy that relied on the motherland of Portugal to provide its economic lifeblood: a steady stream of slaves. Unlike the territories of New Spain, Portuguese Brazil had few gold or silver mines and therefore used its sugar plantations as its principal source of wealth. Sugar, still considered a luxury product in the 18th century, was primarily cultivated in nearly 3,000 plantations on the north coast of Portuguese Brazil, as well as in Demarara (now Guyana) and Suriname. Sugar production was labor intensive, requiring a vast concentration of labor. That made sugar plantations very unhealthy places where both local and imported labor suffered a high death rate from smallpox, malaria, and yellow fever.

In response, Portuguese traders had established a massive trade in slaves from their West African territories, which explains why for much of this time, Portugal was a world leader in the commercialization of slavery. It is sometimes forgotten that of all slaves taken from Africa, only 6 percent wound up in the English colonies of North America. The largest number by far were forced to work in Portuguese Brazil or New Spain, including the French and British Caribbean, where they suffered unspeakable horrors. This also explains why the coastal regions of Portuguese Brazil, where these slaves were kept in appalling conditions, experienced several slave rebellions. In 1605, for example, a slave from the Congo named Zumbi succeeded in establishing a free state in the hinterland of Pernambuco, called Quilombo dos Palmares. At its height, this freemen's state had a population of 30,000 that repeatedly rebuffed frantic attempts by Portuguese forces to conquer them. Only in 1695 did the Portuguese overrun the enclave and re-enslave its survivors.

INDEPENDENCE IN SOUTH AMERICA

FORMER COLONIES

- British, Dutch, French
- Portuguese
- Spanish
- (1822) Year of independence

"THE GRITO DE DOLORES" ("Cry of Dolores"), marking the moment when Miguel Hidalgo y Costilla launched the Mexican War of Independence, is a mural painted by 20th-century artist Juan O'Gorman.

NOTABLE DATES

1763
After the Seven Years' War, France cedes French holdings in North America

1791
Slaves and free blacks in French-controlled Haiti rise in rebellion

1810
Miguel Hidalgo y Costilla launches Mexican War of Independence

1811
Simón Bolívar proclaims the independence of Venezuela

1820
First Christian missionaries arrive in Hawaii

1821
José de San Martín proclaims Peru as an independent state

1858
Queen Victoria sends the first transatlantic telegraph via undersea cable

1861
The Confederate attack on Fort Sumter ignites the American Civil War

1863
Abraham Lincoln issues the Emancipation Proclamation, ending slavery in the United States

1864
Cheyenne and Arapaho Indians are massacred at Sand Creek, Colorado

1865
The Confederacy of America is defeated, ending the Civil War

THIS IMPRESSION of a sugarcane plantation in Brazil was painted by 17th-century Dutch artist Frans Post around 1655.

"THE CORONATION of Emperor Pedro I of Brazil" is the work of an anonymous 19th-century Brazilian artist.

Two years earlier, in 1693, Portuguese explorers finally discovered gold in the southeastern part of the country, soon known as the Minas Gerais ("General Mines"). This reduced Brazil's reliance on sugar cultivation, but gold mining too was an extremely hazardous task. In response, the flow of slaves from West Africa increased, this time to be tasked in the manufacture of sugar as well as the extraction of gold.

Dom Pedro Declares Independence

The ties between the Brazilian elite and Portugal began to fray after the Napoleonic invasion of Spain, and in 1807, the Portuguese court fled Lisbon for Rio de Janeiro on British ships. In 1815, Brazil was formally made part of a new united kingdom that also included Portugal and its southern region of the Algarve. This new entity was short-lived, however, for no sooner had King João VI returned to Portugal than his son Pedro, whom he had appointed as regent, declared Brazil's independence. "Dom Pedro" then established a constitutional monarchy on the Napoleonic model—even declaring himself "Emperor Pedro I." Of course, this was bound to inflame the political turmoil between Brazil's landed gentry and its urban liberals. In 1889, a coup by a group of politicians and officers led by Marshal Deodoro da Fonseca did away with all imperial pretense and established the Republic of Brazil.

In the meantime, the country had seized on another highly successful crop: the coffee bean. By the middle of the 19th century, Brazil was supplying half the world's demand for coffee. But slavery was not abolished until 1888, making Brazil the last nation in the Americas to do so. Soon after, Italian, Spanish, and even Japanese workers found employ on coffee plantations.

Slavery in the United States

In the new republic of the United States of America, the issue of slavery continued to fester as well. Although in 1735, the trustees of the Colonial Commonwealth of Georgia were the first to enact a law prohibiting the importation of slaves in their new colony, enslavement continued to be practiced in the other 12 English colonies well into the 19th century. Modern historians credit a religious revival movement called the Second Great Awakening (after the initial awakening in the mid-18th century) with bringing the issue of slavery to the forefront. This movement was the result of the wholesale destruction of churches and church property during the American Revolution and the fact that many Anglican clergy had fled America following the Declaration of Independence. In response, American believers had little choice but to meet in tents or camps for worship, cobbling together a largely improvised liturgy of prayer, preaching, and hymns. In time, this produced a revival movement that combined Pietist, Presbyterian, and Puritan ideas into the ideal of making America a shining "city upon a hill," a place that could serve as a moral beacon to the world.

The Great Awakening inspired thousands of volunteers to go out and help the poor, proselytize, promote women's rights, and curb excesses such as alcohol abuse. At the same time, preachers such as Charles Finney worked on a clandestine network of safe houses designed to spirit slaves from Southern plantations to havens in the North. Known as the Underground Railroad, this network may have saved as many as 100,000 slaves.

A split between the North, which was rapidly industrializing, and the South, which continued to rely on slave labor working its plantations, became inevitable. The first cracks appeared in the

THESE RUSTY HANDCUFFS were once used to restrain a slave.

HARRIET TUBMAN, who was born into slavery and became a leading American abolitionist who rescued more than 300 slaves, is shown at far left in this portrait from the early 20th century.

"GIVE THEM COLD STEEL BOYS" is an impression of Pickett's Charge during the 1863 Battle of Gettysburg by American illustrator Don Troiani.

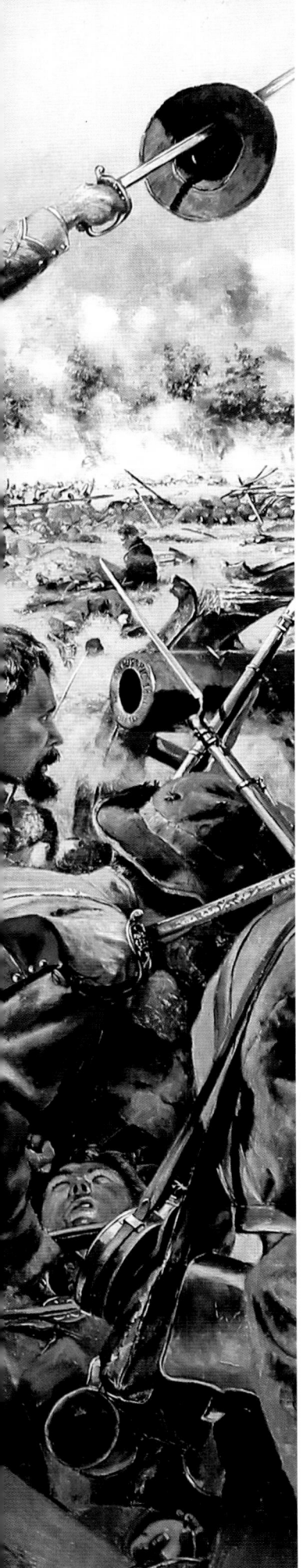

"I SHALL THROW AN OVERWHELMING FORCE ON THEIR ADVANCE . . . CREATE A PANIC AND VIRTUALLY DESTROY THE ARMY. [THEN] THE WAR WILL BE OVER."

GEN. ROBERT E. LEE BEFORE THE BATTLE OF GETTYSBURG

Southern Baptist Convention and the Old School Presbyterians, who broke away from their Northern affiliates over the issue of slavery. A political clash was bound to follow, particularly after the admittance in the 1850s of California, Oregon, and Minnesota as "free states" to the United States. This shifted the balance of power toward the North, much to the alarm of the Southern states.

The American Civil War

The issue came to a head during the presidential election of 1860. While the Southern states supported a pro-slavery Democrat, John Breckenridge, the Northern states coalesced around the Republican Abraham Lincoln. Lincoln did not campaign as a declared abolitionist, but in 1858, he had declared that the republic could not survive as a nation "half slave and half free." In the end, he won the day and was elected to the White House.

The reaction was almost immediate. The Southern states, led by South Carolina, voted to secede from the Union and established the Confederate States of America. Jefferson Davis, a politician from Mississippi who had served in the U.S. Senate and House of Representatives, was chosen as its president. In April 1861, Confederate forces attacked Fort Sumter in Charleston Harbor, igniting the American Civil War—the bloodiest conflict ever fought on American soil.

To avoid an irrevocable split of the nation,

CIVIL WAR PHOTOGRAPHY

The American Civil War was the first major conflict in which photographs captured the shocking violence of warfare, not only in newspapers and magazines but also as album cards, enlarged prints, and even so-called stereographs. It is a little-known fact that some 70 percent of all Civil War photography was taken with stereoscopic lenses. Many photographers used the wet-collodion process to create negative plates to develop an infinite number of prints. Well-known photographers such as Mathew Brady and George Barnard set up traveling darkrooms in canvas-covered wagons and followed the armies as they prepared for the next major clash. Few actually managed to take pictures in the heat of battle, so that most photos from this era usually show a battlefield after the armies had disengaged (at right). Still, pictures such as Timothy O'Sullivan's famous "The Harvest of Death," taken after the Battle of Gettysburg, fully revealed the gruesome reality of soldiers killed in combat.

Lincoln temporized on the slavery issue. He believed, like many in Congress, that the far more numerous Union Army would make short work of the Confederate forces. But the South had superior generals, including Stonewall Jackson, who dealt the North several defeats including his famous victory at Bull Run, Virginia, in July 1861. Moreover, in June 1862, a brilliant strategist, Gen. Robert E. Lee, took command of the Army of Northern Virginia and launched a daring invasion of the North through Maryland. Later that year, a massive clash between the two armies at Antietam left about 23,000 soldiers dead or wounded. This shocking outcome persuaded Lincoln on September 22, 1862, to issue the Emancipation Proclamation, which legally liberated all four million slaves in the rebellious states.

In summer 1863, Lee's battered army tried again to circumvent the Union troops by invading Pennsylvania. This time, however, the Union Army had learned from its mistakes and was now prepared to meet the Confederates at Gettysburg.

Fifth Maine jacket and cap

Although some Union infantry and cavalry units were pushed back, most of the army held firm and ultimately defeated a massive Confederate infantry assault, known ever since as the legendary Pickett's Charge. In all, the three-day battle resulted in 46,000 casualties—the largest toll of any Civil War battle. At the same time, Gen. Ulysses S. Grant captured the last Confederate fortification on the Mississippi River at Vicksburg. It was the turning point. Depleted and outnumbered, Lee led his army back to Virginia.

The writing was on the wall, and yet the South refused to give in. The Union Army then swept through Tennessee, Georgia, and the Carolinas, forcing Lee's surrender at Appomattox on April 9, 1865, mere months after the U.S. Congress passed the 13th Amendment abolishing slavery. President Lincoln was not able to savor the fruits of his victory. He was assassinated at Ford's Theater in Washington, D.C., by a Confederate sympathizer, actor John Wilkes Booth, on April 14, 1865, and died the next day. ◾

THE UNITED STATES CIVIL WAR 1861-1865

BRITISH NORTH AMERICA

WASHINGTON TERRITORY
OREGON
DAKOTA TERRITORY
MINN.
MICH.
WIS.
ME.
VT.
N.H.
N.Y.
MASS.
R.I.
CONN.
NEVADA TERR.
UTAH TERRITORY
NEBRASKA TERRITORY
IOWA
ILL.
IND.
OHIO
PA.
N.J.
DEL.
MD.
CALIFORNIA
COLORADO TERRITORY
KANSAS
MO.
KY.
VA.
PUBLIC LAND STRIP
NEW MEXICO TERRITORY
UNORGANIZED TERRITORY
ARK.
TENN.
N.C.
S.C.
GA.
MISS.
ALA.
LA.
TEXAS
FLA.

Boundary of Confederate States

Antietam (Sharpsburg) Sept. 17, 1862
Gettysburg July 1-3, 1863
1st and 2nd Manassas (Bull Run) July 21, 1861; Aug. 29-30, 1862
Fredericksburg Dec. 13, 1862
Wilderness May 5-6, 1864
Cold Harbor June 1-3, 1864
Chickamauga Sept. 19-20, 1863
Appomattox Court House Apr. 9, 1865
Siege of Petersburg mid June 1864- early Apr. 1865
Shiloh Apr. 6-7, 1862
Ft. Sumter Apr. 12-13, 1861
Chancellorsville May 1-4, 1863
Siege of Vicksburg May 18-July 4, 1863
Chattanooga Nov. 23-25, 1863

PACIFIC OCEAN
ATLANTIC OCEAN
MEXICO

Slave states that seceded
Slave states and regions remaining in the Union
Free states
United States territories
Battle

0 mi 400
0 km 400
Boundaries are as of late 1861.

UNION FORCES on Morris Island, South Carolina, fire 100-pounder Parrott cannons on the Confederate position at Fort Sumter in 1863.

A 1907 PORTRAIT of a young Tamil girl, adorned in jewelry and silk

THE AGE OF COLONIZATION

After the Napoleonic Wars, European powers continued to aggressively expand their spheres of influence in Southeast Asia and Africa as part of the race to obtain sugar, spices, coffee, and rubber—the demand for which would soar with the development of the automobile.

n the 17th and 18th centuries, the primary lure of Southeast Asia had been the quest for spices and tea. Now, with industrialization growing in Great Britain, Germany, and the United States, the demand shifted to rubber, tin, and oil, in addition to sugar, coffee, and cocoa. The development of the steamship, combined with substantial improvements in cannons and musketry, enabled the European powers to vastly extend their colonial control.

It was once again England, the victor of the Napoleonic Wars, that took the lead in this colonization effort, using India as its base. In 1819, British statesman Sir Stamford Raffles struck a deal with a Malay governor to acquire the old Portuguese trading port of "Singapura." Raffles then declared Singapore a tax-free port, which had the desired effect of drawing trading ships from around the region at the expense of Dutch ports in the East Indies. As wealth poured in, Singapore's population exploded from 340 to 10,000 in just five years. By the end of the 19th century, Singapore had become the leading transit point for tin, needed for the newly invented canning process, and rubber, the demand for which was soaring following the development of the automobile. But the port's principal source of revenue was a commodity that would become the scourge of Asia: opium, which accounted for as much as 50 percent of Singapore's revenues.

The Opium Wars

From 1636 onward, the Ming Dynasty of China had been steadily eroded by insurgents who were not native Han Chinese but a group known as the Jurchen, living in today's Chinese provinces of Jilin and Heilongjiang. In time, they would become known as the Manchu. In 1644, they seized Beijing and formally replaced the Ming Dynasty with the new Qing Dynasty. Qing rulers, however, were careful to embrace existing Han customs and Confucian ideals. Emperor Kangxi, who ascended the throne in 1661, lowered taxes and expanded access to education, which endeared him to his Han subjects. Unfortunately, the outbreak of a severe famine in 1796, coupled with a downturn in trade and widespread corruption, had a severe impact on Chinese society. The result was the White Lotus Rebellion, led by Buddhists who denounced the Manchu as foreign invaders. Though

AN OPIUM WEIGHT in the shape of a hamsa, an Asian goose, was made in Burma, today's Myanmar, around 1900.

> # "YOU DO NOT WISH OPIUM TO HARM YOUR OWN COUNTRY, BUT YOU CHOOSE TO BRING THAT HARM TO OTHER COUNTRIES SUCH AS CHINA. WHY?"
>
> **CHINESE GOVERNOR LIN ZEXU TO QUEEN VICTORIA OF GREAT BRITAIN**

ultimately defeated, this revolt left the Qing Dynasty severely weakened and vulnerable to foreign exploitation.

By this time, the British East India Company had developed a lucrative trade in smuggling opium from India into China. By some estimates, the export of opium would increase to nearly 700,000 pounds a year in the early decades of the 19th century. Opium accounted for 16 percent of East India Company receipts, which in turn were used to finance the expansion of Britain's control of India. The impact on the Chinese population, however, was devastating. Between 10 and 12 million Chinese living in the coastal areas, particularly Canton, were addicted. A highly placed Qing official, Governor Lin Zexu of Hunan and Hubei, wrote a letter to Queen Victoria begging the British government to intervene, but the illegal trade continued unimpeded.

The Chinese Daoguang emperor then ordered all the opium contraband to be seized and foreign opium ships to be denied entry into Chinese ports. Britain responded by dispatching a naval force that went on to bombard the port of Dinghai and other Chinese coastal areas. Bereft of a modern navy of its own or the means to defend its cities, China was forced into signing the 1842 Treaty of Nanking (or Nanjing). Under the terms of this odious agreement, Hong Kong Island was ceded to Britain, and five other ports were designated as transshipment areas for British products. In addition, the Chinese emperor was forced to remit reparation payments to the tune of $21 million. It was a humiliating defeat for a nation that had been one of the greatest powers in the world.

The Taiping Rebellion

The treaty's punitive terms further eroded the Chinese economy and destabilized the imperial system. The result was the 1850 Taiping Rebellion, led by an aspiring teacher named Hong Xiuquan who believed his mission was to restore some form of Christianity to China. The rebellion rapidly spread and in 1851 proclaimed a free state, the Taiping Heavenly Kingdom of Great Peace. Here, Hong was worshipped as the brother of Jesus and second Son of God. Notwithstanding these claims, Hong and a younger cousin, Hong Rengan, advocated a number of reforms, including the development of a comprehensive railway (after the

A MANCHU man and woman smoking opium during the final decades of the Qing Dynasty

AN OFFICIAL COURT PORTRAIT depicts the Daoguang emperor, seventh Chinese emperor of the Manchu-led Qing Dynasty.

NOTABLE DATES

1807
British missionary Robert Morrison begins Mandarin version of the Bible

1814
Holland cedes southern Africa to the British Empire

1819
Stamford Raffles acquires port of Singapore from local Malay governor

1837
Queen Victoria assumes the throne at age 18

1839
First of Opium Wars between China and the British Empire

1847
French vessels bombard Da Nang in Vietnam

1853
The Crimean War begins, foreshadowing industrial warfare

1867
The United States acquires Alaska from Russia

1875
Hudson Taylor begins an evangelizing mission in China

1876
King Leopold of Belgium takes Congo as his private preserve

1882
Britain assumes control of Egypt

1883
Vietnam becomes a French protectorate

invention of the steam locomotive in 1825 in Britain), the establishment of private banks, the organization of a national postal system, and the development of steamships for commerce and defense. In 1860, the Taiping came very close to capturing Shanghai before it was defeated and ultimately destroyed.

In the meantime, a civil war had broken out in 1853 between two rival emperors. This did not deter one enterprising official from confiscating a British ship reportedly filled with opium and throwing its crew into prison. Naturally, this outraged the British ambassador, who summoned the British Navy to the Cantonese shores once more. While salvo after salvo reduced much of Canton to ashes, a Chinese mob stormed various Euro-pean shops and buildings and put them to the torch. China, it seemed, was descending into chaos, much of it wrought by the greed of the British Empire.

New negotiations—once again conducted under duress—forced the Chinese in 1858 to accept the Treaty of Tien-Tsin. This treaty not only legalized the opium trade but also gave British traders access to all of China's main cities, where starving laborers were particularly vulnerable to opium exploitation. What's more, Western mis-sionaries were now granted the right to proselytize anywhere in the country and even purchase prop-erty and build churches. This had a beneficial effect in that many of these missionaries built schools and hospitals, often in rural regions where

"WHEN PEOPLE OF THIS EARTH KEEP NOTHING
FOR THEIR PRIVATE USE, BUT GIVE ALL THINGS TO GOD
FOR ALL TO USE IN COMMON, THEN EVERY PLACE
SHALL HAVE EQUAL SHARES, AND EVERYONE
BE CLOTHED AND FED."

HONG XIUQUAN, LEADER OF THE TAIPING REBELLION

no such services had ever existed before. Many Western denominations considered overseas missionary work a moral duty, with the aim of bringing both Christian salvation and the "civilizing" force of European culture to undeveloped regions. As a result of their efforts, by the beginning of the 20th century, there were some 1.4 million Catholics and more than half a million Protestants in China alone.

The Colonization of Africa and Asia

Contrary to British missionaries in China, British and Dutch colonial administrators made little attempt to convert the native populations under their sway. As early as 1835, a church dedicated to St. Andrew was built in Singapore, close to the administrative district, but only for the purpose of serving British colonials. The Dutch too were content to leave local faith traditions in place. The first church to rise in Java was the Blenduk Church, built in 1753 in the late baroque style then still in fashion, primarily to serve colonial adherents of the Dutch Reformed Church. The Dutch government was too busy harvesting valuable commodities from Java and other islands to worry about matters of faith. By the end of the 19th century, Java was producing most of the world's quinine and pepper; more than a third of its rubber; a quarter of its coconut products; and a fifth of its tea, sugar, and

coffee. The advent of the automobile also made it a key provider of oil.

For France, the situation was quite different. Since the French Revolution, it seemed that the nation had trouble deciding in what form it should be governed. After the demise of the Napoleonic Empire, the foppish Louis XVIII was once again

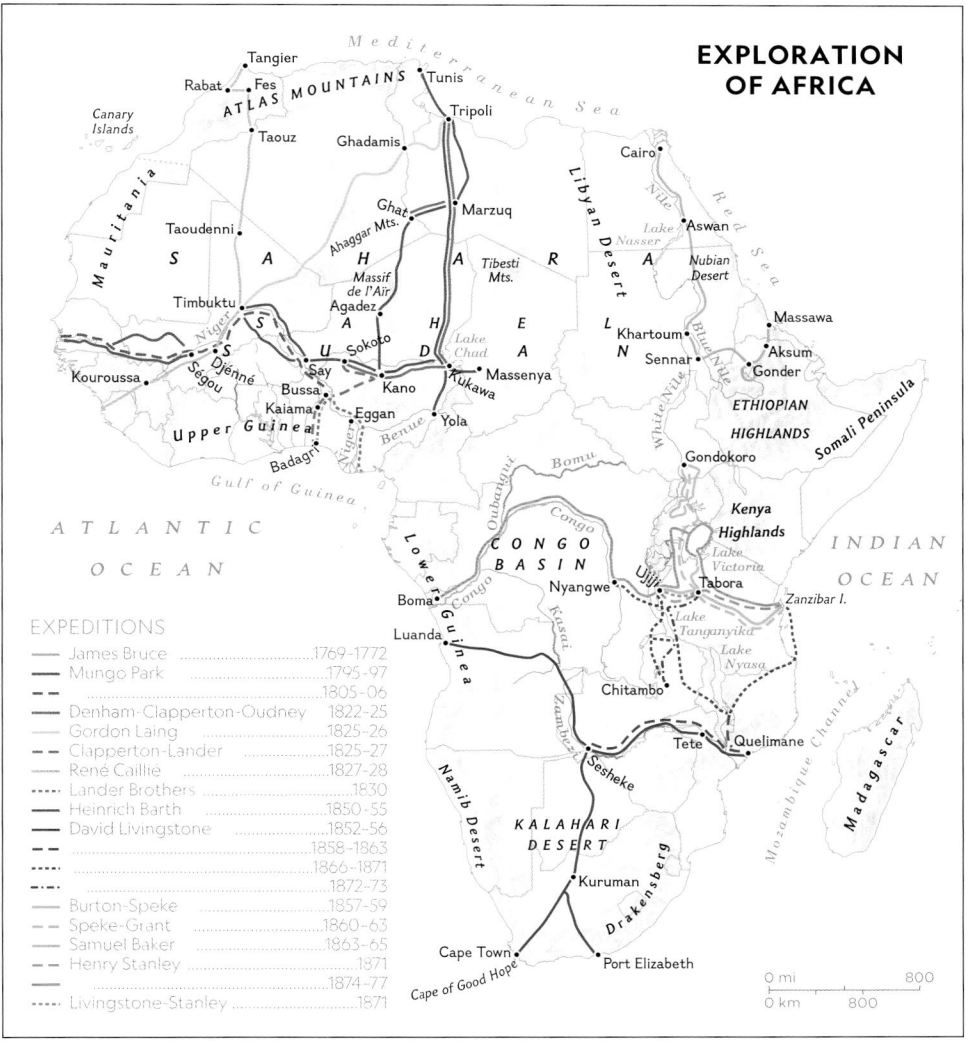

EXPLORATION
OF AFRICA

EXPEDITIONS
James Bruce 1769–1772
Mungo Park 1795–97
....1805–06
Denham-Clapperton-Oudney 1822–25
Gordon Laing 1825–26
Clapperton-Lander 1825–27
René Caillié 1827–28
Lander Brothers 1830
Heinrich Barth 1850–55
David Livingstone 1852–56
....1858–1863
....1866–1871
....1872–73
Burton-Speke 1857–59
Speke-Grant 1860–63
Samuel Baker 1863–65
Henry Stanley 1871
....1874–77
Livingstone-Stanley 1871

A DETAIL of the Benin Plaques, created from the 16th century on, that once decorated the royal palace of the king of Benin. Looted by British forces in 1897, the bronzes are currently being claimed by the Nigerian government.

placed on the French throne in an ill-fated effort to restore the Bourbon Dynasty. That obviously did not sit well with much of the French population. In 1830, King Charles X was toppled and replaced by a constitutional monarchy, led by King Louis-Philippe. But republican sentiment was strong, and soon revolts threatened to paralyze many of the nation's principal cities. In 1848, the king abdicated and a new republic, La Deuxième République, was declared. Ironically, its president was none other than the nephew of Napoleon Bonaparte, Louis Napoleon. Four years later, this politician took a leaf from his uncle's playbook and staged a coup that, amazingly, restored the French Empire, known as Le Second Empire (1852–1870).

Along the way, however, successive French governments—whether of the royal or republican ilk—recognized that France needed to catch up in the colonial race with its European rivals. French troops occupied Algeria in 1830, followed by the conquest of other African colonies, during which more than 150,000 French soldiers and an estimated 300,000 Algerians died. France also set its sights on Vietnam, which had been unified by the Nguyen emperor Gia Long in 1802 with French support. In the meantime, hundreds of French missionaries had fanned out through Southeast Asia in search of souls to save. Their missions now provided the French government with the perfect pretext to intervene militarily. In 1847, French forces attacked Da Nang in retaliation for the presumed persecution of French missionaries by Emperor Tu Duc. Fourteen years later, Napoleon III occu-

pied Saigon. By 1883, Vietnam had become a French protectorate.

In 1887, all of the French possessions in Asia, including Cambodia, were consolidated into a federation known as French Indochina, or Indochine. In 1893, Laos was added as well. This so alarmed the British that it seized Burma to act as a buffer between the French and British spheres of influence.

A similar race for colonial possessions took place in Africa. Holland still held on to large parts of South Africa, including Cape Town, acquired in 1652, but then ceded much of its control to Britain in 1814. King Leopold of Belgium established the Congo as his private preserve in 1876. Britain took control of Egypt in 1882. Two years later, the Conference of Western Powers carved Africa up into British, French, and German spheres.

The British Raj

It has become fashionable to denounce European colonialism as an unmitigated disaster. It is true that many colonial powers were interested only in extracting the resources of the territories under their control while brutally exploiting the native population. But some nuance is in order. While the Dutch and Belgian governments cared little for their subject peoples (until a belated reform movement took hold in the Netherlands in the 1920s), the British did make some effort to improve the standard of living in their dominions. In India, for example, British physicians undertook a major initiative to study the epidemiology of infectious diseases that were ravishing India's provinces and developed a number of medicines in response. As early as 1785, medical departments were set up in Bengal, Madras, and Bombay, with 234 surgeons on staff. In 1835, the first medical college was opened in

Official brochure of French Indochina

THIS OFFICIAL 1853 portrait of Emperor Napoleon III of France was painted by German artist Franz Xaver Winterhalter, who in the mid-19th century was much in demand for portraits of European royalty.

THE CENTRAL POST OFFICE of Saigon, today's Ho Chi Minh City, was designed by Alfred Foulhoux and Gustave Eiffel, the engineer responsible for the Eiffel Tower in Paris.

"THE DAY THE POWER
OF LOVE OVERRULES
THE LOVE OF POWER,
THE WORLD WILL
KNOW PEACE."

MOHANDAS GANDHI,
INDIA'S INDEPENDENCE LEADER

Calcutta, which in the years to come would train hundreds of native physicians and specialists. By 1880, some 1,200 public hospitals and pharmacies were operating in India; 20 years later, the British Raj had secured a hospital for every 330 square miles. Similarly, scores of schools were operating throughout the country, though many of these were run by religious missions.

Beginning in 1853, the British also built India's railway network. By 1860, the Raj (as British colonial India was known) operated the ninth largest railroad network in the world—ahead of the United States and many European countries. While it is true, as some historians have argued, that the development of this network was largely driven by military and commercial considerations, the subcontinent would not have been able to function in the modern era without its railways.

French colonial administrators were less charitable when it came to raising the standard of living in French Indochina. They set out to create beautiful, French-style administrative centers in places like Saigon and Hanoi, some of which have survived to this day. For example, Gustave Eiffel, the engineer who designed the Eiffel Tower for the 1889 International Exposition in Paris, was prevailed on to build Saigon's lovely post office in 1886. Between 1877 and 1880, the French also built a stupendous neo-Romanesque cathedral in the heart of Saigon, using red bricks from Marseilles and stained glass blown in Chartres. In the countryside, however, the French ran large rubber, cocoa, and coffee plantations using local labor as virtual serfs.

SMOKE RISES from chimneys of the Staffordshire Potteries, a producer of ceramic products, in Stoke-on-Trent, Great Britain.

The Industrial Revolution

Before the 1830s, Europe's societies were overwhelmingly agrarian, with most farmers—or peasants—practicing subsistence agriculture, raising a diverse spectrum of crops to feed their families. In the mid-19th century, however, mechanization, made possible by steam power, changed this model forever. These technological changes, which together are referred to as the Industrial Revolution, obliterated the centuries-old apprentice model in which productivity was measured by what human hands could accomplish. Machines could do much of this work better and faster, increasing manufacturing a hundred-fold. All this required labor, however—industrial labor, trained to perform the same mechanical tasks over and over again, often for as much as 10 or 12 hours a day. This demand pulled thousands of farmhands to the cities, transforming places like Britain's Birmingham and Manchester into major metropolitan centers.

Despite the hardship of working in mills or factories (including the egregious exploitation of child labor), the Industrial Revolution did succeed in raising the standards of living after a long decline in the 18th century. Workers' wages rose, albeit slowly, while food costs dropped because of improvements in production and transportation. By the second half of the 19th century, famine and malnutrition had been mostly eradicated. On the downside, the concentration of industrial labor in urban areas led to shantytowns with unsanitary conditions, where disease was often rampant.

Another outcome of this process was that Europe's population began to grow at an unprecedented rate, largely as a result of medical advancement and better nutrition. In England, the population doubled between 1801 and 1850 and then doubled again between 1850 and 1901. Though the Industrial Revolution was relatively slow in coming to France and Germany, their population was growing by leaps and bounds by the 1870s as well. As several historians have noted, were it not for the Industrial Revolution, this population growth would have strained available food supplies in Europe to the breaking point. Mechanization had become an existential necessity.

As part of these changes, a new social class made its appearance. Vastly improved educational opportunities—a result of the Age of Reason—produced a new middle class of professionals, doctors, lawyers, bankers, entrepreneurs, and artisans. In time, this bourgeoisie displaced the traditional role of the nobility and fueled a growing demand for civic services and urban beautification. In Paris, Emperor Napoleon III ordered its medieval center to be destroyed so as to create the wide boulevards, bordered by elegant apartment blocks, that we so admire today. Instead of the cathedral, the nuclei of urban life were now the railway station, the hotel, the theater, and the opera house.

At the same time, new intellectual movements took Europe's cafés and salons by storm. In 1859, British naturalist Charles Darwin published *On the Origin of Species,* based on his observation of the extraordinary life-forms of the Galápagos Islands.

Darwin concluded that life on Earth was the product of a long evolutionary process of natural selection that ultimately produced *Homo sapiens.* Echoing that idea was the theory by a German philosopher named Georg Hegel that humanity was on a constant course of ascendancy. Unlike Kant, Hegel believed that there was no limit to what the human mind could imagine or achieve.

In 1899, an Austrian professor of neuropathology named Sigmund Freud published *Die Traumdeutung* (*The Interpretation of Dreams*), which argued that a person's essential being was not his or her soul, as Christianity believed, but that person's sense of self, or psyche. In Freud's view, a person's individual character was shaped not by a yearning for moral rectitude or salvation but by individual desires rooted in childhood development. His identification of the inner self as the primary motive for human behavior would become the foundation of a new discipline: psychology.

All of these ideas, propelled by a buoyant

THIS 1870 PORTRAIT of Charles Darwin was taken by renowned British photographer Julia Margaret Cameron.

THE RETURN OF THE PAST

The Victorian penchant for delineating history as a sequence of periods produced a desire to dress its buildings in decorative styles of the past. The Industrial Revolution, which allowed the mechanical manufacture of virtually anything, abetted this movement. The result was a series of neo-isms, designed to express the unique character of a building or its civic setting. Neo-Gothic architecture, for example, was deemed appropriate for cathedrals, whereas the neo-Classical style was used for parliamentary buildings and other monuments of Western democracy. Neo-Romanesque would flourish for civic buildings in the American East and Midwest and exert a strong influence on the Chicago school of Louis Sullivan and Frank Lloyd Wright. In Cologne, Germany, the neo-Gothic movement stimulated a drive to finish the city's cathedral (at left), first begun in 1248, while inspiring many other neo-Gothic churches throughout Europe.

FRENCH IMPRESSIONIST
Édouard Manet painted "In the Conservatory" in 1877, depicting his friends, the Guillemets, in an idle moment in the greenhouse of 70 Rue d'Amsterdam, Paris.

"WE ARE NOT INTERESTED IN THE POSSIBILITIES
OF DEFEAT. THEY DO NOT EXIST."

QUEEN VICTORIA OF THE UNITED KINGDOM

economy and wealth pouring in from overseas colonies, produced an era of irrepressible optimism. Contemporary observers saw their age—often known as the Victorian era, after the improbably long reign of Britain's Queen Victoria from 1837 to 1901—as the culmination of all that had passed before, politically, culturally, and morally.

The Franco-German War

This optimism was tested by the reappearance of European wars just when many believed that the thriving European economy had made armed conflict a thing of the past. Among others, Napoleon's fall had stimulated the ascendancy of the Prussian House of Hohenzollern. The Hohenzollern monarchy had ambitions of becoming the dominant power of continental Europe, propelled by a sense of Protestant manifest destiny. In rattling its saber and flexing its militarist muscle, the Hohenzollern crown saw itself as the new leader of an old European struggle: a *Kulturkampf,* or cultural struggle, between nationalist Protestantism and the crumbling power of international Catholicism.

King Wilhelm I, who rose to the Prussian throne in 1861, actively promoted the idea of combining all of the disparate German states into one great empire, *ein Deutsches Reich.* In 1866, he made good on that promise by declaring war on the Austrian Hapsburg Empire, thus gaining control of several German principalities, including Hanover, Hesse-Kassel, and the Free City of Frankfurt. This greatly alarmed Napoleon III, who feared that a German Empire would destabilize the balance of power in Europe.

In 1870, the French emperor persuaded the French parliament to declare war on Prussia. It was

*Pocket watch,
Victorian era*

a serious mistake. Napoleon III did not have the military acumen of his uncle, and French troops were no match for the superbly drilled Prussian Army. On January 28, 1871, Paris fell to German forces. France was humiliated to the core. Its ore-rich region of Alsace-Lorraine, vital to French industry, was annexed. Worse, in the Hall of Mirrors at Versailles, the former symbol of French absolutist hegemony, King Wilhelm I was declared emperor of the new German Reich, combining 27 German kingdoms and principalities into a vast nation-state. Thus were sown the seeds of German militarism of the 20th century.

Devastated, France reverted to a republic once more, its third in less than a century, which became known as the Troisième République. Most Europeans expected the nation to take many decades to recover from this catastrophe. No doubt, many believed that France would be forced to relinquish its role as Europe's center of art, music, and fashion. But amazingly, the opposite happened: France paid off the reparation demands imposed by King Wilhelm in record time and then embarked on a golden age of creative revival known as the belle époque, or the "beautiful age."

In Paris, the era spawned a new art movement, Impressionism, as a reaction against the worn-out historical themes of academic painting. Impressionists like Edouard Manet, Edgar Degas, Berthe Morisot, and Claude Monet embraced the pulse of modern life, painting milliners, washerwomen, ballerinas, and young couples dancing the night away in Parisian *cafés dansants.* Their startling scenes, painted *en plein air* ("in the open air") in rapid brushstrokes and brilliant colors, would lay the foundation for 20th-century modern art. ∎

CHAPTER 9

THE WORLD AT WAR

1900—1950

SOLDIERS OF the U.S. Army's First Infantry Division wade ashore under withering fire at Omaha Beach during the Normandy invasion of June 6, 1944.

CONTENTS

20TH-CENTURY CONFLICTS

Although the 20th century opened on a note of great optimism, an escalating arms race and growing tensions between European states precipitated two devastating world wars. A naval arms race, sparked by the all-metal British battleship *Dreadnought,* led in 1914 to a devastating world war in which some nine million soldiers and at least six million civilians were killed. This Great War, later called World War I, erased the optimism of the Victorian era and showed that deepening economic ties between European nations did not necessarily eliminate the threat of armed conflict. Though sparked by the assassination of Habsburg Archduke Franz Ferdinand by Serbian-trained terrorists, the war was the outcome of long-simmering tensions between the Habsburg Empire and its foe, the Kingdom of Serbia. Interlocking treaty obligations between European nations turned this regional conflict into a major world war.

The Fall of Empires

The Great War differed from previous European conflicts in one important aspect: It was conducted on an industrial scale, abetted by new technologies such as the machine gun, long-range artillery, airplane, telegraph, and even poison gas. When the war finally ended on November 11, 1918, after the arrival of the American Expeditionary Forces, the map of Europe was redrawn in ways that no 19th-century European would have recognized. Four major empires fell: the Russian, Austrian, German, and Turkish Ottoman Empires. The 1919 Treaty of Versailles, negotiated in the same Hall of Mirrors at the palace of Versailles where Emperor Wilhelm I had proclaimed the German Empire in 1871, imposed crippling reparation payments on Germany. This, combined with the Wall Street crash of 1929, eviscerated the German middle class and led to mass unemployment. The political crisis crippled the German Weimar Republic and led to the rise of populist agitator Adolf Hitler. As political instability spread throughout Europe, similar autocratic or fascist regimes appeared in Italy, Spain, and the Balkans, and France's Third Republic was torn between communist and nationalist forces. Great Britain, meanwhile, was distracted by Irish demands for home rule, while in the United States, President Franklin D. Roosevelt was focused on a vast federal work program, known as the New Deal, to stabilize the American economy. In Spain, a group of generals led by Francisco Franco launched a civil war against the democratically elected republican government.

In Russia, the October Revolution of 1917 toppled Tsar Nicholas II and installed a Bolshevik dictatorship led by Vladimir Lenin. After Lenin's death in 1924, fellow revolutionary Joseph Stalin seized power and would rule the Soviet Union with an iron fist until his death in 1953. In China, the 1911 Xinhai Revolution brought an end to the Qing Dynasty and China's 2,000-year history of imperial dynasties. In 1933, Hitler was appointed German chancellor. Six years later, he launched a new war of aggression that would leave no part of the world untouched. This time, the death toll was 75 million people in all theaters, or about 3 percent of the total world population. At war's end, an exhausted world found itself ruled by two nuclear world powers, the United States and the Soviet Union. ∎

A JAPANESE WATCH stopped the moment that an atom bomb exploded over Hiroshima on August 6, 1945.

THE OPTIMISM of a new era was on full display at the Palace of Electricity of the 1900 Universal Exposition in Paris, France.

AN ALBANIAN WOMAN passes through the immigration procedures at Ellis Island, New York, in 1905.

DAWN OF THE 20TH CENTURY

The 20th century opened with the 1900 Universal Exposition in Paris that showcased an astounding range of new technologies. But as the gap between industrialized and agricultural nations widened, unrest spread, China's Qing Dynasty was toppled, and the major powers of Europe launched an arms race.

The 20th century opened on a wave of optimism. In 1900, Paris was once again host to a major world exhibition, the Universal Exposition, in which every major nation on Earth was represented, proudly showcasing its great achievements in dedicated pavilions. More than 50 million people visited the fairgrounds to admire such novelties as the diesel engine, motion pictures, escalators, and gramophones. Many visitors were fascinated by the display of new weapons of war, such as the Maxim machine gun and a recoilless cannon forged by the Krupp works in Germany. Guns like these no longer fired along the gunner's line of sight, straight into an advancing enemy column, as had been the case during the Napoleonic Wars era and the American Civil War. Instead, the propulsive force of its ammunition was such that an explosive shell could be launched on a high trajectory to hit enemy forces many miles in the rear, out of sight of the gunner. This new form of artillery needed an observer, such as an officer perched high in a bell tower, to see the point of impact. Using a field telephone (another new invention), this artillery officer could then provide new coordinates and, once the enemy position was pinpointed, order the gun to fire for effect. It was clear to everyone, and certainly the German High Command, that such long-range artillery would revolutionize modern warfare by extending the battlefield to many miles around. At the same time, this fearsome new weapon would also be capable of inflicting unimaginable damage to surrounding towns and villages, causing scores of civilian casualties.

That the danger of such a conflict was real was reinforced by the tensions that ran underneath the fair's international feeling of goodwill. France was still smarting over its defeat during the Franco-Prussian War and the loss of its provinces of Alsace and Lorraine. Its officer corps was itching for revanche, an opportunity to redeem its humiliation and recover the lost lands. The Germans knew this, of course, and so its High Command had been stealthily working on a plan, developed by Count Alfred Von Schlieffen, to attack France in a vast movement of its infantry through neutral Belgium. The Germans knew that could potentially bring Britain into the war, since Britain and

THE BING COMPANY of Nuremberg, Germany, made this Bingola II gramophone in 1903.

> # "IT IS A TIME WHEN ONE'S SPIRIT IS SUBDUED AND SAD, ONE KNOWS NOT WHY."
>
> MARK TWAIN AND CHARLES DUDLEY WARREN, *THE GILDED AGE*

France had pledged to defend Belgium's neutrality as part of the post-Napoleonic settlement of Europe. But, the Germans reasoned, ever since the Napoleonic Wars, Britain had been content to wallow in "splendid isolation," keeping the meddling of European kings and queens at arm's length.

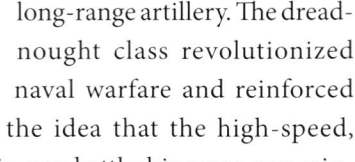

Replica of Wright Flyer, 1903

It was Germany's great misfortune that its pacifist emperor, Frederick III, died after only 90 days in office, succeeded by the bellicose young Wilhelm II. A restless and deeply insecure man, painfully aware of his malformed left arm, the new kaiser was eager to prove himself as a statesman, preferably unhindered by the advice of his more experienced councilors. Among other missteps, the kaiser embarked on a foolhardy expansion of Germany's naval fleet, explicitly challenging Britain for control of the high seas. In the meantime, Britain had developed a revolutionary new battleship, the *Dreadnought,* the first all-metal ship propelled by steam turbines and bristling with long-range artillery. The dreadnought class revolutionized naval warfare and reinforced the idea that the high-speed, big-gun battleship was a war-winning weapon, particularly when a modern Japanese naval force destroyed the Russian Navy at the Battle of Tsushima in 1905. Eventually, however, German politicians had to face the fact that its naval program took a huge economic toll. In 1912, Chancellor Theobald von Bethmann-Hollweg of Germany abandoned the dreadnought race and instead focused on a more insidious new weapon: the submarine.

Even as the naval arms race escalated and the Continent inexorably moved toward war, few people believed that a major conflict was possible. Newspaper editors opined that national economies were now so intertwined that a European war was unthinkable. Inevitably, diplomats would intervene, cooler heads would prevail, and bourses would go on making money.

The Gilded Age

The feeling was shared on the other side of the Atlantic. For the past 30 years, the United States had enjoyed a period known as the Gilded Age, when huge fortunes were made in new industries such as the development of transcontinental railroads. Inspired by the title of a novel by authors Mark Twain and Charles Dudley Warren, the term effectively captures the idea that while on the surface everything seemed glamorous, in reality things were

THE H.M.S. *DREADNOUGHT,* first all-metal, steam-propelled battleship with long-range guns, revolutionized naval warfare in 1906 and launched a worldwide arms race.

532 THE WORLD AT WAR

RAILROAD CREWS from the East and West meet to lay the last rail of the transcontinental Union Pacific Railroad at Promontory Summit, Utah, in 1869.

NOTABLE DATES

1900
The Universal Exposition in Paris opens

1900
The British capture much of South Africa in the Boer War

1900
Western allies put down the Boxer Rebellion in China

1901
U.S. President William McKinley is assassinated

1901
Cuba officially becomes a U.S. protectorate

1901
Australia achieves independence as part of the British Commonwealth

1903
Orville and Wilbur Wright fly the first motorized airplane

1906
Britain launches its all-metal dreadnought, igniting a naval arms race

1907
An unprecedented 1.2 million immigrants enter the United States

1911
The Xinhai Revolution topples the Qing Dynasty of China

1912
The *Titanic* sinks after hitting an iceberg in the Atlantic Ocean

1912
Sun Yat-sen is elected president of the Republic of China

THE NEW YORK PUBLIC LIBRARY, completed by New York firm Carrère & Hastings in 1911, is one of the foremost buildings in the Beaux Arts style that exemplified the Gilded Age.

EMPIRES IN 1900

- American (U.S.)
- British
- Danish
- Dutch
- French
- German
- Italian
- Japanese
- Ottoman
- Portuguese
- Russian
- Spanish

quite different. While it is true that the rapid industrialization of the North and West of the United States led to an average wage growth between 1860 and 1890 of 60 percent, with annual wages peaking at $425 in 1890, much of this productivity was sustained by child labor and the exploitation of poor immigrants from eastern Europe. As a result, wealth became increasingly concentrated in wealthy enclaves of the major cities, while millions lived in abject poverty.

The West in particular experienced unprecedented rates of growth in sectors such as farming, mining, and the cultivation of large herds of cattle. Despite major recessions in 1873, 1882, and 1893, the American economy kept growing, except in the southern states. The South had yet to recover from the devastation of the American Civil War and remained largely bound to the cultivation of crops such as cotton and tobacco, with little industrialization taking place.

The construction of railroads was one of the prime movers of American economic activity, with its attendant need for heavy industries such as steel and coal. The first transcontinental railroad was inaugurated in 1869, linking the farming

and ranching output in the West with the high demand for food in cities in the Midwest and the East. By the mid-1890s, the United States had effectively bypassed Great Britain as the leading industrial nation in the world. To sustain this economic growth required capital, however, and this led to an increasing consolidation of leading industries. By 1900, much of America's economic activity, including steel, oil, telephone, farming, and cattle, was held by a handful of monopolies such as Standard Oil and American Telephone and Telegraph Company. While these businesses offered plenty of opportunities for young, educated workers, they also stifled competition.

Nevertheless, the growing railroad network unlocked major parts of America as never before. For the first time, middle-class families could travel through their state and across the country, which in turn produced the development of an entirely new industry, spawning untold numbers of hotels, restaurants, and entertainment venues. Suddenly the "big city" was in everyone's reach. Cities like Chicago, Kansas City, and Winnipeg in Canada became huge rail centers where meat, wheat, and other perishable food products could

THE BRASS CANDLESTICK TELEPHONE, with a separate transmitter and receiver, was introduced in the late 1890s and remained in use through the 1940s.

be stored and shipped in refrigerated railroad cars across the country. As a result, the average American diet improved markedly, with prices dropping as a result of the growing food supply.

American prosperity attracted waves of immigrants in unprecedented numbers, particularly from eastern and southern Europe. In 1907, a peak year, more than 1.2 million immigrants entered the country, often prodded by religious, racial, or political persecution at home. As a result, America's religious constellation changed. Catholics had already become the country's largest denomination in 1850, but by 1890 their population tripled, largely as a result of immigration from Europe. This led to tensions, particularly in the South, with the formation of groups like the Ku Klux Klan that actively promoted discrimination against Catholics, Jews, and African Americans.

The Pan American Exposition

The Gilded Age found its culmination in the 1901 Pan American Exposition, held in Buffalo, New York, with the aim of fostering "commercial well-being and understanding among the American Republics." Following in the astounding success of the Columbian Exposition of 1893 in Chicago, the fair was conceived as a showcase of magnificent pavilions, built in the neoclassical style known as beaux arts. Among its highlights was the first large-scale deployment of electric lights that illuminated the grounds at night—thrilling everyone who saw it.

On September 5, 1901, President William McKinley decided to visit the grounds. A day after delivering a speech in which he praised such

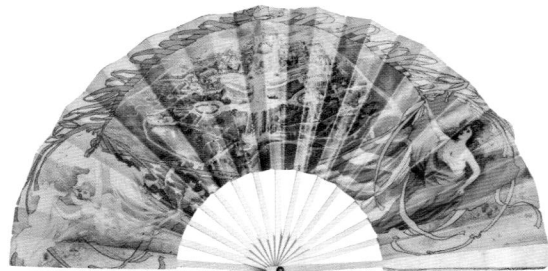

THIS COLORFUL FAN was sold as a souvenir during the 1901 Pan-American Exposition in Buffalo, New York.

A BIRD'S-EYE VIEW of the 1901 Pan-American Exposition in Buffalo, New York, depicts a series of sumptuous neoclassical pavilions arrayed around a series of large pools and canals.

expositions as "timekeepers of progress [that] record the world's advancement," he was shot in the stomach by an anarchist named Leon Czolgosz. A steelworker by trade, Czolgosz had lost his job in the recession of 1893. Though the wound was not immediately fatal, the president died eight days later of gangrene. He was succeeded by Vice President Theodore Roosevelt. On October 29, 1901, Czolgosz was executed in the electric chair, an event that was later reenacted in a film shot by the Edison Studios.

A watch from a Titanic *victim*

The *Titanic*

Two major events served as a reminder that rapid industrialization came at a cost. In 1912 came the shocking news that the R.M.S. *Titanic,* a vast new ocean liner built by the White Star Line, had floundered on its maiden voyage from Southampton to New York. Like the *Dreadnought,* the *Titanic* was the product of a mind-set that believed that new technology knew no bounds and that bigger was always better. Built at the Harland and Wolff shipyard in Belfast, the *Titanic* was designed by Thomas Andrews as the largest ship afloat at the time. On its first and only voyage, it carried 2,223 passengers and crew in three classes. The first-class accommodation was designed to trump anything that had been available on liners before, including a swimming pool, a gymnasium, and a choice of top-class restaurants. The liner was also equipped with remotely activated watertight compartments and doors, which prompted the press to call it "unsinkable." Indeed, the ship carried only enough lifeboats for 1,178 people, about half the number of passengers and crew onboard.

On April 14, 1912, four days after leaving the port of Southampton, the *Titanic* struck an iceberg that cut a deep gash in its starboard side and, fatefully, exposed five of its 16 watertight compart-

THE FIRST FLIGHT

Fascinated by the possibility of motorized flight since the 1890s, two bicycle builders from Ohio, Orville and Wilbur Wright, decided to try to realize the dream that had fascinated humankind since the days of Leonardo da Vinci. They built a wind tunnel and started to test various models of gliders with the goal of creating a wing that could lift a person. The result was the Wright Flyer (at left), a manned glider built of spruce wood and equipped with a 12-horsepower gasoline engine driving twin propellers. On December 17, 1903, Orville was able to fly this contraption from Kitty Hawk on North Carolina's Outer Banks. Though the flight lasted only 12 seconds, covering a distance of 120 feet, the Wright Brothers demonstrated the feasibility of powered flight in a heavier-than-air machine. The world would never be the same. Just 11 years later, during World War I, airplanes developed into fighter and bomber aircraft equipped with machine guns.

ments to the sea. At 2:20 a.m., less than three hours after the collision, the ship broke in half and sank, taking more than 1,500 souls with it to the depths of the Atlantic Ocean. The news shocked the world and prompted numerous government inquiries that led to new rules of maritime safety. The remains of the *Titanic* were discovered in 1985 at a depth of 12,415 feet. Since then, numerous explorations have recorded the wreck's increasing disintegration.

The Chinese Revolution

Another event that made world headlines took place in China in 1911. Throughout the first decade of the century, China was riven by numerous plots to overthrow the Qing Dynasty. As we saw, China had been forced to accept humiliating terms after the Opium Wars, which exposed it to

foreign exploitation and laid bare its vulnerability to modern arms, including battleships. Throughout the remainder of the 19th century, Qing emperors tried to improve the fighting ability of the once redoubtable Imperial Army, but China's defeat during the first Sino-Japanese War of 1895 demonstrated that only a drastic reform of China's feudal society could raise the nation to modern standards. This was indeed the aim of a new program initiated by the Guangxu emperor in 1898, known as the Hundred Days' Reform. A coup led by the ultraconservative Empress Dowager Cixi, however, toppled the emperor and brought the reform movement to a halt.

Two years later, the empress threw her support behind the Boxer Rebellion, a popular revolt against all foreign influences in China, including Christian missionaries. In response, a coalition of

THE REMAINS of the *Titanic* were discovered in 1985 off the coast of Newfoundland at a depth of more than two miles.

"IF WE DO NOT EARNESTLY PROMOTE NATIONALISM
AND WELD TOGETHER OUR FOUR HUNDRED MILLIONS
INTO A STRONG NATION, WE FACE A TRAGEDY."

SUN YAT-SEN, FOUNDER OF REPUBLICAN CHINA

eight nations, including the United States, tsarist Russia, Britain, and France, launched an invasion with a combined force of 20,000 troops. They handily defeated the Imperial Army, freed the besieged Westerners who had sought refuge in the diplomatic quarter, and engaged in the wholesale plunder of Beijing and its surrounding territory. Western troops were stationed in Beijing while reparation payments of $333 million were imposed on the Chinese government.

From that time forward, China was in ferment, with various revolutionary groups agitating to topple the Qing Dynasty, some of whom sought to restore a monarchy led by the ethnic majority Han. A charismatic physician named Sun Yat-sen, however, had a different aim: to reconstitute China

as a modern republic. In 1905, he was able to consolidate a number of revolutionary groups with his Xingzhonghui ("Revive China") movement, which soon became the dominant revolutionary force. In response, the Qing Dynasty tried to refashion itself as a constitutional monarchy, abrogating the autocratic power of the emperor, but it was all too little, too late. By December 1911, the revolutionary forces were in possession of the strategic city of Nanjing. On January 1, 1912, Sun Yat-sen, head of the newly formed Kuomintang (Nationalist People's Party) was elected as the first president of the Republic of China. Two months later, on February 12, 1912, the last Qing emperor formally abdicated, and the nation's 2,000-year imperial history came to an end. ■

THE PACIFIC AND EAST ASIA
SEPTEMBER 1, 1940

SPHERE OF INFLUENCE

American (U.S.)
British
Dutch
French (Vichy)
Japanese
Russian
No strong alliances

1940 features are shown.

CHILD REFUGEES from the Boxer Rebellion were brought to safety by a priest, Father Quilloux, during the Battle of Tientsin, China, in 1900.

THE FIRST WORLD WAR

World War I was the largest conflict up to that time. Although the combatants predicted that the war would be over "before the leaves fell from the trees," the introduction of new mechanized arms ensured that the conflict would last four years, forever erasing the optimism and stability of Old Europe.

I n the summer of 1914, most people in France, Britain, and Belgium had never heard of Franz Ferdinand, heir to the Habsburg throne of Austria-Hungary. In 1867, the ancient Habsburg Empire had morphed into a large, multinational realm anchored on the merger of two major entities: the Austrian Empire and the Hungarian kingdom. Led by Emperor Franz Joseph in Vienna, one of the longest-reigning monarchs in history, the so-called dual monarchy ruled over a vast swath of Europe in which 12 languages were spoken. This unwieldy state was slowly torn apart by ethnic tensions among Slovaks, Croats, Serbs, and other ethnicities.

The powder keg of ethnic tensions exploded on June 28, 1914, when Archduke Franz Ferdinand and his morganatic wife, Sophie, were assassinated by Serbian-trained terrorists in Sarajevo. Kaiser Wilhelm II of Germany, brimming with indignation, demanded that Austria exact revenge against Serbia, lest its passivity be mistaken for weakness. By the time Austria finally issued an ultimatum to Serbia, Tsar Nicholas II of Russia, the traditional protector of the Slavs of Serbia, had also begun to rattle his sword, which forced France to join the fray, for France and Russia had recently concluded a joint defensive pact. As a result, the diplomacy on which so many Europeans had pinned their hopes never materialized. The generals, their mobilization schedules, and the fear of being taken by surprise eliminated any chance for diplomats to intervene. This was the great tragedy of early 20th-century Europe: Its kingdoms were locked in the grip of treaty obligations that were supposed to secure the peace yet served only to thrust the continent into war.

Some modern historians, however, believe that a major European war was inevitable, notwithstanding the deep commercial ties among Germany, Britain, and France. They argue that on a continent that was now armed to the teeth by the Industrial Revolution and torn by competing nationalistic and imperialist aims, the European powers were bound to come to blows.

For the next three years, the nations of Europe did their best to destroy one another. On the Western Front, which ran from the North Sea

A HELMET and goggles worn by French aviators during air battles between German and Allied airmen

> "WHEN YOU MARCH INTO FRANCE,
> LET THE LAST MAN ON THE RIGHT BRUSH THE
> [ENGLISH] CHANNEL WITH HIS SLEEVE."
>
> ALFRED VON SCHLIEFFEN,
> ARCHITECT OF THE GERMAN INVASION OF FRANCE

to the Swiss frontier, the Allied forces of France and Britain launched offensives that were invariably rebuffed by German defenses running four to five miles deep. Between 1914 and 1917, a thousand men would die daily in the Ypres sector alone. On the opening day of the Passchendaele Offensive of 1917, the British suffered more than 100,000 casualties. By that time, such numbers were commonplace. The war simply refused to end. It grew until it consumed all the treasure and men that the nations had to offer, killing soldiers as fast as the ships and trains and trucks could carry them to the battlefields. The only redemptive aspect of the war, if indeed there was one, is that in the trenches, the differences between Protestant

BRITISH SOLDIERS line up in a communication trench along the Western Front during World War I.

and Catholic victims and caretakers dissolved. Nuns, chaplains, and pastors, aided by heroic members of the Red Cross, tended to the needs of the wounded without regard for their nationality or religious affiliation.

The Zimmermann Telegram

The war took a dramatic turn in 1917 when German foreign secretary Arthur Zimmermann sent a secret telegram to the Mexican government. Wilhelmine diplomacy, never known for subtlety, had come up with a plan to persuade Mexico to join the war on the side of imperial Germany. Such a move, it was believed, would tie down American troops at its southern border and discourage the United States from entering the Great War. As an incentive, Zimmermann assured the Mexican government that Kaiser Wilhelm II, after Germany's inevitable victory, would look favorably on Mexico's claims on territories lost to the United States, such as Texas, Arizona, and New Mexico.

Unfortunately, Herr Zimmermann didn't know that the eavesdropping services of British intelligence could read Germany's cable traffic. When a transcript of the so-called Zimmermann Telegram was forwarded to Washington, D.C., it created an uproar. Already, the United States had been on the brink of declaring war after a German U-boat torpedoed a civilian liner, the *Lusitania,* in 1915, with massive loss of life. For the American public, it underscored the barbaric way in which the kaiser saw fit to wage war. The Zimmermann Telegram was the final straw. On April 2, 1917, a deeply vexed President Wilson asked Congress to declare war on Germany and Austria. Thus, America officially became a belligerent on the side of the Allies.

A RARE COLOR PHOTOGRAPH shows *poilus,* French infantry, with their sky-blue uniforms and tattered regimental flag

NOTABLE DATES

1914
Archduke Franz Ferdinand of Austria-Hungary is assassinated in Sarajevo

1914
Germany invades Belgium and France, igniting World War I

1915
Germans launch chlorine gas attack against Allied line near Ypres, Belgium

1915
Ottoman commander Mustafa Kemal rebuffs the Allied invasion at Gallipoli

1915
German U-boat sinks the British ocean liner *Lusitania,* killing 1,198

1915
First transcontinental telephone call between San Francisco and New York

1916
Battle of the Somme results in 1.1 million total casualties from both sides

1917
United States declares war on Germany after release of Zimmermann Telegram

1917
October Revolution leads Russia to seek armistice with Imperial Germany

1918
The war ends with an armistice

"WE INTEND TO BEGIN ON THE FIRST OF FEBRUARY UNRESTRICTED SUBMARINE WARFARE. WE SHALL ENDEAVOR IN SPITE OF THIS TO KEEP THE UNITED STATES OF AMERICA NEUTRAL."

ZIMMERMANN TELEGRAM TO THE MEXICAN GOVERNMENT

The Russian Revolution

Ever since Peter the Great had ascended the throne of Russia in 1682, its emperors or tsars (a title derived from Caesar) had tried to open Russia's windows to the West and benefit from the great economic, cultural, and technological innovations emerging from Europe. But ultimately, rulers like Catherine the Great lacked the political strength to abolish Russia's deeply entrenched feudal system. By the late 19th century, when illiteracy was being erased in much of western Europe, the literacy rate in the Russian Empire was less than 24

Romanov Tercentenary Box, 1913

percent. Many in the Russian elite did not see the need to educate the masses; even Russian author Leonid Tolstoy described one his peasant characters in *War and Peace,* a man named Platon Karataev, as the "eternal personification of the spirit of simplicity and truth."

Alexander II, who was crowned tsar in 1855, formally abolished serfdom in 1861, allowing 23 million peasants to own the land they toiled on. Pressing his reforms against a staunchly conservative nobility, the tsar sold Alaska to the United States in 1867 and moved toward changing Russia's absolutist monarchy to a constitutional

CATHERINE PALACE in Tsarskoye Selo, designed in 1752 by Italian architect Bartolomeo Rastrelli, is a superb example of the Russian rococo style. Largely destroyed by Nazi forces during World War II, the palace has been partly restored.

ONE OF THE LAST official family portraits of Romanov Tsar Nicholas II shows him with Tsarina Alexandra and their four daughters—Olga, Tatiana, Maria, and Anastasia—and son, Alexei, the Tsarevitch. They were murdered by Bolshevik agents in 1918.

"THERE ARE NO MORALS IN POLITICS;
THERE IS ONLY EXPEDIENCY."

VLADIMIR LENIN, FOUNDER OF RUSSIAN COMMUNIST PARTY

one. Unfortunately, he was assassinated in 1881 before many of his reforms could bear fruit.

Shocked by the brazen murder of his father, Tsar Alexander III resolutely abandoned any further attempts at reforms and reaffirmed the Russian Crown as an autocracy. Similar values were imparted on his son, the future Nicholas II, who ascended the throne in 1894. Thus, as Russia confronted the great challenges of the early 20th century, it found itself ruled by a weak and deeply reactionary autocrat.

The belated arrival of Russian industrialization did not fail to foster an educated middle class that soon bridled against the lack of personal freedoms. Some of these movements were organized

World War I Russian cap

around social democratic principles, with the aim of producing reforms through peaceful means. Others, including the Bolsheviks, were inspired by Marxism and believed that only a radical political overthrow could create an equitable society.

In January 1905, a large crowd marched to the Winter Palace in St. Petersburg to present the tsar with a petition for reforms. Mounted Cossacks opened fire and killed more than a hundred unarmed demonstrators. This "Bloody Sunday" massacre created an outcry and forced Nicholas II to accept modest reforms, including the establishment of a parliament, the duma, as Russia's legislative body.

For the Bolshevik Party, led by Vladimir Lenin,

THE BIRTH OF MARXISM

Marxism, first espoused in a pamphlet called *The Communist Manifesto* by two 19th-century German theorists, Friedrich Engels and Karl Marx (at right), argued that modern society was driven by a growing class struggle between the poor and elites over control of a nation's wealth or "capital." This phenomenon, for which he coined the term "capitalism," was bound to run its course, said Marx. Its internal contradictions would eventually lead to self-destruction and the emergence of a new social order, which he called socialism. In this new utopia, all resources and wealth would be shared, all class distinctions would be eradicated, and all power would be distributed. For many who were disenchanted with organized religion, Marxism was a heady tonic. Here was not only an ideology but also a practical program to create a society where all were equal. Though the impact of Marxism would not be felt until the 20th century, many historians have called Marx one of the most influential figures in modern history.

> # "DURING THE YEARS OF THE SO-CALLED PEACE, POLITICS HAVE ONLY A MEANING: TO PREPARE FOR TOTAL WAR."
>
> **GERMAN GENERAL ERICH LUDENDORFF**

these reforms fell far short. Russia's decision to enter World War I on the side of its ally, France, created the opportunity he was looking for. The poorly trained Russian Army did not fare well against German forces, in part because most of its military signals were sent without code, thus giving the Germans advance notice of Russian strategy. By 1917, the situation in St. Petersburg was dire, with long food lines snaking through the city. After the outbreak of a spontaneous revolt, the Cossacks refused to intervene. In March, Nicholas II was forced to abdicate, and a provisional government was formed. However, the new administration, led by Alexander Kerensky, vowed to continue to fight in the Great War.

The Germans then offered Lenin safe passage from his exile in Switzerland and inserted him into Russia "like a bacillus," where, in October 1917, he led another revolution. This time, the Bolsheviks succeeded in taking control of the country. Monarchist forces, aided by Western powers, tried to intervene, but their White Army was defeated by Lenin's newly formed Red Army. In July 1918,

Tsar Nicholas II, Tsarina Alexandra, and their five children were brutally murdered, shocking much of Europe. Earlier that same year, Lenin had signed the Treaty of Brest-Litovsk with Germany, ending Russia's involvement in the First World War. In 1922, the former Russian Empire became the Union of Soviet Socialist Republics, or U.S.S.R.

The Final Offensive

Having transferred much of their forces from the Eastern Front to the West, German generals Hindenburg and Ludendorff now threw all their might behind one last offensive in the West, before the arrival of the American Expeditionary Forces could tilt the balance. The much-vaunted Ludendorff Offensive failed against staunch Allied opposition, however, and by October 1918, a million American soldiers were in action on the Western Front. At that time, Germany's civilian government, under pressure from a new Allied offensive and because strikes were spreading throughout Germany's cities, sought to negotiate an armistice. On November 9, Kaiser Wilhelm II abdicated the German throne and fled on a train to Holland, where he was given asylum. Two days later, at the 11th hour on the 11th day of the 11th month of 1918, the armistice went into effect, and the Great War came to an end. U.S. forces had suffered 320,000 casualties, compared to the 6.2 million men lost by France, and the 7.2 million men killed, maimed, or missing in Germany. ■

"BLOODY SUNDAY Massacre" refers to events of January 22, 1905, when the Imperial Guard opened fire on a large group of unarmed demonstrators led by Russian Orthodox priest Father Georgy Gapon.

CROWDS IN LONDON celebrate the Armistice of November 11, 1918, which brought the hostilities of World War I to an end.

"MIGRANT MOTHER" by photographer Dorothea Lange is a portrait of Florence Owens Thompson, a 32-year-old mother of seven, whose livelihood was devastated by the Great Depression.

THE INTERBELLUM

The period between the two world wars was a time of great cultural activity, with Paris regaining its role as the center of art, music, and fashion. But the Wall Street crash of 1929 put millions out of work and spawned the rise of nationalist regimes in Italy, Germany, Japan, and other nations.

The interbellum, the decades between the two world wars, was a period of intense activity on numerous fronts. The impact of World War I was most deeply felt in the battle zones, particularly in France, Belgium, Italy, as well as Austria-Hungary, Serbia, and Russia. Of the five empires that went to war in the name of God and country, four ceased to exist: the Orthodox Russian Empire, the Protestant German Empire, the Catholic Austro-Hungarian Empire, and the Muslim Ottoman Empire. Only the British Empire remained in existence, but its economic and political foundations were severely battered by the human and financial tolls of the war. Almost immediately after the cessation of hostilities in November 1918, the issue of home rule in Ireland rose again, with the Protestant North (or Ulster) pitted against the largely Catholic Irish South. And from 1929 onward, India's Congress, spurred by Mohandas Gandhi, began to agitate for independence.

Elsewhere, the violence continued. During and after the Great War, the tottering Ottoman Empire massacred more than a million Armenians. Greece invaded Asia Minor but was pushed back by the Turkish army under Mustafa Kemal. Tremendous destruction was visited on the people of Asia Minor, and priceless monuments were destroyed. Kemal, better known as Atatürk, went on to topple the Ottoman sultan and establish the modern republic of Turkey.

Foremost on the minds of many was the idea of preventing a conflict on the scale of the Great War at any cost. That was the aim of the Treaty of Versailles, signed in 1919: to guarantee the peace. But crushing terms were imposed on the new German state, known informally as the Weimar Republic, including the loss of 25,000 square miles of territory and billions of dollars in reparations. These all but ensured that another world war would become inevitable.

The Treaty of Versailles also inspired the formation of a worldwide organization to arbitrate any future conflicts. The brainchild of U.S. President

THE *LIFE* MAGAZINE cover of February 18, 1928, shows a couple dancing the Charleston during the Roaring Twenties.

> "I HAVE NO PATIENCE WITH THE MODERN NEUROTIC
> GIRL WHO JAZZES FROM MORNING TO NIGHT,
> SMOKES LIKE A CHIMNEY, AND USES LANGUAGE WHICH
> WOULD MAKE A . . . FISHWOMAN BLUSH!"
>
> AGATHA CHRISTIE, *THE MURDER ON THE LINKS*

Woodrow Wilson, the so-called League of Nations was formally established in Geneva in 1920 and eventually numbered 58 member nations. Much to Wilson's regret, however, the United States never joined, thus depriving this body of the authority it so desperately needed. Indeed, the United States had now emerged as the world's leading superpower, not in the least because both France and Britain were heavily indebted to America because of their war expenditures.

The Revival of the 1920s

Much of Europe as well as North America now enjoyed a decade of boundless economic and cultural prosperity that is often referred to as the Roaring Twenties. Affluent Americans once again returned to Europe for their "grand tour" of European capitals or to winter along the Riviera in France. As a result, the period from the 1920s to the 1930s has been called the "second golden age of the ocean liners." France, Britain, Germany, and Italy all competed in offering the fastest, most luxurious vessels in which passengers (even those in second and third class) could make the transatlantic crossing in comfort. A daredevil American pilot, Charles Lindbergh, stunned the world in 1927 when he made the first solo crossing of the Atlantic Ocean in his single-engine *Spirit of St. Louis* monoplane.

The Great War had also made a deep impact on writers, artists, and musicians. Rejecting all academic traditions and their penchant for naturalism, they embarked on developing new, reductive ideas that sought more authentic forms of artistic expression. This prompted not only a late flowering of fauvism and cubism, but also new movements such as Dada, surrealism, futurism, and German expressionism. Perhaps the most influential of these currents was cubism. Inspired by the artwork of Paul Cézanne, cubism sought to reduce three-dimensional illusion to a collage of elementary forms. This meant that objects—such as a human figure, a musical instrument, or a landscape—could be broken down into highly abstracted forms and reassembled into a collage, sometimes as seen from multiple vantage points. Picasso's "Les Demoiselles d'Avignon" from 1907 is often considered a seminal work of cubism, as is Georges Braque's "Baigneuse" of 1908.

The need to rebuild many of Europe's devastated towns also prompted entirely new forms of

SPANISH ARTIST Salvador Dalí became a popular icon of the surrealist movement between the two world wars.

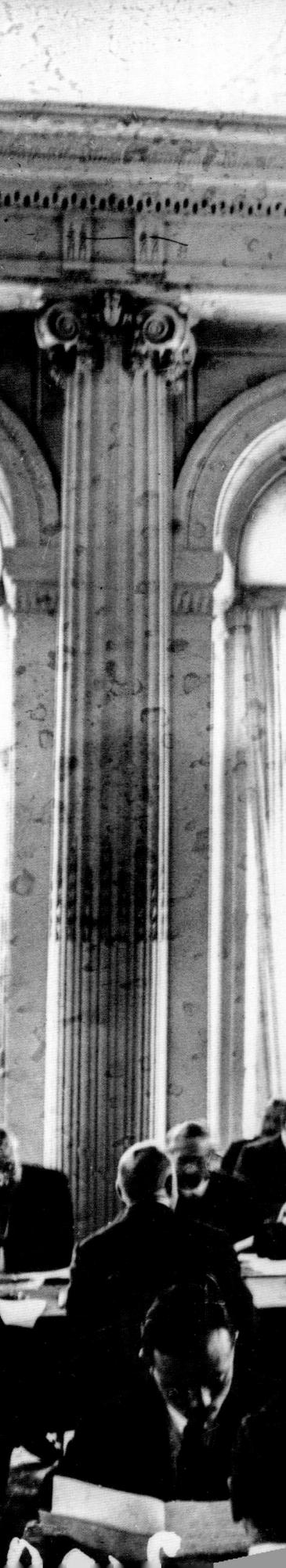

THE TREATY OF VERSAILLES, negotiated by representatives of the principal belligerents in the Hotel Trianon-Palace in Versailles, imposed punitive terms on Germany that all but doomed its democratic Weimar Republic, founded at the end of World War I.

NOTABLE DATES

1919

Versailles Peace Treaty is signed in Paris

1919

Ottoman Turkey initiates systematic persecution of Armenians

1919

Walter Gropius founds the Bauhaus in Weimar, Germany

1920

The United States prohibits the sale of alcohol

1921

Adolf Hitler takes control of National Socialist (Nazi) party of Germany

1922

Benito Mussolini seizes power in Italy

1923

The Charleston becomes the rage in dance halls around the world

1924

Henry Ford's moving assembly line produces half of the world's motor cars

1927

Charles Lindbergh flies solo across the Atlantic in the *Spirit of St. Louis*

1929

Wall Street Crash leads to Great Depression throughout the world

1933

Franklin Delano Roosevelt becomes 32nd president of the United States

1935

On eve of Spanish Civil War, Nativity facade of Barcelona's Sagrada Família is finished

IN 1927, American aviator Charles Lindbergh captivated the world with his thrilling solo flight across the Atlantic, flying from New York to Paris in slightly more than 33 hours in a monoplane, the *Spirit of St. Louis.*

modern architecture. Rejecting the derivative ornamental styles of the past, architects such as German designer Walter Gropius and French architect Le Corbusier formulated a new aesthetic of utilitarian forms shaped by exposed steel, glass, and concrete. Gropius's Bauhaus in Weimar, founded in 1919, became a major center of modernist design and practice until Hitler closed the school.

In bars, music halls, and theaters, jazz ruled supreme with musicians such as Louis Armstrong and Duke Ellington. The Charleston, a dance named for Charleston, South Carolina, became the rage of dance halls after it was introduced by composer James P. Johnson in the 1923 Broadway show *Runnin' Wild*. In Italy, where fascist leader Benito Mussolini seized power in 1922, a group of Italian artists, poets, and musicians had developed another movement, futurism, that sought an art form that

Jazz bass saxophone

was always modern, dynamic, and disruptive—such as a car, an airplane, or a gun. Another movement, known as surrealism, held that spontaneous dreams, visions, or hallucinations could serve as principal motifs for figurate art. Artists like André Breton, Giorgio de Chirico, and Salvador Dalí believed that the subconscious and the irrational held the key to the next transformative stage in Western art; indeed, they believed that an overreliance on rationalism, shaped by bourgeois values, had led to the outbreak of World War I.

At first, the Soviet Union was a fertile ground for modern art movements as well. Russian avant-garde artists such as Vasiliy Kadinsky, Alexander Archipenko, and Kazimir Malevich experimented with suprematism, productivism, and constructivism from a uniquely Russian perspective. But in the 1920s, the Soviet government began to

INDIA'S ROAD TO INDEPENDENCE

O f all of Britain's colonial possessions, India was its crown jewel, its Raj. But since the mid-1910s, an Indian lawyer named Mohandas Gandhi (at right) had made it his mission to strive for India's independence. Known as Mahatma—an honorific meaning "Great Soul," bestowed on him by his followers—Gandhi pursued this goal through peaceful resistance known as *satyagraha*. A leader of the Indian National Congress from 1920, Gandhi urged his fellow Indians to become self-reliant by defying the British-imposed salt tax and boycotting English textiles, favoring homespun instead. He also resisted India's support for Britain in World War II, for which he was put in prison. In 1947, at long last, his dream of Indian independence became a reality, but not how he had envisioned. India's Hindu and Muslim populations, often at loggerheads, were separated into two nations: India and Pakistan. The religious friction that prompted the partition continues to this day. Now armed with nuclear weapons, India and Pakistan often clash, particularly over control of Kashmir Province.

signal that these experiments were going too far, and by 1932, the Soviet Communist Party had imposed a soulless socialist realism on all artistic activity in the U.S.S.R.

The Great Depression

The Wall Street crash of October 1929 brought a swift end to the exuberance of the 1920s and quickly spread unemployment and financial despair throughout North America and much of the rest of the developed world. Though the roots of the crash have been endlessly debated, economists agree that by the end of the 1920s, speculation in steel, construction, and manufacturing far exceeded the actual value that these sectors represented. The London Stock Exchange crash in September further eroded confidence in overseas investments, prompting investors to exit the markets. Large-scale stock purchases by industrialist John D. Rockefeller and other financial giants failed to stem the tide. By 1932, the Dow had lost 89 percent of its value.

The Wall Street crash devastated the American economy as well as that of many nations around the world that had come to rely on U.S. capital and trade. Between 1929 and 1932, international trade dropped by as much as 70 percent. Workers and farmers suffered in equal measure as construction dried up and crop prices fell by about 60 percent. The United States responded with a series of tariffs, including the 1930

A 1930S SIGN identifies a project from the Works Progress Administration (WPA), developed by President Franklin D. Roosevelt as part of the New Deal program to combat unemployment in the wake of the Great Depression.

A PHOTO OF UNEMPLOYED MEN queuing up for a soup kitchen in New York captures the despondent mood in 1930, at the height of the Great Depression.

MEMBERS OF the National Socialist German Workers Party (NSDAP), also known as the *Nationalsozialistische Bewegung,* or Nazi Party, march with their leader, Adolf Hitler, to protest the Treaty of Versailles.

> "YOU WERE GIVEN THE CHOICE BETWEEN WAR AND DISHONOR. YOU CHOSE DISHONOR AND YOU WILL HAVE WAR."

WINSTON CHURCHILL DENOUNCING NEVILLE CHAMBERLAIN'S
APPEASEMENT POLICY TOWARD HITLER

Smoot-Hawley Tariff Act, which according to some historians served to stifle international trade and exacerbate the Great Depression.

By the time Franklin D. Roosevelt succeeded Herbert Hoover as president, the overall U.S. economy had shrunk by an astonishing 31 percent. In response, President Roosevelt offered a New Deal, whereby national wealth and income would be more equitably shared. Vast public works, such as the Tennessee Valley Authority and other projects funded by the Works Progress Administration, created nearly nine million jobs for Americans.

Of all European nations, Germany was hit hardest by the financial crisis. The German Republic, governed by a constitutional assembly based in Weimar, did not have the resources to mount such massive public works. President Herbert Hoover called for a temporary halt on the war reparations that Germany was still paying under the terms of the Versailles Treaty, which was reluctantly agreed to in France (which depended on the steady flow of German payments to bolster its own economy). But the growing failures of German and Austrian banks, beginning with the Creditanstalt in Vienna, failed to stop the spiral and brought ever greater political instability.

Throughout the early 1930s, Communist and ultra-nationalist demonstrators came to blows in many German cities. Soothing words that things were bound to get better were the only thing that Weimar politicians could offer in return. This created an opportunity for an Austrian ideologue and postcard illustrator named Adolf Hitler. In 1921, Hitler had become the leader of the NSDAP, the National Socialist German Workers Party. Two years later, he tried unsuccessfully to stage a coup against the Weimar Republic. He was arrested and put in a (rather comfortable) prison, where in 1924 he wrote his manifesto, *Mein Kampf* (*My Struggle*).

The outrageous terms of the Treaty of Versailles were the cause of Germany's ills, Hitler wrote, and were compounded by Jewish control of the nation's levers of power and the threat of a Communist takeover. This combustible mix of anti-Semitism (which had always been just below the surface in 19th-century Europe), fear of communism, and German nationalist sentiment propelled Hitler to power in 1933, when President Hindenburg of Germany asked him to form a government as chancellor. But after a suspicious fire at the Reichstag, the German Parliament, and Hindenburg's untimely death, Hitler pushed through the 1933 Ermächtigungsgesetz (Enabling Act), which gave him full dictatorial powers. ∎

HITLER, chancellor of the Weimar Republic, used a fire at the German Reichstag, or Parliament, in February 1933 to push through the 1933 Enabling Act that created the Nazi police state.

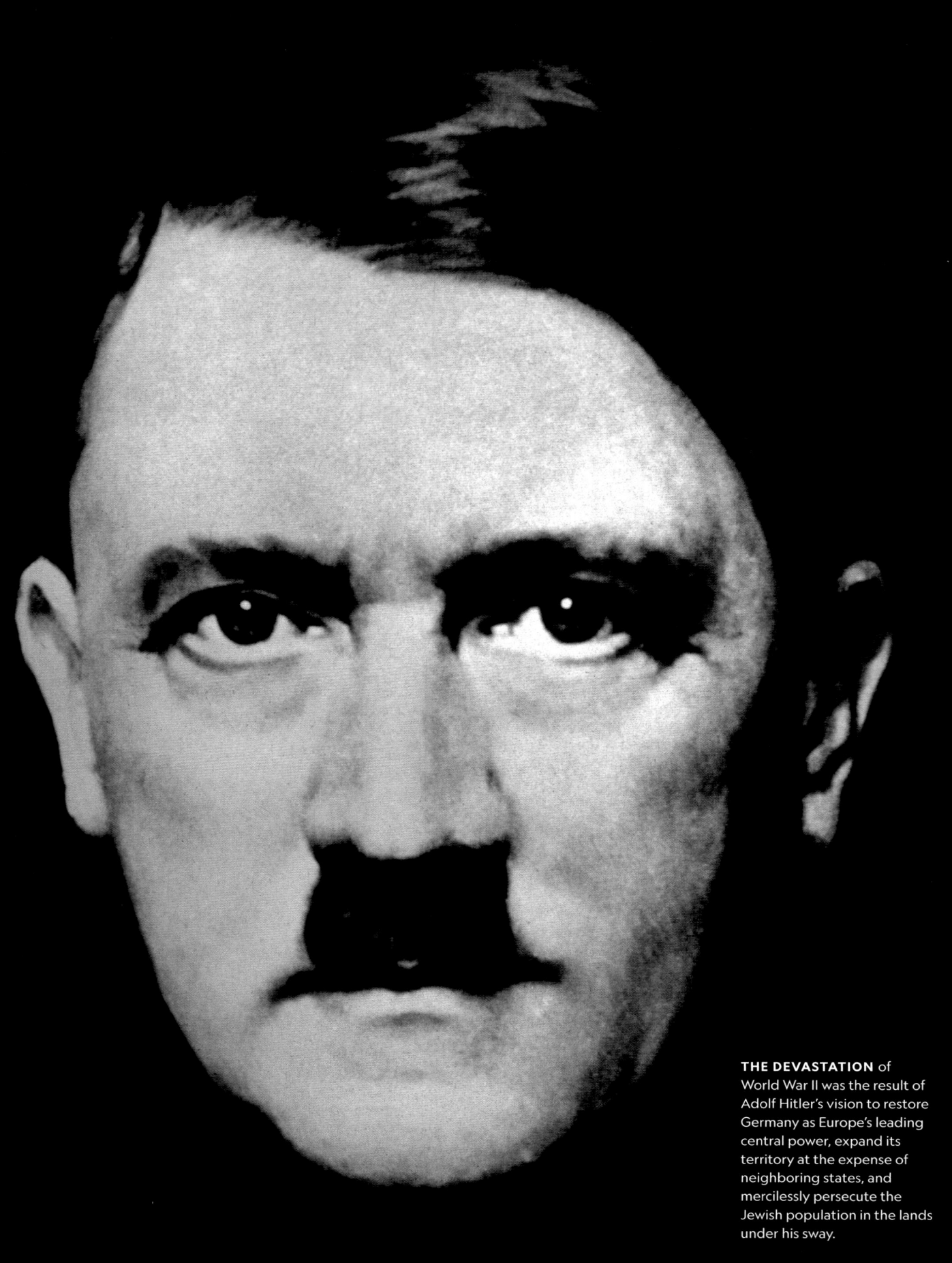

THE DEVASTATION of World War II was the result of Adolf Hitler's vision to restore Germany as Europe's leading central power, expand its territory at the expense of neighboring states, and mercilessly persecute the Jewish population in the lands under his sway.

THE SECOND
WORLD WAR

World War II was the most destructive conflict in human history, spanning the globe and leaving very few nations untouched. After Nazi Germany conquered much of Europe, a massive effort by the Allies—Britain, the United States, and the U.S.S.R—liberated the continent and left Germany in ruins.

In many ways, World War II was foreshadowed by the Spanish Civil War, which became an intensely violent clash between left-wing Republicans and right-wing Nationalists. During the Great War, Spain had profited handsomely from trading with the belligerents. But the end of the war plunged the country into a deep recession. As unemployment and poverty spread, prompting numerous strikes, the Spanish Army suffered a grave defeat at the hands of Berber insurgents in Spanish Morocco. This played into the hands of certain right-wing circles in the Spanish military, which had been waiting for a pretext to stage a coup. In 1923, these officers, led by Gen. Miguel Primo de Rivera, toppled the constitutional government and seized power. The junta immediately launched a crusade against anyone suspected of socialist or communist sympathies. But when King Alfonso XIII was finally prevailed upon to call for elections in 1931, a coalition of socialist and liberal republicans came to power. Soon after, the monarchy was abolished in favor of the Second Spanish Republic. King Alfonso fled the country, as did many noblemen and wealthy conservatives who joined a party

called the Falange Española y de las Juntas de Ofensiva Nacional-Sincicalista, or "Falange" for short. In July 1936, Falangist officers, including Gen. Francisco Franco, seized control of Spanish Morocco and launched a full-fledged invasion of Spain. The Spanish Civil War had begun.

While the Republicans seemed to have the upper hand initially, the momentum shifted to the Nationalists when German dictator Adolf Hitler ordered German air and armored forces to intervene on the side of the Falange. When separatists in the Basque provinces and Catalonia seized the opportunity to agitate for independence, Franco asked the German Condor Legion, a force of Luftwaffe fighters and bombers, to attack a Basque village named Guernica. The Luftwaffe complied, staging the type of terror bombing that later would become a major feature of World War II. It inspired one of Picasso's best-known masterpieces, "Guernica," which he completed just two months later in his Paris studio.

Although thousands of European volunteers, known as the International Brigades, had flocked

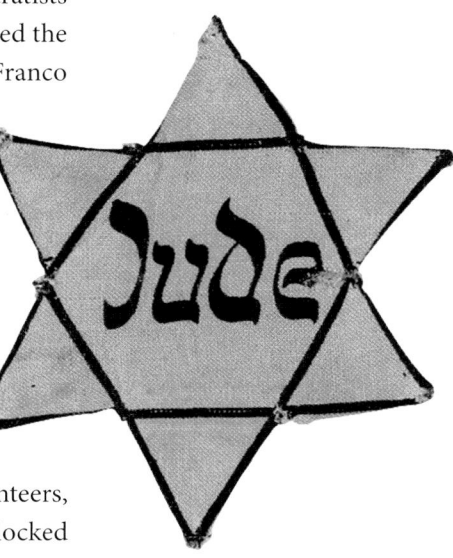

FROM 1941 ON, all Jews in German-ruled territories older than six were forced to wear a badge with the yellow Star of David marked "Jew," so as to increase their marginalization in society.

> "TO MAKE WAR ALL YOU NEED IS INTELLIGENCE.
> BUT TO WIN YOU NEED TALENT AND MATERIAL."
>
> ERNEST HEMINGWAY, *FOR WHOM THE BELL TOLLS*

to the Republican side, Franco was in control of much of the country by 1938. He sealed his victory with large-scale reprisals against anyone suspected of Republican sympathies. Though Spain has yet to make an official reckoning of the toll, estimates range from 30,000 to 100,000 killed, with thousands more sent to forced labor camps. Scores were still in prison when the Franco regime fell in 1975, and it took the 1977 Amnesty Law to set all remaining political prisoners free.

Spanish Civil War hand grenade

Crises Around the World

Beginning in 1935, Hitler had embarked on an aggressive program to seize European territory through intimidation rather than military power. In 1935, he engineered a plebiscite in the heavily industrialized Saar region, which, under the terms of the Versailles Treaty, was occupied by France and Britain. The plebiscite overwhelmingly supported a return to German sovereignty, which was approved by the League of Nations. In 1938, Hitler took the next step by forcing the Anschluss, the political union of Austria and Germany, again without a shot being fired. He then set his sights on another region, the Sudetenland territory of Czechoslovakia. This time, German forces mobilized, but during the infamous conference in Munich on September 30, 1938, Prime Minister Neville Chamberlain of Great Britain caved in to Hitler's demands. After the war, Chamberlain was vilified for his "appeasement" of Hitler, but some modern historians argue that the respite gave Britain the necessary time to build up its forces. This included the critical development of the Royal Air Force (RAF) and modern fighters such as the Hawker Hurricane and the

THE 1937 CANVAS "GUERNICA" by Spanish artist Pablo Picasso became a rallying cry against the horror of the Spanish Civil War—specifically the bombing by the German Condor Legion, a force of Luftwaffe fighters and bombers.

MALE AND FEMALE MILITIA FIGHTERS gather to march at the beginning of the Spanish Civil War in July 1936.

NOTABLE DATES

1936

Spanish Civil War erupts as Nationalists under Franco invade Spain from Morocco

1939

Ocean liner *St. Louis,* carrying 937 German Jews, is denied entry into the U.S. and Canada

1939

Nazi Germany and the U.S.S.R. sign the Non-Aggression Pact

1939

Nazi Germany invades Poland, igniting World War II

1941

Imperial Japanese forces bomb the American fleet at Pearl Harbor, Hawaii

1942

The Battle of Midway is the turning point in the war in the Pacific

1942

he Battle of Stalingrad stems the German invasion of the Soviet Union

1944

British and American forces invade German-occupied Europe at Normandy

1944

Count von Stauffenberg attempts to assassinate Hitler at his Wolf's Lair headquarters

1945

The Philippines are liberated by forces led by General Douglas MacArthur

1945

Soviet forces capture Berlin after Hitler commits suicide, ending World War II in Europe

1945

The U.S. drops atomic bombs on Hiroshima and Nagasaki, resulting in Japan's surrender

JAPANESE TROOPS cheer their capture of a Shanghai railroad station during the Japanese invasion of China in November 1937.

Supermarine Spitfire. Indeed, less than six months after the Munich Agreement, Hitler invaded the rest of Czechoslovakia anyway. Britain and France were now compelled to pledge their defense of Poland, which Hitler had identified as his next acquisition.

In the meantime, major changes had taken place in Japan. After two centuries of relative seclusion under the rule of the shogunate, the country had opened its windows to the West and embraced rapid industrialization. In 1889, it declared itself an empire and by 1910 had seized control of Taiwan and Korea. After Emperor Hirohito ascended the throne in 1926, the Japanese government adopted a militarist doctrine known as Hokushin-ron, aggressive military conquest. Its aim was to provide Japan with critical national resources, such as rice, steel, oil, and rubber, that the nation lacked to sustain its growing population.

In 1931, Japan invaded the northeastern part of China known as Manchuria and installed a puppet regime with Puyi, the last Qing emperor, as a figurehead. Six years later, Japan invaded China proper, prompting a three-way conflict of Japanese forces, Chinese nationalists led by Gen. Chiang Kai-shek, and Chinese communists led by Mao Zedong. On December 13, 1937, Japanese soldiers initiated a six-week massacre in Nanjing in which as many as 200,000 civilians were killed.

Next, Japan set its sights on the oil-rich Dutch East Indies, French Indochina, and British Malaya. To do so, however, the Japanese government realized that it first had to deal a knockout blow to its main military opponent in the Pacific. That happened to be the fleet of the U.S. Navy. Accelerating matters was the decision by President Roosevelt to impose an embargo on all oil exports to Japan because of its occupation of Indochina. This made Tokyo's quest for resources—including oil—even more stringent. Thus, the two nations slowly moved toward war.

Nazi bronze eagle from Nuremberg

The Outbreak of World War II

In 1939, as the world enjoyed its last months of peace, New York was the host city of a World's Fair, heir to the Universal Exhibitions of the 19th century. The theme of the fair was the future. Its opening ceremony was broadcast locally by the RCA Corporation using the new medium of television. Other technological inventions showcased by the exhibitors included such novelties as air-conditioning, nylon, and color photography. One of the pavilions hosted a computing machine developed by IBM, using punched cards. One of the most popular attractions, however, was the surrealist pavilion with the theme of the "Dream of Venus." Designed by Salvador Dalí, who by now was one of the most popular European artists in the United States, its entrance featured a pair of women's legs surmounted by a cutout of Botticelli's "Birth of Venus," and scantily clad women inside.

The fair was still in full swing when the Wehrmacht, the German Army, invaded Poland on September 1, 1939. As a result of a Non-Aggression

WINSTON CHURCHILL'S soaring rhetoric and firm resolve sustained Great Britain in the dark days when it was the only nation to resist the Nazi conquest of Europe.

A HEINKEL HE 111 BOMBER of the German Luftwaffe prepares to jettison its bombs over the East End of London during the Blitz of September 1940.

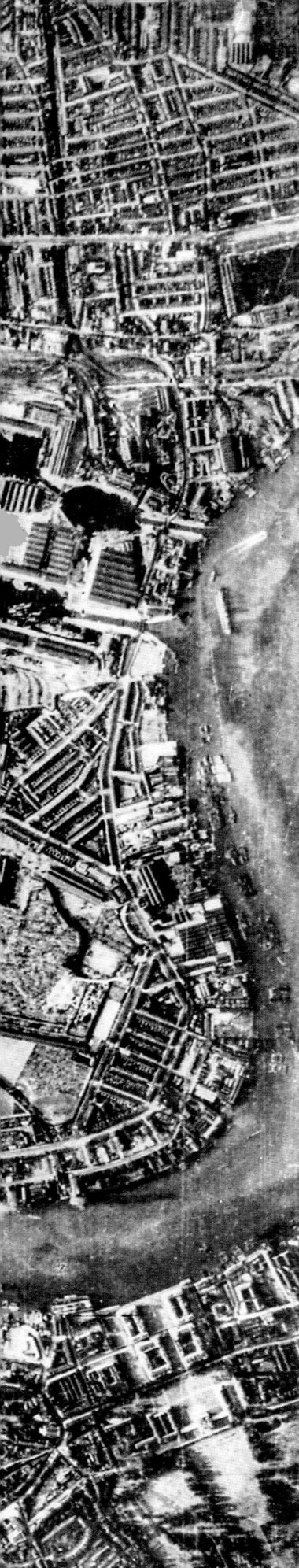

"NEVER IN THE FIELD OF HUMAN CONFLICT WAS SO MUCH OWED BY SO MANY TO SO FEW."

WINSTON CHURCHILL'S TRIBUTE TO RAF PILOTS DURING THE BATTLE OF BRITAIN

Pact with the Soviet Union, Hitler and Soviet leader Joseph Stalin carved up Poland into German and Russian territories. The Western Allies, France and Britain, had no choice but to declare war on Nazi Germany, even though psychologically they were wholly unprepared for another European conflict. When the Allies failed to launch any offensives, Hitler decided to reckon with them once and for all. A coordinated attack by German air and land forces, which quickly became known as blitzkrieg or "lightning war,"

took control of Holland, Belgium, and northern France in less than six weeks. The German population, which had anticipated another drawn-out conflict, was overjoyed, and Hitler's popularity rose to new heights. Impressed with Hitler's victory, Japan and Italy joined Nazi Germany in the Tripartite Pact, a military alliance that pledged to come to each other's aid if attacked. Only Britain, now led by Prime Minister Winston Churchill, remained obstinate in its resistance. Attempts by the German Luftwaffe to subdue the Royal Air

WORLD WAR II EUROPEAN THEATER

- Allied controlled areas
- Axis controlled areas
- Neutral nations
- Greatest area under Axis military occupation Nov. 1942
- → Allied advance
- ✳ Major battle

A COLORIZED PHOTO of the U.S.S. *West Virginia* after it was hit by nine torpedoes evokes the shock of the Japanese attack on Pearl Harbor on December 7, 1941.

Force during the Battle of Britain failed, however, boosting British morale. In late 1940, Hitler was forced to postpone plans for the invasion of Great Britain.

Meanwhile, the German dictator's attention had shifted to the east. On June 22, 1941, Hitler launched Operation Barbarossa, invading his nominal ally, the Soviet Union. Hitler had high hopes for a swift victory, but after initial successes, the Wehrmacht invasion became bogged down in the face of stiffening resistance and the fearsome Russian winter. The German army was finally checked at the Battle of Stalingrad, the gateway to the oil fields of the Caucasus, in early 1943. This was the turning point of the war. From this moment, Soviet, British, and U.S. forces steadily rolled back the Wehrmacht's grip on Russia and North Africa. After the successful Allied invasion of Normandy in June 1944, most German generals knew that the war was lost, but their oath of loyalty to Hitler kept many of them committed to fanatical resistance.

The War in the Pacific

On December 7, 1941, a Japanese fleet of aircraft carriers launched a surprise attack on the U.S. Navy base at Pearl Harbor, Hawaii. While several American battleships were damaged or destroyed, the U.S. carrier fleet was at sea and thus spared from destruction. Japanese forces went on to capture most European colonies in Southeast Asia, including Singapore, Hong Kong, Malaya, and the oil-rich Dutch East Indies. Thousands of Westerners, including nuns and missionaries, were imprisoned in the territories they conquered. Many prisoners, including children, died as a result of maltreatment. Surprisingly, indigenous Protestant or Catholic churches were largely left unmolested as long as they abstained from any political activity. As a result, untold numbers of downed

A NAZI shield identified the Hotel Meurice on the Rue de Rivoli in Paris as headquarters of the German occupation authorities.

THE CHURCH AND THE HOLOCAUST

Many Protestant and Catholic German clergy were initially drawn to Hitler's vision of a prosperous state, based on the rule of law and order. The Vatican had always identified communist atheism as its greatest threat. Cardinal Eugenio Pacelli, Vatican secretary of state (and future Pope Pius XII), even negotiated a concordat with the Hitler regime that secured full religious freedom for German Catholics. The German Protestant Church, however, split into the *Deutsche Christen* (German Christian) movement, which sympathized with the Nazi regime, and the *Bekennende Kirche* (Confessional Church), which remained loyal to democratic principles. As Nazi terror deepened and persecution of Jews escalated (at right), dissidents such as Martin Niemöller and Dietrich Bonhoeffer led the Protestant opposition. In 1937, Pope Pius XI could not remain silent, denouncing the excesses of Nazi racial laws. During the Holocaust, when millions of Jews perished in concentration camps, Catholic priests saved thousands of Jews, though the exact number is subject to debate.

> "WE ONLY HAVE TO KICK IN THE DOOR AND THE WHOLE ROTTEN STRUCTURE WILL COME CRASHING DOWN."
>
> **ADOLF HITLER**
> **BEFORE THE INVASION OF THE SOVIET UNION**

airmen and Allied soldiers were rescued by Asian church organizations and kept hidden from the Japanese.

Using its precious carriers, the United States struck back at the Battle of Midway in 1942. From that point on, U.S. forces moved from island to island to liberate Japanese-held territories in the Pacific, at a horrific cost in casualties. After the successful American liberation of the Philippines, when much of the Japanese Navy lay at the bottom of the sea, the Japanese unleashed one last, desperate weapon: waves of kamikaze suicide pilots, trained to fly their planes straight into American ships. Fearful that in the face of such suicidal tactics, an invasion of the Japanese homeland could claim up to half a million American lives, President Harry Truman (who had succeeded President Roosevelt upon his death in April 1945) made the controversial decision to drop an atomic bomb on the Japanese city of Hiroshima. Three days later, another atomic bomb devastated the city of Nagasaki, and Japan capitulated at last.

Meanwhile, Soviet forces had pushed into Germany and surrounded the German capital of Berlin. On April 30, 1945, Hitler committed suicide.

The Aftermath

Many people who lived through those days describe being deeply affected by the

A HIGHLY CLASSIFIED DOCUMENT from July 1943 offered a preliminary version of the Allied invasion of Normandy, France, on D-Day.

BARRAGE BALLOONS float over Omaha Beach while landing ships unload tanks and troops on D-Day, June 6, 1944, after the British and American forces' successful invasion of Normandy .

AMERICAN SERVICEMEN and servicewomen celebrate the surrender of Japanese forces on August 15, 1945, in front of the Red Cross Club in Paris.

"THE PEOPLES OF THIS WORLD MUST UNITE OR THEY WILL PERISH."

J. ROBERT OPPENHEIMER,
DESIGNER OF THE ATOM BOMB

unfathomable destruction wrought by the atom bomb on the city of Hiroshima on August 6, 1945. The idea that a single bomb could cause more than 150,000 casualties while leveling more than 60 percent of a modern city seemed to raise humankind's penchant for self-immolation to an entirely new level. Nonetheless, a genuine sense of relief prevailed among the Allies. Though this is perhaps difficult to imagine, given the deep aversion to nuclear weapons today, in 1945 the atom bomb became the subject of pride and a symbol of complete American military hegemony.

World War II was the largest and deadliest war ever fought on the planet. Historians estimate that more than 100 million uniformed men and women fought in 30 countries, and somewhere between 50 and 80 million people, civilian and military, died in the conflagration.

Like President Wilson before him, President Roosevelt had sought to create a world body that would be able to intervene and arbitrate peacefully in the conflict of nations. His vision became a reality with the foundation of the United Nations, which convened as the UN Conference in San Francisco on April 25, 1945, just two weeks after Roosevelt's death.

Germany was partitioned into western and eastern zones, governed by the Western Allies and the Soviet Union. This division became permanent in 1949 when the Soviets created a Communist state, the Deutsche Demokratische Republik (German Democratic Republic, DDR), in the eastern zone, with its capital in Berlin. The Allies nurtured the western zone into a parliamentary democracy under the name of the Bundesrepublik Deutschland (Federal Republic of Germany), with its capital in Bonn. ∎

A PHOTO OF HIROSHIMA reveals the devastation wrought by the bomb dropped by an American B-29 on August 6, 1945. **ABOVE:** U.S. military newspaper *Stars and Stripes* proclaims Hitler's death on May 2, 1945.

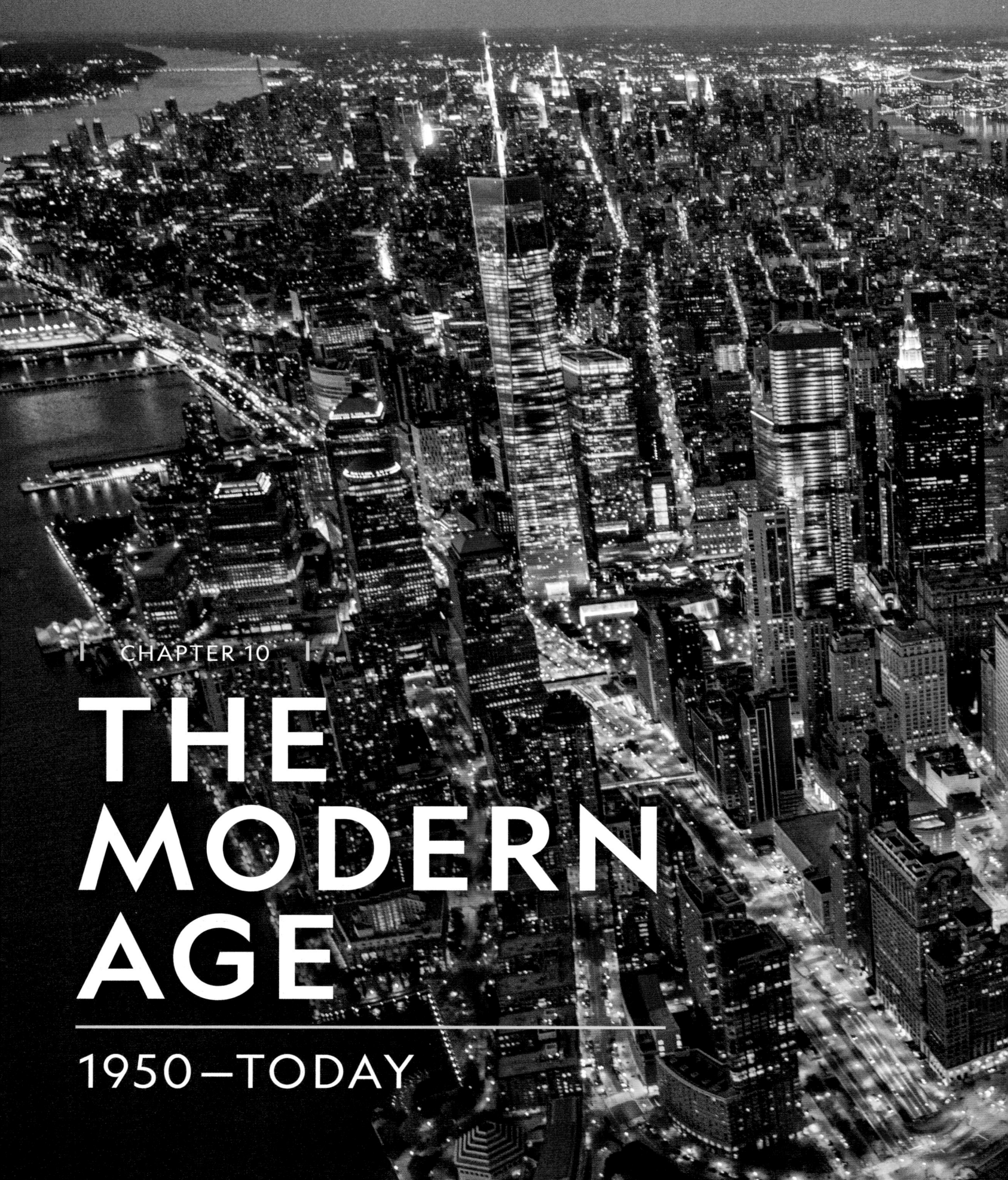

CHAPTER 10

THE MODERN AGE

1950—TODAY

A NIGHTTIME VIEW of Manhattan shows the metropolis with the proud new World Trade Center soaring to the skies at left

CONTENTS

THE AMERICAN CENTURY

The postwar era saw a world split by the Cold War rivalry between the United States and the U.S.S.R, the formation of the European Union, and the emergence of China as a new world power. But above all, the modern age has witnessed the rapid rise of new science and technology that has brought the world closer than ever before. Through much of the 20th century, the United States led the rest of the world in scientific and technological development, as well as in manufacturing and entertainment. The lifestyle celebrated in American films became a benchmark for many peoples around the world as they sought to recover from the destruction of World War II. Part of the reason is that the United States emerged relatively unscathed from the war. None of its homeland had been occupied, and none of its cities had been bombed or damaged. At the same time, the massive mobilization of American industry for the war effort had eliminated the economic woes of the post-Depression era, reaching a level of efficiency and productivity unmatched by any other nation.

For example, by 1950, American companies were producing nearly three-quarters of all automobiles in the world. To accommodate this explosion of automotive travel, President Dwight D. Eisenhower, who had served as Supreme Commander of Allied forces in World War II, launched an ambitious project: to build the interstate highway system that today still serves as the backbone of transportation across the United States.

The Marshall Plan

Europe needed much more time to recover from the immense destruction of the war. In response, the United States developed the Marshall Plan, a project to assist in the rebuilding of European cities, trade, farming, and industry with funds that eventually would total more than $13 billion (the equivalent of $140 billion today). The Marshall Plan, named after U.S. Secretary of State (and former Chief of Staff) George Marshall, was not without political motives. By actively supporting the restoration of European economies, the United States hoped to forestall the encroachment of Soviet-style communism, particularly among the labor movements of France, Italy, and Greece. The Soviet Union recognized this, of course, and refused any American support. It also forced countries now under its sway, including Poland, Hungary, and Czechoslovakia, to reject the funding.

Meanwhile, the last major colonial power, Great Britain, reluctantly oversaw the dismantling of its once powerful empire as nation after nation demanded independence. France too lost most of its possessions, though it fought a bitter civil war in Algeria and tenuously tried to hang on to its control of Vietnam, thus triggering the Vietnam War.

After escalating tensions between the superpowers throughout the 1960s, the decade of the 1970s was notable for efforts to establish a détente between the United States and the U.S.S.R. By 1985, the U.S.S.R. was brought to the brink of economic ruin, partly because of the escalating arms race initiated by U.S. President Ronald Reagan. In response, the new Soviet leader, Mikhail Gorbachev, introduced reforms that unleashed the simmering resentment against the Soviet yoke throughout the Eastern-bloc nations. ■

THIS PRESSURE SUIT was worn by astronaut Neil Armstrong during the 1969 Apollo 11 mission to the moon.

MARILYN MONROE,
Hollywood's reigning star
of the silver screen in the
1950s and early 1960s,
poses for celebrity
photographer Michael
Ochs during a 1952
publicity shoot.

AN AMERICAN infantry soldier in camouflage paint, hardened by combat in Vietnam, poses with a picture of his sweetheart on his helmet.

THE SPREAD OF THE
COLD WAR

President Roosevelt had hoped that the wartime alliance of the United States, Britain, and the Soviet Union would outlast Nazi Germany's defeat and secure the peace. But Stalin's enslavement of Eastern Europe and his blockade of Berlin's Western sectors launched an era of Cold War hostility.

n February 1945, the Allied leaders—President Franklin D. Roosevelt, Prime Minister Winston Churchill, and Soviet leader Josef Stalin—met at Yalta on the Crimea to decide the shape of the postwar world. Each came with his own agenda. Stalin was determined to keep any European countries liberated by the Soviet Army under his control. Roosevelt was focused on two other priorities: to secure Stalin's military support for the American invasion of Japan and safeguard the formation of his coveted United Nations organization. Churchill, who realized that Britain was now the junior member of the Allied forces, was determined to have free and fair elections in Poland—Polish freedom being the very reason that Britain had declared war on Germany—and to ensure that Greece did not fall to the Eastern bloc. All three leaders signed a document, the Yalta Agreement, that called for each liberated nation to determine its own destiny through free elections, though Stalin had no intention to adhere to that agreement in Eastern Europe and Churchill was determined to retain the British Empire.

By now, Roosevelt was gravely ill. Journalists were shocked by his physical appearance. When he returned to the United States to brief Congress on March 1, the president declared, "I come from the Crimea with a firm belief that we have made a start on the road to a world of peace." But Soviet secret police were already busy arresting Polish leaders so as to eliminate any opposition to the installation of a Communist government. Other agents were laying the groundwork for a similar Communist takeover in Romania, Hungary, Albania, Czechoslovakia, and East Germany. More than a month after his address to Congress, Roosevelt died of a brain hemorrhage and was succeeded by his vice president, Harry Truman.

Meanwhile, Winston Churchill had lost the 1945 British election to Labor leader Clement Attlee. In a speech at Westminster College in Fulton, Missouri, Churchill declared, "From Stettin in the Baltic to Trieste in the Adriatic, an iron curtain has descended across the continent." He was exactly right, and the term Iron Curtain has been used ever since to distinguish the free Western nations from those living under the Soviet yoke in Eastern Europe.

THIS HELMET, worn by an American soldier during the Vietnam War, is preserved by the Massachusetts Vigil Society.

> "AFTER THE MOSCOW CONFERENCE LAST DECEMBER, RUSSIA BEGAN TO MAKE A 'COLD WAR' ON BRITAIN AND THE BRITISH EMPIRE."
>
> GEORGE ORWELL, ENGLISH NOVELIST AND ESSAYIST

Growing Tensions in Berlin

Others now woke up to the danger, including a diplomat named George Kennan who urged the Truman administration to adopt a policy of "containment" against the growing Soviet encroachment of the free world. But Stalin was one step ahead: In June 1948, he suddenly blocked all highway traffic from West Germany to Berlin, which had to travel via a special corridor through East Germany. At the time, Berlin was still organized in four separate sectors: one controlled by the Russians and the other three governed by Britain, the United States, and France. Within days, West Berlin faced an acute shortage of food, fuel, and medicine. In response, the Allied air forces launched the Berlin Airlift to bring badly needed supplies to the besieged city. At its peak, a cargo plane landed at Berlin Tempelhof Airport every 45 seconds. The Soviets finally lifted the blockade almost a year later, on May 12, 1949. Fearing a trick, however, the airlift continued for another four months. The Berlin blockade dashed any hope that the United States and U.S.S.R. could find a way to coexist in peace, as Roosevelt had hoped.

In response, both the United States and the U.S.S.R. began to arm themselves once more. In the West, this led in 1949 to the formation of NATO (North Atlantic Treaty Organization) alliance of 10 European countries as well as the United States and Canada, while the Soviets formed the Warsaw Pact of East European forces, under command of Soviet military leadership.

At this time, Berlin was not yet a divided city; East German citizens could freely enter West Berlin and make their way to West Germany and freedom. The result was a brain drain of thousands of doctors, scientists, and other professionals,

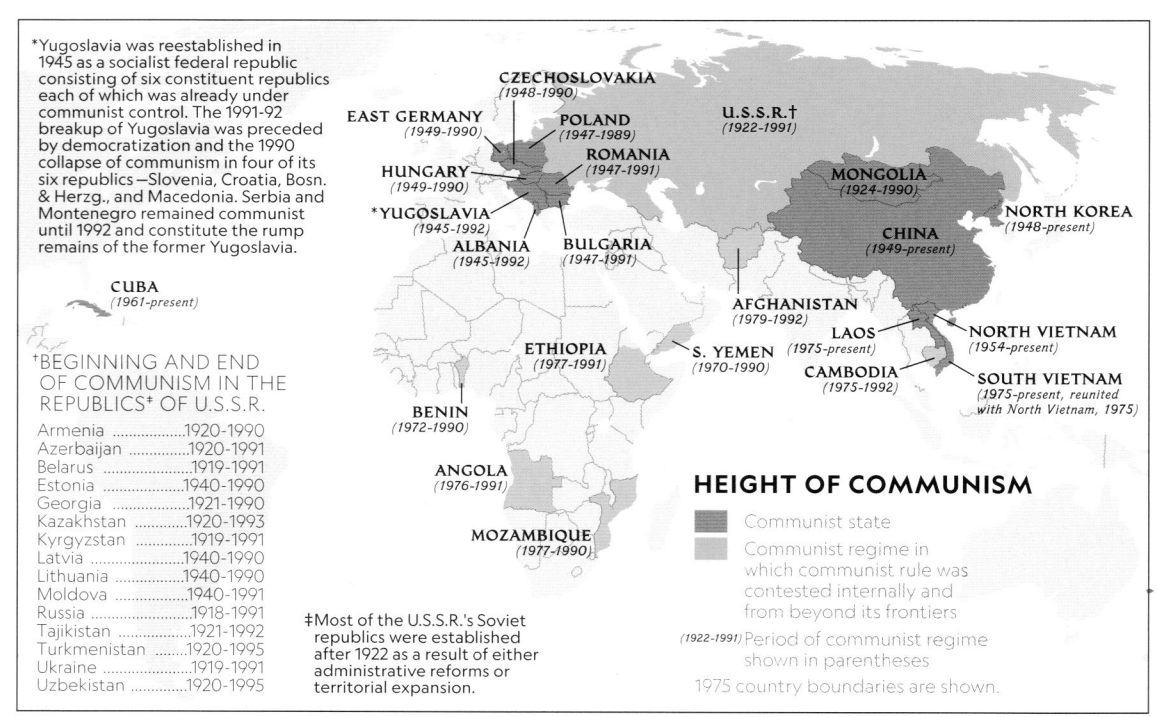

*Yugoslavia was reestablished in 1945 as a socialist federal republic consisting of six constituent republics each of which was already under communist control. The 1991-92 breakup of Yugoslavia was preceded by democratization and the 1990 collapse of communism in four of its six republics—Slovenia, Croatia, Bosn. & Herzg., and Macedonia. Serbia and Montenegro remained communist until 1992 and constitute the rump remains of the former Yugoslavia.

CZECHOSLOVAKIA
(1948-1990)

EAST GERMANY
(1949-1990)

POLAND
(1947-1989)

U.S.S.R.†
(1922-1991)

ROMANIA
(1947-1991)

HUNGARY
(1949-1990)

MONGOLIA
(1924-1990)

*YUGOSLAVIA
(1945-1992)

ALBANIA
(1945-1992)

BULGARIA
(1947-1991)

NORTH KOREA
(1948-present)

CHINA
(1949-present)

CUBA
(1961-present)

AFGHANISTAN
(1979-1992)

LAOS
(1975-present)

NORTH VIETNAM
(1954-present)

ETHIOPIA
(1977-1991)

S. YEMEN
(1970-1990)

CAMBODIA
(1975-1992)

SOUTH VIETNAM
(1975-present, reunited with North Vietnam, 1975)

†BEGINNING AND END OF COMMUNISM IN THE REPUBLICS‡ OF U.S.S.R.

Armenia	1920-1990
Azerbaijan	1920-1991
Belarus	1919-1991
Estonia	1940-1990
Georgia	1921-1990
Kazakhstan	1920-1993
Kyrgyzstan	1919-1991
Latvia	1940-1990
Lithuania	1940-1990
Moldova	1940-1991
Russia	1918-1991
Tajikistan	1921-1992
Turkmenistan	1920-1995
Ukraine	1919-1991
Uzbekistan	1920-1995

BENIN
(1972-1990)

ANGOLA
(1976-1991)

MOZAMBIQUE
(1977-1990)

‡Most of the U.S.S.R.'s Soviet republics were established after 1922 as a result of either administrative reforms or territorial expansion.

HEIGHT OF COMMUNISM

◼ Communist state

◼ Communist regime in which communist rule was contested internally and from beyond its frontiers

(1922-1991) Period of communist regime shown in parentheses

1975 country boundaries are shown.

BRITISH PRIME MINISTER
Winston Churchill, a visibly
ailing president Franklin D.
Roosevelt, and Soviet
premier Joseph Stalin
gather at the pivotal Yalta
Conference, February 4–11,
1945, to determine the
shape of postwar Europe.

NOTABLE DATES

1946
Despite the promise of free
elections, the Iron Curtain
descends over Eastern Europe

1948
Marshall Plan begins, funding
the recovery of European
nations

1949
NATO is established in Europe

1949
Mao Zedong's Communists
take over China

1950
North Korea invades South,
igniting the Korean War

1954
French colonial forces are
defeated at Dien Bien Phu,
Vietnam

1956
Soviet forces crush the
Hungarian Uprising

1961
East Germany builds Berlin
Wall to divide East and
West Berlin

1962
The Cuban Missile Crisis
pushes U.S. and U.S.S.R. to
brink of war

1968
Tet Offensive is a turning
point in the Vietnam War

1968
Prague Spring prompts Soviet
invasion of Czechoslovakia

1972
Strategic Arms Limitation
Talks (SALT) slow nuclear
arms race

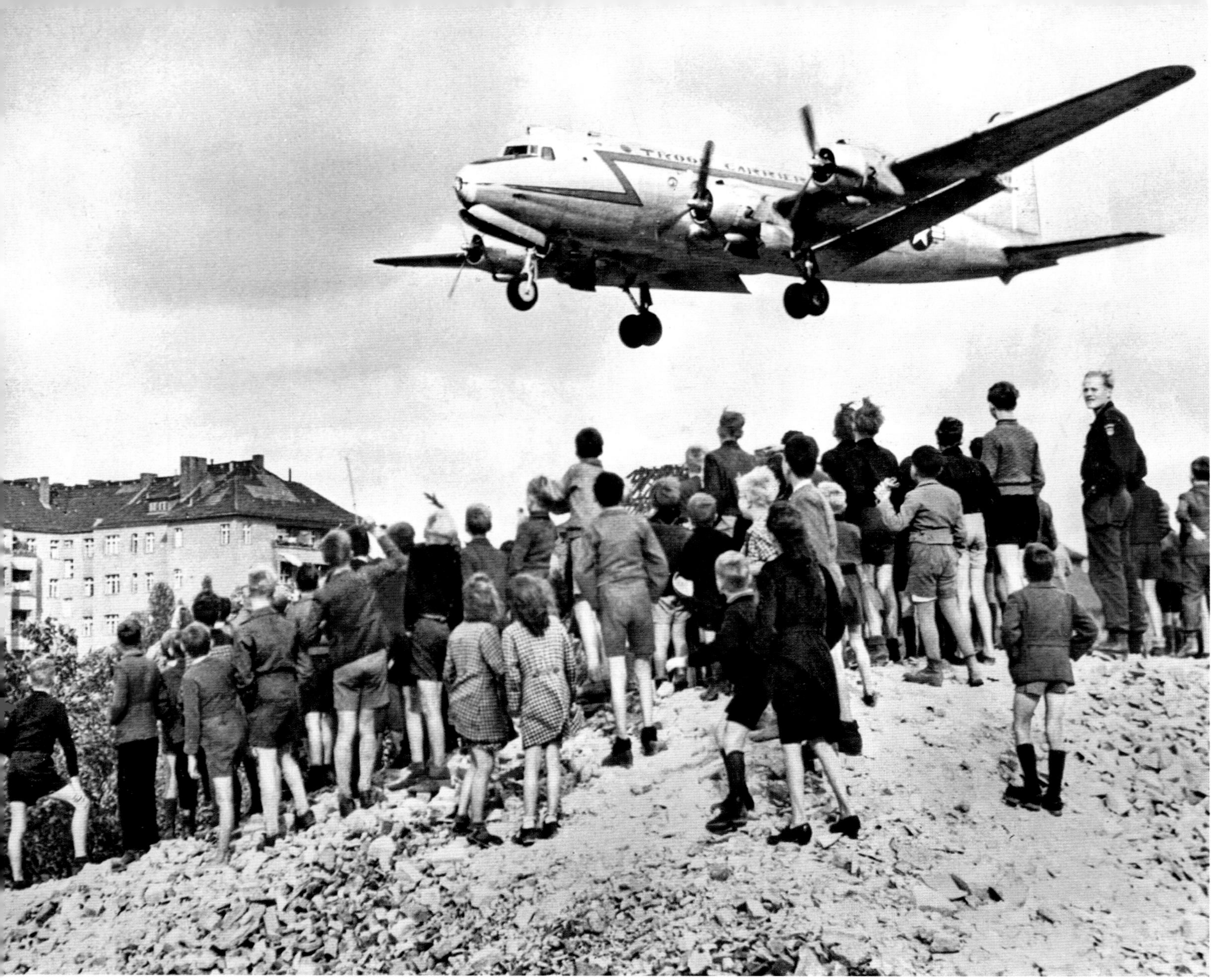

FOLLOWING THE SOVIET BLOCKADE of West Berlin, Allied air forces launched the Berlin Airlift that at its peak brought a cargo plane to Berlin's Tempelhof Airport every 45 seconds.

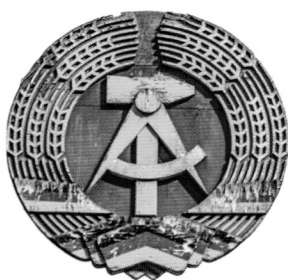

East Germany emblem

as well as scores of East German families. Modern estimates suggest that between 1949 and 1961, some three and a half million East German citizens made their way from East to West Berlin, totaling some 20 percent of the East German population. This led to acute labor shortages in the German Democratic Republic (GDR), not to mention international embarrassment.

In response, East German leader Walter Ulbricht ordered that the flow of emigrants be stopped. Without warning, East German soldiers began to barricade the dividing line between East and West Berlin during the night of August 12, 1961, followed by a brick wall. Eventually the space between East and West would become a no-man's-land filled with land mines, subjected to constant surveillance from guard posts placed along the wall. Any East German citizen who attempted to cross it was unceremoniously gunned down.

The East Rises in Revolt

The oppressed people of Eastern Europe did not accept the Soviet yoke quietly. Nations such as Poland, Hungary, and Czechoslovakia had tasted the freedom of a parliamentary democracy between the two world wars and yearned to restore it. In October 1956, the Hungarian leadership caved in to intense public pressure and granted freedom of speech, inviting an open debate of

A WEST BERLIN policeman stands before East German workers building the Berlin Wall in August 1961. The wall was put up to keep East Germans from fleeing the oppressive Communist regime of the German Democratic Republic.

A YOUNG STUDENT mounts a disabled Soviet tank during the 1968 Warsaw Pact invasion of Czechoslovakia, during which the U.S.S.R. sought to crush the Prague Spring.

badly needed economic reforms. The Soviet response was swift: On November 4, the new Soviet Premier, Nikita Khrushchev, ordered the Red Army to invade Hungary. The Soviet forces crushed the revolt in one bloody week, which caused the deaths of 2,500 Hungarians and 700 Soviet troops. Hungary's premier, Imre Nagy, was arrested and executed in 1958.

In 1968, Czechs rose in a popular uprising that became known as the Prague Spring, led by Communist Party leader Alexander Dubček. His aim was to create a compromise between communist ideals and basic human rights, which he termed "socialism with a human face." For seven months, the world held its breath, wondering whether this time, the Soviet leadership—now led by Leonid Brezhnev—would allow matters to take their course. The Prague Spring inspired spontaneous revolts around Europe, often led by students who clamored for an end to American intervention in Southeast Asia.

But on August 21, 1968, the Soviet Army was once more called in to intervene, and the Prague Spring was crushed—dashing the hopes of millions who thought perhaps the Cold War was coming to an end. Dubček was removed from office and in 1970 expelled from the Czech Communist Party, after which he was posted to the Forestry Service in Slovakia.

The Korean War

It was in Southeast Asia, however, that superpower tensions finally erupted in outright war. Here, both Korea and Vietnam were trying to recover from Japanese occupation and reconstitute themselves as autonomous nations. Long controlled by

"WAR IS NOT ONLY A CONTEST OF STRENGTH, BUT ALSO A TEST OF MORALITY AND ETHICS."

KIM IL-SUNG,
FOUNDER OF THE DEMOCRATIC PEOPLE'S REPUBLIC OF KOREA (NORTH KOREA)

China and annexed by Japan since 1910, Korea was particularly eager to affirm its independence. After declaring war on Japan as President Roosevelt had hoped, however, Soviet troops occupied the country's North, above the 38th parallel, while American forces liberated the South. The United Nations then granted both the U.S.S.R. and the United States the right to develop a trustee government in their respective territories. This division became permanent when talks to unify the nation went nowhere. As in the case of Germany, the Soviets established a Communist regime in Korea's North, while the United States created a multiparty state on the Western model in the South.

Thus, the stage was set for a proxy war, in which the Soviets could test Western resolve in defending its interests in Southeast Asia. In June 1950, North Korea's Communist dictator, Kim Il-sung, invaded the South with tanks, artillery, and other arms provided by the U.S.S.R. The United Nations Security Council promptly authorized a military invasion—its first—in order to restore the situation pro ante. Since most of the troops would be supplied by the United States, Gen. Douglas MacArthur was placed in command of the UN forces. But the intervention did not go according to plan, and North Korean forces were able to capture much of South Korea's territory. MacArthur then launched an amphibious assault behind enemy lines at Inchon, some 20 miles west of South Korea's capital of Seoul. The attack sent North Korean forces into a hasty retreat. The UN forces went in pursuit until they came close to the Yula River border with China.

China was then just recovering from its bitter civil war between the Kuomintang forces led by Chiang Kai-shek and Communist troops led by Mao Zedong. Although Mao's army had emerged victorious, sending Chiang Kai-shek in exile to Taiwan, Mao's grip on power remained tenuous. Sensing that the UN forces might try to invade China and restore a pro-West regime, Mao ordered his army to launch a preemptive attack on UN forces in Korea. Bitter fighting ensued, often in appalling

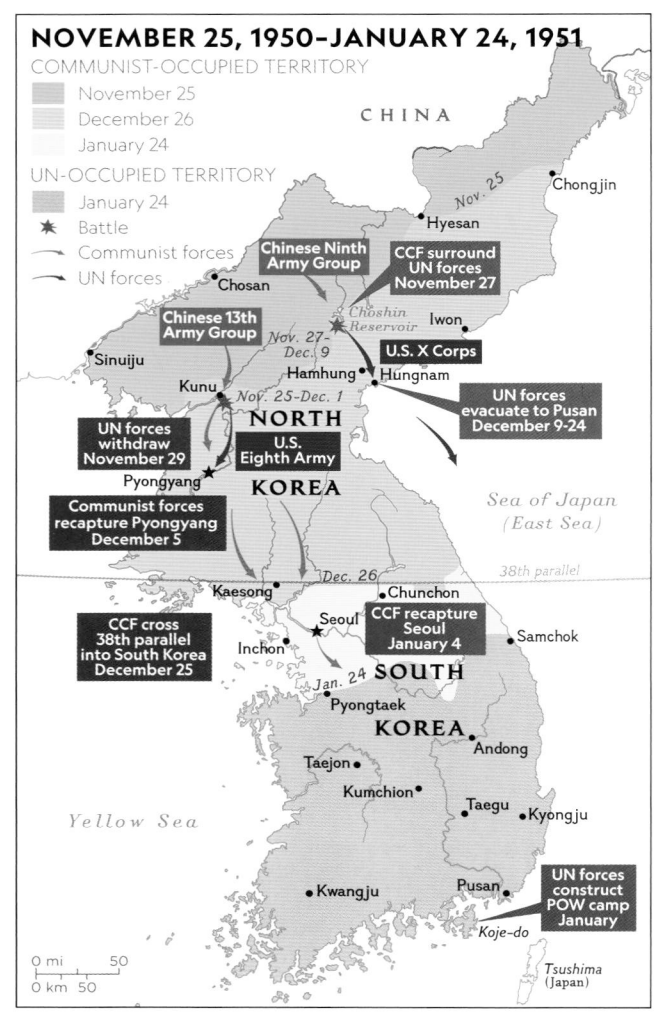

NOVEMBER 25, 1950–JANUARY 24, 1951

COMMUNIST-OCCUPIED TERRITORY
- November 25
- December 26
- January 24

UN-OCCUPIED TERRITORY
- January 24
- ★ Battle
- Communist forces
- UN forces

CHINA

Chongjin
Nov. 25
Hyesan
Chinese Ninth Army Group
CCF surround UN forces November 27
Chosan
Choshin Reservoir
Iwon
Chinese 13th Army Group
Nov. 27-Dec. 9
U.S. X Corps
Sinuiju
Hamhung
Hungnam
Kunu
Nov. 25-Dec. 1
UN forces evacuate to Pusan December 9-24
UN forces withdraw November 29
NORTH
U.S. Eighth Army
KOREA
Pyongyang
Sea of Japan (East Sea)
Communist forces recapture Pyongyang December 5
38th parallel
Kaesong
Dec. 26
Chunchon
Seoul
CCF recapture Seoul January 4
Samchok
CCF cross 38th parallel into South Korea December 25
Inchon
Jan. 24
SOUTH
Pyongtaek
KOREA
Andong
Taejon
Kumchion
Taegu
Kyongju
Yellow Sea
Kwangju
Pusan
UN forces construct POW camp January
Koje-do
Tsushima (Japan)

0 mi 50
0 km 50

AN EXHAUSTED Korean girl with her baby brother on her back passes a stalled American M-26 tank during operations near Haengju, Korea, in June 1951.

winter conditions, during which the city of Seoul changed hands four times. Newly developed fighter jets—American Sabres versus Soviet-built MiGs—fought lethal dogfights in the air. At long last, an armistice agreement was signed on July 27, 1953, creating a demilitarized zone (DMZ) between North and South Korea. However, no peace treaty was signed, and so the two nations technically remained at war through the 20th and the early 21st century. Following a meeting between President Moon Jae-in and North Korean leader Kim Jong-un in 2018, both leaders pledged to negotiate an end to the war, but the tensions between the two nations remain high.

Zippo lighter from the Vietnam War

The Vietnam War

During World War II, 26 nations had signed the Atlantic Charter issued by Roosevelt and Churchill in 1941, which gave each nation the right to choose its form of government. Among them was France's president, Charles de Gaulle, who had led the Free French forces during World War II. But like Great Britain, de Gaulle was determined to hang on to French colonial possessions in Asia, which he felt were of vital importance to help France recover from German occupation. In this, he was firmly opposed by Ho Chi Minh, leader of a militia known as the Vietminh, who had fought against the Japanese in close liaison with the American Office of Strategic Services (the forerunner of the Central Intelligence Agency). In September 1945, Ho Chi Minh proclaimed the Democratic Republic of Vietnam with a speech inspired by the American Declaration of Independence. The French, however, vowed to resist, and in late 1946, war broke out in the Vietnamese peninsula. The conflict would last 29 years.

THE TELEVISED WAR

The Vietnam War was the first major conflict to be covered by television, with footage of the fighting broadcast within days or sooner. Thus, the American public was far more engaged with this war than the Korean War of just a decade earlier. Television coverage also galvanized resistance against the Vietnam War and increasingly traumatized the nation, particularly when American casualties exceeded 50,000. On February 27, 1968, CBS anchor Walter Cronkite (at left), widely regarded as the most authoritative voice on television, announced that in his opinion, the war could no longer be won. "It is increasingly clear to this reporter that the only rational way out then will be to negotiate," Cronkite said on air, "not as victors, but as an honorable people who lived up to their pledge to defend democracy, and did the best they could." When President Johnson heard of the broadcast, he said, "If I've lost Cronkite, I've lost Middle America."

WOUNDED MARINE Gunnery Sergeant Jeremiah Purdie reaches out to a wounded comrade after the intense firefight for control of Hill 484 near "Landing Zone Mack" northwest of Cam Lô, Quang Trị Province, in central Vietnam.

"IT SEEMS NOW MORE CERTAIN THAN EVER
THAT THE BLOODY EXPERIENCE OF VIETNAM
IS TO END IN A STALEMATE."

CBS ANCHOR WALTER CRONKITE AFTER THE 1968 TET OFFENSIVE

Now supported by the Soviet Union, Ho's forces unleashed a devastating guerrilla war on French colonial troops that culminated in 1954 in a crushing French defeat at Dien Bien Phu. By then, 80 percent of the French war effort in Indochina was funded by the U.S. government, including the provision of carrier-based aircraft, pilots, artillery, and support forces. President Dwight Eisenhower's secretary of state, John Foster Dulles, believed that it was America's mission to contain and deter Soviet influence anywhere in the world, and particularly in resource-rich Southeast Asia. Eisenhower explained this doctrine as the "domino theory": If one country in Southeast Asia was allowed to become Communist, others would follow.

Vietnam protest button from 1969

Mere weeks after Dien Bien Phu, the Geneva Conference temporarily partitioned Vietnam at the 17th parallel, similar to the way Korea had been divided between a Communist North and a Western-supported South. North Vietnam, supported by both the Soviet Union and Communist China, would be governed from its capital in Hanoi, while South Vietnam would be ruled by a Catholic politician, Ngo Dinh Diem, in Saigon. An election was to be held in 1956 to establish the final political makeup of the country, but Diem canceled the vote, knowing that Ho Chi Minh would probably win. He did order a plebiscite in South Vietnam, which was rigged to give him 98.2 percent of the vote. Ho responded by ordering his North Vietnamese guerrillas, the Vietcong, to infiltrate the south and liberate it at the earliest opportunity. Thus began the second phase of the Vietnam War.

Subsequent U.S. presidents, including John F. Kennedy and Lyndon B. Johnson, found there was no alternative but to support the corrupt regime in the South, lest all of Vietnam fall under the Communist yoke. Thus, the United States became gradually mired in a war that it had no hope of winning, given the broad sympathies among rural Vietnamese for Ho and their widespread hatred of the corruption in Saigon. As the war escalated, so too did American involvement; by 1968, more than 500,000 American soldiers were fighting both the Vietcong and North Vietnamese army regulars all across the South. American commanders, including General William Westmoreland, repeatedly signaled that the war was winnable and that the Vietcong were increasingly on the defensive. But the North's Tet Offensive of 1968 put paid to that notion when its forces attacked some 100 towns and villages across South Vietnam and even besieged the American Embassy in Saigon.

Still, it would take another four years before North Vietnam's Le Duc Tho and American national security adviser Henry Kissinger negotiated the Paris Peace Accords that formally ended hostilities. Despite the truce, North and South continued to fight, and in April 1975, victorious North Vietnamese troops entered Saigon. Of the 2.7 million Americans who served in uniform in Vietnam, 58,220 were killed and more than 300,000 were wounded. The number who suffered disabling wounds or amputations was 300 percent higher than during World War II. As many as two million civilians were killed on both sides. ■

IN THIS FEBRUARY 1, 1968, photo by Eddie Adams that shocked the world, South Vietnamese Brig. Gen. Nguyen Ngoc Loan executes a Vietcong prisoner, Nguyen Van Lem, illustrating the wanton horror of the Vietnam War.

SOVIET COSMONAUT
Valentina Tereshkova
became the first woman in
space during a 1963 solo
mission in a Vostok 6
spacecraft.

THE AGE OF SCIENCE AND
TECHNOLOGY

World War II stimulated the development of new science and technology, much of which was converted to peacetime, such as jet airliners and spacecraft. The 20th century also saw breakthroughs in new materials, medicine, and physics, and modern transportation fostered a global economy.

By turning to private industry to galvanize the war effort, all the major combatants of World War II spurred scientific discovery on an unprecedented scale. One of the major outcomes was the use of penicillin, discovered in 1928 by Scottish scientist Alexander Fleming and produced en masse in 1940 to combat infections as a result of war wounds. Commodity shortages also led to the invention of synthetic fuels, rubber, and nylon as a substitute for silk. Other inventions include radar, the dynamo-powered flashlight, the electronic computer, and the "jerrycan" (named after petrol containers used by German soldiers, or "Jerrys"). Wartime research also accelerated the development of plastics for a host of household applications.

In the 1950s, two doctors, Jonas Salk and Albert Sabin, developed vaccines to combat polio, a disease that had sometimes reached epic proportions earlier in the 20th century. Similar vaccines were developed to help eradicate smallpox, measles, and cholera—all illnesses that had claimed countless victims around the world.

The 1953 mapping of human DNA by Francis Crick and James Watson opened up a whole new world in medicine as well as in law enforcement. Little known today is that their discovery drew heavily from the work of other researchers, including a British female chemist, Rosalind Franklin. Unfortunately, her contribution was not recognized when both men were awarded the 1962 Nobel Prize in physiology or medicine.

Another breakthrough was the development of organ transplants. The most famous transplant pioneer was South African surgeon Christiaan Barnard, who performed the first human heart transplant in 1967. Less known is American plastic surgeon Joseph Murray, who in 1954 accomplished the first successful kidney transplant on identical twins. Today, organ transplants have become such a key feature of modern medicine that wait times for a new heart average 190 days, and the search for a kidney donor may take almost three years.

Just as old diseases were eradicated, or at least contained, new illnesses emerged. AIDS (acquired

ASTRONAUTS Virgil Grissom, Edward White, and Roger Chaffee, the ill-fated crew of Apollo 1, pose before the Saturn V launch vehicle.

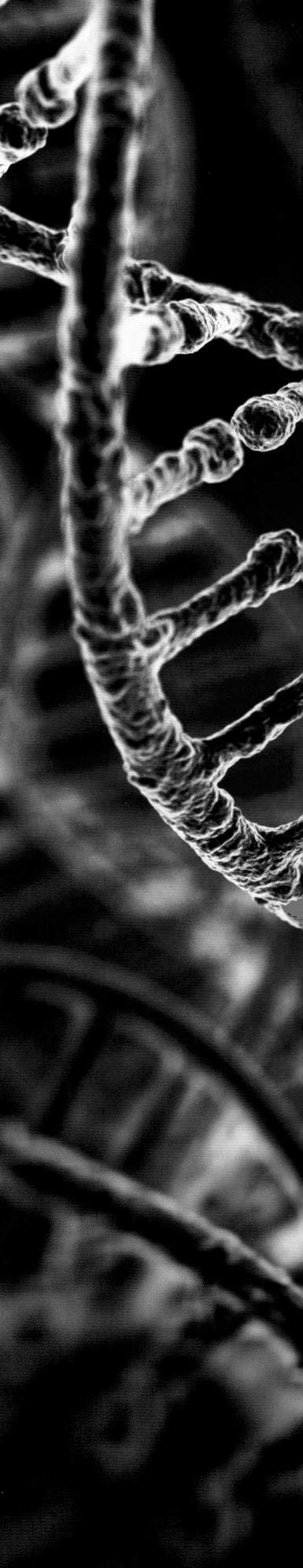

> "HIV DOES NOT MAKE PEOPLE DANGEROUS TO KNOW, SO YOU CAN SHAKE THEIR HANDS AND GIVE THEM A HUG. HEAVEN KNOWS THEY NEED IT."

DIANA, PRINCESS OF WALES

immunodeficiency syndrome) is a potentially fatal condition caused by the human immunodeficiency virus (HIV). AIDS, which is usually transmitted through the direct exchange of bodily fluids, has become the scourge of many nations, particularly in eastern and southern Africa. Since AIDS was identified in the early 1980s, the disease has claimed an estimated 32 million deaths worldwide and continues to spread. There is no cure, though a new class of antiretroviral drugs can help contain the disease and reduce the chance of death.

In developed countries such as the United States, another threat is posed by the growing addiction to opioids. Originally developed for pain relief, many prescribers initially underestimated their intense addictive effect. Today, it is estimated that 0.8 percent of the world population has become dependent on opioid drugs. In the United States alone, opioid addiction kills an average of 128 people a day, according to 2019 statistics by the National Institutes of Health. As a result, the life expectancy of American adult men has actually declined from 76.2 years to 76.1 years.

Modern Transportation

Another unique product of World War II research was the jet engine and the pressurized cabin, which allows an airplane to fly above 10,000 feet without the need for oxygen masks. This led to the development of pressurized passenger aircraft with jet propulsion, rather than piston engines, which can fly nonstop across the Atlantic. The first jet airliner was the Comet, developed by the British de Havilland company, which had its maiden flight in 1949. When metal fatigue caused several airplanes to crash, the American Boeing Company

THE PAST MEETS THE MODERN AGE as three Sudanese policemen on camels inspect a brand-new de Havilland Comet, the world's first commercial jet airliner, at the Khartoum airport in 1952.

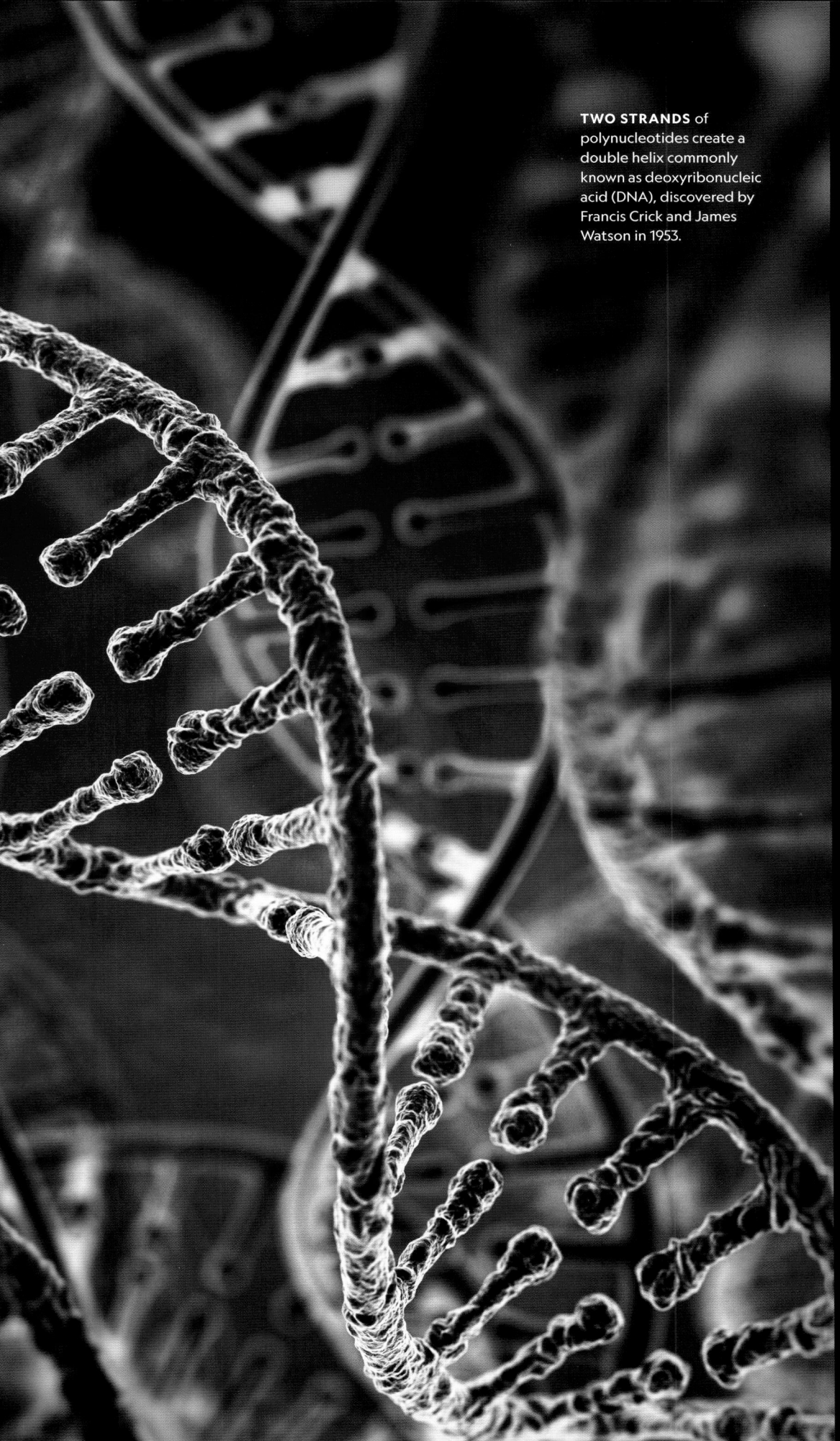

TWO STRANDS of polynucleotides create a double helix commonly known as deoxyribonucleic acid (DNA), discovered by Francis Crick and James Watson in 1953.

NOTABLE DATES

1953
Francis Crick and James Watson discover double-helix structure of DNA

1957
The Soviet Union launches Sputnik, the first artificial satellite

1967
Christiaan Barnard performs the first human heart transplant

1969
Apollo 11 astronaut Neil Armstrong is first man to walk on the moon

1978
First test-tube baby is born

1981
First U.S. space shuttle *Columbia* makes its maiden flight

1981
French TGV high-speed rail service begins

1990
Hubble Space Telescope is put into orbit

1994
Channel tunnel between Britain and France is opened

1996
British geneticists clone an adult sheep named Dolly

2008
Large Hadron Collider opens near Geneva

2017
Oldest *Homo sapiens* fossil, 300,000 years old, is found in North Africa

SINCE 2008, China has been creating a rail network of more than 18,000 miles of special high-speed track.

took the lead with its sleek four-engine 707, introduced in 1957.

In the 1960s, the British Aircraft Corporation and the French Aérospatiale company joined to create a supersonic airliner, the Concorde. Notwithstanding its sleek lines and a cruising speed at more than twice the speed of sound, the Concorde was a commercial failure. Its high operating cost ensured that only the wealthy could afford the average fare of $7,995 (about $12,500 today) to fly from New York to London in three and a half hours. After an Air France Concorde crashed in 2000, killing all passengers and crew on board, the model was retired in 2003.

Today, wide-body jets, low-cost airlines, and bigger airports have transformed international travel. During the 2010s, half a million people were in the air at any given moment, circling the globe. Growing concerns about the carbon footprint of jet aircraft and ecological damage to nature destinations are creating a greater awareness for the need for sustainable travel, however.

High-Speed Rail

Ecological concerns as well as the increasing congestion of the European airspace prompted several nations to look for alternatives to air travel. The answer was high-speed rail, the idea of laying special track to allow a train to travel at 150 miles an hour or more. Japan took an early lead in 1964 with the development of the Tokaido Shinkansen, the bullet train, eventually whisking passengers

"THE CONCORDE IS GREAT. IT GIVES YOU
THREE EXTRA HOURS TO FIND YOUR LUGGAGE."

BOB HOPE, AMERICAN COMEDIAN

from Tokyo to Osaka in two and a half hours. France then created a network of Trains à Grande Vitesse (high-speed trains). Today, the TGV track covers more than 1,640 miles. Germany, Italy, Spain, Denmark, and Sweden soon followed suit. China too has been creating an extensive high-speed rail network, laying more than 18,000 miles of special track since 2008—more than the combined total of high-speed lines in the rest of the world, serving more than 1.7 billion passengers a year.

Regrettably, high-speed rail has lagged in the United States. A compromise solution is Amtrak's Acela Express, which runs from Boston to Washington, D.C., on mostly regular track. California has begun developing a high-speed rail link from Los Angeles to San Francisco, but funding and appropriation problems in the wake of the COVID-19 pandemic have cast doubt on its timely completion.

The Channel Tunnel

The most impressive venture of the postwar era, however, was the construction of a railway tunnel between Great Britain and France, called the "Chunnel" for short. Construction began in 1988 with the aim of drilling a tunnel some 250 feet beneath the seabed of the English Channel. While English crews started digging near Folkestone, Kent, French crews set out from Coquelles, near Pas-de-Calais. Eleven special boring machines cut through the soft chalk of the seabed, creating two rail tunnels and a service tunnel with a length of 31 miles each. On December 1, 1990, the English

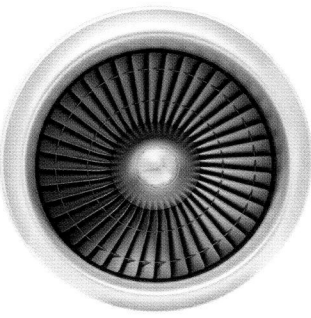

IN THE 1950S and 1960s, the turbofan jet engine revolutionized the airline industry, making international travel affordable for millions of passengers.

THE AGE OF JET TRAVEL

Although it was soon matched by the Douglas DC-8 and the Convair Coronado, the Boeing 707 was a stunning commercial success that inaugurated the age of jet travel. Similar passenger jet aircraft followed, including the three-engine 727 (1963), two-engine 737 (1967), and double-deck 747 jumbo jet, which first flew in 1969. In response, several European aerospace companies formed Airbus Industrie in 1970, after the French and British had developed the supersonic Concorde in the 1960s (at right). The result was the A300 wide body, which revolutionized intercontinental travel by relying on only two engines. In 1987, Airbus introduced the twin-engine A320, the first of so-called fly-by-wire aircraft. in which cockpit controls are transmitted electronically rather than through mechanical controls. In 2005, Airbus produced the full-length, double-deck A380. But Boeing's introduction of a successor to the best-selling 737 jet, the 737 MAX, was delayed after two MAX aircraft crashed as a result of the malfunctioning of its MCAS guidance software.

"A TRAIN RIDE FROM LONDON TO PARIS VIA THE 'CHUNNEL' EMITS 90% LESS GREENHOUSE GASES THAN THE EQUIVALENT SHORT-HAUL FLIGHT."

JOE MINIHANE, TRAVEL WRITER

and French crews met in the middle, shaking hands through a narrow opening. According to the BBC, a tunnel worker named Graham Fagg was the first man "to cross the Channel by land in 8,000 years."

Today, thousands of travelers cross the tunnel every day in Eurostar trains at speeds approaching 186 mph, covering the distance from London to Paris in 2 hours 15 minutes.

The Space Race

For much of the postwar era, the world was held in thrall by another major engineering challenge: the conquest of space. In this, the Soviet Union had taken an early lead by launching the world's first artificial satellite, Sputnik ("travel companion") in 1957. Though it orbited only for three weeks before its batteries died, Sputnik shocked the Western world at the height of the Cold War. It also created an acute crisis in the American engineering community.

Alarmed, in 1958, the U.S. Congress voted the National Aeronautics and Space Act, establishing NASA as the preeminent center of American space exploration. As part of this venture, NASA incorporated several other research institutes, including the Army Ballistic Missile Agency. Here, German scientist Wernher von Braun, designer of Hitler's V-2 rocket, was working on ballistic missiles for America's nuclear deterrent.

NASA's initial attempts to get a rocket into Earth's orbit failed, however, creating an even greater distance from the Soviet space program.

WITH A DIAMETER of more than 27 feet, the South Rail Boring Machine burrows its way deep under the floor of the English Channel on its journey to France.

IN FEBRUARY 1984, *Challenger* shuttle astronaut Bruce McCandless became the first American astronaut to float untethered in space, using a jet-propelled backpack.

"WE CHOOSE TO GO TO THE MOON IN THIS DECADE AND DO THE OTHER THINGS, NOT BECAUSE THEY ARE EASY, BUT BECAUSE THEY ARE HARD."

PRESIDENT JOHN F. KENNEDY ANNOUNCING THE APOLLO PROGRAM

Meanwhile, the Soviets succeeded in sending a probe to the moon in September 1959, followed by the spectacular launch of the first human being into orbit, cosmonaut Yuri Gagarin, in April 1961. This feat was followed two years later by the first woman in space, Valentina Tereshkova, in the spacecraft Vostok 6. At that time, it was believed that the U.S.S.R. had an almost insurmountable advantage in space technology, with major consequences for the Cold War and the security of the West.

Newly elected President John F. Kennedy decided to confront this superiority. In a May 25, 1961, speech to Congress, he announced that he was committing the United States to landing a man on the moon before the end of the 1960s. At the time, it seemed an almost impossible task: The U.S. space community lacked the technology to fulfill such an ambitious mission. But as Kennedy had anticipated, it was only by formulating a bold objective that Americans could catch up with the Soviets. In February 1962, NASA placed the first American astronaut in orbit with the successful launch of a Mercury capsule piloted by John Glenn. The subsequent Mercury and Gemini programs allowed astronauts to learn to maneuver in space before NASA embarked on the Apollo program that would carry three astronauts to the moon. In January 1967, however, the program suffered a tragic setback when, during a test on the ground, the capsule of Apollo 1 caught fire, killing all three men on board. Three months later, the Soviet Soyuz-1 spacecraft malfunctioned in space and crashed to Earth near Karabutak, Russia, killing cosmonaut Vladimir Komarov. The space race had become deadly.

The Apollo Program

After a thorough investigation, NASA plowed on with the Apollo program. Though Apollo 8 was originally intended to test the Apollo lunar module in Earth orbit, NASA planners changed the mission and sent the crew, led by Frank Borman, on the first manned flight to the moon. While orbiting its pockmarked surface, the astronauts read the first verses from the Book of Genesis, moving many on Earth to tears. One anonymous telegram read that Apollo 8 had "saved 1968"—a dark year otherwise marked by the devastating Tet Offensive in Vietnam, the Soviet suppression of the Prague Spring, as well as the assassinations of Senator Robert F. Kennedy and civil rights leader Martin Luther King, Jr. Even the Soviet newspaper *Pravda* was compelled to salute the "outstanding achievement of American space sciences and technology." Today, many historians agree that the flight of Apollo 8 was a turning point in the arms race.

Finally, on July 20, 1969, astronaut Neil Armstrong became the first human to set foot on the moon. Just three weeks earlier, a Soviet N-1 booster rocket had exploded on the launchpad, forever ending Russia's hopes to beat the Americans to the moon.

In the 1970s, NASA embarked on a new project: to develop a reusable orbital space shuttle that could deliver any number of satellites and return safely to Earth. The first space shuttle flew in 1981, but two spacecraft were lost as a result of technical malfunctions: *Challenger* in 1986 and *Columbia* in 2003. In 2011, the last space shuttle was retired from service. Since then, American space exploration has shifted to private companies such as SpaceX, as well as joint ventures with other government space agencies, including the European Space Agency. ∎

THE INITIAL Soviet lead in the space race became a major factor in the propaganda of the Cold War era.

**BELGIAN-BORN
BRITISH ACTRESS**
Audrey Hepburn
epitomized the glamour
and fashion of the early
1960s in the Hollywood
film *Breakfast at Tiffany's.*

THE RISE
OF MEDIA AND GLOBALIZATION

Some of the most prominent movements in the 20th century were the development of mass media and communications, bringing people around the globe closer together than ever before. The impact of the internet was the most profound, disrupting existing business while creating entirely new endeavors.

The first major mass medium was cinema, introduced as a series of film shorts in Paris by the Lumière brothers in 1895. It was only in the 1920s that motion pictures found their voice with synchronized sound, first pioneered in the motion picture *The Jazz Singer.* It was quickly adopted by Walt Disney to produce the first sound cartoon, *Steamboat Willie,* in 1928.

Cinema then rapidly grew in popularity around the world. It became the dominant mass medium between the wars, with stars such as Errol Flynn, Charles Chaplin, Greta Garbo, Gary Cooper, and Carole Lombard. Germany was at the forefront of avant-garde films with *Das Cabinet des Dr. Caligari* (1920), while Soviet director Sergei Eisenstein created a new cinematic vocabulary with films such as *Battleship Potemkin* (1925) and *Alexander Nevsky* (1938).

After World War II, Hollywood became the dominant source of filmed entertainment, though Hollywood itself experienced a profound change. The so-called studio system, whereby a studio retained a captive pool of directors, screenwriters, and actors, was abandoned, allowing them to work as free agents. In the 1960s, directors also quietly ended the Production Code, an unwritten law that put limits on the use of foul language, violence, and sex, resulting in films such as Arthur Penn's *Bonnie and Clyde* (1967) and Sam Peckinpah's *The Wild Bunch* (1969).

Hollywood has been able to hold on to its leading role in filmed entertainment with blockbusters such as *Avatar* (2009) and the *Star Wars* series, in both theaters and via streaming platforms.

Radio and Television

Shortly after World War I, another mass medium emerged, known as the wireless in Britain and radio in the United States. During the so-called Golden Age of Radio, this medium began to experiment with a range of new program formats, from news broadcasts to quiz shows, variety shows, and what today we call "scripted drama."

In the late 1930s, another mass medium made its appearance: television. Although the American General Electric Corporation planned to initiate daily television broadcasts as early as 1928, it was the German Telefunken company that launched the first television broadcast in 1936, covering the

THE FIRST electronic mass medium of the 20th century was radio, known as the wireless in Britain.

> "NOBODY REALLY KNEW WHAT TELEVISION WAS SUPPOSED TO BE LIKE; THE NETWORKS WHO OWNED THE TECHNOLOGY DIDN'T HAVE A CLUE AS TO HOW TO PROGRAM IT."

CHARLTON HESTON, FILM AND TV STAR

Olympic Games in Berlin. As a medium, however, television found itself imitating radio because of the same technical limitations: the inability to prerecord shows for later broadcast. Thus, early television embraced live theater and drama just as early radio had done, with shows like *Kraft Television Theater, Playhouse 90,* and CBS's *Studio One.*

Cinema, the leading 20th-century medium

In due course, television became one of the most successful media platforms of the 20th century. Part of its rapid penetration was due to the GI Bill of Rights, which gave war veterans access to higher education as well as low-interest loans for homes or small business. It also became a major competitor to another source of entertainment: movies. In response, the American film community began to produce lavish color epics in wide-screen Cinemascope, so as to compete with the small black-and-white screen at home.

Television was a major catalyst in bringing the civil rights movement of the 1960s to the attention to the American public. Now that nearly 90 percent of all American households owned a TV set,

EUROPEAN CINEMA

In reaction to the carefully staged cinematography of Hollywood, French and Italian filmmakers of the 1970s moved out of the studio and onto the street—making films in real-life locations. The French called it *la Nouvelle Vague,* "the New Wave," bringing fame to the likes of Brigitte Bardot (at left). Film directors Jean-Luc Godard, Claude Chabrol, and François Truffaut became auteurs, not just directing but also writing screenplays, editing films, and serving as producers. In Italy, a similar movement, "neorealism," used working-class characters rather than professional actors in films such as Roberto Rossellini's *Rome, Open City* and Federico Fellini's *La Strada.* Still, European audiences flocked to American movies, which were usually produced with more glamorous stars. By the 1990s, Hollywood was producing 70 percent of the world's television content and 80 percent of the world's theatrical features. In response, many countries established quotas that sought to limit American films in favor of homegrown features.

THE *STAR WARS* motion picture franchise was launched in 1977 with the first movie of the saga, directed by George Lucas and starring Mark Hamill, Carrie Fisher, and Harrison Ford.

NOTABLE DATES

1941
FCC develops NTSC standard for black and white television

1951
UNIVAC, the first commercial computer, comes online

1955
Opening of Disneyland is first live coast-to-coast broadcast in U.S.

1956
Ampex develops broadcast-quality videotape

1960
The Kennedy-Nixon debate is televised nationwide

1960
Jean-Luc Godard's New Wave film *Breathless* is released

1967
Most of U.S. network TV switches to color

1969
ARPANET, forerunner of the internet, is developed

1977
The Apple II computer is launched

1977
Star Wars grosses $775 million at box office worldwide

1996
FCC approves high-definition standard for television

2007
Apple releases a consumer smartphone, the iPhone

A 1950S computer technician operates a computer console of one of the early IBM mainframe computers, known as an electronic data processing machine.

"MAY NOT MACHINES CARRY OUT SOMETHING WHICH OUGHT TO BE DESCRIBED AS THINKING, BUT WHICH IS VERY DIFFERENT FROM WHAT A MAN DOES?"

ALAN TURING, BRITISH COMPUTER SCIENTIST

the country could witness the shocking scenes of violent clashes between civil rights protesters and the police in places like Selma, Birmingham, and Little Rock. For civil rights leader Martin Luther King, Jr., the television camera became "[his] chosen instrument," as an NBC correspondent put it, exposing the Jim Crow segregation policies of the South. The growing public outcry led to the Civil Rights Act of 1964.

The Age of the Computer

As influential as television and cinema was the development of the computer—an idea as old as human civilization. The abacus, essentially a counting frame, was developed in Sumer as early as the third millennium B.C.E. But it was not until the 1801 invention of an automatic loom using punched cards by Joseph-Marie Jacquard that a machine could execute complex tasks previously performed by a human being. The punch card system inspired American inventor Herman Hollerith to create an electromechanical machine to process the data from the 1890 U.S. Census. He went on to found the Tabulating Machine Company in 1896, which eventually became known as IBM.

In 1936, Alan Turing, a British mathematician, began work on a computational machine that during World War II was able to break the Enigma code that the German Navy used. His work was matched by German scientist Konrad Zuse, who in 1941 created the first programmable computer, the Z3. The Nazi regime did not recognize its potential, however, and two years later, the Z3 was destroyed during a bombing attack on Berlin. The next development came in the United States with the first programmable electronic digital computer, known as the ENIAC, in 1946, followed by UNIVAC, the first commercial computer, in 1951. The ENIAC weighed 30 tons and could perform 5,000 operations a second. Large mainframe computers such as these could be operated only with a special binary programming language, such as COBOL or FORTRAN. What's more, they took up a lot of room, often in special air-conditioned spaces.

The breakthrough invention of the integrated circuit or computer chip, such as the Motorola 68000 microprocessor, made it possible for computers to become increasingly miniaturized. In the late 1970s, this led to the development of the first personal computers such as the Commodore PET and Radio Shack's TRS-80. But since most people did not know or understand any computer languages, their impact was limited. This changed in 1977, when Steve Wozniak and Steve Jobs introduced a computer with a graphical user interface

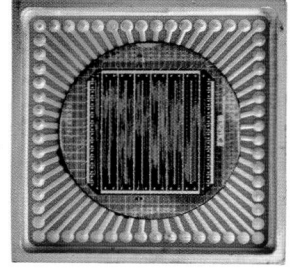

THE APPLE II, originally designed and built by Steve Jobs and Steve Wozniak in 1976, was the first mass-marketed personal computer. **ABOVE:** An early integrated circuit, or microchip, designed by Howard Aiken in 1957.

> "WITHOUT SOUNDING TOO CLICHÉ, THE INTERNET IS REALLY THE BIRTH OF THE GLOBAL MIND."
>
> **TERENCE MCKENNA,**
> **AMERICAN MYSTIC AND AUTHOR**

that made its use easy and transparent for consumers. When their Apple II became a big success, IBM, long a manufacturer of office mainframes, responded with the IBM PC in 1981. So immediate was the impact of these machines that *Time* magazine named the home computer the 1982 "Machine of the Year."

The Birth of the Internet

These early computers were used for simple tasks such as word processing and spreadsheets. But it was soon recognized that computers could also serve as communication terminals if they could be connected to a network. The internet was born in 1969 as a private system known as ARPANET, enabling researchers and developers to share data. This was done by formatting data groups in "packets" that could be transmitted via ordinary phone lines and decoded using so-called modems (MODulation and DEModulation). As ARPANET and a number of other networks began to proliferate, system designers recognized the need to link these systems together, known as "internetworking." France took the lead by creating a nationwide network called Minitel, delivered in French, that was offered free to every phone subscriber.

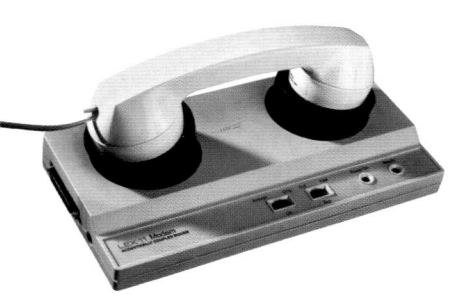

AT THE BEGINNING of the internet age, personal computers used a 300-band acoustic coupler modem to transmit computer data over telephone lines.

THE INTERNET, which was born in 1969 as a private system known as ARPANET, has fundamentally changed the way the world does business, while social media allow anyone to instantly publish text, images, or video for a global audience.

A KARENNI WOMAN in Myanmar takes a selfie with her friend. In many parts of the Third World, mobile technology and Wi-Fi connectivity have leapfrogged more traditional forms of communications, such as two-wire phone lines or coaxial cable.

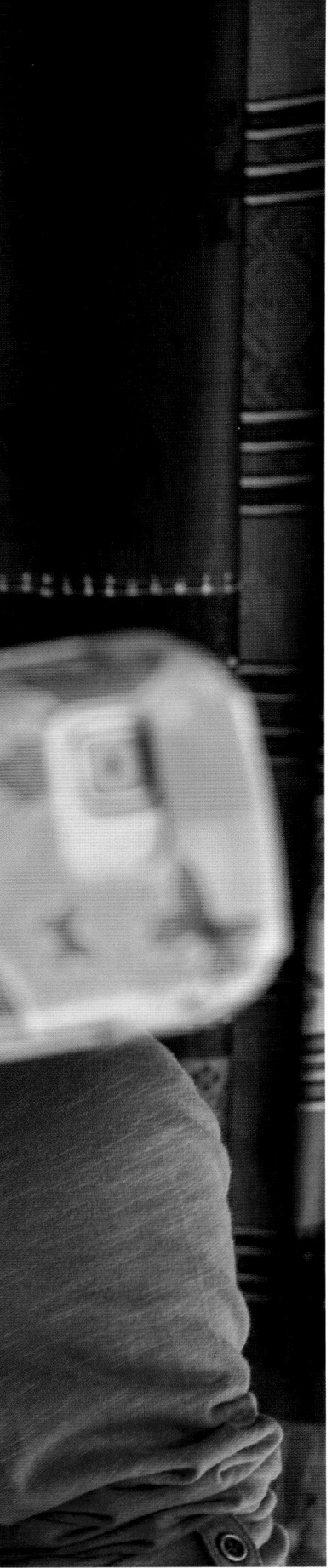

In the 1990s, however, new protocols began to replace such dedicated systems with a network that could truly go global: the World Wide Web. But like home computers, the Web needed a graphical user interface to allow people without computer training to "browse" the growing number of databases available on this network. Some of the earliest browsers were Netscape, Altavista, and Microsoft's Internet Explorer. The problem that these services faced was how to make money if the browsers were to be offered for free. In the early 2000s, a company named Google solved that problem by linking key word searches to sponsored advertising. Today, the market value of tech companies like Google and Microsoft is routinely valued at around $1 trillion each.

The Smartphone Revolution

During the first two decades of the 21st century, the internet transformed the way humans communicated with one another, conducted their business, and shopped for goods. Social media such as YouTube, Facebook, and Instagram now have billions of subscribers all over the world. Much of this revolution involved not only computers but also an entirely new class of technology: the smartphone. This device was made possible by the development of cellular technology that enabled consumers to make phone calls via a radio frequency link rather than conventional landlines. In the mid- to late 1990s, several companies developed so-called personal digital assistants (PDAs) such as the Apple Newton, the PalmPilot, and the Pocket PC, but their weight, bulkiness, and limited cellular access sharply limited their appeal. Japan's products were the exception. Here mobile phones rapidly gained in Web connectivity because of a dedicated mobile internet platform created by Japanese wireless provider NTT. By 2002, NTT's DoCoMo mobile service had an estimated 40 million subscribers.

Taking its cue from the Japanese model, a Canadian company launched the first true line of smartphones in North America under the BlackBerry brand. These mobile devices soon gained a rapid following, particularly in the business community, but their high price and subscriber cost made them less attractive for consumers. Apple's Steve Jobs recognized this opportunity and in 2007 launched the iPhone as the first truly integrated smartphone designed for consumer use.

The iPhone—and a host of similar devices built by Korean and Chinese imitators—has transformed human society. Today, there are about 8.3 billion subscribers of wireless devices (in a total world population of 7.7 billion). In many parts of the Third World, mobile technology and Wi-Fi connectivity have leapfrogged conventional land-based telephony systems, giving users in remote or rural regions access to information they never enjoyed before.

Apple iPhone

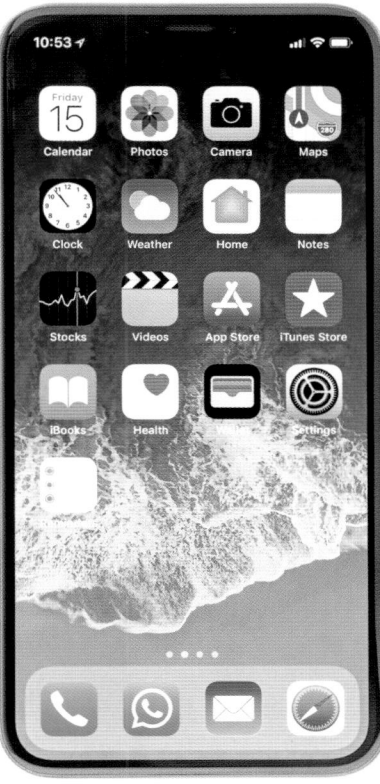

The rapid growth of online transactions has allowed scores of independent entrepreneurs to break into market sectors previously dominated by large retail actors. A 2019 study found a marked correlation between female entrepreneurship and single parenthood—an important phenomenon at a time when a growing number of single women are raising children. At the same time, the internet has opened up a range of e-government functions that invite greater participation by citizens while providing online access to a plethora of traditional government services. In sum, modern life is unthinkable without the World Wide Web. ∎

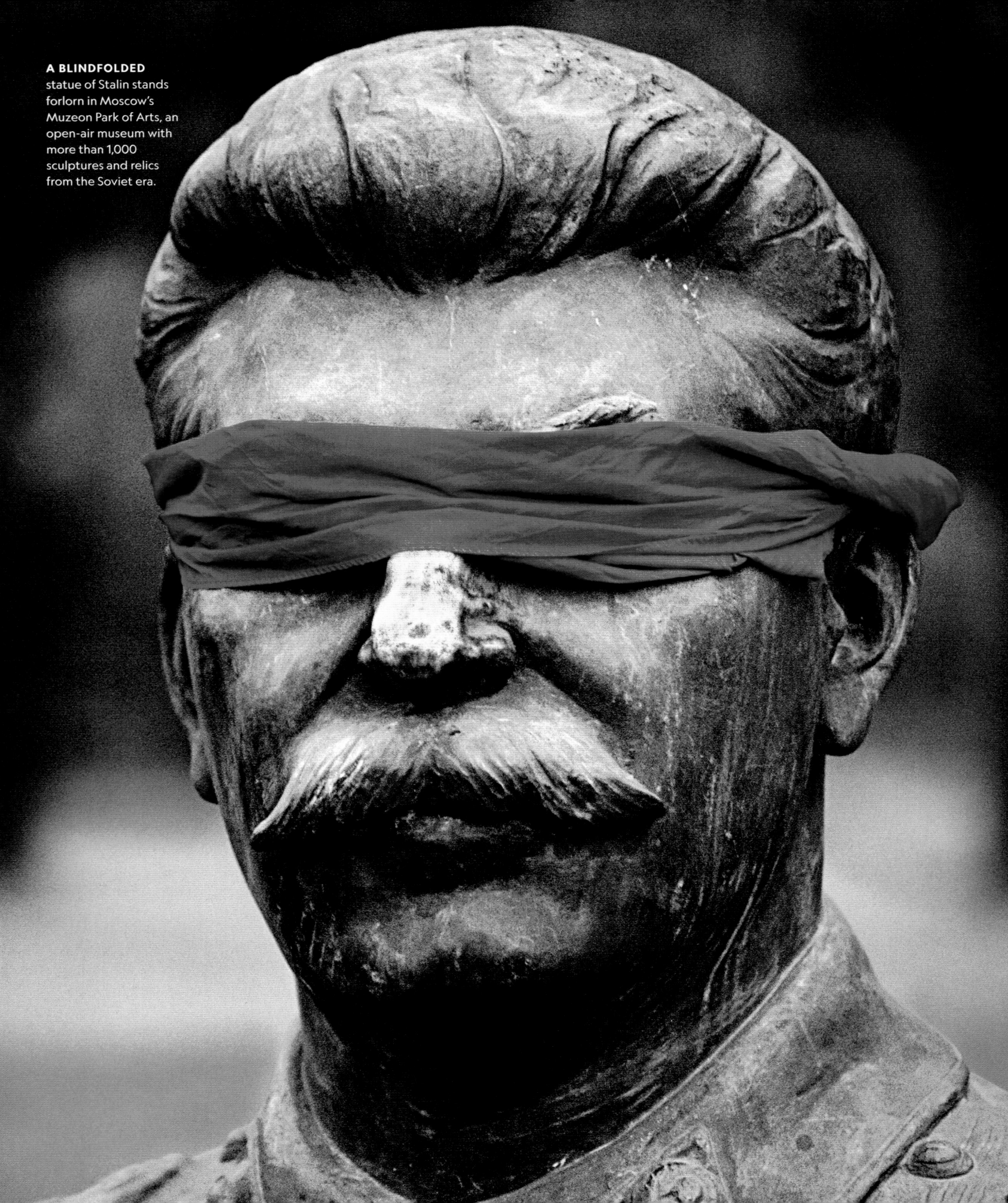

A BLINDFOLDED statue of Stalin stands forlorn in Moscow's Muzeon Park of Arts, an open-air museum with more than 1,000 sculptures and relics from the Soviet era.

THE MULTIPOLAR
WORLD

With the fall of the Soviet Union and the rise of China, the 21st century is facing a multipolar world. A key factor is the global economy, which has fueled prosperity as well as greater inequality. At the same time, nations must confront the threat of climate change, pandemics, and shrinking resources.

Many had hoped that the fall of the Soviet bloc would usher in a new era of peace and prosperity. But the dawn of the 21st century saw a new world order in which bipolar Cold War tensions were replaced with a growing multipolar complexity, driven by the conflicting forces of the global economy and a growing desire to reassert individual sovereignty and national identity. While overall global prosperity has increased, it has also created greater inequality between the developed and the developing world while driving a widening gap between a wealthy elite and the vast majority of middle- and lower-income families in First World nations.

The Threat of Terrorism

Another key factor that is threatening global stability is terrorism. Terrorist acts in the service of political goals are nothing new, of course. Countless leaders as well as innocent citizens have been killed to advance particular ideological goals since the exploits of the Hashshashin against the Sunni caliphs of the 11th-century Seljuk Empire. In the 1970s, for example, the West was rocked by a spate of terrorist attacks that often involved the hijacking of airplanes or the assassination of prominent figures. Italy had the *Brigate Rosse* (Red Brigades), and Germany was tormented by the Baader-Meinhof Gang, while in 1970, several airliners were hijacked by Palestinian militants and blown up in the Jordanian Desert.

Even so, the world was unprepared for the intense violence of the attacks of September 11, 2001, in which a group of mostly Saudi militants flew hijacked planes into the World Trade Center and the Pentagon. A fourth hijacked plane was aiming for the capital of Washington, D.C., but crashed in a Pennsylvania field after passengers heroically tried to take control of the aircraft. In response, U.S. leaders launched military invasions of Afghanistan and Iraq that, while successfully capturing the mastermind of the 9/11 attacks, al Qaeda's Osama bin

A 1988 propaganda poster celebrated the achievements of the Soviet Union and the irresistible march of Marxism. Three years later, the U.S.S.R. had ceased to exist.

"MR. GORBACHEV, TEAR DOWN THIS WALL!"

PRESIDENT RONALD REAGAN AT THE BRANDENBURG GATE IN WEST BERLIN

Laden, also destabilized the Middle East.

Two other important developments are the rise of China as a global economic and military power and a resurgent Russia that tries to reassert its former role on the world stage through cyberterrorism and so-called asynchronous warfare.

Fire helmet from the World Trade Center

Latin America

During the past 50 years, the countries of Latin America have experienced grave challenges of their own. Many were ruled by military juntas through the 1960s and 1970s that tried to stem the growing influence of Soviet-inspired communism. These included the junta that in 1973 overthrew the democratically elected government of Marxist Salvador Allende of Chile and the 1976 coup that brought a ruthless group of generals to power in Argentina, led by Jorge Rafael Videla. Brazil had succumbed to a military dictatorship in 1964. Only Mexico and Venezuela remained beacons of parliamentary democracy, though their economies became overly reliant on their oil revenues.

At the same time, Latin America's economy was rapidly changing from one vested in mining and agriculture to one relying on growing industrialization and manufacturing. This, in turn, created a demand for imported raw materials, leading to large foreign debts. These changes also spurred a growing urban resistance

THE FALL OF THE IRON CURTAIN

Prompted by the reforms of Soviet President Mikhail Gorbachev, leaders in Hungary and Poland gradually reduced state control of their populations. In 1989, the feared East German *Volkspolizei*, or "People's Police," stood by while East German citizens breached the Berlin Wall, reuniting the city for the first time since 1961 (at left). In Romania, furious protests led to the fall of dictator Nicolae Ceauşescu and his wife, Elena. Czechoslovakia, meanwhile, achieved its freedom through a nonviolent transition of power known as the Velvet Revolution. Faced with these developments, Gorbachev refused to intervene. Outraged, an ultraconservative group of Marxist-Leninist hardliners staged a coup against the Soviet leader in August 1991, which failed. Meanwhile, unrest among the individual republics of the U.S.S.R. continued to grow, and on December 26, 1991, the Soviet Union formally ceased to exist.

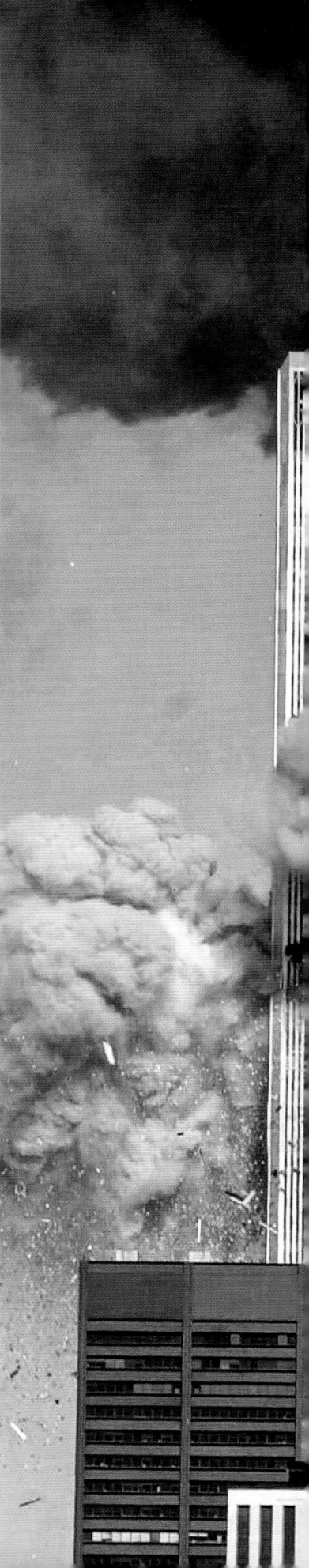

UNITED AIRLINES Flight 175, piloted by al Qaeda terrorists, crashes into the south tower of the World Trade Center in New York at 9:03 a.m. on September 11, 2001.

NOTABLE DATES

1953
Six nations create the European Coal and Steel Community (ECSC)

1957
ECSC members create the European Economic Community (EEC)

1967
Five Asian nations form the Association of Southeast Asian Nations (ASEAN)

1978
Deng Xiaoping moves China toward a socialist market economy

1989
Fall of the Berlin Wall

1993
Maastricht Treaty creates a single market known as the European Union

1999
The euro is introduced as common currency in 11 countries

2002
International Criminal Court begins operations in The Hague, Netherlands

2011
Protesters take to the streets in the Middle East during Arab Spring

2020
The United Kingdom leaves the European Union

2020
COVID-19 pandemic wreaks global havoc

NICARAGUAN CONTRA rebels train in a camp near Yamales, Honduras, as part of a CIA-financed bid to topple the revolutionary Sandinista regime in Nicaragua.

to traditional landowning elites who always had enjoyed strong political influence.

The worsening global economy of the early 1980s, staggering national debts, and growing popular unrest left the military juntas little choice but to negotiate a return to democratic rule. In 1982, Brazil held its first national elections in 20 years. The following year, Argentines went to the polls and chose Raúl Alfonsín the first democratically elected president since 1976. Alfonsín promptly ordered a government investigation into the disappearance of up to 30,000 men and women

during Videla's rule. Peru also returned to democracy in 1979, as did Bolivia in 1982. In 1989, General Pinochet of Chile was ousted after losing a plebiscite by 54 percent of the vote.

During the administration of President Ronald Reagan, however, Central America became a battleground between pro-American forces and revolutionary movements supported by the Soviet Union. The United States firmly allied itself with the military juntas of El Salvador and Guatemala, while fomenting rebellion (by the so-called contras) against the revolutionary

Sandinista regime in Nicaragua. In doing so, it often ignored the intense suffering of farmers and peasants during these civil wars. Thousands of indigenous communities throughout Central America were displaced or destroyed. Only in the late 1980s was President Óscar Arias of Costa Rica able to get the various ruling factions to sign the Esquipulas Peace Agreement, which laid the basis for bringing the regional civil wars to an end. In recognition of this, Arias was awarded the 1987 Nobel Peace Prize.

Today, the nations of Latin America face new political and economic challenges. As in other parts of the world, Latin Americans are dismayed that few of the blessings of a global economy are shared by the population at large. In response, new populist parties came to power in Brazil, Argentina, and Mexico between 2017 and 2019.

Many hope that Brazil, long the economic engine of the region, will lead the continent out of its prolonged slump. But the reluctance of Brazilian leaders to intervene in the rampant deforestation of the Amazon rainforest runs the risk of tarnishing Brazil's reputation and damages its chances of an economic recovery. Therefore, many business leaders in the region have pinned their hopes on a trade deal between MERCOSUR (a trade bloc consisting of Brazil, Argentina, Paraguay, and Uruguay) and the European Union to vouchsafe the continent's economic future.

Africa

No other continent has seen so many changes in the postwar era as Africa. Although it suffered little devastation during World War II (except for Libya and Tunisia, the site of prolonged battles between the Allies and the German Afrika Korps), its disengagement from European colonialism was

THE NOBEL PEACE PRIZE is awarded each year to those who have worked for "fraternity between nations."

A BUSY SHOPPING street in Lagos, Nigeria's largest city and one of the fastest-growing urban centers in the world

"I LEARNED THAT COURAGE WAS NOT THE ABSENCE OF FEAR, BUT THE TRIUMPH OVER IT."

NELSON MANDELA, FIRST BLACK PRESIDENT OF SOUTH AFRICA

difficult and protracted. Both France and Great Britain had hoped to restore control of their African colonies at the end of the war, notwithstanding their signing of the Atlantic Charter that allowed all nations to choose their government. Thus, the very continent where humanity began some 200,000 years ago achieved its independence only at considerable cost, further exacerbated by Cold War proxy wars. These efforts peaked in 1960, "The Year of Africa," when 17 African nations declared their independence. President Charles de Gaulle of France, however, clung to French control of Algeria, prompting a vicious civil war in which 7,000 French soldiers and 77,000 Algerian revolutionary fighters died.

By 1974, all of the nations of West Africa had achieved their independence, but the enmity of this process and the lack of a proper political transition ensured that many of these countries would suffer from corruption, tribal nepotism, and economic decline. The political instability soon invited insurgency groups in Nigeria, Sierra Leone, Liberia, and the Ivory Coast, often as superpower proxies.

British colonies did not fare much better. A key catalyst was the 1952 overthrow of the monarchy in Egypt, long a de facto British protectorate, and the rise of Gamal Nasser as a model of the modern African leader. After the ill-fated British invasion of Egypt during the Suez Crisis of 1956, which brought Britain to the brink of bankruptcy, its disengagement from its colonial possessions in Africa accelerated. In 1957, Ghana became the first sub-Saharan African nation to gain independence. Three years later, British Minister Harold Macmillan delivered a speech in South Africa in which he spoke of the "wind of change blowing

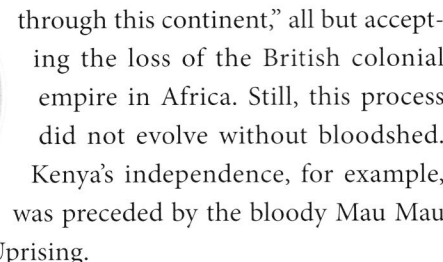

1984 anti-apartheid badge

through this continent," all but accepting the loss of the British colonial empire in Africa. Still, this process did not evolve without bloodshed. Kenya's independence, for example, was preceded by the bloody Mau Mau Uprising.

Rhodesia and South Africa

Over the preceding centuries, many Western families—including Dutch and British citizens—had settled in the colonial possessions of their nations to cultivate large estates while nurturing a strong bond with the land. These white farmers watched with alarm as their former homelands began to divest themselves from their colonies, believing that widespread chaos and violence between whites and blacks were likely to follow—as it did, for example, in Belgian Congo in 1960. In 1965, a former Royal Air Force pilot and white African farmer named Ian Smith declared himself head of an independent Rhodesia, to be ruled by a white minority. The result was a 14-year conflict known as the Bush War among Ian Smith's minority government, the Zimbabwe African National Union, and the Zimbabwe People's Revolutionary Army—each supported to some degree by the United States, Russia, and China. The conflict ended with the formation of independent Zimbabwe under ZANU leader Robert Mugabe in 1980.

A similar process was taking place in South Africa. Here, its predominantly Dutch farmer community (known as Boers) had formed the Union of South Africa in 1910 as a dominion within the British Empire. Its white minority government then proceeded to marginalize the majority Black population with a segregationist policy called apartheid ("separateness") so as to preempt any takeover by the Black African major-

ity. As the standard of living rose for whites, Black Afrikaners were deliberately disadvantaged in housing, education, and employment. In 1961, South Africa's ruling National Party severed all relations with the British and began to pursue apartheid with a vengeance, cracking down on any form of dissent, including the anti-apartheid African National Congress (ANP) led by Nelson Mandela. Mandela himself was arrested in 1962 and held in prison for 26 years.

As international condemnation of its apartheid policies grew, the South African leadership began to arm itself with nuclear weapons so as to deter any foreign invasion. But severe international sanctions brought the Far Right government to its knees. After Mandela was released in 1990, a new government led by President F. W. de Klerk rolled back the onerous apartheid rules, dismantled its nuclear weapons, and held universal elections in 1994. In a sign of hope and reconciliation, Nelson Mandela was elected the nation's first Black president.

Modern Africa

Today, Africa is not only the second most populous continent in the world; its population of

NELSON MANDELA campaigns in Cape Town during South Africa's first democratic election in 1994. He was elected as the nation's first black head of state and served until 1999.

SAMBURU WOMEN in traditional dress gather in a classroom north of Nairobi, Kenya, to learn how to operate a computer tablet.

1.3 billion is also the youngest, with a median age of 19.7 (as compared to the worldwide median age of 30.9). What's more, Africa is blessed with abundant natural resources. And yet the continent is also the world's poorest and least developed region, in part because of its endemic corruption, tribalism, lack of education, and limited access to foreign capital. The region is also frequently riven by tribal conflicts, such as the Rwandan genocide against the Tutsi, Twa, and Hutu tribes in 1990.

Another economic impediment is the poor quality of roads between its towns and cities, which means that transporting goods can cost five times more in Africa than in the United States. Visa requirements, even among neighboring nations, are another obstacle, particularly since the continent is carved up in no fewer than 54 separate countries. There are, however, positive signs that better times are ahead. The discovery of oil and gas has made Equatorial Guinea one of the richest countries in Africa. The Africa 2020 project, led by France's President Emmanuel Macron, aims to

former Ottoman Province of Palestine, governed as a British Mandate since the Great War, would be partitioned into a Jewish and an Arab state. At the time, Palestine was populated by 56,000 Jews and 644,000 Arabs, but tensions between Arab and Jewish settlements had led to outright guerrilla warfare in the 1930s. While Britain originally supported the idea of a Jewish homeland in Palestine, that sentiment changed during World War II, when British support swung to the Arab side so as not to incite an Arab uprising while British forces were fighting German forces in North Africa. Jewish immigration to Palestine was curtailed.

Following the discovery of Nazi concentration camps and the full extent of the Holocaust, in which six million Jews perished, world opinion swept back in favor of granting both Jews and Arabs their own states in Palestine. As violence between the two factions escalated, Britain was desperate to relinquish its mandate over the territory.

At midnight on May 14, 1948, the British Mandate expired, and an exultant David Ben-Gurion proclaimed the State of Israel, becoming its first prime minister. The next day, a coalition of Arab nations including Egypt, Iraq, and Jordan staged a multipronged invasion of the young Israeli state with the aim of driving all Jewish inhabitants into the sea. Remarkably, they did not succeed. However, some 600,000 Arabs had left their homes, either under duress or voluntarily, in the belief that Arab victory was inevitable. They settled in refugee camps in bordering states, many of them still in existence today. When an armistice was reached after months of bitter conflict, Israeli

ACROSS THE GLOBE, the logo of the United Nations, adopted in 1946, is a sign of hope, encompassing nine international UN agencies that work for the betterment of humankind.

overcome tribalism by developing a sense of a pan-African identity through art, science, education, and entrepreneurship. Even more hopeful is the 2019 launch of the African Continental Free Trade Agreement (AfCFTA), which economists hope will eliminate intra-African tariffs and create a free trade zone across the continent.

The Middle East Conflict

In 1947, the newly formed United Nations voted for a plan, known as Resolution 181, whereby the

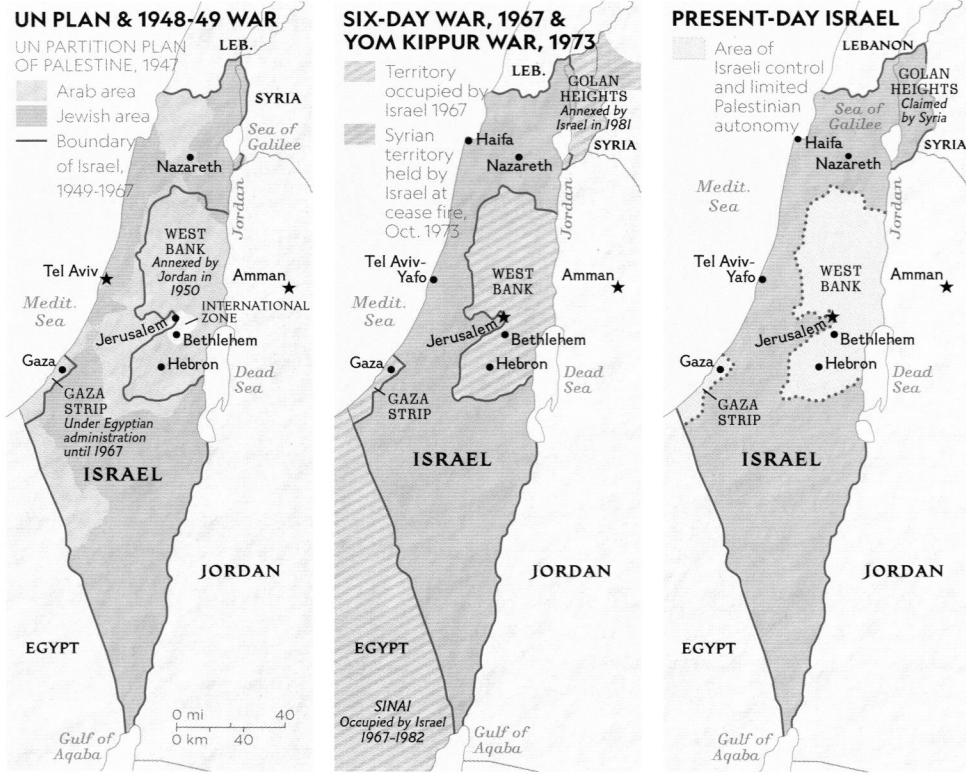

UN PLAN & 1948-49 WAR

UN PARTITION PLAN
OF PALESTINE, 1947

Arab area

Jewish area

Boundary
of Israel,
1949-1967

LEB.

SYRIA

Sea of Galilee

Nazareth

Jordan

WEST
BANK
Annexed by
Jordan in
1950

Amman ★

Tel Aviv ★

*Medit.
Sea*

INTERNATIONAL
ZONE

Jerusalem • Bethlehem

Gaza

• Hebron

*Dead
Sea*

GAZA
STRIP
Under Egyptian
administration
until 1967

ISRAEL

JORDAN

EGYPT

0 mi   40
0 km   40

*Gulf of
Aqaba*

**SIX-DAY WAR, 1967 &
YOM KIPPUR WAR, 1973**

Territory
occupied by
Israel 1967

Syrian
territory
held by
Israel at
cease fire,
Oct. 1973

LEB.

GOLAN
HEIGHTS
Annexed by
Israel in 1981

• Haifa

Nazareth

SYRIA

Tel Aviv-
Yafo •

*Medit.
Sea*

WEST
BANK

Amman ★

Jerusalem • Bethlehem

Gaza •

• Hebron

*Dead
Sea*

GAZA
STRIP

ISRAEL

JORDAN

EGYPT

*SINAI
Occupied by Israel
1967-1982*

*Gulf of
Aqaba*

PRESENT-DAY ISRAEL

Area of
Israeli control
and limited
Palestinian
autonomy

LEBANON

GOLAN
HEIGHTS
Claimed
by Syria

*Sea of
Galilee*

• Haifa

Nazareth

SYRIA

Tel Aviv-
Yafo •

*Medit.
Sea*

WEST
BANK

Amman ★

Jerusalem • Bethlehem

Gaza •

• Hebron

*Dead
Sea*

GAZA
STRIP

ISRAEL

JORDAN

EGYPT

*Gulf of
Aqaba*

**NIGHT VISION
GOGGLES** were widely
deployed during night
operations of the 1991
Gulf War, pitting a
coalition of 36 nations
against Iraq's annexation
of Kuwait.

forces had not only secured the territory allotted to them under the UN Partition Plan but also taken possession of almost 60 percent of the proposed Arab state, including Galilee and parts of the Negev. The Kingdom of Jordan, meanwhile captured the remaining half, including the West Bank and the Old City of Jerusalem.

Two more wars would follow: the 1967 Six Day War that gave Israel control of the West Bank and Jerusalem and the 1973 Yom Kippur War in which Israel came very close to defeat. But President Anwar Sadat of Egypt, who had succeeded Gamal Nasser in 1970, realized that acquiescence in Israel's existence was inevitable. Egypt's limited victory in the Yom Kippur War, when it retook much of the Sinai Peninsula, gave him the political credibility to seek peace. After a dramatic 1977 visit to Israel, Sadat entered negotiations with U.S. President Jimmy Carter and Israeli prime minister Menachem Begin that led to the 1979 Peace Treaty between Egypt and Israel. For this, Sadat was ostracized by much of the Arab world and assassinated by Islamic militants in

1981. In 1994, however, Jordan's King Hussein followed suit, signing a peace treaty with Israel's prime minister, Yitzhak Rabin, under auspices of U.S. President Bill Clinton.

The peace treaties shifted the balance of power in the Middle East. Israel, previously the underdog, now became a major economic and military power, even though the hostility of other states, including Iraq and Iran, remained undiminished.

The Persian Gulf Wars

In 1991, U.S. President George H. W. Bush and Britain's prime minister, Margaret Thatcher, led a coalition of 35 nations in a military attack on Iraq for its annexation of Kuwait. In just 100 hours of ground war, the coalition forces commanded by Gen. Norman Schwarzkopf of the United States decimated Iraqi troops and armor, ending with a cease-fire. Iraq's dictator, Saddam Hussein, however, was allowed to remain in power, much to the regret of some. Indeed, after the al Qaeda terror attacks of September 11, 2001, President George W. Bush (son of President George H. W. Bush) sought a UN mandate to invade Iraq once more, based on intelligence, largely discredited since, that Saddam Hussein was involved in the 9/11 attacks and had stockpiled an arsenal of chemical weapons. Although no UN support was forthcoming, the United States did invade Iraq in 2003, toppling Saddam Hussein. The invasion also incited a civil war between Iraq's Sunni minority and Shiite majority that would last for more than a decade. Few American strategists, however, realized that Hussein's regime, no matter how odious, had served as a major deterrent to Iran's ambitions in the region. That deterrent was now gone.

Until 1979, Iran had been a staunch U.S. ally, led by the Shah Mohammed Reza Pahlavi. But the shah's excessive lifestyle and his brutal suppression of dissent led in 1978 to a revolution led by

CAMELS DESPERATELY search for water and untainted shrubs while the oil fields of southern Kuwait burn on the horizon.

Ayatollah Ruhollah Khomeini. Persia now became the Islamic Republic of Iran. Today, with a population of 82 million kept in check by an Islamic theocracy, Iran continues to nurture the hope of becoming the leading power in the Middle East. With Iraq now governed by a Shiite majority, that nation has changed from an enemy to one of Iran's closest allies, further abetting Iranian ambitions.

To bolster its military prowess, Iran embarked on a plan to develop nuclear weapons. This program was temporarily suspended by a 2015 deal with the United States and five other world powers: China, Russia, France, the United Kingdom, and the European Union. Under terms of this deal, Iran agreed to limit its nuclear activities and allow international inspectors to verify its compliance, in return for the lifting of crippling economic sanctions. But in 2018, President Donald Trump abrogated the deal, prompting Iran to resume its nuclear development while escalating its proxy wars against Western interests in the region.

The Arab Spring

In 2010, a 26-year-old Tunisian named Mohamed Bouazizi was trying to sell his crop of vegetables from a cart in Sidi Bouzid, some 190 miles south of Tunis, as he had been doing for the past seven years. As the sole breadwinner of a family of eight, he had many mouths to feed. But on December 17, an officer confiscated his cart and his produce, claiming that he did not have the proper license. Bouaziz, who was used to the corrupt ways of the Tunisian regime led by President Zine El Abidine Ben Ali, first offered to pay a fine. When this was refused, an altercation ensued, Bouaziz was struck, and strenuous attempts to recover his vegetables were refused. The young man then returned to police headquarters, doused himself with paint thinner, and set himself on fire.

In previous periods, incidents such as this, though tragic, would not have merited much media attention beyond the local newspapers. But this was 2010, when much of the world's news was no longer transmitted through news agencies but through social media such as Twitter, Facebook, and YouTube. When the young man's immolation led to riots, scenes of angry young men smashing shop windows and being beaten by the police quickly spread through the Arab world. The result was a series of popular revolts that in 2011 cascaded through North Africa and the Middle East, threatening the grip of decades-old autocratic regimes throughout the region. Street protests erupted in Morocco, Iraq, Lebanon, Jordan, Kuwait, Algeria, and Oman. The long-time dictatorship of Colonel Muammar Gaddafi in Libya was toppled, as was the rule of President Ali Saleh in Yemen. President Abdelaziz Bouteflika of Algeria was forced to resign. In Egypt, mass demonstrations led to the Egyptian Revolution and the overthrow of Hosni Mubarak, who had ruled Egypt for 30 years. In 2019, longtime President Omar al-Bashir of Sudan was ousted in a coup.

But the Arab Spring did not succeed in producing the long-awaited wave of democracy and economic equity to the region. Popular elections in Egypt brought the Muslim Brotherhood to power, whose president, Mohamed Morsi, tried to turn Egypt into an Islamic republic, marginalizing Coptic Christians and other minority groups. After only one year in office, Morsi was overthrown by General Abdel Fattah El-Sisi as part of a 2013 military coup. Sisi has since ruled in increasingly autocratic fashion, suppressing dissent and freedom of speech. Meanwhile, the dynastic autocracies of the United Arab Emirates and Saudi Arabia survived intact, as did the more moderate monarchies of Morocco and Jordan.

The World Today

During the third decade of the 21st century, the world will face numerous challenges, some of them predictable and others new and unfamiliar. In a multipolar world, in which the century-long preeminence of the United States is being challenged, many nations will find themselves in either an Anglophile orbit (including the United States, Canada, Britain, and Australia), a Sinophile sphere of influence (including China and much of

✦✦✦✦✦✦✦✦✦✦✦✦✦✦✦✦✦✦✦✦✦✦✦✦

THE SYRIAN CIVIL WAR

Nowhere was the impact of the Arab Spring more tragic than in Syria (at left), where the people rose in revolt against Bashar al-Assad, whose family had ruled Syria since 1971. Several factions joined the fight, including Kurds, Sunni rebels, the terrorist group ISIS, and the Salafi jihadist al-Nusra Front. The result was a devastating civil war where both Iran and Russia rallied to al-Assad's side, supporting the regime with arms, tanks, and air strikes. The Syrian civil war became the deadliest of the 21th century, killing 560,000 Syrians while displacing more than half the country's population. Of these, more than a million tried to flee to Europe, usually by boat to Greece and Italy, causing an acute immigration crisis for the European Union. Overall, the "migrant crisis" of 2015–2017 involved not only Syrians (46.7 percent) but also Afghans (20.0 percent) and Iraqi citizens (9.4 percent), according to UN estimates. Thousands of migrants died when their overloaded boats sank in the Mediterranean Sea.

SUPPORTERS OF Mohamed Morsi, leader of the Muslim Brotherhood, protest against Egypt's autocratic regime of Hosni Mubarak during protests that led to the Egyptian revolution of 2011.

A POLAR BEAR swims amid the dwindling ice floes off the coast of Greenland. Greenland's ice melt is accelerating at an alarming rate according to a consortium of 89 polar experts, having shed some 3.8 trillion metric tons of ice since 1995.

Southeast Asia), or that of the European Union, diminished as it is by Britain's decision to leave the EU. But regardless of their geographical or geopolitical positions, all countries will face common problems and opportunities.

Perhaps the most important challenge that every nation on Earth has to contend with is climate change. The idea that carbon dioxide in the atmosphere absorbs infrared radiation, thus trapping heat, was suggested as early as the late 19th century. But few scientists anticipated the rapid growth in carbon dioxide emissions as a result of the use of fossil fuels such as coal and gas. The quadrupling of the human population during the 20th century, despite two world wars, accelerated the trend where today, humankind emits 20 times the amount of carbon dioxide released at the beginning of the 20th century. Much as some may

want to deny the cause, the fact that the Earth is warming is indisputable, as attested by the growing number of extreme weather patterns such as widespread flooding in the United States and wildfires in Australia. Increasing deforestation, particularly in the Amazon, has accelerated the trend. A 2019 study suggests that by 2050, several major coastal cities around the world will be largely inundated, including Miami, Atlantic City, Shanghai, and Mumbai. Reversing this trend is painful, particularly for developing nations that need access to low-cost fossil fuels to catch up with the First World.

The COVID-19 Pandemic

Another major challenge is the growing danger of pandemics as a result of ongoing globalization. Between 2004 and 2020, air travel more than

"WE CAN SAY WITH CONFIDENCE THAT JULY IS ALWAYS WARMER THAN JANUARY . . . SIMILARLY, WE CAN SAY WITH CONFIDENCE THAT THE 2080S WILL BE WARMER THAN THE 2000S."

PAUL WILLIAMS, CLIMATE SCIENTIST

doubled, from 1.9 billion to 4.7 billion passengers. This rapid increase contributed to a perfect storm in 2020, when an outbreak of the coronavirus (COVID-19) in Wuhan, the capital of Hubei Province in China, was disseminated to the rest of the world. The increase in air travel may explain why COVID-19 spread much more quickly than the pandemic of a similar acute respiratory disease, SARS-CoV, in the early 2000s. The impact of that pandemic was largely limited to Asia, with 648 deaths in China and Hong Kong compared with only four in the United States.

Though the Chinese government of President Xi claims it acted quickly to isolate Wuhan, by January 29, 2020, the COVID-19 strain had spread to all provinces of mainland China, as well as South Korea. The World Health Organization warned that the high transmission rate of COVID-19 would pose a genuine threat to the world, but few governments in the West took immediate action. On February 1, for example, the Trump administration announced restrictions on travel from China but not yet from other countries. The limited availability of test kits further delayed the response, so that by the time the U.S. government sharply curtailed inbound air travel in March and many cities declared a "stay-at-home" order, the virus had already spread to all 50 states. In response, much of American—and indeed, global—economic activity ground to a halt at a level not seen since the 1929 Depression.

Pandemics are not new, of course. Much of Europe and the Near East suffered grievously from a smallpox epidemic in the late second century, which some historians believe hastened the decline of the Roman Empire. The outbreak in 1347 of the Black Death is estimated to have killed a third of the European population. And in 1918, the influenza pandemic carried off at least 50 million people, more than all combatants and civilians killed during World War I.

Other than the horrific death toll, past pandemics may also give a glimpse of how long it takes for affected areas to recover. While the Roman smallpox epidemic devastated trade links across the Mediterranean—as evidenced by the sharp decline of shipwrecks from this period—the high mortality rate of the Black Death led to a radical redistribution of arable lands, which in turn boosted incomes, population growth, and urbanization. The sharp decline of trading centers such as Siena allowed Florence to increase its market share, thus laying the foundation for the Florentine Renaissance.

In modern times, such silver linings are more difficult to discern, particularly because manufacturing has become heavily dependent on suppliers from around the globe. According to *Fortune*

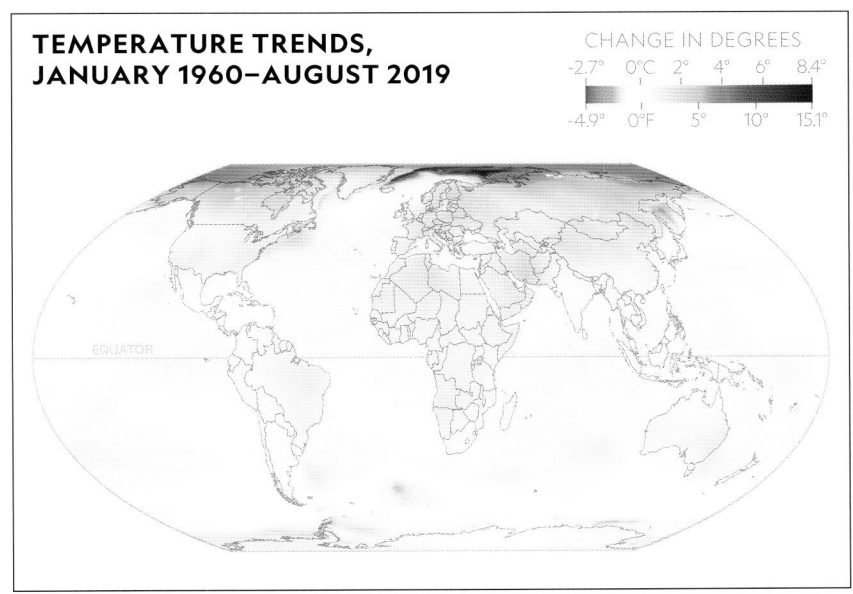

TEMPERATURE TRENDS, JANUARY 1960–AUGUST 2019

CHANGE IN DEGREES
-2.7° 0°C 2° 4° 6° 8.4°
-4.9° 0°F 5° 10° 15.1°

EQUATOR

DISINFECTION TECHNICIANS try to sanitize a market in Seoul, South Korea, as the COVID-19 outbreak spread across Asia and the rest of the world in 2020.

magazine, nearly 50 percent of a typical 2019 American automobile consists of parts produced outside the United States. This is why many economists expect that the COVID-19 pandemic and the massive worker layoffs will accelerate another trend: the shift from human workers to automated systems run by artificial intelligence (AI). Unlike human beings, robots are impervious to pandemics. Nor will AI algorithms replace only blue-collar jobs. According to some reports, lawyers, insurance underwriters, accountants, and even medical professionals will be at risk as well. As a case in point, pilots flying a Boeing 777 on long-haul flights reported they spend only an average of seven minutes actually flying the plane. One study by consulting firm McKinsey, published before the coronavirus outbreak, suggested that by 2030, a third of America's workforce could be displaced by AI-based automation.

Climate change and the growing vulnerability to pandemics have one other thing in common: They cannot be solved by a single nation alone. These phenomena threaten all people on the planet. That should prompt the world to join in a massive endeavor to combat it. Only by reaching across the fault lines of political ideology, culture, religion, or ethnicity can we vouchsafe life on Earth for many generations to come. ■

COVID-19, or the coronavirus disease caused by the novel virus, created the world's worst health crisis since World War I.

SCHOOLGIRLS IN Tamil Nadu, India, prepare to celebrate the birth anniversary of Mohandas Gandhi, a founder of modern India, during the October 2 national holiday known as Gandhi Jayanti.

HAS HUMANKIND PROGRESSED?

Today, it is tempting to look back on the first two decades of the 21st century and point to things that did not happen. The outbreak of democracy and freedom in the 1990s, from the Eastern bloc to Africa and Latin America, did not produce a golden age of world peace, as many had hoped. Today, new proxy wars are brewing among Russia, China, and the West, even though many of these are fought in cyberspace rather than the jungles of East Africa or Central America. The Arab Spring did not bring about a wave of democracy in the Middle East other than simply installing a new brand of autocratic regimes. The defeat of al Qaeda and ISIS in situ reduced but did not eliminate the cancer of global terrorism. What's more, the outbreak of COVID-19 exposed the vulnerability of a modern world utterly dependent on global travel and trade. And rather than raising the living standard of families around the world, the global economy continues to concentrate much of its wealth and capital in a narrow elite.

Still, in many ways humankind has advanced. As we saw in the Introduction, most people in the early 19th century lived in ways that were not significantly different from the days of the Roman Empire, nearly 2,000 years earlier. The horse was the primary mode of transportation. The principal source of illumination was the wax candle. Most European cities were dangerous at night, for they were plunged in darkness. Information was transmitted by handwritten mail, with transfer times measured in the distance a horse could travel in a day—usually between 15 and 20 miles. Seaborne traffic was dependent on favorable winds.

By the end of the 19th century, all of these axioms of human activity had been transformed. Major cities were lit at night by gaslight, soon to be replaced by electric illumination. For the first time in history, rail networks and the steam-driven locomotive made long-distance travel affordable for millions. At the same time, the steam-driven turbine transformed seagoing traffic. Despite the hardship of working in mills or factories (including the exploitation of child labor), the Industrial Revolution caused the standard of living to rise after its long decline in the 18th century. Meanwhile, the cost of food dropped because of improvements in production and transportation, thus improving the diet and health of the general population.

These tangible improvements continue in our day. After literacy rates began to rise in the Victorian era, 86 percent of the world population can now read and write. *New York Times* columnist Nicholas Kristof points out that every day, 200,000 new people gain access to fresh, piped water, and 650,000 people are able to connect to the internet for the first time. As recently as 1981, world poverty rates hovered around 42 percent; today, that number is down to 10 percent, in part because of the internet and the rise of countless philanthropic organizations. In the 20th century, NATO and the Warsaw Pact held more than 60,000 nuclear weapons. Today, that number is down to 14,000. And while there are still a number of conflicts raging in various parts of the globe, there were many more just 30 years ago. In addition, the world has made significant progress in providing education for girls in developing nations and promoting gender equality in the workplace of the developed world.

The work is far from done. Too many places in the world still suffer from famine, inequality, or the ravages of civil war. Pandemics and climate change are an existential threat. But on the whole, the planet has advanced, albeit in fits and starts. As Harvard psychologist Steven Pinker wrote, progress is a slow but steady process of problem solving. As long as we stay focused on that task, the world can look forward to a better future. ∎

GENERAL REFERENCE

Braudel, Fernand. *A History of Civilizations.* Penguin Books, 1995.

Briggs, Amy (Ed.). *History at a Glance: Illustrated Time Lines from Prehistory to the Present Day.* National Geographic, 2020.

Gott, J. Richard, and Robert J. Vanderbei. *Sizing Up the Universe: The Cosmos in Perspective.* National Geographic, 2011.

Harari, Yuval Noah. *Sapiens: A Brief History of Humankind.* Harper Perennial, 2018.

Hyslop, Stephen G. et al. (Eds.), *Eyewitness to History: From Ancient Times to the Modern Era.* National Geographic, 2013.

Kagan, Neil (Ed.). *Concise History of the World: An Illustrated Timeline.* National Geographic, 2006.

Marr, Andrew. *A History of the World.* Pan Books, 2013.

ANCIENT CIVILIZATIONS

Baines, John, and Jaromír Málek. *Cultural Atlas of Ancient Egypt.* Andromeda Oxford, 2000.

Bertman, Stephen. *Life in Ancient Mesopotamia.* Oxford University Press, 2005.

Collon, Dominique. *Ancient Near Eastern Art.* Trustees of the British Museum, 1995.

Hunt, Norman Bancroft. *Historical Atlas of Ancient Mesopotamia.* Thalamus Publishing, 2004.

Isbouts, Jean-Pierre. *The Biblical World: An Illustrated Atlas.* National Geographic Society, 2007.

Roaf, Michael. *Cultural Atlas of Mesopotamia and the Ancient Near East.* Andromeda Oxford, 2004.

Roberts, J. A. G. *A Concise History of China.* Harvard University Press, 1999.

ANTIQUITY

Adkins, Leslie and Roy. *Handbook to Life in Ancient Rome.* Oxford University Press, 1998.

Beard, Mary. *SPQR: A History of Ancient Rome.* Liveright, 2016.

Browning, Robert (Ed.). *The Greek World.* Thames & Hudson, 1999.

Ebrey, Patricia Buckley. *The Cambridge Illustrated History of China.* Cambridge University Press, 2010.

Isbouts, Jean-Pierre. *Archaeology of the Bible.* National Geographic Society, 2016.

Isbouts, Jean-Pierre. *In the Footsteps of Jesus: A Chronicle of His Life and the Origins of Christianity.* National Geographic Society, 2012

Magness, Jodi. *The Archaeology of the Holy Land, from the Destruction of Solomon's Temple to the Muslim Conquest.* Cambridge University Press, 2012.

Smith, Bradley, and Wan-go Weng. *China: A History in Art.* Doubleday, 1976.

THE MEDIEVAL WORLD

Frankopan, Peter. *The Silk Roads: A New History of the World.* Vintage, 2017.

Grant, Edward. *God and Reason in the Middle Ages.* Cambridge University Press, 2001.

Hannam, James. *The Genesis of Science: How the Christian Middle Ages Launched the Scientific Revolution.* Regnery Publishing, 2014.

Hourani, Albert. *A History of the Arab Peoples.* Faber & Faber, 2013.

Isbouts, Jean-Pierre. *From Moses to Muhammad: The Shared Origins of Judaism, Christianity and Islam.* Pantheon, 2011.

Isbouts, Jean-Pierre. *The Story of Christianity.* National Geographic Society, 2014.

Jordan, Michael. *Islam: An Illustrated History.* Carlton Books, 2002.

Logan, Donald. *A History of the Church in the Middle Ages.* Taylor & Francis, 2012.

Trautmann, Thomas. *India: Brief History of a Civilization.* Oxford University Press, 2015.

EARLY MODERN HISTORY

Atkinson, Rick. *The British Are Coming.* Holt, 2019

Brooke-Hitching, Edward. *The Golden Atlas: The Greatest Explorations, Quests and Discoveries on Maps.* Simon & Schuster, 2018

Cook, Don. *The Long Fuse: How England Lost the American Colonies, 1760–1785.* Atlantic Monthly Press, 1995.

Gilmour, David. *The British in India: Three Centuries of Ambition and Experience.* Penguin Books, 2019.

Popkin, Jeremy D. *A New World Begins: The History of the French Revolution.* Basic Books, 2019.

Taylor, Alan. *American Colonies: The Settling of North America.* Penguin Books, 2001

FURTHER READING

Zinn, Howard. *A People's History of the United States: 1492 to Present.* HarperCollins, 2005

MODERN HISTORY

Aitkin, H. G. J. *The Continuous Wave: Technology and the American Radio, 1900–1932.* Princeton University Press, 1985.

Beevor, Antony. *The Second World War.* Back Bay, 2013.

Benz, Wolfgang. *A Concise History of the Third Reich.* University of California Press, 2006.

Edgerton, G. R. (Ed.). *The Columbia History of American Television.* Columbia University Press, 2007.

Gandhi, Rajmohan. *Gandhi: The Man, His People, and the Empire.* University of California Press, 2008.

Keegan, John. *An Illustrated History of the First World War.* Knopf, 2001.

Hastings, Max. *Vietnam: An Epic Tragedy, 1945–1975.* Harper, 2018.

Isbouts, Jean-Pierre. *Charlton Heston's Hollywood: 50 Years in American Film.* GT Publishing, 1998.

Pinker, Steven. *Enlightenment Now: The Case for Reason, Science, Humanism, and Progress.* Viking, 2018.

Westwood, John. *The History of the Middle East Wars.* JG Press, 2002.

ABOUT THE AUTHOR

DR. JEAN-PIERRE ISBOUTS is a historian and doctoral professor in the Human Development Ph.D. program at Fielding Graduate University in Santa Barbara, California. He has published widely on the origins of human civilization, including two best sellers: *The Biblical World,* published by the National Geographic Society in 2007, and *In the Footsteps of Jesus,* published by the National Geographic Society in 2012. His other books include *From Moses to Muhammad: The Shared Origins of Judaism, Christianity and Islam* (Pantheon, 2010); *The Story of Christianity,* published by the National Geographic Society in 2014; *Archaeology of the Bible,* published by the National Geographic Society in 2016; *The Da Vinci Legacy,* published by Apollo Publishers in 2019; and his upcoming book, *The Birth of America as Told by the Maps of the Era.* An award-winning filmmaker, Dr. Isbouts has also produced a number of programs, including *Charlton Heston's Voyage Through the Bible* (GoodTimes, 1998), *The Quest for Peace* (Hallmark, 2003), *Walt: The Man Behind the Myth* (Disney/Buena Vista, 2018), and *The Search for the Last Supper* (PBS, 2019). He and his wife, Cathie, live in Santa Monica, California. His website is www.jpisbouts.org.

ACKNOWLEDGMENTS

Ultimate Visual History of the World is the culmination of many years of research into a subject that has fascinated me for much of my career as a historian: How new ideas have propelled humankind throughout history.

Once again, I must thank Lisa Thomas, head of National Geographic's Book Division, and Bridget Hamilton, editorial manager, for initiating the concept for this book and for their strong and unerring support throughout. In the same breath, I express my deep gratitude to my wonderful editor, Barbara Payne. Many thanks are also due to the superb creative team for this book, including Carol Norton for her elegant design and beautiful layouts, Matt Propert and Uliana Bazar for their excellent photo research, Debbie Gibbons and Jerome Cookson for their wonderful maps, Sharon Moore for her diligent fact checking, and Beverly Miller for her sensitive and incisive copyedit.

In writing this book I have profited from the research of many other scholars too numerous to mention, though I have tried to identify them in the Further Reading section.

Thanks are due to my literary manager, Peter Miller, and his staff at Global Lion Intellectual Property Management. And finally, I express my deepest gratitude to my wonderful wife, Cathie, who continues to be my muse and indefatigable companion on our many journeys across our planet.

Jean-Pierre Isbouts

Cover (top to bottom): model by Charlie James (#1489/1 a-d), photo by Kyla Bailey, UBC Museum of Anthropology, Vancouver, Canada; Universal History Archive/UIG/Bridgeman Images; Bill Ballenberg/NG Image Collection; Bruce Dale/NG Image Collection; Fred Ward/NG Image Collection. Spine: British Museum, London/Werner Forman Archive/Bridgeman Images. Back Cover (left to right): Pantheon Studios, Inc.; Ashmolean Museum, University of Oxford/HIP/Art Resource, NY; Germanisches Nationalmuseum, Nuremberg/Bridgeman Images; akg-images/Heritage-Images/CM Dixon, photographed at British Museum, London; National Air and Space Museum, Washington, DC/Bridgeman Images.

1, Kenneth Garrett/National Geographic Image Collection; 2-3, MediaProduction/Getty Images; 4, Pantheon Studios, Inc.; 6-7, Heritage Images/Getty Images; 8-9, Kent Kobersteen/National Geographic Image Collection ; 10, Ami Vitale/National Geographic Image Collection; 11, Jean Pierre Courau/Museo Nacional de Arqueología y Etnología, Guatemala City/Bridgeman Images.

Chapter 1: Prehistory-3000 B.C.E.
12-13, NASA, ESA, and The Hubble Heritage Team (STScI/AURA); Acknowledgment: J. Gallagher (University of Wisconsin), M. Mountain (STScI), and P. Puxley (National Science Foundation); 14, James Cohen/Shutterstock; 15, Delmarty/Andia/Alamy Stock Photo; 16, © 2021, John Gurche; 17, Kenneth Garrett/National Geographic Image Collection; 18, Bruno Compagnon/Alamy Stock Photo; 18-19, Robert C. Magis/National Geographic Image Collection; 20, Babak Tafreshi/National Geographic Image Collection; 21, Vincent J. Musi/National Geographic Image Collection; 22-3, Vincent J. Musi/National Geographic Image Collection; 23 (UP), Sisse Brimberg/National Geographic Image Collection; 23 (LO), Alex Saberi/National Geographic Image Collection; 24, Vincent J. Musi/National Geographic Image Collection; 24-5, Jim Richardson/National Geographic Image Collection; 26, Heritage Image Partnership Ltd/Alamy Stock Photo; 27, Zev Radovan/BibleLandPictures/Alamy Stock Photo; 28, Pantheon Studios, Inc.; 28-9, Robert Hoetink/Alamy Stock Photo; 30, Lynn Abercrombie/National Geographic Image Collection; 31 (UP), Pantheon Studios, Inc.; 31 (LO), Peter Horree/Alamy Stock Photo; 32, akg-images/Bible Land Pictures/www.BibleLandPictures; 32-3, Georg Gerster/Science Source; 34, Pantheon Studios, Inc.; 34-5, Matt Moyer/National Geographic Image Collection; 36, DEA/G. Dagli Orti/De Agostini via Getty Images; 37, Georg Gerster/Science Source; 38, akg-images/Bible Land Pictures; 39, akg-images/De Agostini Picture Lib./G. Dagli Orti. Location: Private collection; 40 (UP), © The Trustees of the British Museum/Art Resource, NY; 40 (LO), Pantheon Studios, Inc.; 40-1, Michael Hampshire/National Geographic Image Collection; 43 (UP), The Iraq Museum, Baghdad/De Agostini Picture Library/M. Carrieri/Bridgeman Images; 43 (LO), Cagan Sekercioglu/National Geographic Image Collection; 44, Archaeological Museum, Aleppo, Syria/A. Dagli Orti/De Agostini Picture Library/Bridgeman Images; 44-5, Kenneth Garrett/National Geographic Image Collection; 46-7, akg-images/Balage Balogh/archaeologyillustrated.com; 47, Pantheon Studios, Inc.; 48, Pantheon Studios, Inc.; 49 (UP), Chris Bradley/Design Pics Inc/National Geographic Image Collection; 49 (LO), Private Collection/G. Dagli Orti/De Agostini Picture Library/Bridgeman Images; 50-1, Essam Al-Sudani/AFP via Getty Images; 52 (UP), Pantheon Studios, Inc.; 52 (LO), Pictures from History/Bridgeman Images; 53, Pantheon Studios, Inc.; 54, akg-images/De Agostini Picture Lib./G. Dagli Orti. Location: Paris (France), Musée Du Louvre; 55 (UP), Private Collection/© Christie's Images/Bridgeman Images; 55 (LO), akg-images/De Agostini Picture Lib./G. Dagli Orti; 56, Pantheon Studios, Inc.; 56-7, Babak Tafreshi/National Geographic Image Collection; 58, akg-images/De Agostini Picture Lib./M. Carrieri. Location: Baghdad, National Museum of Iraq; 59, © The Trustees of the British Museum/Art Resource, NY; 60 (UP), akg-images/De Agostini Picture Lib./G. Dagli Orti; 60 (LO), Balage Balogh/Archaeology Illustrated; 60-1, Pantheon Studios, Inc.; 62-3, Balage Balogh/Archaeology Illustrated; 63 (UP), akg-images/Liszt Collection; 63 (LO), British Museum, London/Pictures from History/Bridgeman Images; 64, Pantheon Studios, Inc.; 64-5, Balage Balogh/Archaeology Illustrated; 66, Kenneth Garrett/National Geographic Image Collection; 67, Private Collection/© Look and Learn /Bridgeman Images; 68 (UP), Sandro Vannini; 68 (LO), Bill Ellzey/National Geographic Image Collection; 68-9, Jennylynn Fields/SPYD Photography/National Geographic Your Shot; 70-1, Theerawat Kaiphanlert/

Getty Images; 71, Kenneth Garrett/National Geographic Image Collection; 72-3 (ALL), Kenneth Garrett/National Geographic Image Collection; 75, Kenneth Garrett/National Geographic Image Collection; 76, LatitudeStock/Chris and Sally Gable/Alamy Stock Photo; 76-7, Yann Arthus-Bertrand/Getty Images.

Chapter 2: 3000-1500 B.C.E.
78-9, Maurizio Rellini/Sime/eStock Photo; 80, Shanghai Museum, China/Pictures from History/David Henley/Bridgeman Images; 81, Hannu Viitanen/123RF; 82, DEA/A. Dagli Orti/De Agostini via Getty Images; 83, Metropolitan Museum of Art, New York/Bridgeman Images; 84, Robert Kawka/Alamy Stock Photo; 84-5, Pictures from History/Bridgeman Images; 86, Imaginechina-Tuchong/Alamy Stock Photo; 87 (UP), Granger.com - All rights reserved; 87 (LO), Liu Xiaoyang/China Images/Alamy Stock Photo; 88, Robert Harding Productions/National Geographic Image Collection; 88-9, Nadeem Khawar/Getty Images; 90 (UP), Nadeem Khawar/Getty Images; 90 (LO), National Museum of India, New Delhi, India/Bridgeman Images; 91, Pantheon Studios, Inc.; 92, National Archaeological Museum, Athens, Greece/De Agostini Picture Library/G. Nimatallah/Bridgeman Images; 93, NYPL/Science Source; 94-5 (BOTH), Ken Geiger/National Geographic Image Collection; 96-7, Gerard Sioen/Gamma-Rapho via Getty Images; 97 (UP), Ashmolean Museum, University of Oxford, UK/Bridgeman Images; 97 (LO), Pantheon Studios, Inc.; 98, National Archaeological Museum, Athens, Greece/De Agostini Picture Library/G. Nimatallah/Bridgeman Images; 98-9, Stefano Brozzi/Sime/eStock Photo; 100, Private Collection/© Look and Learn/Bridgeman Images; 101, Pantheon Studios, Inc.; 102 (UP), Pantheon Studios, Inc.; 102 (CTR), Archaeological Museum of Rethymno, Crete, Greece/Archivio J. Lange/De Agostini Picture Library/Bridgeman Images; 102 (LO), National Archaeological Museum, Athens, Greece/Tarker/Bridgeman Images; 102-3, Heracles Kritikos/Shutterstock.com; 104-5, Pecold/Shutterstock.com; 105, Pantheon Studios, Inc.; 106 (UP), Michael Runkel/robertharding/National Geographic Image Collection; 106 (LO), Pantheon Studios, Inc.; 107, Olimpio Fantuz/Sime/eStock Photo; 108, akg-images/Pictures From History; 109, akg-images/CDA/Guillemot. Location: Paris, Musée Guimet, from the Camondo collection; 110 (UP), O. Louis Mazzatenta; 110 (LO), akg-images/Bildarchiv Steffens; 110-1, O. Louis Mazzatenta/National Geographic Image Collection; 112-3, O. Louis Mazzatenta/National Geographic Image Collection; 113, Pantheon Studios, Inc.; 114 (UP), Pantheon Studios, Inc.; 114 (LO), akg-images/Liszt Collection; 114-5, O. Louis Mazzatenta/National Geographic Image Collection; 116-7, William Albert Allard/National Geographic Image Collection; 117 (UP), Luisa Ricciarini/Bridgeman Images; 117 (LO), Costfoto/Barcroft Media via Getty Images; 118, Musée Du Louvre, Paris, France/G. Dagli Orti /De Agostini Picture Library/Bridgeman Images; 119, Pantheon Studios, Inc.; 120, National Archaeological Museum, Florence, Italy/Luisa Ricciarini/Bridgeman Images; 120-1, Pantheon Studios, Inc.; 122, © A. Dagli Orti/De Agostini Picture Library/Bridgeman Images; 123 (UP), Egyptian National Museum, Cairo, Egypt/© Sandro Vannini/Bridgeman Images; 123 (LO), Tarker/Bridgeman Images; 124, Metropolitan Museum of Art, Gift of Edward S. Harkness, 1917; 124-5, Erich Lessing/Art Resource, NY; 126-7, Nathan Benn; 127 (UP), Jonathan O'Rourke/Alamy Stock Photo; 127 (LO), Prisma/UIG/Getty Images; 128-9 (BOTH), Pantheon Studios, Inc.

Chapter 3: 1500-500 B.C.E.
130-1, Kenneth Garrett/National Geographic Image Collection; 132, Fitzwilliam Museum, University of Cambridge, UK/Bridgeman Images; 133, Kenneth Garrett/National Geographic Image Collection; 134, Gordon Wiltsie/National Geographic Image Collection; 135, bpk Bildagentur/Museum fuer Asiatische Kunst, Staatliche Museen, Berlin, Germany/Iris Papadopoulos/Art Resource, NY; 136 (UP), Ashmolean Museum, University of Oxford/HIP/Art Resource, NY; 136 (LO), Steve McCurry; 136-7, Dinodia/Bridgeman Images; 138-9, Steve McCurry/Magnum Photos; 139 (UP), Tokyo National Museum, Japan/Pictures from History/Bridgeman Images; 139 (LO), © British Library Board. All Rights Reserved/Bridgeman Images; 140 (UP), Pantheon Studios, Inc.; 140 (LO), Private Collection/© Christie's Images/Bridgeman Images; 140-1, Paul Chesley/National Geographic Image Collection; 142, akg-images/Roland & Sabrina Michaud. Location: Private collection; 143, © RMN-Grand Palais/Art Resource, NY; 144 (UP), Fred Ward; 144 (LO), Ira Block/National Geographic Image Collection; 144-5, akg-images/Pictures From History;

146 (UP), Liz Jurey/National Geographic Your Shot; 146 (LO), Pantheon Studios, Inc.; 147 (UP), Pantheon Studios, Inc.; 147 (LO), Melodious Vision/Getty Images; 148, Kenneth Garrett/National Geographic Image Collection; 149, akg-images. Location: Hildesheim, Germany, Roemer-und Pelizaeus-Museum; 150, akg-images. Location: Hildesheim, Germany, Roemer-und Pelizaeus-Museum; 150-1, Nathan Benn; 152-3, Richard Maschmeyer/robertharding/National Geographic Image Collection; 153, Pantheon Studios, Inc.; 154, akg-images/WHA/World History Archive; 154-5, Kenneth Garrett/National Geographic Image Collection; 156-7, Michael Melford/National Geographic Image Collection; 157, Metropolitan Museum of Art/Art Resource, NY; 159, Anna Gett Photography/Getty Images; 160, Pantheon Studios, Inc.; 161, Private Collection/© Zev Radovan/Bridgeman Images; 162, akg-images/Fototeca Gilardi; 162-3, Duby Tal/Albatross/Alamy Stock Photo; 164, akg-images/De Agostini/Archivio J. Lange; 165 (UP), Private Collection/© Zev Radovan/Bridgeman Images; 165 (LO), Joe Daniel Price/Getty Images; 166 (BOTH), Pantheon Studios, Inc.; 166-7, akg-images/Heritage Images/Fine Art Images. Location: Art Gallery of New South Wales, Australia; 168-9, akg-images/Balage Balogh/archaeologyillustrated.com; 169, akg-images/Heritage-Images/CM Dixon; 170 (UP), © The Trustees of the British Museum/Art Resource, NY; 170 (LO), © RMN-Grand Palais/Art Resource, NY; 171, Scarborough Borough Council, North Yorkshire, UK/Bridgeman Images; 172-3, Pantheon Studios, Inc.; 173, akg-images/Bible Land Pictures/Zev Radovan; 174, akg-images/Bible Land Pictures; 175, © The Trustees of the British Museum/Art Resource, NY; 176, Erich Lessing/Art Resource, NY; 176-7, Jane Sweeney/Art Directors + TRIP/Alamy Stock Photo; 178, Image copyright © The Metropolitan Museum of Art. Image source: Art Resource, NY; 180-1, Erich Lessing/Art Resource, NY; 181 (UP), Scala/Art Resource, NY; 181 (LO), Pantheon Studios, Inc.; 182-3, Private Collection/A. Dagli Orti/De Agostini Picture Library/Bridgeman Images; 184, Richard Alexander Cooke III; 185, Private Collection/© Boltin Picture Library/Bridgeman Images; 186, Dallas Museum of Art, Texas/Dallas Art Association Purchase, The Art Museum League Fund/Bridgeman Images; 186-7, Kenneth Garrett/Danita Delimont/Alamy Stock Photo; 188-9, akg-images/De Agostini Picture Lib./G. Dagli Orti; 189 (UP), akg-images/Liszt Collection; 189 (LO), James L. Stanfield/National Geographic Image Collection; 190, akg-images/Liszt Collection; 190-1, Richard Schlecht/National Geographic Image Collection; 192, Photo12/Universal Images Group via Getty Images; 193, Kenneth Garrett/National Geographic Image Collection; 194 (UP), Pantheon Studios, Inc.; 194 (LO), Jim Richardson/National Geographic Image Collection; 194-5, Keenpress/National Geographic Image Collection; 196-7, Jim Richardson/National Geographic Image Collection; 197 (UP), James P. Blair/National Geographic Image Collection; 197 (LO), akg-images/jh-Lightbox_Ltd./John Hios. Location: Aegean wall painting in Akrotiri, West House; 198 (UP), Robert Clark/National Geographic Image Collection; 198 (LO), Archaeological Museum, Istanbul, Turkey/De Agostini Picture Library/Bridgeman Images; 199, Robert Clark/National Geographic Image Collection; 200-1, akg-images/Balage Balogh/archaeologyillustrated.com; 201, James P. Blair/National Geographic Image Collection; 202, akg-images/IAM/World History Archive; 203, akg-images/Z.Radovan/BibleLandPictures.com; 204 (UP), Erich Lessing/Art Resource, NY; 204 (LO), akg-images/Heritage Images/Fine Art Images. Location: National Gallery, London; 204-5, Simon Norfolk; 207 (UP), akg-images/Balage Balogh/archaeologyillustrated.com; 207 (LO), akg-images. Location: Teheran, Iran, National Museum; 208, Pantheon Studios, Inc.; 208-9, Simon Norfolk; 210-1, Simon Norfolk; 211 (UP), Pantheon Studios, Inc.; 211 (LO), Peter Langer/Design Pics Inc/National Geographic Image Collection.

Chapter 4: 500 B.C.E.-300 C.E.
212-3, ollirg/Shutterstock; 214, O. Louis Mazzatenta/National Geographic Image Collection; 215, Pantheon Studios, Inc.; 216, Taranto, Museo Archeologico Nazionale/G. Dagli Orti/De Agostini Picture Library/Bridgeman Images; 217, Musei Capitolini, Rome, Italy/Bridgeman Images; 218, Peter Horree/Alamy Stock Photo; 218-9, Pantheon Studios, Inc.; 220-1, Stanley Meltzoff/Silverfish Press/National Geographic Image Collection; 221, Arthur M. Sackler Museum, Harvard University Art Museums,USA/Bequest of David M. Robinson/Bridgeman Images; 222 (UP), Reynold Mainse/Design Pics Inc/National Geographic Image Collection; 222 (LO), Pantheon Studios, Inc.; 222-3, Simon Norfolk; 224-5, Reynold Mainse/Design Pics

Inc/National Geographic Image Collection; 225, Pantheon Studios, Inc.; 226, National Archaeological Museum, Athens, Greece/Bridgeman Images; 226-7, Poike/Getty Images; 228, Gordon Gahan/National Geographic Image Collection; 229 (UP), Bridgeman Images; 229 (LO), Pantheon Studios, Inc.; 230-1, Universal Images Group/Getty Images; 232-3, Vatican Museums and Galleries, Vatican City/Bridgeman Images; 233, Art Gallery of South Australia, Adelaide, Australia, Gift of the Rt. Honourable, the Earl of Kintore 1893/Bridgeman Images; 234, Robbie Shone/National Geographic Image Collection; 235, Kenneth Garrett/National Geographic Image Collection; 236 (UP), Egyptian Museum, Cairo/Werner Forman Archive/Bridgeman Images; 236 (LO), Kenneth Garrett/National Geographic Image Collection; 236-7, John Frumm/hemis.fr/Alamy Stock Photo; 238-9, Randy Olson/National Geographic Image Collection; 239, Private Collection/Photo © Heini Schneebeli/Bridgeman Images; 240 (UP), akg-images/Jean-Louis Nou. Location: Carthage, Tunisia, National Museum; 240 (LO), NickolayV/Getty Images; 240-1, Yoshio Tomii/Getty Images; 242, Winfield Parks/National Geographic Image Collection; 243, Lloyd K. Townsend/National Geographic Image Collection; 244-5 (BOTH), O. Louis Mazzatenta/National Geographic Image Collection; 246, O. Louis Mazzatenta/National Geographic Image Collection; 246-7, Pictures from History/Bridgeman Images; 248-9, Darrell Gulin/Getty Images; 249 (UP), Pantheon Studios, Inc.; 249 (LO), O. Louis Mazzatenta/National Geographic Image Collection; 250, Pantheon Studios, Inc.; 250-1, Sybil Sassoon/robertharding/National Geographic Image Collection; 252, Blaine Harrington III/Getty Images; 253 (UP), Pictures from History/Bridgeman Images; 253 (LO), Musée Cernuschi, Paris, France/De Agostini Picture Library/Bridgeman Images; 254, James L. Stanfield/National Geographic Image Collection; 254-5, Bibliothèque nationale, Paris, France/© Archives Charmet/Bridgeman Images; 256-7, Massimo Bassano/National Geographic Image Collection; 257, akg-images/Liszt Collection; 258, Pantheon Studios, Inc.; 260-1, Diane Cook and Len Jenshel/National Geographic Image Collection; 261 (UP), akg-images/Pictures From History; 261 (LO), Museo Nazionale, Rome, Italy/Bridgeman Images; 262, akg-images/UIG/PHAS. Location: Archaelogical Museum of Naples, Italy; 263, akg-images/Liszt Collection; 264, Pantheon Studios, Inc.; 264-5, Xantana/Getty Images; 266-7, Ken Gillham/robertharding/National Geographic Image Collection; 267 (UP), Granger.com - All rights reserved; 267 (LO), Pantheon Studios, Inc.; 269 (UP), George F. Mobley/National Geographic Image Collection; 269 (LO), Robert Kawka/Alamy Stock Photo; 270-1, Olmoroz/Getty Images; 271, Pantheon Studios, Inc.; 272 (UP), Pantheon Studios, Inc.; 272 (LO), Paolo Verzone; 272-3, Dinodia Photos/Alamy Stock Photo; 274, Tetra Images/Getty Images; 275, Pantheon Studios, Inc.; 276 (UP), James L. Stanfield/National Geographic Image Collection; 276 (LO), Pantheon Studios, Inc.; 276-7, George Steinmetz/National Geographic Image Collection; 280 (UP), Pantheon Studios, Inc.; 280 (LO), George Steinmetz/National Geographic Image Collection; 281, Musée des Beaux-Arts, Lyon, France/Bridgeman Images; 282-3, akg-images. Location: Baltimore, Maryland, Walters Art Gallery; 283, Pantheon Studios, Inc.; 284, George Steinmetz/National Geographic Image Collection; 284-5, Giovanni Simeone/Sime/eStock Photo; 286-7 (BOTH), Ira Block/National Geographic Image Collection; 288 (UP), Bill Ballenberg; 288 (LO), Robert Clark/National Geographic Image Collection; 288-9, John Elk/Getty Images; 290-1 (BOTH), Ira Block/National Geographic Image Collection; 292 (UP), akg-images/François Guénet. Location: Mexico City, Museo Nacional de Antropología; 292 (LO), akg-images/WHA/World History Archive; 292-3, Photo by Enrico Ferorelli, art enhancement by digital artist Doug Stern; 294, Kenneth Garrett/National Geographic Image Collection; 295 (UP), Kumar Sriskandan/Alamy Stock Photo; 295 (LO), akg-images/Andrea Baguzzi. Location: Guatemala, Museo Nacional de Arqueología; 296 (UP), Jean Pierre Courau/Museo de Arqueología, Guatemala/Bridgeman Images; 296 (LO), akg-images/De Agostini Picture Lib./G. Dagli Orti. Location: Mexico City, Anthropology Museum; 296-7, Paul Nicklen/National Geographic Image Collection.

Chapter 5: 300-900 C.E.
298-9, Chanachai Panichpattanakij/Getty Images; 300, Luca Tettoni/robertharding/National Geographic Image Collection; 301, Pantheon Studios, Inc.; 302, Matt Brandon/Design Pics Inc/National Geographic Image Collection; 303, © RMN-Grand Palais/Art Resource, NY; 304 (UP), Pantheon Studios, Inc.; 304 (LO), Musée

des Beaux-Arts et d'Archeologie, Besancon, France/Bridgeman Images; 304-5, Richard T. Nowitz/National Geographic Image Collection; 306-7, Pantheon Studios, Inc.; 307 (UP), Pantheon Studios, Inc.; 307 (LO), akg-images/Werner Forman Archive/N.J Saunders; 308, The Israel Museum, Jerusalem/Bridgeman Images; 309, Vatican Museums and Galleries, Vatican City/De Agostini Picture Library/Bridgeman Images; 312 (UP), Metropolitan Museum of Art, New York, USA/Bridgeman Images; 312 (LO), Church of the Multiplication, Tabgha, Israel/Bridgeman Images; 313, Louvre, (Museum), Paris, France/Art Resource, NY; 314, Tetra Images/Getty Images; 315, Museum of the Treasury, St. Peter's Basilica, Vatican/Scala/Art Resource, NY; 316, G. Dagli Orti/De Agostini Picture Library/Bridgeman Images; 317, Pantheon Studios, Inc.; 318 (UP), akg-images/Liszt Collection; 318 (LO), Pictures From History/CPA Media Pte Ltd/Alamy Stock Photo; 318-9, akg-images/Jean-Louis Nou; 320 (UP), Ashmolean Museum, University of Oxford, UK/Bridgeman Images; 320 (LO), Alex Webb; 321, Pictures from History/Bridgeman Images; 322, Private Collection/Look and Learn/Illustrated Papers Collection/Bridgeman Images; 323, 4X-image/Getty Images; 324, Tony Law/Redux; 324-5, Qixin Chen/Getty Images; 326, Ashmolean Museum, University of Oxford, UK/Bridgeman Images; 327, akg-images/De Agostini Picture Library. Location: Washington, D.C., Smithsonian Institution; 328-9, Anneliese Possberg/National Geographic Your Shot; 329 (UP), Saint Louis Art Museum, Missouri, USA/Museum purchase/Bridgeman Images; 329 (LO), Pantheon Studios, Inc.; 330, Museum of Fine Arts, Houston, Texas, USA/Museum purchase funded by Brown Foundation Accessions Endowment Fund/Bridgeman Images; 330-1, Werner Forman Archive/National Palace Museum, Taipei/ HIP/Art Resource, NY; 332-3, Sean Pavone/Getty Images; 333, akg-images/Liszt Collection; 334-5 (BOTH), Pictures from History/Bridgeman Images; 336, De Agostini Picture Library/G. Nimatallah/Bridgeman Images; 337, Pantheon Studios, Inc.; 338, Pantheon Studios, Inc.; 339, Germanisches Nationalmuseum, Nuremberg, Germany/Bridgeman Images; 340 (UP), akg-images/De Agostini Picture Lib./G. Dagli Orti; 340 (LO), Aurelian Images/Alamy Stock Photo; 340-1, Louvre Museum, Paris/Pictures from History/Bridgeman Images; 342 (UP), Louvre Museum, Paris/© Photo Josse/Bridgeman Images; 342 (LO), Private Collection/© Tallandier/Bridgeman Images; 343, akg-images. Location: Washington, D.C., National Gallery of Art; 344-5, Michael Runkel/robertharding/National Geographic Image Collection; 345 (UP), Pictures from History/Bridgeman Images; 345 (LO), British Library/Science Source; 346 (UP), www.BibleLandPictures.com/Alamy Stock Photo; 346 (LO), Private Collection/PVDE/Bridgeman Images; 347, Chuck David Photography; 348-9, Private Collection/The Stapleton Collection/Bridgeman Images; 350, Afriandi/Getty Images; 351, akg-images/Philippe Maillard. Location: Sèvres, France, Musée National de Céramique; 352, Pantheon Studios, Inc.; 352-3, Thomas J. Abercrombie/National Geographic Image Collection; 354, Reuters/Sigit Pamungkas; 355, akg-images/Jean-Louis Nou. Location: Fès, Morocco, Musée Dar Batha; 356, akg-images/Universal Images Group; 357, Private Collection/Photo © Christie's Images/Bridgeman Images; 358, © Tallandier/Bridgeman Images; 359 (UP), akg-images/Philippe Maillard. Location: Damascus, Syria, National Museum; 359 (LO), Allan Baxter/Getty Images; 360, National Maritime Museum, Greenwich, London; 360-1, Aaron Huey/National Geographic Image Collection; 362-3, Chateau de Versailles, France/Bridgeman Images; 363, akg-images. Location: California, Los Angeles County Museum of Art; 364, Pantheon Studios, Inc.; 365, akg-images/Pictures From History; 366 (UP), akg-images/Pictures From History; 366 (LO), Chris Bradley/Design Pics Inc/National Geographic Image Collection; 366-7, Keith Levit/Perspectives/Design Pics Inc/Alamy Stock Photo; 368-9, B.O'Kane/Alamy Stock Photo; 370 (UP), akg-images/François Guénet. Location: Private collection; 370 (LO), © Santiago Urquijo/Getty Images; 370-1, Kenneth Garrett/National Geographic Image Collection.

Chapter 6: 900-1400

372-3, Emad Aljumah/Getty Images; 374, © Photo Josse/Bridgeman Images; 375, Luca Tettoni/robertharding/National Geographic Image Collection; 376, Galleria degli Uffizi, Florence, Tuscany, Italy/Universal History Archive/UIG /Bridgeman Images; 377, akg-images/Fototeca Gilardi; 378, Royal Armouries, Leeds, UK/Bridgeman Images; 378-9, Versailles, Chateau Museum/© Photo Josse/Bridgeman Images; 380-1, Château de Versailles, France/Bridgeman Images; 381 (UP), Deutsches Historisches Museum, Berlin, Germany/© DHM/Bridgeman Images;

381 (LO), Pantheon Studios, Inc.; 382-3, © Gerard Degeorge/Bridgeman Images; 384, Château de Versailles, France/Bridgeman Images; 385 (UP), akg-images. Location: Leipzig, Germany, Universitätsbibliothek; 385 (LO), akg-images/A.F. Kersting; 386, akg-images/Pictures From History; 386-7, Dean Conger/National Geographic Image Collection; 388, Martin Gray/National Geographic Image Collection; 389 (UP), Luca Tettoni/robertharding/National Geographic Image Collection; 389 (LO), akg-images/Pictures From History; 390, Robert Clark/National Geographic Image Collection; 390-1, Paul Chesley/National Geographic Image Collection; 392 (UP), Pictures From History/CPA Media Pte Ltd/Alamy Stock Photo; 392 (LO), The Picture Art Collection/Alamy Stock Photo; 393, akg-images/Roland and Sabrina Michaud. Location: Private collection; 394, James L. Stanfield/National Geographic Image Collection; 395 (LE), Private Collection/© Look and Learn/Bridgeman Images; 395 (RT), Pictures from History/Bridgeman Images; 396-7, Nicolas Reynard/National Geographic Image Collection; 398, Museo di San Marco, Florence, Italy/© Nicolò Orsi Battaglini/Bridgeman Images; 399, Pictures from History/Bridgeman Images; 400, © Fine Art Images/Heritage Image Partnership Ltd/Alamy Stock Photo; 400-1, © RMN-Grand Palais/Art Resource, NY; 402-3, Joe Daniel Price/Getty Images; 403, Pantheon Studios, Inc.; 404, Private Collection/© Philip Mould Ltd, London/Bridgeman Images; 404-5, Pantheon Studios, Inc.; 406, © Vanni Archive/Art Resource, NY; 407 (UP), University of Barcelona, Spain/Index Fototeca/Bridgeman Images; 407 (LO), Pantheon Studios, Inc.; 408, Alfredo Dagli Orti/Art Resource, NY; 408-9, gbarm/Getty Images; 410-1, Pantheon Studios, Inc.; 412, © Photo Josse/Bridgeman Images; 413, Private Collection/Photo © Peter Nahum at The Leicester Galleries, London/Bridgeman Images; 414, akg-images/Heritage-Images/CM Dixon. Location: London, England, British Museum; 415, Museo Nacional De Antropología, Mexico City/© A. De Gregorio/De Agostini Picture Library/Bridgeman Images; 416, Album/Alamy Stock Photo; 416-7, David Hiser/National Geographic Image Collection; 418-9 (BOTH), Kenneth Garrett/National Geographic Image Collection; 420-1, Greg Vaughn/Getty Images; 421 (UP), British Museum, London/Werner Forman Archive/Bridgeman Images; 421(LO), Werner Forman Archive/Bridgeman Images; 422 (UP), Robert Clark/National Geographic Image Collection; 422 (LO), Pantheon Studios, Inc.; 422-3, traumlichtfabrik/Getty Images.

Chapter 7: 1400-1700

424-5, Museo Maritimo Torre del Oro (Navy Museum), Seville, Spain/G. Dagli Orti/De Agostini Picture Library/Bridgeman Images; 426, Pantheon Studios, Inc.; 427, Bob Sacha/National Geographic Image Collection; 428, Pantheon Studios, Inc.; 429, akg-images/WHA/World History Archive; 430, Universal History Archive/UIG/Bridgeman Images; 430-1, Jill Schneider/National Geographic Image Collection; 432, Musée des Augustins, Toulouse, France/Bridgeman Images; 434, Erich Lessing/Art Resource, NY; 434-5, André Durenceau/National Geographic Image Collection; 436-7, Louvre, Paris, France/Bridgeman Images; 437, Schlossmuseum, Weimar, Germany/Bridgeman Images; 438 (UP), Deutsches Historisches Museum, Berlin, Germany/Bridgeman Images; 438 (LO), Bridgeman Images; 439, akg-images. Location: Eisenach, Germany, Wartburg Castle; 440-1, Taylor Kennedy/National Geographic Image Collection; 441 (UP), Museo Archeologico, Naples, Italy/Luisa Ricciarini/Bridgeman Images; 441 (LO), akg-images. Location: Nuremberg, Germany, Germanisches Museum; 444-5, Real Academia de Bellas Artes de San Fernando, Madrid, Spain/Bridgeman Images; 446, Pantheon Studios, Inc.; 447, Ira Block/National Geographic Image Collection; 448, akg-images; 448-9, Majority World/UIG/Bridgeman Images; 450, Private Collection/Bridgeman Images; 451, Richard Schlecht/National Geographic Image Collection; 453, Engelbrecht, Martin (1684-1756)/Bibliothèque nationale, Paris, France/Bridgeman Images; 454, Robert Clark/National Geographic Image Collection; 454-5, Krista Rossow/National Geographic Image Collection; 456 (UP), Ira Block/National Geographic Image Collection; 456 (LO), Pantheon Studios, Inc.; 457 (UP), Benjawan Sittidech/Getty Images; 457 (LO), Museum of New Zealand Te Papa Tongarewa, Wellington, New Zealand/Purchased 1953/Bridgeman Images; 458 (UP), Paul Chesley/Getty Images; 458 (LO), Museo Archeologico, Naples, Italy/Luisa Ricciarini/Bridgeman Images; 459 (UP), De Agostini Picture Library/Bridgeman Images; 459 (LO), Private Collection/Index Fototeca/Bridgeman Images; 460, Kunsthistorisches Museum, Vienna, Austria/Bridgeman Images; 461, G. Dagli Orti/De Agostini Picture Library/

Bridgeman Images; 462, akg-images/Rabatti & Domingie. Location: Florence, Italy, Museo Stibbert; 462-3, Pantheon Studios, Inc.; 464-5, Wien Museum Karlsplatz, Vienna, Austria/Ali Meyer/Bridgeman Images; 465 (UP), Pantheon Studios, Inc.; 465 (LO), Joe Daniel Price/Getty Images; 466-7, Amos Chapple/Getty Images; 468, Tretyakov Gallery, Moscow, Russia/Bridgeman Images; 469 (UP), Pictures from History/David Henley/Bridgeman Images; 469 (LO), akg-images/Liszt Collection; 470, akg-images/Liszt Collection; 471 (UP), Pictures from History/Bridgeman Images; 471 (LO), Freer Gallery of Art, Smithsonian Institution/Bridgeman Images; 472-3, Victoria & Albert Museum, London, UK/Bridgeman Images; 473, Indianapolis Museum of Art at Newfields, USA/Gift of Mr. and Mrs. Eli Lilly/Bridgeman Images; 474, Victoria & Albert Museum, London, UK/Bridgeman Images; 474-5, Michael S. Lewis/National Geographic Image Collection.

Chapter 8: 1700-1900

476-7, Château de Versailles, France/Bridgeman Images; 478, Gift of John Sanderson du Mont, New York State Society of the Cincinnati, 1994; 479, Virginia Historical Society, Richmond, Virginia, USA/Bridgeman Images; 480, Louvre, Paris, France/Photo © Leonard de Selva/Bridgeman Images; 481, Pantheon Studios, Inc.; 482, Bibliothèque des Arts Décoratifs, Paris, France/© Archives Charmet/Bridgeman Images; 482-3, Neue Nationalgalerie, Berlin, Germany/De Agostini Picture Library/Bridgeman Images; 484, yongyuan/Getty Images; 485, Copyright 2020 The Society of the Cincinnati, Washington, D.C.; 486-7, Private Collection/Art Resource, NY; 488 (UP), National Portrait Gallery, London, UK/De Agostini Picture Library/Bridgeman Images; 488 (LO), Buyenlarge Archive/UIG/Bridgeman Images; 489, Delaware Art Museum, Wilmington, USA/Howard Pyle Collection/Bridgeman Images; 490-1, Château de Versailles, France/Bridgeman Images; 491, Deutsches Historisches Museum, Berlin, Germany/© DHM/Bridgeman Images; 492, Comedie Francaise, Paris/Photo Josse/Bridgeman Images; 492-3, Antiquarian Images/Alamy Stock Photo; 494-5 (ALL), Pantheon Studios, Inc.; 496, Pantheon Studios, Inc.; 497 (UP), National Army Museum, London/Bridgeman Images; 497 (LO), Francis Apesteguy/Getty Images; 498-9, Private Collection/Bridgeman Images; 499, Private Collection/© Don Troiani/Bridgeman Images; 500, Bridgeman Art Library/Image Partner/GettyImages; 501, Private Collection/Photo © Don Troiani/Bridgeman Images; 502, © A. Dagli Orti/De Agostini Picture Library/Bridgeman Images; 502-3, Museo Nacional de Historia, Castillo de Chapultepec, Mexico/Jean Pierre Courau/Bridgeman Images © 2020 Estate of Juan O'Gorman/Artists Rights Society (ARS), New York; 504, Louvre, Paris, France/De Agostini Picture Library/Bridgeman Images; 505, Universal History Archive/UIG/Bridgeman Images; 506, Roman Milert/Alamy Stock Photo; 506-7, National Geographic Image Collection; 508-9, Private Collection/Bridgeman Images; 509, Library of Congress Prints and Photographs Division/Timothy H. O'Sullivan; 510, © Don Troiani/Bridgeman Images; 510-11, Library of Congress Prints and Photographs Division/Haas & Peale; 512, Eliza Scidmore/National Geographic Image Collection; 513, Pictures from History/Bridgeman Images; 514-5 (BOTH), Pictures from History/Bridgeman Images; 516, akg-images/Pictures From History; 518 (UP), Pantheon Studios, Inc.; 518 (LO), Private Collection/© Archives Charmet/Bridgeman Images; 519, Château de Versailles, France/Bridgeman Images; 520-1, Walter Bibikow/Getty Images; 522, Print Collector/Getty Images; 523 (UP), The Stapleton Collection/Bridgeman Images; 523 (LO), Westend61/Dirk Wüstenhagen/GettyImages; 524-5, Pantheon Studios, Inc.; 525, Private Collection/© Paul Freeman/Bridgeman Images.

Chapter 9: 1900-1950

526-7, U.S. National Archives; 528, Brian Brake/Science Source; 529, Universal History Archive/UI/Bridgeman Images; 530, akg-images/Lewis W. Hine; 531, akg-images/Interfoto; 532 (UP), Science & Society Picture Library/Getty Images; 532 (LO), Peter Newark Military Pictures/Bridgeman Images; 532-3, Andrew J. Russell/The Beinecke Rare Book and Manuscript Library, Yale University; 534, Pantheon Studios, Inc.; 535, t-woo/Getty Images; 536, akg-images/Jean Tholance. Location: Paris, France, Les Arts Décoratifs; 536-7, Everett Collection/Bridgeman Images; 538 (UP), Bruce Dale/National Geographic Image Collection; 538 (LO), Pantheon Studios, Inc.; 539, Walden Media; 540-1, LOC/Science Source; 542, Private Collection/Peter Newark Historical Pictures/Bridgeman Images; 543, Private Collection/Photo © Don Troiani/Bridgeman Images; 544, Hulton Archive/Getty Images; 544-5, Léon

GIMPEL - Paris, the celebration of the flags, 114th Infantry, July 14, 1917. Autochrome glass plate,, 9×12cm. Collection Société française de photographie (coll. SFP). (frSFP_0806im_A_0145); 546, Photo © Derek Bayes/Bridgeman Images; 547, Pantheon Studios, Inc.; 548-9, Pantheon Studios, Inc.; 549 (UP), West Point Museum, New York, USA/Photo © Don Troiani/Bridgeman Images; 549 (LO), Bettmann/Getty Images; 550, Pantheon Studios, Inc.; 550-1, Universal History Archive/UIG/Bridgeman Images; 552, Library of Congress Prints and Photographs Division/Dorothea Lange; 553, Private Collection/Peter Newark American Pictures/Bridgeman Images; 554, Bettmann/Getty Images; 554-5, Archives Larousse, Paris, France/Bridgeman Images; 556-7, Bettmann/Getty Images; 557 (UP), Claus Alwin Vogel/Getty Images; 557 (LO), Rolls Press/Popperfoto via Getty Images; 558, dovate/Getty Images; 558-9, PhotoQuest/Getty Images; 560-1, Universal History Archive/UIG/Bridgeman Images; 561, Historica Graphica Collection/Heritage Images/Getty Images; 562, Photo © Archivio GBB/Bridgeman Images; 563, United States Holocaust Memorial Museum Collection, Gift of Mali Fenigstein; 564 (UP), imv/Getty Images; 564 (LO), Paolo Woods and Gabriele Galimberti. Artwork © 2020 Estate of Pablo Picasso/Artists Rights Society (ARS), New York; 564-5, Keystone/Getty Images; 566-7, ullstein bild via Getty Images; 567 (UP), Kenneth W. Rendell, The International Museum of World War II; 567 (LO), © Yousuf Karsh; 568-9, Imperial War Museums/Getty Images; 570, U.S. National Archives/Army Signal Corps Collection; 571 (UP), Kenneth W. Rendell, The International Museum of World War II; 571 (LO), Alexander Vorontsov/Galerie Bilderwelt/Getty Images; 572, Kenneth W. Rendell, The International Museum of World War II; 572-3, U.S. National Archives; 574, Hulton Archive/Getty Images; 575 (LE), Universal History Archive/UIG/Bridgeman Images; 575 (RT), Peter Horree/Alamy Stock Photo.

Chapter 10: 1950-Today

576-7, George Steinmetz; 578, National Air and Space Museum, Washington DC, USA/Bridgeman Images; 579, Michael Ochs Archives/Getty Images; 580, Photo Media/ClassicStock/Getty Images; 581, Bill O'Leary/The Washington Post via Getty Images; 582-3, J. T. Vintage/Bridgeman Images; 584 (UP), Bridgeman Images; 584 (LO), Michael Glatt/Danita Delimont/Getty Images; 585, Everett Collection/Bridgeman Images; 586-7, Josef Koudelka/Magnum Photos; 588-9, RV Spencer/Interim Archives/Getty Images; 590 (UP), Frank Zeller/AFP via Getty Images; 590 (LO), CBS Photo Archive/Getty Images; 590-1, Larry Burrows/The LIFE Picture Collection/Getty Images; 592, Stuart Lutz/Gado/Getty Images; 592-3, AP Photo/Eddie Adams; 594, Photo © B.A.Tafreshi/Novapix/Bridgeman Images; 595, NASA; 596, PNA Rota/Stringer/Getty Images; 596-7, iLexx/Getty Images; 598, Michael Yamashita; 599 (UP), spooh/Getty Images; 599 (LO), David Parker/BWP Media/Getty Images; 600-1, qaphotos.com/Alamy Stock Photo; 602, Encyclopaedia Britannica/UIG/Bridgeman Images; 603, Universal History Archive/UIG/Bridgeman Images; 604, Paramount Pictures/Courtesy of Getty Images; 605, Valerie Loiseleux/Getty Images; 606 (UP), Valerie Loiseleux/Getty Images; 606 (LO), Hulton Archive/Getty Images; 606-7, The Advertising Archives/Alamy Stock Photo; 608, GraphicaArtis/Getty Images; 609 (LE), Science & Society Picture Library/Getty Images; 609 (RT), Henry Groskinsky/The LIFE Picture Collection/Getty Images; 610, Science & Society Picture Library/Getty Images; 610-1, NicoElNino/Getty Images; 612-3, Tino Soriano/National Geographic Image Collection; 613, bombuscreative/Getty Images; 614, Gerd Ludwig/National Geographic Image Collection; 615, Museum of the Revolution, Moscow, Russia/Bridgeman Images; 616 (UP), Ira Block/National Geographic Image Collection; 616 (LO), Gerard Malie/AFP via Getty Images; 616-7, Spencer Platt/Getty Images; 618, Cindy Karp/The LIFE Images Collection/Getty Images; 619 (UP), Ragnar Singsaas/Getty Images; 619 (LO), Martin Roemers; 620, ©The Trustees of the British Museum. All rights reserved.; 621, Susan Winters Cook/Getty Images; 622-3, Ciril Jazbec/National Geographic Image Collection; 623, Kevin Wheal/Alamy Stock Photo; 624, Becart/Getty Images; 625, Wally McNamee/Corbis via Getty Images; 626-7, Steve McCurry; 628, Andrea Bruce/NOOR; 628-9, Daniel Berehulak/Getty Images; 630, Andy Mann/National Geographic Image Collection; 632-3, REUTERS/Kim Hong-Ji; 633, Centers for Disease Control; 634, Rena Effendi; 635, Walter Myers/Stocktrek Images/National Geographic Image Collection.

Since 1888, the National Geographic Society has funded more than 14,000 research, conservation, education, and storytelling projects around the world. National Geographic Partners distributes a portion of the funds it receives from your purchase to National Geographic Society to support programs including the conservation of animals and their habitats.

Get closer to National Geographic Explorers and photographers, and connect with our global community. Join us today at nationalgeographic.com/join

For rights or permissions inquiries, please contact National Geographic Books Subsidiary Rights: bookrights@natgeo.com

ISBN: 978-1-4262-2189-7

Printed in Hong Kong

22/PPHK/2